Collins

STREET FINDER
GLASGOW

D0589819

Contents

Key to street map symbols	1
Key to street map pages	2-3
City centre map	4-5
Street maps	6-145
Local information	146-165
Rail network map	166-167
Key to route planning map symbols	168
Key to route planning map pages	169
Route planning maps	170-173
Index to place names	174-175
Index to street names	176-270

Collins

Published by Collins
An imprint of HarperCollins Publishers
77-85 Fulham Palace Road, Hammersmith, London W6 8JB

www.collins.co.uk

Mapping generated from Collins Bartholomew digital databases

Printed in China

ISBN 978 0 00 718466 8
ISBN 0 00 718466 2   Imp 003   RI11727   NDB

e-mail: roadcheck@harpercollins.co.uk

Key to street map symbols **1**

M73 ▬ ▬ ▬	Motorway/under construction or proposed
A74	Primary road dual/single
A89	A Road dual/single
B763	B Road dual/single
	Other road dual/single
▬ ▬ ▬ ▬	Road under construction
‑ ‑ ‑ ‑ ‑ ‑	Road tunnel

→ Toll	One-way street/Toll
	Restricted access street
	Pedestrian street
═══ ‑‑‑‑‑	Minor road/Track
‑‑‑‑‑ _FB_	Footpath/Footbridge
	Unitary authority boundary
	Postcode boundary

——————	Railway line
✕ ‑┐ ┌‑	Level crossing/Railway tunnel
⇥ ⇥	Main/Other railway station

Ⓢ	Subway station
●	Bus/Coach station
‑‑‑‑‑‑‑‑‑‑	Pedestrian ferry

◢	Leisure/Tourism
◢	Shopping/Retail
◢	Administration/Law
◢	Education

◢	Hospital
◢	Industry/Commerce
◢	Notable building
◢	Major religious building

■	Health centre
■ Pol	Police station
■ PO	Post Office
■ Lib	Library
■	Fire station/Crematorium/Ambulance station/Community centre

+ ☾ ✿	Church/Mosque/Synagogue
🎥 🎭	Cinema/Theatre
⊠	Hotel
𝒊 𝒊	Tourist information centre (all year/seasonal)
Ⓟ	Car park

	Wood/Forest
	Park/Garden/Recreation ground
	Public open space

⚑	Golf course
♱♱♱	Cemetery
	Built up area

15⁵	National Grid number
16 ◣	Page continuation number

For general map abbreviations see list on page 176

SCALE 1:15,840 4 inches to 1 mile (6.3 cm to 1 km)

0	1/4	1/2	3/4	1 mile

0	1/4	1/2	3/4	1	1 1/4	1 1/2 kilometres

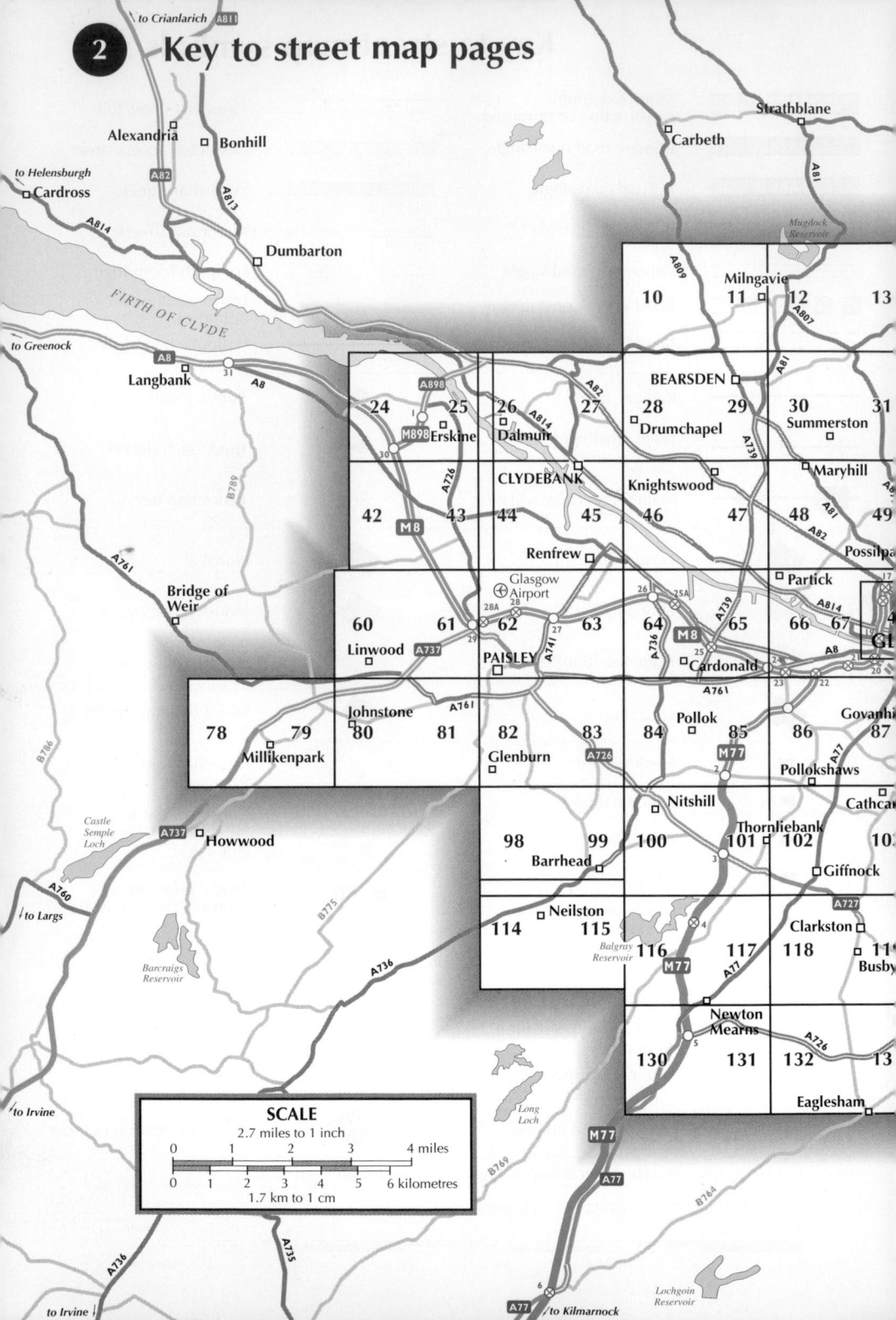

to Crianlarich A811

Alexandria □ Bonhill □

to Helensburgh
□ Cardross

A82

A813

Strathblane □

□ Carbeth

A81

Mugdock
Reservoir

A814

□ Dumbarton

FIRTH OF CLYDE

to Greenock

A8

□ Langbank

A8

31

Milngavie
10 | 11 □ | 12 | 13

A809

A807

BEARSDEN □

A898

24 | 25 | 26 | 27

28 | 29 | 30 | 31

Erskine Dalmuir

M898

Drumchapel □

A814

A82

Summerston

CLYDEBANK

Knightswood

□ Maryhill

A761

A726

42 | 43 | 44 | 45

46 | 47 | 48 | 49

M8

A739

A81

A82

Possilpa

Renfrew □

Bridge of
Weir

Glasgow
Airport

Partick □

28A

17

A814

60 | 61 | 62 | 63

64 | 65 | 66 | 67

B789

Linwood

A737

27

26

25A

M8

A739

Gl

29

PAISLEY

A741

A736

25

A8

Cardonald

20

23 | 22

Johnstone

A761

A761

Govanhi

78 | 79 | 80 | 81

82 | 83 | 84 | 85

86 | 87

B786

Millikenpark

Glenburn

Pollok □

A77

Pollokshaws

A726

M77

2

Castle
Semple
Loch

A737 □ Howwood

Nitshill □

Cathca

98 | 99 | 100 | 101

102 | 10

Thornliebank

A760

to Largs

Barrhead

3

□ Giffnock

Barcraigs
Reservoir

B775

A736

Neilston □

A727

114 | 115

116 | 117 | 118 | 11

Clarkston □

Busby

M77

A77

4

Balgray
Reservoir

to Irvine

A736

Newton
Mearns

130 | 131 | 132 | 13

5

A726

Long
Loch

Eaglesham □

SCALE

2.7 miles to 1 inch

0   1   2   3   4 miles

0 1 2 3 4 5 6 kilometres

1.7 km to 1 cm

B769

M77

A77

to Irvine

A736

A735

Lochgoin
Reservoir

6

A77 / to Kilmarnock

B764

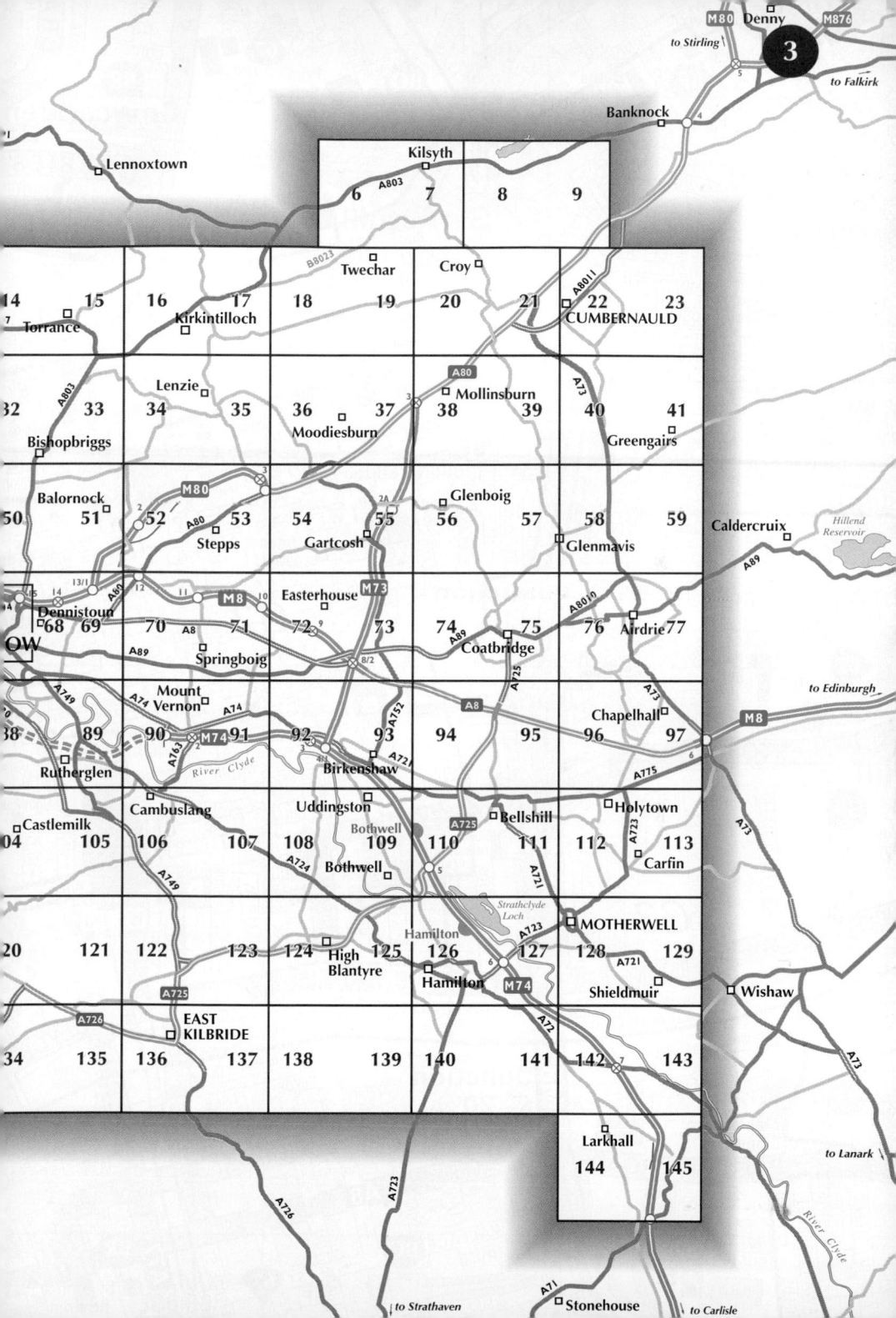

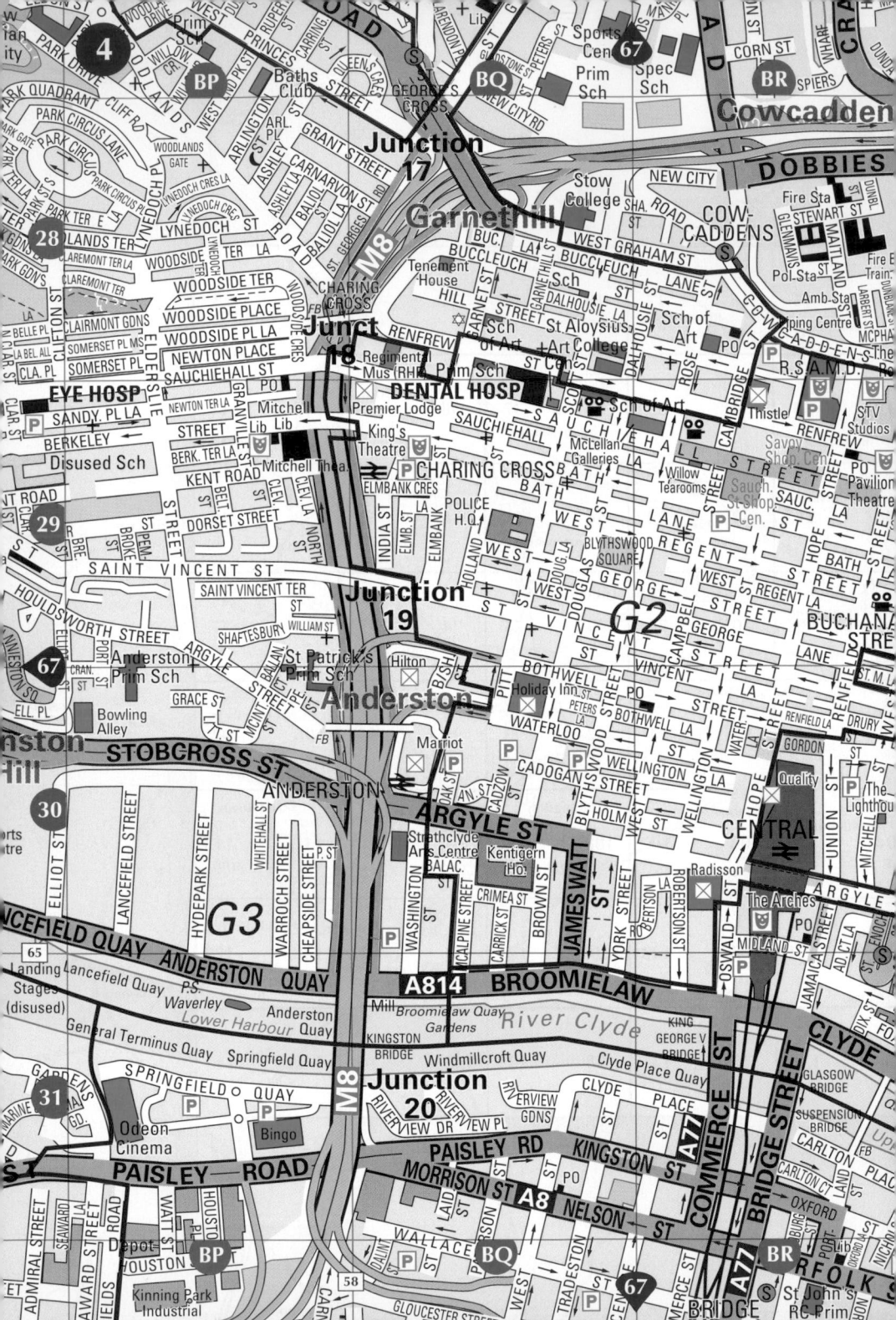

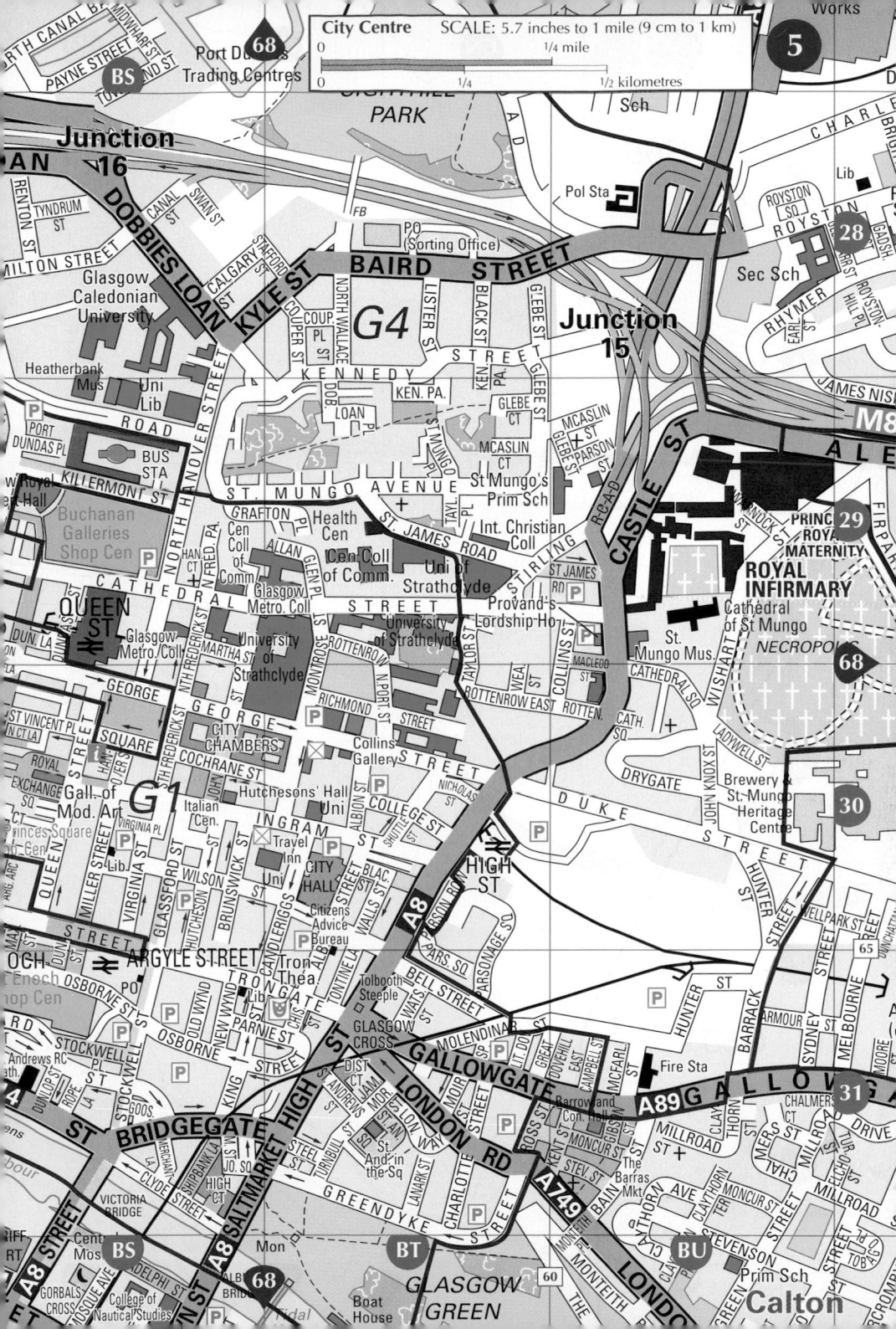

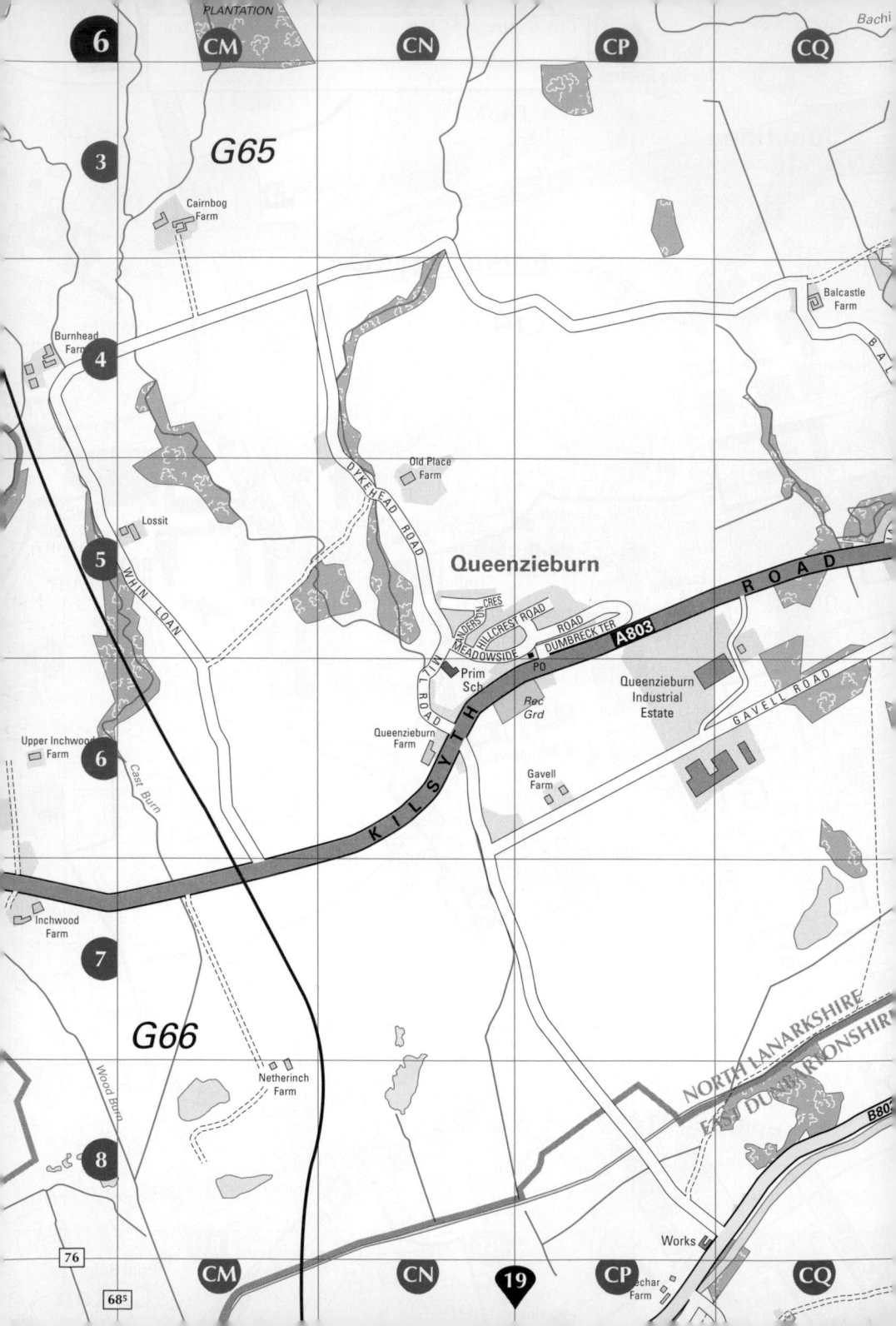

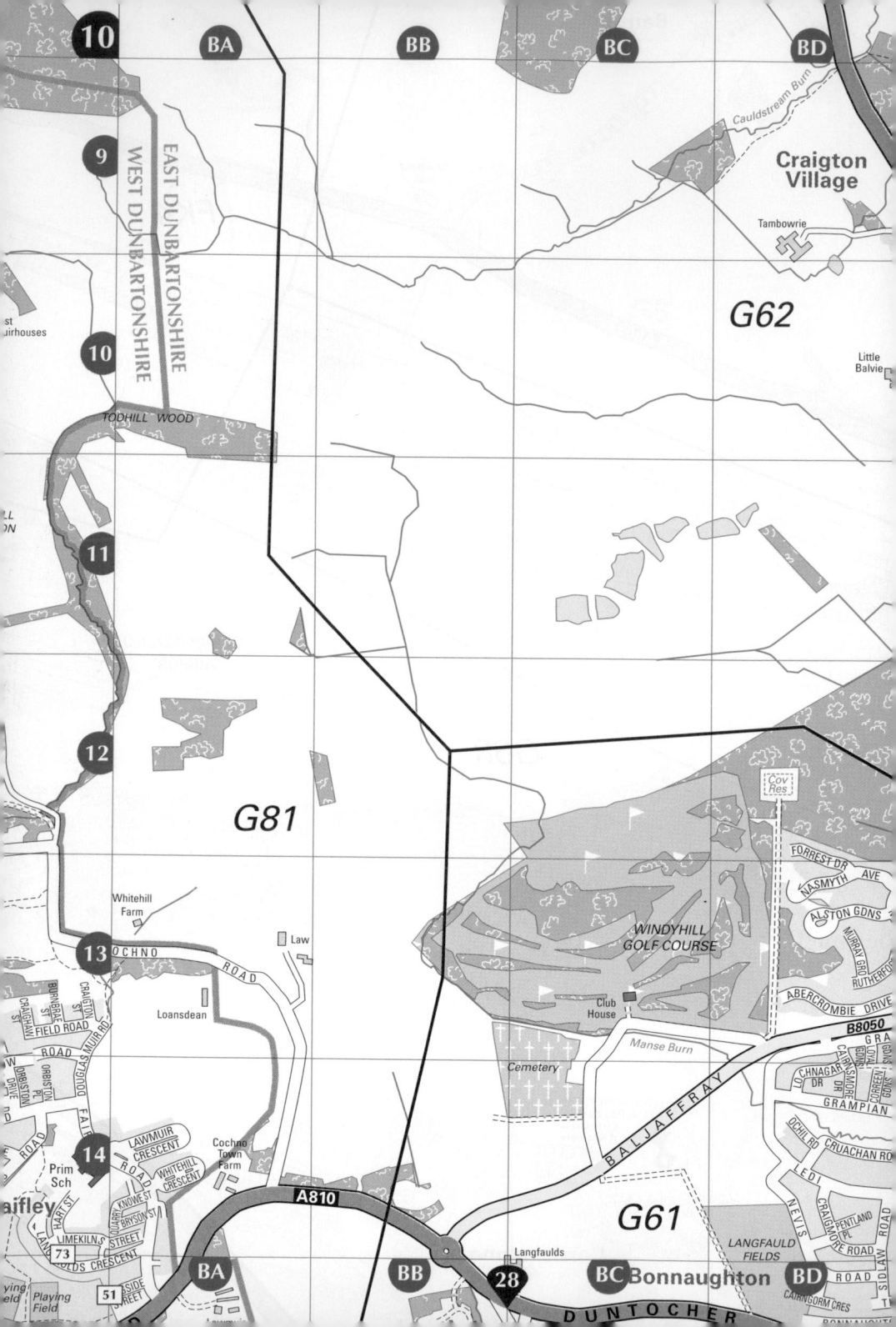

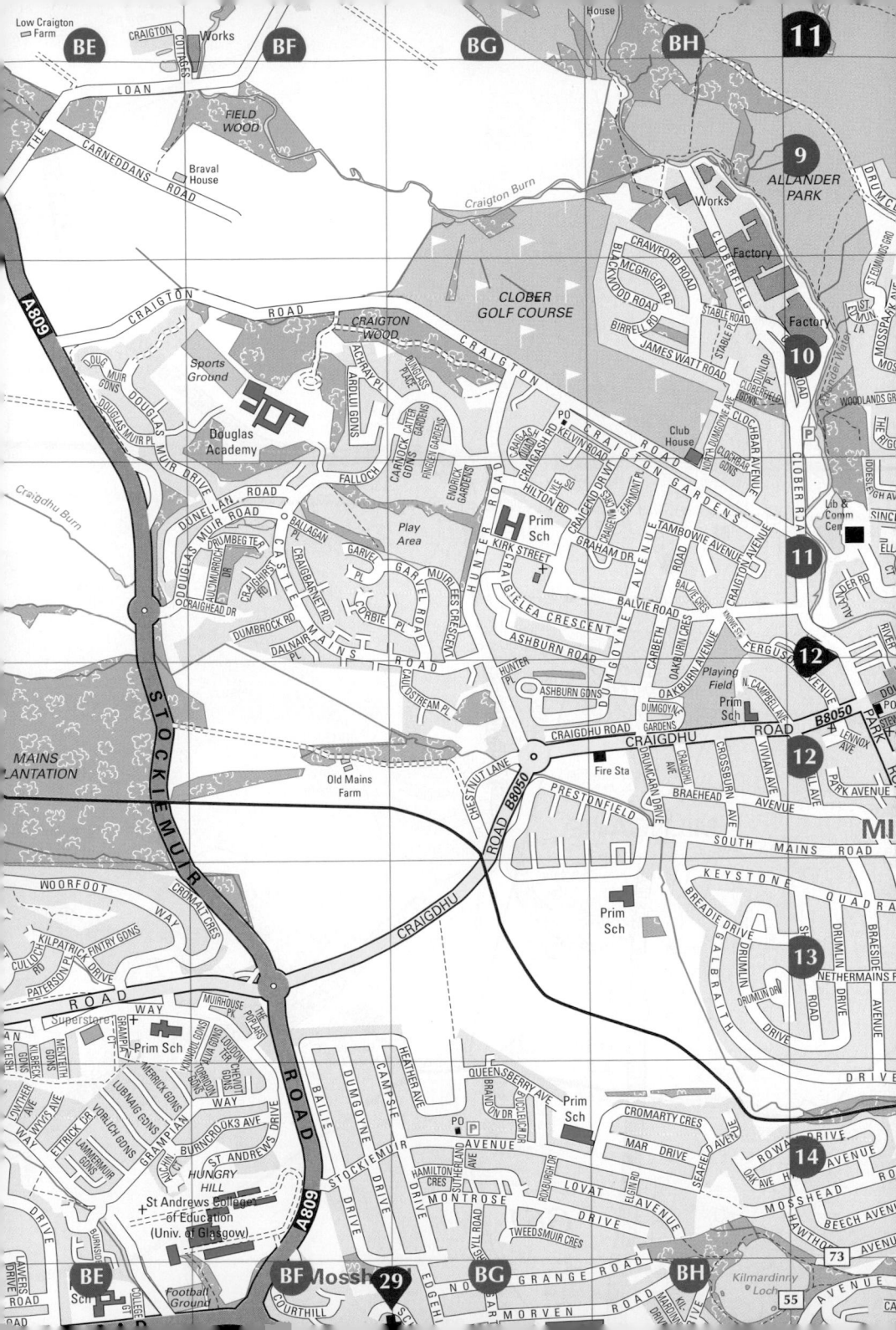

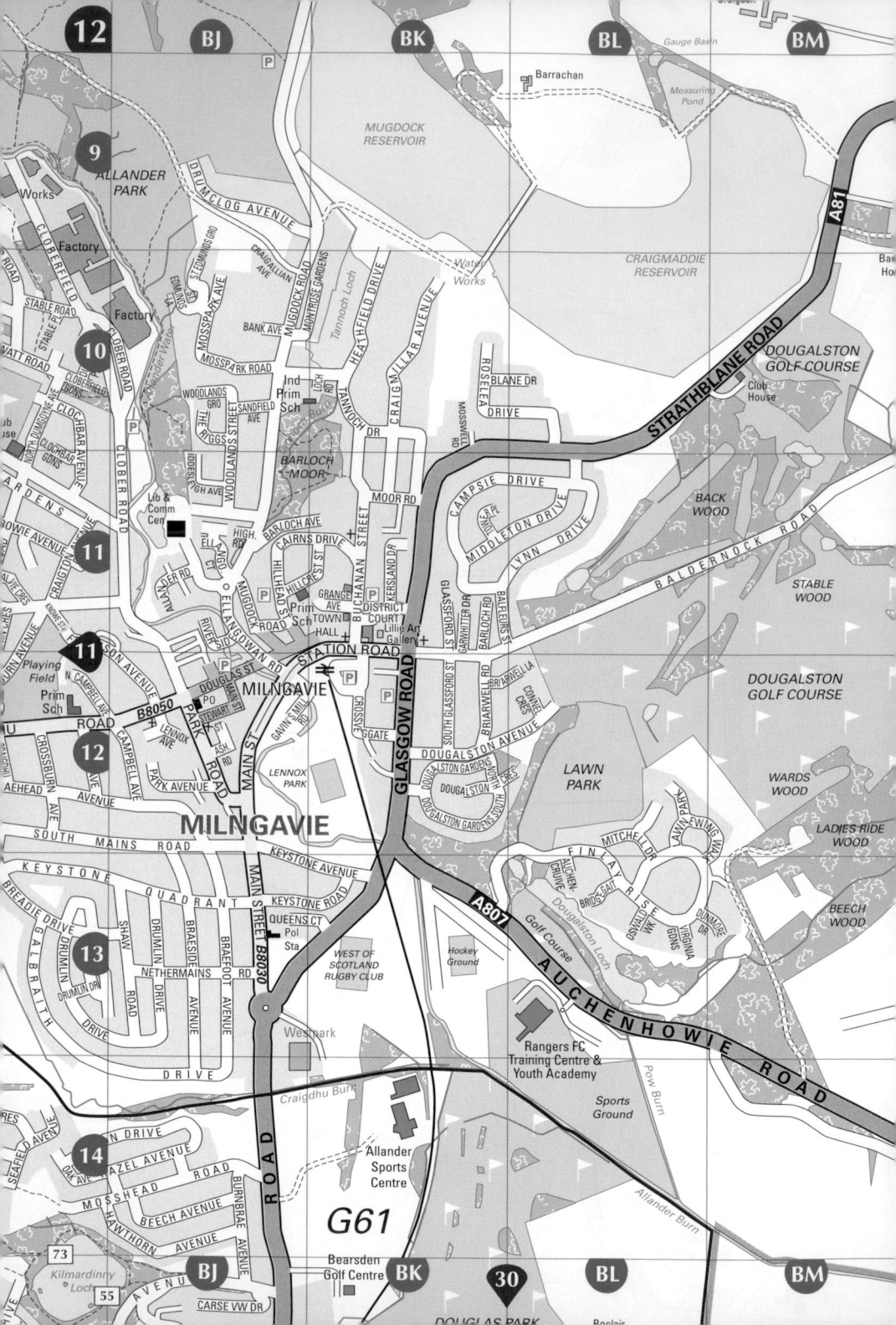

73

BW   BX   BY   BZ   **15**

G66

9

Upper
Carlestoun

Red Burn

Langshot

10

Guardbank

Acre
Valley

Leitchbank

Drumbayne

East
Balgrochan
Farm

ACRE VALLEY ROAD

East
Balgrochan

Red Burn

11

Carlston

CAMPSIE

Balgrochan

West
Balgrochan Farm

WEST BALGROCHAN RD

NEVIS DR

KINGS PL

SCHOOL ROAD

MILL CRES

16

**West
Balgrochan**

WARDEND ROAD

BLAIR
GDNS

MAITLAND DRIVE

CAMPBELL PL

BUCHANAN
PL

Rec
Grd

WALDRONHILL DR

PARK CRES

Playing
Field

12

MORAY DR

WALLACE GDNS

ATHOLL AVE

WEST RD

Prim
Sch

B822

CORMACK AVE

Torrance

Meadowbank
Farm

Tower
Farm

Glenside

TOWER ROAD

MAIN STREET

HAWTHORN ST

VIOLA PL

GUTHRIE PL

DALRIADA

CORMACK AVE

ROSEHILL ROAD

KELVIN VIEW

CRAIGMADDIE
GDNS

ALLANDER
DR

SMEATON AVE

CLYDE AVE

DUND
AVE

CHARLOTTE
AVE

FORTH ROAD

JOHN MAITLAND DR

MCMILLAN DR

QUEEN'S VW

CRAIGMARLOCH AVE

NITHDALE

MORRISON
GDNS

FIRBANK AVE

KELVIN PL

13

Kelvinbridge
Roundabout

A807

River Kelvin

TORRANCE ROAD

Bogton
House

Forth & Clyde Canal

14

73

BW   BX   **33**   BY   BZ

63

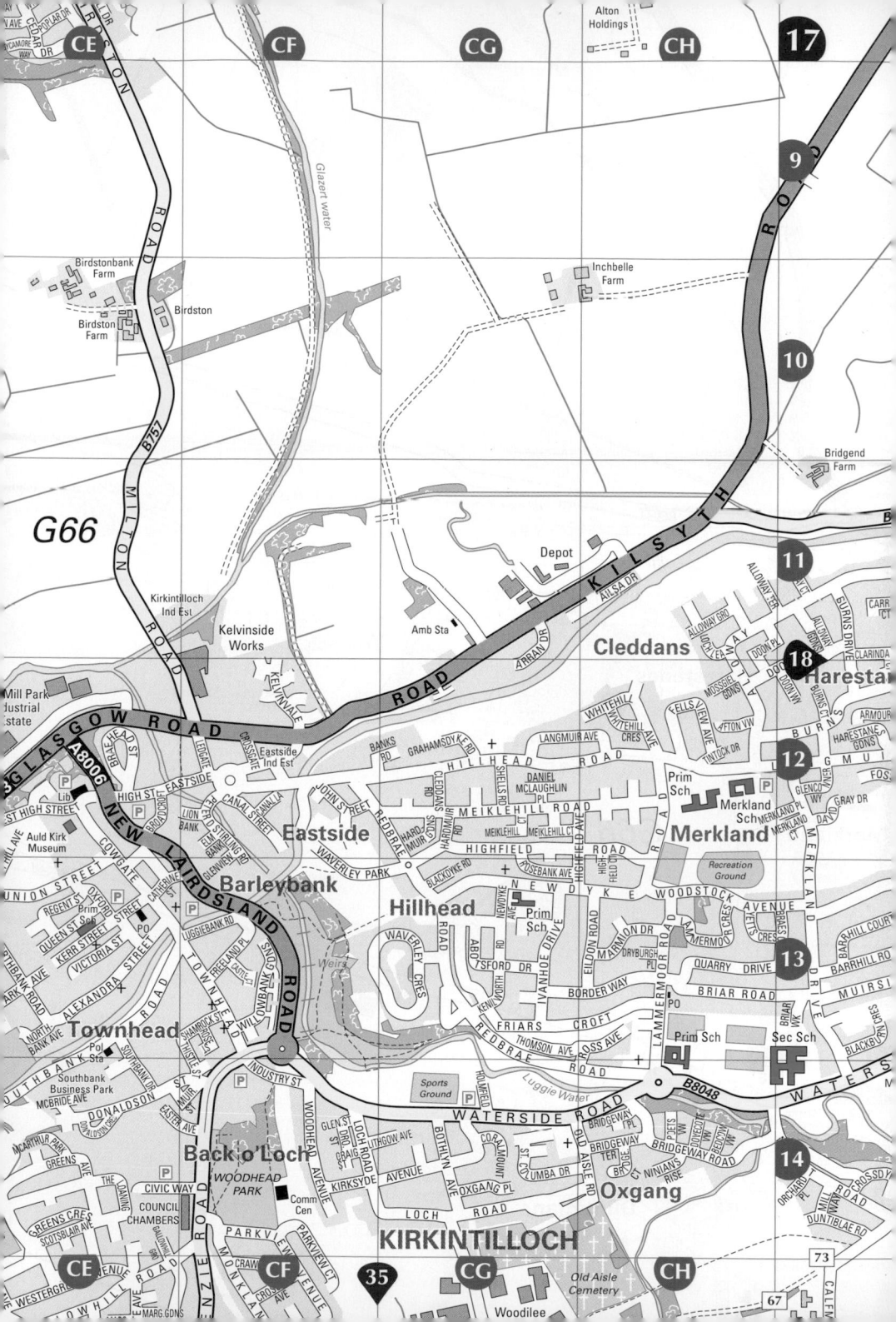

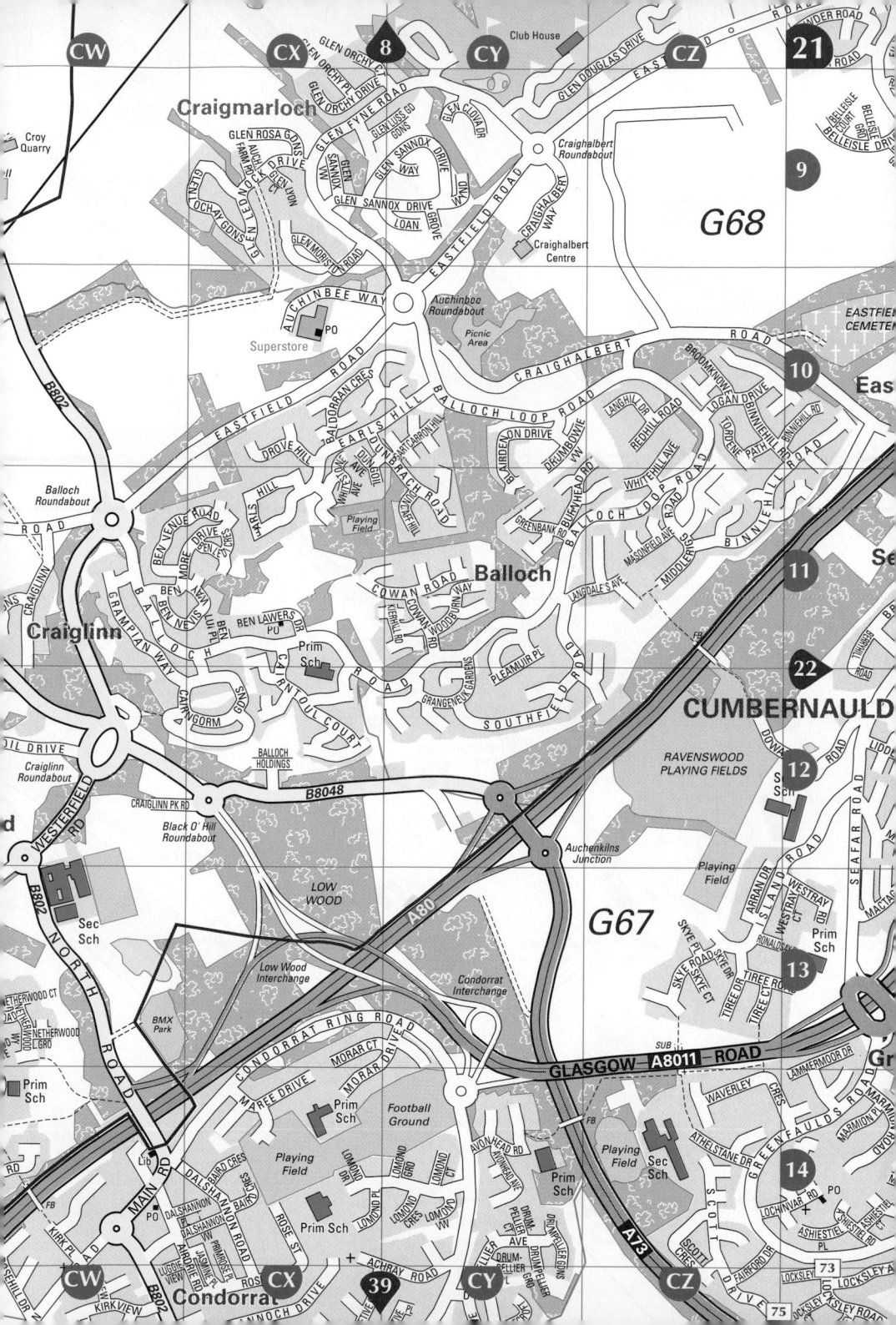

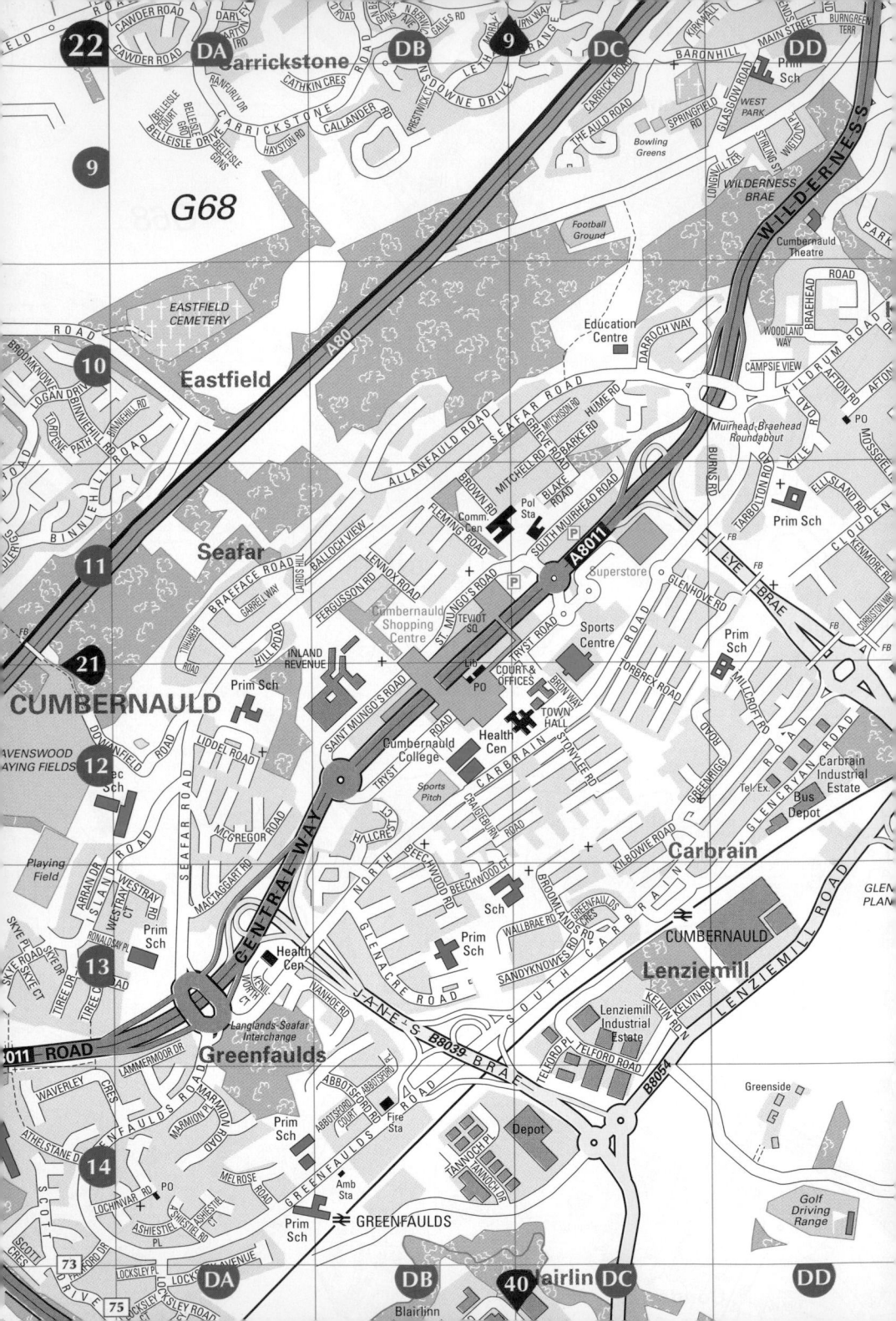

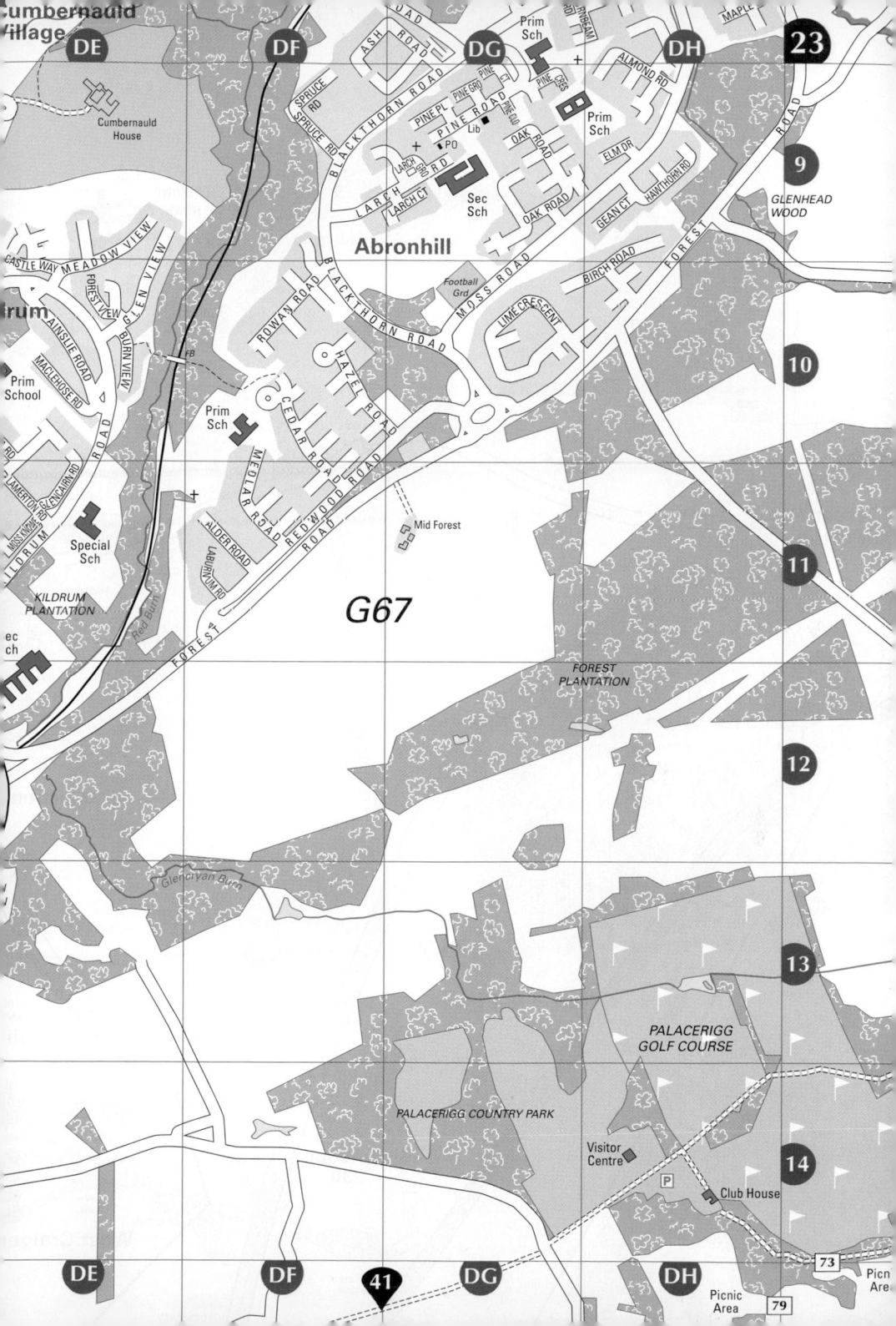

Cumbernauld Village

DE DF DG DH **23**

9

Cumbernauld House

Prim Sch

Prim Sch

ASH ROAD

SPRUCE RD
SPRUCE RD

BLACKTHORN ROAD

PINE PL
PINE GRO
PINE ROAD
LARCH RD
LARCH CT

PO
Lib

OAK ROAD

OAK ROAD

ELM DR

GEAN CT

HAWTHORN RD

BIRCH ROAD

ALMOND RD

MAPLE

FOREST ROAD

GLENHEAD WOOD

Sec Sch

Abronhill

MOSS ROAD

Football Grd

LIME CRESCENT

10

CASTLE WAY MEADOW VIEW

drum

FOREST VIEW

GLEN VIEW

BURN VIEW

AINSLIE ROAD

MACLEHOSE RD

Prim School

ROAD

LAMBERTON RD
GLENCAIRN RD

MOSSWOOD

DRUM

Special Sch

KILDRUM PLANTATION

ec ch

ROWAN ROAD

HAZEL ROAD

BLACKTHORN ROAD

Prim Sch

CEDAR ROAD

MEDLAR ROAD

REDWOOD ROAD

ALDER ROAD

LABURNUM RD

Red Burn

FB

FOREST

Mid Forest

11

G67

FOREST PLANTATION

12

Glencryan Burn

13

PALACERIGG GOLF COURSE

PALACERIGG COUNTRY PARK

Visitor Centre

P

Club House

14

73

DE DF **41** DG DH

Picnic Area 79 Picn Are

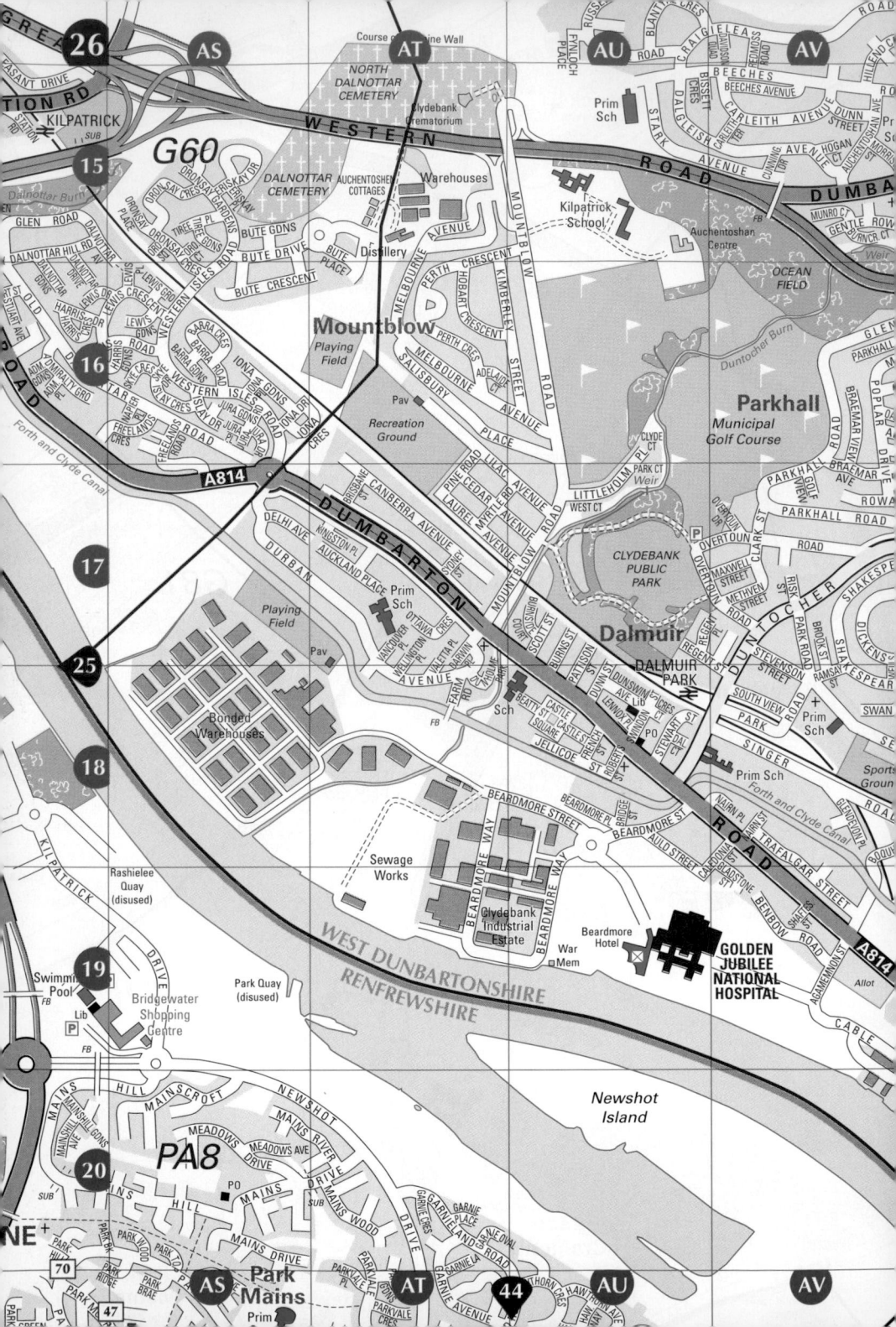

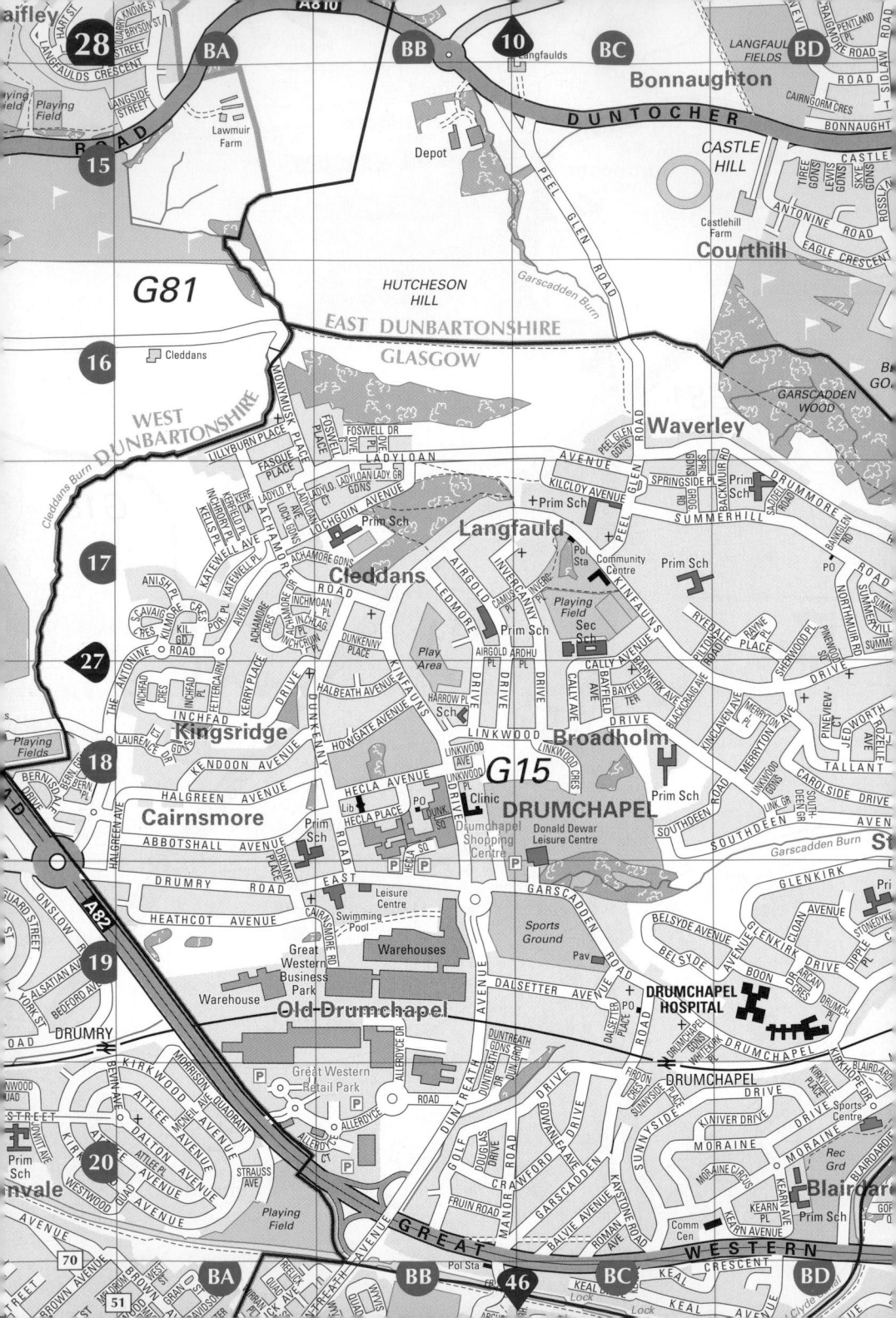

BN **BP** **13** **BQ** **BR** **31**

15

G62

River Kelvin

G64

16

Buchley Farm

HEN ROAD

East Millichen

17

Factory

ROAD

BALMUILDY

Wester Balmuidy Farm

32

18

Works

G23

Blackhill Farm

19

BLACKHILL ROAD

Parkholm Farm

Lochfauld Farm

LOCHFAULD ROAD

Forth and Clyde Canal

BLACKHILL COTTAGES

20

CASTLE

LAMBHILL CEMETERY

70 CASTL

59

Prim Sch

SHIELDAIG ROAD

BN WESTERN NECROPOLIS **BP** **49** **BQ** POSSIL LOCH (Bird Sanctuary) **BR**

ST KENTIGERN'S

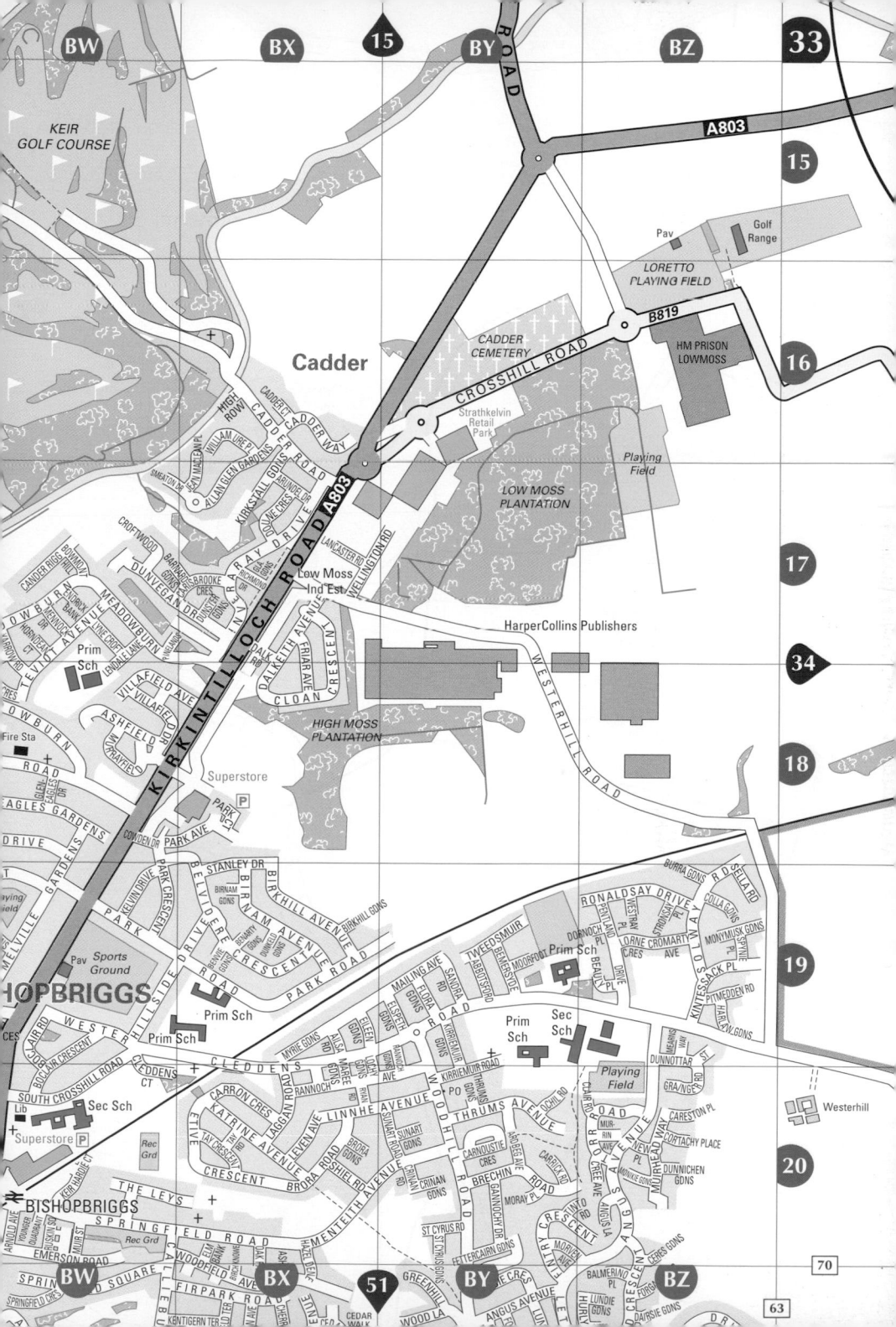

34

CA

GLASGOW BRIDGE

CB

16

CC

CD

T
Gre

15

A803

Golf
Range

Prim
Sch

BROOM GARDENS

High
Gallowhill

Meiklehill
Farm

CYPRESS DRIVE

CONIFER PL

ALDER AVENUE

ALMOND DRIVE

Prim Sch

TTO
G FIELD

HM PRISON
LOWMOSS

16

Bearhill
Farm

PINEWOOD CT

PINEWOOD PL

PINEWOOD

BOGHEAD

THORNWOOD DR

OAK DRIVE

JUNIPER

MAPLE

BIRCH

AVENUE

ROAD

PINEWOOD RD

GLEN GDNS

ALMOND'S

POPLAR DR

SPRUCE DRIVE

BLACK

HORN

AVE

ASH GROVE

LABURNUM

BLACK

GLENWOOD
RD

GLEN

PL

GLENWOOD

GLEN CT

GROVE

Sch

CROSSHILL ROAD

HEATHER DRIVE

FOREST
GDNS

FOREST PL

HEATHER GDNS

17

Playing
Field

B819

G64

33

B812

18

CRO

EAST DUNBARTONSHIRE

NORTH LANARKSHIRE

GADLOCH

BURRA GDNS

R D

SELLAR RD

COLLA GDNS

SOLWAY

DRIVE

MONYMUSK GDNS

SPYNI

ROBROYSTON ROAD

Parkhillhead

19

KINTESSACK PL

PITMEDDEN RD

HARE...W. GDNS

MART...

AVE

Rushyhill

MEARNS

WYND

NOTTAR

GRANGE RD

CARESTON PL

Westerhill

CORTACHY PLACE

20

DUNNICHEN
GDNS

...S GDNS

70

63

CA

CB

52

CC

CD

DRI

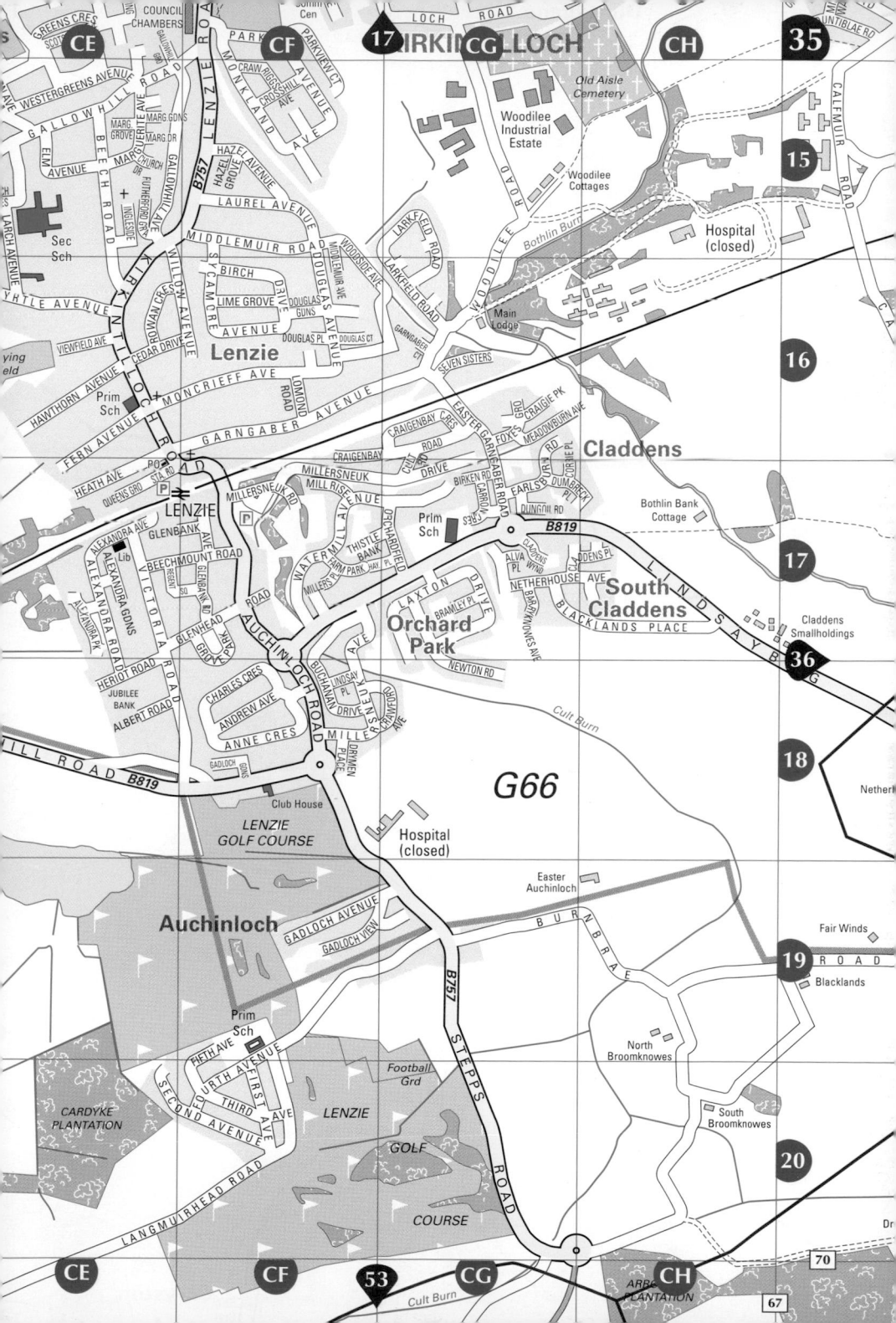

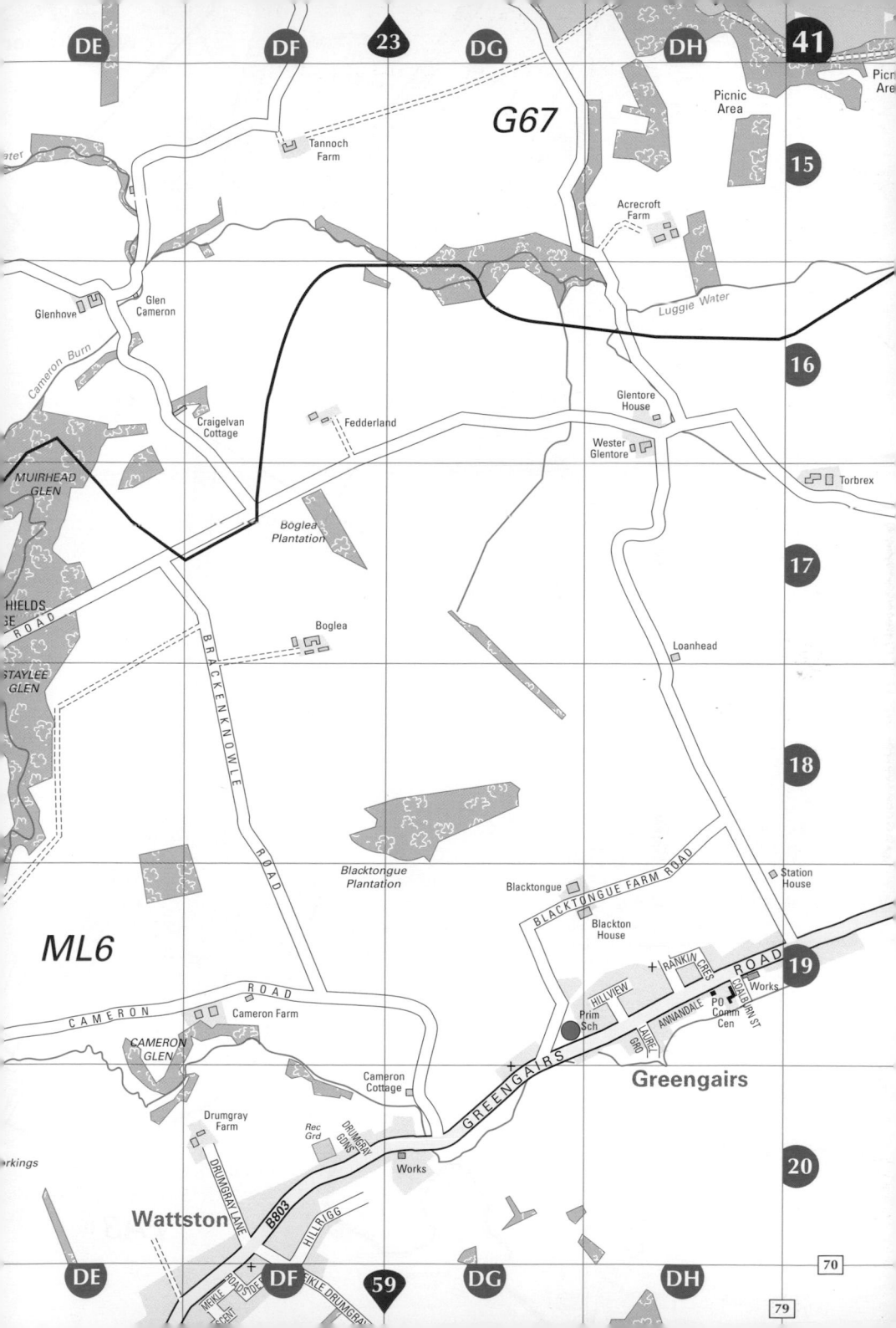

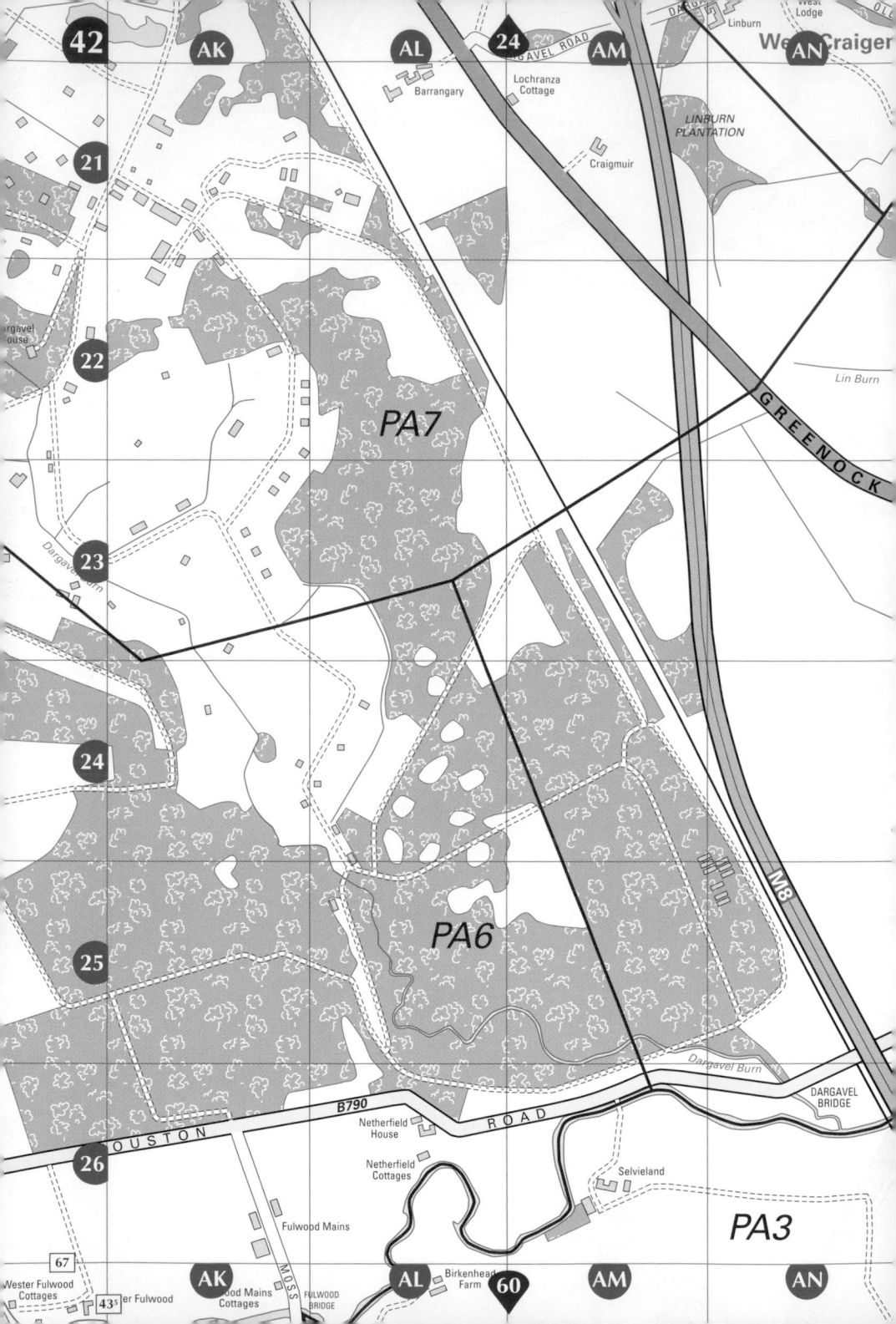

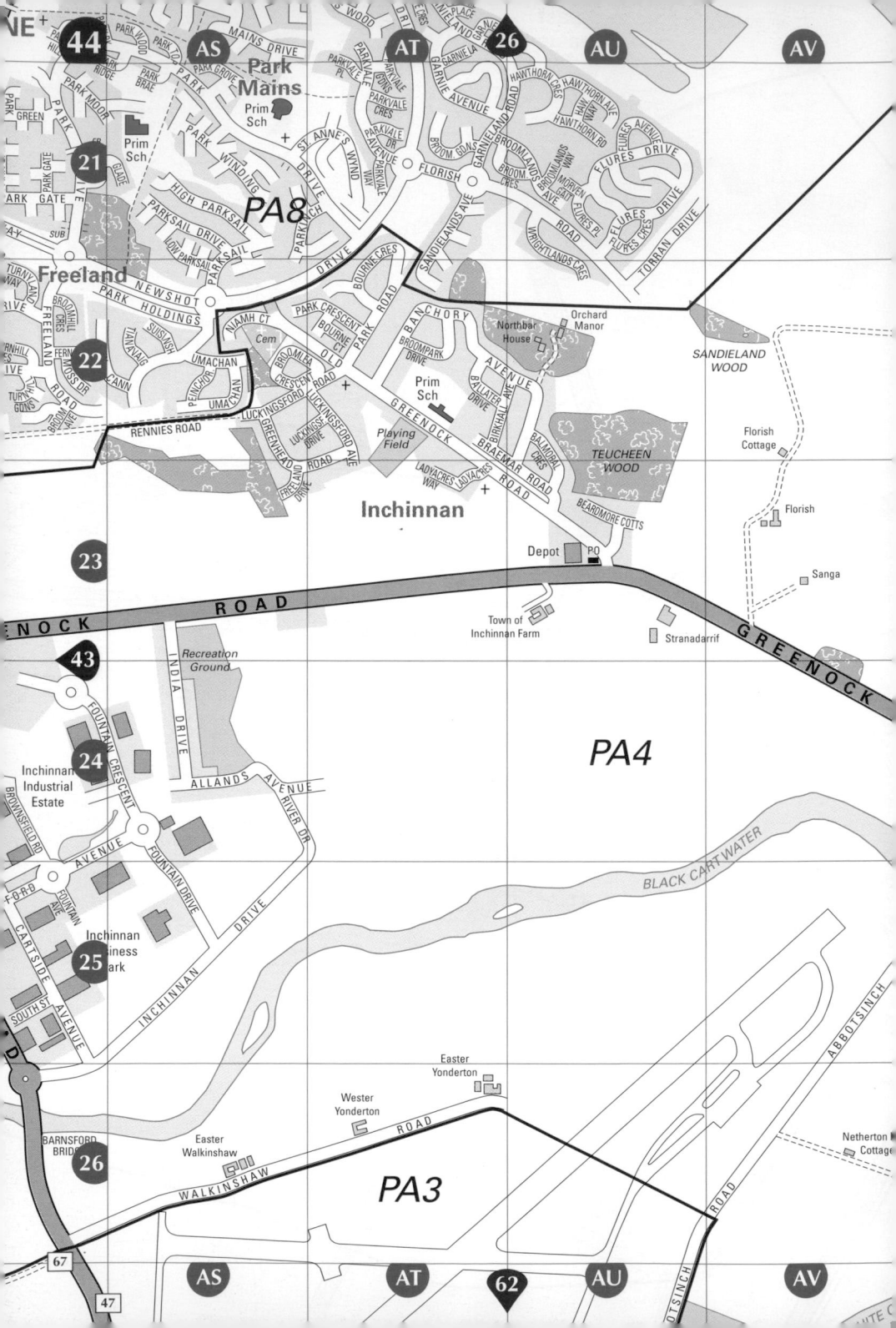

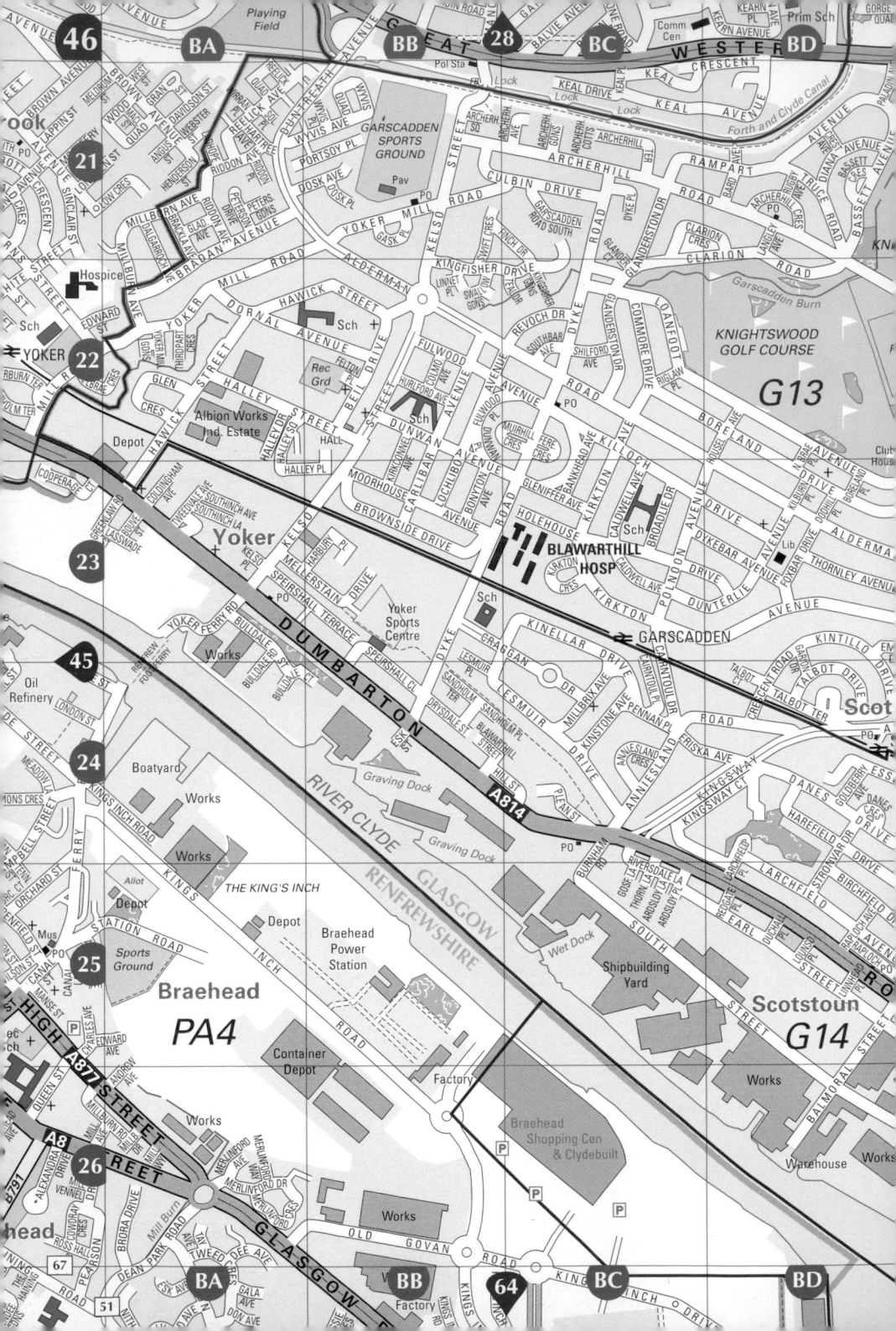

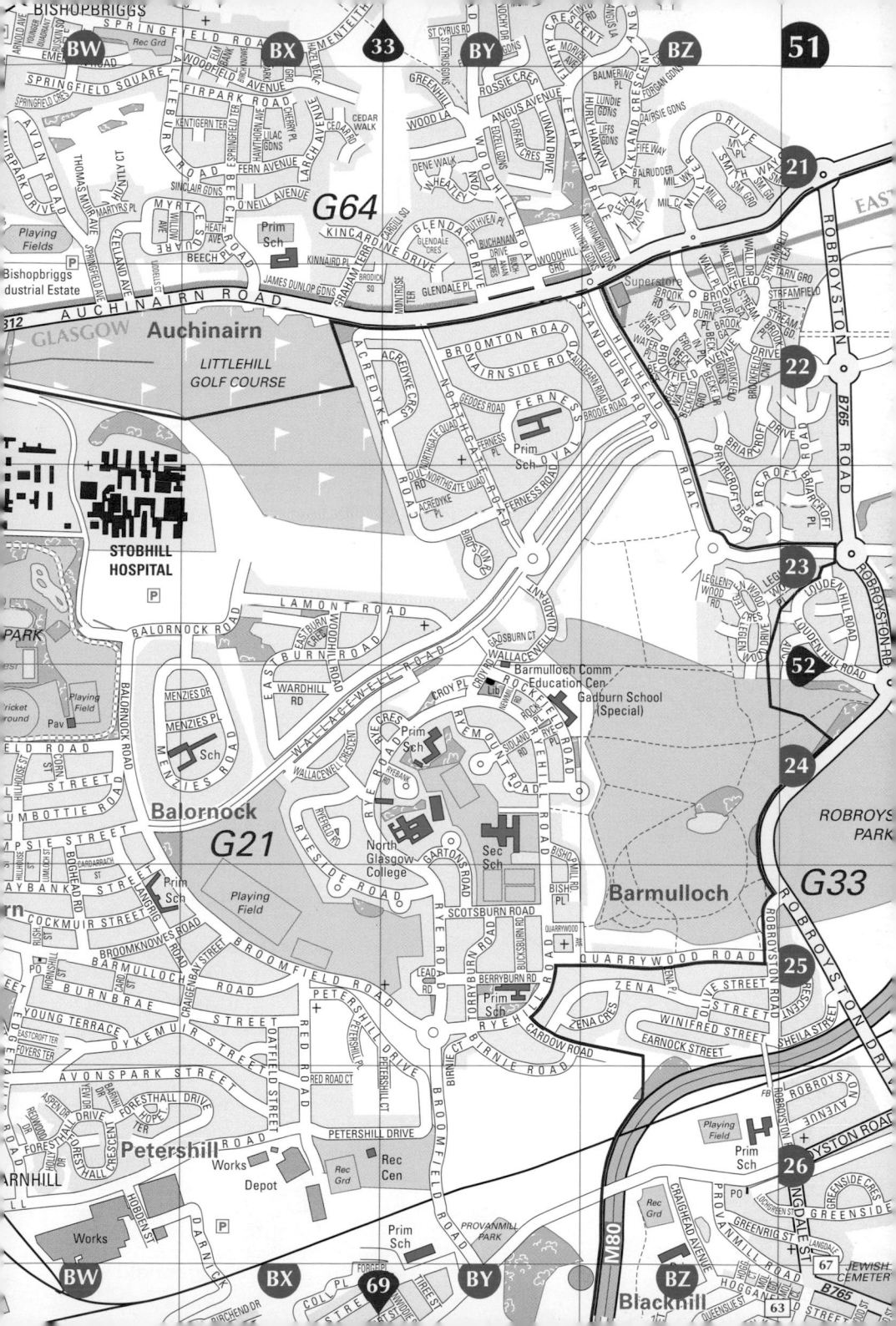

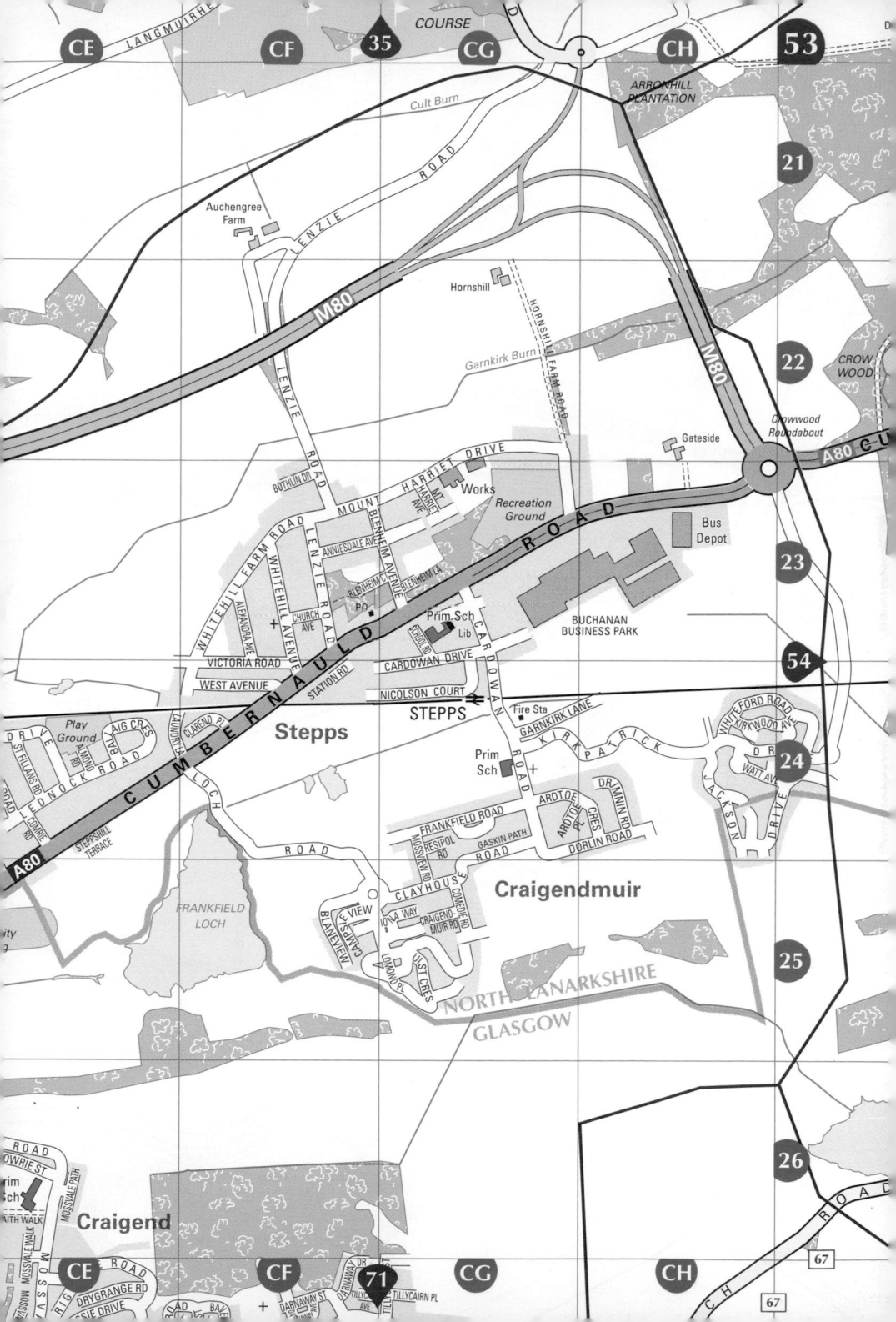

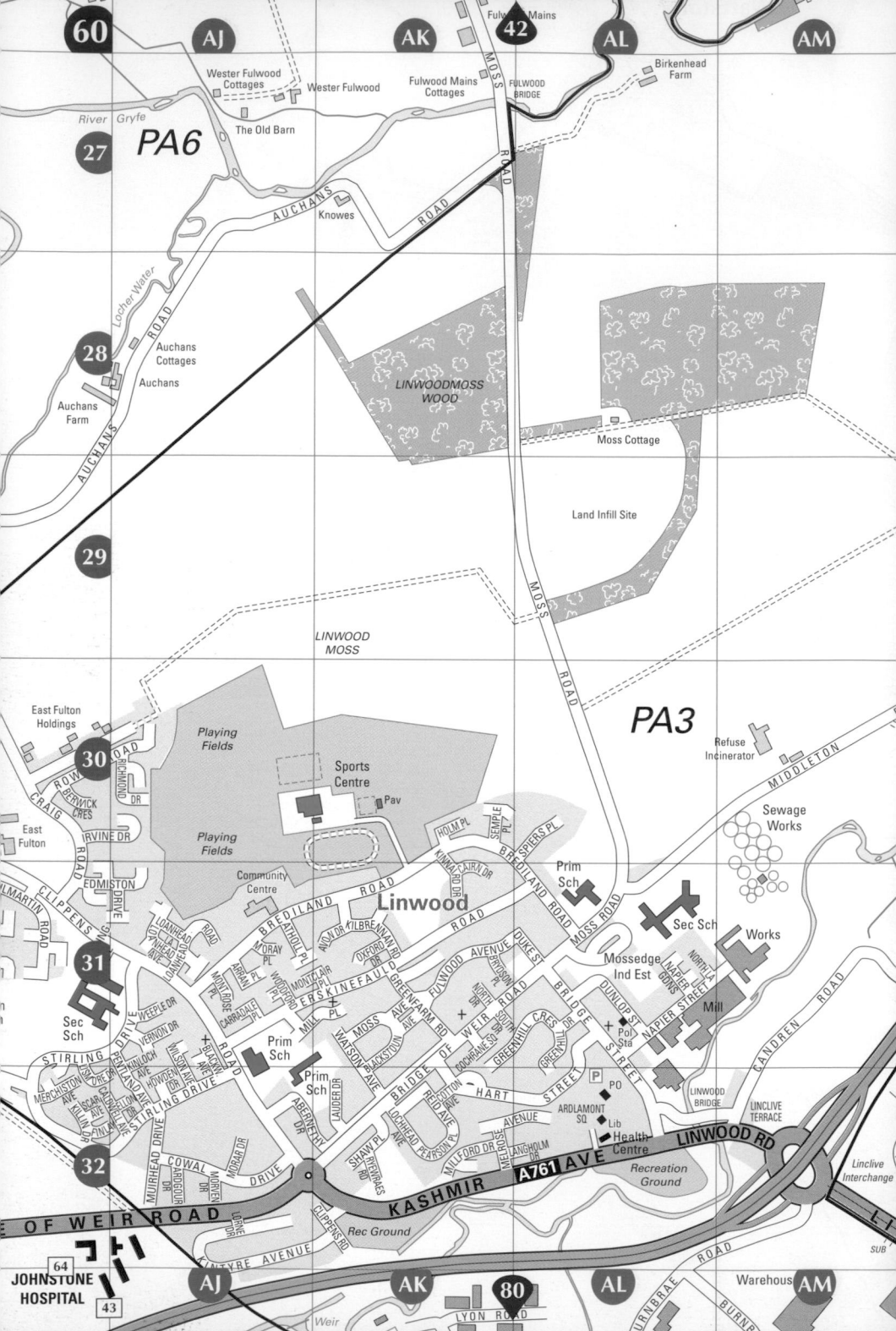

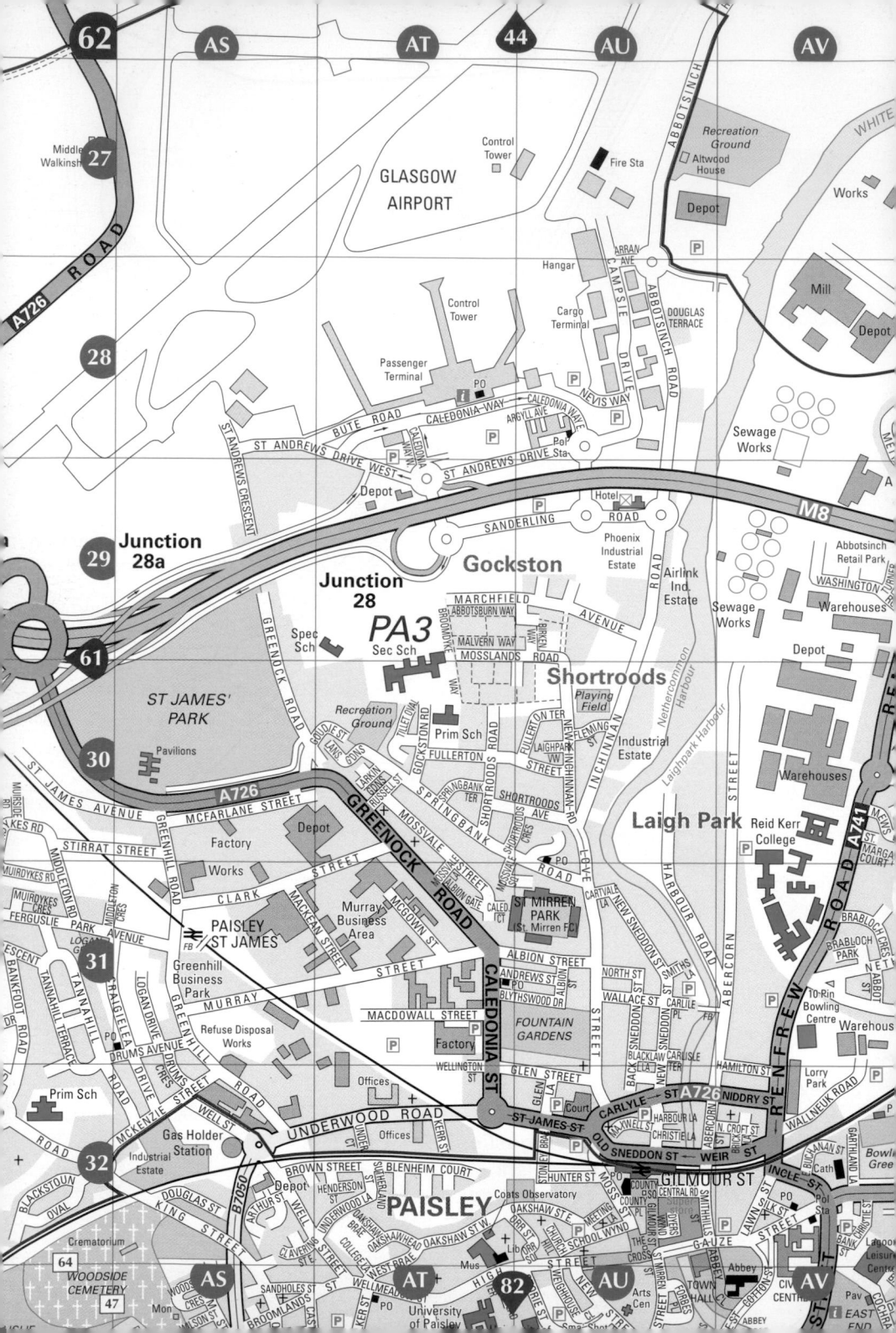

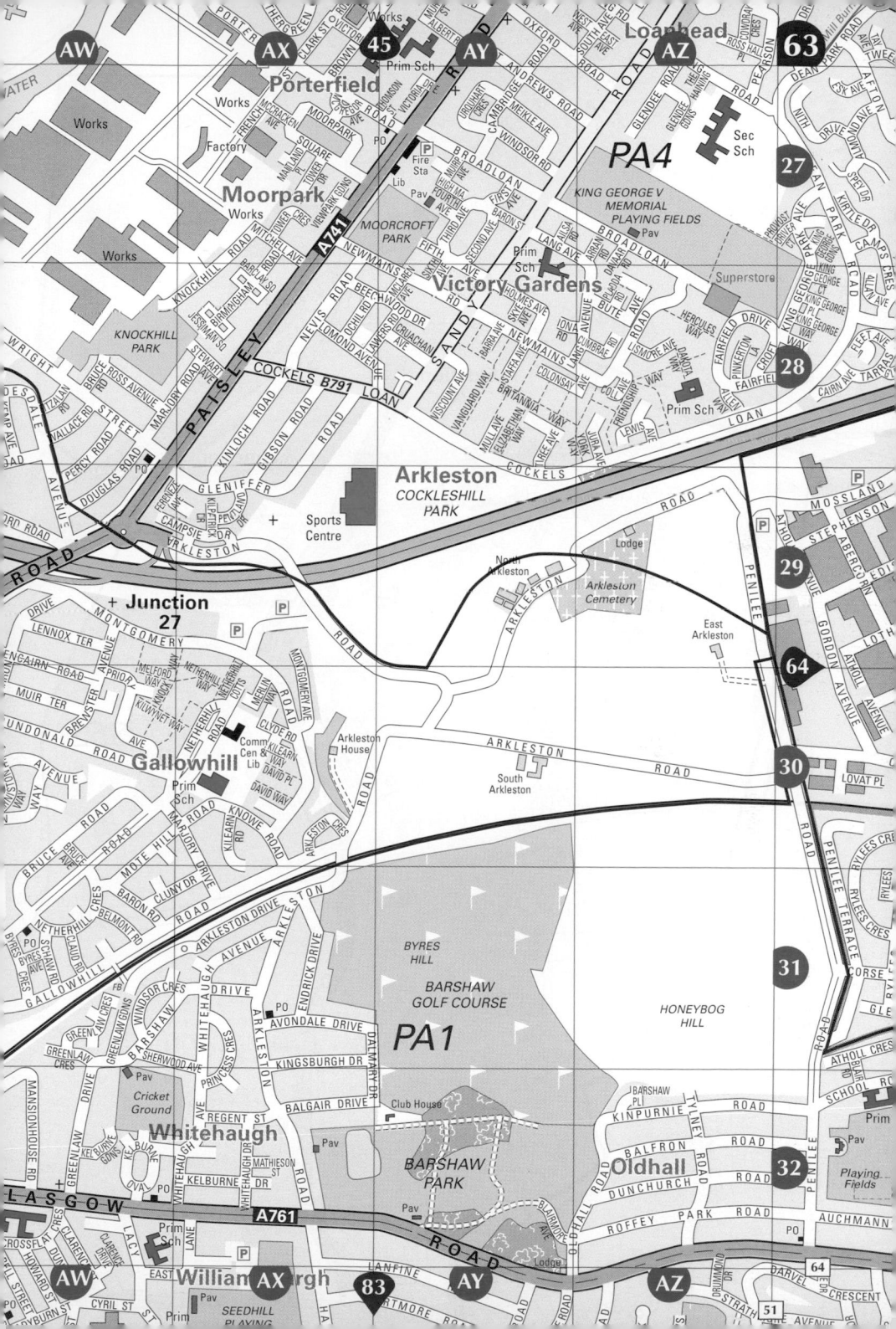

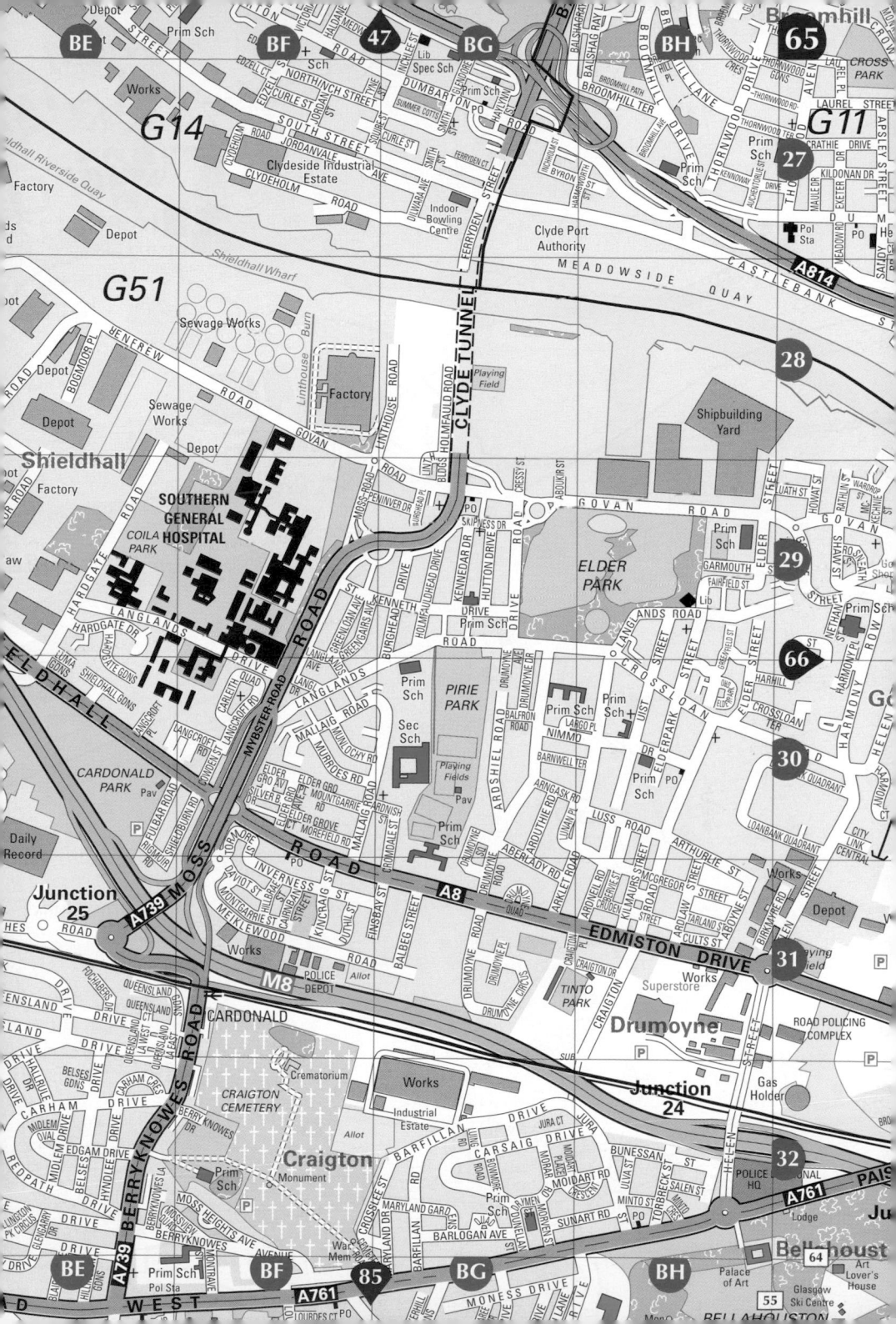

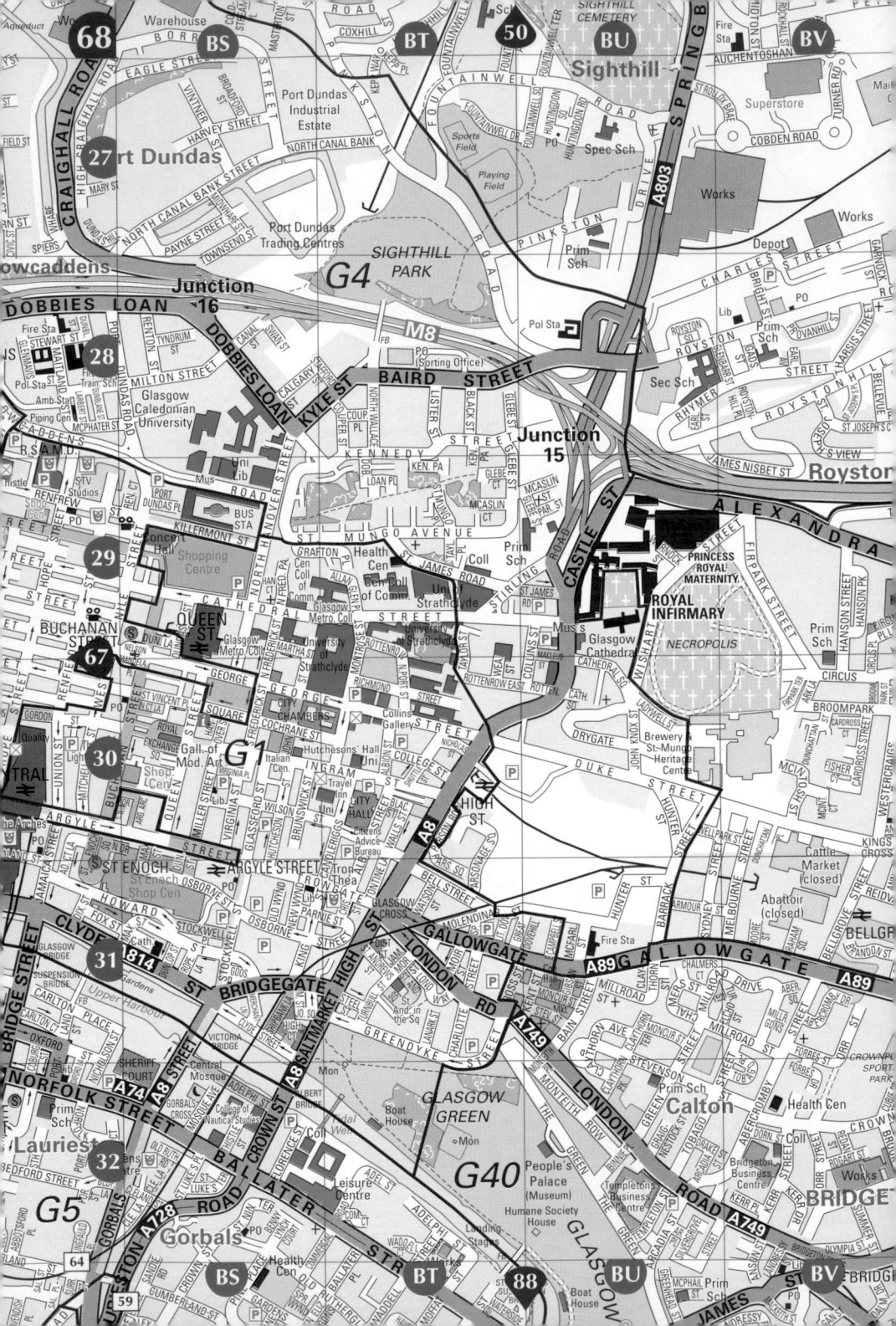

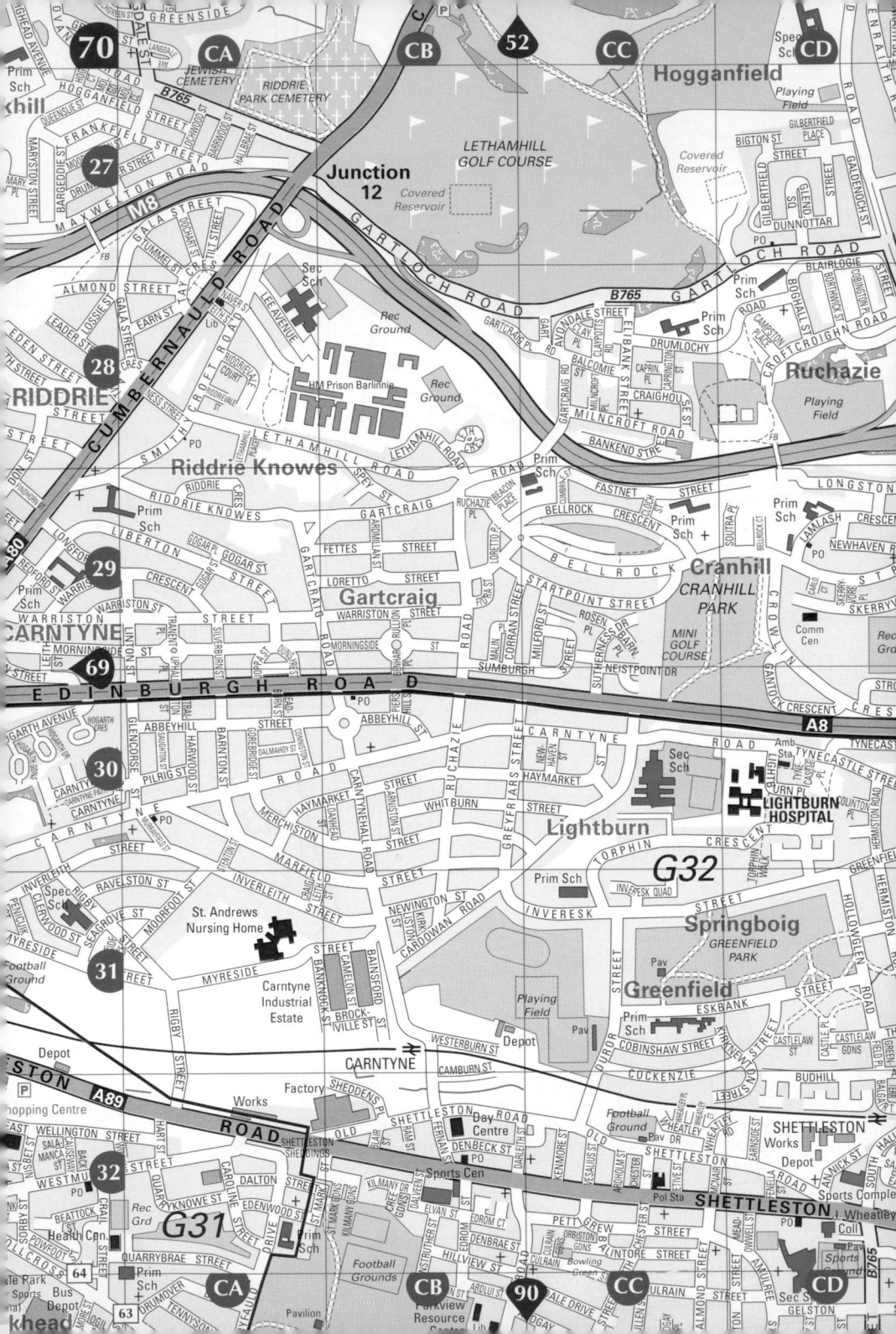

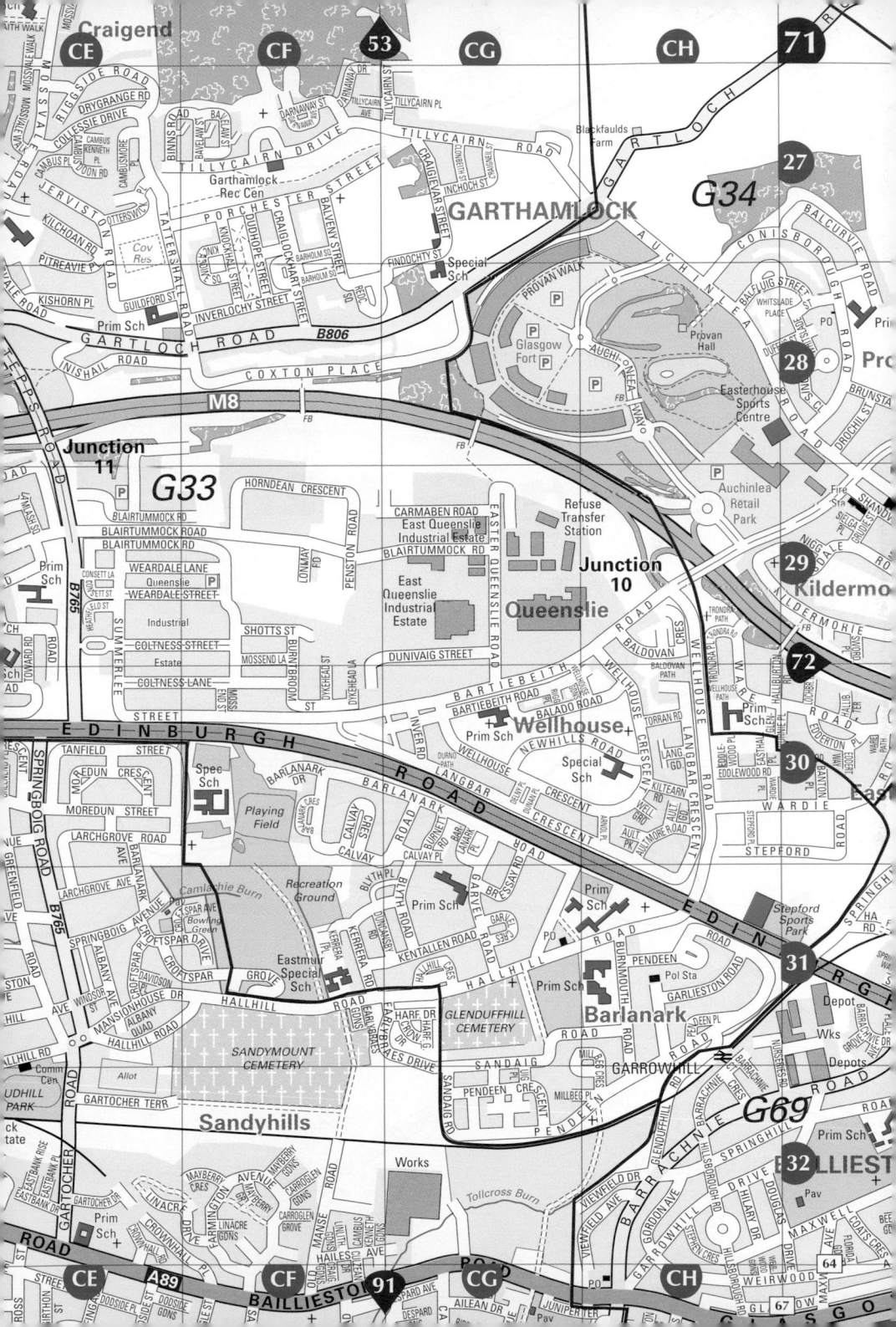

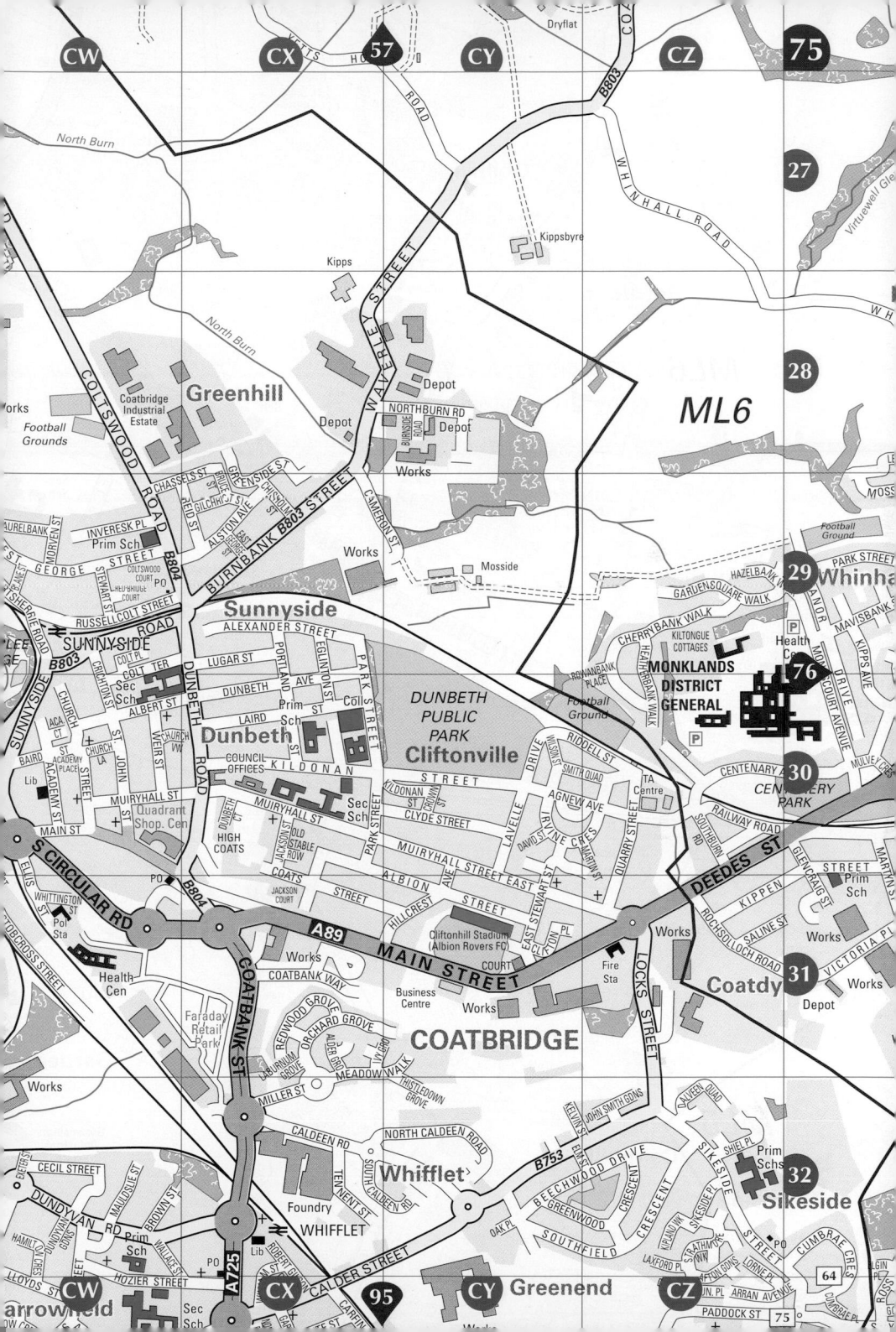

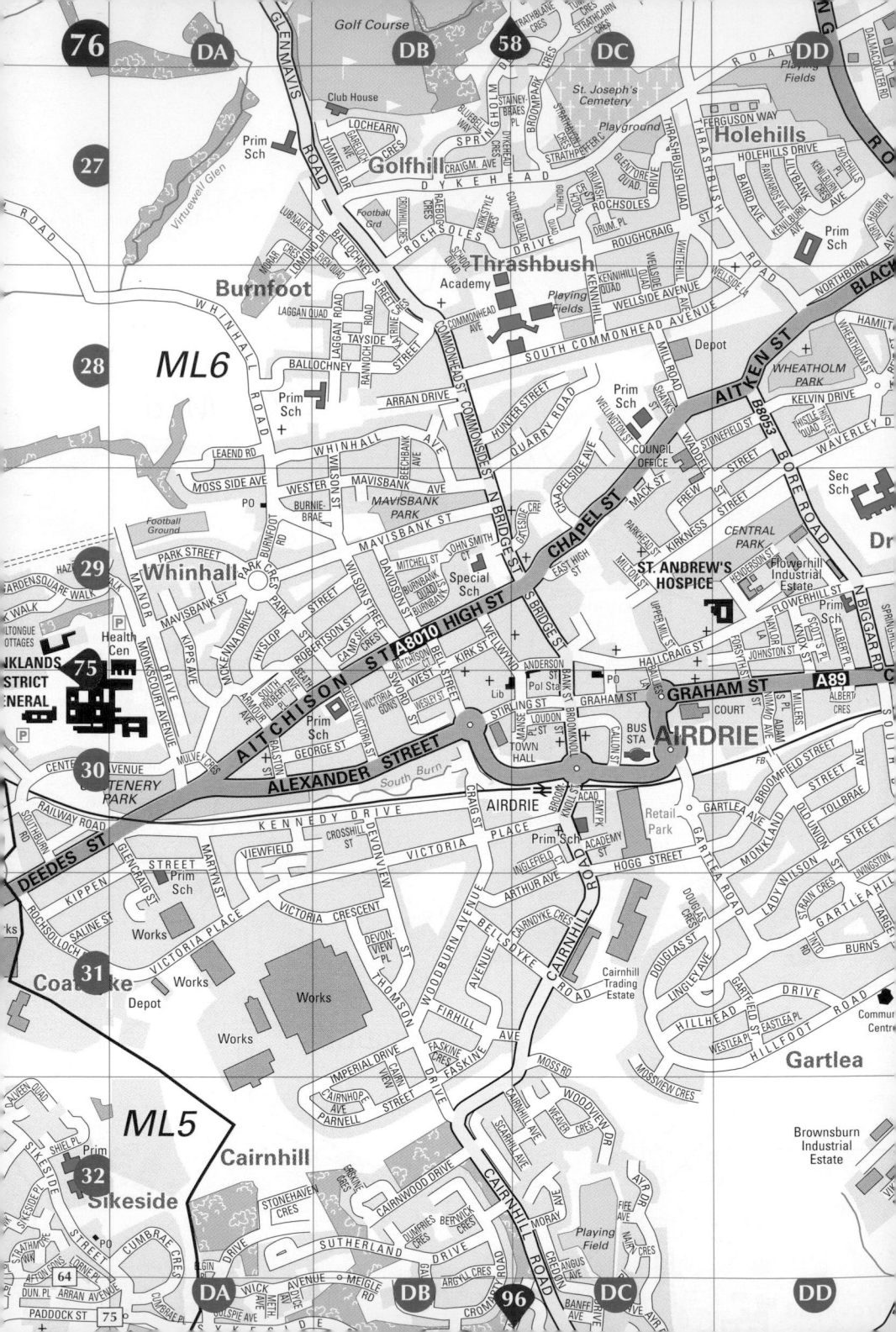

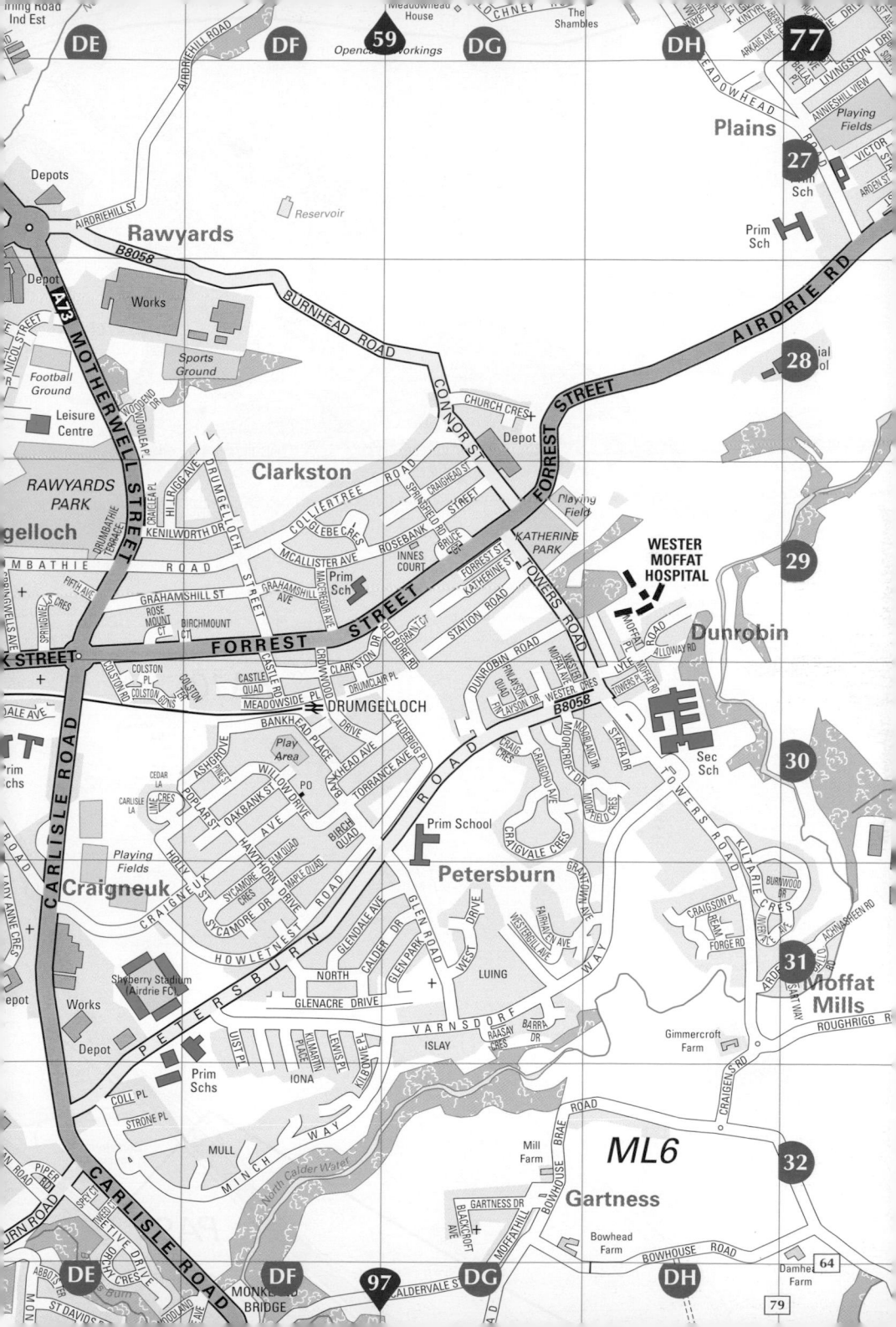

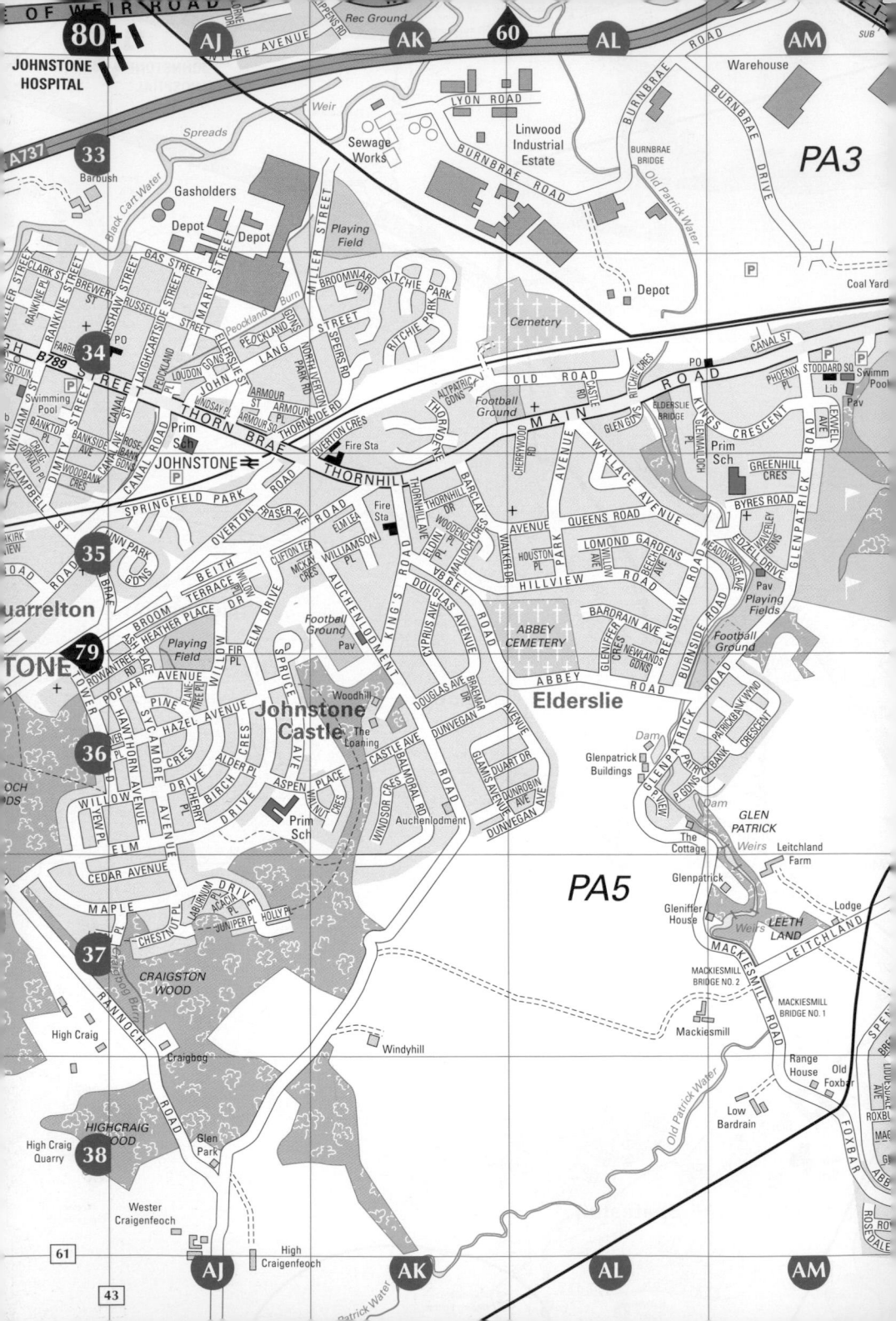

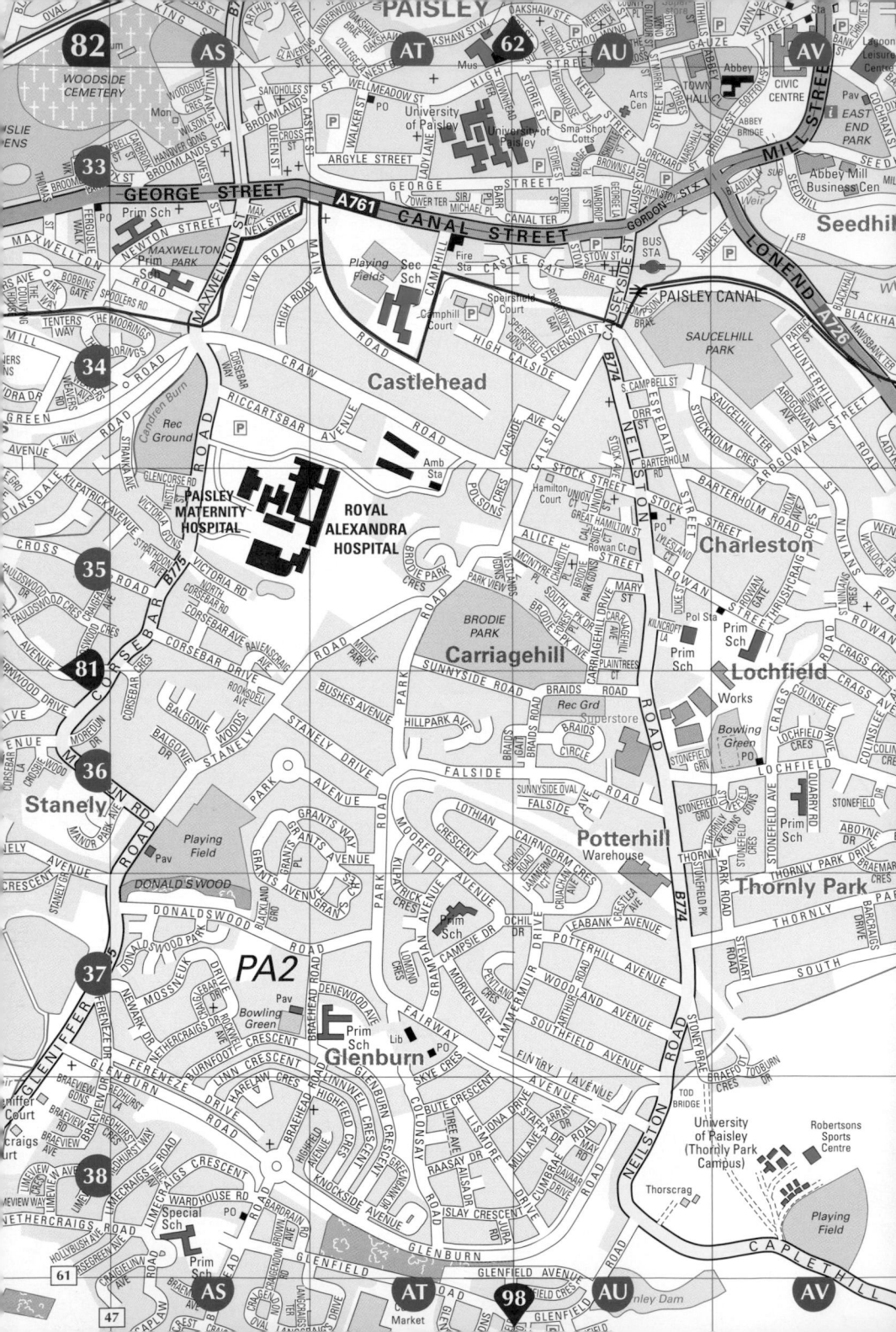

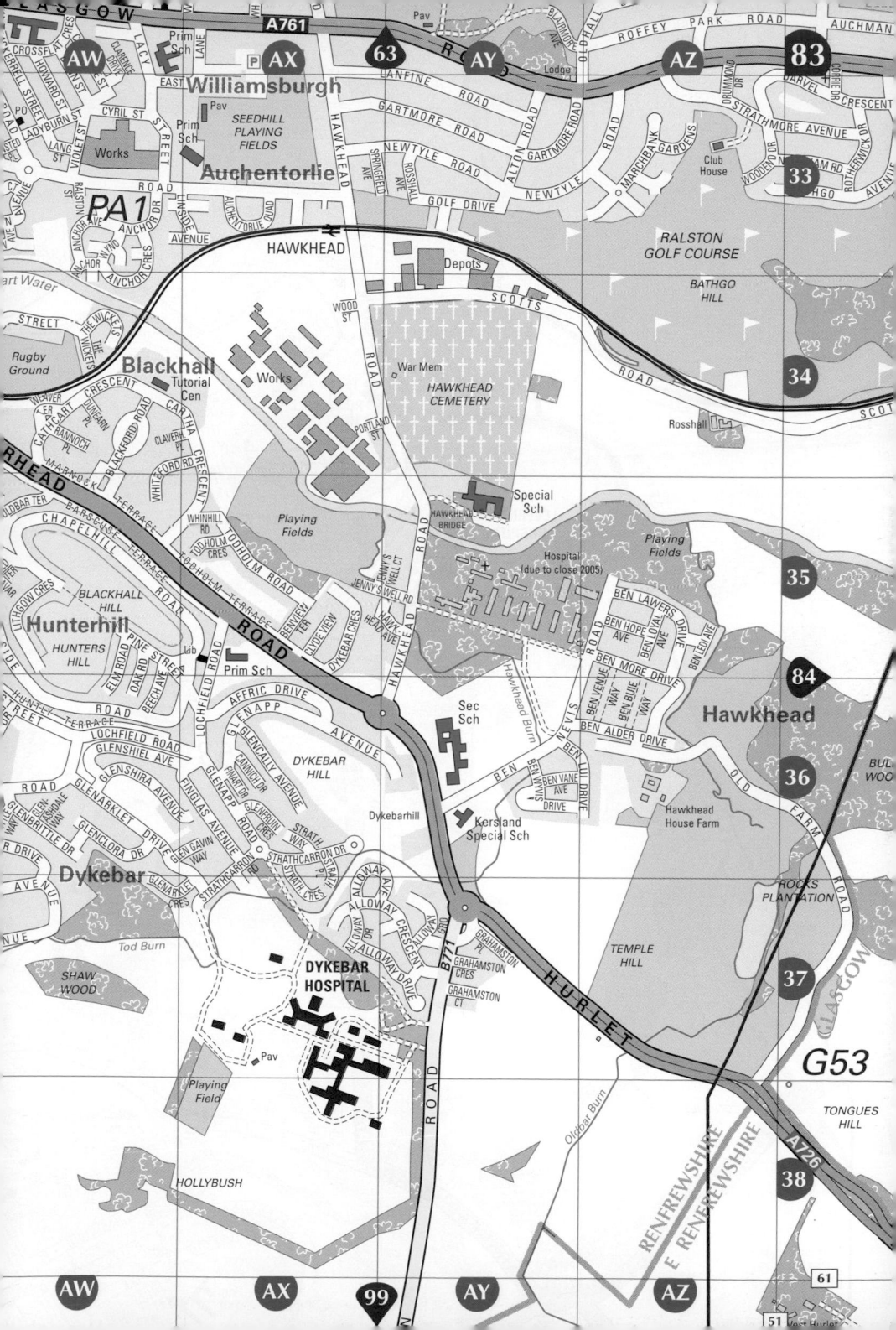

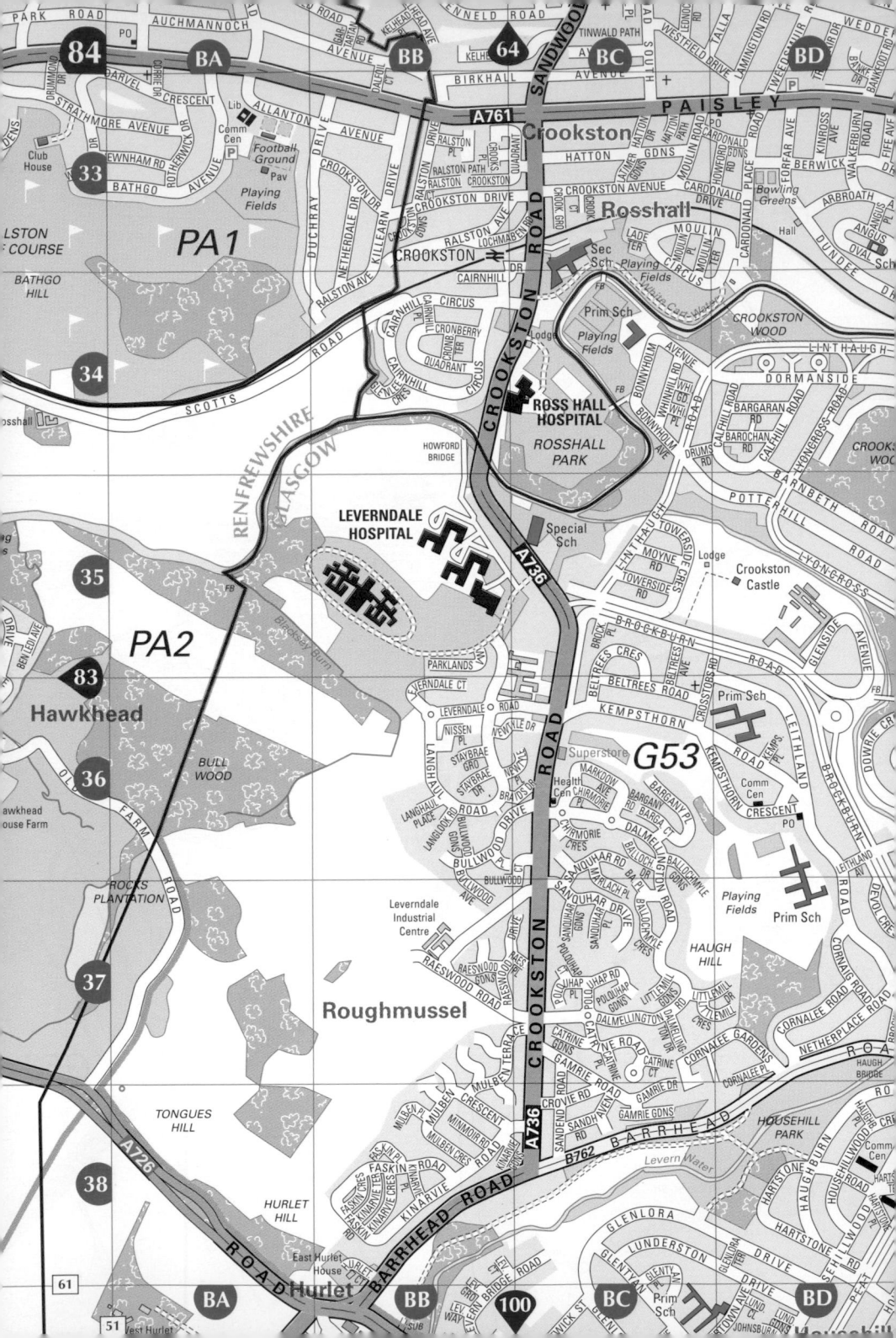

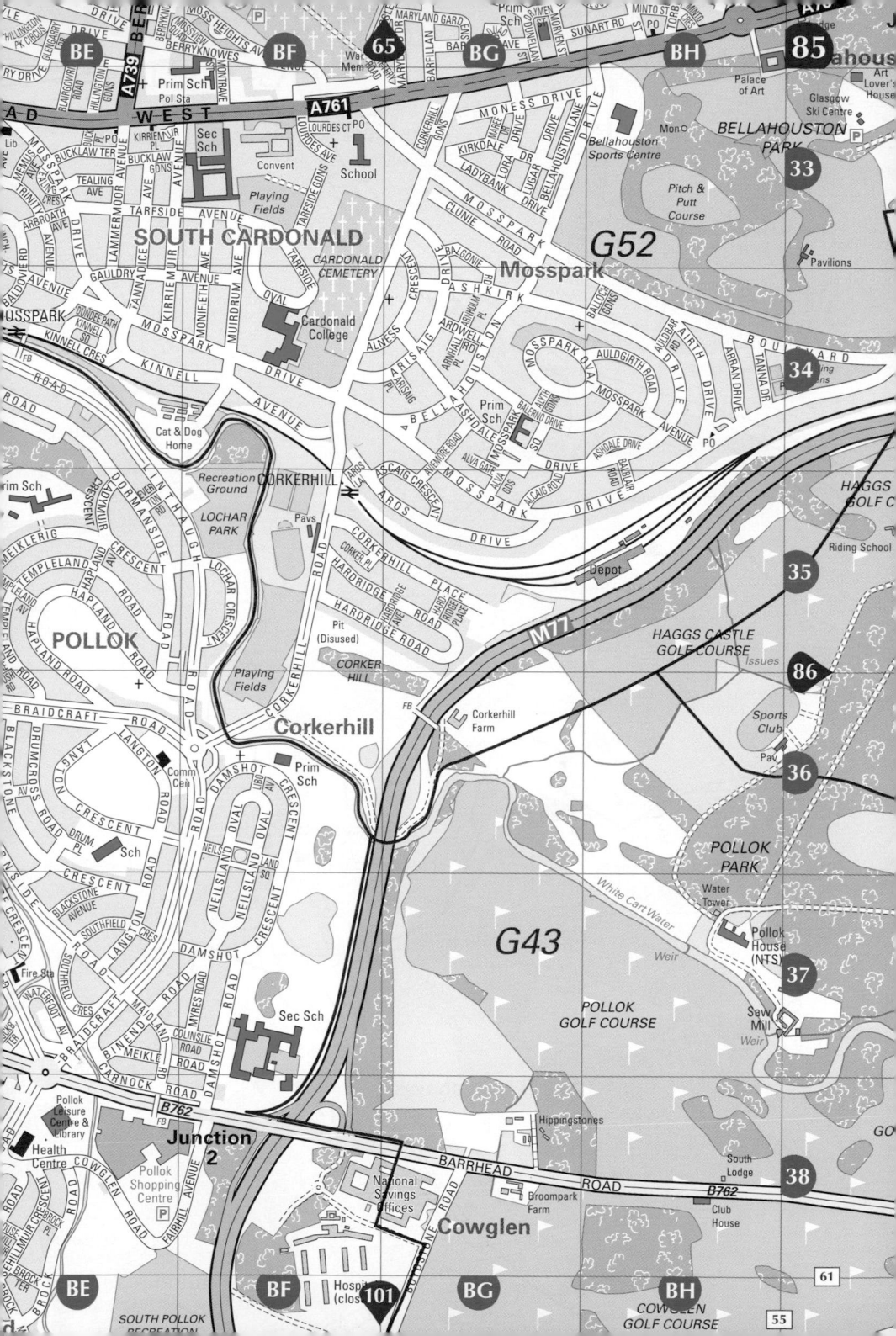

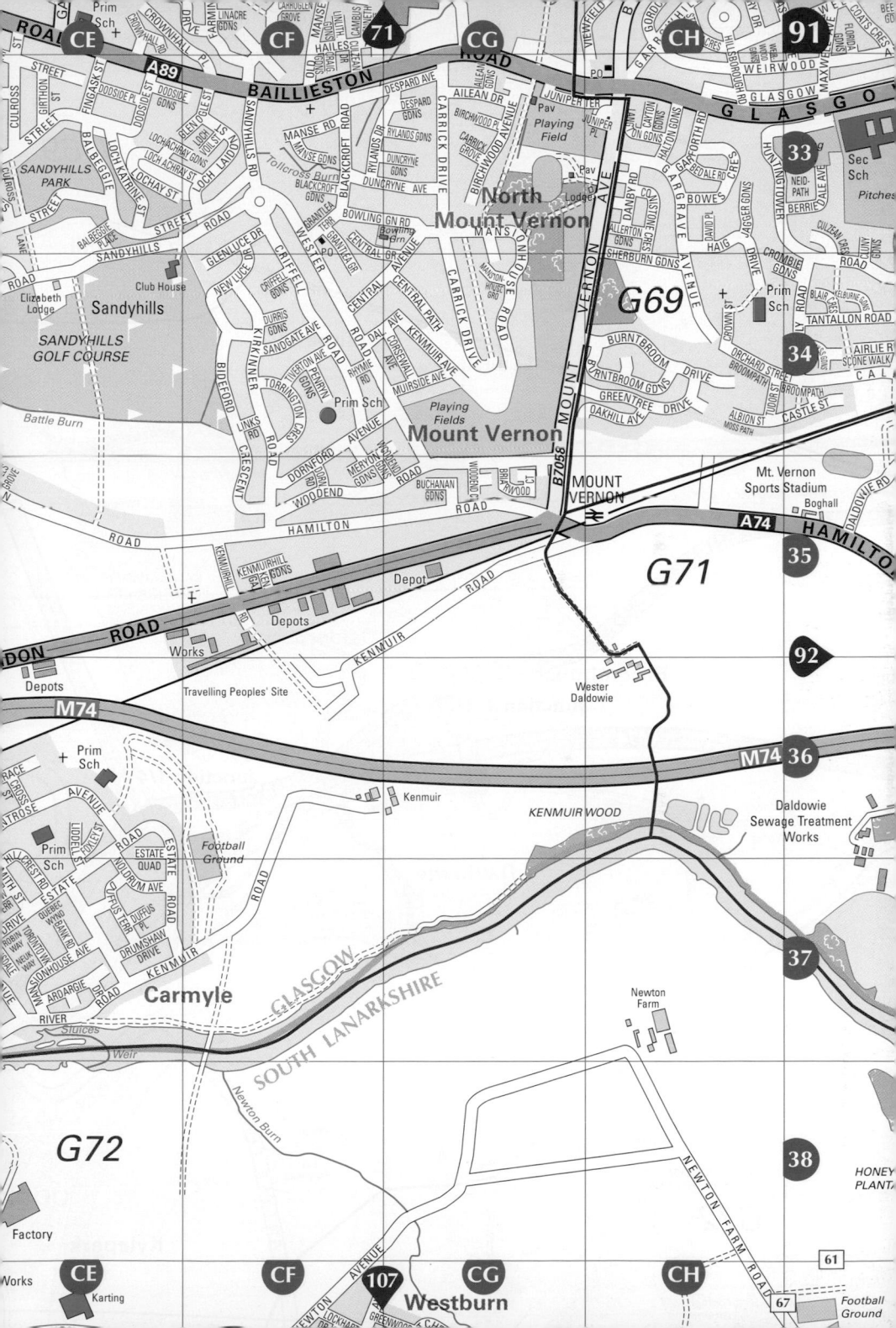

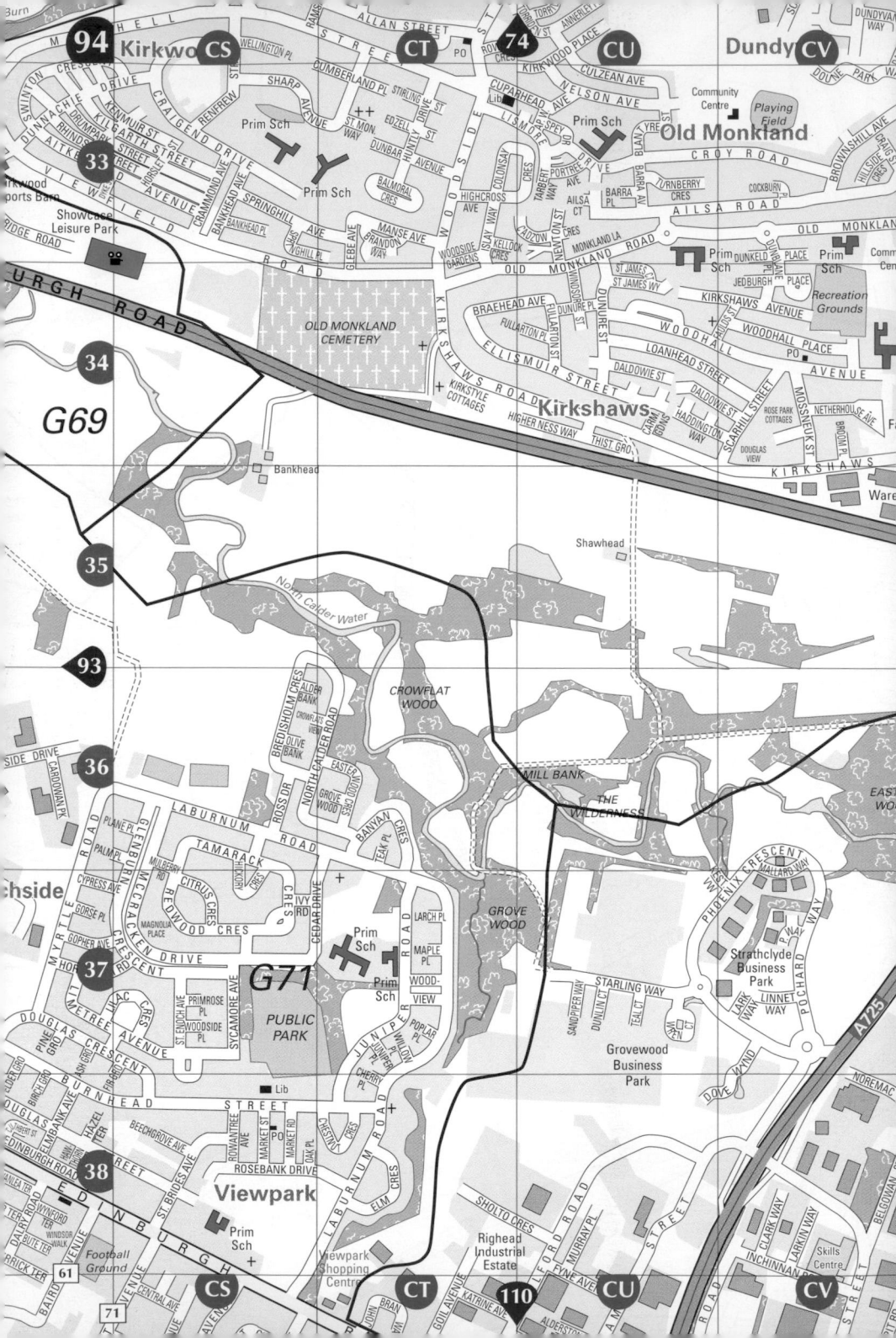

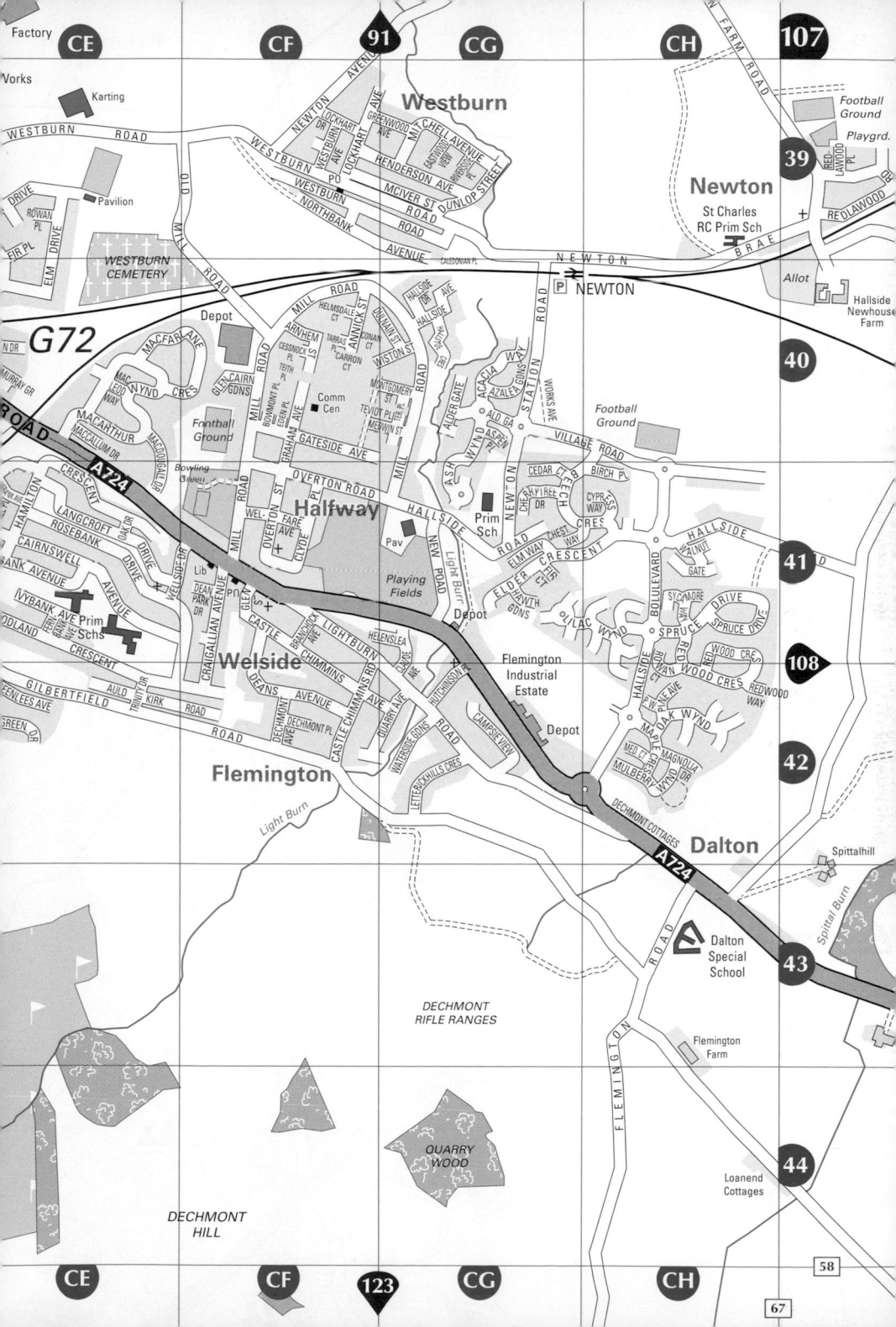

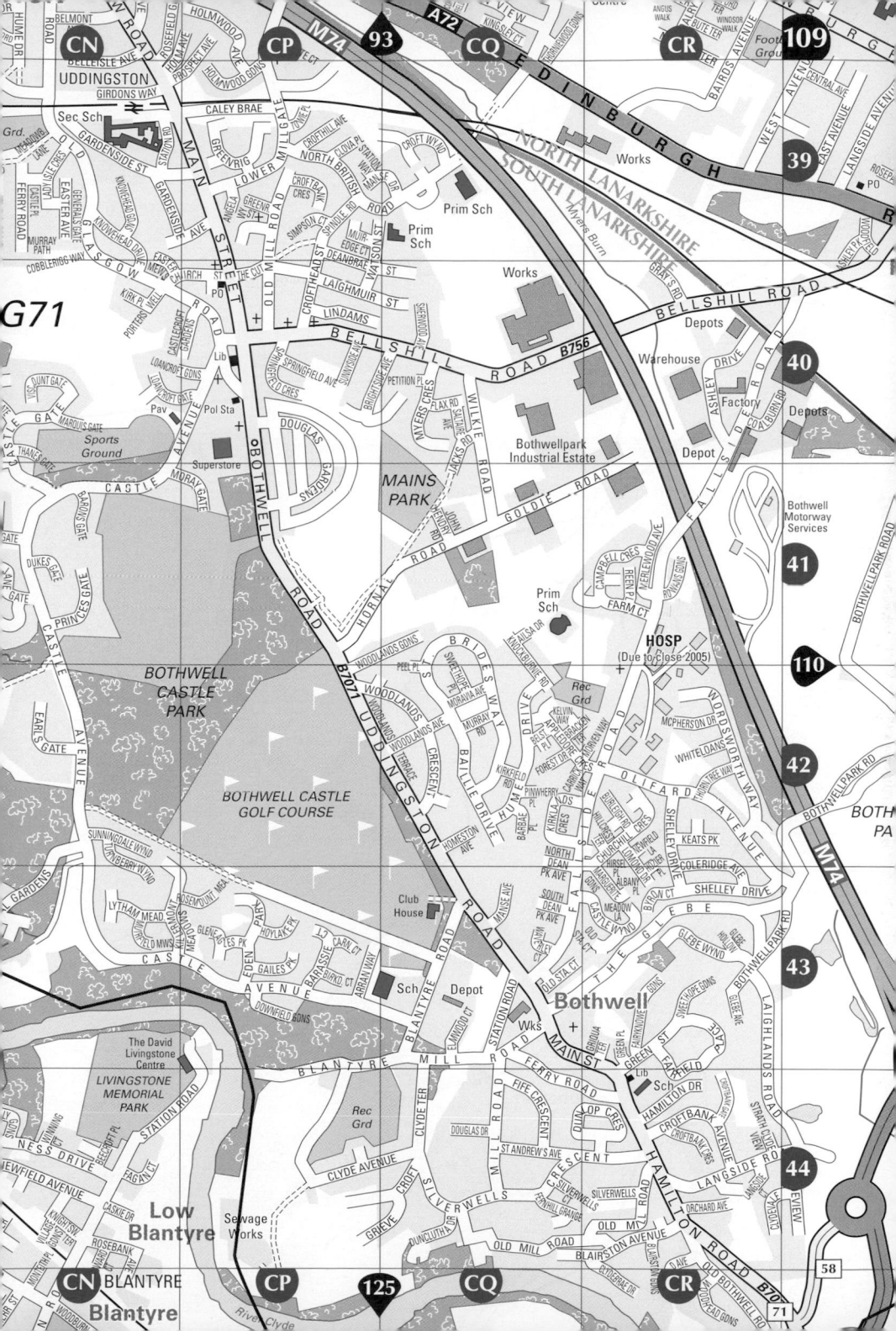

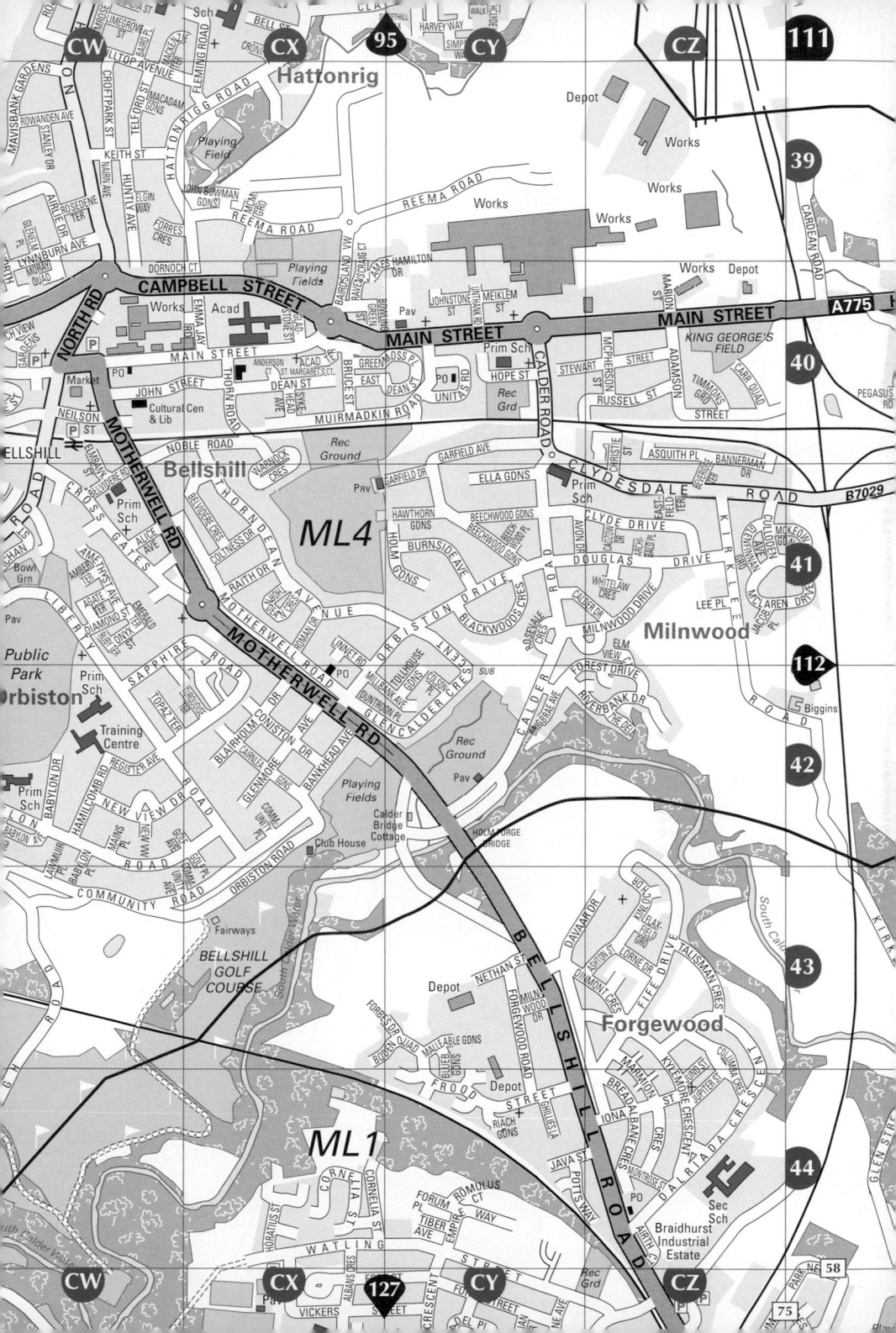

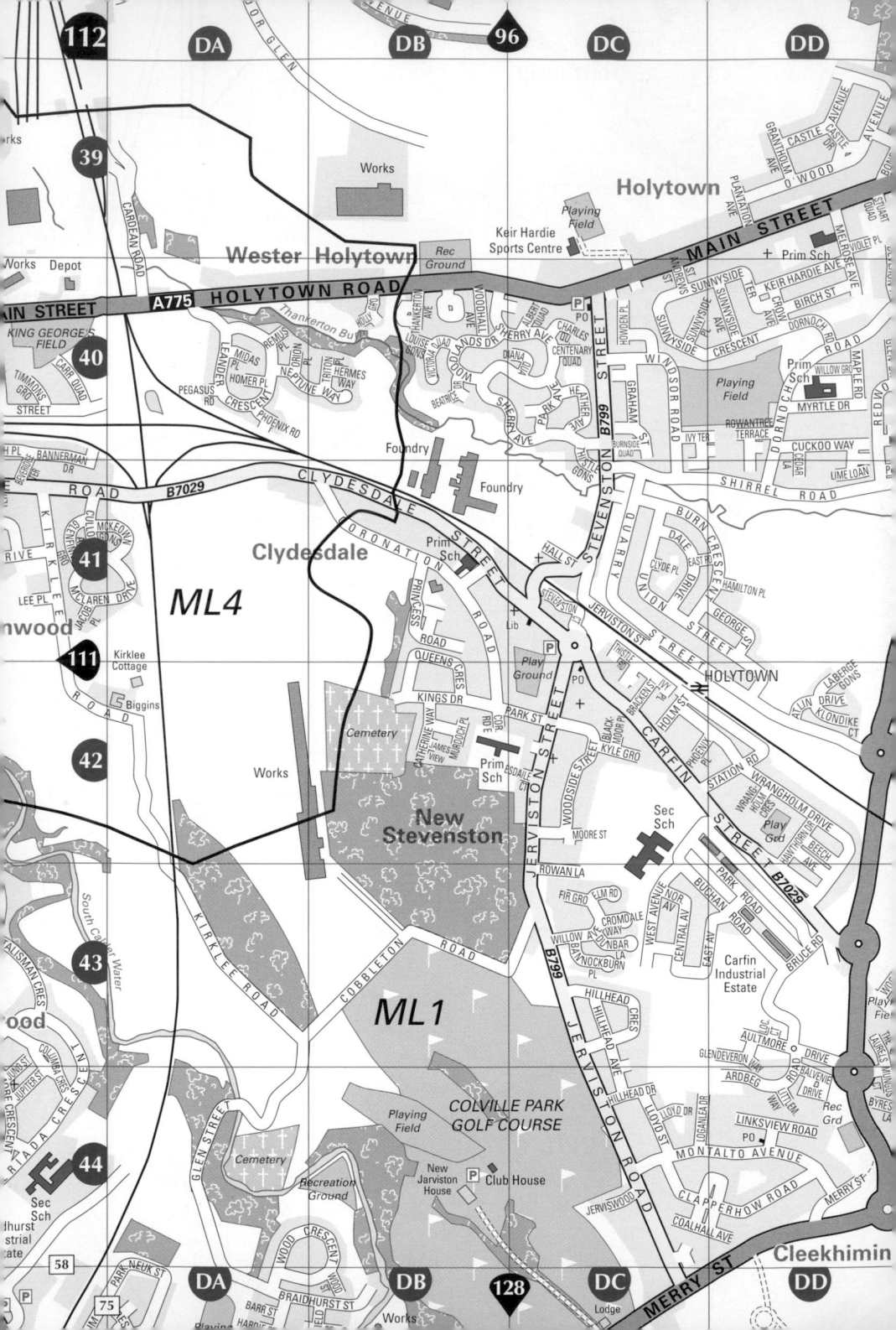

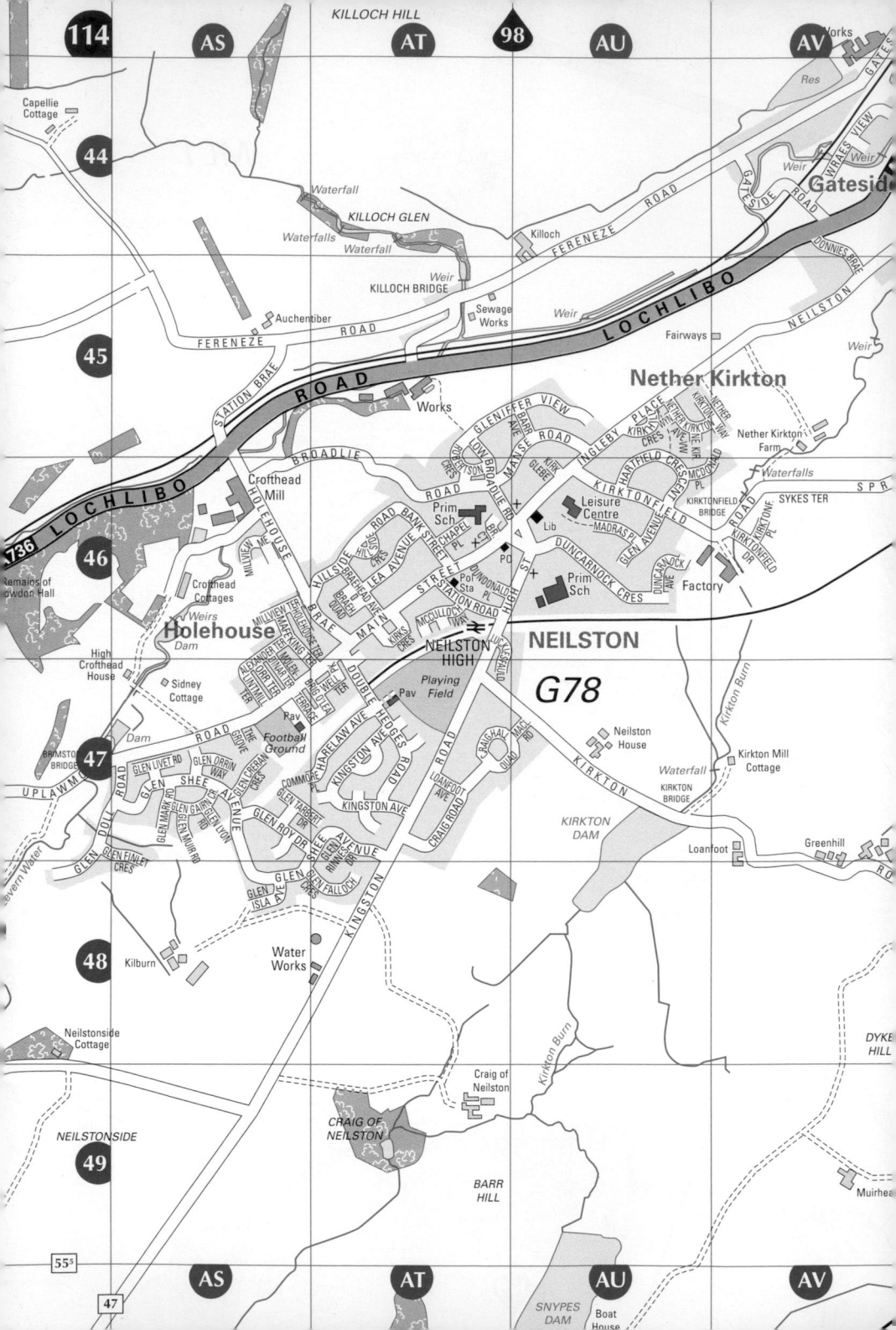

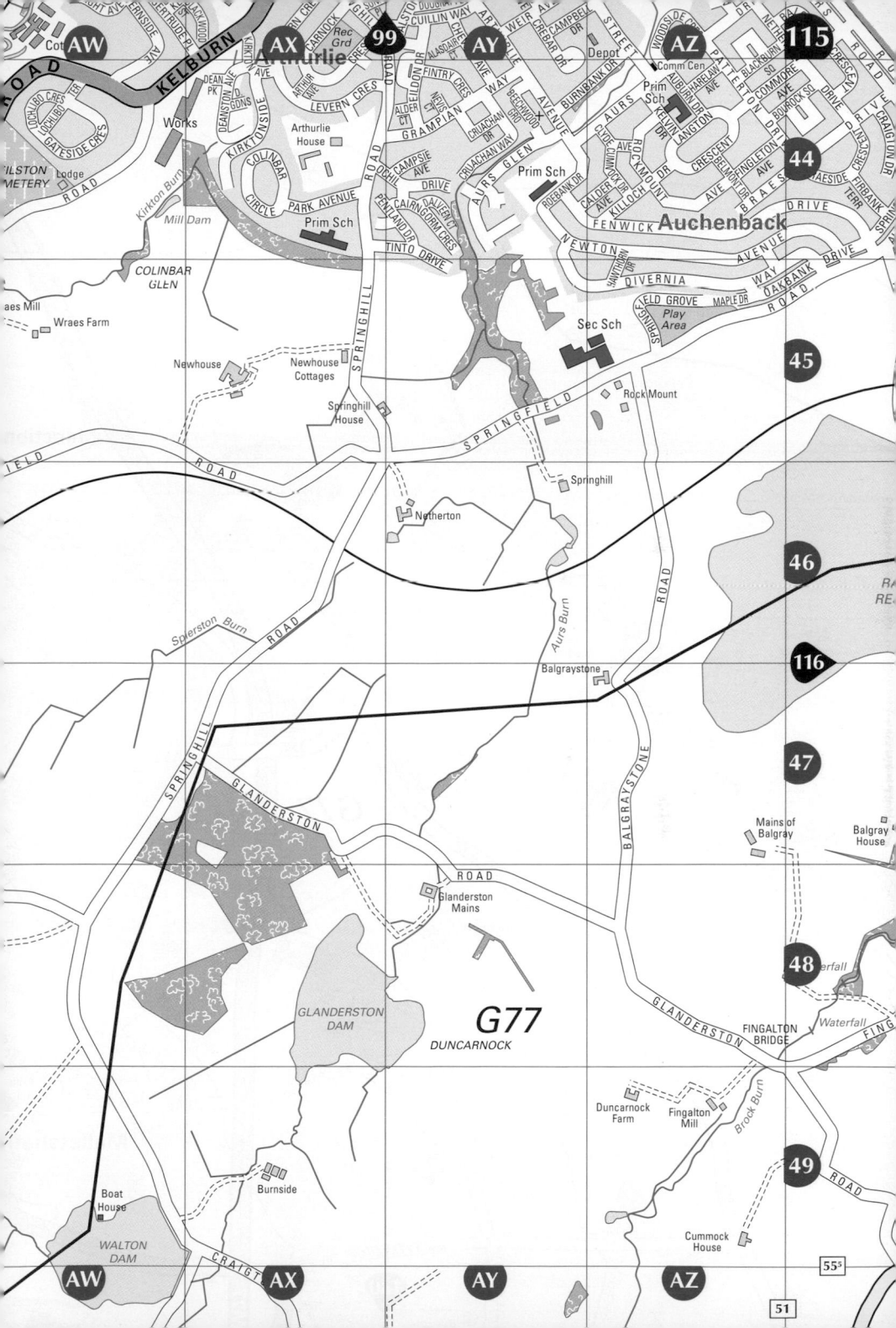

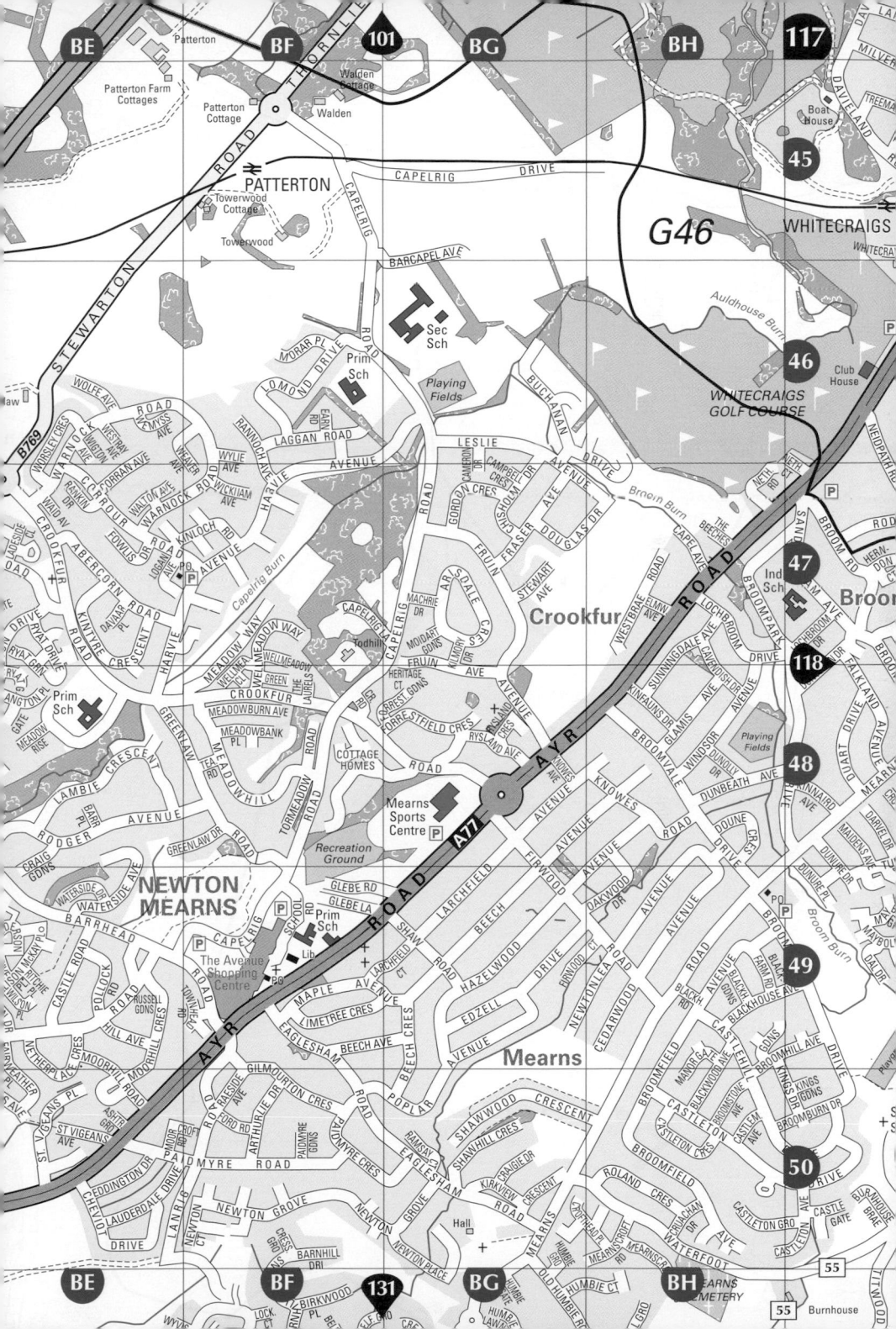

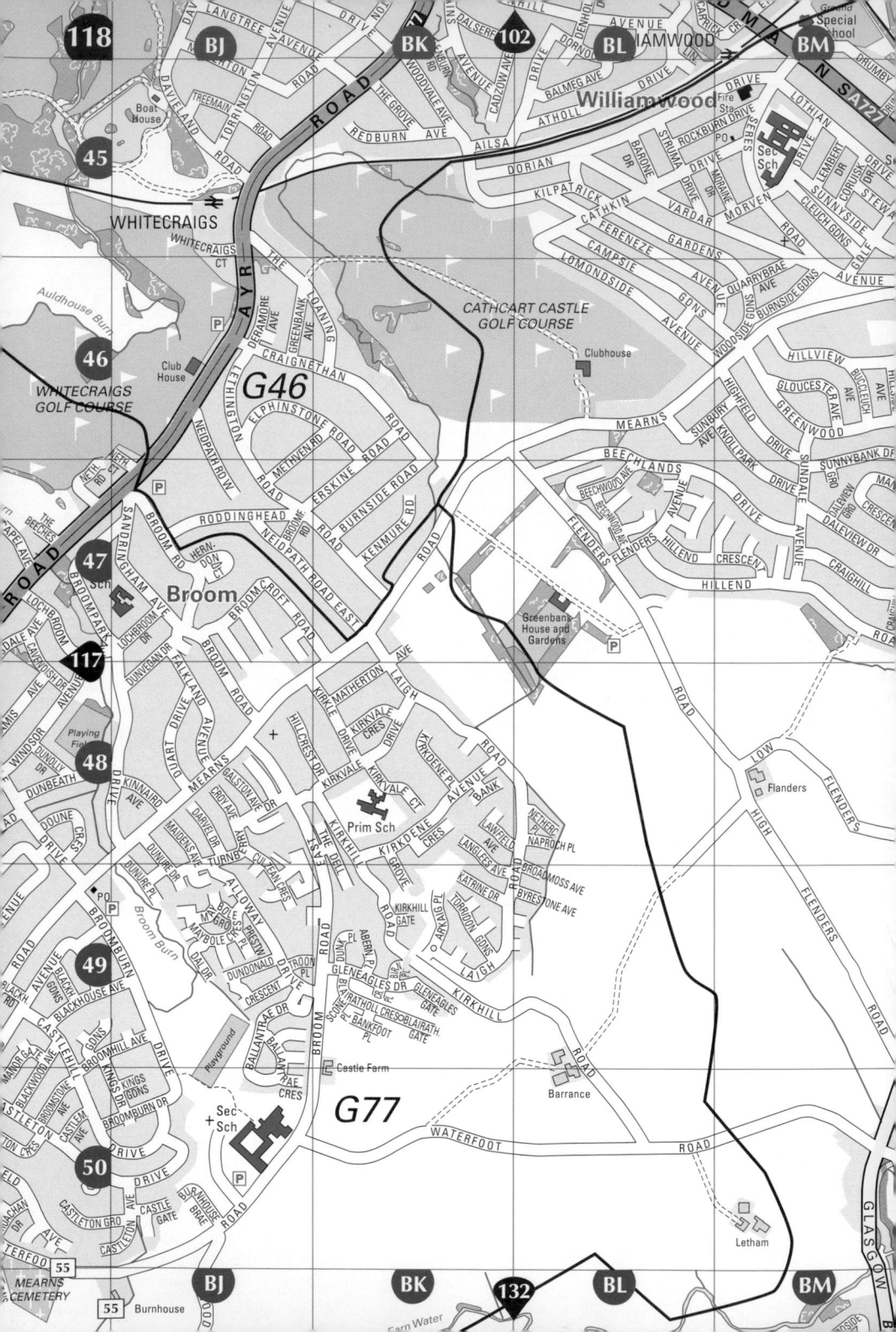

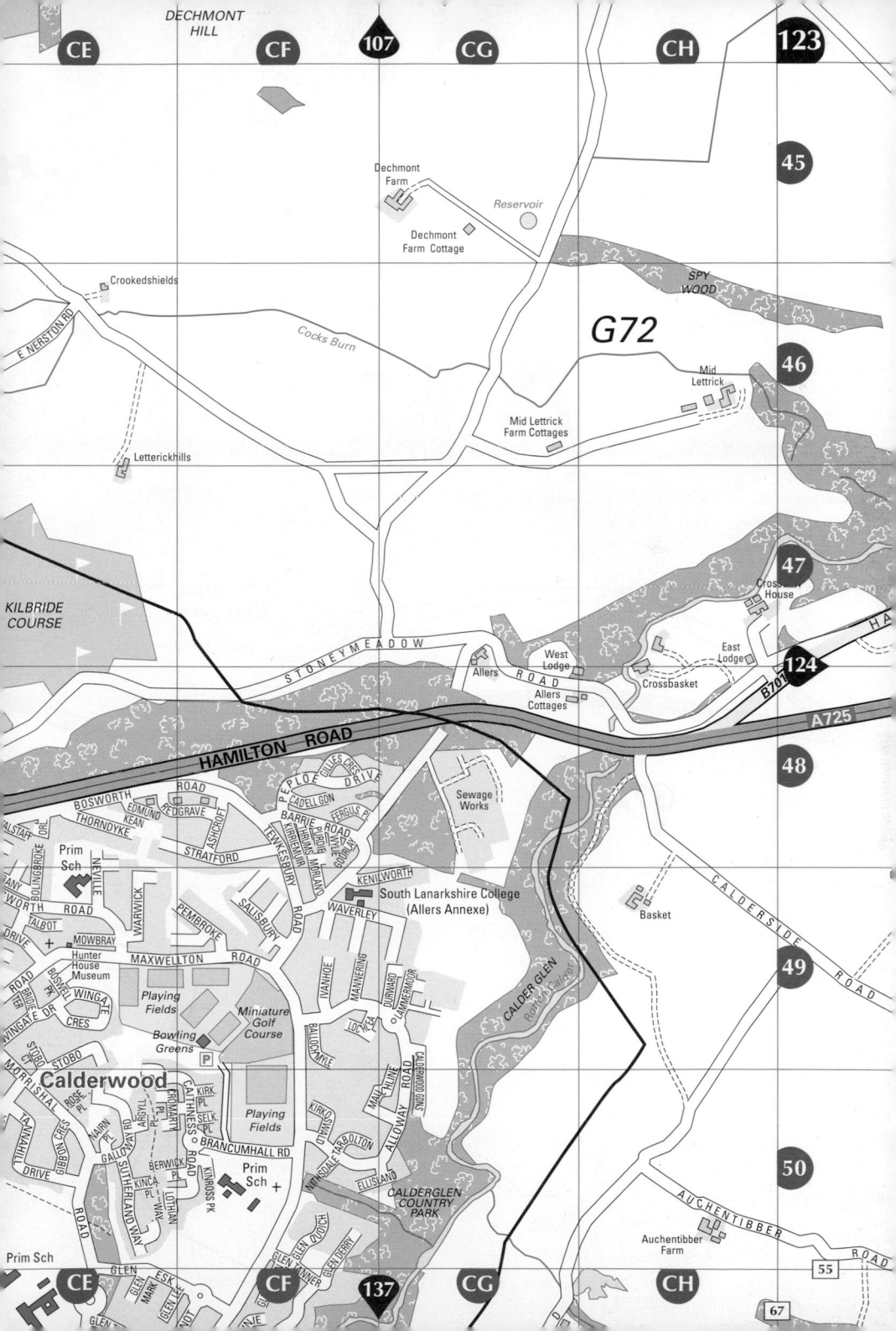

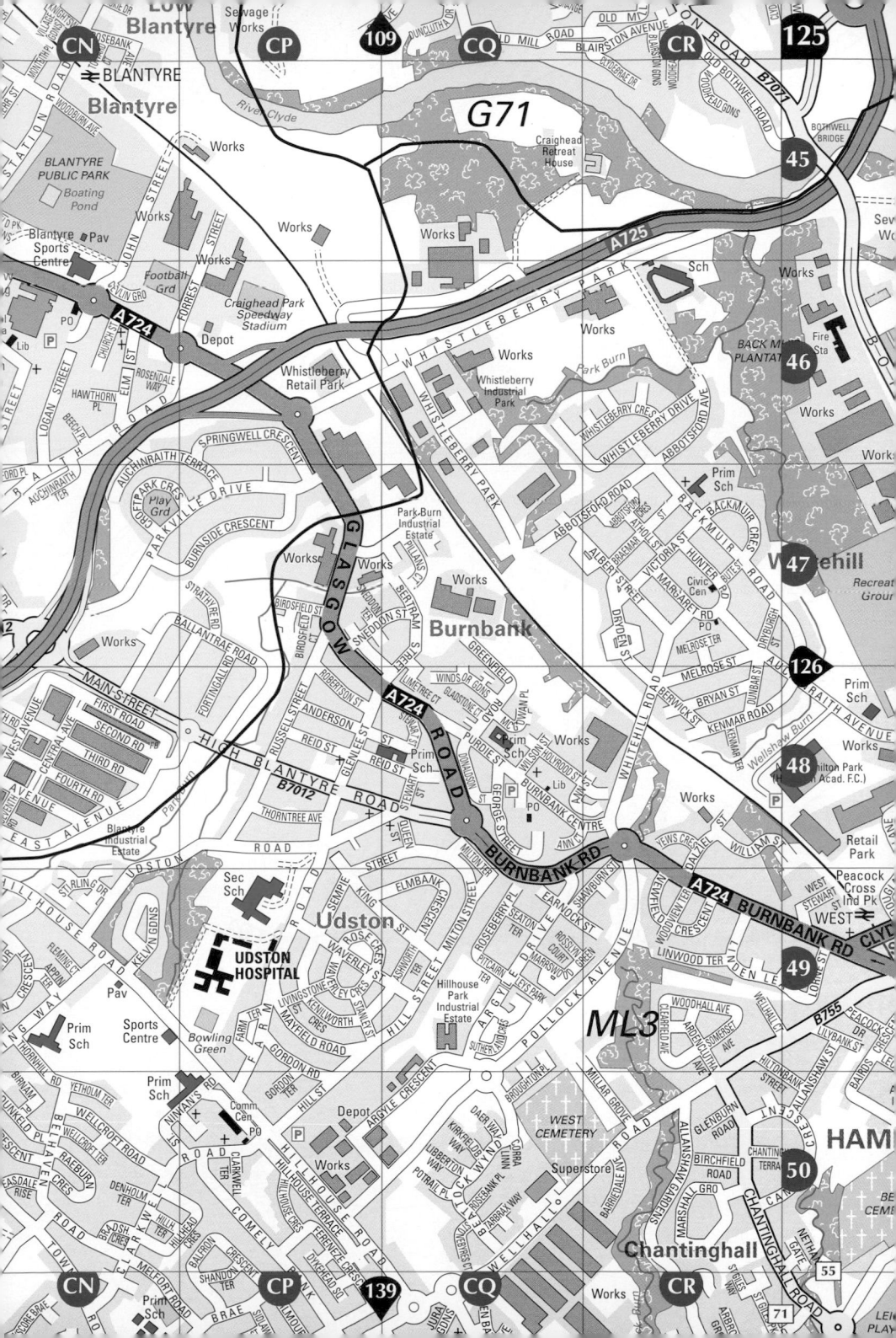

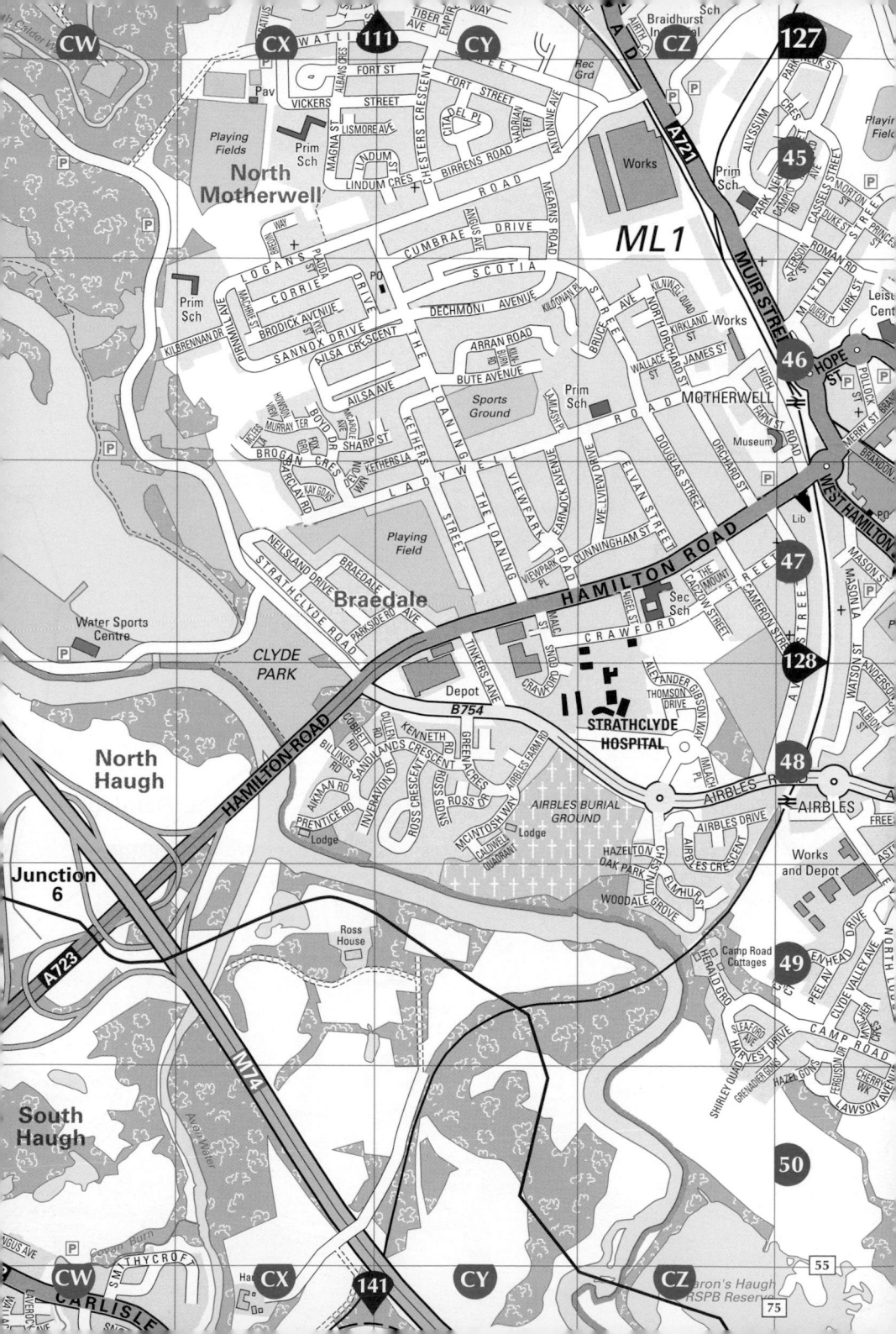

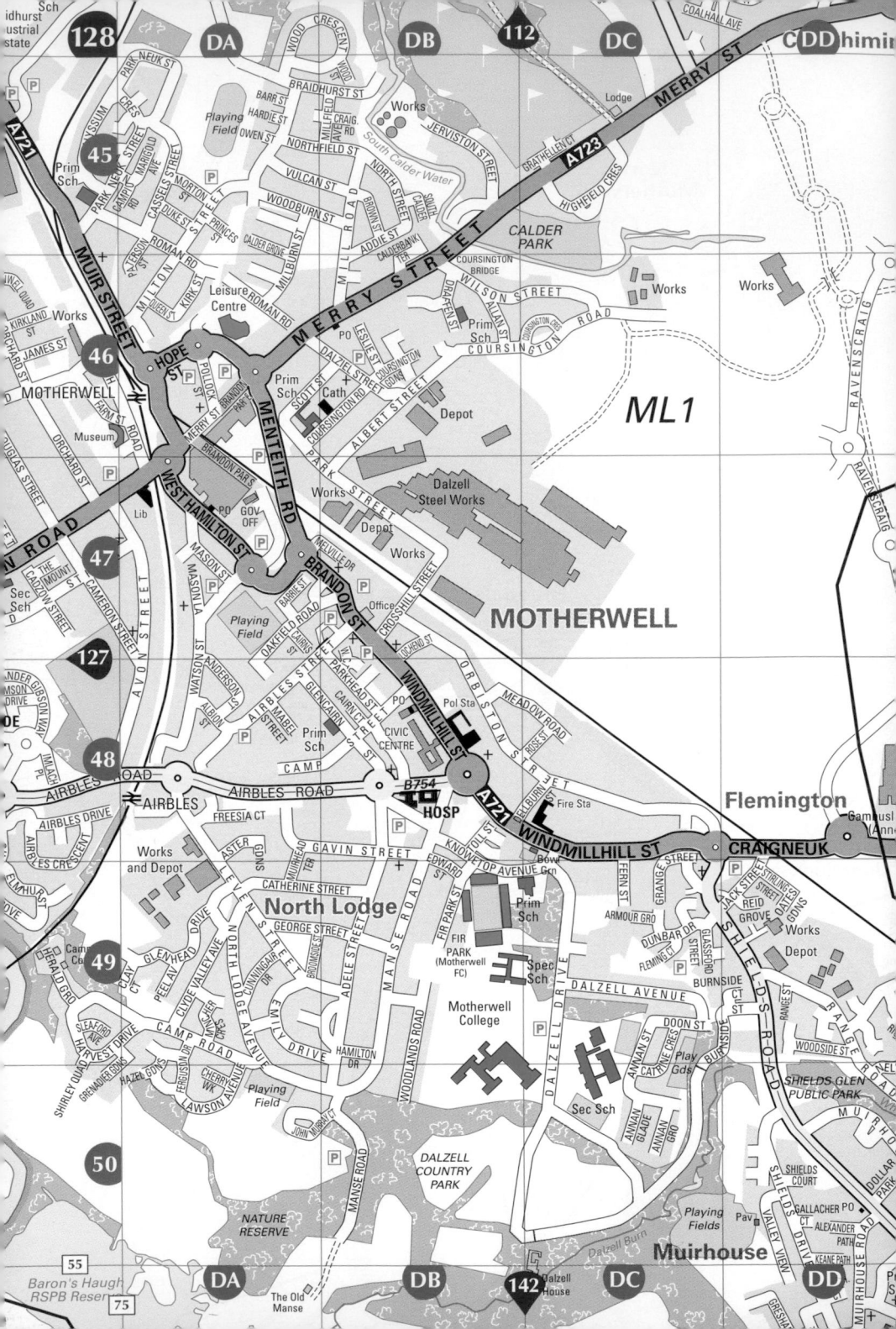

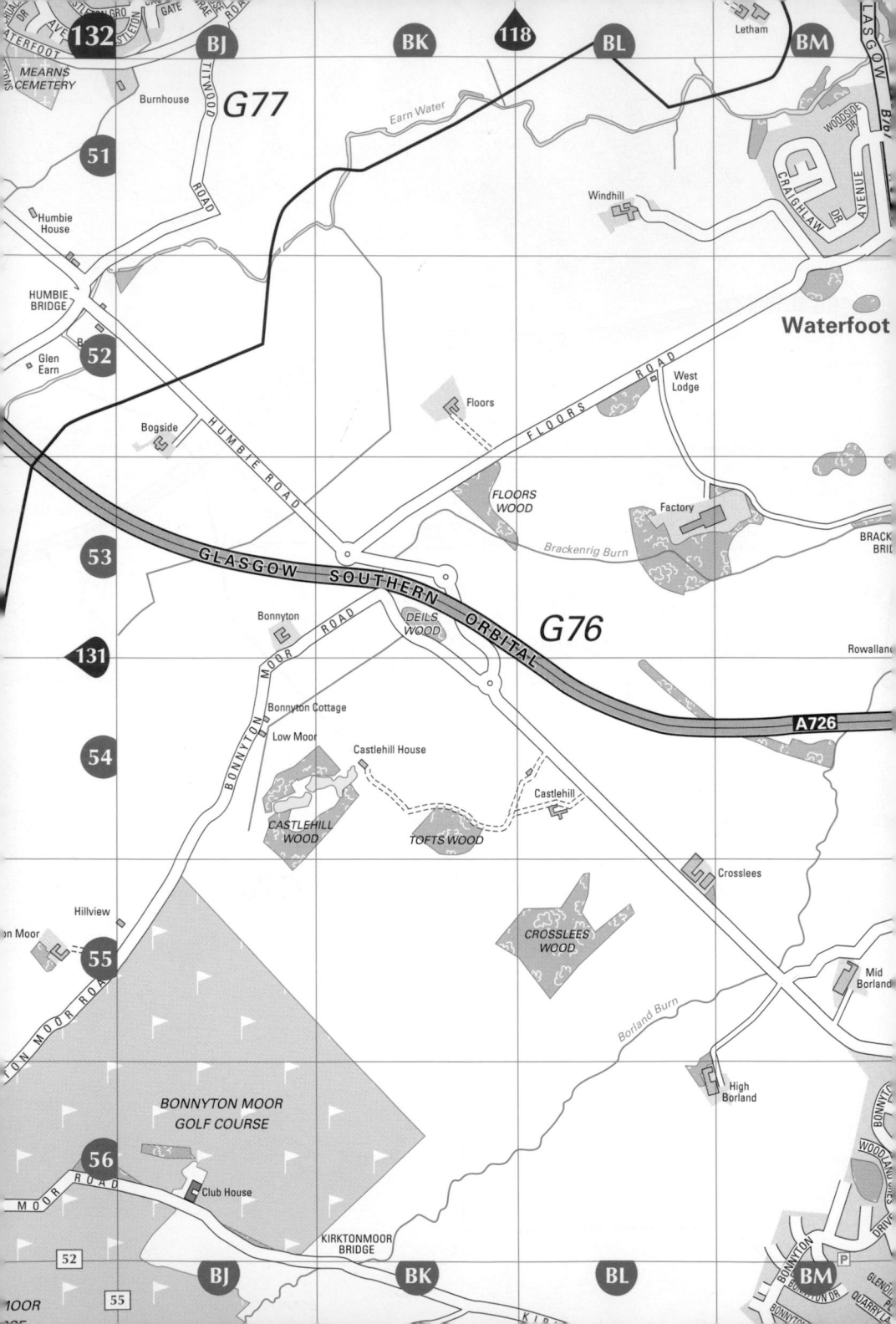

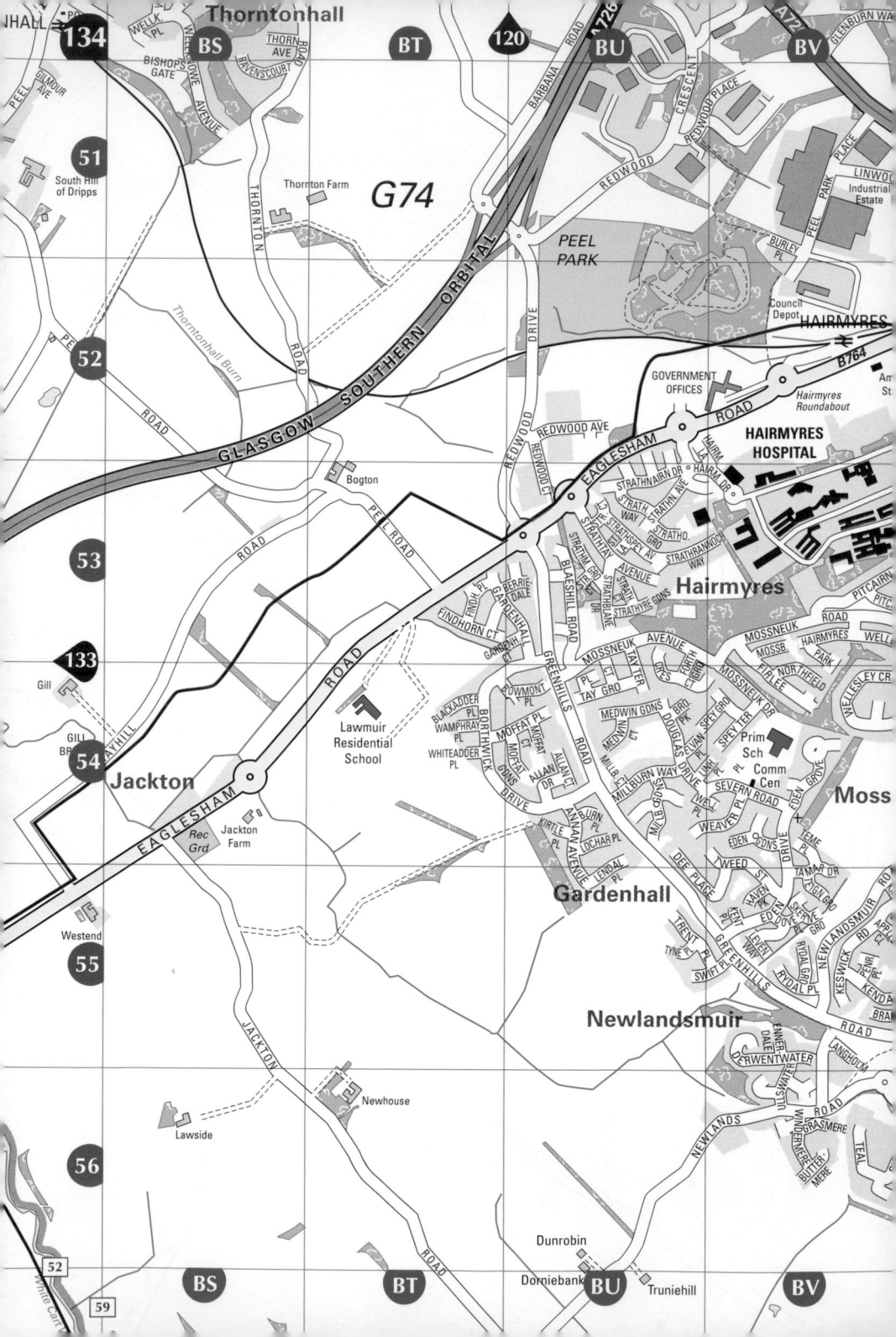

Thorntonhall

134

BS

BT

120

BU

BV

WELLK PL
BISHOPS GATE
WILLOWE AVENUE
THORN AVE
THORNTON ROAD
RAVENSCOURT
BARBANA ROAD
A726
A72?
GLENBURN WA

51

South Hill
of Dripps

Thornton Farm

G74

REDWOOD PLACE
REDWOOD
CRESCENT
PEEL
PARK
PLACE
BURLEY PL
LINWO
Industrial
Estate

GILMOUR AVE
PEEL

Thorntonhall Burn

THORNTON ROAD

Council
Depot

HAIRMYRES

52

PEEL ROAD

GLASGOW SOUTHERN ORBITAL

Bogton

REDWOOD DRIVE

REDWOOD AVE

REDWOOD CT

GOVERNMENT
OFFICES

EAGLESHAM ROAD

Hairmyres
Roundabout

B764
Am
St

**HAIRMYRES
HOSPITAL**

STRATHNAIRN DR
STRATHN AVE
STRATHD.
STRATHSEY AV
STRATH WAY
STRATH GRO
STRATHRANNOCH WAY

Hairmyres

53

PEEL ROAD

ROAD

FINDHORN CT

HINDI
BERRIE-DALE
GARRENHALL PL
GAMBHIL
PL
POWMONT PL
BLAESHILL ROAD
GREENHILLS
MOSSNEUK
PL
TAY TER
TAY GRO
FIRTH
TREE
MOSSNEUK AVENUE
MOSSNEUK DR
MOSS B.
PITCAIRN
PITC.
ROAD
HAIRMYRES
PARK
WELLE
FIRLEE
MOSSNEUK DR
NORTHFIELD
WELLESLEY CR

133

Gill

GILL BR

HAYHILL

Lawmuir
Residential
School

BLACKADDER PL
WAMPHRAY PL
WHITEADDER PL
BORTHWICK PL
MOFFAT PL
MOFFAT CT
ALLAN CT
ALLAN DR
MEDWIN GDNS
MEDWIN PL
BRO.
PK.
DOUGLAS DRIVE
SPEY GRO
EVAN
LINDI
SPEY TER
GROVE
Prim
Sch
Comm
Cen

54

Jackton

EAGLESHAM ROAD

Rec
Grd

Jackton
Farm

KIRTLE PL
ANNAN AVENUE
BURN PL
LOCHAR PL
KENT PL
LENDAL PL
MILLBURN WAY
MILL B.
WAL
WEAVER PL
EDEN GDNS
SEVERN ROAD
EDEN DR
DEE PLACE
WEED
TAMAR DR
TEME

Moss

Gardenhall

HAVEN PL
SKENE
EDE
GROVE
NEWLANDSMUIR
RD
SHIN GRO
KESWICK RD
RIDAL GRO

55

Westend

JACKTON

TRENT PL
TYNE PL
SWIFT PL
GREENHILLS
RYDAL PL
VIDAL GRO
KENDA

Newlandsmuir

56

Newhouse

Lawside

NEWLANDS ROAD
FINNER DALE
DERWENTWATER
ULSTWATER
WINDERMERE
BUTTER-MERE
LANGHOLM
GRASMERE
TEAL
ROAD

52

White Cart

59

Dunrobin

Dorniebank

BS

BT

BU

Truniehill

BV

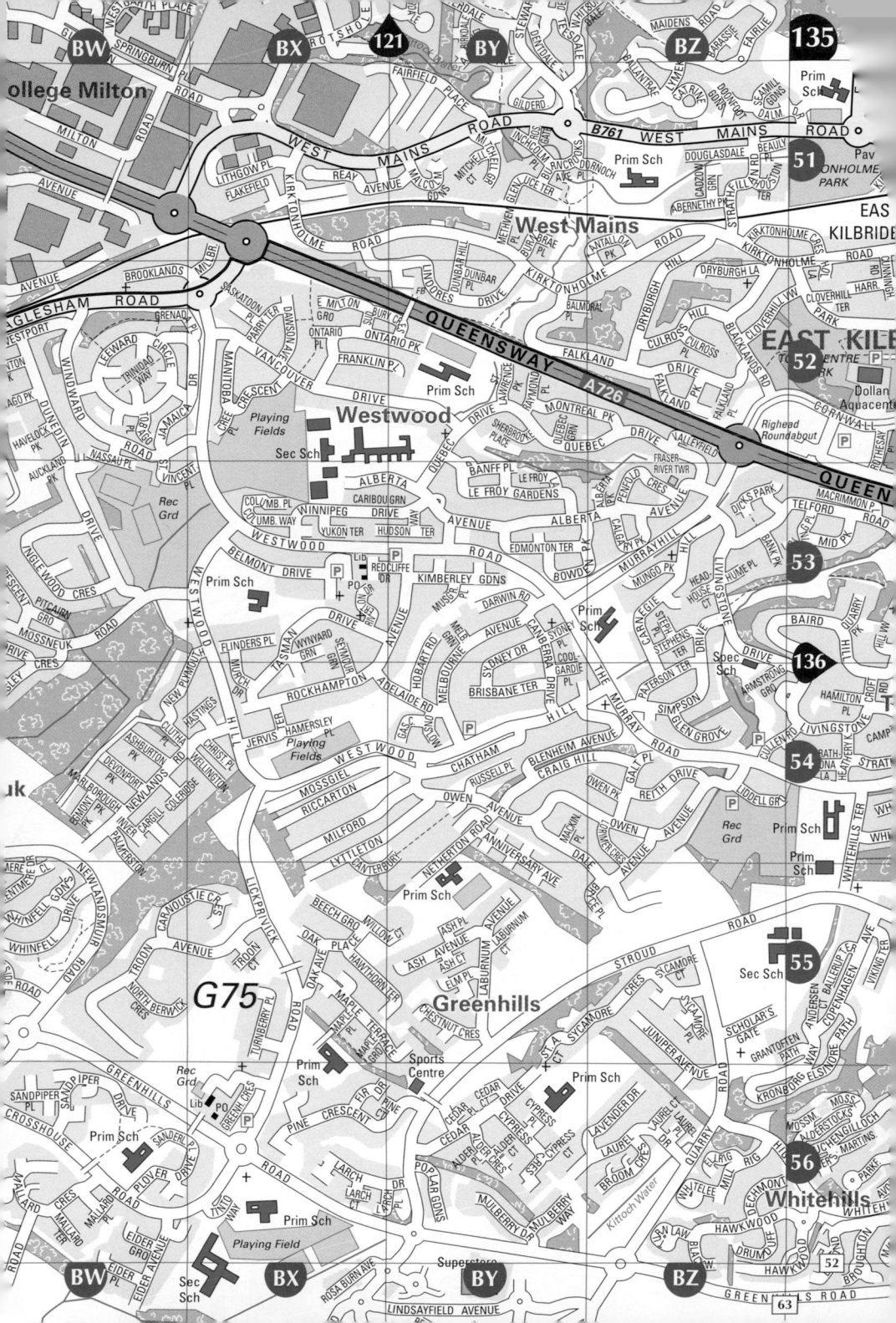

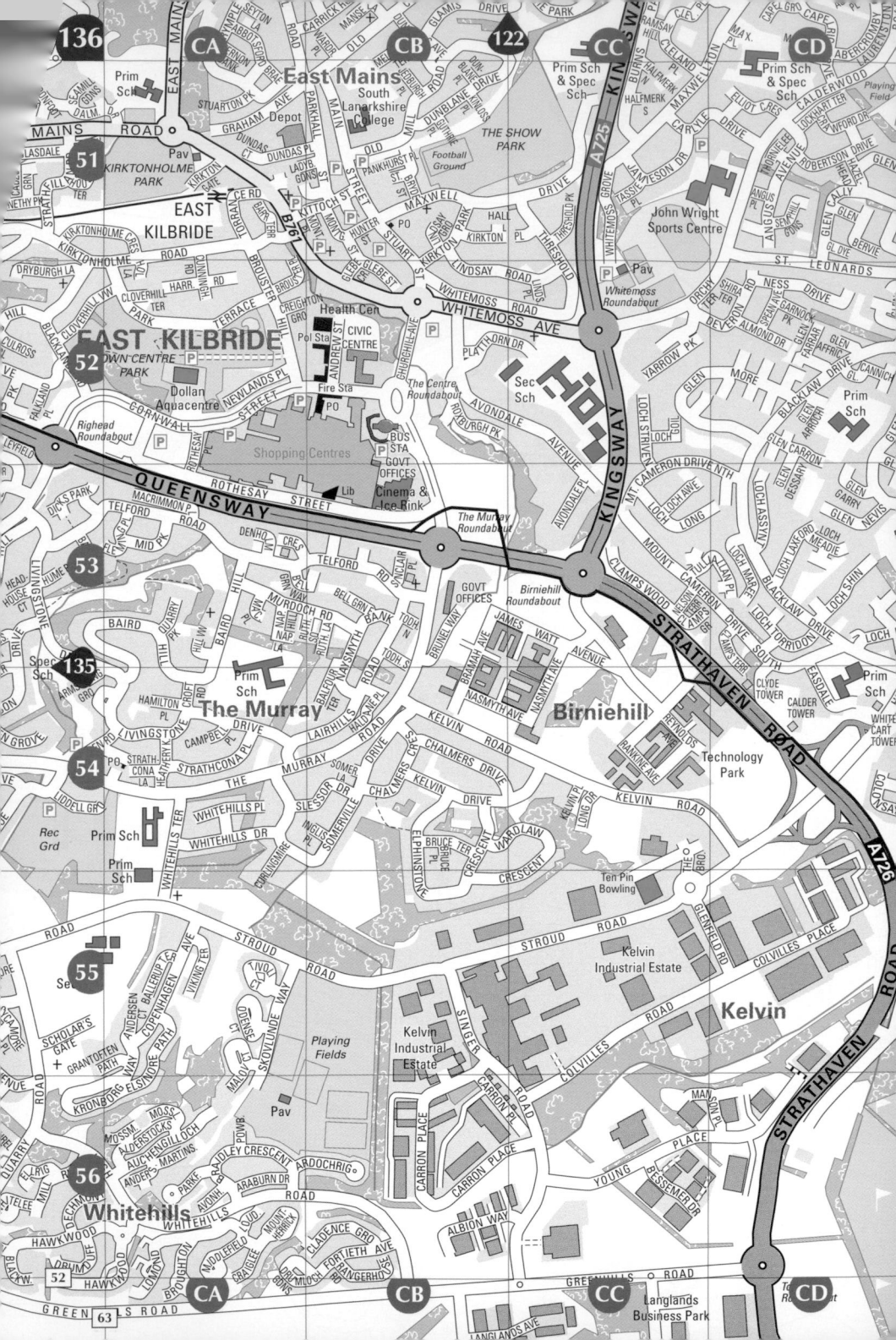

138 CJ **CK** 124 **CL** **CM**

Clyde Cottage

Springbank

51

Dykehead

Broomhouse

TURNBERRY DR
MUIR
BARNHILL
DAVINGTON
STATION
DUNURE
ALLOWAY
GDNS
KILMONGTON
AIL

Greenblairs

PARKNEUK ROAD

G72

Park
View

Newfield

Cov.
Res.

52

Braehead
Cottage

Cov.
Res.

Muirmains

Stewartfield

Earnock Burn

53

Laigh
Muirhouses

Wellbrae
Cottages

137

MUTTONHO

54

Highmuir
Houses

G74

55

Rotten Burn

G75

Devonhill

56

muir

52

East
Drumloch

67

CJ **CK** **CL** **CM**

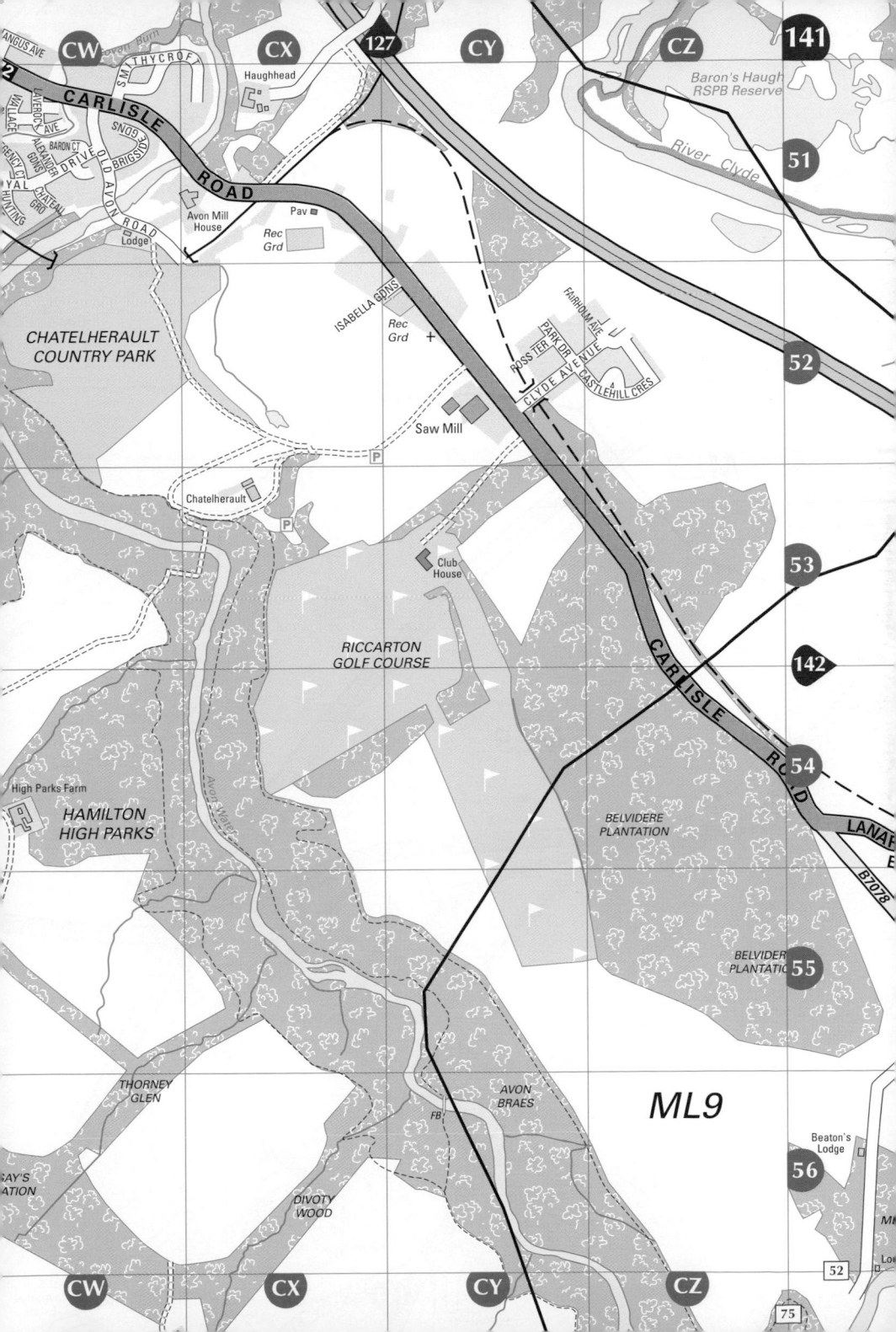

Glasgow information

Contents

History & development   147
Local information   148-151
Places of worship   151
Architecture, museums & shops 152-153
Sport & recreation   154-156
Entertainment   156-157
Strathclyde further education 157-158
Hospitals   158-160
Tourist information   160-162
Weather   162
Parks & gardens   163
Transport   164
Glasgow International Airport   165
Strathclyde Passenger Transport map 166-167

History & development

The City of Glasgow began life as a makeshift hamlet of huts huddled round a 6thC church, built by St. Mungo on the banks of a little salmon river – the Clyde. It was called Gleschow, meaning 'beloved green place' in Celtic. The cathedral was founded in 1136; the university, the second oldest in Scotland, was established in the 15thC; and in 1454 the flourishing medieval city wedged between the cathedral and the river was made a Royal burgh. The city's commercial prosperity dates from the 17thC when the lucrative tobacco, sugar and cotton trade with the New World flourished. The River Clyde, Glasgow's gateway to the Americas, was dredged, deepened and widened in the 18thC to make it navigable to the city's heart.

By the 19thC, Glasgow was the greatest shipbuilding centre in the world. From the 1820s onwards, it grew in leaps and bounds westwards along a steep ridge of land running parallel with the river. The hillside became encased in an undulating grid of streets and squares. Gradually the individualism, expressed in one-off set pieces characteristic of the 18thC and early 19thC, gave way to a remarkable coherent series of terraced squares and crescents of epic proportions – making Glasgow one of the finest of Victorian cities. But the price paid for such rapid industrialisation, the tremendous social problems manifest in the squalor of some of the worst of the 19thC slums, was high. Today the city is still the commercial and industrial capital of the West of Scotland. The most notorious of the slums have been cleared but the new buildings lack that sparkling clenchfisted Glaswegian character of the 19thC. Ironically, this character was partially destroyed when the slums were cleared for it wasn't the architecture that had failed, only the bureaucrats, who designated such areas as working class ghettos.

Districts

Little remains of medieval Glasgow, which stood on the wedge of land squeezed between the Cathedral and the River Clyde. Its business centre was The Cross, a space formed by the junction of several streets with the tall, square Tolbooth Steeple, 1626, in the middle. Opposite is Trongate, an arch astride a footpath, complete with tower and steeple salvaged from 17thC St. Mary's Church which was destroyed by fire in 1793.

The centre of 20thC Glasgow is George Square, a tree-lined piazza planned in 1781 and pinned down by more than a dozen statues including an 80 foot high Doric column built in 1837 to carry a statue of Sir Walter Scott. Buildings of interest include the monumental neo-Baroque City Chambers 1883-88 which takes up the east side and the Merchants' House 1874, on the west. To the south of the square, in a huddle of narrow streets, is the old Merchant City. Of interest here is the elegant Trades Hall, 85 Glassford Street, built by Robert Adam in 1794.

An elegant Ionic portico stands on a rusticated ground storey flanked by domed towers. Hutcheson's Hall, 158 Ingram Street, is a handsome Italianate building designed by David Hamilton in 1805. Nearby is the Gallery of Modern Art (GOMA), previously Stirling's Library, but originally an 18thC private residence, it became the Royal Exchange in 1827 when the Corinthian portico was added. To the north west is Kelvingrove, Victorian Glasgow at its best. This area is built around a steep saddle of land, landscaped by Paxton in 1850 and lined along its edge with handsome terraces.

Last but not least are the banks of the River Clyde. From Clyde Walkway on the north bank in Glasgow Green you can see: the Suspension Bridge of 1871 with its pylons in the form of triumphal arches; 17thC Merchants' Steeple; the Gothic Revival St. Andrew's R.C. Cathedral of 1816; the church, built 1739, in nearby St. Andrew's Square is a typical copy of London's St. Martin-in-the-Fields.

Local information

Useful information
Area of City 79 sq. miles (approx)

Population (Glasgow City 1999) 611,440

Electricity 240 volts A.C.

Emergency Services
Police, Fire and Ambulance. Dial 999 on any telephone.

Licensing Hours
Public Houses
City Centre
Daily except Sundays 11 a.m. – 12 midnight
Sundays 12.30 p.m. – 12 midnight

Restaurants, hotels and public houses with catering facililities; same as above but can be extended for drinks with meals.

Tourist Information Centres
11 George Square, G2 1DY
0141 204 4400

Town Hall, 9a Gilmour Street,
Paisley, PA1 1DD
0141 889 0711

Glasgow International Airport (Abbotsinch),
Paisley, PA3 2ST
0141 848 4440

Road Chef Services, M74 Northbound,
Hamilton, ML 6JW
01698 285590

Help & advice
Chamber of Commerce
30 George Square, G2 1EQ
0141 204 2121

Citizens Advice Bureaus
Airdrie
Resource Centre,
14 Anderson Street, Airdrie, ML6 0AA
01236 754 109

Barrhead
216 Main Street, Barrhead, G78 1SN
0141 881 2032

Bellshill
6 Hamilton Road, Bellshill, ML4 1AQ
01698 748 615

Clydebank
34 Alexander Street, Clydebank, G81 1RZ
0141 952 7921

Coatbridge
Unit 10, Fountain Business Park,
Ellis Street, Coatbridge, ML5 3AA
01236 421 447/ 8

Cumbernauld
3rd Floor, 2 Annan House, Annan Way,
Cumbernauld, G67 1DP
01236 723 201

East Dunbartonshire
5, Dalrymple Court, Townhead,
Kirkintilloch, G66 3AA
0141 578 0160/ 1

East Kilbride
24 Cornwall Way, East Kilbride, G74 1JR
01 355 263698

Glasgow Albion Street
48 Albion Street, G1 1LH
0141 552 5556

Glasgow Bridgeton
35 Main Street, Bridgeton, G40 1QB
0141 554 0336

Glasgow Castlemilk
27 Dougrie Drive, Castlemilk,
G45 9AD
0141 634 0338

Glasgow Drumchapel
49 Dunkenny Square, Drumchapel, G15 8NE
0141 944 2612 / 0205

Glasgow Easterhouse
46 Shandwick Square, Easterhouse, G34 9DT
0141 771 2328

Glasgow Maryhill
1145 Maryhill Road, G20 9AZ
0141 946 6373

Glasgow Parkhead
1361-1363 Gallowgate, G31 4DN
0141 554 0004

Greater Pollok
Unit 17, Pollok Shopping Centre,
45 Cowglen Road, G53 6ER
0141 876 4573

Motherwell & Wishaw
32 Civic Square, Motherwell, ML11 1TP
01698 251981/ 259389

Paisley
45 George Street, Paisley, PA1 2JY
0141 889 2121

Rutherglen & Cambuslang
School House, 2 McCallum Avenue,
Rutherglen, G73 3AL
0141 647 5100

Consumer Advice Centre
231 George Street, G1 1RX
0141 287 6681

Customs and Excise
21 India Street, G2 4PZ
0141 221 3828

Enable
(Organisation for people with learning
disabilities)
6th Floor
7 Buchanan Street, G1 3HL
0141 226 4541

H.M. Immigration Office
Festival Court,
200 Brand Street, Govan, G51 1AR
0141 419 1256

Housing aid and advice
Shelter, 53 St. Vincent Crescent, G3 8NQ
0141 221 8995

Lost property
Trains – There is a railway switchboard
number that will put you through to Lost
Property (at any station). 0141 335 3276
Buses – Office of bus company
Elsewhere in City – Strathclyde Police.
Lost Property Department,
173 Pitt Street, G2 4JS
0141 532 2000

Registrar of Births, Deaths and Marriages
1 Martha Street, G1 1JJ
0141 287 7652

Marriages only:
22 Park Circus, G3 6BE
0141 287 8350
Hours: Monday 9.15 a.m. – 5.00p.m.
Tuesday to Friday 9.15 a.m. – 4.00 p.m.
Births must be registered within twenty one
days, deaths within eight days and marriages
within three days. The Registrar should be
consulted at least one month before intended
date of marriage.

Children First
c/o Learning & Teaching Scotland,
74 Victoria Crescent Road,
G12 9JN
0141 334 2547

RNID - Royal National Institute for the Deaf
Floor 3, Crowngate Business Centre
Brook Street, G40 3AP
0141 554 0053
0141 550 5750 (textphone)

Shopmobility
Book a free battery powered wheelchair or
scooter, or request a guide at the following:
Buchanan Galleries and Saint Enoch
Shopping Centres 0141 354 0416
Braehead Shopping Centre 0141 885 4630
The Paisley Centre 0141 889 0441
Hamilton, 8-14 Lamb Street 01698 459955

**SSPCA-Scottish Society for the Prevention of
Cruelty to Animals**
0131 339 0111

Helplines

Childline 0800 1111
Missing Persons 0500 700 70
NSPCC Child Protection 0808 800 5000
ParentLine Scotland 0808 800 2222

Samaritans 08457 90 90 90
Rape Crisis Federation 0115 934 8474
RSPCA 0870 55 55 999
Victim Support 0131 668 4486

Media

British Broadcasting Corporation
Queen Margaret Drive, G12 8DG
0141 339 8844

Scottish Television
200 Renfield Street, G2 3PR
0141 300 3000

Morning Daily Newspapers
Daily Record
40 Anderston Quay, G3 8DA.
0141 248 7000

The Herald
200 Renfield Street, G2 3PR
0141 302 7000

Scottish Daily Express
Park House, Park Circus Place,
G3 6AF
0141 332 9600

The Scotsman
Regent Court, 70 West Regent Street, G2 2QZ
0141 236 6410

Evening Daily Newspapers
Evening Times
200 Renfield Street, G2 3PR
0141 302 7000

Sunday Newspapers
Scotland on Sunday
Regent Court, 70 West Regent Street G2 2QZ
0141 236 6410

Sunday Herald
200 Renfield Street,G2 3PR
0141 302 7000

Scottish Sunday Express
Park House, Park Circus Place, G3 6AF
0141 332 9600

Sunday Mail
40 Anderston Quay, G3 8DA
0141 248 7000

Sunday Post
144 Port Dundas Road, G4 0HZ
0141 332 9933

Post Offices

City Branch Office
87-91 Bothwell Street, G2 7AA
Monday – Friday 9.00a.m. – 5.30p.m.

Hope Street Branch Office
228 Hope Street, G2 3PN
Monday – Thursday 8.30a.m. – 5.30p.m.
Friday - 9.00a.m. – 5.30p.m.
Saturday - 8.30a.m. – 5.30p.m.

St. Vincent Street Branch Office
47 St. Vincent Street, G2 5QX
Monday to Friday 8.30a.m. – 5.45p.m.
Saturdays 9a.m. – 5.30p.m.

Post Office Counters Ltd
0845 722 3344

Local Government

East Dunbartonshire
Tom Johnston House,
Civic Way, Kirkintilloch, G66 4TJ
0141 578 8000

East Renfrewshire
Eastwood Park,
Rouken Glen Road, Giffnock, G46 6UG
0141 577 3000

Glasgow City
City Chambers, George Square, G2 1DU
0141 287 2000

North Lanarkshire
Civic Centre, Motherwell, ML1 1TW
01698 302222

Renfrewshire
North Building, Cotton Street, Paisley,
PA1 1BU
0141 842 5000

South Lanarkshire
Almada Street,
Hamilton, ML3 0AA
01698 454444

West Dunbartonshire
Garshake Road
Dumbarton
G82 3PU
01389 737000

Places of worship

Glasgow Cathedral is a perfect example of pre-Reformation Gothic architecture. Begun in 1238, it has a magnificent choir and handsome nave with shallow projecting transepts. On a windy hill to the east is the Necropolis, a cemetery with a spiky skyline of Victoriana consisting of pillars, temples and obelisks, dominated by an 1825 Doric column carrying the statue of John Knox. Other churches of interest: Landsdowne Church built by J.

Honeyman in 1863; St. George's Tron Church by William Stark 1807; Caledonian Road Church, a temple and tower on top of a storey-high base, designed by Alexander Thomson in 1857; a similar design is to be found at the United Presbyterian Church, St. Vincent Street, 1858, but on a more impressive scale; Queen's Cross Church 1897 is an amalgam of Art Nouveau and Gothic Revival by the brilliant Charles Rennie Mackintosh.

Churches within central Glasgow:
Church of Scotland
Glasgow Cathedral- St. Mungo,
Castle Street, G4

Renfield St. Stephen's Church,
262 Bath Street, G2

St. Columba Church (Gaelic),
300 St. Vincent Street, G3

St. George's Tron Church,
165 Buchanan Street, G1

Baptist
Adelaide Place Church,
209 Bath Street, G2

Episcopal Church in Scotland
Cathedral Church of St. Mary,
300 Great Western Road, G4

First Church of Christ Scientist
Berkeley Street, G3

Free Church of Scotland
265 St. Vincent Street, G2

German Speaking Congregation
Services held at 7 Hughenden Terrace, G12

Greek Orthodox Cathedral
St. Luke's, 27 Dundonald Road, G12

Islamic Centre
Glasgow Central Mosque,
Mosque Avenue, G5

Jewish Orthodox Synagogue
Garnethill Hebrew Congregation,
129 Hill Street, G3

Methodist
Woodlands Church,
229 Woodlands Road, G3

Roman Catholic
St. Andrew's Cathedral,
90 Dunlop Street, G1

St. Aloysius' Church,
27 Hill Street, G3

Unitarian Church
72 Berkeley Street, G3

United Free
Candlish Wynd, 62 Daisy Street, G42

Architecture, museums & shops

Interesting Buildings

Victorian Glasgow was extremely eclectic architecturally. Good examples of the Greek Revival style are Royal College of Physicians 1845, by W.H. Playfair and the Custom House 1840, by G.L. Taylor. The Queen's Room 1857, by Charles Wilson, is a handsome temple used now as a Christian Science church. The Gothic style is seen at its most exotic in the Stock Exchange 1877, by J. Burnet.

The new Victorian materials and techniques with glass, wrought and cast iron were also ably demonstrated in the buildings of the time. Typical are: Gardener's Stores 1856, by J. Baird; the Buck's Head, Argyle Street, an amalgam of glass and cast iron; and the Egyptian Halls of 1873, in Union Street, which has a masonry framework. Both are by Alexander Thomson. The Templeton Carpet Factory 1889, Glasgow Green, by William Leiper, is a Venetian Gothic building complete with battlemented parapet.

The great genius of Scottish architecture is Charles Rennie Mackintosh whose major buildings are in Glasgow. In the Scotland Street

University of Glasgow

School 1904–6, he punctuated a 3-storey central block with flanking staircase towers in projecting glazed bays. His most famous building – Glasgow School of Art 1897–9 – is a magnificent Art Nouveau building of taut stone and glass; the handsome library, with its gabled facade, was added later in 1907–9.

The Clyde Auditorium at the SECC

Galleries & Museums

Scotland's largest tourist attraction, The Burrell Collection, is situated in Pollok Country Park, Haggs Road and has more than 8,000 objects, housed in an award winning gallery. The Museum and Art Gallery, Kelvingrove Park (Re-opens 2006), Argyle Street, a palatial sandstone building with glazed central court, has one of the best municipal collections in Britain; superb Flemish, Dutch and French paintings, drawings, prints, also ceramics, silver, costumes and armour, as well as a natural history section.

The McLellan Galleries in Sauchiehall Street provide an important venue for touring and temporary art exhibitions. Provand's Lordship c1471, in Castle Street, is Glasgow's oldest house and is now a museum of furniture and household items dating from the 16th – 18thC. Pollok House, Pollok Country Park, a handsome house designed by William Adam in 1752, has paintings by William Blake and a notable collection of Spanish paintings, including works by El Greco.

Kelvingrove Art Gallery and Museum

Princes Square Shopping Centre

The Museum of Transport, housed in Kelvin Hall, Bunhouse Road, has a magnificent collection of trams, cars, model ships, bicycles, horse-drawn carriages and 7 steam locos. The People's Palace, Glasgow Green built 1898 with a huge glazed Winter Garden, has a lively illustrated history of the city. But the oldest museum in Glasgow is the Hunterian Museum, University of Glasgow, University Avenue, opened in 1807, it has a fascinating collection of manuscripts, early painted books, as well as some fine archaeological and geological exhibits.

Streets & Shopping

The Oxford Street of Glasgow is Sauchiehall (meaning 'willow meadow') Street. This together with Buchanan Street, The Buchanan Galleries Shopping Centre, Argyle Street, Princes Square and St. Enoch Centre form the main shopping area. Here you will find the department stores, boutiques and general shops. All three streets are largely pedestrianised, but the most exciting is undoubtedly Buchanan Street. Of particular interest is the spatially elegant Argyll Arcade 1828, the Venetian Gothic-style Stock Exchange 1877, the picturesque Dutch gabled Buchanan Street Bank building 1896 and the Glasgow Royal Concert Hall (opened 1990). In Glasgow Green is The Barras, the city's famous street market, formed by the junction of London Road and Kent Street.

Sport & recreation

East Dunbartonshire

The Allander Sports Complex
Milngavie Road, Bearsden, G61 3DF
0141 942 2233

The Leisuredrome
147 Balmuildy Road, Bishopbriggs, G64 3HD
0141 772 6391

East Renfrewshire

Barrhead Sports Centre
Main Street, Barrhead, G78 1SW
0141 580 1174

Eastwood Recreational Centre
Eastwood Park, Rouken Glen Road,
Giffnock, G46 6UG
0141 577 4956

Neilston Leisure Centre
Main Street, Neilston, G78 3NN
0141 577 4811

Glasgow City

Alexandra Sports Hall
Alexandra Parade, G31
0141 556 1695

Auchinlea Recreation Centre
Auchinlea Road, G34 9PQ
0141 771 7600

Barlia Sports Complex
Glenwood Path, G45 9UD
0141 634 5474

Bellahouston Leisure Centre
Bellahouston Drive, G52 1HH
0141 427 9090

Castlemilk Pool
137 Castlemilk Drive, G45 9UG
0141 634 8254

Castlemilk Sports Centre
10 Dougrie Road, G45 9NF
0141 634 8187

Crownpoint Road Sports Complex
183 Crownpoint Road, G40 2AL
0141 554 8274

Drumchapel Pool
199 Drumry Road East, G15 8NS
0141 944 5812

Easterhouse Pool
5 Bogbain Road, G34 9DU
0141 771 7978

Easterhouse Sports Centre
Auchinlea Road, G34 9PQ
0141 771 1963

Glasgow Green Football Centre
Kings Drive, G40 1HB
0141 554 7547

Gorbals Leisure Centre
275 Ballater Street, G5 0YP
0141 429 5556

Holyrood Sports Centre
600 Aikenhead Road, G42 0PD
0141 423 9431

Kelvin Hall International Sports Arena
1445 Argyle Street, G3 8AW
0141 357 2525

North Woodside Leisure Centre
Braid Square, G4 9YB
0141 332 8102

Palace of Art (Bellahouston Park)
Paisley Road West, G52
0141 427 5180

Pollok Leisure Pool
27 Cowglen Road, G53 6EW
0141 881 3313

Scotstoun Leisure Centre
72 Danes Drive, G14 9HD
0141 959 4000

Springburn Leisure Centre
10 Kay Street, G21 1JY
0141 557 5878

Springburn Park Synthetic Pitch
Broomfield Road, G21
0141 557 1692

Tollcross Park Leisure Centre
Wellshot Road, G32 7QR
0141 763 2345

Whitehill Pool
240 Onslow Drive, G31 2QF
0141 551 9969

Yoker Sports Centre
2 Speirshall Terrace, G13 0LN
0141 959 8386

North Lanarkshire
Airdrie Leisure Centre
Motherwell Street, Airdrie, ML6 7HU
01236 762871

Aquatec,
Menteith Road, Motherwell, ML1 1AZ
01698 276464

Birkenshaw Sports Barn
Fourth Street, Tannochside, G71 6AU
01698 815872

Broadwood Stadium,
1 Ardgoil Drive, Cumbernauld, G68 9NE
01236 451351

Coatbridge Outdoor Sports Centre
Langloan Street, Coatbridge, ML5 1ER
01236 812472

Coatbridge College Leisure Centre
Park Street, Coatbridge, ML5 3LY
01236 440 213

Iain Nicolson Recreation Centre
Chryston Road, Chryston, G69 9NA
0141 779 2835

John Smith Pool
Stirling Street, Airdrie, ML6 0AH
01236 750130

Keir Hardie Sports Centre
Main Street, Holytown, ML1 4TP
01698 833803

Kilsyth Swimming Pool
1 Airdrie Street, Kilsyth, G65 9JE
01236 822334

Sir Matt Busby Sports Complex
50 Main Street, Bellshill, ML4 3DP
01698 747466

Time Capsule
100 Buchanan Street, Coatbridge, ML5 1DL
01236 422242

Wishaw Sports Centre
Alexander Street, Wishaw, ML2 0HQ
01698 355821

Renfrewshire
Elderslie Leisure Centre
Stoddard Square, Elderslie, PA 9AS
01505 328133

Erskine Swimming Pool
Bridgewater Shopping Centre, Erskine,
PA8 7AA
0141 812 0044

Johnstone Swimming Pool
Ludovic Square, Johnstone, PA5 8EE
01505 322 954

Lagoon Leisure Centre
Christie Street, Paisley, PA1 1NB
0141 889 4000

Linwood Sports Complex
Brediland Road, Linwood, PA3 3RA
01505 329461

McMaster Sports Centre
Thomas Shanks Park, Greenend Avenue,
Johnstone, PA5
01505 335 171

Renfrew Victory Baths
Inchinnan Road, Renfrew, PA4 8ND
0141 886 2088

South Lanarkshire
Blantyre Sports Centre
Glasgow Road, Blantyre, G72 0JS
01698 821767

Burnhill Recreation Centre
Toryglen Road, Rutherglen, G73 1JH
0141 643 0327

Dollan Aqua Centre
Brouster Hill, East Kilbride, G74 1AF
01355 260000

Duncanrig Sports Centre
Alberta Avenue, East Kilbride, G75 8HX
01355 248922

Hamilton Palace Sports Ground
Motehill, Hamilton, ML3 6BY
01698 424101

Hamilton Water Palace
35 Almada Street, Hamilton, ML3 0HQ
01698 459950

Halfway Recreation Centre
New Road, Cambuslong, G72 7PU
0141 641 4158

John Wright Sports Centre
Calderwood Road, East Kilbride, G74 3EU
01355 237731

Larkhall Leisure Centre
Broomhill Road, Larkhall, ML9 1QP
01698 881742

Rutherglen Pool
Greenhill Road, Rutherglen, G73 2SS
0141 647 4530

Greenhills Sport Centre
Stroud Road, East Kilbride, G75 0YA
01355 221003

West Dunbartonshire
Antonine Sports Centre
Roman Road, Duntocher, Clydebank, G81 6BT
01389 878972

The Play Drome
2 Abbotsford Road, Clydebank, G81 1PA
0141 951 4321

Entertainment

As Scotland's commercial and industrial capital, Glasgow offers a good choice of leisure activities. The city now has many theatres where productions include serious drama, pantomime, pop and musicals. The Theatre Royal, Hope Street is Scotland's only opera house and has been completely restored to its full Victorian splendour. The Royal Scottish National Orchestra gives classical music concerts at the Glasgow Royal Concert Hall between October and April and is the venue for the proms in June. Cinemas are still thriving in Glasgow, as are the many public houses, some of which provide meals and live entertainment. In the city centre and Byres Road, West End,

there is a fair number of restaurants where traditional home cooking, as well as international cuisines, can be sampled. More night life can be found at the city's nightclubs, discos and dance halls.

Outdoors, apart from the many parks and nature trails, there is Calderpark Zoological Gardens, situated 6 miles from the centre between Mount Vernon and Uddingston. Here you may see white rhinos, black panthers and iguanas among many species. Departing from Anderston Quay, you can also cruise down the Clyde in 'P.S. Waverley' – the last sea-going paddle-steamer in the world.

Cinemas
Glasgow Film Theatre 12 Rose Street, G3 6RB. 0141 332 8128

Grosvenor Ashton Lane, G12 8SJ
0141 339 4298

IMAX 50 Pacific Quay, G51 1EA
0141 420 5000

Odeon Springfield Quay, Paisley Road, G5 8NP. 08705 050007

Odeon 56 Renfield Street, G2 1NF
08705 050007

Showcase Barrbridge Road, Bargeddie, G69 7TZ. 01236 438 880

Showcase Phoenix Business Park, Paisley, PA1 2BH. 0141 887 0011

UCI Clyde Shopping Centre, Britannia Way, Clydebank, G81 2RZ. 08700 10 20 30

UGC The Forge Shopping Centre, 1221 Gallowgate, G31 4EB. 08701 555136

UGC 145-159 West Nile Street, G1 2RL 08709 070789

Theatres

Arches Theatre
30 Midland Street, G1 4PR
09010 220300

Citizens' Theatre
119 Gorbals Street, G5 9DS
0141 429 0022

King's Theatre
297 Bath Street, G2 4JN
0845 330 3511

Mitchell Theatre and Moir Hall
Granville Street, G3
0141 287 5511

New Athenaeum Theatre (R.S.A.M.D.)
100 Renfrew Street, G2 3DB
0141 332 5057

Pavilion Theatre
121 Renfield Street, G2 3AX
0141 332 1846

Theatre Royal
282 Hope Street, G2 3QA
0845 330 3511

Tramway
25 Albert Drive, G41 2PE
0845 330 3511

Tron Theatre
63 Trongate, G1 5HB
0141 552 4267

Halls

Glasgow Royal Concert Hall
2 Sauchiehall Street, G2 3NY
0141 353 8000

Henry Wood Hall,
73 Claremont Street, G3 7JB
0141 225 3555

Scottish Exhibition Conference Centre,
G3 8YW
0141 248 3000

For more information about the following G.C.C. halls contact;
Cultural and Leisure Services,
3rd Floor, 20 Trongate, G1 5ES.
0141 287 8931
City Halls, Candleriggs, G1
Couper Institute, 86 Clarkston Road, G44
Langside Hall, 5 Langside Avenue, G41
Partick Burgh Hall, 9 Burgh Hall Street, G11
Shettleston Hall, Wellshot Road, G32
Woodside Hall, Glenfarg Street, G20

Strathclyde further education

Anniesland College
19 Hatfield Drive, G12 OYE
0141 357 3969

Bell College
Almada Street, Hamilton, ML3 0JB
01698 283100

Cardonald College of Further Education
690 Mosspark Drive, G52 3AY
0141 272 3333

Central College of Commerce
300 Cathedral Street, G1 2TA
0141 552 3941

Clydebank College
Kilbowie Road, Clydebank, G81 2AA
0141 952 7771

Coatbridge College
Kildonan Street, Coatbridge, ML5 3LS
01236 422316

Cumbernauld College
Tryst Road, Town Centre, Cumbernauld,
G67 1HU
01236 731811

Glasgow Caledonian University
70 Cowcaddens Road, G4 0BA
0141 331 3000

Glasgow Metropolitan College :
Glasgow College of Building and Printing
60 North Hanover Street, G1 2BP
0141 332 9969
Glasgow College of Food Technology
230 Cathedral Street, G1 2TG
0141 552 3751

Glasgow College of Nautical Studies
21 Thistle Street, G5 9XB
0141 565 2500

John Wheatley College
1346 Shettleston Road, G32 9AT
0141 778 2426

Langside College
50 Prospecthill Road, G42 9LB
0141 649 4991

North Glasgow College
110 Flemington Street, G21 4BX
0141 558 9001

Motherwell College
Dalzell Drive, Motherwell, ML1 2DD
01698 232 323

Reid Kerr College,
Renfrew Road, Paisley, PA3 4DR
0141 581 2222

Royal Scottish Academy of Music & Drama,
100 Renfrew Street, G2 3DB
0141 332 4101

Scotus College
2 Chesters Road, Bearsden, G61 4AG
0141 943 1995

South Lanarkshire College
Hamilton Road, Cambuslang, G72 7BS
0141 641 6600

Stow College
43 Shamrock Street, G4 9LD
0141 332 1786

University of Glasgow
University Avenue, G12 8QQ
0141 339 8855

University of Paisley
High St, Paisley, PA1 2BE
0141 848 3000

University of Strathclyde
16 Richmond Street, G1 1XQ
0141 552 4400

Hospitals

Acorn Street Day Hospital
23 Acorn Street, Bridgeton, G40 4AA
0141 556 4789

Airbles Road Hospital
(formerly Adult Day Hosp)
49 Airbles Road, Motherwell, ML1 2TP
01698 269336

Alexander Hospital
Blair Road, Coatbridge, ML5 2EP
01236 422661

Blawarthill Hospital
129 Holehouse Drive, Blawarthill, G13 3TG
0141 211 9000

Caird House Hospital
Caird Street, Hamilton, ML3 0AL
01698 540182

Coathill Hospital
Hospital Street, Coatbridge, ML5 4DN
01698 245000

Drumchapel Hospital
129 Drumchapel Road, G15 6PX
0141 211 6000

Dykebar Hospital
Grahamston Road, Paisley, PA2 7DE
0141 884 5122

Erskine
Bishopton, PA7 5PU
0141 812 1100

Gartnavel General Hospital
1053 Great Western Road, G12 0YN
0141 211 3000

Gartnavel Royal Hospital
1055 Great Western Road, G12 0XH
0141 211 3600

Glasgow Dental Hospital and School
378 Sauchiehall Street, G2 3JZ
0141 211 9600

Glasgow Nuffield Hospital
25 Beaconsfield Road, G12 0PJ
0141 334 9441

Glasgow Royal Infirmary
82-84 Castle Street, G4 0SF
0141 211 4000

Golden Jubilee National Hospital
Beardmore Street, Clydebank, G81 4HX
0141 951 5000

Hairmyres Hospital
Eaglesham Road, East Kilbride, G75 8RG
01355 585000

Hawkhead Hospital (Due to close 2005)
Hawkhead Road, Paisley, PA2 7BL
0141 889 8151

Homeopathic Hospital
1053 Great Western Road, G12 0XQ
0141 211 1600

Johnstone Hospital
Bridge of Weir Road, Johnstone, PA5 8YX
01505 331471

Kirklands Hospital (Due to close 2005)
Fallside Road Bothwell, G71 8BB
01698 245000

Leverndale Hospital
510 Crookston Road, G53 7TU
0141 211 6400

Lightburn Hospital
966 Carntyne Road, G32 6ND
0141 211 1500

Mansionhouse Unit
Mansionhouse Road, G41 3DX
0141 201 6000/6146

Mearnskirk House
Newton Mearns, G77 5RZ
0141 616 3742

Merchiston Hospital (Due to close 2005)
Barochan Road, Brookfield, Johnstone,
PA5 8TY
01505 328261

Monklands District General Hospital
Monkscourt Avenue, Airdrie, ML6 0JS
01236 748748

Paisley Maternity Hospital
Corsebar Road, Paisley, PA2 9PN
0141 887 9111

Parkhead Hospital
81 Salamanca Street, G31 5ES
0141 211 8300

Parkview Resource Centre
152 Wellshot Road, G32 7AX
0141 303 8800

Princess Royal Maternity Hospital
16 Alexandra Parade, G31 2ER
0141 211 5400

Queen Mother's Hospital
Yorkhill, G3 8SJ
0141 201 0550

Red Deer Day Hospital
Alberta Avenue, Westwood, East Kilbride,
G75 8NH
01355 244254

Ross Hall Hospital
221 Crookston Road, G52 3NQ
0141 810 3151

Royal Alexandra Hospital
Corsebar Road, Paisley, PA2 9PN
0141 887 9111

Royal Hospital for Sick Children
Yorkhill, G3 8SJ
0141 201 0000

St Andrew's Hospice
Henderson Street, Aidrie, ML6 6DJ
01236 766951

Southern General Hospital
1345 Govan Road, G51 4TF
0141 201 1100

Strathclyde Hospital
Airbles Road, Motherwell, ML1 3BW
01698 245000

Stobhill Hospital
133 Balornock Road, G21 3UW
0141 201 3000

Udston Hospital
Farm Road, Burnbank, Hamilton, ML3 9LA
01698 245000

Victoria Infirmary
Langside Road, G42 9TY
0141 201 6000

Victoria Memorial Cottage Hospital
Glasgow Road, Kilsyth, G65 9AG
01236 822172

Wester Moffat Hospital
Towers Road, Airdrie, ML6 8LW
01236 763377

Western Infirmary
Dumbarton Road, Partick, G11 6NT
0141 211 2000

Tourist information

Art Gallery and Museum, Kelvingrove
(Closed for Refurbishment until 2006)
Kelvingrove. 0141 287 2700.
This fine national art collection contains superb paintings and sculptures, silver and ceramic, European armour, weapons and firearms, clothing, and furniture.

Botanic Garden
730 Great Western Road. 0141 334 2422.
The gardens were formed in 1817 to provide a source of plant material for use in teaching medicine and botany. Today specialist plant collections include exotic Australian tree and ferns, orchids and tropical begonias.

The Burrell Collection
Pollok Country Park. 0141 649 7151.
This award winning building houses a world-famous collection gifted to Glasgow by Sir William Burrell. Visitors can see art objects from Iraq, Egypt, Greece and Italy. Tapestries, furniture, textiles, ceramics, stained glass and sculptures from medieval Europe, and drawings from the 15th to 19th centuries.

Glasgow Cathedral
Cathedral Square. 0141 552 6891.
The only Scottish mainland medieval cathedral to have survived the Reformation complete. Notable features are the elaborately vaulted crypt, the stone screen and the unfinished Blackadder Aisle.

City Chambers
George Square. 0141 287 2000.
The City Chambers is the headquarters of Glasgow City Council and arguably Glasgow's finest example of Victorian architecture. The building was opened in 1888 by Queen Victoria and to this day has preserved all its original features.

The Tall Ship at Glasgow Harbour
Stobcross Road. 0141 339 0631.
The principal attraction is an opportunity to board the 103-year-old restored sailing ship Glenlee, the only Clyde-built sailing ship afloat in the UK. The Pumphouse Building (1877) also houses exhibitions.

Fossil Grove
Victoria Park. 0141 950 1448.
Glasgow's oldest tourist attraction discovered by accident and now designated a Site of Special Scientific Interest. Fossil tree trunks from around 330 million years ago are preserved in situ.

Gallery of Modern Art
Queen Street. 0141 229 1996.
The elegant Royal Exchange building displays works by living artists from across the world. It is arranged in four themed areas: Earth, Fire, Water and Air.

House for an Art Lover
Bellahouston Park. 0141 354 4449.
A house designed in 1901 by Charles Rennie Mackintosh but only built between 1989 and 1996. Exhibition and film showing the construction. Sculpture park. Situated in parkland adjacent to magnificent Victorian walled gardens.

Hunterian Art Gallery
82 Hillhead Street. 0141 330 5431.
A prestigious art gallery housing many important works by old masters, impressionists and Scottish paintings from the 18th century to present. Also houses the Mackintosh House, a reconstructed interior of the architect's own house in Glasgow using original furniture, prints and designs.

Hunterian Museum
University of Glasgow. 0141 330 4221.
Scotland's first public museum was established in 1807 based on the vast collections of Dr William Hunter (1718 – 83). Many items from his valuable collections are on display together with new and exciting additions. See displays of dinosaurs from Scotland, Romans in Scotland, geology, archaeology, the history of science and coins.

The Lighthouse
11 Mitchell Lane. 0141 225 8414.
The Lighthouse, Scotland's Centre for Architecture, Design and the City, is the long-term legacy of Glasgow 1999 UK City of Architecture and Design. It is the imaginative conversion of Charles Rennie Mackintosh's first public commission and is located in the heart of the city centre.

Museum of Transport
Kelvin Hall. 0141 287 2700.
The history of transport on land and sea with vehicles from horse-drawn carriages to motor cycles, fire engines, railway engines, steam and motor cars. Also a re-creation of a typical 1938 Glasgow street.

Necropolis
Behind Glasgow Cathedral. 0141 287 3961.
Remarkable and extensive burial ground laid out in 1833, with numerous elaborate tombs of 19th century illustrious Glaswegians and others.

People's Palace
Glasgow Green. 0141 554 0223.
Opened in 1898, this collection displays the story of Glasgow and its people, and its impact on the world from 1175 to the present day. A number of important collections, photographs, film sequences and reminiscences bring to life the city's past.

Piping Centre
30–34 McPhater Street. 0141 353 0220.
A national and international centre of excellence of the bagpipes and its music. Housed in a fine listed building.

Pollok House
Pollok Country Park. 0141 616 6410.
The house was built in 1740 and extended in 1890 by Sir John Stirling Maxwell. The house contains a renowned collection of paintings and furnishings appropriate for an Edwardian country house.

Provand's Lordship
3 Castle Street. 0141 553 2557.
The oldest dwelling in Glasgow, built in 1471 as a manse for the St Nicholas Hospital.

St Mungo Museum of Religious Life and Art
2 Castle Street. 0141 553 2557.
A unique museum exploring the universal themes of life, death and the hereafter through beautiful and evocative art objects associated with different religious faiths.

Glasgow School of Art
167 Renfrew Street. 0141 353 4526.
Glasgow School of Art is Charles Rennie Mackintosh's architectural masterpiece. The Mackintosh Building continues to be admired and respected and has taken its place as one of the most influential and significant structures of the 20th century.

Glasgow Science Centre
Pacific Quay. 0141 420 5000.
Features exhibits devoted to modern science and a planetarium. The centre highlights Glasgow's past, present and future.

Scotland Street School
225 Scotland Street. 0141 287 0513.
A magnificent building with twin leaded towers and Glasgow-style stone carving designed by Charles Rennie Mackintosh in 1904. Now housing a permanent exhibition on the history of education.

Tenement House
145 Buccleuch Street. 0141 333 0183.
A typical late Victorian Glasgow tenement flat, retaining many original features and possessions of the woman who lived here for 50 years give a fascinating glimpse of life in the early 20th century.

Weather

The City of Glasgow is on the same latitude as the City of Moscow, but because of its close proximity to the warm Atlantic shores, and the prevailing westerly winds, it enjoys a more moderate climate. Summers are generally cool and winters mostly mild, this gives Glasgow fairly consistent summer and winter temperatures. Despite considerable cloud the city is sheltered by hills to the south-west and north and the average rainfall for Glasgow is usually less than 40 inches per year. The following table shows the approximate average figures for sunshine, rainfall and temperatures to be expected in Glasgow throughout the year.

Weather forecasts
For the west and central Scotland:
Weathercall 09068 232 791 (60p per min)
The Glasgow Weather Centre (Meteorological

Month	Hours of Sunshine	Inches of Rainfall	Temperature C		
			Ave. Max.	Ave. Min.	High/Low
January	36	3.8	5.5	0.8	-18
February	62	2.8	6.3	0.8	-15
March	94	2.4	8.8	2.2	21
April	147	2.4	11.9	3.9	22
May	185	2.7	15.1	6.2	26
June	181	2.4	17.9	9.3	30
July	159	2.9	18.6	10.8	29
August	143	3.5	18.5	10.6	31
September	106	4.1	16.3	9.1	-4
October	76	4.1	13.0	6.8	-8
November	47	3.7	8.7	3.3	-11
December	30	4.2	6.5	1.9	-12

Parks & gardens

There are over 70 public parks within the city. The most famous is Glasgow Green. Abutting the north bank of the River Clyde, it was acquired in 1662. Of interest are the Winter Gardens attached to the People's Palace. Kelvingrove Park is an 85-acre park laid out by Sir Joseph Paxton in 1852. On the south side of the city is the 148-acre Queen's Park, Victoria Road, established 1857–94. Also of interest: Rouken Glen, Thornliebank, with a spectacular waterfall, walled garden, nature trail and boating facilities; Victoria Park, Victoria Park Drive, with its famous Fossil Grove, flower gardens and yachting pond. In Great Western Road are the Botanic Gardens. Founded in 1817, the gardens' 42 acres are crammed with natural attractions, including the celebrated Kibble Palace glasshouse with its fabulous tree ferns, exotic plants and white marble Victorian statues.

University tower from Kelvingrove Park

Botanic Gardens
730 Great Western Road, G12.

Hogganfield Park
Cumbernauld Road, G33.

Glasgow Green
Greendyke Street, G40.

Kelvingrove Park
Sauchiehall Street, G3.

King's Park
325 Carmunnock Road, G44.

Linn Park
Clarkston Road, G44.

Pollok Country Park
Pollokshaws Road, G43

Queen's Park
Victoria Road, G42.

Rouken Glen Park
Rouken Glen Road, G46.

Springburn Park
Broomfield Road, G21.

Tollcross Park
461 Tollcross Road, G32.

Victoria Park
Victoria Park Drive North, G14.

Transport

The City of Glasgow has one of the most advanced, fully integrated public transport systems in the whole of Europe. The Strathclyde Transport network consists of: the local railway network, the local bus services and the fully modernised Glasgow Subway, with links to Glasgow International Airport and the Steamer and car ferry services.

See the Strathclyde Passenger Transport (SPT) rail network map on pages 166-167 and for information contact them on 0141 332 6811.

Bus Services
Long Distance Coach Service
Citylink 08705 505050
National Express 08705 808080
Scottish Citylink Coaches Ltd and National Express provide rapid services to London and most parts of Scotland.

Local Bus Services
Traveline Scotland (timetable only)
0870 6082608

A comprehensive network of local bus services is provided by a variety of operators within the City of Glasgow and also direct to a number of surrounding towns. These services depart from City Centre bus stops or from Buchanan Bus Station, Killermont Street, G2. 0141 333 3708

Railway Services
National Rail (timetable only): 08457 484 950
ScotRail (telesales only): 08456 550033
Arriva Trains Northern: 08706 023322
G.N.E.R. (timetable & telesales): 08457 225225
Virgin (timetable & telesales): 08457 222333

ScotRail trains serve over 170 stations in Glasgow and Strathclyde (see map on pages 166-167) and operate to most destinations in Scotland.

Arriva Trains Northern, G.N.E.R. & Virgin operate services to England.

Use Glasgow Queen Street station for services to the north east of Glasgow and use Glasgow Central station for services to the west and south of Glasgow and England.

Parking
Car Parking in the central area of Glasgow is controlled. Parking meters are used extensively and signs indicating restrictions are displayed at kerbsides and on entry to the central area.

Traffic Wardens are on duty. There are a large number of car parks throughout the city centre, many of which are open 24 hours a day. See the mapping section for locations.

Taxis
Glasgow has over 1400 traditional London type taxis, all licensed by the Glasgow District Council. At the time of publishing, a three mile journey costs approximately £5. The total price of each journey is shown on the meter and is calculated by distance or time or a combination of both. The major taxi companies offer City tours at fixed prices, listing the places of interest to be visited, leaflets are available at all major hotel reception areas. Tours vary from 1 to 3 hours and in price between £15 and £45. A tour "Glasgow by Night" is also available.

Any passenger wishing to travel to a destination outside the Glasgow District Boundary should ascertain from the driver the fare to be charged.

Complaints
Any complaints regarding the conduct of a taxi driver should be addressed to:
The Taxi Enforcement Officer,
City Building Department,
73 Hawthorn Street, G22 6HY.
0141 287 3326

Glasgow International Airport

Located eight miles (13km) west of Glasgow alongside the M8 motorway at Junction 28 & 28A this airport is linked by a bus service to Buchanan Bus Station, which runs every 15 minutes from 6.30am – 6.00pm Monday to Saturday and every 30 minutes at off peak times. There is a frequent coach service linking the Airport with all major bus and rail terminals in the city. Coach and bus tickets along with rail information can be obtained from the SPT travel desk, door 5 on the ground floor.

Car parking is available with a graduated scale of charges.

The Airport telephone number 0141 887 1111

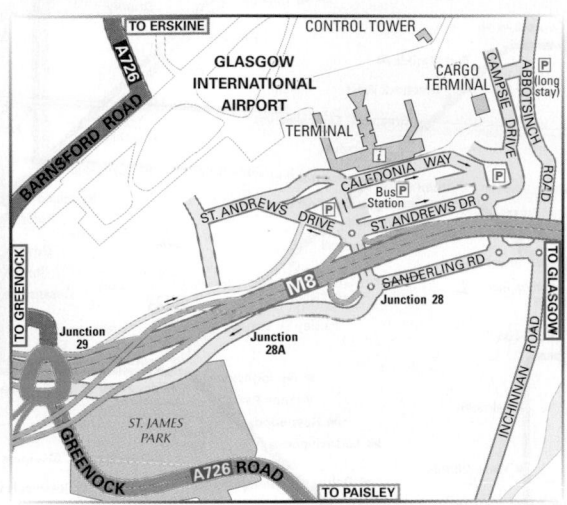

Airlines

Aer Lingus Flights to: Dublin
Reservations 08450 844 444
Air Canada Flights to: Toronto
Reservations 08705 247226
British Airways Flights to: Belfast Birmingham, Bristol, Gatwick, Heathrow, Londonderry, Manchester, Southampton and Inter Scottish Routes
Reservations 0845 77 333 77
British European Flights to: Birmingham
Reservations 08705 676 676
British Midland Flights to: East Midlands, Heathrow, Jersey, Copenhagen, Leeds Bradford, and Manchester

Reservations 0870 607 0555
Continental Flights to: New York
Reservations 0800 776 464
Easy Jet Flights to: Belfast and Luton
Reservations 0870 600 0000
Go Flights to: Belfast, East Midlands and Stansted
Reservations 0870 607 6543
Icelandair Flights to: Reykjavik
Reservations 08457 581 111
KLM U.K. Flights to: Amsterdam
Reservations 08705 074 074
Manx Airlines Flights to: Isle of Man
Reservations 08457 256 256

Prestwick International Airport

Also offers access to Glasgow via a 45 minute train journey. Flights from and to Brussels, Dublin, Frankfurt, Oslo, Paris and Stansted,. Discounted rail fares to Glasgow Central station are available for air passengers.

Prestwick International Airport 01292 511000

Ryanair
Reservations 0871 246 0000

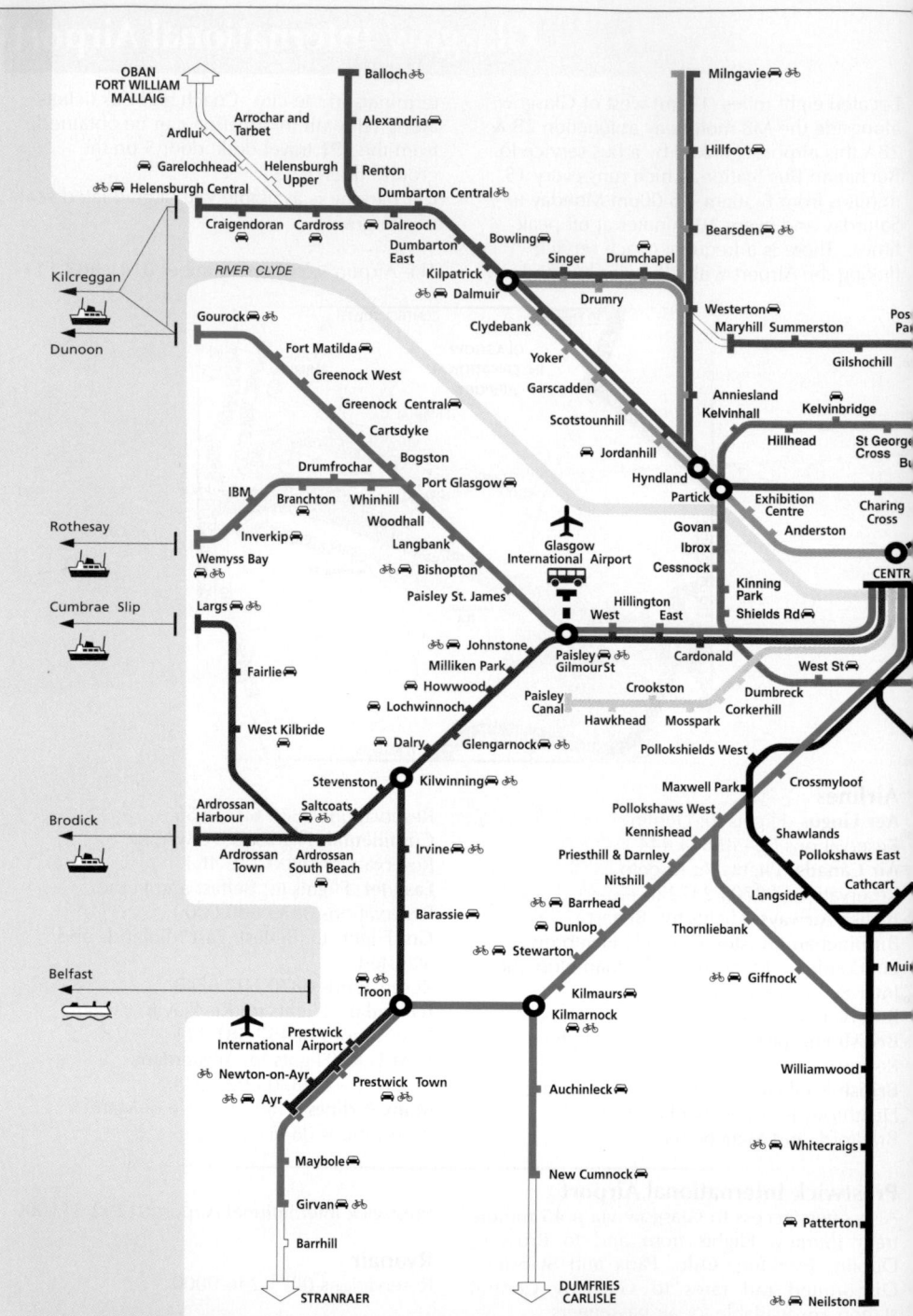

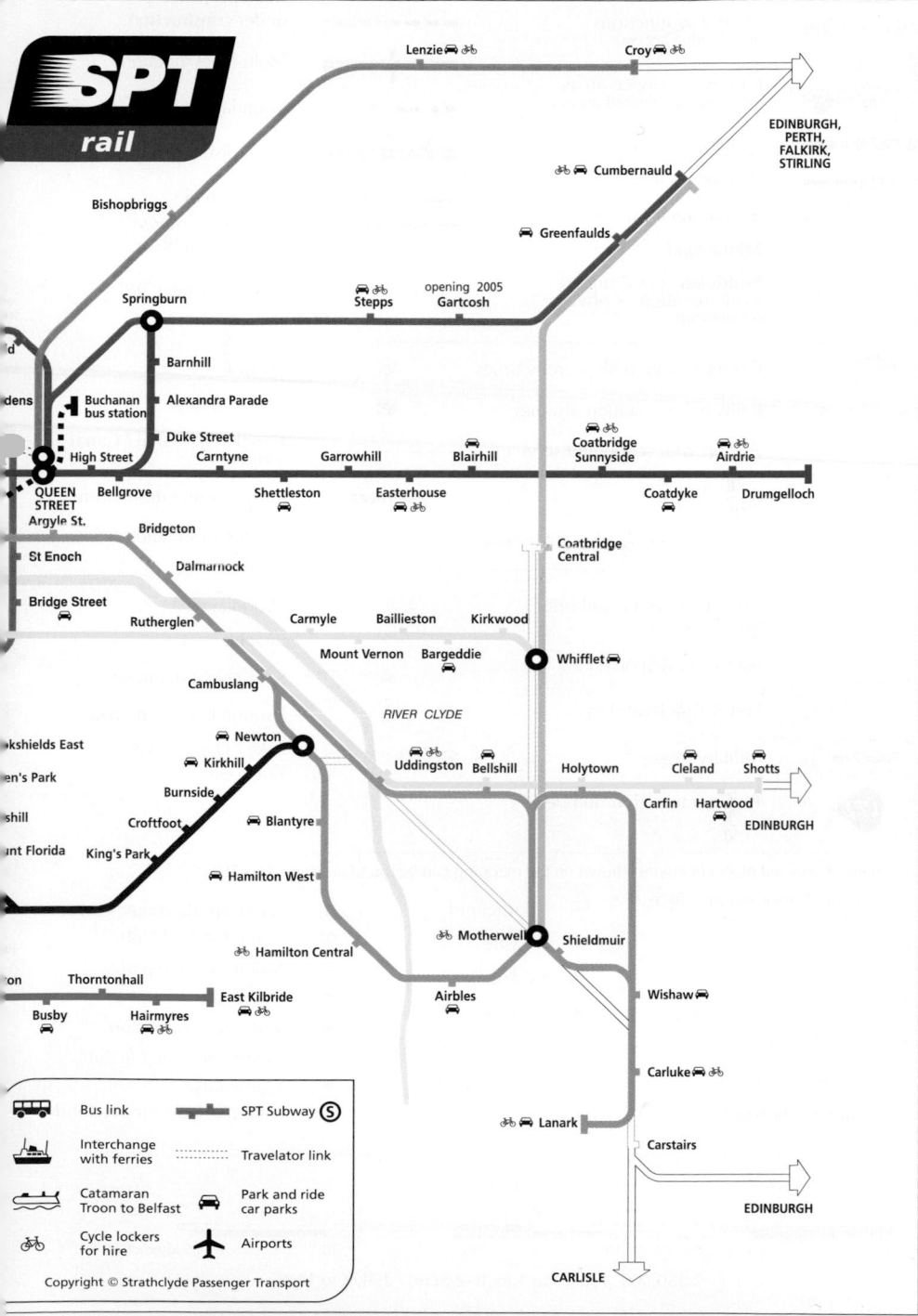

SPT *rail*

Lenzie · Croy

EDINBURGH,
PERTH,
FALKIRK,
STIRLING

Cumbernauld

Bishopbriggs

Greenfaulds

Springburn

Stepps · opening 2005 Gartcosh

Barnhill

Alexandra Parade

Buchanan bus station

Duke Street

High Street · Carntyne · Garrowhill · Blairhill · Coatbridge Sunnyside · Airdrie

QUEEN STREET · Bellgrove · Shettleston · Easterhouse · Coatdyke · Drumgelloch

Argyle St.

St Enoch · Bridgeton · Dalmarnock · Coatbridge Central

Bridge Street

Rutherglen · Carmyle · Baillieston · Kirkwood

Mount Vernon · Bargeddie · Whifflet

Cambuslang

RIVER CLYDE

...kshields East · Newton

...en's Park · Kirkhill · Uddingston · Bellshill · Holytown · Cleland · Shotts

Burnside · Carfin · Hartwood

...shill · Croftfoot · Blantyre · EDINBURGH

...nt Florida · King's Park

Hamilton West

Motherwell · Shieldmuir

Hamilton Central · Wishaw

...on · Thorntonhall · East Kilbride · Airbles

Busby · Hairmyres · Carluke

Lanark

Carstairs

EDINBURGH

CARLISLE

Bus link · SPT Subway **S**

Interchange with ferries · Travelator link

Catamaran Troon to Belfast · Park and ride car parks

Cycle lockers for hire · Airports

Copyright © Strathclyde Passenger Transport

M8	Motorway
10 **9**	Motorway junctions (full, limited access)
◆ Stirling ◆ Harthill Hamilton	Motorway service areas (off road, full, limited access)
A80	Primary route dual / single
A89	'A' road dual / single
B806	'B' road dual / single
	Minor road
=========	Restricted access due to road condition or private ownership

==== ====	Road projected or under construction
⊗	Multi-level junction
	Roundabout
4	Road distance in miles
	Road tunnel
>>	Steep hill (arrows point downhill)
✕ Toll	Level crossing / Toll

Zeebrugge 17½ hrs — Car ferry route with journey times

○———○ Railway line / station / tunnel

✈ Airport with scheduled services

Ⓗ Heliport

Ⓟ Park and Ride

Canal / Dry canal / Canal tunnel

Built up area

□ □ □ Town / Village / Other settlement

Peterhead Primary route destination

☼ Seaside destination

·—·—·—·— County / Unitary Authority boundary

National / Regional Park

Forest Park boundary

Danger Zone — Military range

172 Page continuation number

Woodland

Beach

·468 Spot height (metres)

▲491 Summit height (metres)

Lake / Dam / River / Waterfall

More details of selected places of interest shown on the mapping can be found on pages 160-162

i *i*	Tourist information office (all year / seasonal)	✕1738	Battlefield	✕	Major sports venue
+++•+++	Preserved railway	▦	Castle	⚽	Major football club
m	Ancient monument	❀	Garden		Motor racing circuit
✝	Ecclesiastical building	⚘	Country park		University
⌂	Historic house (with or without garden)	➤	Nature reserve		Wildlife park or Zoo
▥	Museum / Art gallery	✿	Theme park	★	Other interesting feature
£	Factory shop village	⚑	Racecourse	⚑	Golf course
				(NTS)	National Trust for Scotland

SCALE

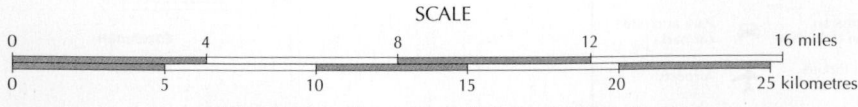

0   4   8   12   16 miles

0   5   10   15   20   25 kilometres

1:250,000 4 miles to 1 inch (2.5cm) / 2.5km to 1cm

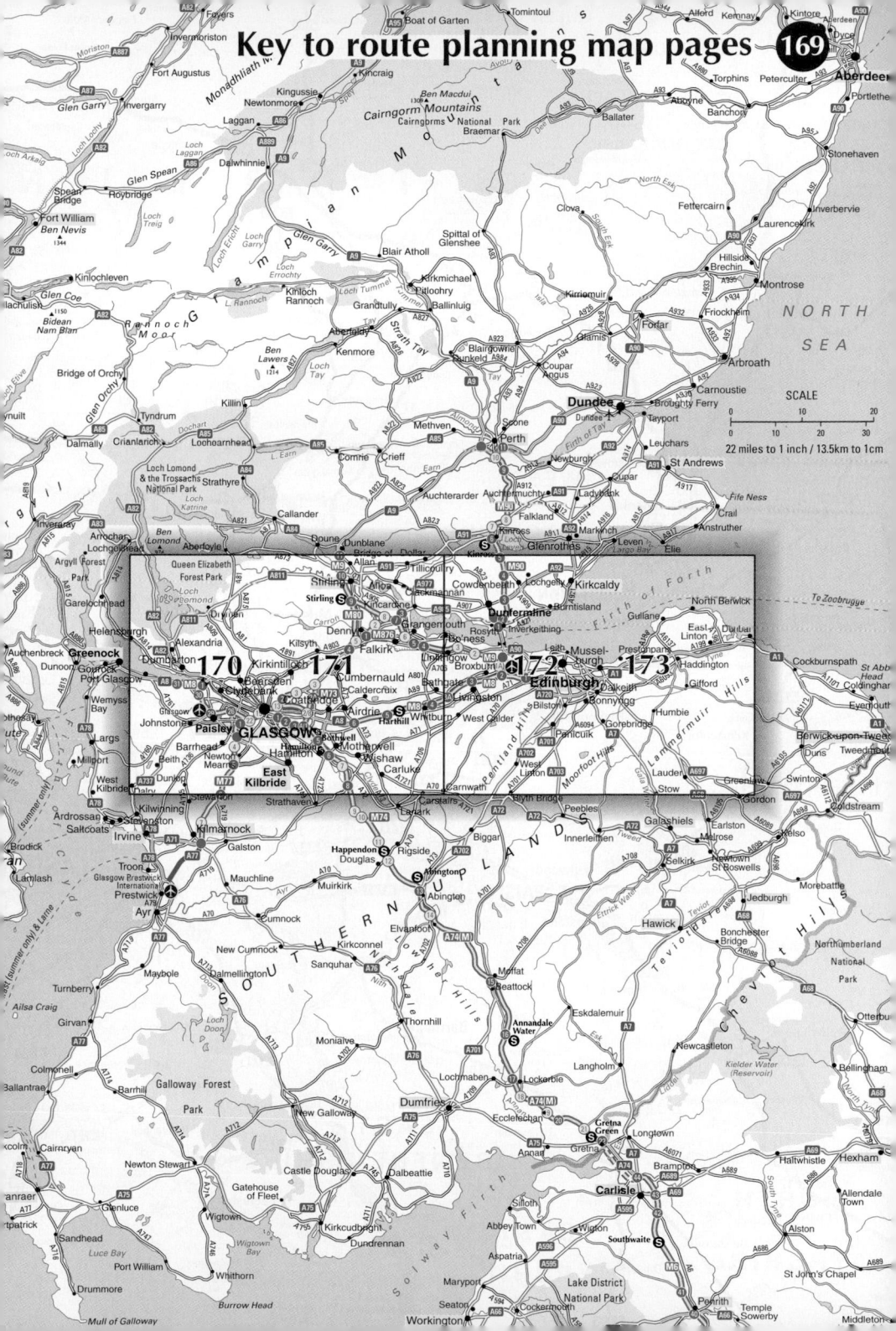

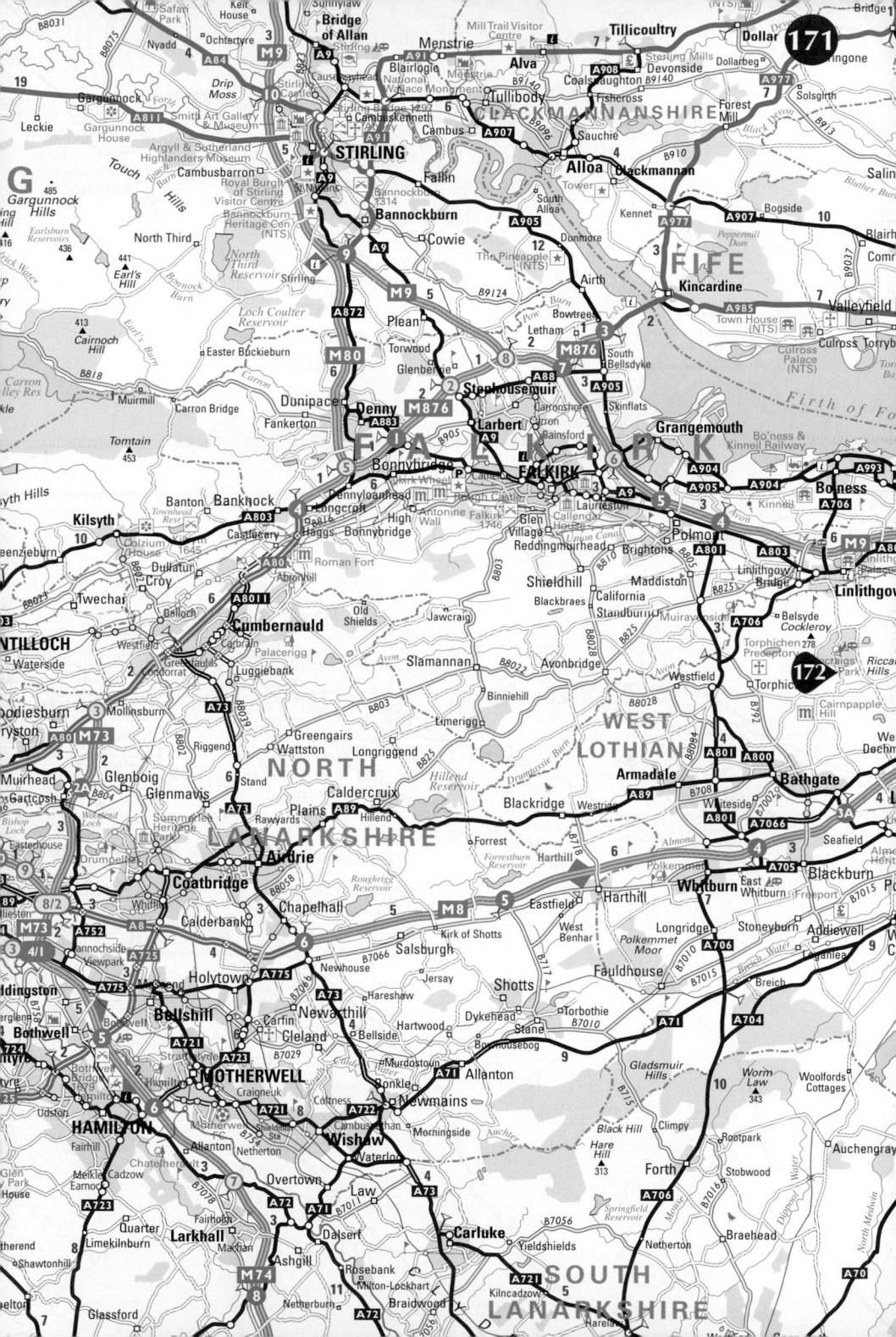

Index to place names

A

Abronhill	23	DF9
Acre	30	BK20
Airdrie	76	DC30
Anderston	4	BP30
Annathill	38	CU19
Anniesland	47	BG23
Arden	101	BG42
Arkleston	63	AY29
Arthurlie	99	AX44
Ashgillhead	145	DG60
Auchenback	99	AZ44
Auchenshuggle	90	CB35
Auchentorlie	83	AX33
Auchinairn	51	BW22
Auchinloch	35	CE19
Auldhouse	102	BL39

B

Back o'Loch	17	CF14
Baillieston	71	CH32
Balgrayhill	50	BV23
Balloch	21	CY11
Balmalloch	7	CS4
Balmore	14	BU13
Balmore Haughs	14	BT14
Balornock	51	BW24
Bankhead	88	BV38
Bardowie	13	BR14
Bargarran	25	AP18
Bargeddie	73	CN32
Barlanark	71	CH31
Barleybank	17	CF13
Barmulloch	51	BZ25
Barnellan	13	BQ12
Barrhead	99	AW42
Barrowfield	95	CW33
Barrwood	8	CV5
Battlefield	87	BQ38
Bearsden	29	BF17
Bellahouston	66	BJ32
Bellshill	111	CW41
Birkenshaw, G71	93	CP36
Birkenshaw, ML9	144	DD62
Birniehill	136	CC54
Bishopbriggs	32	BV19
Bishoploch	72	CL28
Blackhall	83	AW34
Blackhill	69	BZ27
Blackwood	20	CT12
Blairdardie	28	BD20
Blairhill	74	CU30
Blairlinn	40	DC15
Blairtummock	72	CJ29
Blantyre	125	CN45
Blochairn	69	BW28
Blysthwood	45	AY24
Boclair	30	BK17
Bonnaughton	28	BC15
Bothwell	109	CQ43
Bothwellhaugh	110	CU44
Bowerwalls	100	BA41
Bowhouse	105	BW42
Braedale	127	CX47
Braehead	46	BA25
Braeside	104	BV42
Brediland	81	AQ35
Bridgend	37	CN18
Bridgeton	68	BV32
Broadholm	28	BC18
Broadwood	20	CV12
Broom	118	BJ47
Broomhill	47	BH26
Broomhouse	92	CJ36

Brownsburn	96	DD33
Burnbank	125	CQ47
Burnfoot	76	DA28
Burnhead	145	DE58
Burnside	105	BY41
Busby	119	BR48

C

Cadder, G23	49	BP22
Cadder, G64	33	BX16
Cadzow	140	CU53
Cairnhill	76	DA32
Cairnsmore	28	BA18
Calderbank	96	DC34
Calderbraes	93	CN37
Calderpark	92	CL35
Calderwood	123	CE50
Calton	68	BU32
Cambuslang	106	CB39
Camlachie	69	BX31
Canniesburn	29	BH18
Carbrain	22	DC12
Cardonald	64	BD32
Cardowan	53	CF24
Carfin	113	DE43
Carmunnock	120	BU45
Carmyle	91	CE37
Carnbroe	95	CY34
Carntyne	69	BZ29
Carriagehill	82	AT35
Carrickstone	22	DA9
Cartside	79	AF36
Castlehead	82	AT34
Castlemilk	104	BU42
Castleton	104	BS43
Cathcart	103	BQ39
Cathkin	105	BZ43
Ceekhimin	112	DD44
Cessnock	66	BL31
Chantinghill	125	CR50
Chapelhall	97	DG34
Charleston	82	AU35
Chryston	54	CL21
Claddens	35	CH16
Clarkston, G76	118	BM46
Clarkston, ML6	77	DF29
Cleddans, G15	28	BB17
Cleddans, G66	17	CH11
Cliftonville	75	CY30
Clydebank	27	AW20
Clydesdale	112	DA41
Coatbridge	75	CY31
Coatdyke	75	CZ31
College Milton	135	BW51
Colston	50	BU22
Commonhead	73	CN29
Condorrat	39	CW15
Coresford	79	AE37
Corkerhill	85	BF36
Courthill	28	BC15
Cowcaddens	4	BR28
Cowglen	85	BG38
Cowlairs	50	BT25
Craigend	53	CE26
Craigendmuir	53	CG25
Craiglinn	21	CW11
Craigmarloch	21	CW9
Craigneuk, ML2	129	DF49
Craigneuk, ML6	77	DE31
Craigton	65	BF32
Craigton Village	10	BD9
Cranhill	70	CC29
Cranston Hill	67	BN30
Croftfoot	104	BV39

Crookfur	117	BG47
Crookston	84	BC33
Crosshill, G42	87	BQ36
Crosshill, G69	72	CM32
Crossmill	99	AY41
Crossmyloof	86	BM35
Croy	20	CV9
Cumbernauld	21	CZ12

D

Dalbeth	90	CA35
Daldowie	92	CK37
Dalmarnock	89	BW35
Dalmuir	26	AU17
Dalshannon	39	CW15
Dalton	107	CH42
Darnley	101	BE41
Deaconsbank	101	BE43
Dennistoun	69	BW29
Dovecothall	99	AZ42
Dowanhill	48	BL26
Drumchapel	28	BB18
Drumgelloch	76	DD29
Drumoyne	65	BH31
Drumpellier	74	CS31
Drumry	27	AY19
Dullatur	9	CZ7
Dumbreck	86	BK33
Dunbeth	75	CX30
Dundyvan	74	CV32
Dunrobin	77	DH29
Duntiblane	18	CJ14
Duntocher	27	AX15
Dykebar	83	AW37

E

Eaglesham	133	BN56
Earnock	139	CN52
East Balgrochan	15	BY11
East Craigend	25	AQ20
Easterhouse	72	CL29
Eastfield	22	DA10
Easthall	72	CJ30
East Kilbride	135	BZ52
East Mains	136	CA51
East Shawhead	95	CX35
Eastside	17	CF12
Eastwood	102	BJ39
Eddlewood	140	CT54
Elderslie	80	AL36
Erskine	25	AR20
Erskine Harbour	25	AQ17

F

Fairhill	140	CS53
Fallside	110	CS40
Ferguslie Park	61	AP32
Fernhill	105	BX42
Finnieston	66	BM29
Firhill	49	BQ25
Flemington, G72	107	CF42
Flemington, ML1	128	DD48
Fluchter	13	BR11
Forgewood	111	CZ43
Foxbar	81	AP37
Freeland	44	AS22
Fullarton	90	CD35

G

Gallowhill	63	AW30
Gardenhall	134	BU55
Garnethill	4	BQ28

Garnkirk	54	CJ23
Garrowhill	71	CG32
Gartcosh	55	CP24
Gartcraig	70	CB29
Garthamlock	71	CG27
Gartlea	76	DD31
Gartness	77	DG32
Gartsherrie	74	CV28
Gateside	98	AV44
Germiston	69	BX27
Giffnock	102	BM43
Gilshochill	48	BM22
Glenboig	56	CU23
Glenburn	82	AT37
Glengowan	144	DA58
Glenmavis	58	DA25
Glenwood	104	BU43
Gockston	62	AT29
Golfhill	76	DB27
Gorbals	68	BS32
Govan	66	BJ30
Govanhill	87	BQ35
Greenend	95	CY33
Greenfaulds	22	DA13
Greenfield	70	CC31
Greenfoot	57	CW22
Greengairs	41	DH20
Greenhill	75	CX28
Greenhills	135	BY55
Greenlees	106	CD42
Greens, The	16	CD14

H

Haghill	69	BY30
Hairmyres	134	BU53
Halfway	107	CF41
Hallside	107	CH41
Haltonrig	111	CX39
Hamilton	126	CS50
Hamiltonhill	49	BR25
Hangingshaw	88	BS37
Hardgate	27	AY15
Hareleeshill	144	DD60
Harestanes	18	CJ12
Hawkhead	83	AZ36
Hayston	16	CC13
High Balmalloch	7	CS4
High Blantyre	124	CL47
High Burnside	105	BY41
High Gallowhill	34	CC15
High Knightswood	47	BG21
Highland Park	7	CS3
High Possil	49	BR21
Hillhead, G12	49	BN26
Hillhead, G66	17	CG13
Hillington	64	BC31
Hillpark	102	BL40
Hogganfield	70	CC27
Holehills	76	DD27
Holehouse	114	AS46
Holytown	112	DC39
Househillwood	100	BD39
Howgill	103	BR43
Hunterhill	83	AW35
Hunt Hill	20	CS12
Hurlet	100	BA39
Hutchesontown	88	BS34
Hyndland	48	BJ26

I

Ibrox	66	BK31
Inchinnan	44	AT23

J

Jackton	134	BS54
Jenny Lind	101	BF43
Johnstone	79	AH36
Johnstone Castle	80	AJ36
Jordanhill	47	BG24

K

Kelvin	136	CD55
Kelvindale	48	BK23
Kelvingrove	66	BM28
Kelvinhaugh	66	BK28
Kelvinside	48	BK25
Kennishead	101	BG40
Kessington	30	BJ17
Kilbarchan	78	AD34
Kilbowie	27	AX19
Kildermorie	72	CJ29
Kildrum	22	DD10
Killermont	30	BK19
Kilsyth	7	CR5
King's Park	104	BT39
Kingsridge	28	BA18
Kingston	67	BP32
Kinning Park	66	BM32
Kirkhill	102	CD40
Kirkintilloch	17	CG14
Kirklandneuk	45	AW26
Kirkshaws	94	CU34
Kirkwood	74	CS32
Knightswood	47	BE22
Kylepark	92	CM38

L

Laigh Crosshill	92	CL33
Laigh Park	62	AU30
Laighstonehall	140	CS51
Lambhill	49	BQ22
Langfauld	28	BB17
Langloan	74	CU32
Langmuir, G66	18	CK12
Langmuir, G69	93	CP33
Langside	87	BN37
Larkhall	144	DD58
Laurieston	67	BR32
Lenzie	35	CF16
Lenziemill	22	DC13
Lightburn	70	CC30
Linburn	24	AN19
Linndale	104	BS42
Linnvale	27	AZ20
Linwood	60	AK31
Little Earnock	139	CQ52
Loanhead	45	AZ26
Lochfield	82	AV36
Low Blantyre	109	CN44
Low Waters	140	CU52
Luggiebank	40	DC15

M

Machan	144	DC59
Malletsheugh	116	BD50
Mansewood	102	BK40
Marnoch	56	CS22
Maryhill	48	BK22
Meadowhill	144	DD57
Mearns	117	BG49
Meikle Earnock	140	CS54
Meikleriggs	81	AQ34
Merkland	17	CH12
Merrylee	102	BM41
Millarston	81	AP34
Millerston, G33	52	CC25
Millerston, G76	119	BN49
Millheugh	144	DA59

Millikenpark	79	AE36
Milngavie	12	BJ12
Milnwood	111	CZ41
Milton	50	BS22
Milton of Campsie	16	CD9
Mollinsburn	38	CT17
Moodiesburn	36	CM19
Moorpark	63	AX27
Mosshead	29	BF15
Mossneuk	134	BV54
Mosspark	85	BG34
Motherwell	128	DB47
Mountblow	26	AT16
Mount Ellen	55	CN23
Mount Florida	87	BR38
Mount Vernon	91	CG34
Muirend	103	BN41
Muirhead, G69 (Baillieston)	92	CL33
Muirhead, G69 (Chryston)	54	CM22
Muirhouse	128	DC50
Murray, The	136	CA54

N

Neilston	114	AU46
Nerston	122	CB49
Nether Kirkton	114	AU45
Netherlee	103	BQ43
Netherton, G13	47	BH21
Netherton, ML2	143	DE52
Newarthill	113	DI41
Newlands	103	BN39
Newlandsmuir	134	DU55
New Monkland	58	DA24
New Stevenston	112	DB42
Newton	107	CH39
Newton Mearns	117	BE49
Nitshill	100	BB40
North Barr	25	AQ18
North Barrwood	7	CV4
North Cardonald	64	BD29
Northfield	6	CQ4
North Haugh	127	CW48
North Kelvin	49	BN25
North Lodge	128	DA49
North Motherwell	127	CX45
North Mount Vernon	91	CG33

O

Old Drumchapel	28	BA19
Oldhall	63	AZ32
Old Kilpatrick	25	AQ15
Old Monkland	94	CU33
Orbiston	111	CW42
Orchard Park, G46	102	BJ42
Orchard Park, G66	35	CG17
Oxgang	17	CH14

P

Paisley	62	AT32
Parkhall	26	AV16
Parkhead	89	BZ33
Parkhouse	50	BT23
Park Mains	44	AS21
Partick	66	BK27
Partickhill	48	BK26
Penilee	64	BB31
Petersburn	77	DG31
Petershill	51	BW26
Philipshill	120	BU49
Pinewood	29	BE18
Pollok	85	BE35

Pollokshaws	86	BK38
Pollokshields	86	BM34
Polmadie	88	BT35
Port Dundas	67	BR27
Port Eglinton	87	BP33
Porterfield	63	AX27
Possilpark	50	BS24
Potterhill	82	AU36
Priesthill	100	BD39
Provanhall	72	CJ28
Provanmill	69	BY27

Q

Quarrelton	79	AH35
Queenslie	71	CG29
Queenzieburn	6	CN5

R

Radnor Park	27	AW18
Raploch	144	DB59
Rashielee	25	AQ19
Ravenscraig	129	DE47
Rawyards	77	DE27
Renfrew	45	AY26
Riddrie	69	BZ28
Riddrie Knowes	70	CA29
Riggend	40	DD20
Robroyston	52	CA23
Rogerfield	72	CL30
Rosehall	95	CX33
Rosshall	84	BC33
Rossland	24	AL19
Roughmussel	84	BB37
Roystonhill	68	BV29
Ruchazie	70	CD28
Ruchill	49	BP24
Rutherglen	89	BX37

S

St. Leonards	137	CE52
Sandyhills	71	CF32
Scotstoun	46	BD25
Scotstounhill	46	BD24
Seafar	22	DA11
Seedhill	82	AV33
Shawfield	88	BV36
Shawhead	95	CW34
Shawlands	86	BL36
Sheddens	119	BP46
Shettleston	90	CC33
Shieldhall	65	BE29
Shirrel	95	CX38
Shortroods	62	AU30
Sighthill	68	BU27
Sikeside	75	CZ32
Silvertonhill	140	CV51
Simshill	104	BS41
South Barrwood	8	CV6
South Cardonald	85	BE33
South Claddens	35	CH17
South Haugh	127	CW50
South Nitshill	100	BC41
South Westerton	29	BF19
Spateston	79	AF38
Spittal	104	BV40
Springboig	70	CC31
Springburn	50	BV25
Springhall	105	BZ41
Springhill	99	AY43
Stamperland	119	BP45
Stand	58	DD23
Stanely	81	AR36
Stepps	53	CF24
Stewartfield	121	BY49
Stonedyke	28	BD18
Strathbungo	87	BN35

Strutherhill	144	DB61
Summerlee	74	CV30
Summerston	30	BM20
Sunnyside	75	CX29
Swinton	72	CL31

T

Tannochside	93	CR37
Temple	47	BH21
Templecross	104	BV43
Thornliebank	101	BH42
Thornly Park	82	AV37
Thorntonhall	120	BS50
Thrashburn	76	DB28
Tintock	18	CL11
Tollcross	90	CB34
Torrance	15	BY12
Toryglen	88	BT37
Townhead	17	CE13
Tradeston	67	BQ32
Twechar	19	CP10

U

Uddingston	92	CM38
Udston	125	CP49

V

Vicarland	106	CC41
Victory Gardens	63	AY28
Viewpark	94	CS38

W

Wardlawhill	89	BY38
Waterfoot	132	BM52
Wattston	41	DE20
Waverley	28	BC16
Waverley Park	86	BK36
Wellhouse	71	CG30
Welside	107	CF42
West Arthurlie	99	AW43
West Balgrochan	15	BW12
Westburn	107	CG39
Westcastle	104	BT41
West Craigend	24	AN20
Wester Holytown	112	DA40
Westermains	16	CC13
Westerton	29	BG19
Westerwood	9	DB7
Westfield, G65	7	CR5
Westfield, G68	38	CU15
West Mains	135	BY51
Westwood	135	BX52
Whifflet	75	CY32
Whinhall	76	DA29
Whitecrook	45	AZ21
Whitehaugh	63	AW32
Whitehill	125	CR47
Whitehills	135	BZ56
Whiteinch	47	BG26
Whitlawburn	106	CA42
Williamsburgh	83	AX33
Williamwood	118	BL45
Windlaw	104	BT43
Wishaw	129	DG50
Woodside	67	BQ27
Wyndford	48	BM24

Y

Yoker	46	BA23
Yorkhill	66	BM28

Index to street names

General abbreviations

All	Alley	Conv	Convent	Gdns	Gardens	Mus	Museum	Sq	Square
Allot	Allotments	Cor	Corner	Govt	Government	N	North	St.	Saint
Amb	Ambulance	Coron	Coroners	Gra	Grange	NTS	National Trust	St	Street
App	Approach	Cors	Corners	Grd	Ground		for	Sta	Station
Arc	Arcade	Cotts	Cottages	Grds	Grounds	Scotland		Sts	Streets
Av	Avenue	Cov	Covered	Grn	Green	Nat	National	Sub	Subway
Ave	Avenue	Crem	Crematorium	Grns	Greens	PH	Public House	Swim	Swimming
Bdy	Broadway	Cres	Crescent	Gro	Grove	PO	Post Office	TA	Territorial
Bk	Bank	Ct	Court	Gros	Groves	Par	Parade		Army
Bldgs	Buildings	Cts	Courts	Gt	Great	Pas	Passage	TH	Town Hall
Boul	Boulevard	Ctyd	Courtyard	Ho	House	Pav	Pavilion	Tenn	Tennis
Bowl	Bowling	Dep	Depot	Hos	Houses	Pk	Park	Ter	Terrace
Br	Bridge	Dev	Development	Hosp	Hospital	Pl	Place	Thea	Theatre
C of S	Church of	Dr	Drive	Hts	Heights	Pol	Police	Trd	Trading
	Scotland	Dws	Dwellings	Ind	Industrial	Prec	Precinct	Twr	Tower
Cath	Cathedral	E	East	Int	International	Prim	Primary	Twrs	Towers
Cem	Cemetery	Ed	Education	Junct	Junction	Prom	Promenade	Uni	University
Cen	Central,	Elec	Electricity	La	Lane	Pt	Point	Vil	Villas
	Centre	Embk	Embankment	Las	Lanes	Quad	Quadrant	Vil	Villa
Cft	Croft	Est	Estate	Lib	Library	RC	Roman	Vw	View
Cfts	Crofts	Ex	Exchange	Ln	Loan		Catholic	W	West
Ch	Church	Exhib	Exhibition	Lo	Lodge	Rd	Road	Wd	Wood
Chyd	Churchyard	FB	Footbridge	Lwr	Lower	Rds	Roads	Wds	Woods
Cin	Cinema	FC	Football Club	Mag	Magistrates	Rec	Recreation	Wf	Wharf
Circ	Circus	Fld	Field	Mans	Mansions	Res	Reservoir	Wk	Walk
Cl	Close	Flds	Fields	Mem	Memorial	Ri	Rise	Wks	Works
Clo	Close	Fm	Farm	Mkt	Market	S	South	Yd	Yard
Co	County	Gall	Gallery	Mkts	Markets	Sch	School		
Coll	College	Gar	Garage	Ms	Mews	Sec	Secondary		
Comm	Community	Gdn	Garden	Mt	Mount	Shop	Shopping		

Post town abbreviations

Air.	Airdrie	Ersk.	Erskine	Pais.	Paisley
Bell.	Bellshill	Ham.	Hamilton	Renf.	Renfrew
Bish.	Bishopton	John.	Johnstone	Wis.	Wishaw
Clyde.	Clydebank	Lark.	Larkhall		
Coat.	Coatbridge	Moth.	Motherwell		

Locality abbreviations

Abbots.	Abbotsinch	Deac.	Deaconsbank	Linw.	Linwood
Baill.	Baillieston	Dunt.	Duntocher	M. of Cam.	Milton of Campsie
Barr.	Barrhead	E.Kil.	East Kilbride	Millik.	Millikenpark
Bears.	Bearsden	Eagle.	Eaglesham	Miln.	Milngavie
Birk.	Birkenshaw	Elder.	Elderslie	Mood.	Moodiesburn
Bishop.	Bishopbriggs	Gart.	Gartcosh	Muir.	Muirhead
Blan.	Blantyre	Giff.	Giffnock	Neil.	Neilston
Both.	Bothwell	Glenb.	Glenboig	New Stev.	New Stevenston
Calder.	Calderbank	Glenm.	Glenmavis	New.	Newarthill
Camb.	Cambuslang	Green.	Greengairs	Newt. M.	Newton Mearns
Carm.	Carmunnock	Hous.	Houston	Old Kil.	Old Kilpatrick
Chap.	Chapelhall	How.	Howwood	Ruther.	Rutherglen
Chry.	Chryston	Inch.	Inchinnan	Thornlie.	Thornliebank
Clark.	Clarkston	Kilb.	Kilbarchan	Thornton.	Thorntonhall
Cumb.	Cumbernauld	Kirk.	Kirkintilloch	Torr.	Torrance
Cumb.V.	Cumbernauld Village	Lenz.	Lenzie	Udd.	Uddingston

This index contains streets that are not named on the map due to insufficient space. For each of these cases the nearest street that does appear on the map is listed in *italics*.

A

Abbey Cl, Pais. PA1	62	AU32
Abbeycraig Rd, G34	72	CM28
Abbeydale Way, (Ruther.) G73	105	BY42
off Neilvaig Dr		
Abbey Dr, G14	47	BG25
Abbeygreen St, G34	73	CN28
Abbeyhill St, G32	70	CA30
Abbey Mill Business Cen, Pais. PA1	82	AV33
Abbey Pl, Air. ML6	97	DE33
Abbey Rd, (Elder.) John. PA5	80	AK35

Abbey Wk, (Baill.) G69	73	CP32
off Sunnyside Dr		
Abbey Wk, Lark. ML9	144	DD57
off Carrick Pl		
Abbotsburn Way, Pais. PA3	62	AT29
Abbotsford, (Bishop.) G64	33	BY19
Abbotsford Av, (Ruther.) G73	89	BX38
Abbotsford Av, Ham. ML3	125	CR46
Abbotsford Av, Lark. ML9	144	DC60
Abbotsford Brae, (E.Kil.) G74	122	CA50
Abbotsford Ct, (Cumb.) G67	22	DB14
Abbotsford Cres, Ham. ML3	125	CR47

Abbotsford Cres, Pais. PA2	80	AM38
Abbotsford Dr, (Kirk.) G66	17	CG13
Abbotsford La, Bell. ML4	110	CV39
off Cochrane St		
Abbotsford Pl, G5	67	BR32
Abbotsford Pl, (Cumb.) G67	22	DB14
Abbotsford Pl, Moth. ML1	112	DD40
off Ivy Ter		
Abbotsford Rd, (Bears.) G61	29	BE15
Abbotsford Rd, (Cumb.) G67	22	DB14
Abbotsford Rd, (Chap.) Air. ML6	97	DG36

Name	Page	Grid
Abbotsford Rd, Clyde. G81	27	AX20
Abbotsford Rd, Ham. ML3	125	CQ47
Abbotshall Av, G15	28	BA18
Abbotsinch Retail Pk, Pais. PA3	62	AV29
Abbotsinch Rd, Pais. PA3	62	AU27
Abbotsinch Rd, Renf. PA4	44	AV25
Abbots Ter, Air. ML6	97	DE33
Abbot St, G41	87	BN36
off Frankfort St		
Abbot St, Pais. PA3	62	AV31
Abbott Cres, Clyde. G81	45	AZ21
Aberconway St, Clyde. G81	45	AY21
Abercorn Av, G52	64	BA29
Abercorn Cres, Ham. ML3	140	CU51
Abercorn Dr, Ham. ML3	126	CV50
Abercorn Pl, G23	31	BN20
Abercorn Rd, (Newt. M.) G77	117	BE47
Abercorn St, Pais. PA3	62	AV31
Abercrombie Cres, (Baill.) G69	73	CP32
Abercrombie Dr, (Bears.) G61	10	BD13
Abercrombie Pl, (Kilsyth) G65	7	CR4
Abercromby Cres, (E.Kil.) G74	122	CD50
Abercromby Dr, G40	68	BV31
Abercromby Pl, (E.Kil.) G74	122	CD50
Abercromby Sq, G40	68	BV31
Abercromby St, G40	68	BV32
Aberdalgie Gdns, G34	72	CK29
Aberdalgie Path, G34	72	CK29
Aberdalgie Rd, G34	72	CK29
Aberdeen Rd, Air. ML6	97	DF33
off Stirling Rd		
Aberdour St, G31	69	BY30
Aberfeldy Av, (Plains) Air. ML6	59	DH26
Aberfeldy St, G31	69	BY30
Aberfoyle St, G31	69	BY30
Aberlady Rd, G51	65	BG31
Abernethy Dr, (Linw.) Pais. PA3	60	AJ32
Abernethy Pk, (E.Kil.) G74	135	BZ51
Abernethy Pl, (Newt. M.) G77	118	BK49
Abernethy St, G31	69	BY30
Aberuthven Dr, G32	90	CD34
Abiegail Pl, (Blan.) G72	108	CM44
Aboukir St, G51	65	BG29
Aboyne Dr, Pais. PA2	82	AV36
Aboyne St, G51	65	BH31
Acacia Dr, (Barr.) G78	99	AW40
Acacia Dr, Pais. PA2	81	AR36
Acacia Pl, John. PA5	80	AJ37
Acacia Way, (Camb.) G72	107	CG40
Academy Ct, Coat. ML5	75	CW30
off Academy St		
Academy Pk, G51	86	BL33
Academy Pk, Air. ML6	76	DC30
Academy Pl, Coat. ML5	75	CW30
off Baird St		
Academy Rd, (Giff.) G46	102	BL43
Academy St, G32	90	CD33
Academy St, Air. ML6	76	DC30
Academy St, Coat. ML5	75	CW30
Academy St, Lark. ML9	144	DC58
Academy Ter, Bell. ML4	111	CX40
Acer Cres, Pais. PA2	81	AQ36
Acer Gro, (Chap.) Air. ML6	97	DG34
Achamore Cres, G15	28	BA17
Achamore Dr, G15	28	BA17
Achamore Rd, G15	28	BA17
Achray Dr, Pais. PA2	81	AQ36
Achray Pl, (Miln.) G62	11	BF10
Achray Pl, Coat. ML5	74	CS28
Achray Rd, (Cumb.) G67	21	CX14
Acorn Ct, G40	88	BV33
Acorn St, G40	88	BV33
Acre Dr, G20	30	BK20
Acredyke Cres, G21	51	BY22
Acredyke Pl, G21	51	BY23
Acredyke Rd, G21	51	BX22
Acredyke Rd, (Ruther.) G73	88	BV37
Acre Rd, G20	30	BK20
Acres, The, Lark. ML9	144	DD59
Acre Valley Rd, (Torr.) G64	15	BX11
Adam Av, Air. ML6	76	DD30
Adams Ct La, G1	4	BR31
Adamslie Cres, (Kirk.) G66	16	CC13
Adamslie Dr, (Kirk.) G66	16	CC13
Adamson St, Bell. ML4	111	CZ40
Adams Pl, (Kilsyth) G65	7	CT5
Adamswell St, G21	50	BU26
Adamswell Ter, (Mood.) G69	37	CQ19
Addie St, Moth. ML1	128	DB45
Addiewell Pl, Coat. ML5	95	CW33
Addiewell St, G32	70	CC30
off Cardowan Rd		
Addison Gro, (Thornlie.) G46	101	BH41
Addison Pl, (Thornlie.) G46	101	BH41
Addison Rd, G12	48	BM25
Addison Rd, (Thornlie.) G46	101	BH41
Adelaide Ct, Clyde. G81	26	AT16
Adelaide Rd, (E.Kil.) G75	135	BX54
Adele St, Moth. ML1	128	DB49
Adelphi St, G5	68	BT32
Admiral St, G41	67	BN32
Admiralty Gdns, (Old Kil.) G60	25	AR16
Admiralty Gro, (Old Kil.) G60	25	AR16
Admiralty Pl, (Old Kil.) G60	25	AR16
Advie Pl, G42	87	BR37
Affric Dr, Pais. PA2	83	AX36
Afton Cres, (Bears.) G61	30	BK18
Afton Dr, Renf. PA4	64	BA27
Afton Gdns, (Blan.) G72	124	CK47
Afton Gdns, Coat. ML5	95	CZ33
Afton Rd, (Cumb.) G67	22	DD10
Afton St, G41	87	BN37
Afton St, Lark. ML9	145	DE59
Afton Vw, (Kirk.) G66	17	CH12
Agamemnon St, Clyde. G81	26	AV19
Agate Ter, Bell. ML4	111	CW41
Agnew Av, Coat. ML5	75	CY30
Agnew Gro, Bell. ML4	110	CT40
Agnew La, G42	87	BQ36
Aigas Cotts, G13	47	BH24
off Fern La		
Aikenhead Rd, G42	87	BR34
Aikenhead Rd, G44	104	BS39
Aikman Pl, (E.Kil.) G74	122	CD50
Aikman Rd, Moth. ML1	127	CX48
Ailean Dr, G32	91	CG33
Ailean Gdns, G32	91	CG33
Aillort Pl, (E.Kil.) G74	122	CA50
Ailort Av, G44	103	BQ40
off Lochinver Dr		
Ailsa Av, (Ashgill) Lark. ML9	145	DH61
Ailsa Av, Moth. ML1	127	CX46
Ailsa Ct, Coat. ML5	94	CU33
Ailsa Ct, Ham. ML3	138	CM52
Ailsa Cres, Moth. ML1	127	CX46
Ailsa Dr, G42	87	BP38
Ailsa Dr, (Giff.) G46	118	BK45
Ailsa Dr, (Kirk.) G66	17	CH11
Ailsa Dr, (Both.) G71	109	CQ41
Ailsa Dr, (Ruther.) G73	104	BW40
Ailsa Dr, Clyde. G81	27	AY15
Ailsa Dr, Pais. PA2	82	AT38
Ailsa Pl, Coat. ML5	94	CV33
Ailsa Rd, (Bishop.) G64	33	BX19
Ailsa Rd, Coat. ML5	94	CU33
Ailsa Rd, Renf. PA4	63	AY27
Ainslie Av, G52	64	BC29
Ainslie Rd, G52	64	BC29
Ainslie Rd, (Cumb.) G67	23	DE10
Airbles Cres, Moth. ML1	127	CZ48
Airbles Dr, Moth. ML1	127	CZ48
Airbles Fm Rd, Moth. ML1	127	CY48
Airbles Rd, Moth. ML1	127	CZ48
Airbles St, Moth. ML1	128	DA48
Airdale Av, (Giff.) G46	102	BL43
Airdriehill Rd, Air. ML6	77	DE27
Airdriehill St, Air. ML6	77	DE27
Airdrie Rd, (Kilsyth) G65	7	CT5
Airdrie Rd, (Cumb.) G67	38	CT17
Airdrie Rd, Air. ML6	77	DH28
Aird's La, G1	5	BS31
off Bridgegate		
Airgold Dr, G15	28	BB17
Airgold Pl, G15	28	BB17
Airlie Av, (Bears.) G61	11	BG14
off Montrose Dr		
Airlie Dr, Bell. ML4	111	CW39
Airlie Gdns, (Ruther.) G73	105	BZ41
Airlie La, G12	48	BK25
Airlie Rd, (Baill.) G69	92	CJ34
Airlie St, G12	48	BJ26
Airlink Ind Est, Pais. PA3	62	AU29
Airlour Rd, G43	103	BN40
Airth Ct, Moth. ML1	111	CZ44
Airth Dr, G52	85	BH34
Airth La, G52	85	BH34
off Mosspark Dr		
Airth Pl, G52	85	BH34
off Mosspark Dr		
Airthrey Av, G14	47	BG26
Airthrey La, G14	47	BG25
off Airthrey Av		
Airth Way, (Cumb.) G68	20	CU13
Airyligg Dr, (Eagle.) G76	133	BN56
Aitchison Ct, Air. ML6	76	DB29
Aitchison St, Air. ML6	76	DA30
Aitkenhead Av, Coat. ML5	93	CR33
Aitkenhead Rd, (Udd.) G71	93	CQ36
Aitkenhead Rd, (Chap.) Air. ML6	97	DF35
Aitken Rd, Ham. ML3	140	CU54
Aitken St, G31	69	BY30
Aitken St, Air. ML6	76	DD28
Alasdair Ct, (Barr.) G78	99	AY43
Albans Cres, Moth. ML1	127	CX45
Albany, (E.Kil.) G74	123	CE49
Albany Av, G32	71	CE31
Albany Cotts, G13	47	BH24
off Fern La		
Albany Cres, Moth. ML1	112	DB40
off Thankerton Av		
Albany Dr, (Ruther.) G73	105	BX39
Albany Pl, (Both.) G71	109	CR43
off Marguerite Gdns		
Albany Quad, G32	71	CE31
Albany Rd, Ham. ML3	140	CS53
off Annsfield Rd		
Albany St, G40	89	BW33
Albany St, Coat. ML5	74	CU30
Albany Ter, (Camb.) G72	106	CA42
Albany Way, Pais. PA3	62	AU29
off Abbotsburn Way		
Albany Wynd, Lark. ML9	144	DD57
off Duncan Graham St		
Alba Way, Ham. ML3	140	CS55
Alberta Av, (E.Kil.) G75	135	BX53
Alberta Av, Coat. ML5	74	CV29

Alberta Cres, (E.Kil.) G75	135	BY53
off Alberta Av		
Alberta Pk, (E.Kil.) G75	135	BZ53
Alberta Pl, (E.Kil.) G75	135	BZ53
off Alberta Av		
Albert Av, G42	87	BQ36
Albert Br, G1	68	BS32
Albert Br, G5	68	BS32
Albert Cres, Air. ML6	76	DD30
Albert Cross, G41	87	BP34
Albert Dr, G41	86	BL35
Albert Dr, (Bears.) G61	30	BK18
Albert Dr, (Ruther.) G73	105	BX40
Albert Dr, Lark. ML9	144	DD59
Albert Pl, Air. ML6	76	DD29
Albert Quad, Moth. ML1	112	DC40
off Sherry Av		
Albert Rd, G42	87	BQ36
Albert Rd, (Lenz.) G66	35	CE18
Albert Rd, Clyde. G81	27	AW18
Albert Rd, Renf. PA4	45	AY26
Albert St, Coat. ML5	75	CW30
Albert St, Ham. ML3	125	CR47
Albert St, Moth. ML1	128	DB46
Albert Ter, Ham. ML3	125	CQ47
off Albert St		
Albion Gate, G1	5	BT30
off Albion St		
Albion Pl, Pais. PA3	62	AT31
Albion St, G1	5	BT31
Albion St, (Baill.) G69	91	CH34
Albion St, Coat. ML5	75	CX30
Albion St, Moth. ML1	128	DA48
Albion St, Pais. PA3	62	AT31
Albion Way, (E.Kil.) G75	136	CB56
Albion Wks Ind Est, G13	46	BA22
Alcaig Rd, G52	85	BG35
Alder Av, (Kirk.) G66	34	CD16
Alder Av, Ham. ML3	140	CU52
Alder Bk, (Udd.) G71	94	CS36
Alder Ct, (E.Kil.) G75	135	BY56
Alder Ct, (Barr.) G78	99	AY44
Alder Cres, (E.Kil.) G75	135	BY56
Alder Gate, (Camb.) G72	107	CG40
Alder Gro, Coat. ML5	75	CX31
Alder La, (Holytown) Moth.	13	DE40
ML11 off Elm Rd		
Alder La, (New Stev.) Moth.	12	DC42
ML11 off Jerviston St		
Alderman Pl, G13	47	BE23
Alderman Rd, G13	46	BB21
Alder Pl, G43	102	BK40
Alder Pl, (E.Kil.) G75	135	BY56
Alder Pl, John. PA5	80	AJ36
Alder Rd, G43	102	BL40
Alder Rd, (Cumb.) G67	23	DF11
Alder Rd, Clyde. G81	26	AV16
Alderside Pl, (Both.) G71	109	CR42
off Churchill Cres		
Alderstocks, (E.Kil.) G75	136	CA56
Alderston Pl, Bell. ML4	110	CU41
Alderston Way, (Righead Ind.	110	CU39
Est.) Bell. ML4		
Aldersyde Av, Wis. ML2	129	DF49
Aldersyde Gdns, (Udd.) G71	93	CQ38
Aldersyde Pl, (Blan.) G72	108	CL44
Alexander Av, (Kilsyth) G65	19	CN9
Alexander Av, (Udd.) G71	110	CS39
Alexander Av, (Eagle.) G76	133	BN55
Alexander Balfour Gdns, Ham.	140	CT52
ML3 off Morris St		
Alexander Cres, G5	88	BS33
Alexander Gdns, Ham. ML3	141	CW51
Alexander Gibson Way, Moth.	127	CZ47
ML1		
Alexander Path, Moth. ML1	128	DD50
Alexander Pl, (Kirk.) G66	18	CK14
Alexander St, Air. ML6	76	DA30
Alexander St, Clyde. G81	27	AX20
Alexander St, Coat. ML5	75	CX29
Alexander St, Wis. ML2	129	DH50
Alexander Ter, (Neil.) G78	114	AS47
Alexandra Av, (Stepps) G33	53	CF23
Alexandra Av, (Lenz.) G66	35	CE17
Alexandra Ct, G31	69	BX29
Alexandra Cross, G31	69	BX30
Alexandra Dr, Pais. PA2	81	AR34
Alexandra Dr, Renf. PA4	45	AZ26
Alexandra Gdns, (Kirk.) G66	35	CE17
Alexandra Par, G31	5	BU29
Alexandra Pk, (Kirk.) G66	35	CE17
Alexandra Pk St, G31	69	BX30
Alexandra Dr, (Lenz.) G66	35	CE17
Alexandra St, (Kirk.) G66	17	CE13
Alexandria Quad, Moth. ML1	112	DC40
off Main St		
Alford Av, (Kirk.) G66	16	CD13
Alford St, G21	50	BT26
Alfred La, G12	48	BM26
Alfred Ter, G12	49	BN26
Algie St, G41	87	BP37
Algoma Pl, (E.Kil.) G75	135	BX53
off Winnipeg Dr		
Alice Av, Bell. ML4	111	CW41
Alice St, Pais. PA2	82	AU35
Aline Ct, (Barr.) G78	99	AX41
off Lomond Dr		
Alison Lea, (E.Kil.) G74	122	CD50
Allan Av, Renf. PA4	64	BA28
Allan Ct, (E.Kil.) G75	134	BU54
Allandale Av, Moth. ML1	113	DH40
Allandale Path, (Blan.) G72	124	CM46
off Winton Cres		
Allander Av, (Miln.) G62	13	BR14
Allander Dr, (Torr.) G64	15	BW13
Allander Gdns, (Bishop.) G64	32	BV17
Allander Rd, (Bears.) G61	29	BF18
Allander Rd, (Miln.) G62	12	BJ11
Allander St, G22	50	BS25
Allander Wk, (Cumb.) G67	22	DB12
off Cumbernauld Shop Cen		
Allan Dr, (E.Kil.) G75	134	BU54
Allands Av, (Inch.) Renf. PA4	44	AS24
Allanfauld Rd, (Kilsyth) G65	7	CT3
Allanfauld Rd, (Cumb.) G67	22	DB11
Allan Glen Gdns, (Bishop.)	33	BX17
G64		
Allan Pl, G40	89	BX34
Allanshaw Gdns, Ham. ML3	125	CR50
Allanshaw Gro, Ham. ML3	139	CR51
off Allanshaw Gdns		
Allanshaw St, Ham. ML3	126	CS50
Allan St, G40	89	BX35
Allan St, Coat. ML5	74	CT32
Allan St, Moth. ML1	128	DB46
Allanton Av, Pais. PA1	84	BA33
Allanton Dr, G52	64	BD32
Allanton Lea, Ham. ML3	140	CS53
Allendale, (E.Kil.) G74	135	BY51
Allen Way, Renf. PA4	63	AZ28
Allerdyce Ct, G15	28	BA20
Allerdyce Dr, G15	28	BB20
Allerdyce Rd, G15	28	BB20
Allershaw Pl, Wis. ML2	143	DH53
Allershaw Rd, Wis. ML2	143	DH53
Allerton Gdns, (Baill.) G69	91	CH33
Alleysbank Rd, (Ruther.) G73	89	BX36
Allison Av, Ersk. PA8	25	AP19
Allison Dr, (Camb.) G72	106	CC39
Allison Pl, G42	87	BQ35
off Prince Edward St		
Allison Pl, (Gart.) G69	55	CN25
Allison Pl, (Newt. M.) G77	117	BE49
Allison St, G42	87	BQ35
Allnach Pl, G34	73	CN29
Alloway Av, Pais. PA2	83	AX37
Alloway Ct, (Kirk.) G66	18	CJ11
Alloway Cres, (Ruther.) G73	104	BV40
Alloway Cres, Pais. PA2	83	AX37
Alloway Dr, (Kirk.) G66	17	CH12
Alloway Dr, (Ruther.) G73	104	BV40
Alloway Dr, (Newt. M.) G77	118	BJ49
Alloway Dr, Clyde. G81	27	AY18
Alloway Dr, Pais. PA2	83	AX37
Alloway Gdns, (Kirk.) G66	18	CJ11
Alloway Gdns, Ham. ML3	138	CM52
Alloway Gro, (Kirk.) G66	17	CH11
Alloway Gro, Pais. PA2	83	AY37
Alloway Quad, (Kirk.) G66	18	CJ12
Alloway Rd, G43	102	BM39
Alloway Rd, (E.Kil.) G74	123	CG50
Alloway Rd, Air. ML6	77	DH29
Alloway St, Lark. ML9	145	DE59
Alloway Ter, (Kirk.) G66	17	CH11
Alloway Wynd, Moth. ML1	113	DG41
off Kirkoswald Rd		
Almada La, Ham. ML3	126	CT49
off Almada La		
Almada La, Ham. ML3	126	CT49
Almada St, Ham. ML3	126	CS49
Alma St, G40	69	BW32
Almond Av, Renf. PA4	64	BA27
Almond Bk, (Bears.) G61	29	BE19
Almondbank, (Plains) Air. ML6	59	DH26
off Arondale Rd		
Almond Cres, Pais. PA2	81	AP35
Almond Dr, (Kirk.) G66	34	CD16
Almond Dr, (E.Kil.) G74	136	CD52
Almond Dr, Bish. PA7	24	AK19
Almond Pl, Coat. ML5	74	CT28
Almond Pl, Moth. ML1	112	DD40
off Cuckoo Way		
Almond Rd, G33	53	CE24
Almond Rd, (Bears.) G61	29	BF19
Almond St, G33	69	BZ28
Almond Vale, (Udd.) G71	93	CQ38
off Hamilton Vw		
Almond Way, Moth. ML1	128	DA50
off Ferguson Dr		
Alness Cres, G52	85	BF34
Alness St, Ham. ML3	140	CT52
Alness Ter, Ham. ML3	140	CT51
Aloa Way, Lark. ML9	145	DE60
off Blair Atholl Dr		
Alpine Gro, (Udd.) G71	93	CP38
Alsatian Av, Clyde. G81	27	AZ19
Alsh Ter, Ham. ML3	139	CQ52
Alston Av, Coat. ML5	75	CX29
Alston Gdns, (Bears.) G61	10	BD13
Alston La, G40	5	BU31
off Claythorn St		
Altnacraig Gdns, (Mood.) G69	37	CQ18
Alton Rd, Pais. PA1	83	AY33
Altpatrick Gdns, (Elder.) John.	80	AK34
PA5		
Altyre St, G32	90	CB34
Alva Gdns, G52	85	BG35
Alva Gdns, (Bears.) G61	11	BF13

Name	Page	Grid
Alva Gate, G52	85	BG34
Alva Pl, (Lenz.) G66	35	CG17
Alwyn Ct, (E.Kil.) G74	122	CA50
Alwyn Dr, (E.Kil.) G74	122	CA50
Alyssum Cres, Moth. ML1	127	CZ45
Alyth Cres, (Clark.) G76	119	BQ45
Alyth Gdns, G52	85	BG34
Alyth Gdns, (Clark.) G76	119	BQ45
Ambassador Way, Renf. PA4	63	AZ28
off Cockels Ln		
Amber Ter, Bell. ML4	111	CW41
Ambleside, (E.Kil.) G75	134	BV55
Ambleside Ri, Ham. ML3	140	CS55
Amethyst Av, Bell. ML4	111	CW41
Amisfield St, G20	49	BN24
Amochrie Dr, Pais. PA2	81	AQ37
Amochrie Glen, Pais. PA2	81	AQ37
Amochrie Rd, Pais. PA2	81	AP37
Amochrie Way, Pais. PA2	81	AP36
Amulree Pl, G32	90	CC33
Amulree St, G32	70	CD32
Ancaster Dr, G13	47	BH23
Ancaster La, G13	47	BH23
off Great Western Rd		
Anchor Av, Pais. PA1	83	AW33
Anchor Cres, Pais. PA1	83	AW34
Anchor Dr, Pais. PA1	83	AW33
Anchor La, G1	5	BS30
off St. Vincent Pl		
Anchor Wynd, Pais. PA1	83	AW34
Ancroft St, G20	49	BQ26
Ancrum St, G32	70	CD32
Andersen Ct, (E.Kil.) G75	136	CA55
Anderside, (E.Kil.) G75	136	CA56
Anderson Av, (Kilsyth) G65	7	CR4
Anderson Ct, Bell. ML4	111	CX40
Anderson Cres, (Kilsyth) G65	6	CN5
Anderson Dr, (Newt. M.) G77	117	BE49
Anderson Dr, Renf. PA4	45	AZ25
Anderson Gdns, (Blan.) G72	109	CN44
off Station Rd		
Anderson La, Air. ML6	76	DC29
off Chapel St		
Anderson St, G11	66	BK27
Anderson St, Air. ML6	76	DC29
Anderson St, Ham. ML3	125	CP48
Anderson St, Moth. ML1	128	DA48
Anderston Cross Cen, G2	4	BQ30
Anderston Quay, G3	4	BP31
Andrew Av, (Lenz.) G66	35	CF18
Andrew Av, Renf. PA4	46	BA26
Andrew Dr, Clyde. G81	45	AY21
Andrew Sillars Av, (Camb.) G72	106	CD40
Andrews St, Pais. PA3	62	AT31
Andrew St, (E.Kil.) G74	136	CB52
Anford Pl, (Blan.) G72	125	CN47
Angela Way, (Udd.) G71	109	CP39
Angle Gate, G14	47	BF25
Angus Av, G52	84	BD33
Angus Av, (Bishop.) G64	51	BY21
Angus Av, (E.Kil.) G74	136	CD51
Angus Av, Air. ML6	76	DC32
Angus Av, Ham. ML3	127	CW50
Angus Av, Moth. ML1	127	CY45
Angus Gdns, (Udd.) G71	93	CP37
Angus La, (Bishop.) G64	33	BZ20
Angus Oval, G52	84	BD33
Angus Pl, G52	84	BD33
Angus Pl, (E.Kil.) G74	136	CD51
Angus St, G21	50	BU25
Angus St, Clyde. G81	46	BA21
Angus Wk, (Udd.) G71	93	CR38
Anish Pl, G15	28	BA17
Annan Av, (E.Kil.) G75	134	BU54
Annan Ct, Coat. ML5	74	CV31
off Kirk St		
Annan Cres, (Chap.) Air. ML6	97	DF36
off Callander Rd		
Annandale, (Green.) Air. ML6	41	DH19
Annandale Dr, G42	87	BR34
Annandale Ter, (Old Kil.) G60	26	AS15
off Dalnottar Av		
Annan Dr, (Bears.) G61	29	BE18
Annan Dr, (Ruther.) G73	89	BZ38
Annan Glade, Moth. ML1	128	DC50
Annan Gro, Moth. ML1	128	DC50
Annan Pl, John. PA5	79	AE37
Annan St, G42	87	BQ37
Annan St, Moth. ML1	128	DC49
Annan Way, (Cumb.) G67	22	DB12
off Cumbernauld Shop Cen		
Annbank Gdns, (Annathill) Coat. ML5	38	CU19
Annbank Pl, G31	68	BV31
Annbank St, G31	68	BV31
Annbank St, Lark. ML9	144	DB58
Ann Ct, Ham. ML3	126	CQ48
Anne Av, Renf. PA4	45	AZ25
Anne Cres, (Lenz.) G66	35	CF18
Annerley Ct, Coat. ML5	74	CU32
off Torriden St		
Annerley Pl, Coat. ML5	74	CU32
Annette St, G42	87	BQ35
Annfield Gdns, (Blan.) G72	108	CK44
Annfield Pl, G31	68	BV30
Annick Dr, (Bears.) G61	29	BE18
Annick Ind Est, G32	71	CE32
Annick St, G32	70	CD32
Annick St, (Camb.) G72	107	CF40
Anniesdale Av, (Stepps) G33	53	CF23
Anniesland Cres, G14	46	BC24
Anniesland Ind Est, G13	47	BG21
Anniesland Mans, G13	47	BH23
off Ancaster Dr		
Anniesland Rd, G13	46	BD24
Anniesland Rd, G14	46	BC24
Annieston, (Kilsyth) G65	19	CP9
Anniversary Av, (E.Kil.) G75	135	BY54
Annsfield Rd, Ham. ML3	140	CS54
Ann St, Ham. ML3	125	CQ48
Ansdell Av, (Blan.) G72	124	CL46
Anson St, G40	88	BV33
Anson Way, Renf. PA4	63	AY28
off Britannia Way		
Anstruther St, G32	90	CB33
Anthony St, G2	4	BQ30
Antigua Way, (E.Kil.) G75	135	BW52
off Leeward Circle		
Anton Cres, (Kilsyth) G65	7	CU5
Antonine, (Kirk.) G66	18	CK11
Antonine Av, Moth. ML1	127	CY45
Antonine Gdns, Clyde. G81	27	AW15
Antonine Rd, (Bears.) G61	28	BD15
Antonine Rd, (Dullatur) G68	9	CZ7
Antonine Rd,The, G15	28	BA18
Antrim La, Lark. ML9	144	DD57
off Roselea St		
Anwoth St, G32	90	CC34
Apartments,The (Giff.) G46	102	BK44
off Milverton Rd		
Apollo Path, Moth. ML1	112	DD40
off Maple Rd		
Appin Ct, (Kirk.) G66	18	CK12
off Moray Pl		
Appin Cres, G31	69	BX30
Appin Rd, G31	69	BX30
Appin Ter, (Ruther.) G73	105	BZ41
Appin Ter, Ham. ML3	125	CN49
Appin Way, (Both.) G71	109	CQ42
off Bracken Ter		
Appin Way, (Glenm.) Air. ML6	58	DA25
Appin Way, Coat. ML5	94	CU33
Appleby Cl, (E.Kil.) G75	134	BV55
Appleby St, G22	49	BR26
Applecross Gdns, (Mood.) G69	37	CP18
Applecross Rd, (Kirk.) G66	18	CK12
Applecross St, G4	49	BR26
Appledore Cres, (Both.) G71	109	CQ42
Appleyard Ct, Bell. ML4	110	CV42
off Busby Rd		
Apsley La, G11	66	BJ27
off Apsley St		
Apsley St, G11	66	BJ27
Aqua Av, Ham. ML3	139	CN51
Aqua Ct, Ham. ML3	139	CN51
off Aqua Av		
Araburn Dr, (E.Kil.) G75	136	CA56
Aranthrue Cres, Renf. PA4	45	AY25
Aranthrue Dr, Renf. PA4	45	AY25
off Aranthrue Cres		
Aray St, G20	48	BM22
Arbroath Av, G52	84	BD33
Arbroath Gro, Ham. ML3	139	CR51
Arcadia Pl, G40	68	BU32
Arcadia St, G40	68	BU32
Arcadia St, Bell. ML4	95	CW38
off Primrose Av		
Arcan Cres, G15	28	BD19
Archamore Gdns, G15	28	BA17
Archerfield Av, G32	90	CC35
Archerfield Cres, G32	90	CC35
Archerfield Dr, G32	90	CC35
Archerfield Gro, G32	90	CC35
Archerhill Av, G13	46	BC21
Archerhill Cotts, G13	46	BC21
Archerhill Cres, G13	46	BD21
Archerhill Gdns, G13	46	BC21
Archerhill Rd, G13	46	BC21
Archerhill Sq, G13	46	BB21
Archerhill Ter, G13	46	BC21
Archibald Pl, Bell. ML4	111	CZ41
Arch Way, (Kilsyth) G65	7	CT4
Ardargie Dr, G32	91	CE37
Ardargie Gro, G32	91	CE37
off Ardargie Dr		
Ardargie Pl, G32	91	CE37
off Ardargie Dr		
Ardbeg Av, (Bishop.) G64	33	BY20
Ardbeg Av, (Ruther.) G73	106	CA42
Ardbeg La, G42	87	BQ35
Ardbeg Rd, (Carfin) Moth. ML1	112	DD44
Ardbeg St, G42	87	BQ35
Ardconnel St, (Thornlie.) G46	101	BH41
Arden Av, (Thornlie.) G46	101	BG43
Ardenclutha Av, Ham. ML3	125	CR49
Arden Ct, Air. ML6	75	CZ29
off Monkscourt Av		
Arden Ct, Ham. ML3	140	CT52
Ardencraig Dr, G45	104	BV43
Ardencraig Gdns, G51	105	BW43
Ardencraig Pl, G45	104	BU42
Ardencraig Quad, G45	104	BV43
Ardencraig Rd, G45	104	BS44
Ardencraig St, G45	105	BW42
Ardencraig Ter, G45	104	BV43
Arden Dr, (Giff.) G46	102	BK43
Arden Gro, (Kilsyth) G65	7	CS3

Ardenlea, (Udd.) G71	93	CP38	
Ardenlea St, G40	89	BX34	
Arden Pl, (Thornlie.) G46	101	BG43	
Arden Rd, Ham. ML3	140	CS51	
Arden Ter, Ham. ML3	140	CS51	
Ardery St, G11	66	BJ27	
off Apsley St			
Ardessie Pl, G20	48	BM24	
Ardessie St, G23	30	BM20	
off Torrin Rd			
Ardfern Rd, Air. ML6	77	DH31	
Ardfern St, G32	90	CC34	
Ardgay Pl, G32	90	CC33	
Ardgay St, G32	90	CC33	
Ardgay Way, (Ruther.) G73	105	BX42	
Ardgoil Dr, (Cumb.) G68	20	CV12	
Ardgour Ct, (Blan.) G72	125	CP47	
off Ballantrae Rd			
Ardgour Dr, (Linw.) Pais. PA3	60	AJ32	
Ardgour Par, Moth. ML1	113	DE43	
Ardgowan Av, Pais. PA2	82	AV34	
Ardgowan Ct, Pais. PA2	83	AX34	
off Cartha Cres			
Ardgowan Dr, (Udd.) G71	93	CP38	
Ardgowan St, Pais. PA2	82	AV35	
Ardholm St, G32	70	CC32	
Ardhu Pl, G15	28	BC17	
Ardlamont Sq, (Linw.) Pais. PA3	60	AL32	
Ardlaw St, G51	65	BH31	
Ardle Rd, G43	103	BN40	
Ard Ln, Moth. ML1	112	DC40	
off Howden Pl			
Ardlui Gdns, (Miln.) G62	11	BF10	
Ardlui St, G32	90	CB33	
Ardmaleish Cres, G45	104	BU43	
Ardmaleish Dr, G45	104	BT43	
Ardmaleish Rd, G45	104	BT43	
Ardmaleish St, G45	104	BT43	
Ardmaleish Ter, G45	104	BU43	
Ardmay Cres, G44	88	BS38	
Ardmillan St, G33	70	CB29	
Ardmory Av, G42	88	BT38	
Ardmory La, G42	88	BU38	
Ardmory Pl, G42	88	BU38	
Ardnahoe Av, G42	88	BT37	
Ardnahoe Pl, G42	88	BT37	
Ardneil Rd, G51	65	BH31	
Ardnish St, G51	65	BG30	
Ardoch Gdns, (Camb.) G72	106	CB39	
Ardoch Gro, (Camb.) G72	106	CB39	
Ardochrig, (E.Kil.) G75	136	CA56	
Ardoch Rd, (Bears.) G61	30	BK16	
Ardoch St, G22	50	BS25	
Ardoch Way, (Chry.) G69	37	CP19	
off Braeside Av			
Ardo Gdns, G51	66	BJ32	
off Hinshelwood Dr			
Ard Rd, Renf. PA4	45	AX25	
Ardshiel Rd, G51	65	BG30	
Ardsloy La, G14	46	BC25	
Ardsloy Pl, G14	46	BC25	
Ard St, G32	90	CC33	
Ardtoe Cres, G33	53	CG24	
Ardtoe Pl, G33	53	CG24	
Arduthie Rd, G51	65	BG30	
Ardwell Rd, G52	85	BG34	
Argosy Way, Renf. PA4	63	AY28	
off Britannia Way			
Argus Av, (Chap.) Air. ML6	97	DE35	
Argyle Cres, (Hillhouse Ind. Est.) Ham. ML3	125	CP50	
Argyle Dr, Ham. ML3	125	CQ49	
Argyle St, G2	4	BQ30	
Argyle St, G3	66	BM28	
Argyle St, Pais. PA1	82	AT33	
Argyll Arc, G2	5	BS30	
Argyll Av, (Abbots.) Pais. PA3	62	AT28	
Argyll Av, Renf. PA4	45	AX25	
Argyll Cres, Air. ML6	96	DB33	
Argyll Gdns, Lark. ML9	144	DD58	
Argyll Pl, (Kilsyth) G65	7	CU5	
Argyll Pl, (E.Kil.) G74	123	CE50	
Argyll Pl, Bell. ML4	110	CV42	
Argyll Rd, (Bears.) G61	29	BG15	
Argyll Rd, Clyde. G81	27	AY20	
Arisaig Dr, G52	85	BG34	
Arisaig Dr, (Bears.) G61	30	BK18	
Arisaig Pl, G52	85	BG34	
Arisdale Cres, (Newt. M.) G77	117	BG47	
Arkaig Av, (Plains) Air. ML6	59	DH26	
Arkaig Pl, (Newt. M.) G77	118	BK49	
Ark La, G31	68	BV30	
Arkleston Ct, Pais. PA3	63	AX29	
off Montgomery Rd			
Arkleston Cres, Pais. PA3	63	AX30	
Arkleston Dr, Pais. PA1	63	AX31	
Arkleston Rd, Pais. PA1	63	AX31	
Arkleston Rd, Pais. PA3	63	AX30	
Arkleston Rd, Renf. PA4	63	AW29	
Arkle Ter, (Camb.) G72	106	CB42	
Arklet Rd, G51	65	BG31	
Arkwrights Way, Pais. PA1	81	AR34	
off Turners Av			
Arlington Pl, G3	4	BP28	
Arlington St, G3	4	BP28	
Armadale Ct, G31	69	BW29	
Armadale Path, G31	69	BW29	
Armadale Pl, G31	69	BW29	
Armadale St, G31	69	BW30	
Armine Path, Moth. ML1	113	DE41	
off Glenburn Av			
Armour Av, Air. ML6	76	DA30	
Armour Ct, (Kirk.) G66	18	CJ12	
Armour Ct, (Blan.) G72	124	CK47	
Armour Dr, (Kirk.) G66	18	CJ12	
Armour Gdns, (Kirk.) G66	18	CJ12	
off Armour Ct			
Armour Gro, Moth. ML1	128	DC49	
Armour Pl, (Kirk.) G66	18	CJ12	
Armour Pl, John. PA5	80	AJ34	
Armour Pl, Moth. ML1	113	DE41	
off Glenburn Av			
Armour Sq, John. PA5	80	AJ34	
Armour St, G31	5	BU31	
Armour St, John. PA5	80	AJ34	
Armstrong Cres, (Udd.) G71	93	CQ37	
Armstrong Gro, (E.Kil.) G75	135	BZ54	
Arnbrae Rd, (Kilsyth) G65	7	CR4	
Arngask Rd, G51	65	BG30	
Arnhall Pl, G52	85	BG34	
Arnhem St, (Camb.) G72	107	CF40	
Arnholm Pl, G52	85	BG34	
Arnisdale Pl, G34	72	CJ29	
Arnisdale Rd, G34	72	CJ29	
Arnisdale Way, (Ruther.) G73	105	BX42	
off Shieldaig Dr			
Arniston St, G32	70	CB30	
Arniston Way, Pais. PA3	63	AW30	
Arnold Av, (Bishop.) G64	33	BW20	
Arnold St, G20	49	BQ23	
Arnol Pl, G33	71	CH30	
Arnott Dr, Coat. ML5	95	CW33	
Arnott Quad, Moth. ML1	111	CY44	
off Frood St			
Arnott Way, (Camb.) G72	106	CC39	
Arnprior Cres, G45	104	BT42	
Arnprior Gdns, (Chry.) G69	37	CP19	
off Braeside Av			
Arnprior Quad, G45	104	BT41	
Arnprior Rd, G45	104	BT41	
Arnprior St, G45	104	BT41	
Arnside Av, (Giff.) G46	102	BL42	
Arnwood Dr, G12	48	BJ24	
Arondale Rd, Air. ML6	59	DH26	
Aron Ter, (Camb.) G72	106	CB42	
Aros Dr, G52	85	BF35	
Aros La, G52	85	BF35	
Arran, (E.Kil.) G74	137	CE52	
Arran Av, Coat. ML5	95	CZ33	
Arran Av, (Abbots.) Pais. PA3	62	AU27	
Arran Dr, (Giff.) G46	102	BK43	
Arran Dr, G52	85	BH34	
Arran Dr, (Kirk.) G66	17	CG12	
Arran Dr, (Cumb.) G67	21	CZ13	
Arran Dr, Air. ML6	76	DB28	
Arran Dr, (Glenm.) Air. ML6	58	DB24	
Arran Dr, John. PA5	79	AF36	
Arran Dr, Pais. PA2	82	AU38	
Arran Gdns, Ham. ML3	140	CU52	
Arran La, (Chry.) G69	37	CQ19	
Arran Path, Lark. ML9	145	DE60	
off Bannockburn Dr			
Arran Pl, Clyde. G81	27	AY19	
Arran Pl, (Linw.) Pais. PA3	60	AJ31	
Arran Rd, Moth. ML1	127	CY46	
Arran Rd, Renf. PA4	63	AZ27	
Arran Ter, (Ruther.) G73	104	BV40	
off Carrick Rd			
Arran Vw, (Kilsyth) G65	7	CT5	
off Murray Av			
Arranview St, (Chap.) Air. ML6	97	DG36	
Arran Way, (Both.) G71	109	CP43	
Arrochar Ct, G23	48	BM21	
Arrochar Dr, G23	30	BM20	
Arrochar Path, G23	30	BM20	
off Chatton St			
Arrochar St, G23	48	BM21	
Arrol Pl, G40	89	BX33	
Arrol Rd, G40	89	BW33	
Arrol St, G52	64	BA30	
Arrotshole Ct, (E.Kil.) G74	121	BX49	
Arrotshole Rd, (E.Kil.) G74	121	BX50	
Arrowsmith Av, G13	47	BF21	
Arthur Av, (Barr.) G78	99	AX44	
Arthur Av, Air. ML6	76	DB31	
Arthurlie Av, (Barr.) G78	99	AY43	
Arthurlie Dr, (Giff.) G46	102	BL44	
Arthurlie Dr, (Newt. M.) G77	117	BF50	
Arthurlie Gdns, (Barr.) G78	99	AY43	
Arthurlie St, G51	65	BH30	
Arthurlie St, (Barr.) G78	99	AY43	
Arthur Pl, (Clark.) G76	119	BN47	
off Eaglesham Rd			
Arthur Rd, Pais. PA2	82	AU37	
Arthur St, G3	66	BM28	
Arthur St, (Clark.) G76	119	BN47	
Arthur St, Pais. PA1	62	AS32	
Arundel Dr, G42	87	BQ38	
Arundel Dr, (Bishop.) G64	33	BX17	
Asbury Ct, (Linw.) Pais. PA3	60	AL32	
off Melrose Av			
Ascaig Cres, G52	85	BF35	
Ascog Rd, (Bears.) G61	29	BH19	
Ascog St, G42	87	BO35	
Ascot Av, G12	47	BH23	
Ascot Ct, G12	48	BJ23	
Ash Av, (E.Kil.) G75	135	BY55	

Ashbank Cres, (Chap.) Air. 97 DG34
ML6
Ashburn Gdns, (Miln.) G62 11 BG12
Ashburn Ln, Lark. ML9 144 DD57
Ashburn Rd, (Miln.) G62 11 BG11
Ashburton La, G12 48 BK23
Ashburton Pk, (E.Kil.) G75 135 BW54
Ashburton Rd, G12 48 BJ23
Ashby Cres, G13 29 BG20
Ash Ct, (E.Kil.) G75 135 BY55
Ashcroft, (E.Kil.) G74 123 CF48
Ashcroft Dr, G44 104 BU40
Ashdale Dr, G52 85 BG34
Ashdene St, G22 49 BR22
Asher Rd, (Chap.) Air. ML6 97 DG35
Ashfield, (Bishop.) G64 33 BW18
Ashfield Rd, (Miln.) G62 12 BJ12
Ashfield Rd, (Clark.) G76 119 BN47
Ashfield St, G22 50 BS25
Ashgillhead Rd, (Ashgill) Lark. 145 DG60
ML9
Ashgill Pl, G22 50 BS23
Ashgill Rd, G22 49 BR22
Ash Gro, (Bishop.) G64 33 BX20
Ash Gro, (Kirk.) G66 34 CD16
Ashgrove, (Mood.) G69 37 CP19
off Deepdene Rd
Ashgrove, Air. ML6 77 DF30
Ashgrove, Coat. ML5 95 CW33
Ashgrove Rd, Bell. ML4 95 CX38
Ashgrove St, G40 89 BW35
Ashiestiel Ct, (Cumb.) G67 22 DA14
Ashiestiel Pl, (Cumb.) G67 22 DA14
Ashiestiel Rd, (Cumb.) G67 22 DA14
Ashkirk Dr, G52 85 BG34
Ashkirk Dr, (Ashgill) Lark. ML9 145 DH61
off Rosslyn Rd
Ashland Av, Ham. ML3 140 CT54
Ashlea Dr, (Giff.) G46 102 BM41
Ashlea Gdns, (Plains) Air. ML6 59 DH26
Ashley Dr, (Both.) G71 109 CR40
Ashley La, G3 4 BP28
Ashley Pk, (Udd.) G71 110 CS40
Ashley Pl, (Blan.) G72 124 CL45
Ashley St, G3 4 BP28
Ashmore Rd, G43 103 BP40
Ashmore Rd, G44 103 BP40
Ash Pl, (E.Kil.) G75 135 BY55
Ash Pl, John. PA5 80 AJ35
Ash Rd, (Baill.) G69 92 CJ34
Ash Rd, Clyde. G81 26 AV16
Ashton Gdns, (Gart.) G69 55 CP23
Ashton Grn, (E.Kil.) G74 136 CA51
off Dalrymple Dr
Ashton La, G12 66 BM27
Ashton La N, G12 66 BM27
off Ashton La
Ashton Rd, G12 66 BM27
Ashton Rd, (Ruther.) G73 89 BW36
Ashton St, Moth. ML1 111 CZ43
Ashton Way, Pais. PA2 81 AN37
Ashtree Ct, (Old Kil.) G60 25 AQ15
Ashtree Gro, (Newt. M.) G77 117 BE50
Ashtree Rd, G43 86 BL37
Ashvale Cres, G21 50 BU24
Ash Wk, (Ruther.) G73 105 BY42
Ash Wk, Moth. ML1 112 DD40
off Elm Rd
Ashwood, Wis. ML2 143 DG52
Ashwood Gdns, G13 47 BH24
Ashworth Ter, Ham. ML3 125 CQ49
Ash Wynd, (Camb.) G72 107 CG41

Aspen Dr, G21 51 BW26
Aspen Pl, (Camb.) G72 107 CG40
Aspen Pl, John. PA5 80 AJ36
Aspen Way, Ham. ML3 140 CU51
Asquith Pl, Bell. ML4 111 CZ40
Aster Dr, G45 105 BW42
Aster Gdns, G53 101 BE42
off Waukglen Cres
Aster Gdns, Moth. ML1 128 DA48
Athelstane Dr, (Cumb.) G67 21 CZ14
Athelstane Rd, G13 47 BE22
Athena Way, (Udd.) G71 93 CQ38
Atholl Gdns, G12 48 BL26
Athole La, G12 48 BL26
Atholl Av, G52 64 BA29
Atholl Av, (Torr.) G64 15 BX12
Atholl Ct, (Kirk.) G66 18 CK12
Atholl Ct, (Blan.) G72 125 CP47
off Ballantrae Rd
Atholl Cres, Pais. PA1 64 BA31
Atholl Dr, (Giff.) G46 118 BL45
Atholl Gdns, (Bears.) G61 11 BG14
Atholl Gdns, (Bishop.) G64 32 BV18
Atholl Gdns, (Ruther.) G73 106 CA42
Atholl La, (Mood.) G69 37 CQ19
Atholl Pl, Coat. ML5 95 CX34
Atholl Pl, (Linw.) Pais. PA3 60 AJ31
Atholl St, Ham. ML3 125 CR47
Atholl Ter, (Udd.) G71 93 CP36
Atlas Ind Est, G21 50 BV25
Atlas Pl, G21 50 BV26
Atlas Rd, G21 50 BU25
Atlas Sq, G21 50 BV25
off Ayr St
Atlas St, Clyde. G81 45 AX21
Atlin Dr, (New Stev.) Moth. 112 DD42
ML1
Attercliffe Av, Wis. ML2 143 DE51
Attlee Av, Clyde. G81 28 BA20
Attlee Pl, Clyde. G81 28 BA20
Attow Rd, G43 102 BK40
Auburn Dr, (Barr.) G78 99 AZ44
Auchans Rd, (Hous.) John. PA6 60 AJ27
Auchenbothie Cres, G33 51 BZ23
Auchenbothie Pl, G33 52 CA24
off Auchenbothie Cres
Auchencrow St, G34 72 CM29
Auchencruive, (Miln.) G62 12 BL13
Auchendavie Rd, G66 18 CK11
Auchendavie Steading, (Kirk.) 18 CL11
G66
Auchengeich Rd, (Mood.) G69 36 CM17
Auchengilloch, (E.Kil.) G75 136 CA56
Auchengreoch Av, John. PA5 79 AF37
Auchengreoch Rd, John. PA5 79 AF37
Auchengreoch Rd, (How.) 79 AF37
John. PA9
Auchenhowie Rd, (Miln.) G62 12 BL13
Auchenkilns Holdings, (Cumb.) 39 CZ15
G67
Auchenkilns Junct, (Cumb.) 21 CY13
G67
Auchenlodment Rd, John. PA5 80 AK35
Auchentibber Rd, (Blan.) G72 123 CH50
Auchentorlie Quad, Pais. PA1 83 AX33
Auchentorlie St, G11 65 BH27
Auchentoshan Av, Clyde. G81 26 AV15
Auchentoshan Ter, G21 68 BV27
Auchentoshan Cotts, (Old Kil.) 26 AT15
G60
Auchinairn Gdns, (Bishop.) 51 BZ21
G64
Auchinairn Rd, (Bishop.) G64 51 BW22

Auchinbee Fm Rd, (Cumb.) 21 CX9
G68
Auchinbee Roundabout, 21 CY10
(Cumb.) G68
Auchinbee Way, (Cumb.) G68 21 CX10
Auchincampbell Rd, Ham. 126 CT50
ML3
Auchineden Ct, (Bears.) G61 11 BE14
Auchingill Path, G34 72 CM28
off Auchingill Rd
Auchingill Pl, G34 72 CM28
Auchingill Rd, G34 72 CL28
Auchingramont Rd, Ham. ML3 126 CT49
Auchinlea Retail Pk, G34 71 CH28
Auchinlea Rd, G34 71 CH27
Auchinlea Way, G34 71 CG28
Auchinleck Av, G33 52 CA23
Auchinleck Cres, G33 52 CA23
Auchinleck Dr, G33 52 CA23
Auchinleck Gdns, G33 52 CA23
Auchinleck Rd, G33 52 CB22
Auchinloch Rd, (Lenz.) G66 35 CF17
Auchinloch St, G21 50 BV26
Auchinraith Av, Ham. ML3 125 CR47
Auchinraith Rd, (Blan.) G72 124 CM47
Auchinraith Ter, (Blan.) G72 125 CN47
Auchintibber Ct, (Blan.) G72 125 CN47
off Ballantrae Rd
Auchinvole Cres, (Kilsyth) G65 7 CR5
Auchmannoch Av, Pais. PA1 64 BA32
Auckland Pk, (E.Kil.) G75 135 BW53
Auckland Pl, Clyde. G81 26 AT17
Auckland St, G22 49 BR26
Auldbar Rd, G52 85 BH34
Auldbar Ter, Pais. PA2 83 AW35
Auldburn Rd, G43 102 BK39
Auldburn Rd, G43 102 BK39
Auldearn Rd, G21 51 BY22
Auldgirth Rd, G52 85 BH34
Auldhame St, Coat. ML5 74 CU29
Auldhouse Av, G43 102 BK39
off Thornliebank Rd
Auldhouse Ct, G43 102 BK39
off Stoneside Dr
Auldhouse Gdns, G43 102 BK39
Auldhouse Rd, G43 102 BL39
Auldhouse Ter, G43 102 BM39
Auld Kirk Rd, (Camb.) G72 107 CE42
Auldmurroch Dr, (Miln.) G62 11 BF11
Auld Rd, The (Cumb.) G67 22 DC9
Aulds Brae, Air. ML6 76 DC29
off Chapel St
Auld St, Clyde. G81 26 AU18
Auldton Ter, (Ashgill) Lark. ML9 145 DH60
Aultbea St, G22 49 BR21
Aultmore Dr, (Carfin) 112 DD43
Moth. ML1
Aultmore Gdns, G33 71 CH30
Aultmore Pk, G33 71 CH30
Aultmore Rd, G33 71 CH30
Aursbridge Cres, (Barr.) G78 99 AZ43
Aursbridge Dr, (Barr.) G78 99 AZ43
Aurs Cres, (Barr.) G78 99 AZ43
Aurs Dr, (Barr.) G78 99 AZ44
Aurs Glen, (Barr.) G78 99 AY44
Aurs Pl, (Barr.) G78 100 BA43
Aurs Rd, (Newt. M.) G77 116 BB47
Aurs Rd, (Barr.) G78 99 AZ43
Austen La, G13 47 BG24
off Skaterig La
Austen Rd, G13 47 BG24
Austine Dr, Ham. ML3 140 CU54
Avenel Rd, G13 29 BG20

Avenue, The (Kilb.) John. PA10 78 AD35
off Low Barholm
Avenue End Rd, G33 52 CD25
Avenuehead Rd, (Chry.) G69 37 CQ20
Avenuepark St, G20 49 BN25
Avenue Shop Cen, The 117 BF49
(Newt. M.) G77
Avenue St, G40 69 BW32
Avenue St, (Ruther.) G73 89 BX36
Aviemore Gdns, (Bears.) G61 30 BK16
Aviemore Rd, G52 85 BG35
Avoch Dr, (Thornlie.) G46 101 BG42
Avoch St, G34 72 CK28
off Dubton St
Avon Av, (Bears.) G61 30 BK18
Avonbank Cres, Ham. ML3 140 CU53
Avonbank Rd, (Ruther.) G73 88 BV38
Avonbank Rd, Lark. ML9 144 DA59
Avonbrae Cres, Ham. ML3 140 CU53
Avonbridge Dr, Ham. ML3 126 CV50
Avondale Av, (E.Kil.) G74 136 CB52
Avondale Dr, Pais. PA1 63 AX31
Avondale Pl, (E.Kil.) G74 136 CC53
Avondale St, G33 70 CC28
Avon Dr, (Bishop.) G64 51 BW21
off Avon Rd
Avon Dr, Bell. ML4 111 CY41
Avon Dr, (Linw.) Pais. PA3 60 AK31
Avonhead, (E.Kil.) G75 136 CA56
Avonhead Av, (Cumb.) G67 21 CY14
Avonhead Gdns, (Cumb.) G67 21 CY14
Avonhead Pl, (Cumb.) G67 21 CY14
off Avonhead Av
Avonhead Rd, (Cumb.) G67 21 CY14
Avon Pl, Coat. ML5 74 CT28
Avon Pl, Lark. ML9 144 DD62
Avon Rd, (Giff.) G46 102 BK43
Avon Rd, (Bishop.) G64 51 BW21
Avon Rd, Lark. ML9 144 DC61
Avonside Gro, Ham. ML3 126 CV50
Avonspark St, G21 51 BW26
Avon St, Ham. ML3 126 CU50
Avon St, Lark. ML9 144 DB58
Avon St, Moth. ML1 128 DA48
Avon Wk, (Cumb.) G67 22 DB12
off Cumbernauld Shop Cen
Aylmer Rd, G43 103 BP39
Ayr Dr, Air. ML6 96 DC33
Ayr Rd, (Giff.) G46 118 BJ46
Ayr Rd, (Newt. M.) G77 117 BG48
Ayr Rd, Lark. ML9 145 DF60
Ayr St, G21 50 BU26
Ayton Pk N, (E.Kil.) G74 122 CD50
Ayton Pk S, (E.Kil.) G74 122 CD50
Aytoun Dr, Ersk. PA8 25 AP18
Aytoun Rd, G41 86 BM34
Azalea Gdns, (Camb.) G72 107 CG40

B
Babylon Av, Bell. ML4 111 CW42
Babylon Dr, Bell. ML4 111 CW42
Babylon Pl, Bell. ML4 111 CW43
Babylon Rd, Bell. ML4 110 CV42
Backbrae St, (Kilsyth) G65 7 CS5
Back Causeway, G31 69 BZ32
Backmuir Cres, Ham. ML3 125 CR47
Backmuir Pl, Ham. ML3 125 CR47
off Backmuir Rd
Backmuir Rd, G15 28 BD17
Backmuir Rd, Ham. ML3 125 CR47
Back o'Barns, Ham. ML3 126 CV49
off Church St

Back o'Hill Rd, (Torr.) G64 14 BU11
Back Row, Ham. ML3 126 CU49
Back Sneddon St, Pais. PA3 62 AU32
Badenheath Pl, (Cumb.) G68 38 CT16
Badenheath Ter, (Cumb.) G67 38 CT17
Badenoch Rd, (Kirk.) G66 18 CK12
Bagnell St, G21 50 BV24
Bahamas Way, (E.Kil.) G75 135 BW52
off Leeward Circle
Bailie Dr, (Bears.) G61 11 BF14
Baillie Dr, (Both.) G71 109 CQ42
Baillie Dr, (E.Kil.) G74 122 CD49
Baillie Pl, (E.Kil.) G74 122 CD49
Baillies La, Air. ML6 76 DC30
off Graham St
Baillieston Rd, G32 91 CF33
Baillieston Rd, (Udd.) G71 92 CK34
Baillie Wynd, (Udd.) G71 93 CQ37
Bainsford St, G32 70 CB31
Bain Sq, G40 5 BU31
off Bain St
Bain St, G40 5 BU31
Baird Av, G52 64 BA29
Baird Av, Air. ML6 76 DD27
Baird Av, (Strutherhill Ind. Est.) 144 DD61
Lark. ML9
Baird Ct, Clyde. G81 27 AW19
Baird Cres, (Cumb.) G67 21 CX14
Baird Dr, (Bears.) G61 29 BF16
Baird Dr, Ersk. PA8 25 AP18
Baird Hill, (E.Kil.) G75 136 CA53
Baird Pl, Bell. ML4 95 CW38
Bairds Av, (Udd.) G71 109 CR39
Bairds Brae, G4 49 BR26
Bairds Cres, Ham. ML3 126 CS50
Bairdsland Vw, Bell. ML4 111 CX40
Baird St, G4 5 BT28
Baird St, Coat. ML5 75 CW30
Baker Pl, G41 87 BN36
off Baker St
Baker St, G41 87 BN36
Bakewell Rd, (Baill.) G69 72 CJ32
Balaclava St, G2 4 BQ30
Balado Rd, G33 71 CG30
Balbeggie Pl, G32 91 CE33
Balbeggie St, G32 91 CE33
Balbeg St, G51 65 BG31
Balblair Rd, G52 85 BH34
Balcarres Av, G12 48 BL24
Balcary Pl, (Chap.) Air. ML6 97 DG36
Balcastle Gdns, (Kilsyth) G65 7 CR4
Balcastle Rd, (Kilsyth) G65 6 CQ4
Balcomie St, G33 70 CC28
Balcomie Ter, Ham. ML3 139 CR53
off Balmore Dr
Balcurvie Rd, G34 72 CJ27
Baldernock Rd, (Miln.) G62 12 BL11
Baldinnie Rd, G34 72 CK29
Baldorran Cres, (Cumb.) G68 21 CX10
Baldovan Cres, G33 71 CH29
Baldovan Path, G33 71 CH30
Baldovie Rd, G52 85 BE34
Baldragon Rd, G34 72 CK28
Baldric Rd, G13 47 BE23
Baldwin Av, G13 47 BF21
Balerno Dr, G52 85 BG34
Balfearn Dr, (Eagle.) G76 133 BN56
Balfleurs St, (Miln.) G62 12 BK11
Balfluig St, G34 71 CH28
Balfour St, G20 48 BM23
Balfour Ter, (E.Kil.) G75 136 CB54
Balfour Wynd, Lark. ML9 144 DD60
off Fir Bk Av

Balfron Cres, Ham. ML3 125 CP50
Balfron Rd, G51 65 BG30
Balfron Rd, Pais. PA1 63 AZ32
Balgair Dr, Pais. PA1 63 AX32
Balgair Pl, G22 49 BR25
Balgair St, G22 49 BR24
Balgair Ter, G32 70 CD32
Balglass Gdns, G22 49 BR25
Balglass St, G22 49 BR25
Balgonie Av, Pais. PA2 81 AQ36
Balgonie Dr, Pais. PA2 82 AS36
Balgonie Rd, G52 85 BG33
Balgonie Wds, Pais. PA2 82 AS36
Balgownie Cres, (Thornlie.) 102 BJ43
G46
Balgraybank St, G21 50 BV25
Balgray Cres, (Barr.) G78 99 AZ43
Balgrayhill Rd, G21 50 BV24
Balgray Rd, (Newt. M.) G77 116 BC48
Balgraystone Rd, (Newt. M.) 115 AZ47
G77
Balintore St, G32 70 CC32
Baliol La, G3 4 BP28
Baliol St, G3 4 BP28
Baljaffray Rd, (Bears.) G61 10 BC14
Ballagan Pl, (Miln.) G62 11 BF11
Ballaig Av, (Bears.) G61 29 BF16
Ballaig Cres, (Stepps) G33 53 CE24
Ballantay Quad, G45 105 BW42
Ballantay Rd, G45 105 BW42
Ballantay Ter, G45 105 BW42
Ballantrae, (E.Kil.) G74 121 BZ50
Ballantrae Ct, G3 4 BP30
Ballantrae Cres, (Newt. M.) 118 BJ49
G77
Ballantrae Dr, (Newt. M.) G77 118 BJ50
Ballantrae Rd, (Blan.) G72 125 CN47
Ballantrae Wynd, Moth. ML1 112 DD40
off Ivy Ter
Ballantyne Av, G52 64 BC30
Ballater Dr, (Bears.) G61 29 BH19
Ballater Dr, Pais. PA2 82 AV36
Ballater Dr, (Inch.) Renf. PA4 44 AT22
Ballater Pl, G5 88 BT33
Ballater St, G5 68 BS32
Ballater Way, (Glenb.) Coat. 56 CS23
ML5 *off The Oval*
Ballayne Dr, (Chry.) G69 37 CQ18
Ballerup Ter, (E.Kil.) G75 136 CA55
Ballindalloch Dr, G31 69 BW29
Ballindarroch La, G31 69 BW29
off Armadale St
Balloch Gdns, G52 85 BH34
Balloch Holdings, (Cumb.) G68 21 CX12
Balloch Loop Rd, (Cumb.) G68 21 CY10
Ballochmill Rd, (Ruther.) G73 89 BZ37
Ballochmyle, (E.Kil.) G74 123 CF49
Ballochmyle Cres, G53 84 BC37
Ballochmyle Dr, G53 84 BC36
Ballochmyle Gdns, G53 84 BC36
Ballochmyle Pl, G53 84 BC37
Ballochney La, Air. ML6 76 DA28
off Ballochney St
Ballochney Rd, Air. ML6 59 DG26
Ballochney St, Air. ML6 76 DA28
Balloch Rd, (Cumb.) G68 21 CW11
Balloch Roundabout, (Cumb.) 21 CW11
G68
Balloch Vw, (Cumb.) G67 22 DB11
Ballogie Rd, G44 87 BR38
Balmalloch Rd, (Kilsyth) G65 7 CR4
Balmartin Rd, G23 30 BM20
Balmedie, Ersk. PA8 25 AQ19

Name	Page	Grid
Balmeg Av, (Giff.) G46	118	BL45
Balmerino Pl, (Bishop.) G64	51	BZ21
Balmoral Av, (Glenm.) Air. ML6	58	DB24
Balmoral Cres, Coat. ML5	94	CT33
Balmoral Cres, (Inch.) Renf. PA4	44	AU22
Balmoral Dr, G32	90	CD37
Balmoral Dr, (Bears.) G61	30	BJ19
Balmoral Dr, (Camb.) G72	106	CA40
Balmoral Dr, Bish. PA7	24	AL19
Balmoral Gdns, (Udd.) G71	93	CP36
Balmoral Gdns, (Blan.) G72	108	CL43
Balmoral Path, Lark. ML9	145	DE59
off Afton St		
Balmoral Pl, (E.Kil.) G74	135	BY52
Balmoral Rd, (Elder.) John. PA5	80	AK36
Balmoral St, G14	46	BD26
Balmore Dr, Ham. ML3	139	CQ53
Balmore Pl, G22	49	BR23
Balmore Rd, G22	49	BR22
Balmore Rd, G23	31	BQ18
Balmore Rd, (Miln.) G62	31	BP15
Balmore Rd, (Torr.) G64	14	BS13
Balmore Sq, G22	49	BR24
Balmuildy Rd, G23	31	BQ17
Balmuildy Rd, (Bishop.) G64	32	BV18
Balornock Rd, G21	51	BW24
Balornock Rd, (Bishop.) G64	51	BW23
Balruddery Pl, (Bishop.) G64	51	BZ21
Balshagray Av, G11	47	BG26
Balshagray Cres, G14	65	BG27
off Dumbarton Rd		
Balshagray Dr, G11	47	BG26
Balshagray La, G11	65	BH27
Balshagray Pl, G11	47	BH26
off Balshagray Dr		
Baltic Ct, G40	89	BW34
off Baltic St		
Baltic La, G40	89	BW34
Baltic Pl, G40	89	BW33
Baltic St, G40	89	BW33
Balvaird Cres, (Ruther.) G73	89	BW38
Balvaird Dr, (Ruther.) G73	89	BW38
Balvenie Dr, (Carfin) Moth. ML1 *off Ardbeg Rd*	112	DD44
Balvenie St, Coat. ML5	95	CX34
Balveny St, G33	71	CF27
Balvicar Dr, G42	87	BP36
Balvicar St, G42	87	BP36
Balvie Av, G15	28	BC20
Balvie Av, (Giff.) G46	102	BM43
Balvie Cres, (Miln.) G62	11	BH11
Balvie Rd, (Miln.) G62	11	BH11
Banavie La, G11	48	BK26
off Banavie Rd		
Banavie Rd, G11	48	BJ26
Banchory Av, G43	102	BK40
Banchory Av, (Glenm.) Air. ML6	58	DB24
Banchory Av, (Inch.) Renf. PA4	44	AT22
Banchory Cres, (Bears.) G61	30	BJ19
Baneberry Path, (E.Kil.) G74	121	BZ49
Banff Av, Air. ML6	96	DC33
Banff Pl, (E.Kil.) G75	135	BY53
Banff St, G33	70	CD27
off Gilbertfield St		
Bangorshill St, (Thornlie.) G46	101	BH41
Bank Av, (Miln.) G62	12	BJ10
Bankbrae Av, G53	100	BC39
Bankend St, G33	70	CC28
Bankfield Dr, Ham. ML3	140	CT54
Bankfoot Dr, G52	64	BD32
Bankfoot Pl, (Newt. M.) G77	118	BK49
Bankfoot Rd, G52	84	BD33
Bankfoot Rd, Pais. PA3	61	AR31
Bankglen Rd, G15	28	BD17
Bankhall St, G42	87	BR35
Bankhead Av, G13	46	BC23
Bankhead Av, Air. ML6	77	DF30
Bankhead Av, Bell. ML4	111	CX42
Bankhead Av, Coat. ML5	94	CS33
Bankhead Dr, (Ruther.) G73	89	BW38
Bankhead Pl, Air. ML6	77	DF30
Bankhead Pl, Coat. ML5	94	CS33
Bankhead Rd, (Kirk.) G66	18	CJ14
Bankhead Rd, (Ruther.) G73	104	BV39
Bankhead Rd, (Carm.) G76	120	BT46
Bankholm Pl, (Clark.) G76	119	BP48
Banknock St, G32	70	CA31
Bank Pk, (E.Kil.) G75	135	BZ53
Bank Rd, G32	91	CE37
Bankside Av, John. PA5	79	AH34
Banks Rd, (Kirk.) G66	17	CF12
Bank St, G12	67	BN27
Bank St, (Camb.) G72	106	CC39
Bank St, (Barr.) G78	99	AY43
Bank St, (Neil.) G78	114	AT46
Bank St, Air. ML6	76	DC30
Bank St, Coat. ML5	74	CU31
Bank St, Pais. PA1	82	AV33
Banktop Pl, John. PA5	79	AH34
Bank Vw, (Chap.) Air. ML6	97	DF35
Bankview Cres, (Kirk.) G66	16	CC13
Bankview Dr, (Kirk.) G66	16	CC13
Bank Way, Lark. ML9	144	DD57
off Duncan Graham St		
Bannatyne Av, G31	69	BX30
Bannercross Av, (Baill.) G69	72	CJ32
Bannercross Dr, (Baill.) G69	72	CJ32
Bannercross Gdns, (Baill.) G69	72	CJ32
Banner Dr, G13	29	BE20
Bannerman Dr, Bell. ML4	111	CX42
Bannerman Pl, Clyde. G81	27	AX19
Banner Rd, G13	29	BE20
Bannockburn Dr, Lark. ML9	145	DE60
Bannockburn Pl, (New Stev.) Moth. ML1	112	DC43
Bantaskin St, G20	48	BL22
Banton Pl, G33	72	CJ30
Banton Rd, G65	8	CY4
Banyan Cres, (Udd.) G71	94	CT36
Barassie, (E.Kil.) G74	121	BZ50
Barassie Ct, (Both.) G71	109	CP43
Barassie Cres, (Cumb.) G68	9	DB7
Barbados Grn, (E.Kil.) G75	135	BW52
off Leeward Circle		
Barbae Pl, (Both.) G71	109	CQ42
Barbana Rd, (E.Kil.) G74	134	BU51
Barbegs Cres, (Kilsyth) G65	20	CV9
Barberry Av, G53	100	BD43
Barberry Gdns, G53	100	BD43
Barberry Pl, G53	101	BE43
Barbeth Gdns, (Cumb.) G67	39	CX16
Barbeth Pl, (Cumb.) G67	39	CW15
Barbeth Rd, (Cumb.) G67	39	CW15
Barbeth Way, (Cumb.) G67	39	CW15
Barbreck Rd, G42	87	BQ35
off Pollokshaws Rd		
Barcaldine Av, (Chry.) G69	54	CK21
Barcapel Av, (Newt. M.) G77	117	BG46
Barclay Av, (Elder.) John. PA5	80	AK35
Barclay Rd, Moth. ML1	127	CX47
Barclay Sq, Renf. PA4	63	AX28
Barclay St, G21	50	BV24
off Lenzie St		
Barclay St, (Old Kil.) G60	25	AR16
Barcloy Pl, (Chap.) Air. ML6	97	DG36
Barcraigs Dr, Pais. PA2	82	AV37
Bard Av, G13	46	BD21
Bardowie St, G22	49	BR25
Bardrain Av, (Elder.) John. PA5	80	AL35
Bardrain Rd, Pais. PA2	82	AS38
Bardrill Dr, (Bishop.) G64	32	BU20
Bardykes Rd, (Blan.) G72	124	CK45
Barefield St, Lark. ML9	144	DC57
Barfillan Dr, G52	65	BG32
Barfillan Rd, G52	85	BG33
Bargany Ct, G53	84	BC36
Bargany Pl, G53	84	BC36
Bargany Rd, G53	84	BC36
Bargaran Rd, G53	84	BD34
Bargarran Dr, Ersk. PA8	25	AP19
Bargarran Sq, Ersk. PA8	25	AQ18
off Bargarran Rd		
Bargarron Dr, Pais. PA3	63	AW30
Bargeddie St, G33	69	BZ27
Bar Hill Pl, (Kilsyth) G65	7	CR5
Barholm Sq, G33	71	CF27
Barke Rd, (Cumb.) G67	22	DC10
Barkly Ter, (E.Kil.) G75	135	BY53
off Kimberley Gdns		
Barlae Av, (Eagle.) G76	133	BN53
Barlanark Av, G32	71	CE30
Barlanark Cres, G33	71	CF30
Barlanark Dr, G33	71	CF30
Barlanark Pl, G32	70	CD31
Barlanark Pl, G33	71	CG30
Barlanark Rd, G33	71	CF30
Barlandfauld St, (Kilsyth) G65	7	CT5
Barlia Dr, G45	104	BU42
Barlia Gdns, G51	104	BU42
Barlia St, G45	104	BU42
Barlia Ter, G45	104	BV42
Barloch Av, (Miln.) G62	12	BJ11
Barloch Rd, G62	12	BK11
Barloch St, G22	50	BS25
Barlogan Av, G52	65	BG32
Barlogan Quad, G52	65	BG32
Barmulloch Rd, G21	51	BW25
Barnard Gdns, (Bishop.) G64	33	BW17
Barnbeth Rd, G53	84	BD35
Barncluith Rd, Ham. ML3	126	CV50
Barnes Rd, G20	49	BQ23
Barness Pl, G33	70	CC29
Barnes St, (Barr.) G78	99	AX43
Barnett Path, (Blan.) G72	124	CM46
off Selkirk St		
Barnflat St, (Ruther.) G73	89	BX36
Barn Grn, (Kilb.) John. PA10	78	AC34
Barnhill Dr, G21	51	BW26
off Foresthall Dr		
Barnhill Dr, (Newt. M.) G77	117	BF50
Barnhill Dr, Ham. ML3	138	CM51
Barnkirk Av, G15	28	BC17
Barnsford Av, (Inch.) Renf. PA4	43	AR25
Barnsford Rd, (Abbots.) Pais. PA3	61	AQ29
Barnsford Rd, (Inch.) Renf. PA4	43	AQ24
Barns St, Clyde. G81	45	AY21
Barnswood Pl, (Both.) G71	109	CR42
off Burleigh Rd		
Barnton St, G32	70	CA30
Barnwell Ter, G51	65	BG30
Barochan Cres, Pais. PA3	81	AQ33
Barochan Pl, G53	84	BD34
off Barochan Rd		

Street	Page	Grid
Barochan Rd, G53	84	BD34
Barochan Way, Pais. PA3	81	AQ33
Baronald Dr, G12	48	BK23
Baronald Gate, G12	48	BK23
Baronald St, (Ruther.) G73	89	BX36
Baron Ct, Ham. ML3	141	CW51
Barone Dr, (Clark.) G76	118	BL45
Baronhall Dr, (Blan.) G72	124	CL45
Baronhill, (Cumb.) G67	9	DC8
Baron Path, (Baill.) G69	73	CP32
off Campsie Vw		
Baron Rd, Pais. PA3	63	AW31
Baronscourt Dr, Pais. PA1	81	AP33
Baronscourt Gdns, Pais. PA1	81	AP33
Baronscourt Rd, Pais. PA1	81	AP33
Barons Gate, (Both.) G71	109	CN41
Barons Rd, Moth. ML1	143	DE51
Baron St, Renf. PA4	63	AY27
Barony Ct, (Baill.) G69	72	CK31
Barony Dr, (Baill.) G69	72	CK31
Barony Gdns, (Baill.) G69	72	CK32
Barony Pl, (Cumb.) G68	20	CU12
Barony Wynd, (Baill.) G69	72	CK31
Barra Av, Coat. ML5	94	CU33
Barra Av, Renf. PA4	63	AY28
Barrachnie Av, (Baill.) G69	72	CJ31
Barrachnie Ct, (Baill.) G69	71	CH31
Barrachnie Cres, (Baill.) G69	71	CH32
Barrachnie Dr, (Baill.) G69	72	CJ31
Barrachnie Gro, (Baill.) G69	72	CJ31
Barrachnie Pl, (Baill.) G69	72	CJ31
Barrachnie Rd, (Baill.) G69	71	CH32
Barrack St, G4	5	BU31
Barrack St, Ham. ML3	126	CT48
Barra Cres, (Old Kil.) G60	26	AS16
Barra Dr, Air. ML6	77	DG31
Barra Gdns, (Old Kil.) G60	26	AS16
Barra Pl, Coat. ML5	94	CU33
Barra Rd, (Old Kil.) G60	26	AS16
Barraston Rd, (Torr.) G64	14	BV10
Barra St, G20	48	BL21
Barr Av, (Neil.) G78	114	AU45
Barrbridge Rd, (Baill.) G69	93	CR33
Barr Cres, Clyde. G81	27	AX16
Barr Gro, (Udd.) G71	93	CQ37
Barrhead Rd, G43	85	BG38
Barrhead Rd, G53	100	BB39
Barrhead Rd, (Newt. M.) G77	116	BC48
Barrhead Rd, Pais. PA2	82	AV34
Barrhill Ct, (Kirk.) G66	18	CJ13
Barrhill Cres, (Kilb.) John. PA10	78	AD35
Barrhill La, (Kilsyth) G65	19	CP9
Barrhill Rd, (Kirk.) G66	18	CJ13
Barrhill Rd, Ersk. PA8	25	AQ20
Barr Hill Ter, G65	19	CQ9
Barriedale Av, Ham. ML3	125	CR50
Barrie Quad, Clyde. G81	27	AW17
Barrie Rd, G52	64	BC30
Barrie Rd, (E.Kil.) G74	123	CF48
Barrie St, Moth. ML1	128	DA47
Barrington Dr, G4	67	BP27
Barrisdale Rd, G20	48	BM21
Barrisdale Way, (Ruther.) G73	105	BX42
off Shieldaig Dr		
Barrland Dr, (Giff.) G46	102	BL42
Barrland St, G41	87	BQ34
Barrmill Rd, G43	102	BJ40
Barrochan Interchange, John. PA5	79	AG33
Barrowfield St, G40	69	BW32
Barrowfield St, Coat. ML5	95	CW33
Barrpath, (Kilsyth) G65	8	CV6
Barr Pl, (Newt. M.) G77	117	BE48
Barr Pl, Pais. PA1	82	AT33
Barr St, G20	49	BQ26
Barr St, Moth. ML1	128	DA45
Barr Ter, (E.Kil.) G74	136	CA51
Barrwood Pl, (Udd.) G71	93	CQ37
Barrwood St, G33	70	CA27
Barry Gdns, (Blan.) G72	124	CM47
Barscube Ter, Pais. PA2	83	AW35
Barshaw Dr, Pais. PA1	63	AW31
Barshaw Pl, Pais. PA1	63	AZ32
off Kinpurnie Rd		
Barshaw Rd, G52	64	BA31
Barskiven Rd, Pais. PA1	81	AP33
Barterholm Rd, Pais. PA2	82	AU35
Bartholomew St, G40	89	BW34
Bartiebeith Rd, G33	71	CG30
Bartie Gdns, (Ashgillhead) Lark. ML9	145	DG60
Barwood Rd, Ersk. PA8	25	AQ17
Bassett Av, G13	46	BD21
Bassett Cres, G13	46	BD21
Bathgate St, G31	69	BW31
Bathgo Av, Pais. PA1	84	BA33
Bath La, G2	4	BQ29
Bath La W, G3	4	BP29
off North St		
Bath St, G2	4	BQ29
Batson St, G42	87	BR35
Battlefield Av, G42	87	BQ38
Battlefield Cres, G42	87	BQ38
off Battlefield Gdns		
Battlefield Gdns, G42	87	BQ37
Battlefield Rd, G42	87	BQ37
Battle Pl, G41	87	BP37
Battles Burn Dr, G32	90	CC35
Battles Burn Gate, G32	90	CC35
Battles Burn Vw, G32	90	CC35
Bavelaw St, G33	71	CF27
Bayfield Av, G15	28	BC18
Bayfield Ter, G15	28	BC18
Beacon Pl, G33	70	CB29
off Bellrock St		
Beaconsfield Rd, G12	48	BK24
Beard Cres, (Gart.) G69	55	CP24
Beardmore Cotts, (Inch.) Renf. PA4	44	AU23
Beardmore Pl, Clyde. G81	26	AU18
Beardmore St, Clyde. G81	26	AT18
Beardmore Way, G31	69	BX31
Beardmore Way, Clyde. G81	26	AT19
Bearford Dr, G52	64	BD32
Bearsden Rd, G13	47	BH23
Bearsden Rd, (Bears.) G61	47	BH23
Bearsden Shop Cen, (Bears.) G61	30	BJ17
Beaton Rd, G41	87	BN35
Beaton St, Lark. ML9	144	DB57
Beatrice Dr, Moth. ML1	112	DB40
Beatson Wynd, (Udd.) G71	93	CQ36
off Macmillan Gdns		
Beattock St, G31	69	BZ32
Beattock Wynd, Ham. ML3	125	CQ50
Beatty St, Clyde. G81	26	AU18
Beaufort Av, G43	102	BL39
Beaufort Dr, (Kirk.) G66	16	CD13
Beaufort Gdns, (Bishop.) G64	32	BU20
Beauly Dr, Pais. PA2	81	AN36
Beauly Pl, G20	48	BM23
Beauly Pl, (Bishop.) G64	33	BZ19
Beauly Pl, (Chry.) G69	36	CM20
Beauly Pl, (E.Kil.) G74	135	BZ51
Beauly Pl, (Coat.) ML5	95	CX34
Beauly Rd, (Baill.) G69	92	CJ34
Beaumont Gate, G12	48	BL26
Beckfield Cres, G33	51	BZ22
off Brookfield Av		
Beckfield Dr, G33	51	BZ22
Beckfield Gate, G33	51	BZ22
off Brookfield Av		
Beckfield Gro, G33	51	BZ22
Beckfield Pl, G33	51	BZ22
off Brookfield Av		
Beckfield Wk, G33	51	BZ22
off Brookfield Av		
Beckford St, Ham. ML3	126	CS48
Beckford St Business Pk, Ham. ML3	126	CT48
Bedale Rd, (Baill.) G69	91	CH33
Bedcow Vw, (Kirk.) G66	17	CH14
Bedford Av, Clyde. G81	27	AZ19
Bedford La, G5	67	BR32
Bedford St, G5	67	BR32
Bedlay Ct, (Chry.) G69	37	CQ18
Bedlay Pl, (Annathill) Coat. ML5	38	CV20
Bedlay Vw, (Udd.) G71	93	CR36
Bedlay Wk, (Chry.) G69	37	CQ18
off Bedlay Ct		
Beech Av, G41	66	BK32
Beech Av, (Bears.) G61	12	BJ14
Beech Av, (Baill.) G69	72	CJ32
Beech Av, (Camb.) G72	106	CB39
Beech Av, (Ruther.) G73	105	BY41
Beech Av, (Newt. M.) G77	117	BF49
Beech Av, (Elder.) John. PA5	80	AL35
Beech Av, Lark. ML9	145	DE59
Beech Av, Moth. ML1	112	DD42
Beech Av, Pais. PA2	83	AW36
Beechbank Av, Air. ML6	76	DB29
Beech Ct, Coat. ML5	94	CV33
off Ailsa Rd		
Beech Cres, (Camb.) G72	107	CG41
Beech Cres, (Newt. M.) G77	117	BG50
Beech Cres, Moth. ML1	97	DE38
Beech Dr, Clyde. G81	27	AW16
Beeches, The (Blan.) G72	124	CL46
off Burnbrae Rd		
Beeches, The (Newt. M.) G77	117	BH47
Beeches Av, Clyde. G81	26	AV15
Beeches Rd, Clyde. G81	26	AV15
Beeches Ter, Clyde. G81	27	AW15
Beech Gdns, (Baill.) G69	72	CJ32
Beechgrove, (Chry.) G69	37	CP19
Beech Gro, (Gart.) G69	55	CQ24
Beech Gro, (E.Kil.) G75	135	BX55
Beechgrove Av, (Udd.) G71	94	CS38
Beechgrove Quad, Moth. ML1	112	DC40
off Graham St		
Beechgrove St, G40	89	BX35
Beechlands Av, G44	103	BN43
Beechlands Dr, (Clark.) G76	118	BL46
Beechmount Rd, (Lenz.) G66	35	CE17
Beech Pl, (Bishop.) G64	51	BX21
Beech Pl, (Blan.) G72	125	CN46
Beech Rd, (Bishop.) G64	51	BX21
Beech Rd, (Lenz.) G66	35	CE15
Beech Rd, John. PA5	79	AF36
Beech Rd, Moth. ML1	97	DE38
Beech Ter, Lark. ML9	144	DD60
Beechwood, Lark. ML9	142	DC56
Beechwood, Wis. ML2	143	DF52
Beechwood Av, (Ruther.) G73	105	BY39
Beechwood Av, (Clark.) G76	118	BL47
Beechwood Av, Ham. ML3	139	CR53
Beechwood Ct, (Bears.) G61	29	BH18
off Drymen Rd		

Name	Page	Grid
Beechwood Ct, (Cumb.) G67	22	DB13
Beechwood Dr, G11	47	BH25
Beechwood Dr, Coat. ML5	75	CY32
Beechwood Dr, Renf. PA4	63	AX28
Beechwood Gdns, (Mood.) G69	37	CP20
Beechwood Gdns, Bell. ML4	111	CY41
Beechwood Gro, (Barr.) G78	99	AY44
Beechwood La, (Bears.) G61	29	BH18
Beechwood Pl, G11	47	BH25
Beechwood Pl, Bell. ML4	111	CY41
Beechwood Rd, (Cumb.) G67	22	DB12
Bccohworth Dr, Moth. ML1	113	DF43
Beecroft Pl, (Blan.) G72	109	CN44
Beil Dr, G13	46	BB22
Beith Dr. Air. ML6	96	DC33
Beith Rd, John. PA5	80	AJ35
Beith Rd, (How.) John. PA9	78	AD38
Beith Rd, (Kilb.) John. PA10	78	AD38
Beith St, G11	66	BK28
Belford Ct, (Newt. M.) G77	131	BF51
Belford Dr, (Newt. M.) G77	131	BF51
Belgowan St, (Bellshill Ind. Est.) Bell. ML4	94	CV38
Belgrave La, G12	49	BN26
Belgrave St, (Bellshill Ind. Est.) Bell. ML4	110	CV39
Belgrave Ter, G12	49	BN26
Belhaven Ct, (Newt. M.) G77	131	BE51
Belhaven Cres La, G12	48	BL25
off Kensington Rd		
Belhaven Pk, (Muir.) G69	54	CL22
Belhaven Pl, (Newt. M.) G77	131	BF51
Belhaven Rd, Ham. ML3	125	CN50
Belhaven Ter, G12	48	BL25
Belhaven Ter, (Ruther.) G73	105	BY39
Belhaven Ter La, G12	48	BL25
Belhaven Ter W, G12	48	BL25
Belhaven Ter W La, G12	48	BL25
Bellahouston Dr, G52	85	BG34
Bellahouston La, G52	85	BG33
Bellairs Pl, (Blan.) G72	108	CL44
Bellcraig Ct, (Clark.) G76	119	BR48
off Easterton Av		
Bell Dr, (Blan.) G72	124	CL49
Belleisle Av, (Udd.) G71	109	CN39
Belleisle Ct, (Cumb.) G68	22	DA9
Belleisle Dr, (Cumb.) G68	22	DA9
Belleisle Gdns, (Cumb.) G68	22	DA9
Belleisle Gro, (Cumb.) G68	22	DA9
Belleisle St, G42	87	BR36
Bellevue Av, (Kirk.) G66	16	CD13
Bellevue Pl, G21	68	BV28
Bellevue Rd, (Kirk.) G66	16	CD13
Bellfield Ct, (Barr.) G78	99	AX41
off Bellfield Cres		
Bellfield Cres, (Barr.) G78	99	AX41
Bellfield Rd, (Kirk.) G66	16	CD13
Bellfield St, G31	69	BW31
Bellflower Av, G53	100	BD42
Bellflower Ct, (E.Kil.) G74	121	BY50
Bellflower Gdns, G53	101	BE42
Bellflower Gro, (E.Kil.) G74	121	BY50
Bellflower Pl, G53	101	BE42
Bell Grn E, (E.Kil.) G75	136	CB53
Bell Grn W, (E.Kil.) G75	136	CA53
Bellgrove St, G31	68	BV31
Bellisle Ter, Ham. ML3	139	CR53
off Pitreavie Ct		
Bellrock Ct, G33	70	CD29
Bellrock Cres, G33	70	CC29
Bellrock Path, G33	70	CD29
off Bellrock St		
Bellrock St, G33	70	CC29
Bellscroft Av, (Ruther.) G73	88	BV38
Bellsdyke Rd, Air. ML6	76	DB31
Bellsfield Dr, (Blan.) G72	124	CM47
Bellshaugh Ct, G12	48	BL24
Bellshaugh Gdns, G12	48	BL24
Bellshaugh La, G12	48	BL24
Bellshaugh Pl, G12	48	BL24
Bellshaugh Rd, G12	48	BL24
Bellshill N Ind Est, Bell. ML4	110	CV39
Bellshill Rd, (Both.) G71	110	CT43
Bellshill Rd, (Udd.) G71	109	CP40
Bellshill Rd, Bell. ML4	110	CT43
Bellshill Rd, Moth. ML1	111	CY43
Bellside Rd, (Chap.) Air. ML6	97	DG35
Bell St, G1	5	BT31
Bell St, G4	5	BT31
Bell St, Air. ML6	76	DB29
Bell St, Bell. ML4	95	CX38
Bell St, Clyde. G81	45	AZ22
Bell St, Renf. PA4	45	AZ25
Bell St, Wis. ML2	129	DH50
Belltrees Cres, Pais. PA3	81	AQ33
Bellview Ct, Renf. PA4	45	AZ25
Bellvue Cres, Bell. ML4	110	CU41
Bellvue Way, Coat. ML5	95	CZ33
Bellwood St, G41	87	BN38
Bellziehill Rd, Bell. ML4	110	CU40
Belmar Ct, (Linw.) Pais. PA3	60	AL32
off Langholm Dr		
Belmont Av, (Udd.) G71	93	CN38
Belmont Ct, (Kirk.) G66	17	CF14
off Willowbank Gdns		
Belmont Cres, G12	49	BN26
Belmont Dr, (Giff.) G46	102	BK42
Belmont Dr, (Ruther.) G73	89	BX38
Belmont Dr, (E.Kil.) G75	135	BX53
Belmont Dr, (Barr.) G78	99	AZ44
Belmont La, G12	49	BN26
Belmont Rd, G21	50	BV23
Belmont Rd, (Camb.) G72	106	CA41
Belmont Rd, Pais. PA3	63	AW31
Belmont St, G12	49	BN26
Belmont St, (Kilsyth) G65	7	CS4
Belmont St, Clyde. G81	45	AX21
Belmont St, Coat. ML5	74	CT28
Belses Dr, G52	65	BE32
Belses Gdns, G52	65	BE32
Belstane Pl, (Both.) G71	109	CQ42
Belstane Rd, G67	40	DB16
Belsyde Av, G15	28	BC19
Beltane St, G3	4	BP29
Beltrees Av, G53	84	BC35
Beltrees Cres, G53	84	BC36
Beltrees Rd, G53	84	BC36
Belvidere Cres, (Bishop.) G64	33	BX19
Belvidere Cres, Bell. ML4	111	CX41
Belvidere Rd, Bell. ML4	111	CW41
Belvoir Pl, (Blan.) G72	124	CM45
Bemersyde, (Bishop.) G64	33	BY19
Bemersyde Av, G43	102	BK40
Bemersyde Pl, Lark. ML9	144	DC60
Bemersyde Rd, Pais. PA2	80	AM37
Ben Aigan Pl, G53	101	BE41
Ben Alder Dr, Pais. PA2	83	AZ36
Benalder St, G11	66	BL28
Benarty Gdns, (Bishop.) G64	33	BX19
Benbecula, (E.Kil.) G74	137	CE52
Benbow Rd, Clyde. G81	26	AV19
Ben Buie Way, Pais. PA2	83	AZ36
Bencroft Dr, G44	104	BU40
Ben Donich Pl, G53	101	BF41
off Ben Vorlich Dr		
Ben Edra Pl, G53	101	BF41
off Ben Vorlich Dr		
Benford Av, Moth. ML1	113	DF41
Benford Knowe, Moth. ML1	113	DG41
Bengairn St, G31	69	BY30
Bengal Pl, G43	86	BL38
off Christian St		
Bengal St, G43	86	BL38
Ben Garrisdale Pl, G53	101	BF41
off Ben Vorlich Dr		
Ben Glas Pl, G53	101	BF40
off Ben Vorlich Dr		
Benhar Pl, G33	70	CB30
Benholm St, G32	90	CB34
Ben Hope Av, Pais. PA2	83	AZ35
Ben Laga Pl, G53	101	BF41
off Ben Vorlich Dr		
Ben Lawers Dr, (Cumb.) G68	21	CX11
Ben Lawers Dr, Pais. PA2	83	AZ35
Ben Ledi Av, Pais. PA2	83	AZ35
Ben Ledi Cres, (Cumb.) G68	21	CX11
Ben Loyal Av, Pais. PA2	83	AZ35
Ben Lui Dr, Pais. PA2	83	AY36
Ben Lui Pl, G53	101	BF41
off Ben Vorlich Dr		
Ben Lui Pl, (Cumb.) G68	21	CX11
Ben Macdui Gdns, G53	101	BF41
Ben More Dr, G68	21	CW11
Ben More Dr, Pais. PA2	83	AZ35
Benmore St, G21	50	BV23
Bennan Sq, G42	88	BS35
Benn Av, Pais. PA1	83	AW33
Ben Nevis Rd, Pais. PA2	83	AY36
Ben Nevis Way, (Cumb.) G68	21	CW11
Benny Lynch Ct, G5	68	BS32
Ben Oss Pl, G53	101	BE41
Benson St, Coat. ML5	95	CW33
Benston Pl, John. PA5	79	AG36
off Craigview Av		
Benston Rd, John. PA5	79	AG36
Bent Cres, (Udd.) G71	110	CS39
Benthall St, G5	88	BT33
Bentinck St, G3	67	BN28
Bent Rd, (Chap.) Air. ML6	97	DF34
Bent Rd, Ham. ML3	126	CS50
Bents Rd, (Baill.) G69	72	CK32
Ben Uird Pl, G53	101	BF41
Ben Vane Av, Pais. PA2	83	AY36
Ben Venue Rd, (Cumb.) G68	21	CW11
Ben Venue Way, Pais. PA2	83	AZ36
Benvie Gdns, (Bishop.) G64	33	BX19
Benview Rd, (Clark.) G76	119	BN46
Benview St, G20	49	BP25
Benview Ter, Pais. PA2	83	AX35
Ben Vorlich Dr, G53	101	BF41
Ben Vorlich Pl, G53	101	BF41
Ben Wyvis Dr, Pais. PA2	83	AY36
Berelands Cres, (Ruther.) G73	88	BU38
Berelands Pl, (Ruther.) G73	88	BV38
Beresford Av, G14	47	BG25
Berkeley St, G3	67	BN29
Berkeley Ter La, G3	4	BP29
Berkley Dr, (Blan.) G72	108	CL44
Bernadette Cres, Moth. ML1	113	DF43
Bernard Path, G40	89	BW33
Bernard St, G40	89	BW33
Bernard Ter, G40	89	BW33
Berneray St, G22	50	BS22
Bernisdale Dr, G15	27	AZ18
Bernisdale Gdns, G15	27	AZ18
Bernisdale Pl, G15	27	AZ18
Berridale Av, G44	103	BQ39
Berriedale, (E.Kil.) G75	134	BT53

Name	Page	Grid
Berriedale Av, (Baill.) G69	92	CJ33
Berryburn Rd, G21	51	BY25
Berry Dyke, (Kirk.) G66	18	CK14
off Burnbrae Rd		
Berryhill Dr, (Giff.) G46	102	BK43
Berryhill Rd, (Giff.) G46	102	BK44
Berryhill Rd, (Cumb.) G67	22	DA11
Berryknowe, (Kirk.) G66	18	CK14
off Alexander Pl		
Berryknowe Av, (Chry.) G69	54	CL22
Berryknowes Av, G52	65	BE32
Berryknowes Dr, G52	65	BF32
Berryknowes La, G52	65	BE32
Berryknowes Rd, G52	65	BE32
Bertram St, G41	87	BN36
Bertram St, Ham. ML3	125	CQ47
Bertram St, Lark. ML9	145	DE60
off Keir Hardie Rd		
Bertrohill Ter, G33	71	CE30
off Stepps Rd		
Bervie St, G51	65	BH31
Berwick Cres, Air. ML6	76	DB32
Berwick Dr, G52	84	BD33
Berwick Dr, (Ruther.) G73	105	BZ39
Berwick Pl, (E.Kil.) G74	123	CE50
Berwick Pl, Coat. ML5	95	CX34
Berwick Pl, Coat. ML5	95	CX34
Berwick St, Ham. ML3	125	CR48
Bessemer Dr, (E.Kil.) G75	136	CC56
Betula Dr, Clyde. G81	27	AW16
Bevan Gro, John. PA5	79	AF35
Beveridge Ter, Bell. ML4	111	CZ41
Beverley Rd, G43	102	BM39
Bevin Av, Clyde. G81	27	AZ20
Bideford Cres, G32	91	CF34
Biggar Rd, Moth. ML1	97	DH38
Biggar St, G31	69	BX31
Bigton St, G33	70	CD27
Billings Rd, Moth. ML1	127	CX48
Bilsland Ct, G20	49	BR24
Bilsland Dr, G20	49	BP24
Binend Rd, G53	85	BE37
Binniehill Rd, (Cumb.) G68	21	CZ11
Binnie Pl, G40	68	BU32
Binns Rd, G33	71	CE27
Birch Av, (Clark.) G76	119	BP47
Birch Brae, Ham. ML3	140	CU52
Birch Ct, Coat. ML5	94	CV33
off Ailsa Rd		
Birch Cres, (Clark.) G76	119	BP47
Birch Cres, John. PA5	80	AJ36
Birch Dr, (Lenz.) G66	35	CF16
Birch Dr, (Camb.) G72	107	CE39
Birchend Dr, G21	69	BX27
Birchend Pl, G21	69	BW27
Birchfield Dr, G14	46	BD25
Birchfield Rd, Ham. ML3	125	CR50
Birch Gro, (Udd.) G71	93	CR38
Birchgrove, Lark. ML9	142	DC56
Birch Knowe, (Bishop.) G64	51	BX21
Birchlea Dr, (Giff.) G46	102	BM41
Birchmount Ct, Air. ML6	77	DE29
off Forrest St		
Birch Pl, (Blan.) G72	124	CM45
Birch Pl, (Camb.) G72	107	CH41
Birch Quad, Air. ML6	77	DF30
Birch Rd, (Cumb.) G67	23	DG10
Birch Rd, Clyde. G81	27	AW17
Birch St, G5	88	BT34
off Silverfir St		
Birch St, Moth. ML1	112	DD40
Birch Vw, (Bears.) G61	30	BJ16
Birchview Dr, (Clark.) G76	119	BP49
Birchwood Av, G32	91	CG33
Birchwood Dr, Pais. PA2	81	AQ36
Birchwood Pl, G32	91	CG33
Birdsfield Ct, Ham. ML3	125	CP47
off Birdsfield St		
Birdsfield Dr, (Blan.) G72	124	CM47
Birdsfield St, Ham. ML3	125	CP47
Birdston Rd, G21	51	BY23
Birgidale Rd, G45	104	BT43
Birgidale Ter, G45	104	BT43
Birkdale, (E.Kil.) G74	121	BY50
Birkdale Ct, (Both.) G71	109	CP43
Birkdale Cres, (Cumb.) G68	9	DB7
Birkdale Wd, (Cumb.) G68	9	DC7
Birken Rd, (Lenz.) G66	35	CG17
Birkenshaw Ind Est, (Udd.) G71	93	CN35
Birkenshaw Rd, (Gart.) G69	56	CS21
Birkenshaw St, G31	69	BX30
Birkenshaw Way, Pais. PA3	62	AU29
Birkhall Av, G52	84	BB33
Birkhall Av, (Inch.) Renf. PA4	44	AT22
Birkhall Dr, (Bears.) G61	29	BH19
Birkhill Av, (Bishop.) G64	33	BX19
Birkhill Gdns, (Bishop.) G64	33	BX19
Birkhill Rd, Ham. ML3	140	CT54
Birkmyre Rd, G51	65	BH31
Birks Rd, Lark. ML9	144	DD62
Birks Rd, Renf. PA4	63	AX27
off Tower Dr		
Birkwood Pl, (Newt. M.) G77	131	BF51
Birkwood St, G40	89	BX35
off Dalmarnock Rd		
Birmingham Rd, Renf. PA4	63	AX28
Birnam Av, (Bishop.) G64	33	BX19
Birnam Cres, (Bears.) G61	30	BK16
Birnam Gdns, (Bishop.) G64	33	BX19
Birnam Pl, (Newt. M.) G77	118	BK49
Birnam Pl, Ham. ML3	125	CN50
Birnam Rd, G31	89	BZ34
off London Rd		
Birness Dr, G43	86	BM37
Birness St, G43	86	BM38
off Pleasance St		
Birnie Ct, G21	51	BY26
Birniehill Roundabout, (E.Kil.) G74	136	CC53
Birnie Rd, G21	51	BY25
Birnock Av, Renf. PA4	64	BA28
Birrell Rd, (Miln.) G62	11	BH10
Birrens Rd, Moth. ML1	127	CY45
Birsay Rd, G22	49	BR22
Bishopdale, (E.Kil.) G74	121	BY50
Bishop Gdns, (Bishop.) G64	32	BU19
Bishop Gdns, Ham. ML3	140	CU54
Bishopmill Pl, G21	51	BY25
Bishopmill Rd, G21	51	BY24
Bishopsgate Dr, G21	50	BU22
Bishopsgate Gdns, G21	50	BU22
Bishopsgate Pl, G21	50	BU22
Bishopsgate Rd, G21	50	BU22
Bishops Pk, (Thornton.) G74	119	BR50
Bishop St, G3	4	BQ30
Bissett Cres, Clyde. G81	26	AU15
Blackadder Pl, (E.Kil.) G75	134	BT54
Blackbog Rd, Air. ML6	40	DB19
Blackbraes Rd, (E.Kil.) G74	122	CD49
Blackburn Cres, (Kirk.) G66	18	CJ13
Blackburn Sq, (Barr.) G78	99	AZ44
Blackburn St, G51	66	BM31
Blackbyres Ct, (Barr.) G78	99	AZ41
Blackbyres Rd, (Barr.) G78	99	AY39
Blackcraig Av, G15	28	BC18
Blackcroft Av, Air. ML6	77	DG32
Blackcroft Gdns, G32	91	CF33
Blackcroft Rd, G32	91	CF33
Blackdyke Rd, (Kirk.) G66	17	CG13
Blackfarm Rd, (Newt. M.) G77	117	BH49
Blackfaulds Rd, (Ruther.) G73	88	BU37
Blackford Rd, Pais. PA2	83	AW34
Blackfriars St, G1	5	BT30
Blackhall Ct, Pais. PA2	83	AX34
off Cartha Cres		
Blackhall La, Pais. PA1	82	AV34
Blackhall St, Pais. PA1	82	AV34
Blackhill Cotts, G23	31	BQ20
Blackhill Pl, G33	70	CA27
off Maxwelton Rd		
Blackhill Rd, G23	31	BN19
Blackhouse Av, (Newt. M.) G77	117	BH49
Blackhouse Gdns, (Newt. M.) G77	117	BH49
Blackhouse Rd, (Newt. M.) G77	117	BH49
Blackie St, G3	66	BM29
Blackland Gro, Pais. PA2	82	AS37
Blacklands Pl, (Lenz.) G66	35	CG17
Blacklands Rd, (E.Kil.) G74	135	BZ52
Blacklaw Dr, (E.Kil.) G74	136	CD52
Blacklaw La, Pais. PA3	62	AU31
Blackmoor Pl, Moth. ML1	112	DC42
Blackmoss Dr, Bell. ML4	111	CW41
off Hamilton Rd		
Blackness St, Coat. ML5	95	CX34
Black O' Hill Roundabout, (Cumb.) G68	21	CW12
Blackstone Av, G53	85	BE37
Blackstone Cres, G53	85	BE36
Blackstone Rd, Pais. PA3	61	AQ29
Blackstoun Av, (Linw.) Pais. PA3	60	AK32
Blackstoun Oval, Pais. PA3	61	AR32
Blackstoun Rd, Pais. PA3	61	AQ32
Black St, G4	5	BT28
Black St, Air. ML6	76	DD28
Blackswell La, Ham. ML3	126	CV50
Blackthorn Av, (Kirk.) G66	34	CC16
Blackthorn Gro, (Kirk.) G66	34	CD16
Blackthorn Rd, (Cumb.) G67	23	DF9
Blackthorn Rd, (Udd.) G71	94	CS37
off Redwood Cres		
Blackthorn St, G22	50	BU24
Blacktongue Fm Rd, (Green.) Air. ML6	41	DG19
Blackwood, (E.Kil.) G75	135	BZ56
Blackwood Av, (Newt. M.) G77	117	BH50
Blackwood Av, (Linw.) Pais. PA3	60	AJ31
Blackwood Rd, (Miln.) G62	11	BH9
Blackwood Rd, G68	20	CT12
Blackwood Roundabout, (Cumb.) G68	20	CV11
Blackwoods Cres, (Mood.) G69	37	CP19
Blackwoods Cres, Bell. ML4	111	CY53
Blackwoods Gdns, Moth. ML1	111	CY44
off Frood St		
Blackwood St, G13	47	BG22
Blackwood St, (Barr.) G78	99	AX43
Blackwood Ter, John. PA5	79	AF37
Bladda La, Pais. PA1	82	AV33
Blades Ct, (Gart.) G69	55	CQ23
Bladnoch Dr, G15	29	BE19
Blaeloch Av, G45	104	BS44
Blaeloch Dr, G45	103	BR44
Blaeloch Ter, G45	103	BR44
Blaeshill Rd, (E.Kil.) G75	134	BU53

Blairatholl Av, G11 48 BJ26
Blairatholl Cres, (Newt. M.) 118 BK49
G77
Blair Atholl Dr, Lark. ML9 145 DE60
Blairatholl Gdns, G11 48 BJ26
Blairatholl Gate, (Newt. M.) 118 BK49
G77
Blairbeth Dr, G44 87 BR38
Blairbeth Pl, (Ruther.) G73 105 BW40
off Drumilaw Rd
Blairbeth Rd, (Ruther.) G73 105 BW40
Blairbeth Ter, (Ruther.) G73 105 BY40
off Blairbeth Rd
Blairbuie Dr, G20 48 BL22
Blair Cres, (Baill.) G69 92 CJ34
Blairdardie Dr, G15 28 BD20
Blairdardie Rd, G13 28 BD20
Blairdardie Rd, G15 28 BD20
Blairdenan Av, (Mood.) G69 37 CP18
Blairdenon Dr, (Cumb.) G68 21 CY11
Blair Gdns, (Torr.) G64 15 BX12
Blair Gdns, (Newt. M.) G77 118 BD40
Blairgowrie Rd, G52 85 BE33
Blairgrove Ct, Coat. ML5 74 CU31
Blairhall Av, G41 87 BP37
Blairhill Av, (Kirk.) G66 36 CJ15
Blairhill Pl, Coat. ML5 74 CU30
Blairhill St, Coat. ML5 74 CU30
Blairholm Dr, Bell. ML4 111 CX42
Blairlinn Ind Est, (Cumb.) G67 40 DB15
Blairlinn Rd, (Cumb.) G67 40 DB15
Blairlinn Vw, (Cumb.) G67 40 DC15
Blairlogie St, G33 70 CD28
Blairmore Av, Pais. PA1 63 AY32
Blairpark Av, Coat. ML5 74 CU29
Blair Path, Moth. ML1 128 DB48
off Toll St
Blair Rd, Coat. ML5 74 CU31
Blair Rd, Pais. PA4 64 BA31
Blairston Av, (Both.) G71 109 CQ44
Blairston Gdns, (Both.) G71 109 CR44
Blair St, G32 70 CB32
Blairtum Dr, (Ruther.) G73 105 BX40
Blairtummock Rd, G33 71 CE29
Blake Rd, (Cumb.) G67 22 DC11
Blane Dr, (Miln.) G62 12 BK10
Blanefield Gdns, G13 47 BH21
Blane St, Coat. ML5 75 CW29
Blaneview, (Stepps) G33 53 CF25
Blantyre Ct, Ersk. PA8 25 AQ18
Blantyre Ferme Rd, (Udd.) 108 CL39
G71
Blantyre Gdns, (Cumb.) G68 20 CU12
Blantyre Ind Est, (Blan.) G72 125 CN48
Blantyre Mill Rd, (Both.) G71 109 CP44
Blantyre Rd, (Both.) G71 109 CQ43
Blantyre St, G3 66 BM28
Blantyre St, Coat. ML5 94 CU33
Blaven Ct, (Baill.) G69 92 CL33
Blawarthill St, G14 46 BB24
Bleasdale Ct, Clyde. G81 27 AX19
Blenheim Av, (Stepps) G33 53 CF23
Blenheim Av, (E.Kil.) G75 135 BY54
Blenheim Ct, (Stepps) G33 53 CF23
Blenheim Ct, (Kilsyth) G65 7 CT4
Blenheim Ct, Pais. PA1 62 AT32
Blenheim La, (Stepps) G33 53 CG23
Blochairn Rd, G21 69 BW28
Bluebell Gdns, G45 105 BW43
Bluebell Gdns, Moth. ML1 111 CY43
off Malleable Gdns
Bluebell Wk, Moth. ML1 112 DC42
off Thistle Rd

Bluebell Way, Air. ML6 76 DB27
Bluevale St, G31 69 BW31
Blyth Pl, G33 71 CF31
Blyth Rd, G33 71 CG31
Blythswood Av, Renf. PA4 45 AZ25
Blythswood Ct, G2 4 BQ30
off Cadogan St
Blythswood Dr, Pais. PA3 62 AT31
Blythswood Retail Pk, Renf. 45 AX25
PA4
Blythswood Rd, Renf. PA4 45 AY24
Blythswood Sq, G2 4 BQ29
off Blythswood St
Blythswood St, G2 4 BQ30
Bobbins Gate, Pais. PA1 81 AR34
Boclair Av, (Bears.) G61 29 BH17
Boclair Cres, (Bears.) G61 30 BJ17
Boclair Cres, (Bishop.) G64 33 BW20
Boclair Rd, (Bears.) G61 30 BJ17
Boclair Rd, (Miln.) G62 30 BM15
Boclair Rd, (Bishop.) G64 33 BW19
Boclair St, G13 47 BG21
Boden Ind Est, G40 89 BX33
Boden Quad, Moth. ML1 111 CX43
Boden St, G40 89 BW33
Bodmin Gdns, (Chry.) G69 37 CP18
off Gartferry Rd
Bogany Ter, G45 104 BU43
Bogbain Rd, G34 72 CJ29
Boggknowe, (Udd.) G71 92 CM37
Boghall Rd, (Udd.) G71 92 CJ35
Boghall St, G33 70 CD28
Boghead Rd, G21 51 BW24
Boghead Rd, (Kirk.) G66 34 CC16
Bogleshole Rd, (Camb.) G72 90 CA38
Bogmoor Pl, G51 65 BE28
Bogmoor Rd, G51 65 BE29
Bogside Pl, (Baill.) G69 72 CL30
off Whamflet Av
Bogside Rd, G33 52 CC24
Bogside Rd, (Kilsyth) G65 7 CT6
Bogside Rd, (Ashgill) Lark. 145 DG62
ML9
Bogside St, G40 89 BX33
Bogs Vw, Bell. ML4 110 CV42
Bogton Av, G44 103 BP41
Bogton Av La, G44 103 BP41
Boleyn Rd, G41 87 BN35
Bolingbroke, (E.Kil.) G74 123 CE49
Bolivar Ter, G42 88 BS37
Bolton Dr, G42 87 BQ37
Bon Accord Rd, (Clark.) G76 119 BP47
Bon Accord Sq, Clyde. G81 45 AX21
Bonawe St, G20 49 BP25
off Kirkland St
Boness Rd, Moth. ML1 113 DE39
Boness St, G40 89 BX33
Bonhill St, G22 49 BR26
Bonnar St, G40 89 BW34
Bonnaughton Rd, (Bears.) 28 BD15
G61
Bonnyholm Av, G53 84 BC34
Bonnyrigg Dr, G43 102 BJ40
Bonnyton Dr, (Eagle.) G76 132 BM56
Bonnyton La, Ham. ML3 139 CR54
off Loch Grn
Bonnyton Moor Rd, (Eagle.) 132 BJ54
G76
Bonyton Av, G13 46 BB23
Boon Dr, G15 28 BD19
Boquhanran Pl, Clyde. G81 27 AW18
Boquhanran Rd, Clyde. G81 26 AV18
Borden La, G13 47 BG24

Borden Rd, G13 47 BG24
Border Way, (Kirk.) G66 17 CG13
Boreland Dr, G13 46 BC22
Boreland Dr, Ham. ML3 139 CN51
Boreland Pl, G13 46 BD23
Bore Rd, Air. ML6 76 DD28
Borgie Cres, (Camb.) G72 106 CC40
Borland Cres, (Eagle.) G76 133 BN56
off Pollock Av
Borland Dr, Lark. ML9 144 DD61
Borland Rd, (Bears.) G61 30 BJ18
Borron St, G4 50 BS26
Borrowdale, (E.Kil.) G75 134 BV56
off Ullswater
Borthwick Dr, (E.Kil.) G75 134 BT54
Borthwick St, G33 70 CD28
Bosfield Cor, (E.Kil.) G74 122 CB50
Bosfield Pl, (E.Kil.) G74 122 CB50
Bosfield Rd, (E.Kil.) G74 122 CB50
Boswell Ct, G42 87 BP38
Boswell Dr, (Blan.) G72 124 CM46
Boswell Pk, (E.Kil.) G74 123 CE49
Boswell Sq, G52 64 BB30
Bosworth Rd, (E.Kil.) G74 123 CE48
Botanic Cres, G20 48 BM25
Botanic Cres La, G20 48 BM25
Bothlin Dr, (Stepps) G33 53 CF23
Bothlyn Av, (Kirk.) G66 17 CG14
Bothlyn Cres, (Gart.) G69 55 CN22
Bothlyn Rd, (Chry.) G69 54 CM21
Bothwellhaugh Quad, Bell. 110 CV42
ML4 off Strathview Rd
Bothwellhaugh Rd, Bell. ML4 110 CV44
Bothwellhaugh Rd, Moth. ML1 110 CV44
Bothwell La, G2 4 BQ30
Bothwellpark Ind Est, (Udd.) 109 CQ40
G71
Bothwellpark Pl, Bell. ML4 110 CT39
off Philip Murray Rd
Bothwellpark Rd, (Both.) G71 110 CS42
Bothwell Pl, Coat. ML5 74 CV30
Bothwell Pl, Pais. PA2 81 AN37
Bothwell Rd, (Udd.) G71 109 CP40
Bothwell Rd, Ham. ML3 126 CS46
Bothwell St, G2 4 BQ29
Bothwell St, (Camb.) G72 106 CA39
Bothwell St, Ham. ML3 126 CS48
Bothwick Way, Pais. PA2 81 AN37
off Crosbie Dr
Boundary Rd, (Ruther.) G73 88 BU35
off Rutherglen Rd
Bourhill Ct, Wis. ML2 143 DF51
off Netherton Rd
Bourne Ct, (Inch.) Renf. PA4 44 AT22
Bourne Cres, (Inch.) Renf. PA4 44 AT22
Bourne St, Ham. ML3 126 CV50
Bourock Sq, (Barr.) G78 99 AZ44
Bourtree Rd, Ham. ML3 139 CP52
Bouverie St, G14 46 BA23
Bouverie St, (Ruther.) G73 88 BV38
Bowden Dr, G52 64 BD31
Bowden Pk, (E.Kil.) G75 135 BY53
Bower St, G12 49 BN26
Bowes Cres, (Baill.) G69 91 CH33
Bowfield Av, G52 64 BB31
Bowfield Cres, G52 64 BB31
Bowfield Dr, G52 64 BB31
Bowfield Path, G52 64 BB31
off Bowfield Av
Bowfield Pl, G52 64 BB31
Bowfield Ter, G52 64 BB31
off Bowfield Cres
Bowhousebrae Rd, Air. ML6 77 DG32

Bowhouse Rd, Air. ML6	77	DH32
Bowhouse Way, (Ruther.) G73	105	BW41
Bowling Grn La, G14	47	BF26
Bowling Grn Rd, G14	47	BF26
Bowling Grn Rd, G32	91	CF33
Bowling Grn Rd, G44	103	BQ40
off Clarkston Rd		
Bowling Grn Rd, (Chry.) G69	54	CM21
Bowling Grn St, Bell. ML4	111	CX40
Bowling St, Coat. ML5	74	CV30
Bowmanflat, Lark. ML9	144	DC58
off McNeil St		
Bowman St, G42	87	BQ35
Bowmont Gdns, G12	48	BL26
Bowmont Hill, (Bishop.) G64	33	BW17
Bowmont Pl, (Camb.) G72	107	CF40
Bowmont Pl, (E.Kil.) G75	134	BT54
Bowmont Ter, G12	48	BL26
Bowmore Gdns, (Udd.) G71	93	CN37
Bowmore Gdns, (Ruther.)	106	CA42
G73 *off Ardbeg Av*		
Bowmore Rd, G52	65	BG32
Bowyer Vennel, Bell. ML4	110	CV39
Boyd Dr, Moth. ML1	127	CX46
Boydstone Pl, (Thornlie.) G46	101	BH40
Boydstone Rd, G43	101	BG40
Boydstone Rd, (Thornlie.)	101	BG39
G46		
Boydstone Rd, G53	101	BG40
Boyd St, G42	87	BR36
Boylestone Rd, (Barr.) G78	99	AW41
Boyle St, Clyde. G81	45	AZ21
Boyndie Path, G34	72	CK29
Boyndie St, G34	72	CK29
Brabloch Cres, Pais. PA3	62	AV31
Brabloch Pk, Pais. PA3	62	AV31
Bracadale Dr, (Baill.) G69	92	CM33
Bracadale Gdns, (Baill.) G69	92	CM33
Bracadale Gro, (Baill.) G69	92	CL33
Bracadale Rd, (Baill.) G69	92	CL33
Brackenbrae Av, (Bishop.) G64	32	BU19
Brackenbrae Rd, (Bishop.) G64	32	BV20
Brackenhill Dr, Ham. ML3	139	CR54
Brackenhirst Gdns, (Glenm.)	57	CZ24
Air. ML6		
Brackenhirst Rd, (Glenm.)	58	DA23
Air. ML6		
Brackenknowle Rd, Air. ML6	41	DF17
Brackenrig Cres, (Eagle.) G76	133	BN52
Brackenrig Rd, (Thornlie.) G46	101	BG43
Bracken St, G22	49	BR23
Bracken St, Moth. ML1	112	DC42
Bracken Ter, (Both.) G71	109	CQ42
Bracken Way, Lark. ML9	145	DE60
off Morris St		
Brackla Av, G13	46	BA21
Brackla Av, Clyde. G81	46	BA21
Bradan Av, G13	46	BA22
Bradan Av, Clyde. G81	46	BA22
Bradda Av, (Ruther.) G73	105	BY41
Bradfield Av, G12	48	BL24
Bradshaw Cres, Ham. ML3	125	CN50
Brady Cres, (Mood.) G69	37	CQ18
Braedale Av, Air. ML6	76	DD30
Braedale Av, Moth. ML1	127	CX47
Braeface Rd, (Cumb.) G67	22	DA11
Braefield Dr, (Thornlie.) G46	102	BJ42
Braefoot Av, (Miln.) G62	12	BJ13
Braefoot Cres, Pais. PA2	82	AU38
Braehead, (Blan.) G72	124	CM47
Braehead Av, (Miln.) G62	11	BH12
Braehead Av, (Neil.) G78	114	AT46
Braehead Av, Coat. ML5	94	CT34
Braehead Av, Lark. ML9	144	DA59
off Millheugh Brae		
Braehead Dr, Bell. ML4	110	CV41
Braehead Pl, Bell. ML4	110	CV41
Braehead Quad, (Neil.) G78	114	AT46
Braehead Quad, Moth. ML1	113	DF41
off Hillside Cres		
Braehead Rd, (Cumb.) G67	22	DD10
Braehead Rd, (Thornton.) G74	120	BT50
Braehead Rd, Pais. PA2	98	AS39
Braehead Shop Cen, G51	46	BC26
Braehead St, G5	88	BT34
Braehead St, (Kirk.) G66	17	CE12
Braemar Av, Clyde. G81	26	AV16
Braemar Ct, G44	103	BN41
Braemar Cres, (Bears.) G61	29	BH15
Braemar Cres, Pais. PA2	82	AV36
Braemar Dr, (Elder.) John. PA5	80	AK36
Braemar Rd, (Ruther.) G73	106	CA42
Braemar Rd, (Inch.) Renf. PA4	44	AT22
Braemar St, G42	87	BP38
Braemar St, Ham. ML3	125	CR47
Braemar Vw, Clyde. G81	26	AV16
Braemore Gdns, G22	50	BT25
Braemount Av, Pais. PA2	98	AS39
Braes Av, Clyde. G81	27	AZ20
Braeside Av, (Miln.) G62	12	BJ13
Braeside Av, (Mood.) G69	37	CP19
Braeside Av, (Ruther.) G73	89	BY38
Braeside Cres, (Baill.) G69	73	CP32
Braeside Cres, (Barr.) G78	100	BA44
Braeside Dr, (Barr.) G78	99	AZ44
Braeside Gdns, Ham. ML3	140	CU53
Braeside La, Lark. ML9	144	DD57
off Meadowhill St		
Braeside Pl, (Camb.) G72	106	CD41
Braeside Rd, Moth. ML1	113	DF41
Braeside St, G20	49	BP26
Braeside Way, Lark. ML9	144	DD60
off Fisher St		
Braes O'Yetts, (Kirk.) G66	18	CJ13
Braeview Av, Pais. PA2	81	AR38
Braeview Dr, Pais..PA2	81	AR38
Braeview Gdns, Pais. PA2	81	AR38
Braeview Pl, (E.Kil.) G74	122	CC49
Braeview Rd, Pais. PA2	81	AR38
Braid Av, Moth. ML1	113	DH44
Braidbar Ct, (Giff.) G46	102	BL42
off Braidbar Rd		
Braidbar Fm Rd, (Giff.) G46	102	BM41
Braidbar Rd, (Giff.) G46	102	BL42
Braidcraft Pl, G53	85	BE37
off Braidcraft Rd		
Braidcraft Rd, G53	85	BE36
Braidcraft Ter, G53	85	BF36
off Braidcraft Rd		
Braidfauld Gdns, G32	90	CB34
Braidfauld Pl, G32	90	CB35
Braidfauld St, G32	90	CB34
Braidfield Gro, Clyde. G81	27	AX16
Braidfield Rd, Clyde. G81	27	AX16
Braidholm Cres, (Giff.) G46	102	BL42
Braidholm Rd, (Giff.) G46	102	BL42
Braidhurst Ind Est, Moth. ML1	111	CZ44
Braidhurst St, Moth. ML1	128	DA45
Braidley Cres, (E.Kil.) G75	136	CA56
Braidpark Dr, (Giff.) G46	102	BM42
Braids Circle, Pais. PA2	82	AU36
Braids Ct, Pais. PA2	82	AU36
Braids Dr, G53	84	BB36
Braids Gait, Pais. PA2	82	AT36
Braid Sq, G4	67	BQ27
Braids Rd, Pais. PA2	82	AU36
Braid St, G4	67	BQ27
Bramah Av, (E.Kil.) G75	136	CB54
Bramley Pl, (Lenz.) G66	35	CG17
Bramley Pl, Air. ML6	77	DH31
off Fairhaven Av		
Brampton, (E.Kil.) G75	134	BV55
Branchock Av, (Camb.) G72	107	CF41
Brancumhall Rd, (E.Kil.) G74	123	CF50
Brandon Arc, Moth. ML1	128	DA47
Brandon Ct, Moth. ML1	128	DA47
off Brandon Par S		
Brandon Dr, (Bears.) G61	11	BG14
Brandon Gdns, (Camb.) G72	106	CA40
Brandon Par E, Moth. ML1	128	DA46
Brandon Par S, Moth. ML1	128	DA47
Brandon Pl, Bell. ML4	110	CU42
Brandon St, G31	68	BV31
Brandon St, Coat. ML5	94	CU33
off Lismore Dr		
Brandon St, Ham. ML3	126	CU50
Brandon St, Moth. ML1	128	DA47
Brandon Way, Coat. ML5	94	CT33
Brand Pl, G51	66	BL31
Brand St, G51	66	BL31
Brankholm Brae, Ham. ML3	124	CM49
Branklyn Ct, G13	47	BF23
Branklyn Cres, G13	47	BF23
Branklyn Gro, G13	47	BF23
Branklyn Pl, G13	47	BF23
Brannock Av, Moth. ML1	113	DF41
Brannock Pl, Moth. ML1	113	DF41
Brannock Rd, Moth. ML1	113	DF42
Branscroft, (Kilb.) John. PA10	78	AD33
Brassey St, G20	49	BN23
Breadalbane Cres, Moth. ML1	111	CZ44
Breadalbane Gdns, (Ruther.)	105	BZ41
G73		
Breadalbane St, G3	4	BP29
off St. Vincent St		
Breadie Dr, (Miln.) G62	11	BH13
Breamish Pl, (E.Kil.) G75	134	BV55
off Dove Pl		
Brechin Rd, (Bishop.) G64	33	BY20
Brechin St, G3	67	BN29
Breck Av, Pais. PA2	80	AM37
Brediland Rd, Pais. PA2	81	AN36
Brediland Rd, (Linw.) Pais. PA3	60	AJ31
Bredin Way, Moth. ML1	127	CX45
Bredisholm Cres, (Udd.) G71	94	CS36
Bredisholm Dr, (Baill.) G69	92	CL33
Bredisholm Rd, (Baill.) G69	92	CL33
Bredisholm Ter, (Baill.) G69	92	CL33
Bremner Cotts, Clyde. G81	26	AV15
Brenfield Av, G44	103	BP41
Brenfield Dr, G44	103	BP41
Brenfield Rd, G44	103	BP41
Brent Av, (Thornlie.) G46	101	BH40
Brent Ct, (E.Kil.) G74	122	CA50
Brent Dr, (Thornlie.) G46	101	BH40
Brent Gdns, (Thornlie.) G46	102	BJ40
Brent Rd, (Thornlie.) G46	101	BH40
Brent Rd, (E.Kil.) G74	122	CA50
Brent Way, (Thornlie.) G46	101	BH40
Brentwood Av, G53	100	BC41
Brentwood Dr, G53	100	BC41
Brentwood Sq, G53	100	BD41
Brereton St, G42	88	BS36
Bressay, (E.Kil.) G74	122	CA50
Bressay Rd, G33	71	CG31
Breval Ct, (Baill.) G69	92	CL33
Brewery St, John. PA5	79	AH34
Brewster Av, Pais. PA3	63	AW30

Briarbush Way, (Blan.) G72	124	CL46
off Ansdell Av		
Briarcroft Dr, G33	51	BZ22
Briarcroft Pl, G33	52	CA23
Briarcroft Rd, G33	51	BZ23
Briar Dr, Clyde. G81	27	AX17
Briar Gdns, G43	102	BM40
Briar Gro, G43	102	BM40
Briarlea Dr, (Giff.) G46	102	BL41
Briar Neuk, (Bishop.) G64	51	BX21
off Woodfield Av		
Briar Rd, G43	102	BM40
Briar Rd, (Kirk.) G66	17	CH13
Briar Wk, (Kirk.) G66	18	CJ13
Briarwell La, (Miln.) G62	12	BK12
Briarwell Rd, (Miln.) G62	12	BK12
Briarwood Ct, G32	91	CG35
Briarwood Gdns, G32	91	CG35
off Woodend Rd		
Briarwood Rd, Wis. ML2	129	DG49
Brick La, Pais. PA3	62	AV32
off Weir St		
Bridgeburn Dr, (Mood.) G69	37	CN19
Bridgeford Av, Bell. ML4	95	CY38
off Rosebank Rd		
Bridgegait, (Miln.) G62	12	BL13
Bridgegate, G1	5	BS31
Bridgegate Path, G1	5	BS31
off Bridgegate		
Bridge La, Pais. PA2	81	AR34
off Tenters Way		
Bridgend Cres, (Mood.) G69	37	CN19
Bridgend Pl, (Mood.) G69	37	CN19
Bridge of Weir Rd, (Linw.)	60	AK32
Pais. PA3		
Bridge St, G5	4	BR31
Bridge St, (Camb.) G72	106	CC39
Bridge St, Clyde. G81	26	AU18
Bridge St, Ham. ML3	140	CS51
Bridge St, Pais. PA1	82	AU33
Bridge St, (Linw.) Pais. PA3	60	AL31
Bridge St, Wis. ML2	129	DG50
Bridgeton Business Cen, G40	68	BV32
Bridgeton Cross, G40	68	BV32
Bridgeton Shop Cen, Ersk.	26	AS19
PA8		
Bridgeway Ct, (Kirk.) G66	17	CH14
Bridgeway Pl, (Kirk.) G66	17	CH14
Bridgeway Rd, (Kirk.) G66	17	CH14
Bridgeway Ter, (Kirk.) G66	17	CH14
Bridie Ter, (E.Kil.) G74	123	CE49
Brigbrae Av, Bell. ML4	111	CY42
Brigham Pl, G23	49	BN21
off Broughton Rd		
Brighton Pl, G51	66	BK31
Brighton St, G51	66	BK31
Brightside Av, (Udd.) G71	109	CP40
Bright St, G21	68	BV28
Brig O'Lea Ter, (Neil.) G78	114	AS47
Brigside Gdns, Ham. ML3	141	CW51
Brisbane Ct, (Giff.) G46	102	BM42
Brisbane Rd, Bish. PA7	24	AK18
Brisbane St, G42	87	BQ38
Brisbane St, Clyde. G81	26	AT17
Brisbane Ter, (E.Kil.) G75	135	BY54
Britannia Way, Clyde. G81	27	AX19
off Sutherland Rd		
Britannia Way, Renf. PA4	63	AY28
Briton St, G51	66	BK31
Broadcroft, (Kirk.) G66	17	CE12
Broadford St, G4	68	BS27
Broadholm St, G22	49	BR23
Broadleys Av, (Bishop.) G64	32	BV18

Broadlie Ct, (Neil.) G78	114	AT46
Broadlie Dr, G13	46	BC23
Broadlie Rd, (Neil.) G78	114	AS46
Broadloan, Renf. PA4	63	AY27
Broadmoss Av, (Newt. M.)	118	BL49
G77		
Broad Sq, (Blan.) G72	124	CL45
Broad St, G40	68	BV32
Broadwalk, The (E.Kil.) G75	136	CC55
Broadway, The, Wis. ML2	129	DG49
Broadwood Business Pk,	20	CV13
(Cumb.) G68		
Broadwood Dr, G44	103	BR39
Broadwood Roundabout,	20	CV13
(Cumb.) G68		
Brockburn Cres, G53	84	BD37
Brockburn Pl, G53	84	BC35
Brockburn Rd, G53	84	BC35
Brockburn Ter, G53	85	BE37
Brocklinn Pk, (E.Kil.) G75	134	BU54
Brock Oval, G53	101	BE39
Brock Pl, G53	85	BE38
Brock Rd, G53	101	BE39
Brock Ter, G53	85	BE38
Brockville St, G32	70	CB31
Brock Way, (Cumb.) G67	22	DB12
off North Carbrain Rd		
Brodick Av, Moth. ML1	127	CX46
Brodick Dr, (E.Kil.) G74	121	BZ50
Brodick Pl, (Newt. M.) G77	116	BC49
Brodick Sq, (Bishop.) G64	51	BX22
Brodick St, G21	69	BW28
Brodie Gdns, (Baill.) G69	72	CL31
Brodie Pk Av, Pais. PA2	82	AU35
Brodie Pk Cres, Pais. PA2	82	AT35
Brodie Pk Gdns, Pais. PA2	82	AU35
Brodie Pl, (E.Kil.) G74	121	BZ50
Brodie Rd, G21	51	BZ22
Brogan Cres, Moth. ML1	127	CX46
Bron Way, (Cumb.) G67	22	DC12
Brookfield Av, G33	51	BZ22
Brookfield Cor, G33	51	BZ22
Brookfield Dr, G33	51	BZ22
Brookfield Gdns, G33	51	BZ22
off Brookfield Av		
Brookfield Gate, G33	51	BZ22
off Brookfield Av		
Brookfield Pl, G33	51	BZ22
Brookfield Rd, G33	51	BZ22
Brooklands, (E.Kil.) G74	135	BW52
Brooklands Av, (Udd.) G71	93	CN38
Brooklea Dr, (Giff.) G46	102	BL40
Brooklime Dr, (E.Kil.) G74	121	BY49
Brooklime Gdns, (E.Kil.) G74	121	BY49
Brookside St, G40	69	BW32
Brook St, G40	68	BV32
Brook St, Clyde. G81	26	AV17
Broom Av, Ersk. PA8	43	AR22
Broomburn Dr, (Newt. M.)	117	BH49
G77		
Broom Cliff, (Newt. M.) G77	117	BH50
off Castleton Dr		
Broom Cres, (E.Kil.) G75	135	BZ56
Broom Cres, (Barr.) G78	99	AW40
Broomcroft Rd, (Newt. M.)	118	BJ47
G77		
Broom Dr, Clyde. G81	27	AW17
Broom Dr, Lark. ML9	142	DC56
off Maple Dr		
Broomdyke Way, Pais. PA3	62	AT29
Broomfield Av, (Camb.) G72	89	BZ38
off Cambuslang Rd		

Broomfield Av, (Newt. M.)	117	BH50
G77		
Broomfield La, G21	50	BV24
Broomfield Pl, G21	50	BV24
Broomfield Rd, G21	50	BV24
Broomfield Rd, (Giff.) G46	118	BJ47
Broomfield Rd, Lark. ML9	144	DC61
Broomfield St, Air. ML6	76	DD30
Broomfield Ter, (Udd.) G71	93	CP36
Broomfield Wk, (Kirk.) G66	17	CF13
off Willowbank Gdns		
Broom Gdns, (Kirk.) G66	34	CD15
Broomhill Av, G11	65	BH27
Broomhill Av, G32	90	CD37
Broomhill Av, (Newt. M.) G77	117	BH50
Broomhill Ct, Lark. ML9	144	DC59
off Broomhill Rd		
Broomhill Cres, Bell. ML4	110	CV42
off Crofthead Cres		
Broomhill Cres, Ersk. PA8	43	AR22
Broomhill Dr, G11	47	BH26
Broomhill Dr, (Ruther.) G73	105	BX40
Broomhill Fm, Ms, (Kirk.) G66	17	CG12
off Kilsyth Rd		
Broomhill Gdns, G11	47	BH26
Broomhill Gdns, (Newt. M.)	117	BH49
G77		
Broomhill Gate, Lark. ML9	144	DC59
Broomhill La, G11	47	BH26
Broomhill Path, G11	65	BH27
Broomhill Pl, G11	47	BH26
Broomhill Rd, Lark. ML9	144	DB59
Broomhill Ter, G11	65	BH27
Broomhill Vw, Lark. ML9	144	DA59
Broomieknowe Dr, (Ruther.)	105	BX39
G73		
Broomieknowe Gdns,	105	BW39
(Ruther.) G73		
Broomieknowe Rd, (Ruther.)	105	BX39
G73		
Broomielaw, G1	4	BQ31
Broomielaw, G2	4	BQ31
Broomknoll St, Air. ML6	76	DC30
Broomknowe, (Cumb.) G68	21	CZ10
Broomknowes Av, (Kirk.) G66	35	CG17
Broomknowes Rd, G21	51	BW25
Broomlands Av, Ersk. PA8	44	AT21
Broomlands Cres, Ersk. PA8	44	AT21
Broomlands Gdns, Ersk. PA8	44	AT21
Broomlands La, Pais. PA1	81	AR33
Broomlands Rd, (Cumb.) G67	22	DC13
Broomlands St, Pais. PA1	82	AS33
Broomlands Way, Ersk. PA8	44	AU21
Broomlea Cres, (Inch.) Renf.	44	AS22
PA4		
Broomlee Rd, (Cumb.) G67	40	DB15
Broomley Dr, (Giff.) G46	102	BL44
Broomley La, (Giff.) G46	102	BL44
Broomloan Ct, G51	66	BJ32
Broomloan Pl, G51	66	BJ31
Broomloan Rd, G51	66	BJ31
Broompark Av, (Blan.) G72	124	CL47
off Broompark Rd		
Broompark Circ, G31	68	BV29
Broompark Cres, Air. ML6	76	DC27
Broompark Dr, G31	68	BV30
Broompark Dr, (Newt. M.) G77	117	BH47
Broompark Dr, (Inch.) Renf.	44	AT22
PA4		
Broompark La, G31	68	BV30
Broompark Rd, (Blan.) G72	124	CL46
Broompark Rd, Wis. ML2	129	DF49
Broompark St, G31	68	BV30

Broompath, (Baill.) G69	91	CH34
Broom Pl, G43	102	BM40
Broom Pl, Coat. ML5	94	CV34
Broom Pl, Moth. ML1	113	DE41
Broom Rd, G43	102	BM40
Broom Rd, (Newt. M.) G77	118	BJ47
Broom Rd E, (Newt. M.) G77	118	BK49
Broomside Cres, Moth. ML1	128	DB49
off Adele St		
Broomside St, Moth. ML1	128	DA49
Broomstone Av, (Newt. M.)	117	BH50
G77		
Broom Ter, John. PA5	80	AJ35
Broomton Rd, G21	51	BY22
Broomvale Dr, (Newt. M.) G77	117	BH48
Broomward Dr, John. PA5	80	AK34
Brora Cres, Ham. ML3	139	CQ53
off Sherry Dr		
Brora Dr, (Giff.) G46	102	BM43
Brora Dr, (Bears.) G61	30	BK17
Brora Dr, Renf. PA4	46	BA26
Brora Gdns, (Bishop.) G64	33	BX20
Brora La, G33	69	BZ28
off Brora St		
Brora Rd, (Bishop.) G64	33	BX20
Brora St, G33	69	BZ28
Broughton Dr, G23	49	BN21
Broughton Gdns, G23	31	BP20
off Broughton Rd		
Broughton Pl, Coat. ML5	95	CX34
Broughton Pl, Ham. ML3	125	CQ50
Broughton Rd, G23	49	BN21
Brouster Gate, (E.Kil.) G74	136	CB52
off The Plaza Shop Cen		
Brouster Hill, (E.Kil.) G74	136	CA51
Brouster Pl, (E.Kil.) G74	136	CA52
Brown Av, Clyde. G81	46	BA21
Brownhill Rd, G43	102	BK41
Brownlie St, G42	87	BR37
Brown Pl, (Camb.) G72	106	CC39
Brown Rd, (Cumb.) G67	22	DB11
Brownsburn Ind Est, Air. ML6	76	DD32
Brownsburn Rd, Air. ML6	96	DD33
Brownsdale Rd, (Ruther.) G73	88	BV38
Brownsfield Cres, (Inch.) Renf.	43	AR24
PA4		
Brownshill Av, Coat. ML5	94	CV33
Brownside Av, (Camb.) G72	106	CA40
Brownside Av, (Barr.) G78	99	AW40
Brownside Av, Pais. PA2	82	AS38
Brownside Cres, (Barr.) G78	99	AW40
Brownside Dr, G13	46	BB23
Brownside Dr, (Barr.) G78	99	AW40
Brownside Gro, (Barr.) G78	99	AW40
Brownside Ms, (Camb.) G72	106	CA40
Brownside Rd, (Camb.) G72	106	CA40
Brownside Rd, (Ruther.) G73	105	BZ40
Brownsland Ct, (Gart.) G69	55	CP23
Browns La, Pais. PA1	82	AU33
Brown St, G2	4	BQ30
Brown St, Coat. ML5	75	CW32
Brown St, Lark. ML9	144	DC57
Brown St, Moth. ML1	128	DB45
Brown St, Pais. PA1	62	AS32
Brown St, Renf. PA4	63	AX27
Bruce Av, John. PA5	79	AG37
Bruce Av, Moth. ML1	127	CZ46
Bruce Av, Pais. PA3	63	AW30
Bruce Ct, Air. ML6	77	DG29
Brucefield Pl, G34	72	CM29
Bruce Pl, (E.Kil.) G75	136	CB54
Bruce Rd, G41	87	BN33
Bruce Rd, Moth. ML1	112	DD43
Bruce Rd, Pais. PA3	63	AW31
Bruce Rd, Renf. PA4	63	AW28
Bruce's Ln, Lark. ML9	145	DE59
off Wallace Dr		
Bruce St, Bell. ML4	111	CX40
Bruce St, Clyde. G81	27	AX20
Bruce St, Coat. ML5	75	CX29
Bruce Ter, (Blan.) G72	109	CN44
Bruce Ter, (E.Kil.) G75	136	CB54
Brunel Way, (E.Kil.) G75	136	CB53
Brunstane Rd, G34	72	CJ28
Brunswick Ho, Clyde. G81	26	AT15
off Perth Cres		
Brunswick St, G1	5	BS30
Brunton St, G44	103	BQ40
Brunton Ter, G44	103	BP41
Bruntsfield Av, G53	100	BD42
Bruntsfield Gdns, G53	100	BD42
Bryan St, Ham. ML3	125	CR48
Bryce Gdns, Lark. ML9	144	DC57
Bryce Pl, (E.Kil.) G75	135	BZ55
Brydson Pl, (Linw.) Pais. PA3	60	AK31
Bryson Ct, Ham. ML3	140	CT54
Bryson St, Clyde. G81	10	BA14
Buccleuch Av, G52	64	BA29
Buccleuch Av, (Clark.) G76	118	BM46
Buccleuch Dr, (Bears.) G61	11	BG14
Buccleuch La, G3	4	BQ28
Buccleuch St, G3	4	BQ28
Buchanan Av, Bish. PA7	24	AK17
Buchanan Business Pk,	53	CH23
(Stepps) G33		
Buchanan Cres, (Bishop.) G64	51	BY22
Buchanan Cres, Ham. ML3	139	CR51
Buchanan Dr, (Bears.) G61	30	BJ17
Buchanan Dr, (Bishop.) G64	51	BY21
Buchanan Dr, (Lenz.) G66	35	CF18
Buchanan Dr, (Camb.) G72	106	CA39
Buchanan Dr, (Ruther.) G73	105	BX39
Buchanan Dr, (Newt. M.) G77	117	BG46
Buchanan Gdns, G32	91	CG35
Buchanan Gro, (Baill.) G69	72	CK32
Buchanan Pl, (Torr.) G64	15	BX12
Buchanan St, G1	4	BR30
Buchanan St, (Miln.) G62	12	BK11
Buchanan St, (Baill.) G69	92	CK33
Buchanan St, Air. ML6	76	DC30
off Graham St		
Buchanan St, Coat. ML5	74	CV31
Buchanan St, John. PA5	79	AG35
Buchandyke Rd, (E.Kil.) G74	122	CD50
Buchan Grn, (E.Kil.) G74	122	CD50
Buchan Rd, Moth. ML1	112	DC43
Buchan St, G5	67	BR32
off Norfolk St		
Buchan St, Ham. ML3	140	CS53
Buchan Ter, (Camb.) G72	106	CA42
Buchlyvie Gdns, (Bishop.) G64	50	BV21
Buchlyvie Path, G34	72	CL30
Buchlyvie Rd, Pais. PA1	64	BA31
Buchlyvie St, G34	72	CK30
Buckie, Ersk. PA8	25	AQ18
Buckie Wk, Bell. ML4	111	CW39
off Hattonrigg Rd		
Buckingham Ct, Ham. ML3	125	CN49
off Stirling Dr		
Buckingham Dr, G32	90	CD37
Buckingham Dr, (Ruther.) G73	89	BZ38
Buckingham St, G12	48	BM26
Buckingham Ter, G12	48	BM26
Bucklaw Gdns, G52	85	BE33
Bucklaw Pl, G52	85	BE33
Bucklaw Ter, G52	85	BE33
Buckley St, G22	50	BT23
Bucksburn Rd, G21	51	BY25
Buckthorne Pl, G53	100	BD42
Buddon St, G40	89	BY33
Budhill Av, G32	70	CD32
Budshaw Av, (Chap.) Air. ML6	97	DE35
Bulldale Ct, G14	46	BA24
Bulldale Rd, G14	46	BA24
Bulldale St, G14	46	BA23
Buller Cres, (Blan.) G72	108	CL43
Bullionslaw Dr, (Ruther.) G73	105	BZ39
Bulloch Av, (Giff.) G46	102	BM43
Bull Rd, (Clark.) G76	119	BP47
Bullwood Av, G53	84	BB36
Bullwood Ct, G53	84	BB37
Bullwood Dr, G53	84	BB36
Bullwood Gdns, G53	84	BB36
Bullwood Pl, G53	84	BB36
Bunbury Ter, (E.Kil.) G75	135	BY53
off Kimberley Gdns		
Bunessan St, G52	65	BH32
Bunhouse Rd, G3	66	BL28
Burghead Dr, G51	65	BG30
Burghead Pl, G51	65	BG29
Burgher St, G31	69	BY32
Burgh Hall La, G11	66	BK27
Burgh Hall St, G11	66	BK27
Burgh La, G12	48	BM26
Burleigh Pl, Coat. ML5	95	CY34
Burleigh Rd, (Both.) G71	109	CR42
Burleigh St, G51	66	BJ29
Burleigh St, Coat. ML5	95	CX34
Burley Pl, (E.Kil.) G74	134	BV51
Burlington Av, G12	48	BK23
Burmola St, G22	49	BR25
Burnacre Gdns, (Udd.) G71	93	CN38
Burnawn Gdns, G33	51	BZ22
off Brookfield Dr		
Burnawn Gro, G33	51	BZ22
off Brookfield Av		
Burnawn Pl, G33	51	BZ22
off Brookfield Av		
Burnbank Cen, Ham. ML3	125	CQ48
Burnbank Dr, (Barr.) G78	99	AY44
Burnbank Gdns, G20	67	BP27
Burnbank Gdns, Ham. ML3	125	CQ48
off George St		
Burnbank La, G20	67	BP27
off Napiershall St		
Burnbank Pl, G4	5	BU30
Burnbank Pl, G20	67	BQ27
off Burnbank Ter		
Burnbank Quad, Air. ML6	76	DB29
Burnbank Rd, Ham. ML3	125	CQ48
Burnbank St, Air. ML6	76	DB29
Burnbank St, Coat. ML5	75	CX29
Burnbank Ter, G20	67	BP27
Burnbank Ter, (Kilsyth) G65	7	CU4
Burnblea Gdns, Ham. ML3	140	CU51
Burnblea St, Ham. ML3	140	CT51
Burnbrae, (Kilsyth) G65	19	CP10
Burnbrae, Clyde. G81	27	AW15
Burnbrae Av, (Bears.) G61	12	BJ14
Burnbrae Av, (Mood.) G69	37	CQ19
Burnbrae Av, (Linw.) Pais.	60	AL32
PA3 off Bridge St		
Burnbrae Dr, (Ruther.) G73	105	BZ40
off East Kilbride Rd		
Burnbrae Dr, (Linw.) Pais. PA3	80	AM33
Burnbrae Gdns, G53	101	BF39
Burnbrae Pl, (E.Kil.) G74	135	BY51
Burnbrae Rd, (Kirk.) G66	18	CK14
Burnbrae Rd, (Lenz.) G66	35	CG19

Burnbrae Rd, (Chry.) G69	36	CK19
Burnbrae Rd, (Blan.) G72	124	CL46
Burnbrae Rd, (Linw.) Pais. PA3	80	AK33
Burnbrae St, G21	51	BW25
Burnbrae St, Lark. ML9	144	DB58
Burncleuch Av, (Camb.) G72	106	CC41
Burn Cres, (Chap.) Air. ML6	97	DF35
Burn Cres, Moth. ML1	112	DC41
Burncrooks Av, (Bears.) G61	11	BE14
Burncrooks Av, (E.Kil.) G74	135	BY51
Burncrooks Ct, Clyde. G81	26	AV15
Burndyke Ct, G51	66	BK30
Burndyke Sq, G51	66	BL30
Burndyke St, G51	66	BK30
Burnet Rose Ct, (E.Kil.) G74	121	BY49
Burnet Rose Gdns, (E.Kil.) G74	121	BY49
Burnet Rose Pl, (E.Kil.) G74	121	BY49
Burnett Rd, G33	71	CG30
Burnfield Av, (Thornlie.) G46	102	BK41
Burnfield Cotts, (Thornlie.) G46	102	BK41
Burnfield Dr, G43	102	BK41
Burnfield Gdns, (Giff.) G46	102	BL41
Burnfield Rd, G43	102	BJ40
Burnfield Rd, (Thornlie.) G46	102	BK41
Burnfoot Cres, (Ruther.) G73	105	BZ40
Burnfoot Cres, Pais. PA2	82	AS38
Burnfoot Dr, G52	64	BD32
Burnfoot Rd, Air. ML6	76	DA29
Burngreen, (Kilsyth) G65	7	CT5
Burngreen Pk, (Kilsyth) G65	7	CU5
Burnham Rd, G14	46	BC25
Burnham Ter, G14	46	BC25
off Burnham Rd		
Burnhaven, Ersk. PA8	25	AQ19
Burnhead Rd, G43	103	BN40
Burnhead Rd, (Cumb.) G68	21	CY11
Burnhead Rd, Air. ML6	77	DF28
Burnhead Rd, Lark. ML9	145	DE58
Burnhead St, (Udd.) G71	93	CR38
Burnhill Quad, (Ruther.) G73	88	BV37
Burnhill St, (Ruther.) G73	88	BV37
Burnhouse Brae, (Newt. M.) G77	118	BJ50
Burnhouse Cres, Ham. ML3	139	CR52
Burnhouse Rd, Ham. ML3	139	CR52
Burnhouse St, G20	48	BM23
Burniebrae, Air. ML6	76	DA29
Burniebrae Rd, (Chap.) Air. ML6	97	DG34
Burn La, Moth. ML1	112	DC41
off Quarry St		
Burnlip Rd, Air. ML6	57	CW30
Burnmouth Ct, G33	71	CH31
off Pendeen Rd		
Burnmouth Pl, (Bears.) G61	30	BJ16
Burnmouth Rd, G33	71	CH31
Burnock Pl, (E.Kil.) G75	134	BU54
Burnpark Av, (Udd.) G71	92	CM38
Burn Pl, (Camb.) G72	90	CA38
off Burn Ter		
Burns Av, Bish. PA7	24	AK18
Burns Ct, (Kirk.) G66	18	CJ12
Burns Cres, Air. ML6	76	DD31
Burns Dr, (Kirk.) G66	18	CJ11
Burns Dr, John. PA5	79	AG37
Burns Gdns, (Blan.) G72	108	CL44
Burns Gro, (Thornlie.) G46	102	BJ43
Burnside, (Bears.) G61	11	BE14
Burnside Av, (Kirk.) G66	16	CD14
Burnside Av, (Barr.) G78	99	AX41
Burnside Av, (Calder.) Air. ML6	96	DD35
Burnside Av, Bell. ML4	111	CY41
Burnside Ct, (Bears.) G61	11	BE14
off Burnside		
Burnside Ct, (Ruther.) G73	105	BY40
Burnside Ct, Clyde. G81	26	AU17
Burnside Ct, Coat. ML5	74	CV32
off Kirk St		
Burnside Ct, Moth. ML1	128	DD49
Burnside Cres, (Blan.) G72	125	CP47
Burnside Gdns, (Clark.) G76	118	BM46
Burnside Gdns, (Kilb.) John. PA10	78	AD35
Burnside Gate, (Ruther.) G73	105	BY40
off Burnside Rd		
Burnside Gro, John. PA5	79	AG35
Burnside Ind Est, (Kilsyth) G65	7	CS5
Burnside La, Ham. ML3	126	CU50
Burnside Pl, Lark. ML9	144	DD58
Burnside Pl, Pais. PA3	61	AQ30
Burnside Quad, Moth. ML1	112	DC40
off Graham St		
Burnside Rd, (Giff.) G46	118	BK47
Burnside Rd, (Ruther.) G73	105	BY40
Burnside Rd, Coat. ML5	75	CY28
Burnside Rd, (Elder.) John. PA5	80	AL36
Burnside Rd, Moth. ML1	113	DF41
Burnside St, Moth. ML1	128	DC49
Burn Side Vw, Coat. ML5	74	CU32
Burnside Wk, (Bears.) G61	11	BE14
off Burnside		
Burnside Wk, Coat. ML5	74	CU32
Burns La, Air. ML6	97	DF34
off Stirling Rd		
Burns Ln, Lark. ML9	144	DD57
off Duncan Graham St		
Burns Pk, (E.Kil.) G74	136	CC51
Burns Path, Bell. ML4	95	CX38
off Bell St		
Burns Rd, (Kirk.) G66	18	CJ12
Burns Rd, (Cumb.) G67	22	DD10
Burns Rd, Air. ML6	97	DF34
Burns St, G4	67	BR27
Burns St, Clyde. G81	26	AU18
Burns St, Ham. ML3	140	CT51
Burns Way, Moth. ML1	113	DE41
off Glenburn Av		
Burntbroom Dr, (Baill.) G69	91	CH34
Burntbroom Gdns, (Baill.) G69	91	CH34
Burntbroom St, G33	71	CF29
Burn Ter, (Camb.) G72	90	CA38
Burntshields Rd, (Kilb.) John. PA10	78	AA35
Burn Vw, (Cumb.) G67	23	DE10
Burra Gdns, (Bishop.) G64	33	BZ18
Burrells La, G4	5	BU30
Burrelton Rd, G43	103	BP39
Burton La, G42	87	BQ36
off Langside Rd		
Busby Rd, (Carm.) G76	120	BS46
Busby Rd, (Clark.) G76	119	BP46
Busby Rd, Bell. ML4	110	CV42
Bushes Av, Pais. PA2	82	AT36
Busheyhill St, (Camb.) G72	106	CC40
Bute, (E.Kil.) G74	137	CE52
Bute Av, Moth. ML1	127	CY46
Bute Av, Renf. PA4	63	AZ28
Bute Cres, (Old Kil.) G60	26	AS16
Bute Cres, (Bears.) G61	29	BH19
Bute Cres, Pais. PA2	82	AT38
Bute Dr, (Old Kil.) G60	26	AS15
Bute Dr, John. PA5	79	AF36
Bute Gdns, G12	66	BM27
Bute Gdns, G44	103	BP41
Bute Gdns, (Old Kil.) G60	26	AS15
Bute La, G12	66	BM27
off Great George St		
Bute Pl, (Old Kil.) G60	26	AT15
Bute Rd, (Kirk.) G66	18	CK13
Bute Rd, (Abbots.) Pais. PA3	62	AT28
Bute St, Coat. ML5	95	CX33
Bute St, Ham. ML3	125	CR47
Bute Ter, (Udd.) G71	93	CR38
Bute Ter, (Ruther.) G73	105	BW40
Butler Wynd, Bell. ML4	110	CV40
off Cochrane St		
Butterbiggins Rd, G42	87	BQ34
Butterburn Pk, Ham. ML3	140	CT51
Butterfield Pl, G41	87	BQ34
off Pollokshaws Rd		
Buttermere, (E.Kil.) G75	134	BV56
Byars Rd, (Kirk.) G66	16	CD13
Byrebush Rd, G53	85	BE36
Byres Av, Pais. PA3	63	AW31
Byres Cres, Pais. PA3	63	AW31
Byresknowe La, Moth. ML1	112	DD44
Byres Rd, G11	66	BL27
Byres Rd, G12	66	BL27
Byres Rd, (Elder.) John. PA5	80	AM35
Byres Rd, Moth. ML1	113	DG41
Byrestone Av, (Newt. M.) G77	118	BL49
Byron Ct, (Both.) G71	109	CR43
Byron St, G11	65	BG27
Byron St, Clyde. G81	27	AW17
Byshot St, G22	50	BT25

C

Cable Dep Rd, Clyde. G81	26	AV19
Cadder Ct, (Bishop.) G64	33	BX16
Cadder Gro, G20	49	BN22
off Cadder Rd		
Cadder Pl, G20	49	BN22
Cadder Rd, G20	49	BN22
Cadder Rd, G23	49	BN22
Cadder Rd, (Bishop.) G64	33	BX16
Cadder Way, (Bishop.) G64	33	BX16
Cadell Gdns, (E.Kil.) G74	123	CF48
Cadoc St, (Camb.) G72	106	CD40
Cadogan St, G2	4	BQ30
Cadsaw Roundabout, Ham. ML3	126	CV49
Cadzow Av, (Giff.) G46	118	BK45
Cadzow Cres, Coat. ML5	94	CU33
Cadzow Dr, (Camb.) G72	106	CB40
Cadzow Dr, Bell. ML4	111	CZ41
Cadzow Grn, (E.Kil.) G74	135	BZ51
Cadzow Ind Est, Ham. ML3	140	CT53
Cadzow La, Ham. ML3	126	CU49
off Cadzow St		
Cadzow St, G2	4	BQ30
Cadzow St, Ham. ML3	126	CU49
Cadzow St, Lark. ML9	144	DC57
Cadzow St, Moth. ML1	127	CZ47
Caerlaverock Pl, (Blan.) G72	124	CL47
off Broompark Rd		
Caird Dr, G11	66	BK27
Caird Gdns, Ham. ML3	126	CT48
off Caird St		
Caird Pk, Ham. ML3	126	CT48
Caird St, Ham. ML3	126	CS48
Caird Ter, (Bears.) G61	11	BF14
off Grampian Way		
Cairn Av, Renf. PA4	64	BA28
Cairnban St, G51	65	BF31
Cairnbrook Rd, G34	72	CL29
Cairn Ct, (E.Kil.) G74	122	CA49

Cairn Ct, Moth. ML1	128	DB48
Cairncraig St, G31	89	BY33
Cairndow Av, G44	103	BP41
Cairndow Av La, G44	103	BP41
Cairndow Ct, G44	103	BP41
Cairn Dr, (Linw.) Pais. PA3	60	AK31
Cairndyke Cres, Air. ML6	76	DC31
Cairngorm Cres, (Bears.) G61	28	BD15
Cairngorm Cres, (Barr.) G78	99	AY44
Cairngorm Cres, Pais. PA2	82	AU36
Cairngorm Cres, Wis. ML2	129	DH50
Cairngorm Gdns, (Cumb.) G68	21	CW12
Cairngorm Rd, G43	102	BL40
Cairnhill Av, Air. ML6	76	DB32
Cairnhill Circ, G52	84	BB34
Cairnhill Cres, Coat. ML5	95	CZ34
Cairnhill Dr, G52	84	BB34
Cairnhill Pl, G52	84	BB34
Cairnhill Rd, (Bears.) G61	29	BH20
Cairnhill Rd, Air. ML6	76	DB32
Cairnhill Trd Est, Air. ML6	76	DC31
Cairnhope Av, Air. ML6	76	DB32
Cairnlea Dr, G51	66	BK31
Cairnlea Gdns, Bell. ML4	111	CX42
Cairnlea Rd, (Miln.) G62	11	BG12
off Castle Mains Rd		
Cairnmuir Rd, (Camb.) G72	122	CA46
Cairnmuir Rd, (E.Kil.) G74	121	BY48
Cairnoch Hill, (Cumb.) G68	21	CY10
off Dunbrach Rd		
Cairn Pl, (E.Kil.) G74	122	CA49
Cairnryan, (E.Kil.) G74	121	BZ50
Cairns Av, (Camb.) G72	106	CD40
Cairns Dr, (Miln.) G62	12	BJ11
Cairnsmore Dr, (Bears.) G61	10	BD13
Cairnsmore Rd, G15	28	BA19
Cairns Rd, (Camb.) G72	106	CD41
Cairns St, Moth. ML1	128	DA47
Cairn St, G21	50	BV23
Cairnswell Av, (Camb.) G72	107	CE41
Cairnswell Pl, (Camb.) G72	107	CE41
Cairntoul Ct, (Cumb.) G68	21	CX11
Cairntoul Dr, G14	46	BC23
Cairntoul Pl, G14	46	BC23
Cairnview, (Kirk.) G66	18	CK14
Cairn Vw, Air. ML6	76	DB31
Cairnwood Dr, Air. ML6	76	DB32
Caithness Rd, (E.Kil.) G74	123	CF49
Caithness St, G20	49	BP25
Caithness St, (Blan.) G72	124	CL47
Cala Sona Ct, Wis. ML2	143	DG52
Calcots Path, G34	72	CL28
off Auchingill Rd		
Calcots Pl, G34	72	CL28
Caldarvan St, G22	49	BR26
Caldeen Rd, Coat. ML5	75	CX32
Calder Av, (Barr.) G78	99	AY44
Calder Av, Coat. ML5	95	CX33
Calderbank Ter, Moth. ML1	128	DB45
Calderbank Vw, (Baill.) G69	92	CL34
Calderbraes Av, (Udd.) G71	93	CN37
Calder Ct, Coat. ML5	95	CX33
off Whifflet St		
Caldercuilt Rd, G20	48	BL21
Caldercuilt Rd, G23	30	BL20
Calder Dr, (Camb.) G72	106	CC40
Calder Dr, Bell. ML4	111	CY41
Calder Gate, (Bishop.) G64	32	BV17
Calderglen Av, (Blan.) G72	108	CL42
Calderglen Rd, (E.Kil.) G74	137	CF51
Calder Gro, Moth. ML1	128	DA45
Calderigg Pl, Air. ML6	77	DG30
Calderpark Av, (Udd.) G71	92	CK35
Calderpark Cres, (Udd.) G71	92	CK35
Calder Pl, (Baill.) G69	92	CK33
Calder Rd, (Udd.) G71	108	CK40
Calder Rd, Bell. ML4	111	CY42
Calder Rd, Pais. PA3	61	AQ32
Calderside Rd, (Blan.) G72	123	CH49
Calderside Rd, (E.Kil.) G74	137	CG52
Calder St, G42	87	BR35
Calder St, (Blan.) G72	124	CM45
Calder St, (Calder.) Air. ML6	97	DE35
off Main St		
Calder St, Coat. ML5	95	CX33
Calder Twr, (E.Kil.) G74	136	CD54
Caldervale St, Air. ML6	97	DG33
Calder Vw, Ham. ML3	139	CQ53
Calderview, Moth. ML1	128	DB46
off Mill Rd		
Calderview Av, Coat. ML5	95	CZ34
Calderwood Av, (Baill.) G69	92	CJ34
Calderwood Dr, (Baill.) G69	92	CJ34
Calderwood Dr, (Blan.) G72	124	CM47
Calderwood Gdns, (Baill.) G69	92	CJ34
Calderwood Gdns, (E.Kil.) G74	123	CG49
Calderwood Rd, G43	102	BM39
Calderwood Rd, (Ruther.) G73	89	BY38
Calderwood Rd, (E.Kil.) G74	136	CD51
Calderwood Sq, (E.Kil.) G74	122	CD50
Caldwell Av, G13	46	BC23
Caldwell Gro, Bell. ML4	95	CW37
Caldwell Quad, Moth. ML1	127	CY48
Caledonia Av, G5	88	BS34
Caledonia Av, (Ruther.) G73	89	BX37
Caledonia Ct, Pais. PA3	62	AT31
off Mossvale St		
Caledonia Dr, (Baill.) G69	92	CK34
Caledonia Dr, Moth. ML1	113	DG41
Caledonian Av, Bell. ML4	110	CV41
Caledonian Ct, (E.Kil.) G74	136	CA53
off The Plaza Shop Cen		
Caledonian Cres, G12	67	BN27
off Great Western Rd		
Caledonian Pl, (Camb.) G72	107	CG40
Caledonian Rd, Lark. ML9	144	DC58
Caledonia Rd, G5	87	BR33
Caledonia Rd, (Baill.) G69	92	CJ34
Caledonia St, G5	88	BS34
Caledonia St, Clyde. G81	26	AV18
Caledonia St, Pais. PA3	62	AT31
Caledonia Wk, Ham. ML3	140	CU52
off Chatelherault Cres		
Caledonia Way, (Abbots.) Pais. PA3	62	AT28
Caledonia Way E, (Abbots.) Pais. PA3	62	AU28
Caledonia Way W, (Abbots.) Pais. PA3	62	AT28
Caledon La, G12	48	BL26
Caledon St, G12	48	BL26
Caley Brae, (Udd.) G71	109	CP39
Calfhill Rd, G53	84	BD34
Calfmuir Rd, (Kirk.) G66	36	CJ16
Calfmuir Rd, (Chry.) G69	36	CJ16
Calgary Pk, (E.Kil.) G75	135	BZ53
Calgary Pl, (E.Kil.) G75	135	BZ53
off Calgary Pk		
Calgary St, G4	5	BS28
Callaghan Wynd, (Blan.) G72	108	CL44
Callander Ct, (Cumb.) G68	22	DB9
off Callander Rd		
Callander Rd, (Cumb.) G68	22	DB9
Callander Rd, (Chap.) Air. ML6	97	DF36
Callander St, G20	49	BQ26
Callieburn Rd, (Bishop.) G64	33	BW20
Callon St, Air. ML6	76	DC30
Cally Av, G15	28	BC18
Calside, Pais. PA2	82	AU34
Calside Av, Pais. PA2	82	AT34
Calside Ct, Pais. PA2	82	AU35
Calton Entry, G40	5	BU31
off Gallowgate		
Calvay Cres, G33	71	CF30
Calvay Pl, G33	71	CG30
Calvay Rd, G33	71	CF30
Cambourne Rd, (Chry.) G69	37	CP18
Cambridge Av, Clyde. G81	27	AX18
Cambridge Rd, Renf. PA4	63	AY27
Cambridge St, G2	4	BR29
Cambridge St, G3	4	BR29
Camburn St, G32	70	CB31
Cambusdoon Rd, G33	71	CE27
Cambus Kenneth Gdns, G32	71	CF32
Cambuskenneth Pl, G33	71	CE27
Cambuslang Ind Est, G32	90	CC38
Cambuslang Rd, G32	90	CA37
Cambuslang Rd, (Camb.) G72	89	BZ38
Cambuslang Rd, (Ruther.) G73	89	BX36
Cambusmore Pl, G33	71	CE27
Cambus Pl, G33	71	CE27
Camden Ter, G5	88	BS33
Camellia Dr, Wis. ML2	143	DG52
Camelon Cres, (Blan.) G72	124	CM46
Camelon St, G32	70	CB31
Cameron Av, Bish. PA7	24	AK17
Cameron Cotts, Clyde. G81	27	AY15
off Glasgow Rd		
Cameron Ct, (Ruther.) G73	89	BW38
Cameron Ct, Air. ML6	77	DG29
off Station Rd		
Cameron Ct, Clyde. G81	45	AY21
off Cameron St		
Cameron Cres, (Carm.) G76	120	BU46
Cameron Cres, Ham. ML3	125	CR50
Cameron Dr, (Bears.) G61	30	BJ18
Cameron Dr, (Udd.) G71	93	CQ37
Cameron Dr, (Newt. M.) G77	117	BG47
Cameronian Pl, Bell. ML4	110	CV42
Cameronian Roundabout, Ham. ML3	126	CV49
Cameronian Way, Lark. ML9	145	DE60
off Elmbank Dr		
Cameron Path, Lark. ML9	145	DE60
off Stuart Dr		
Cameron Rd, (Green.) Air. ML6	41	DE19
Cameron Sq, Clyde. G81	27	AY15
Cameron St, G52	64	BA30
Cameron St, Clyde. G81	45	AY21
Cameron St, Coat. ML5	75	CX29
Cameron St, Moth. ML1	128	DA47
Cameron Way, (Blan.) G72	124	CM45
Camlachie St, G31	69	BX32
Campbell Av, (Miln.) G62	12	BJ12
Campbell Av, Bish. PA7	24	AK17
Campbell Cres, (Both.) G71	109	CR41
Campbell Cres, (Newt. M.) G77	117	BG47
Campbell Dr, (Bears.) G61	29	BF16
Campbell Dr, (Barr.) G78	99	AY43
Campbell La, Ham. ML3	126	CU49
off Campbell St		
Campbell Pl, (Torr.) G64	15	BX12
Campbell Pl, (E.Kil.) G75	136	CA54
Campbell St, G20	48	BM22
Campbell St, Bell. ML4	111	CW40
Campbell St, Ham. ML3	126	CU50
Campbell St, John. PA5	79	AH35

Campbell St, Renf. PA4	45	AZ25
Camphill, Pais. PA1	82	AT34
Camphill Av, G41	87	BN38
Camphill Av, (Kirk.) G66	17	CE13
Camphill Ct, Pais. PA2	82	AT34
Camphill Gdns, Bish. PA7	24	AL18
Campion Rd, Moth. ML1	127	CZ45
Camp Rd, (Baill.) G69	72	CK32
Camp Rd, (Ruther.) G73	88	BV35
Camp Rd, Moth. ML1	128	DA49
Camps Cres, Renf. PA4	64	BA27
Campsie Av, (Barr.) G78	99	AY44
Campsie Ct, (Kirk.) G66	35	CE15
off Westergreens Av		
Campsie Ct, Lark. ML9	142	DB56
Campsie Cres, Air. ML6	76	DB29
Campsie Dr, (Bears.) G61	11	BF14
Campsie Dr, (Miln.) G62	12	BK11
Campsie Dr, Pais. PA2	82	AT37
Campsie Dr, (Abbots.) Pais. PA3	62	AU28
Campsie Dr, Renf. PA4	63	AW29
Campsie Gdns, (Clark.) G76	118	BL45
Campsie Pl, (Chry.) G69	54	CL21
Campsie Rd, (Torr.) G64	15	BZ11
Campsie Rd, (Kirk.) G66	16	CD12
Campsie Rd, Wis. ML2	129	DG49
Campsie St, G21	50	BV24
Campsie Vw, (Stepps) G33	53	CF25
Campsie Vw, (Kirk.) G66	16	CC13
Campsie Vw, (Cumb.) G67	22	DD10
Campsie Vw, (Baill.) G69	73	CP32
Campsie Vw, (Chry.) G69	54	CL21
Campsie Vw, (Udd.) G71	93	CQ37
Campsie Vw, (Camb.) G72	107	CG42
Campsie Vw, Ham. ML3	139	CP51
Campston Pl, G33	70	CD28
Camp St, Moth. ML1	128	DA48
Camstradden Dr E, (Bears.) G61	29	BE17
Camstradden Dr W, (Bears.) G61	29	BE17
Camus Pl, G15	28	BB17
Canal Av, John. PA5	79	AH35
Canal Bk La, G22	49	BQ21
Canal Gdns, (Elder.) John. PA5 off Canal St	80	AM34
Canal La, (Kirk.) G66	17	CF12
Canal La, Renf. PA4	45	AZ25
Canal Rd, John. PA5	80	AJ35
Canal St, G4	5	BS28
Canal St, (Kirk.) G66	17	CF12
Canal St, Clyde. G81	27	AX20
Canal St, John. PA5	80	AJ34
Canal St, (Elder.) John. PA5	80	AM34
Canal St, Pais. PA1	82	AT33
Canal St, Renf. PA4	45	AZ25
Canal Ter, Pais. PA1	82	AT33
Canberra Av, Clyde. G81	26	AT17
Canberra Ct, (Giff.) G46	103	BN42
Canberra Dr, (E.Kil.) G75	135	BY53
Cander Rigg, (Bishop.) G64	33	BW17
Cander St, Lark. ML9	144	DD61
Candleriggs, G1	5	BT31
Candren Rd, Pais. PA3	81	AQ33
Candren Rd, (Linw.) Pais. PA3	60	AM32
Candren Way, Pais. PA3	61	AQ32
off Ferguslie Pk Av		
Canmore Pl, G31	89	BZ33
Canmore St, G31	89	BZ33
Cannich Dr, Pais. PA2	83	AX36
Canniesburn Rd, (Bears.) G61	29	BF18

Canniesburn Sq, (Bears.) G61	29	BH19
off Switchback Rd		
Canniesburn Toll, (Bears.) G61	29	BH19
off Drymen Rd		
Canonbie Av, (E.Kil.) G74	122	CB49
Canonbie St, G34	72	CM28
Canon Ct, Moth. ML1	113	DF43
Canongate, (E.Kil.) G74	123	CF49
off Ivanhoe		
Canterbury, (E.Kil.) G75	135	BX54
Cantieslaw Dr, (E.Kil.) G74	122	CC50
Canting Way, G51	66	BL30
Canyon Rd, (Netherton Ind. Est.) Wis. ML2	143	DF51
Capel Av, (Newt. M.) G77	117	BH47
Capel Gro, (E.Kil.) G74	122	CD50
Capelrig Dr, (E.Kil.) G74	122	CD50
Capelrig Dr, (Newt. M.) G77	117	BG45
Capelrig La, (Newt. M.) G77	117	BF47
off Capelrig Rd		
Capelrig Rd, (Newt. M.) G77	117	BG47
Capelrig St, (Thornlie.) G46	101	BH41
Caplaw Pl, Wis. ML2	143	DH53
Caplaw Rd, Pais. PA2	98	AS39
Caplethill Rd, (Barr.) G78	82	AV38
Caplethill Rd, Pais. PA2	82	AV38
Caprington Pl, G33	70	CC28
Caprington St, G33	70	CC28
Cara Dr, G51	65	BG29
off St. Kenneth Dr		
Caravelle Way, Renf. PA4	63	AZ20
off Friendship Way		
Carbarns, Wis. ML2	143	DF52
Carbarns E, Wis. ML2	143	DF52
Carbarns Rd, Wis. ML2	143	DF52
Carbarns W, Wis. ML2	143	DF52
Carberry Rd, G41	86	BM35
Carbeth Rd, (Miln.) G62	11	BH12
Carbeth St, G22	49	BR25
Carbisdale St, G22	50	BU24
Carbost St, G23	30	BM20
Carbrain Ind Est, (Cumb.) G67	22	DD12
Carbrook St, G21	69	BW28
Carbrook St, Pais. PA1	82	AS33
Cardarrach St, G21	51	BW24
Cardean Rd, Bell. ML4	112	DA39
Cardell Av, Pais. PA2	81	AQ34
Cardell Cres, (Chap.) Air. ML6	97	DF35
Cardell Dr, Pais. PA2	81	AQ34
Cardell Rd, Pais. PA2	81	AQ34
Cardonald Dr, G52	84	BC33
Cardonald Gdns, G52	84	BC33
Cardonald Pl Rd, G52	84	BD33
Cardowan Dr, (Stepps) G33	53	CG24
Cardowan Dr, (Cumb.) G68	20	CU12
Cardowan Pk, (Udd.) G71	93	CR36
Cardowan Rd, G32	70	CB31
Cardowan Rd, (Stepps) G33	53	CG23
Cardow Rd, G21	51	BY25
Cardrona St, G33	52	CD26
Cardross Ct, G31	68	BV30
Cardross St, G31	68	BV30
Cardwell St, G41	87	BQ33
off Eglinton St		
Cardyke St, G21	51	BW25
Careston Pl, (Bishop.) G64	33	BZ20
Carfin Ind Est, Moth. ML1	112	DD43
Carfin Mill Rd, Moth. ML1	113	DE44
Carfin Rd, Moth. ML1	113	DF42
Carfin Rd, Wis. ML2	129	DE49
Carfin St, G42	87	BR35
Carfin St, Coat. ML5	95	CX33
Carfin St, Moth. ML1	112	DC42

Carfrae St, G3	66	BL29
Cargill Sq, (Bishop.) G64	51	BY21
Carham Cres, G52	65	BE32
Carham Dr, G52	65	BE32
Caribou Grn, (E.Kil.) G75	135	BX53
off Winnipeg Dr		
Carillon Rd, G51	66	BL32
Carisbrooke Cres, (Bishop.) G64	33	BX17
Carlaverock Rd, G43	102	BM39
Carleith Av, Clyde. G81	26	AV15
Carleith Quad, G51	65	BF30
Carleith Ter, Clyde. G81	26	AV15
Carleston St, G21	50	BV25
Carleton Ct, (Giff.) G46	102	BL41
Carleton Dr, (Giff.) G46	102	BL41
Carleton Gate, (Giff.) G46	102	BL41
Carlibar Av, G13	46	BB23
Carlibar Dr, (Barr.) G78	99	AY42
Carlibar Gdns, (Barr.) G78	99	AY42
Carlibar Rd, (Barr.) G78	99	AY42
Carlile Pl, Pais. PA3	62	AU31
Carlisle La, Air. ML6	77	DE30
Carlisle Rd, Air. ML6	77	DE32
Carlisle Rd, Ham. ML3	141	CW51
Carlisle Rd, Lark. ML9	141	CZ53
Carlisle Rd, (Birk.) Lark. ML9	144	DD60
Carlisle St, G21	50	BT25
Carlisle Ter, Pais. PA3	62	AU31
Carlock Wk, G32	71	CE31
off Croftspar Pl		
Carloway Ct, G33	70	CD29
Carlowrie Av, (Blan.) G72	108	CL43
Carlton Ct, G5	4	BR31
Carlton Ct, Ham. ML3	140	CU51
off Johnstone Rd		
Carlton Pl, G5	4	BR31
Carlyle Av, G52	64	BB29
Carlyle Dr, (E.Kil.) G74	136	CC51
Carlyle St, Pais. PA3	62	AU32
Carlyle Ter, (Ruther.) G73	89	BX36
Carlyle Ter, (E.Kil.) G74	136	CD51
off Calderwood Rd		
Carmaben Rd, G33	71	CG29
Carment Dr, G41	86	BM37
Carment La, G41	86	BM37
Carmichael Path, (Glenb.) Coat. ML5 off The Oval	56	CS23
Carmichael Pl, G42	87	BP38
Carmichael St, G51	66	BK31
Carmunnock Bypass, G45	120	BS45
Carmunnock Bypass, G76	120	BS45
Carmunnock La, G44	103	BR40
off Madison Av		
Carmunnock Rd, G44	87	BR38
Carmunnock Rd, G45	104	BS40
Carmunnock Rd, (Busby) G76	104	BS44
Carmunnock Rd, (Kittochside) G76	121	BW48
Carmyle Av, G32	90	CD34
Carmyle Gdns, Coat. ML5	94	CU34
Carna Dr, G44	104	BS40
Carnarvon St, G3	4	BP28
Carnbooth Ct, G45	104	BV43
Carnbroe Rd, Bell. ML4	95	CX37
Carnbroe Rd, Coat. ML5	95	CZ33
Carneddans Rd, (Miln.) G62	11	BE9
Carnegie Hill, (E.Kil.) G75	135	BZ53
off Carnegie Pl		
Carnegie Pl, (E.Kil.) G75	135	BZ53
Carnegie Rd, G52	64	BC30
Carnoch St, G23	30	BM20
off Torrin Rd		

Carnock Cres, (Barr.) G78 99 AX43
Carnock Gdns, (Miln.) G62 11 BG11
Carnock Rd, G53 85 BE37
Carnoustie Ct, (Both.) G71 109 CP43
Carnoustie Cres, (Bishop.) G64 33 BY20
Carnoustie Cres, (E.Kil.) G75 135 BW55
Carnoustie Pl, G5 67 BP32
Carnoustie Pl, Bell. ML4 95 CW38
Carnoustie St, G5 67 BP32
Carnoustie Way, (Cumb.) G68 9 DB7
Carntyne Gdns, G32 70 CA30
off Abbeyhill St
Carntynehall Rd, G32 70 CB30
Carntyne Ind Est, G32 70 CA31
Carntyne Path, G32 69 BZ30
Carntyne Pl, G32 69 BZ30
Carntyne Rd, G31 69 BY31
Carntyne Rd, G32 69 BZ30
Carnwadric Rd, (Thornlie.) G46 101 BG41
Carnwath Av, G43 103 BP39
Caroline St, G31 70 CA32
Carolside Av, (Clark.) G76 119 BN46
Carolside Dr, G15 28 BD18
Carolside Gdns, (Clark.) G76 119 BN46
Carradale Cres, (Cumb.) G68 20 CV13
Carradale Gdns, (Bishop.) G64 33 BY20
off Thrums Av
Carradale Pl, (Linw.) Pais. PA3 60 AJ31
Carradale St, Coat. ML5 74 CV30
off Bowling St
Carrbridge Dr, G20 48 BM23
Carresbrook Av, (Kirk.) G66 36 CK15
Carriagehill Av, Pais. PA2 82 AU35
Carriagehill Dr, Pais. PA2 82 AU36
Carrickarden Rd, (Bears.) G61 29 BH18
Carrick Ct, (Kirk.) G66 18 CJ11
Carrick Cres, (Giff.) G46 102 BL44
Carrick Dr, G32 91 CG34
Carrick Dr, (Ruther.) G73 105 BW40
Carrick Dr, Coat. ML5 74 CT31
Carrick Gdns, (Blan.) G72 124 CM47
Carrick Gdns, Bell. ML4 95 CW37
off Rosegreen Cres
Carrick Gdns, Ham. ML3 139 CN51
Carrick Gro, G32 91 CG33
Carrick Mans, G32 91 CG34
off Carrick Dr
Carrick Pl, Bell. ML4 95 CX37
Carrick Pl, Coat. ML5 74 CT30
Carrick Pl, Lark. ML9 144 DD57
Carrick Rd, (Bishop.) G64 33 BY20
Carrick Rd, (Cumb.) G67 22 DC9
Carrick Rd, (Ruther.) G73 105 BW40
Carrick Rd, (E.Kil.) G74 122 CA50
Carrick Rd, Bish. PA7 24 AL19
Carrickstone Rd, (Cumb.) G68 22 DA9
Carrickstone Roundabout,
(Cumb.) G68 9 DA8
Carrickstone Vw, (Cumb.) G68 9 DB8
Carrick St, G2 4 BQ31
Carrick St, Lark. ML9 145 DE59
Carrick Vw, (Glenb.) Coat. ML5 56 CU23
Carrick Way, (Both.) G71 109 CQ42
Carriden Pl, G33 71 CG30
Carrington St, G4 67 BP27
Carroglen Gdns, G32 71 CF32
Carroglen Gro, G32 71 CF32
Carroll Cres, (New.) Moth. ML1 113 DE43
Carron Ct, (Camb.) G72 107 CF40
Carron Ct, Ham. ML3 139 CR52
Carron Cres, G22 50 BT24
Carron Cres, (Bears.) G61 29 BE18
Carron Cres, (Bishop.) G64 33 BX20

Carron Cres, (Lenz.) G66 35 CG17
Carron Dr, Bish. PA7 24 AL19
Carron La, Pais. PA3 63 AX30
off Kilearn Rd
Carron Pl, G22 50 BT24
Carron Pl, (E.Kil.) G75 136 CB56
Carron Pl, Coat. ML5 74 CT28
Carron St, G22 50 BU24
Carron Way, (Cumb.) G67 22 DB12
off Cumbernauld Shop Cen
Carron Way, Moth. ML1 113 DE41
off Lomond Wk
Carron Way, Pais. PA3 63 AW30
off Priory Av
Carrour Gdns, (Bishop.) G64 32 BV19
Carr Quad, Bell. ML4 111 CZ40
Carsaig Dr, G52 65 BG32
Carsaig Ln, (Glenb.) Coat. ML5 56 CS23
off Dinyra Pl
Carscallan Rd, Ham. ML3 140 CU56
Carsegreen Av, Pais. PA2 81 AR38
Carse Vw Dr, (Bears.) G61 30 BJ15
Carstairs St, G40 89 BW35
Carswell Gdns, G41 87 BN36
Carswell Rd, (Newt. M.) G77 116 BC48
Cartbank Gdns, G44 103 BQ41
off Cartbank Rd
Cartbank Gro, G44 103 BQ41
off Cartbank Rd
Cartbank Rd, G44 103 BQ41
Cartcraigs Rd, G43 102 BK39
Cartha Cres, Pais. PA2 83 AW34
Cartha St, G41 86 BM38
Cartsbridge Rd, (Clark.) G76 119 BN47
Cartside Av, John. PA5 79 AF36
Cartside Av, (Inch.) Renf. PA4 43 AR25
Cartside Dr, (Clark.) G76 119 BQ47
Cartside Pl, (Clark.) G76 119 BP48
Cartside Quad, G42 87 BQ38
Cartside Rd, (Clark.) G76 119 BP48
Cartside St, G42 87 BP38
Cartside Ter, (Kilb.) John. PA10 79 AE35
off Kilbarchan Rd
Cart St, Clyde. G81 45 AX21
Cartvale La, Pais. PA3 62 AU31
Cartvale Rd, G42 87 BP38
Cartview Ct, (Clark.) G76 119 BP47
Caskie Dr, (Blan.) G72 109 CN44
Cassels Gro, Moth. ML1 111 CY44
off Potts Way
Cassels St, Moth. ML1 128 DA45
Cassiltoun Gdns, G45 104 BT43
off Stravanan Rd
Cassley Av, Renf. PA4 64 BB27
Castle Av, (Udd.) G71 109 CN41
Castle Av, (Elder.) John. PA5 80 AK36
Castle Av, Moth. ML1 112 DD39
Castlebank Ct, G13 47 BG23
Castlebank Cres, G11 66 BJ28
Castlebank Gdns, G13 47 BG23
Castlebank St, G11 65 BH27
Castlebank Vil, G13 47 BG23
off Munro Pl
Castlebay Dr, G22 32 BS20
Castlebay Pl, G22 50 BS21
off Castlebay St
Castlebay St, G22 50 BS21
Castlebrae Gdns, G44 103 BR39
Castle Chimmins Av, (Camb.) 107 CF41
G72
Castle Chimmins Rd, (Camb.) 107 CF42
G72
Castle Ct, (Kirk.) G66 17 CF13

Castle Cres, Bish. PA7 24 AK19
Castle Cres N Ct, G1 5 BS30
off Royal Ex Sq
Castlecroft Gdns, (Udd.) G71 109 CN40
Castle Dr, Moth. ML1 112 DD39
Castlefern Rd, (Ruther.) G73 105 BX42
Castlefield Ct, G33 52 CD25
Castlefield Gdns, (E.Kil.) G75 135 BX56
off Pine Cres
Castle Gait, Pais. PA1 82 AT34
Castle Gdns, (Chry.) G69 37 CP20
Castle Gdns, Pais. PA2 81 AQ34
Castle Gate, (Udd.) G71 109 CN40
Castle Gate, (Newt. M.) G77 118 BJ50
Castleglen Rd, (E.Kil.) G74 120 BV49
Castle Gro, (Kilsyth) G65 7 CS3
Castlehill Cres, (Chap.) Air. 97 DG36
ML6
Castlehill Cres, Ham. ML3 141 CY52
Castlehill Cres, Renf. PA4 45 AZ25
off Ferry Rd
Castlehill Dr, (Newt. M.) G77 117 BH49
Castlehill Gdns, Ham. ML3 140 CV51
Castlehill Grn, (E.Kil.) G74 120 BV49
Castlehill Rd, (Bears.) G61 28 BD15
Castlehill Rd, Wis. ML2 143 DH53
Castlehill Vw, (Kilsyth) G65 7 CS3
Castlelaw Gdns, G32 70 CD31
Castlelaw Pl, G32 70 CD31
Castlelaw St, G32 70 CD31
Castle Mains Rd, (Miln.) G62 11 BF11
Castlemilk Arc, G45 104 BU42
Castlemilk Cres, G44 104 BU40
Castlemilk Dr, G45 104 BU43
Castlemilk Rd, G44 88 BU38
Castlemilk Ter, G45 104 BU44
off Castlemilk Dr
Castlemount Av, (Newt. M.) 117 BH50
G77
Castle Pl, (Udd.) G71 109 CN39
Castle Quad, Air. ML6 77 DF30
Castle Rd, (Newt. M.) G77 117 BE49
Castle Rd, Air. ML6 77 DF29
Castle Rd, (Elder.) John. PA5 80 AL34
Castle Sq, Clyde. G81 26 AU18
Castle St, G4 5 BU29
Castle St, G11 66 BL28
Castle St, (Baill.) G69 92 CJ34
Castle St, (Ruther.) G73 89 BW37
Castle St, (Chap.) Air. ML6 97 DF35
Castle St, Clyde. G81 26 AU18
Castle St, Ham. ML3 126 CV49
Castle St, Pais. PA1 82 AS33
Castleton Av, (Bishop.) G64 50 BU22
Castleton Av, (Newt. M.) G77 117 BH50
Castleton Ct, G45 104 BV43
Castleton Ct, (Newt. M.) G77 117 BH50
off Castleton Dr
Castleton Cres, (Newt. M.) G77 117 BH50
Castleton Dr, (Newt. M.) G77 117 BH50
Castleton Gro, (Newt. M.) G77 117 BH50
Castle Vw, Clyde. G81 27 AX18
off Granville St
Castleview Av, Pais. PA2 81 AQ38
Castleview Dr, Pais. PA2 81 AQ38
Castleview Pl, Pais. PA2 81 AQ38
off Castleview Av
Castle Way, (Cumb.) G67 23 DE9
Castle Way, (Baill.) G69 73 CP32
off Dukes Rd
Castle Wynd, (Both.) G71 109 CR43
Cathay St, G22 50 BS21
Cathcart Cres, Pais. PA2 83 AW34

Cathcart Pl, (Ruther.) G73	88	BV38
Cathcart Rd, G42	87	BR37
Cathcart Rd, (Ruther.) G73	88	BU38
Cathedral Sq, G4	5	BU30
Cathedral St, G1	5	BS29
Cathedral St, G4	5	BS29
Catherine Pl, G3	4	BP30
off Hydepark St		
Catherine St, (Kirk.) G66	17	CE13
Catherine St, Moth. ML1	128	DA49
Catherine's Wk, (Blan.) G72	124	CM47
off Victoria St		
Catherine Way, Moth. ML1	112	DB42
Cathkin Av, (Camb.) G72	106	CA39
Cathkin Av, (Ruther.) G73	89	BY38
Cathkin Bypass, (Ruther.) G73	105	BZ42
Cathkin Ct, G45	104	BV43
Cathkin Dr, (Clark.) G76	118	BL45
Cathkin Gdns, (Udd.) G71	93	CN36
off Watling St		
Cathkin Pl, (Camb.) G72	106	CA39
Cathkin Rd, G42	87	BP38
Cathkin Rd, (Udd.) G71	93	CN36
Cathkin Rd, (Ruther.) G73	105	BY43
Cathkin Rd, (Carm.) G76	120	BU45
Cathkin Vw, G32	90	CD37
Cathkinview Pl, G42	87	BQ38
Cathkinview Rd, G42	87	BQ38
Catrine, (E.Kil.) G74	135	BZ51
Catrine Av, Clyde. G81	27	AZ18
Catrine Ct, G53	84	BC37
Catrine Cres, Moth. ML1	128	DC50
Catrine Gdns, G53	84	BC37
Catrine Pl, G53	84	BC37
Catrine Rd, G53	84	BC37
Catrine St, Lark. ML9	145	DE59
Catriona Way, Moth. ML1	112	DD41
off Shirrel Rd		
Catter Gdns, (Miln.) G62	11	BG10
Cauldstream Pl, (Miln.) G62	11	BG12
Caurnie Vw, (Kirk.) G66	36	CL15
Causewayside Cres, G32	90	CC35
Causewayside St, G32	90	CC35
Causeyside St, Pais. PA1	82	AU33
Causeystanes, (Blan.) G72	124	CM46
off Winton Cres		
Cavendish Ct, G5	87	BR33
Cavendish Dr, (Newt. M.) G77	117	BH47
Cavendish Pl, G5	87	BR33
Cavendish St, G5	87	BR33
Cavin Dr, G45	104	BU41
Cavin Rd, G45	104	BU41
Cawder Ct, (Cumb.) G68	9	DA8
off Cawder Rd		
Cawder Pl, (Cumb.) G68	9	DA8
off Cawder Rd		
Cawder Rd, (Cumb.) G68	9	DA8
Cawder Vw, (Cumb.) G68	9	DA8
off Cawder Rd		
Cawder Way, (Cumb.) G68	9	DA8
off Cawder Rd		
Cawdor Cres, Bish. PA7	24	AK19
Cawdor Way, (E.Kil.) G74	121	BZ50
off Dunvegan Pl		
Cayton Gdns, (Baill.) G69	91	CH33
Cecil St, G12	48	BM26
Cecil St, Coat. ML5	75	CW32
Cedar Av, (Udd.) G71	94	CS37
off Douglas Cres		
Cedar Av, Clyde. G81	26	AT17
Cedar Av, John. PA5	79	AH37
Cedar Ct, G20	67	BQ27
Cedar Ct, (Camb.) G72	107	CG41
Cedar Ct, (E.Kil.) G75	135	BY56
Cedar Ct, (Kilb.) John. PA10	78	AC34
Cedar Cres, Ham. ML3	140	CU52
Cedar Dr, (Lenz.) G66	35	CE16
Cedar Dr, (Udd.) G71	94	CS37
Cedar Dr, (E.Kil.) G75	135	BY56
Cedar Gdns, (Ruther.) G73	105	BY41
Cedar Gdns, (New.) Moth. ML1	113	DE41
off Western Av		
Cedar La, Air. ML6	77	DE30
Cedar Pl, (Blan.) G72	124	CL45
Cedar Pl, (E.Kil.) G75	135	BY56
Cedar Pl, (Barr.) G78	115	AZ45
off Divernia Way		
Cedar Rd, (Bishop.) G64	51	BX21
Cedar Rd, (Cumb.) G67	23	DF10
Cedar St, G20	67	BQ27
Cedar Wk, (Bishop.) G64	51	BX21
Cedarwood Av, (Newt. M.) G77	117	BH48
Cedric Pl, G13	47	BF22
Cedric Rd, G13	47	BF22
Celtic St, G20	48	BL22
Cemetery Rd, G52	65	BF32
Cemetery Rd, (Blan.) G72	124	CL47
Centenary Av, Air. ML6	75	CZ30
Centenary Ct, (Barr.) G78	99	AX43
Centenary Ct, Clyde. G81	27	AX20
Centenary Gdns, Coat. ML5	75	CW32
Centenary Gdns, Ham. ML3	140	CU51
off Woodside Wk		
Centenary Quad, Moth. ML1	112	DC40
Central Av, G11	65	BH27
off Broomhill Ter		
Central Av, G32	91	CF34
Central Av, (Udd.) G71	110	CS39
Central Av, (Blan.) G72	125	CN48
Central Av, (Camb.) G72	106	CB39
Central Av, Clyde. G81	27	AW19
Central Av, (Holytown) Moth. ML1 *off Holytown Rd*	112	DB40
Central Av, (New Stev.) Moth. ML1	112	DC43
Central Cres, (Ashgill) Lark. ML9	145	DH61
Central Gro, G32	91	CF33
Central Gro, (Camb.) G72	106	CB39
Central Path, G32	91	CG34
Central Rd, Pais. PA1	62	AU32
Central Sta, G1	4	BR30
Central Way, (Cumb.) G67	22	DA13
Central Way, Pais. PA1	62	AU32
off Central Rd		
Centre, The (Barr.) G78	99	AX43
Centre Pk Ct, Coat. ML5	75	CW31
off South Circular Rd		
Centre Roundabout, The (E.Kil.) G74	136	CB52
Centre St, G5	67	BQ32
Centre St, (Chap.) Air. ML6	97	DE35
Centre St, (Glenb.) Coat. ML5	56	CS23
Centre Way, (Barr.) G78	99	AX42
off North Pk Av		
Ceres Gdns, (Bishop.) G64	33	BZ20
Cessnock Pl, (Camb.) G72	107	CF40
Cessnock Rd, G33	52	CC24
Cessnock St, G51	66	BL31
Chalmers Ct, G40	5	BU31
Chalmers Cres, (E.Kil.) G75	136	CB54
Chalmers Dr, (E.Kil.) G75	136	CB54
Chalmers Gate, G40	5	BU31
off Claythorn St		
Chalmers Pl, G40	5	BU31
off Claythorn St		
Chalmers St, G40	5	BU31
Chalmers St, Clyde. G81	27	AX20
Chamberlain La, G13	47	BG24
Chamberlain Rd, G13	47	BG23
Chancellor St, G11	66	BK27
Chantinghall Rd, Ham. ML3	125	CR50
Chantinghall Ter, Ham. ML3	125	CR50
Chapel Ct, (Ruther.) G73	88	BV37
off Western Av		
Chapel Cres, Ham. ML3	140	CT55
Chapelcross Av, Air. ML6	76	DC28
off Chapelside Av		
Chapelhall Ind Est, (Chap.) Air. ML6	97	DF33
Chapelhill Rd, Pais. PA2	83	AW35
Chapelknowe Rd, Moth. ML1	113	DF44
Chapel Pl, (Neil.) G78	114	AT46
Chapel Rd, Clyde. G81	27	AW15
Chapelside Av, Air. ML6	76	DC29
Chapelside Rd, (E.Kil.) G74	122	CC47
Chapel St, G20	49	BN24
Chapel St, (Ruther.) G73	88	BV37
Chapel St, Air. ML6	76	DC29
Chapel St Ind Est, G20	49	BN23
Chapelton Av, (Bears.) G61	29	BH17
Chapelton Gdns, (Bears.) G61	29	BH17
Chapelton Rd, (Cumb.) G67	39	CY15
Chapelton St, G22	50	BS23
Chaplet Av, G13	47	BE21
Chapman Av, (Glenb.) Coat. ML5	56	CS23
Chapman St, G42	87	BQ35
off Allison St		
Chappell St, (Barr.) G78	99	AX42
Charing Cross, G2	4	BP28
Charing Cross La, G3	4	BP29
off Granville St		
Charles Av, Renf. PA4	45	AZ25
Charles Cres, (Lenz.) G66	35	CF18
Charleson Row, (Kilsyth) G65	20	CV10
Charles Path, (Chap.) Air. ML6	97	DF35
off Kennelburn Rd		
Charles Quad, Moth. ML1	112	DC40
Charles St, G21	5	BU28
Charles St, (Kilsyth) G65	7	CT4
Charles St, Wis. ML2	129	DE49
Charlotte Av, (Torr.) G64	15	BX13
Charlotte La, G1	5	BT31
off London Rd		
Charlotte La S, G1	5	BT31
off Charlotte St		
Charlotte La W, G1	5	BT31
off London Rd		
Charlotte Path, Lark. ML9	144	DC59
off Margaretvale Dr		
Charlotte Pl, Pais. PA2	82	AU35
Charlotte St, G1	5	BT31
Charnwood Av, John. PA5	79	AF37
Chartwell Rd, Bish. PA7	24	AK18
Chassels St, Coat. ML5	75	CW29
Chateau Gro, Ham. ML3	141	CW51
Chatelherault Av, (Camb.) G72	106	CA40
Chatelherault Cres, Ham. ML3	140	CU53
Chatelherault Wk, Ham. ML3	140	CU52
off Chatelherault Cres		
Chatham, (E.Kil.) G75	135	BY54
Chatton St, G23	30	BM20
Chatton Wk, Coat. ML5	95	CY35
Cheapside St, G3	4	BP31
Chelmsford Dr, G12	48	BK24
Cherry Bk, (Kirk.) G66	34	CD16
Cherrybank Rd, G43	103	BP40
Cherrybank Wk, Air. ML6	75	CZ29

Cherry Cres, Clyde. G81 27 AW17
Cherry Gro, (Baill.) G69 73 CR31
Cherryhill Vw, Lark. ML9 144 DB59
Cherry Pl, (Bishop.) G64 51 BX21
Cherry Pl, (Udd.) G71 94 CT37
Cherry Pl, John. PA5 80 AJ36
Cherryridge Dr, (Baill.) G69 73 CQ31
Cherrytree Cres, Lark. ML9 142 DC56
Cherrytree Dr, (Camb.) G72 107 CG41
Cherrytree Dr, (Camb.) G72 107 CG41
Cherry Wk, Moth. ML1 128 DA50
Cherrywood Rd, (Elder.) John. 80 AL34
PA5
Chesterfield Av, G12 48 BJ24
Chesters Cres, Moth. ML1 127 CY45
Chesters Pl, (Ruther.) G73 88 BV38
Chesters Rd, (Bears.) G61 29 BF16
Chester St, G32 70 CC32
Chestnut Cres, (Udd.) G71 94 CT38
Chestnut Cres, (E.Kil.) G75 135 BY55
Chestnut Cres, Ham. ML3 140 CU51
Chestnut Dr, (Kirk.) G66 34 CD15
Chestnut Dr, Clyde. G81 26 AV16
Chestnut Gro, (Gart.) G69 56 CS23
Chestnut Gro, (Blan.) G72 124 CL45
Chestnut Gro, Lark. ML9 142 DC56
Chestnut Gro, Moth. ML1 127 CZ48
Chestnut La, (Miln.) G62 11 BG12
Chestnut Pl, John. PA5 80 AJ37
Chestnut St, G22 50 BT24
Chestnut Way, (Camb.) G72 107 CG41
Cheviot Av, (Barr.) G78 99 AY43
Cheviot Ct, Air. ML6 76 DD27
Cheviot Cres, Wis. ML2 129 DH49
Cheviot Dr, (Newt. M.) G77 117 BE50
Cheviot Gdns, (Bears.) G61 11 BF14
off Grampian Way
Cheviot Rd, G43 102 BL40
Cheviot Rd, Ham. ML3 140 CV51
Cheviot Rd, Lark. ML9 145 DE59
off Burnhead Rd
Cheviot Rd, Pais. PA2 82 AT36
Cheviot St, (Blan.) G72 124 CL46
Chirmorie Cres, G53 84 BC36
Chirmorie Pl, G53 84 BC36
Chirnside Ct, (Blan.) G72 125 CP48
off Fortingall Rd
Chirnside Pl, G52 64 BC31
Chirnside Rd, G52 64 BC31
Chisholm Av, Bish. PA7 24 AL18
Chisholm Dr, (Newt. M.) G77 117 BG47
Chisholm Pl, Moth. ML1 142 DD51
Chisholm St, G1 5 BT31
Chisholm St, Coat. ML5 75 CX29
Chrighton Grn, (Udd.) G71 93 CQ37
Chriss Av, Ham. ML3 140 CT54
Christchurch Pl, (E.Kil.) G75 135 BX54
Christian St, G43 86 BL38
Christie La, Pais. PA3 62 AU32
Christie Pl, (Camb.) G72 106 CC40
Christie St, Bell. ML4 111 CZ41
Christie St, Pais. PA1 62 AV32
Christopher St, G21 69 BW27
Chryston Business Cen, (Chry.) 54 CL21
G69
Chryston Rd, (Kirk.) G66 36 CK15
Chryston Rd, (Chry.) G69 54 CM21
Chryston Rd, (Mood.) G69 36 CM16
Church Av, (Stepps) G33 53 CF23
Church Av, (Ruther.) G73 105 BY40
Church Cres, Air. ML6 77 DG28
Church Dr, (Kirk.) G66 35 CE15
Church Hill, Pais. PA1 62 AU32
Churchill Av, (E.Kil.) G74 136 CB52

Churchill Av, John. PA5 79 AE37
Churchill Cres, (Both.) G71 109 CR42
Churchill Dr, G11 48 BJ26
Churchill Dr, Bish. PA7 24 AK18
Churchill Pl, (Kilb.) John. PA10 78 AC34
Churchill Way, (Bishop.) G64 32 BV20
Church La, (Kilsyth) G65 7 CT5
off Church St
Church La, Coat. ML5 75 CW30
Church Pl, (Old Kil.) G60 25 AQ15
Church Rd, (Giff.) G46 102 BL43
Church Rd, (Muir.) G69 54 CL22
Church Rd, (Clark.) G76 119 BP47
Church St, G11 66 BL27
Church St, (Kilsyth) G65 7 CT5
Church St, (Baill.) G69 92 CK33
Church St, (Udd.) G71 109 CN40
Church St, (Blan.) G72 125 CN46
Church St, Clyde. G81 27 AW18
Church St, Coat. ML5 75 CW30
Church St, Ham. ML3 126 CU49
Church St, John. PA5 79 AH34
Church St, (Kilb.) John. PA10 78 AC34
Church St, Lark. ML9 144 DC58
Church St, Moth. ML1 113 DH41
Church Vw, (Camb.) G72 90 CC38
Church Vw, Coat. ML5 75 CW30
Church Vw Gdns, Bell. ML4 111 CW40
Circus Dr, G31 68 BV30
Circus Pl, G31 68 BV30
Circus Pl La, G31 68 BV29
Citadel Pl, Moth. ML1 127 CY45
Citrus Cres, (Udd.) G71 94 CS37
Cityford Cres, (Ruther.) G73 104 BV39
Cityford Dr, (Ruther.) G73 88 BV38
City Link Cen, G51 66 BJ30
Civic St, G4 67 BR27
Civic Way, (Kirk.) G66 17 CE14
Clachan Dr, G51 65 BG29
off Skipness Dr
Claddens Pl, (Lenz.) G66 35 CG17
Claddens Quad, G22 50 BS23
Claddens St, G22 49 BR23
Claddens Wynd, (Kirk.) G66 35 CG17
Cladence Gro, (E.Kil.) G75 136 CB56
Clairinsh Gdns, Renf. PA4 63 AY28
off Sandy Rd
Clairmont Gdns, G3 4 BP28
Clair Rd, (Bishop.) G64 33 BZ20
Clamp Rd, Wis. ML2 129 DE49
Clamps Gro, (E.Kil.) G74 136 CC53
Clamps Ter, (E.Kil.) G74 136 CD53
Clamps Wd, (E.Kil.) G74 136 CC53
Clanrye Dr, Coat. ML5 95 CW33
Clapperhow Rd, Moth. ML1 112 DC44
Claremont Av, (Kirk.) G66 16 CD12
Claremont Dr, (Miln.) G62 12 BJ11
off Clober Rd
Claremont Gdns, (Miln.) G62 12 BJ11
off Clober Rd
Claremont Pas, G3 4 BP28
off Claremont Ter
Claremont Pl, G3 4 BP28
off Claremont Ter
Claremont St, G3 67 BN29
Claremont Ter, G3 4 BP28
Claremont Ter La, G3 67 BN28
Claremount Av, (Giff.) G46 102 BL43
Clarence Dr, G11 48 BJ26
Clarence Dr, G12 48 BJ26
Clarence Dr, Pais. PA1 63 AW32
Clarence Gdns, G11 48 BJ26
Clarence La, G12 48 BK26

Clarence St, Clyde. G81 27 AX18
Clarence St, Pais. PA1 63 AW32
Clarendon La, G20 67 BQ27
off Clarendon St
Clarendon Pl, G20 67 BQ27
Clarendon Pl, (Stepps) G33 53 CF24
Clarendon Rd, Wis. ML2 143 DG52
Clarendon St, G20 67 BQ27
Clare St, G21 69 BW27
Clarinda Ct, (Kirk.) G66 18 CJ11
Clarinda Pl, Moth. ML1 113 DE42
Clarion Cres, G13 46 BC21
Clarion Rd, G13 46 BC21
Clark Pl, (Torr.) G64 15 BY13
Clark Pl, (Newt. M.) G77 116 BD49
Clarkston Av, G44 103 BP41
Clarkston Dr, Air. ML6 77 DF30
Clarkston Rd, G44 103 BP41
Clarkston Rd, (Clark.) G76 119 BN45
Clarkston Toll, (Clark.) G76 119 BN45
Clark St, Air. ML6 76 DD30
Clark St, Clyde. G81 26 AV17
Clark St, John. PA5 79 AH34
Clark St, Pais. PA3 62 AS31
Clark St, Renf. PA4 45 AX26
Clark Way, (Bellshill Ind. Est.) 94 CV38
Bell. ML4
Clarkwell Rd, Ham. ML3 139 CN51
Clarkwell Ter, Ham. ML3 125 CP50
Clathic Av, (Bears.) G61 30 BJ17
Claude Av, (Camb.) G72 107 CG42
Claude St, Lark. ML9 144 DC58
Claud Rd, Pais. PA3 63 AW31
Clavens Rd, G52 64 BA31
Claverhouse Pl, Pais. PA2 83 AW34
Claverhouse Rd, G52 64 BB30
Clavering St E, Pais. PA1 62 AS32
Clavering St W, Pais. PA1 62 AS32
off King St
Clay Ct, Moth. ML1 128 DA49
Clay Cres, Bell. ML4 95 CX38
Clayhouse Rd, G33 53 CG25
Claypotts Pl, G33 70 CC28
Claypotts Rd, G33 70 CC28
Clay Rd, Bell. ML4 95 CX38
Clayslaps Rd, G3 66 BM28
Claythorn Av, G40 68 BU32
Claythorn Circ, G40 5 BU31
off Claythorn Av
Claythorn Ct, G40 5 BU31
off Claythorn Pk
Claythorn Pk, G40 68 BU32
Claythorn St, G40 5 BU31
Claythorn Ter, G40 5 BU31
Clayton Path, Bell. ML4 95 CX38
off Ashgrove Rd
Clayton Ter, G31 68 BV30
Clearfield Av, Ham. ML3 125 CR49
Cleddans Cres, Clyde. G81 27 AY15
Cleddans Rd, (Kirk.) G66 17 CG12
Cleddans Rd, Clyde. G81 27 AX16
Cleddans Vw, (Glenm.) Air. ML6 58 DA25
Cleddans Vw, Clyde. G81 27 AY18
off Kirkoswald Dr
Cleddens Ct, (Bishop.) G64 33 BW19
Cleddens Ct, Air. ML6 75 CZ29
off Monkscourt Av
Cleeves Pl, G53 100 BD40
Cleeves Quad, G53 100 BC40
Cleeves Rd, G53 100 BC40
Cleghorn St, G22 49 BR26
Cleish Av, (Bears.) G61 11 BE13
Cleland La, G5 68 BS32

Cleland Pl, (E.Kil.) G74	122	CC50
Cleland Rd, (Cleland) Moth.	113	DE44
ML1 off Chapelknowe Rd		
Cleland St, G5	68	BS32
Clelland Av, (Bishop.) G64	51	BW21
Clem Attlee Gdns, Lark. ML9	144	DD59
off Machan Rd		
Clerwood St, G32	69	BZ31
Cleuch Gdns, (Clark.) G76	118	BM45
Cleveden Cres, G12	48	BK24
Cleveden Cres La, G12	48	BK24
Cleveden Dr, G12	48	BK24
Cleveden Dr, (Ruther.) G73	105	BY39
Cleveden Dr La, G12	48	BL25
off Mirrlees Dr		
Cleveden Gdns, G12	48	BL24
Cleveden La, G12	48	BK23
Cleveden Pl, G12	48	BK23
Cleveden Rd, G12	48	BK23
Cleveland La, G3	4	BP29
Cleveland St, G3	4	BP29
Clifford Gdns, G51	66	BK32
Clifford La, G51	66	BL32
Clifford Pl, G51	66	BM31
off Clifford St		
Clifford St, G51	66	BK32
Cliff Rd, G3	4	BP28
Clifton Pl, G3	67	BN28
off Clifton St		
Clifton Pl, Coat. ML5	75	CY31
Clifton Rd, (Giff.) G46	102	BK42
Clifton St, G3	67	BN28
Clifton Ter, (Camb.) G72	106	CA42
Clifton Ter, John. PA5	80	AJ35
Clincarthill Rd, (Ruther.) G73	89	BW38
Clincart Rd, G42	87	BR37
Cloan Av, G15	28	BD19
Cloan Cres, (Bishop.) G64	33	BX18
Clober Fm La, (Miln.) G62	11	BG10
off Craigton Rd		
Cloberfield, (Miln.) G62	11	BH9
Cloberfield Gdns, (Miln.) G62	11	BH10
Cloberhill Rd, G13	29	BE20
Clober Rd, (Miln.) G62	11	BH10
Clochbar Av, (Miln.) G62	11	BH10
Clochbar Gdns, (Miln.) G62	11	BH10
Clochoderick Av, (Kilb.) John.	78	AD35
PA10		
Cloch St, G33	70	CC29
Clockenhill Pl, Moth. ML1	113	DG41
Cloister Av, Air. ML6	97	DE33
Clonbeith St, G33	71	CG27
Closeburn St, G22	50	BS24
Cloth St, (Barr.) G78	99	AY43
Clouden Rd, (Cumb.) G67	22	DD11
Cloudhowe Ter, (Blan.) G72	108	CL44
Clouston Ct, G20	49	BN25
off Fergus Dr		
Clouston La, G20	49	BN25
Clouston St, G20	48	BM25
Clova Pl, (Udd.) G71	109	CP39
Clova St, (Thornlie.) G46	101	BH41
Clove Mill Wynd, Lark. ML9	144	DA59
Cloverbank Gdns, G21	69	BW28
Cloverbank St, G21	69	BW28
Clovergate, (Bishop.) G64	32	BU20
Cloverhill Pl, (Chry.) G69	54	CL21
Cloverhill Ter, (E.Kil.) G74	136	CA52
Cloverhill Vw, (E.Kil.) G74	135	BZ52
Clunie Pl, Coat. ML5	95	CX34
Clunie Rd, G52	85	BG33
Cluny Av, (Bears.) G61	30	BJ19
Cluny Dr, (Bears.) G61	30	BJ19

Cluny Dr, (Newt. M.) G77	116	BD48
Cluny Dr, Pais. PA3	63	AW31
Cluny Gdns, G14	47	BG25
Cluny Gdns, (Baill.) G69	92	CJ33
Cluny Vil, G14	47	BG25
off Westland Dr		
Clutha Pl, (E.Kil.) G75	135	BW54
Clutha St, G51	66	BM31
off Paisley Rd W		
Clyde Av, (Torr.) G64	15	BX13
Clyde Av, (Both.) G71	109	CP44
Clyde Av, (Barr.) G78	99	AZ44
Clyde Av, Ham. ML3	141	CY52
Clydebank Business Pk, Clyde.	27	AW19
G81		
Clydebank Ind Est, Clyde. G81	26	AT19
Clydebrae Dr, (Both.) G71	109	CR44
Clydebrae St, G51	66	BK29
Clyde Ct, Clyde. G81	26	AU16
Clyde Cres, (Blan.) G72	124	CM45
Clyde Dr, Bell. ML4	111	CY41
Clydeford Dr, G32	90	CA34
Clydeford Dr, (Udd.) G71	93	CN38
Clydeford Rd, (Camb.) G72	90	CC37
Clydeholm Rd, G14	65	BF27
Clydeholm Ter, Clyde. G81	45	AZ22
Clyde La, Moth. ML1	112	DC41
off Quarry St		
Clydeneuk Dr, (Udd.) G71	92	CM38
Clyde Pl, G5	4	BQ31
Clyde Pl, (Cumb.) G67	22	DB11
off Cumbernauld Shop Cen		
Clyde Pl, (Camb.) G72	107	CF41
Clyde Pl, John. PA5	79	AE37
Clyde Pl, Moth. ML1	112	DC41
Clyde Rd, Pais. PA3	63	AX30
Clyde Shop Cen, Clyde. G81	27	AY20
Clydeside Expressway, G3	66	BL29
Clydeside Expressway, G14	66	BN29
Clydeside Ind Est, G14	65	BF27
Clydeside Rd, (Ruther.) G73	88	BV35
Clydesmill Dr, G32	90	CC38
Clydesmill Gro, G32	90	CC38
Clydesmill Ind Est, G32	90	CC37
Clydesmill Pl, G32	90	CC37
Clydesmill Rd, G32	90	CB37
Clyde St, G1	4	BR31
Clyde St, Clyde. G81	45	AY21
Clyde St, Coat. ML5	75	CY30
Clyde St, Renf. PA4	45	AZ24
Clyde Ter, (Both.) G71	109	CQ44
Clyde Ter, Moth. ML1	143	DE51
Clyde Twr, (E.Kil.) G74	136	CD54
Clyde Tunnel, G14	65	BG28
Clyde Tunnel, G51	65	BG28
Clydevale, (Both.) G71	109	CR44
Clyde Valley Av, Moth. ML1	128	DA49
Clydeview, (Both.) G71	110	CS44
Clyde Vw, Ham. ML3	139	CR52
Clyde Vw, Pais. PA2	83	AX35
Clydeview La, G11	65	BH27
off Broomhill Ter		

Clydeview Shop Cen, (Blan.)	125	CN46
G72		
Clydeview Ter, G32	90	CD37
Clyde Wk, (Cumb.) G67	22	DB11
off Cumbernauld Shop Cen		
Clyde Way, (Cumb.) G67	22	DB11
off Cumbernauld Shop Cen		
Clyde Way, Pais. PA3	63	AX30
off Clyde Rd		
Clynder St, G51	66	BK31
Clyth Dr, (Giff.) G46	102	BM43
Coach Cl, (Kilsyth) G65	8	CW5
Coach Pl, (Kilsyth) G65	7	CU6
Coach Rd, (Kilsyth) G65	8	CV6
Coalburn Rd, (Both.) G71	109	CR40
Coalburn St, (Green.) Air. ML6	41	DH19
Coalhall Av, Moth. ML1	112	DC44
Coalhill St, G31	69	BX32
Coatbank St, Coat. ML5	75	CX31
Coatbank Way, Coat. ML5	75	CX31
Coatbridge Ind Est, Coat. ML5	75	CW28
Coatbridge Rd, (Baill.) G69	73	CN32
Coatbridge Rd, (Gart.) G69	55	CQ25
Coatbridge Rd, (Glenm.) Air.	57	CZ26
ML6		
Coatbridge Rd, (Glenb.) Coat.	56	CV24
ML5		
Coathill St, Coat. ML5	95	CW33
Coats Cres, (Baill.) G69	72	CJ32
Coats Dr, Pais. PA2	81	AR34
Coatshill Av, (Blan.) G72	108	CL44
Coats St, Coat. ML5	75	CX30
Cobbett Rd, Moth. ML1	127	CX48
Cobblerigg Way, (Udd.) G71	109	CN40
Cobden Rd, G21	68	BV27
Cobbleton Rd, Moth. ML1	112	DB43
Cobington Pl, G33	70	CD28
Cobinshaw St, G32	70	CC31
Coburg St, G5	67	BR32
Cochno St, Clyde. G81	45	AY21
Cochrane Ct, (Miln.) G62	12	BL13
off Finlay Ri		
Cochranemill Rd, John. PA5	79	AE36
Cochrane Sq, (Linw.) Pais. PA3	60	AK31
Cochrane St, G1	5	BS30
Cochrane St, (Barr.) G78	99	AX43
Cochrane St, Bell. ML4	110	CV39
Cochran St, Pais. PA1	82	AV33
Cockburn Pl, Coat. ML5	94	CV33
Cockels Ln, Renf. PA4	63	AX28
Cockenzie St, G32	70	CC32
Cockhill Way, Bell. ML4	110	CT39
off Philip Murray Rd		
Cockmuir St, G21	51	BW25
Coddington Cres, (Holytown)	96	DB38
Moth. ML1		
Cogan Pl, (Barr.) G78	99	AX43
off Cogan St		
Cogan Rd, G43	102	BL39
Cogan St, G43	86	BL38
Cogan St, (Barr.) G78	99	AX43
Colbert St, G40	88	BV34
Colbreggan Ct, Clyde. G81	27	AY15
Colbreggan Gdns, Clyde. G81	27	AY15
Colbreggan Pl, Clyde. G81	27	AY15
off Glasgow Rd		
Colchester Dr, G12	48	BJ23
Coldingham Av, G14	46	BA23
Coldstream Dr, (Ruther.) G73	105	BZ39
Coldstream Dr, Pais. PA2	81	AQ36
Coldstream Pl, G21	50	BS26
Coldstream Rd, Clyde. G81	27	AX20
Coldstream St, (Blan.) G72	124	CM46

Colebrooke La, G12	49	BN26
off Colebrooke St		
Colebrooke Pl, G12	49	BN26
Colebrooke St, G12	49	BN26
Colebrooke Ter, G12	49	BN26
Colebrook St, (Camb.) G72	106	CC39
Coleridge, (E.Kil.) G75	135	BW54
Coleridge Av, (Both.) G71	109	CR42
Colfin St, G34	72	CL28
Colgrain Av, G20	49	BQ23
Colgrain Ter, G20	49	BQ23
Colgrave Cres, G32	90	CB34
Colinbar Circle, (Barr.) G78	99	AX44
Colinslee Av, Pais. PA2	82	AV36
Colinslee Cres, Pais. PA2	82	AV36
Colinslee Dr, Pais. PA2	82	AV36
Colinslie Rd, G53	85	BE37
Colinton Pl, G32	70	CD30
Colintraive Av, G33	52	CB25
Colintraive Cres, G33	52	CA26
Coll, (E.Kil.) G74	137	CE53
Colla Gdns, (Bishop.) G64	33	BZ19
Coll Av, Renf. PA4	63	AZ28
College Gate, (Bears.) G61	29	BE15
College La, Pais. PA1	62	AT32
College St, G1	5	BT30
Collessie Dr, G33	71	CE27
Collier St, John. PA5	79	AH34
Colliertree Rd, Air. ML6	77	DF29
Collina St, G20	48	BL23
Collins St, G4	5	BU30
Coll Lea, Ham. ML3	139	CP52
Coll Pl, G21	69	BX27
Coll Pl, Air. ML6	77	DE32
Collree Gdns, G34	72	CL30
off Easterhouse Rd		
Coll St, G21	69	BW27
Collylinn Rd, (Bears.) G61	29	BG17
Colmonell Av, G13	46	BB22
Colonsay, (E.Kil.) G74	136	CD54
Colonsay Av, Renf. PA4	63	AY28
Colonsay Cres, Coat. ML5	94	CT33
Colonsay Dr, (Newt. M.) G77	116	BD48
Colonsay Rd, G52	65	BG32
off Barfillan Dr		
Colonsay Rd, Pais. PA2	82	AT38
Colquhoun Av, G52	64	BC30
Colquhoun Dr, (Bears.) G61	29	BF16
Colson Pl, Bell. ML4	111	CY42
Colston Av, (Bishop.) G64	50	BV22
Colston Dr, (Bishop.) G64	50	BV22
Colston Gdns, (Bishop.) G64	50	BU22
Colston Gdns, Air. ML6	77	DE30
Colston Gro, (Bishop.) G64	50	BV22
Colston Path, (Bishop.) G64	50	BU22
Colston Pl, (Bishop.) G64	50	BU22
Colston Pl, Air. ML6	77	DE30
Colston Rd, (Bishop.) G64	50	BU22
Colston Rd, Air. ML6	77	DE30
Colston Ter, Air. ML6	77	DE30
Colt Av, Coat. ML5	74	CU28
Coltmuir Av, (Bishop.) G64	50	BU21
off Coltmuir Dr		
Coltmuir Cres, (Bishop.) G64	50	BU21
Coltmuir Dr, (Bishop.) G64	50	BU21
Coltmuir Gdns, (Bishop.) G64	50	BU21
Coltmuir St, G22	49	BR23
Coltness Dr, Bell. ML4	111	CX41
Coltness La, G33	71	CE30
Coltness St, G33	71	CE29
Coltpark Av, (Bishop.) G64	50	BU21
Coltpark La, (Bishop.) G64	50	BU21
Colt Pl, Coat. ML5	75	CW29
Coltsfoot Dr, G53	100	BD42
off Waukglen Dr		
Coltswood Ct, Coat. ML5	75	CW29
Coltswood Rd, Coat. ML5	75	CW28
Colt Ter, Coat. ML5	75	CW30
Columba, Clyde. G81	27	AZ19
off Onslow Rd		
Columba Cres, Moth. ML1	111	CZ43
Columba Path, (Blan.) G72	124	CL45
off Glenfruin Rd		
Columba St, G51	66	BK30
Columbia Pl, (E.Kil.) G75	135	BX53
Columbia Way, (E.Kil.) G75	135	BX53
Colvend Dr, (Ruther.) G73	105	BX42
Colvend La, G40	88	BV34
Colvend St, G40	88	BV34
Colville Ct, Moth. ML1	113	DE44
Colville Dr, (Ruther.) G73	105	BZ39
Colvilles Pl, (E.Kil.) G75	136	CD55
Colvilles Rd, (E.Kil.) G75	136	CC56
Colwood Av, G53	100	BC41
Colwood Gdns, G53	100	BC42
Colwood Path, G53	100	BC41
off Parkhouse Rd		
Colwood Pl, G53	100	BC42
Colwood Sq, G53	100	BC41
Colzium Vw, (Kilsyth) G65	7	CU5
Combe Quad, Bell. ML4	110	CU42
off Brandon Pl		
Comedie Rd, G33	53	CG25
Comely Bk, Ham. ML3	125	CP50
Comelypark Pl, G31	69	BW31
off Comelypark St		
Comelypark St, G31	68	BV31
Commerce St, G5	67	BR32
Commercial Ct, G5	68	BT32
Commercial Rd, G5	88	BS33
Commercial Rd, (Barr.) G78	99	AY42
Common Grn, Ham. ML3	126	CU49
Commonhead Av, Air. ML6	76	DB28
Commonhead La, Air. ML6	76	DB28
off Whinhall Av		
Commonhead Rd, G34	72	CM29
Commonhead St, Air. ML6	76	DB28
Commonside St, Air. ML6	76	DB28
Commore Av, (Barr.) G78	99	AZ44
Commore Dr, G13	46	BC22
Commore Pl, (Neil.) G78	114	AS47
Community Av, Bell. ML4	111	CX43
off Community Rd		
Community Pl, Bell. ML4	111	CX42
Community Rd, Bell. ML4	110	CV42
Comrie Cres, Ham. ML3	124	CM50
Comrie Rd, G33	53	CE24
Comrie St, G32	90	CD34
Conan Ct, (Camb.) G72	107	CF40
Cona St, (Thornlie.) G46	101	BG41
Condor Glen, (Holytown) Moth. ML1	96	DA38
Condorrat Ring Rd, (Cumb.) G67	21	CX14
Condorrat Rd, G67	39	CX17
Condorrat Rd, (Glenm.) Air. ML6	57	CZ22
Congress Rd, G3	66	BM30
Congress Way, G3	67	BN30
Conifer Pl, (Kirk.) G66	34	CD15
Conisborough Cl, G34	72	CJ28
Conisborough Path, G34	71	CH27
off Conisborough Rd		
Conisborough Rd, G34	71	CH27
Coniston, (E.Kil.) G75	134	BV56
off Ullswater		
Coniston Cres, Ham. ML3	140	CS55
Coniston Dr, Bell. ML4	111	CX42
Coniston Cres, (Baill.) G69	91	CH33
Connal St, G40	89	BX34
Connel Cres, (Miln.) G62	12	BL12
Conniston St, G32	70	CA30
Connollys Land, Clyde. G81	27	AW15
off Dumbarton Rd		
Connor Rd, (Barr.) G78	99	AX42
Connor St, Air. ML6	77	DG28
Conon Av, (Bears.) G61	29	BE18
Consett La, G33	71	CE29
Consett St, G33	71	CE29
Constarry Rd, (Kilsyth) G65	20	CU9
Contin Pl, G12	48	BM24
Convair Way, Renf. PA4	63	AZ28
off Lismore Av		
Conval Way, Pais. PA3	62	AT29
off Abbotsburn Way		
Cook St, G5	67	BQ32
Coo La, (Eagle.) G76	133	BN56
Coolgardie Grn, (E.Kil.) G75	135	BY54
off Westwood Hill		
Coolgardie Pl, (E.Kil.) G75	135	BY54
Cooperage Ct, G14	45	AZ23
Cooperage Pl, G3	66	BL29
Coopers Well La, G11	66	BL28
off Dumbarton Rd		
Coopers Well St, G11	66	BL28
Copenhagen Av, (E.Kil.) G75	136	CA55
Copland Pl, G51	66	BK30
Copland Quad, G51	66	BK31
Copland Rd, G51	66	BK31
Coplaw Ct, G42	87	BQ34
Coplaw St, G42	87	BQ34
Copperfield La, (Udd.) G71	93	CQ38
Coppice, The, Ersk. PA8	44	AT21
off Newshot Dr		
Coralmount Gdns, (Kirk.) G66	17	CG14
Corbett Ct, G32	90	CB34
Corbett St, G32	90	CB34
Corbie Pl, (Miln.) G62	11	BF11
Corbiston Way, (Cumb.) G67	22	DD11
Cordiner La, G44	87	BR38
Cordiner St, G44	87	BR38
Corkerhill Gdns, G52	85	BG33
Corkerhill Pl, G52	85	BF35
Corkerhill Rd, G52	85	BF36
Corlaich Av, G42	88	BU38
Corlaich Dr, G42	88	BU38
Cormack Av, (Torr.) G64	15	BY12
Cornaig Rd, G53	84	BD37
Cornalee Gdns, G53	84	BC37
Cornalee Pl, G53	84	BD38
Cornalee Rd, G53	84	BD37
Cornelia St, Moth. ML1	111	CX44
Cornhill Dr, Coat. ML5	74	CV29
Cornhill St, G21	51	BW24
Cornish Ct, Coat. ML5	74	CV29
off Gilmour Pl		
Cornock Cres, Clyde. G81	27	AX18
Cornock St, Clyde. G81	27	AX18
Corn St, G4	67	BR27
Cornwall Av, (Ruther.) G73	105	BZ40
Cornwall Ct, (E.Kil.) G74	136	CB52
off The Plaza Shop Cen		
Cornwall St, G41	66	BM32
Cornwall St, (E.Kil.) G74	136	CA52
Cornwall St S, G41	86	BM33
Cornwall Way, (E.Kil.) G74	136	CB52
off The Plaza Shop Cen		
Coronation Av, Lark. ML9	144	DC61
Coronation Cres, Lark. ML9	144	DC61

Coronation Pl, (Gart.) G69 55 CN22
Coronation Pl, Lark. ML9 144 DD61
Coronation Rd, Bell. ML4 112 DB41
Coronation Rd, Moth. ML1 112 DB41
Coronation Rd E, Moth. ML1 112 DB42
Coronation Way, (Bears.) G61 29 BH19
Corpach Pl, G34 72 CM28
Corra Linn, Ham. ML3 125 CQ50
Corran Av, (Newt. M.) G77 117 BE47
Corran St, G33 70 CB29
Correen Gdns, (Bears.) G61 10 BD14
Corrie Brae, (Kilsyth) G65 7 CS4
Corrie Ct, Ham. ML3 139 CP51
Corrie Dr, Moth. ML1 127 CX46
Corrie Dr, Pais. PA1 84 BA33
Corrie Gro, G44 103 BP41
Corrie Pl, (Lenz.) G66 35 CG17
Corrie Rd, (Kilsyth) G65 7 CS4
Corrie Vw, (Cumb.) G68 20 CV13
Corrieview Cotts, (Kilsyth) G65 19 CN9
  off Melrose Gdns
Corrie Way, Lark. ML9 144 DD59
Corrour Rd, G43 86 BM38
Corrour Rd, (Newt. M.) G77 117 BE47
Corsebar Av, Pais. PA2 82 AS35
Corsebar Cres, Pais. PA2 82 AS36
Corsebar Dr, Pais. PA2 82 AS35
Corsebar La, Pais. PA2 81 AR36
Corsebar Rd, Pais. PA2 81 AR36
Corsebar Way, Pais. PA2 82 AS34
Corseford Av, John. PA5 79 AE37
Corsehill Path, G34 72 CL29
Corsehill Pl, G34 72 CL29
Corsehill St, G34 72 CL29
Corselet Rd, G53 100 BD42
Corse Rd, G52 64 BA31
Corsewall Av, G32 91 CG34
Corsewall St, Coat. ML5 74 CU29
Corsford Dr, G53 101 BE39
Corsock Av, Ham. ML3 139 CN51
Corsock St, G31 69 BY30
Corston St, G33 69 BZ29
Cortachy Pl, (Bishop.) G64 33 BZ20
Coruisk Dr, (Clark.) G76 118 BM45
Coruisk Way, Pais. PA2 81 AN37
  off Spencer Dr
Corunna St, G3 67 BN29
Coshneuk Rd, G33 52 CD24
Cosy Neuk, Lark. ML9 145 DE60
Cottage Homes, (Newt. M.) G77 117 BF48
Cottar St, G20 49 BN22
Cotton Av, (Linw.) Pais. PA3 60 AK32
Cotton St, G40 88 BV35
Cotton St, Pais. PA1 82 AV33
Cotton Vale, Moth. ML1 113 DG44
Coulin Gdns, G22 50 BT25
Coulter Av, Coat. ML5 74 CU29
Countess Way, (Baill.) G69 73 CQ32
  off Park Rd
Counting Ho, The, Pais. PA1 81 AR34
  off Turners Av
County Av, (Camb.) G72 89 BZ38
County Pl, Pais. PA1 62 AU32
County Sq, Pais. PA1 62 AU32
Couper Pl, G4 5 BT28
Couper St, G4 5 BT28
Coursington Cres, Moth. ML1 128 DC46
Coursington Gdns, Moth. ML1 128 DB46
Coursington Pl, Moth. ML1 128 DB46
  off Albert St
Coursington Rd, Moth. ML1 128 DA46
Courthill, (Bears.) G61 29 BF15

Courthill Av, G44 103 BR40
Courthill Cres, (Kilsyth) G65 7 CU5
Coustonhill St, G43 86 BL38
  off Pleasance St
Coustonholm Rd, G43 86 BM37
Couther Quad, Air. ML6 76 DB27
Covanburn Av, Ham. ML3 140 CV52
Covenant Cres, Lark. ML9 144 DD59
Covenant Pl, Wis. ML2 143 DE51
Coventry Dr, G31 69 BX29
Cowal Cres, (Kirk.) G66 18 CK12
Cowal Dr, (Linw.) Pais. PA3 60 AJ32
Cowal Rd, G20 48 BK22
Cowal St, G20 48 BL22
Cowan Cl, (Barr.) G78 99 AZ41
Cowan Cres, (Barr.) G78 99 AZ43
Cowan La, G12 67 BN27
Cowan Rd, (Cumb.) G68 21 CX11
Cowan St, G12 67 BN27
Cowan Wilson Av, (Blan.) G72 124 CM45
Cowan Wynd, (Udd.) G71 93 CQ37
Cowcaddens Rd, G4 4 BR28
Cowcaddens St, G2 4 BR28
  off Renfield St
Cowden Dr, (Bishop.) G64 33 BW18
Cowdenhill Circ, G13 47 BF21
Cowdenhill Pl, G13 47 BF21
Cowdenhill Rd, G13 47 BF21
Cowden St, G51 65 BF30
Cowdray Cres, Renf. PA4 45 AZ26
Cowell Vw, Clyde. G81 27 AX18
  off Granville St
Cowgate, (Kirk.) G66 17 CE12
Cowglen Rd, G53 85 BE38
Cowlairs Rd, G21 50 BU25
Coxdale Av, (Kirk.) G66 16 CD13
Coxhill St, G21 50 BT26
Coxton Pl, G33 71 CF28
Coylton Cres, Ham. ML3 139 CN52
Coylton Rd, G43 103 BN40
Crabb Quad, Moth. ML1 111 CY44
  off Frood St
Cragdale, (E.Kil.) G74 121 BY50
Craggan Dr, G14 46 BB23
Crags Av, Pais. PA2 82 AV36
Crags Cres, Pais. PA2 82 AV35
Crags Rd, Pais. PA2 82 AV36
Cragwell Pk, (Clark.) G76 120 BU46
Craigallian Av, (Miln.) G62 12 BJ10
Craigallian Av, (Camb.) G72 107 CF42
Craiganour La, G43 102 BL39
Craiganour Pl, G43 102 BL39
  off Holeburn Rd
Craigard Pl, (Ruther.) G73 105 BZ42
Craigash Quad, (Miln.) G62 11 BG10
Craigash Rd, (Miln.) G62 11 BG11
Craigbank Cres, (Eagle.) G76 133 BN55
Craigbank Dr, G53 100 BC39
Craigbank Gro, (Eagle.) G76 133 BN55
Craigbank Rd, Lark. ML9 144 DC61
Craigbank St, Lark. ML9 144 DC60
Craigbarnet Av, (Torr.) G64 15 BW13
  off Allander Dr
Craigbarnet Cres, G33 52 CD25
Craigbarnet Rd, (Miln.) G62 11 BF11
Craigbo Av, G23 48 BM21
Craigbo Ct, G23 48 BM21
  off Craigbo Rd
Craigbo Dr, G23 48 BM21
  off Craigbo Rd
Craigbog Av, John. PA5 79 AF36
Craigbo Pl, G23 48 BM21
Craigbo Rd, G23 30 BM20

Craigbo St, G23 30 BM20
  off Craigbo Rd
Craigburn Ct, (Ashgill) Lark. 145 DH60
  ML9
Craigburn St, Ham. ML3 140 CT53
  off Tullymet Rd
Craig Cres, (Kirk.) G66 18 CK14
  off Burnbrae Rd
Craigdhu Av, (Miln.) G62 11 BH12
Craigdhu Av, Air. ML6 77 DG30
Craigdhu Rd, (Bears.) G61 11 BG13
Craigdhu Rd, (Miln.) G62 11 BH12
Craigdonald Pl, John. PA5 79 AH34
Craigellan Rd, G43 102 BM39
Craigelvan Av, (Cumb.) G67 38 CV15
Craigelvan Ct, (Cumb.) G67 38 CV15
Craigelvan Dr, (Cumb.) G67 38 CV15
Craigelvan Gdns, (Cumb.) G67 38 CV15
Craigelvan Gro, (Cumb.) G67 38 CV15
Craigelvan Pl, (Cumb.) G67 38 CV15
Craigelvan Vw, (Cumb.) G67 38 CV15
Craigenbay Cres, (Lenz.) G66 35 CG16
Craigenbay Rd, (Lenz.) G66 35 CF16
Craigenbay St, G21 51 BX25
Craigencart Ct, Clyde. G81 28 AV15
  off Gentle Row
Craigend Cres, (Miln.) G62 11 BH11
Craigend Dr, Coat. ML5 94 CS33
Craigend Dr W, (Miln.) G62 11 BG11
Craigendmuir Rd, G33 53 CG25
Craigendmuir St, G33 69 BZ27
Craigendon Oval, Pais. PA2 98 AS39
Craigendon Rd, Pais. PA2 82 AS38
Craigend Pl, G13 47 BG23
Craigend Rd, (Cumb.) G67 38 CU16
Craigends Dr, (Kilb.) John. PA10 78 AC34
Craigend St, G13 47 BG23
Craigend Vw, (Cumb.) G67 38 CV16
Craigenfeoch Av, John. PA5 79 AF36
Craigens Rd, Air. ML6 77 DH32
Craigfaulds Av, Pais. PA2 81 AR35
Craigfell Ct, Ham. ML3 139 CN51
Craigflower Gdns, G53 100 BC41
Craigflower Rd, G53 100 BC41
Craig Gdns, (Newt. M.) G77 117 BE49
Craighalbert Rd, (Cumb.) G68 21 CY10
Craighalbert Roundabout, 21 CY9
  (Cumb.) G68
Craighalbert Way, (Cumb.) G68 21 CY9
Craighall Quad, (Neil.) G78 114 AT47
Craighall Rd, G4 67 BR27
Craighead Av, G33 51 BZ26
Craighead Dr, (Miln.) G62 11 BE11
Craighead Rd, Bish. PA7 24 AK19
Craighead St, (Barr.) G78 99 AX43
Craighead St, Air. ML6 77 DG29
Craighead Way, (Barr.) G78 99 AX43
Craig Hill, (E.Kil.) G75 135 BY54
Craighill Dr, (Clark.) G76 118 BM47
Craighill Gro, (Clark.) G76 118 BM47
Craighirst Rd, (Miln.) G62 11 BF11
Craighlaw Av, (Eagle.) G76 132 BM51
Craighlaw Dr, (Eagle.) G76 132 BM51
Craighouse St, G33 70 CC28
Craigiebar Dr, Pais. PA2 82 AS37
Craigieburn Gdns, G20 48 BK21
Craigieburn Rd, (Cumb.) G67 22 DB12
Craigie Dr, (Newt. M.) G77 117 BG50
Craigiehall Av, Ersk. PA8 43 AQ22
Craigiehall Cres, Ersk. PA8 43 AQ22
Craigiehall Pl, G51 66 BM31
Craigiehall St, G51 66 BM31
  off Craigiehall Pl

Craigiehall Way, Ersk. PA8	43	AQ22
Craigie La, Lark. ML9	144	DD57
off Duncan Graham St		
Craigielea Ct, Renf. PA4	45	AY25
off Kirklandneuk Rd		
Craigielea Cres, (Miln.) G62	11	BG11
Craigielea Dr, Pais. PA3	61	AR31
Craigielea Pk, Renf. PA4	45	AY26
Craigielea Rd, Renf. PA4	45	AY26
Craigielea St, G31	69	BW29
Craigie Pk, (Lenz.) G66	35	CG16
Craigie St, G42	87	BQ35
Craigievar Pl, (Newt. M.) G77	116	BD48
Craigievar St, G33	71	CG27
Craigknowe Rd, (Blan.) G72	108	CL43
Craiglea Pl, Air. ML6	77	DE29
Craiglea Ter, (Plains) Air. ML6	59	DH26
Craigleith St, G32	70	CA31
Craiglinn, (Cumb.) G68	21	CW11
Craiglinn Pk Rd, (Cumb.) G68	21	CW12
Craiglinn Roundabout, (Cumb.) G68	21	CW12
Craiglockhart St, G33	71	CF27
Craigmaddie Gdns, (Torr.) G64	15	BW13
Craigmaddie Rd, (Miln.) G62	13	BQ13
Craigmaddie Ter La, G3	67	BN28
off Derby St		
Craigmarloch Av, (Torr.) G64	15	BX13
Craigmillar Av, (Miln.) G62	12	BK10
Craigmillar Rd, G42	87	BQ38
Craigmochan Av, Air. ML6	76	DB27
Craigmont Dr, G20	49	BN24
Craigmont St, G20	49	BN23
Craigmore Pl, Coat. ML5	94	CU34
off Haddington Way		
Craigmore Rd, (Bears.) G61	10	BD14
Craigmore St, G31	69	BY31
Craigmore Wynd, Lark. ML9	144	DD57
off Duncan Graham St		
Craigmount Av, Pais. PA2	98	AS39
Craigmount St, (Kirk.) G66	17	CF14
Craigmuir Cres, G52	64	BB31
Craigmuir Gdns, (Blan.) G72	124	CK47
off Craigmuir Rd		
Craigmuir Pl, G52	64	BA31
Craigmuir Rd, G52	64	BA31
Craigmuir Rd, (Blan.) G72	124	CK48
Craigneil St, G33	71	CG27
Craigneith Ct, (E.Kil.) G74	123	CG49
off Lammermoor		
Craignethan Gdns, G11	66	BK27
off Lawrie St		
Craignethan Rd, (Giff.) G46	118	BJ46
Craigneuk Av, Air. ML6	77	DE31
Craigneuk St, Moth. ML1	128	DD48
Craigneuk St, Wis. ML2	128	DD48
Craignure Cres, Air. ML6	77	DG30
Craignure Rd, (Ruther.) G73	105	BX42
Craigpark, G31	69	BW30
Craigpark Dr, G31	69	BW30
Craigpark Ter, G31	69	BW30
off Craigpark		
Craigpark Way, (Udd.) G71	93	CQ38
off Newton Dr		
Craig Pl, (Newt. M.) G77	116	BD48
Craig Rd, G44	103	BQ40
Craig Rd, (Neil.) G78	114	AT47
Craigs Av, Clyde. G81	27	AY15
Craigsheen Av, (Carm.) G76	120	BT46
Craigside Ct, (Cumb.) G68	20	CV14
Craigside Pl, (Cumb.) G68	20	CV14
Craigside Rd, (Cumb.) G68	20	CV14
Craigson Pl, Air. ML6	77	DH31

Craigstone Vw, (Kilsyth) G65	8	CV5
Craigston Pl, John. PA5	79	AH35
Craigston Rd, John. PA5	79	AG35
Craig St, (Blan.) G72	125	CN47
Craig St, Air. ML6	76	DB30
Craig St, Coat. ML6	94	CV33
Craigton Av, (Miln.) G62	11	BH11
Craigton Av, (Barr.) G78	100	BA44
Craigton Cres, (Newt. M.) G77	116	BD48
Craigton Dr, G51	65	BH31
Craigton Dr, (Newt. M.) G77	117	BE48
Craigton Dr, (Barr.) G78	100	BA44
Craigton Gdns, (Miln.) G62	11	BG10
Craigton Pl, G51	65	BG31
Craigton Pl, (Blan.) G72	108	CM44
Craigton Rd, G51	65	BH31
Craigton Rd, (Miln.) G62	11	BG10
Craigvale Cres, Air. ML6	77	DG30
Craigvicar Gdns, G32	91	CF33
Craigview Av, John. PA5	79	AF37
Craigview Rd, Moth. ML1	128	DB45
Craigview Ter, John. PA5	79	AF36
off Craigview Av		
Craigwell Av, (Ruther.) G73	105	BZ39
Crail St, G31	69	BZ32
Crammond Av, Coat. ML5	94	CS33
Cramond Av, Renf. PA4	64	BA27
Cramond St, G5	88	BT35
Cramond Ter, G32	70	CD32
Cranborne Rd, G12	48	BJ24
Cranbrooke Dr, G20	48	BM22
Cranston St, G3	4	BP29
Cranworth La, G12	48	BM26
Cranworth St, G12	48	BM26
Crarae Av, (Bears.) G61	29	BG19
Crarae Pl, (Newt. M.) G77	116	BC48
Crathes Ct, G44	103	BN41
Crathie Dr, G11	66	BJ27
Crathie Dr, (Glenm.) Air. ML6	58	DB25
Crathie La, G11	66	BJ27
off Exeter Dr		
Crathie Pl, (Newt. M.) G77	118	BK49
off Gleneagles Dr		
Crawford Av, (Lenz.) G66	35	CG18
Crawford Cres, (Udd.) G71	93	CN38
Crawford Cres, (Blan.) G72	108	CM44
Crawford Dr, G15	28	BB20
Crawford Dr, (E.Kil.) G74	136	CD51
Crawford Gdns, Moth. ML1	127	CY48
Crawford Hill, (E.Kil.) G74	136	CD51
off Crawford Dr		
Crawford La, G11	66	BJ27
off Crawford St		
Crawford Path, G11	66	BJ27
off Crawford St		
Crawford Rd, (Miln.) G62	11	BH9
Crawford St, G11	66	BJ27
Crawford St, Ham. ML3	125	CQ48
off Greenfield Rd		
Crawford St, Moth. ML1	127	CZ47
Crawfurd Dr, Pais. PA3	61	AR31
Crawfurd Gdns, (Ruther.) G73	105	BY41
Crawfurd Rd, (Ruther.) G73	105	BX41
Crawriggs Av, (Kirk.) G66	35	CF15
Craw Rd, Pais. PA2	82	AS34
Crebar Dr, (Barr.) G78	99	AY43
Crebar St, (Thornlie.) G46	101	BG41
Credon Dr, Air. ML6	76	DC32
Credon Gdns, (Ruther.) G73	105	BY41
Cree Av, (Bishop.) G64	33	BZ20
Cree Gdns, G32	70	CB32
Cree Pl, (E.Kil.) G75	135	BX52
Creighton Gro, (E.Kil.) G74	136	CA52

Creran Ct, Ham. ML3	139	CQ52
Creran Dr, Renf. PA4	45	AX25
Crescent, The (Clark.) G76	119	BQ48
Crescent, The, Clyde. G81	26	AU18
off Stewart St		
Crescent Ct, Clyde. G81	26	AU18
Crescent Rd, G13	46	BD24
Crescent Rd, G14	46	BD24
Cressdale Av, G45	104	BT43
Cressdale Ct, G45	104	BT43
Cressdale Dr, G45	104	BT43
Cressland Dr, G45	104	BT44
Cressland Pl, G45	104	BT44
Cresswell Gro, (Newt. M.) G77	117	BF50
Cresswell La, G12	48	BM26
Cresswell Pl, (Newt. M.) G77	131	BG51
Cresswell St, G12	48	BM26
Cressy St, G51	65	BG29
Crest Av, G13	46	BD21
Crestlea Av, Pais. PA2	82	AU37
Creswell Ter, (Udd.) G71	109	CN39
off Kylepark Dr		
Crichton Ct, G45	104	BV43
Crichton Pl, G21	50	BU25
off Crichton St		
Crichton St, G21	50	BU25
Crichton St, Coat. ML5	75	CW29
Crieff Av, (Chap.) Air. ML6	97	DF36
Crieff Ct, G3	4	BP29
off North St		
Criffell Gdns, G32	91	CF34
Criffell Rd, G32	91	CF33
Criffel Path, Moth. ML1	113	DE42
off Martin Pl		
Crighton Wynd, Bell. ML4	110	CT40
off Thomson Dr		
Crimea St, G2	4	BQ30
Crimond Pl, (Kilsyth) G65	7	CR4
Crinan Cres, Coat. ML5	74	CT28
Crinan Gdns, (Bishop.) G64	33	BY20
Crinan Pl, Bell. ML4	111	CX41
off Linnet Rd		
Crinan Pl, Coat. ML5	74	CT28
off Crinan Cres		
Crinan Rd, (Bishop.) G64	33	BY20
Crinan St, G31	69	BX29
Cripps Av, Clyde. G81	27	AZ20
Croft, Lark. ML9	144	DB59
Croftbank Av, (Both.) G71	109	CR44
Croftbank Cres, (Both.) G71	109	CR44
Croftbank Cres, (Udd.) G71	109	CP39
Croftbank Gate, (Both.) G71	109	CR44
Croftbank St, G21	50	BV25
Croftburn Dr, G44	104	BT41
Croftcot Av, Bell. ML4	110	CV42
Croftcroighn Rd, G33	70	CD28
Croftend Av, G44	104	BU39
Croftfoot Cres, G45	105	BW41
Croftfoot Dr, G45	104	BV41
Croftfoot Pl, (Gart.) G69	55	CQ23
off Inchnock Av		
Croftfoot Quad, G45	104	BU41
Croftfoot Rd, G44	104	BT41
Croftfoot Rd, G45	104	BT41
Croftfoot St, G45	105	BW41
off Tormusk Rd		
Croftfoot Ter, G45	104	BV41
Crofthead Cotts, (Neil.) G78	114	AS46
Crofthead Cres, Bell. ML4	110	CV42
Crofthead Pl, (Newt. M.) G77	117	BG50
Crofthead Pl, Bell. ML4	110	CV42
Crofthead St, (Udd.) G71	109	CP40
Crofthill Av, (Udd.) G71	109	CP39

Street	Page	Grid
Crofthill Rd, G44	104	BU40
Crofthouse Dr, G44	104	BU41
Croftmont Av, G44	104	BU41
Croftmoraig Av, (Mood.) G69	37	CQ17
Crofton Av, G44	104	BT41
Croftpark Av, G44	104	BS41
Croftpark Cres, (Blan.) G72	125	CN47
Croftpark St, Bell. ML4	111	CW39
Croft Pl, Lark. ML9	144	DB58
Croft Rd, (Torr.) G64	14	BU13
Croft Rd, (Camb.) G72	106	CD40
Croft Rd, (E.Kil.) G75	136	CA54
Croft Rd, Lark. ML9	144	DB58
Croftside Av, G44	104	BU41
Croftspar Av, G32	71	CE31
Croftspar Ct, G32	71	CF31
off Croftspar Gro		
Croftspar Dr, G32	71	CE31
Croftspar Gate, G32	71	CF31
off Croftspar Gro		
Croftspar Gro, G32	71	CE31
Croftspar Pl, G32	71	CE31
Croft Way, Renf. PA4	63	AZ28
Croftwood, (Bishop.) G64	33	BW17
Croftwood Av, G44	104	BT41
Croftwood Rd, Ham. ML3	140	CS52
Croft Wynd, (Udd.) G71	109	CQ39
Crogal Cres, (Chap.) Air. ML6	97	DF35
Cromalt Cres, (Bears.) G61	11	BE13
Cromarty Av, G43	103	BP39
Cromarty Av, (Bishop.) G64	33	BZ19
Cromarty Cres, (Bears.) G61	11	BH14
Cromarty Gdns, (Clark.) G76	103	BQ44
Cromarty Pl, (Chry.) G69	36	CM20
Cromarty Pl, (E.Kil.) G74	123	CE50
Cromarty Rd, Air. ML6	96	DB33
Crombie Gdns, (Baill.) G69	92	CJ34
Cromdale St, G51	65	BG31
Cromdale Way, (New Stev.) Moth. ML1	112	DC43
Cromer Gdns, G20	49	BP24
Cromer La, Pais. PA3	62	AT29
off Abbotsburn Way		
Cromer Way, Pais. PA3	62	AT30
off Mosslands Rd		
Crompton Av, G44	103	BR40
Cromptons Gro, Pais. PA1	81	AR34
Cromwell La, G20	67	BQ27
Cromwell St, G20	67	BQ27
Crona Dr, Ham. ML3	125	CN49
Cronberry Quad, G52	84	BB34
Cronberry Ter, G52	84	BB34
Cronin Pl, Bell. ML4	95	CX38
Cronulla Pl, (Kilsyth) G65	8	CV5
Crookedshields Rd, (Camb.) G72	122	CC46
Crookedshields Rd, (E.Kil.) G74	122	CC46
Crookfur Rd, (Newt. M.) G77	117	BE47
Crookston Av, G52	84	BC33
Crookston Ct, G52	84	BC33
Crookston Dr, G52	84	BB33
Crookston Dr, Pais. PA1	84	BB33
Crookston Gdns, G52	84	BB33
Crookston Gro, G52	84	BC33
Crookstonhill Path, G52	84	BB33
off Ralston Pl		
Crookston Path, G52	84	BB33
off Crookston Quad		
Crookston Pl, G52	84	BB33
Crookston Quad, G52	84	BB33
Crookston Rd, G52	84	BB34
Crookston Rd, G53	84	BC37
Crosbie Dr, Pais. PA2	81	AN38
Crosbie La, G20	48	BL21
Crosbie St, G20	48	BL21
Crosbie Wd, Pais. PA2	81	AR36
Cross, The, Pais. PA1	62	AU32
Cross Arthurlie St, (Barr.) G78	99	AX42
Crossbank Av, G42	88	BU36
Crossbank Dr, G42	88	BT36
Crossbank Rd, G42	88	BT36
Crossbank Ter, G42	88	BT36
Crossburn Av, (Miln.) G62	11	BH12
Cross Ct, (Bishop.) G64	32	BV20
off Kenmure Av		
Crossdykes, (Kirk.) G66	18	CJ14
Crossflat Cres, Pais. PA1	63	AW32
Crossford Dr, G23	31	BN20
off Broughton Rd		
Crossgate, (Kirk.) G66	17	CF12
Cross Gates, Bell. ML4	111	CW41
Crossgates St, Lark. ML9	144	DB57
Crosshill Av, G42	87	BR36
Crosshill Av, (Kirk.) G66	35	CF15
Crosshill Dr, (Ruther.) G73	105	BX39
Crosshill Rd, (Bishop.) G64	33	BY16
Crosshill Rd, (Kirk.) G66	34	CD18
Crosshill Sq, (Baill.) G69	92	CL33
off Bredisholm Rd		
Crosshill St, Air. ML6	76	DB30
Cross Hill St, Coat. ML5	93	CR33
off Aitkenhead Av		
Crosshill St, Moth. ML1	128	DB47
Crosshouse Rd, (E.Kil.) G75	135	BW56
Crosslees Ct, (Thornlie.) G46	102	BJ41
off Crosslees Dr		
Crosslees Dr, (Thornlie.) G46	101	BH42
Crosslees Pk, (Thornlie.) G46	101	BH42
Crosslees Rd, (Thornlie.) G46	101	BH43
Crosslee St, G52	65	BF32
Crossloan Rd, G51	65	BH30
Crossloan Ter, G51	65	BH30
Crossmill Av, (Barr.) G78	99	AZ41
Crossmyloof Gdns, G41	86	BM36
Cross Orchard Way, Bell. ML4	111	CW40
off Main St		
Crosspoint Dr, G23	31	BN20
off Invershiel Rd		
Cross Rd, Pais. PA2	81	AR35
Cross Stone Pl, Moth. ML1	128	DB47
off Airbles St		
Cross St, G32	91	CE36
Cross St, Pais. PA1	82	AS33
Crosstobs Rd, G53	84	BC36
Crossveggate, (Miln.) G62	12	BK12
Crossview Av, (Baill.) G69	72	CM32
Crossview Pl, (Baill.) G69	72	CM32
Crovie Rd, G53	84	BC36
Crow Av, Moth. ML1	112	DD40
Crowflats Rd, (Udd.) G71	109	CN39
off Lady Isle Cres		
Crowflats Vw, (Udd.) G71	94	CS36
Crowhall Dr, G32	71	CG31
Crowhill Cres, Air. ML6	76	DB27
Crowhill Rd, (Bishop.) G64	50	BV21
Crowhill St, G22	50	BS23
Crow La, G13	47	BH24
Crowlin Cres, G33	70	CD29
Crown Av, Clyde. G81	27	AW18
Crown Circ, G12	48	BL26
Crown Ct, G1	5	BS30
off Virginia St		
Crown Gdns, G12	48	BL26
Crownhall Pl, G32	71	CE32
Crownhall Rd, G32	71	CE32
Crown Mans, G11	48	BK26
off North Gardner St		
Crownpoint Rd, G40	68	BV32
Crown Rd N, G12	48	BK26
Crown Rd S, G12	48	BK26
Crown St, G5	68	BS32
Crown St, (Baill.) G69	91	CH34
Crown St, (Calder.) Air. ML6	96	DD34
Crown St, Coat. ML5	75	CY30
Crown Ter, G12	48	BK26
Crow Rd, G11	48	BJ26
Crow Rd, G13	47	BH24
Crowwood Cres, (Calder.) Air. ML6	96	DD35
Crowwood Dr, Air. ML6	77	DF29
Crow Wd Rd, (Chry.) G69	54	CK22
Crowwood Rd, (Calder.) Air. ML6	96	DD35
Crowwood Roundabout, (Stepps) G33	53	CH22
Crow Wd Ter, (Chry.) G69	54	CK22
Croy, (E.Kil.) G74	121	BZ50
Croy Av, (Newt. M.) G77	118	BJ48
Croy Pl, G21	51	BY24
Croy Rd, G21	51	BY24
Croy Rd, Coat. ML5	94	CU33
Cruachan Av, Pais. PA2	82	AU37
Cruachan Av, Renf. PA4	63	AY28
Cruachan Dr, (Newt. M.) G77	117	BH50
Cruachan Dr, (Barr.) G78	99	AY44
Cruachan Rd, (Bears.) G61	10	BD14
Cruachan Rd, (Ruther.) G73	105	BZ42
Cruachan St, (Thornlie.) G46	101	BH41
Cruachan Way, (Barr.) G78	99	AY44
Cruden St, G51	65	BH31
Crum Av, (Thornlie.) G46	102	BJ42
Crusader Av, G13	29	BF20
Cubie St, G40	68	BV32
Cuckoo Way, Moth. ML1	112	DD40
Cuilhill Rd, (Baill.) G69	73	CP30
Cuillin Pl, (Chap.) Air. ML6	97	DH36
Cuillin Pl, Lark. ML9	145	DE59
off Burnhead Rd		
Cuillins, The (Mood.) G69	37	CQ17
Cuillins, The (Udd.) G71	93	CN36
Cuillins Rd, (Ruther.) G73	105	BZ42
Cuillin Way, (Barr.) G78	99	AY43
Cuilmuir Ter, (Kilsyth) G65	20	CV9
Cuilmuir Vw, (Kilsyth) G65	8	CV8
Culbin Dr, G13	46	BB21
Cullen, Ersk. PA8	25	AQ18
Cullen La, (E.Kil.) G75	136	CA54
off Cullen Rd		
Cullen Pl, (Udd.) G71	93	CQ37
Cullen Rd, (E.Kil.) G75	135	BZ54
Cullen Rd, Moth. ML1	127	CY48
Cullen St, G32	90	CC33
Cullochrig Rd, Air. ML6	58	DB21
Culloch Rd, (Bears.) G61	11	BE13
Culloden Av, Bell. ML4	111	CZ41
Culloden St, G31	69	BX29
Culrain Gdns, G32	70	CC32
Culrain St, G32	70	CC32
Culross Hill, (E.Kil.) G74	135	BZ52
Culross La, G32	91	CE33
Culross Pl, (E.Kil.) G74	135	BZ52
Culross Pl, Coat. ML5	74	CV30
Culross St, G32	91	CE33
Culross Way, (Mood.) G69	37	CQ18
Cult Rd, (Lenz.) G66	35	CG17
Cults St, G51	65	BH31
Culvain Av, (Bears.) G61	10	BD14
Culzean, (Glenm.) Air. ML6	58	DB24

Culzean Av, Coat. ML5	94	CU33
Culzean Cres, (Baill.) G69	92	CJ33
Culzean Cres, (Newt. M.) G77	118	BJ48
Culzean Dr, G32	91	CF33
Culzean Dr, (E.Kil.) G74	121	BZ50
Culzean Dr, (New.) Moth. ML1	113	DE43
Culzean Pl, (E.Kil.) G74	121	BZ50
Cumberland Pl, G5	88	BS33
Cumberland Pl, Coat. ML5	94	CS33
Cumberland St, G5	67	BR32
Cumbernauld Rd, G31	69	BX30
Cumbernauld Rd, G33	69	BZ28
Cumbernauld Rd, (Cumb.) G67	38	CT17
Cumbernauld Rd, (Chry.) G69	54	CJ22
Cumbernauld Shop Cen, (Cumb.) G67	22	DB11
Cumbrae, (E.Kil.) G74	137	CE52
Cumbrae Ct, Clyde. G81	27	AX19
Cumbrae Cres, Coat. ML5	76	DA32
Cumbrae Dr, Moth. ML1	127	CY45
Cumbrae Pl, Coat. ML5	96	DA33
Cumbrae Rd, Pais. PA2	82	AU38
Cumbrae Rd, Renf. PA4	63	AZ28
Cumbrae St, G33	70	CC29
Cumlodden Dr, G20	48	BL22
Cumming Dr, G42	87	BR37
Cumnock Dr, (Barr.) G78	99	AZ44
Cumnock Dr, Air. ML6	96	DC33
off Maybole Dr		
Cumnock Dr, Ham. ML3	138	CM52
Cumnock Rd, G33	52	CA23
Cunard Ct, Clyde. G81	45	AX21
Cunard St, Clyde. G81	45	AX21
Cunningair Dr, Moth. ML1	128	DA49
Cunningham Dr, (Giff.) G46	103	BN42
Cunningham Dr, Clyde. G81	26	AV15
Cunninghame Rd, (E.Kil.) G74	136	CA51
Cunninghame Rd, (Kilb.) John. PA10	78	AD34
Cunningham Rd, G52	64	BB29
Cunningham Rd, (Ruther.) G73	89	BY36
Cunningham St, Moth. ML1	127	CY47
Cuparhead Av, Coat. ML5	94	CT33
Curfew Rd, G13	29	BF20
Curle St, G14	65	BF27
Curlew Pl, John. PA5	79	AE38
Curling Cres, G44	88	BS38
Curlingmire, (E.Kil.) G75	136	CA55
Curran Av, Wis. ML2	143	DG52
Currie Pl, G20	49	BP23
Currie St, G20	49	BN23
Curtis Av, G44	88	BU38
Curtis Av, (Ruther.) G73	88	BS37
Curzon St, G20	49	BN23
Custom Ho Quay, G1	5	BS31
off Clyde St		
Cut, The (Udd.) G71	109	CP40
Cuthbertson St, G42	87	BQ35
Cuthbert St, (Udd.) G71	93	CR38
Cuthelton Dr, G31	90	CA33
Cuthelton St, G31	89	BZ33
Cuthelton Ter, G31	89	BZ33
Cypress Av, (Udd.) G71	93	CR37
Cypress Av, (Blan.) G72	124	CL45
Cypress Ct, (Kirk.) G66	34	CD15
Cypress Ct, (E.Kil.) G75	135	BY56
Cypress Ct, Ham. ML3	140	CU51
Cypress Cres, (E.Kil.) G75	135	BY56
Cypress Pl, (E.Kil.) G75	135	BY56
Cypress St, G22	50	BT24
Cypress Way, (Camb.) G72	107	CH41
Cyprus Av, (Elder.) John. PA5	80	AK36
Cyprus Gro, (Baill.) G69	73	CR31

Cyril St, Pais. PA1	83	AW33

D

Daer Av, Renf. PA4	64	BA28
Daer Wk, Lark. ML9	144	DC61
Daer Way. Ham. ML3	125	CQ50
Daffodil Way, Moth. ML1	128	DA45
off Alyssum Cres		
Dairsie Ct, G44	103	BP41
off Clarkston Rd		
Dairsie Gdns, (Bishop.) G64	51	BZ21
Dairsie St, G44	103	BP41
Daisy St, G42	87	BR36
Dakota Way, Renf. PA4	63	AZ28
Dalbeattie Braes, (Chap.) Air. ML6	97	DG35
Dalbeth Pl, G32	90	CB35
Dalbeth Rd, G32	90	CB35
Dalcharn Path, G34	72	CJ29
off Kildermorie Rd		
Dalcharn Pl, G34	72	CJ29
off Kildermorie Rd		
Dalcraig Cres, (Blan.) G72	108	CL43
Dalcross La, G11	66	BL27
off Byres Rd		
Dalcross Pas, G11	66	BL27
off Dalcross St		
Dalcross St, G11	66	BL27
Dalcruin Gdns, (Mood.) G69	37	CQ17
Daldowie Av, G32	91	CF34
Daldowie Rd, (Udd.) G71	92	CJ35
Daldowie St, Coat. ML5	94	CU34
Dale Av, (E.Kil.) G75	135	BY54
Dale Ct, Wis. ML2	143	DE51
Dale Dr, Moth. ML1	112	DC41
Dale Path, G40	88	BV33
Dale St, G40	88	BV33
Daleview Av, G12	48	BK23
Daleview Dr, (Clark.) G76	118	BM47
Daleview Gro, (Clark.) G76	118	BM47
Dale Way, (Ruther.) G73	105	BX41
Dalfoil Ct, Pais. PA1	84	BB33
Dalgarroch Av, Clyde. G81	46	BA21
Dalgleish Av, Clyde. G81	26	AU15
Dalhousie Gdns, (Bishop.) G64	32	BV19
Dalhousie La, G3	4	BQ28
Dalhousie Rd, (Kilb.) John. PA10	78	AD35
Dalhousie St, G3	4	BQ28
Dalilea Dr, G34	72	CM28
Dalilea Pl, G34	72	CM28
Dalintober St, G5	67	BQ32
Dalkeith Av, G41	86	BK33
Dalkeith Av, (Bishop.) G64	33	BX18
Dalkeith Rd, (Bishop.) G64	33	BX17
Dalmacoulter Rd, Air. ML6	58	DD26
Dalmahoy St, G32	70	CA30
Dalmally St, G20	49	BP26
Dalmarnock Br, G40	89	BX35
Dalmarnock Br, (Ruther.) G73	89	BX35
Dalmarnock Ct, G40	89	BX34
Dalmarnock Dr, G40	88	BV33
Dalmarnock Rd, G40	88	BV33
Dalmarnock Rd, (Ruther.) G73	89	BX35
Dalmarnock Rd Trd Est, (Ruther.) G73	89	BX36
Dalmary Dr, Pais. PA1	63	AX31
Dalmellington Ct, (E.Kil.) G74	135	BZ51
off Dalmellington Dr		
Dalmellington Ct, Ham. ML3	138	CM52
Dalmellington Dr, G53	84	BC37
Dalmellington Dr, (E.Kil.) G74	135	BZ51
Dalmellington Rd, G53	84	BC37

Dalmeny Av, (Giff.) G46	102	BL42
Dalmeny Dr, (Barr.) G78	99	AW43
Dalmeny Dr, Ham. ML3	140	CT51
off Edward St		
Dalmeny St, G5	88	BU35
Dalmuir Ct, Clyde. G81	26	AU18
Dalnair Pl, (Miln.) G62	11	BF11
Dalnair St, G3	66	BL28
Dalness Pas, G32	90	CC33
off Ochil St		
Dalness St, G32	90	CC34
Dalnottar Av, (Old Kil.) G60	25	AR15
Dalnottar Dr, (Old Kil.) G60	25	AR16
Dalnottar Gdns, (Old Kil.) G60	25	AR15
Dalnottar Hill Rd, (Old Kil.) G60	25	AR15
Dalnottar Ter, (Old Kil.) G60	25	AR15
Dalreoch Av, (Baill.) G69	72	CL32
Dalreoch Path, (Baill.) G69	72	CL31
off Dalreoch Av		
Dalriada Cres, Moth. ML1	111	CZ44
Dalriada Dr, (Torr.) G64	15	BY13
Dalriada St, G40	89	BY33
Dalry Gdns, Ham. ML3	138	CM51
Dalrymple Dr, (E.Kil.) G74	122	CA50
Dalrymple Dr, (Newt. M.) G77	118	BJ49
Dalrymple Dr, Coat. ML5	74	CV32
Dalry Pl, (Chap.) Air. ML6	97	DG36
Dalry Rd, (Udd.) G71	93	CR38
Dalry St, G32	90	CD33
Dalserf Ct, G31	69	BX32
Dalserf Cres, (Giff.) G46	102	BK44
Dalserf Gdns, G31	69	BX32
Dalserf Path, Lark. ML9	145	DE60
off Bannockburn Dr		
Dalserf St, G31	69	BX32
Dalsetter Av, G15	28	BB19
Dalsetter Pl, G15	28	BC19
Dalshannon Pl, (Cumb.) G67	21	CW14
Dalshannon Rd, (Cumb.) G67	21	CX14
Dalshannon Vw, (Cumb.) G67	21	CX14
Dalshannon Way, (Cumb.) G67	21	CW14
Dalsholm Av, G20	48	BK21
Dalsholm Ind Est, G20	48	BK22
Dalsholm Rd, G20	48	BK22
Dalskeith Av, Pais. PA3	61	AQ32
Dalskeith Cres, Pais. PA3	61	AQ32
Dalskeith Rd, Pais. PA3	81	AQ33
Dalswinton Path, G34	72	CM29
Dalswinton Pl, G34	72	CL29
off Dalswinton St		
Dalswinton St, G34	72	CL29
Dalton Av, Clyde. G81	28	BA20
Dalton Hill, Ham. ML3	138	CM51
Dalton St, G31	70	CA32
Dalveen Ct, (Barr.) G78	99	AY44
Dalveen Dr, (Udd.) G71	93	CN37
Dalveen Quad, Coat. ML5	75	CZ32
Dalveen St, G32	70	CB32
Dalveen Way, (Ruther.) G73	105	BY42
Dalwhinnie Av, (Blan.) G72	108	CL43
Daly Gdns, (Blan.) G72	109	CN44
Dalzell Av, Moth. ML1	128	DC49
Dalzell Dr, Moth. ML1	128	DC49
Dalziel Dr, G41	86	BL34
Dalziel Quad, G41	86	BL34
Dalziel Rd, G52	64	BB29
Dalziel St, Ham. ML3	125	CR49
Dalziel St, Moth. ML1	128	DB46
Damshot Cres, G53	85	BF36
Damshot Rd, G53	85	BF38
Danby Rd, (Baill.) G69	91	CH33
Danes Av, G14	47	BE25
Danes Cres, G14	46	BD24

Name	Page	Grid
Danes Dr, G14	46	BD24
Danes La N, G14	47	BE25
off Upland Rd		
Danes La S, G14	47	BE25
off Verona Av		
Daniel McLaughlin Pl, (Kirk.) G66	17	CG12
Dargarvel Av, G41	86	BK33
Dargarvel Path, G41	86	BJ34
off Dumbreck Av		
Dargavel Av, Bish. PA7	24	AK19
Dargavel Rd, Bish. PA7	24	AL20
Dargavel Rd, Ersk. PA8	24	AM20
Darkwood Ct, Pais. PA3	61	AR31
off Darkwood Cres		
Darkwood Cres, Pais. PA3	61	AR31
Darkwood Dr, Pais. PA3	61	AR31
off Darkwood Cres		
Darleith St, G32	70	CB32
Darley Rd, (Cumb.) G68	9	DA8
Darnaway Av, G33	71	CF27
Darnaway Dr, G33	71	CF27
Darnaway St, G33	71	CF27
Darngavel Ct, Air. ML6	75	CZ29
off Monkscourt Av		
Darngavil Rd, Air. ML6	59	DG23
Darnick St, G21	51	BX26
Darnley Cres, (Bishop.) G64	32	BV18
Darnley Gdns, G41	87	BN35
Darnley Ind Est, G53	100	BD41
Darnley Mains Rd, G53	101	BE42
Darnley Path, (Thornlie.) G46	101	BG40
off Kennisholm Av		
Darnley Pl, G41	87	BN35
off Darnley Rd		
Darnley Rd, G41	87	BN35
Darnley Rd, (Barr.) G78	99	AZ42
Darnley St, G41	87	BP35
Darroch, Ersk. PA8	25	AP18
Darroch Way, (Cumb.) G67	22	DC10
Dartford St, G22	49	BR26
Darvel Cres, Pais. PA1	63	AZ32
Darvel Dr, (Newt. M.) G77	118	BJ48
Darwin Pl, Clyde. G81	26	AT17
Darwin Rd, (E.Kil.) G75	135	BY53
Davaar, (E.Kil.) G74	137	CE52
Davaar Dr, Coat. ML5	74	CT30
Davaar Dr, Moth. ML1	111	CY43
Davaar Dr, Pais. PA2	82	AU38
Davaar Pl, (Newt. M.) G77	117	BE47
Davaar Rd, Renf. PA4	63	AZ28
Davaar St, G40	89	BX33
Dava St, G51	66	BJ30
Dave Barrie Av, Lark. ML9	142	DB56
Daventry Dr, G12	48	BJ24
off Dorchester Pl		
David Donnelly Pl, (Kirk.) G66	17	CE13
off Catherine St		
David Gray Dr, (Kirk.) G66	18	CJ12
David Pl, (Baill.) G69	91	CH33
David Pl, Pais. PA3	63	AX30
Davidson Cres, (Kilsyth) G65	19	CP10
Davidson Gdns, G14	47	BG25
off Westland Dr		
Davidson Pl, G32	71	CE31
Davidson St, G40	89	BW35
Davidson St, Air. ML6	76	DB29
Davidson St, Clyde. G81	46	BA21
Davidson St, Coat. ML5	95	CX33
Davidston Pl, (Kirk.) G66	35	CH17
off Netherhouse Av		
David St, G40	69	BW32
David St, Coat. ML5	75	CY30
David Way, Pais. PA3	63	AX30
Davieland Rd, (Giff.) G46	102	BJ44
Davie's Acre, (E.Kil.) G74	120	BV49
Davies Quad, Moth. ML1	111	CZ43
off Kinloch Dr		
Davies Sq, Clyde. G81	27	AW15
Davington Dr, Ham. ML3	138	CM51
Daviot St, G51	65	BF31
Dawson Av, (E.Kil.) G75	135	BX52
Dawson Pl, G4	49	BR26
Dawson Rd, G4	49	BR26
Deaconsbank Av, (Thornlie.) G46	101	BF44
Deaconsbank Cres, (Thornlie.) G46	101	BF44
Deaconsbank Gdns, (Thornlie.) G46 off Deaconsbank Av	101	BG44
Deaconsbank Gro, (Thornlie.) G46	101	BG44
Deaconsbank Pl, (Thornlie.) G46	101	BF44
Deacons Rd, (Kilsyth) G65	7	CT5
Dealston Rd, (Barr.) G78	99	AX41
Deanbrae St, (Udd.) G71	109	CP39
Dean Cres, (Chry.) G69	36	CM20
Dean Cres, Ham. ML3	140	CS52
Deanfield Quad, G52	64	BB31
Dean Pk Dr, (Camb.) G72	107	CF41
Dean Pk Rd, Renf. PA4	64	BA27
Deans Av, (Camb.) G72	107	CF42
Deanside La, G4	5	BT30
off Rottenrow		
Deanside Rd, G52	64	BC29
Deanston Av, (Barr.) G78	99	AX44
Deanston Dr, G41	86	BM37
Deanstone Pl, Coat. ML5	95	CZ34
Deanstone Wk, Coat. ML5	95	CZ35
Deanston Gdns, (Barr.) G78	99	AX44
Deanston Gro, Coat. ML5	94	CU34
off Ellismuir St		
Deanston Pk, (Barr.) G78	99	AX44
Dean St, Bell. ML4	111	CX40
Dean St, Clyde. G81	27	AY20
Deanwood Av, G44	103	BP42
Deanwood Rd, G44	103	BP42
Dechmont, (E.Kil.) G75	135	BZ56
Dechmont Av, (Camb.) G72	107	CF42
Dechmont Av, Moth. ML1	127	CY46
Dechmont Cotts, (Camb.) G72	107	CH42
Dechmont Gdns, (Udd.) G71	93	CN36
off Watling St		
Dechmont Gdns, (Blan.) G72	108	CL44
Dechmont Pl, (Camb.) G72	107	CF42
Dechmont Rd, (Udd.) G71	93	CN36
off Watling St		
Dechmont St, G31	69	BY32
Dechmont St, Ham. ML3	140	CS51
Dechmont Vw, (Udd.) G71	93	CQ38
Dechmont Vw, Bell. ML4	110	CV42
off Caledonian Av		
Dee Av, Pais. PA2	81	AP35
Dee Av, Renf. PA4	46	BA26
Deedes St, Air. ML6	75	CZ31
Dee Dr, Pais. PA2	81	AP36
Dee Path, Lark. ML9	144	DC61
off Riverside Rd		
Dee Path, Moth. ML1	112	DD40
off Deveron Rd		
Deep Dale, (E.Kil.) G74	121	BY50
Deepdene Rd, (Bears.) G61	29	BF18
Deepdene Rd, (Chry.) G69	37	CP19
Dee Pl, (E.Kil.) G75	134	BU54
Dee Pl, John. PA5	79	AE37
Deerdykes Ct N, (Cumb.) G68	38	CU15
Deerdykes Ct S, (Cumb.) G68	38	CU16
Deerdykes Pl, (Cumb.) G68	38	CU15
Deerdykes Rd, (Cumb.) G68	38	CT16
Deerdykes Vw, (Cumb.) G68	38	CT16
Deer Pk Ct, Ham. ML3	140	CT54
Deer Pk Pl, Ham. ML3	140	CU54
off Deer Pk Ct		
Deeside Pl, Coat. ML5	95	CZ33
off Paddock St		
Dee St, G33	69	BZ28
Dee St, Coat. ML5	74	CT27
Dee Ter, Ham. ML3	139	CR53
Delhi Av, Clyde. G81	26	AS17
Dell, The (Newt. M.) G77	118	BK48
Dell, The, Bell. ML4	111	CZ42
Dellburn St, Moth. ML1	128	DB48
Delny Pl, G33	71	CG30
Delvin Rd, G44	103	BQ39
Dempsey Rd, Bell. ML4	110	CV42
Den Bak Av, Ham. ML3	139	CQ51
Denbeck St, G32	70	CB32
Denbrae St, G32	70	CB32
Dene Wk, (Bishop.) G64	51	BY21
Denewood Av, Pais. PA2	82	AT37
Denham St, G22	49	BR26
Denholm Cres, (E.Kil.) G75	136	CA53
Denholm Dr, (Giff.) G46	102	BL44
Denholm Gdns, (E.Kil.) G75	136	CB53
off Telford Rd		
Denholm Ter, Ham. ML3	125	CN50
Denmark St, G22	50	BS25
Denmilne Gdns, G34	72	CL30
Denmilne Path, G34	72	CL30
Denmilne Pl, G34	72	CL30
Denmilne Rd, (Baill.) G69	72	CM30
Denmilne St, G34	72	CL30
Dentdale, (E.Kil.) G74	121	BY50
Deramore Av, (Giff.) G46	118	BJ46
Derby St, G3	67	BN29
Derby Ter La, G3	67	BN28
Derwent Dr, Coat. ML5	74	CS27
Derwent St, G22	49	BR25
Derwentwater, (E.Kil.) G75	134	BV55
Despard Av, G32	91	CF33
Despard Gdns, G32	91	CG33
Deveron Av, (Giff.) G46	102	BM43
Deveron Cres, Ham. ML3	124	CM49
Deveron Rd, (Bears.) G61	29	BE19
Deveron Rd, (E.Kil.) G74	136	CC52
Deveron Rd, Moth. ML1	112	DD39
Deveron St, G33	69	BZ28
Deveron St, Coat. ML5	74	CS28
Devlin Gro, (Blan.) G72	125	CN46
Devol Cres, G53	84	BD37
Devondale Av, (Blan.) G72	108	CM44
Devon Dr, Bish. PA7	24	AL18
Devon Gdns, (Bishop.) G64	32	BV18
Devonhill Av, Ham. ML3	140	CT54
Devon Pl, G41	87	BR33
Devonport Pk, (E.Kil.) G75	135	BW54
Devonshire Gdns, G12	48	BK25
Devonshire Gdns La, G12	48	BK25
off Hyndland Rd		
Devonshire Ter, G12	48	BK25
Devonshire Ter La, G12	48	BK25
Devon St, G5	87	BR33
Devonview Pl, Air. ML6	76	DB31
Devonview St, Air. ML6	76	DB30
Devon Wk, (Cumb.) G68	20	CU13
Devon Way, Moth. ML1	127	CX47
Dewar Cl, (Udd.) G71	93	CQ36
Diamond St, Bell. ML4	111	CW41

Diana Av, G13	46	BD21
Diana Quad, Moth. ML1	112	DB40
Dickens Av, Clyde. G81	26	AV17
Dickens Gro, (New.) Moth. ML1	113	DF43
off Carroll Cres		
Dickson Path, Bell. ML4	110	CV43
off McCallum Gdns		
Dickson St, Lark. ML9	145	DE60
Dicks Pk, (E.Kil.) G75	135	BZ53
Dick St, G20	49	BP26
Differ Av, (Kilsyth) G65	19	CP11
Dilwara Av, G14	65	BG27
Dimity St, John. PA5	79	AH35
Dinard Dr, (Giff.) G46	102	BL41
Dinart St, G33	69	BZ28
Dinduff St, G34	72	CL28
Dinmont Av, Pais. PA2	81	AP36
off Montrose Rd		
Dinmont Cres, Moth. ML1	111	CY43
Dinmont Pl, G41	87	BN36
off Norham St		
Dinmont Rd, G41	86	BM36
Dinmont Way, Pais. PA2	81	AP36
off Ivanhoe Rd		
Dinwiddie St, G21	69	BY27
Dinyra Pl, (Glenb.) Coat. ML5	56	CS23
Dipple Pl, (Glenb.) G15	28	BD19
Dirleton Dr, G41	87	BN37
Dirleton Dr, Pais. PA2	81	AQ36
off Tantallon Dr		
Dirleton Gate, (Bears.) G61	29	BF19
Dirleton Pl, G41	87	BN37
Divernia Way, (Barr.) G78	115	AZ45
Dixon Av, G42	87	BR36
Dixon Pl, (E.Kil.) G74	121	BX50
Dixon Rd, G42	87	BR36
Dixons Blazes Ind Est, G5	88	BS34
Dixon St, G1	4	BR31
Dixon St, Coat. ML5	95	CX33
Dixon St, Ham. ML3	126	CT50
Dixon St, Pais. PA1	82	AV33
Dobbies Ln, G4	4	BR28
Dobbies Ln Pl, G4	5	BT29
Dochart Av, Renf. PA4	64	BA28
Dochart Dr, Coat. ML5	74	CT27
Dochart St, G33	70	CA27
Dock St, Clyde. G81	45	AZ22
Dodhill Pl, G13	46	BD23
Dodside Gdns, G32	91	CE33
Dodside Pl, G32	91	CE33
Dodside Rd, (Newt. M.) G77	116	BD47
Dodside St, G32	91	CE33
Dolan St, (Baill.) G69	72	CK32
Dollar Pk, Moth. ML1	128	DD50
Dollar Ter, G20	48	BL21
Dolphin Rd, G41	86	BM35
Dominica Grn, (E.Kil.) G75	135	BW52
off Leeward Circle		
Donaldson Av, (Kilsyth) G65	7	CT6
Donaldson Cres, (Kirk.) G66	17	CE14
Donaldson Dr, Renf. PA4	45	AZ26
off Ferguson St		
Donaldson Grn, (Udd.) G71	93	CR37
Donaldson Pl, (Kirk.) G66	17	CE14
off Thistle St		
Donaldson Rd, Lark. ML9	145	DE60
Donaldson St, (Kirk.) G66	17	CE14
Donaldson St, Ham. ML3	125	CQ48
Donaldswood Pk, Pais. PA2	82	AS37
Donaldswood Rd, Pais. PA2	82	AS37
Donald Ter, Ham. ML3	140	CS52
off Dean Cres		
Donald Way, (Udd.) G71	93	CQ38

Don Av, Renf. PA4	64	BA27
Doncaster St, G20	49	BQ25
Don Ct, Ham. ML3	139	CQ53
Don Dr, Pais. PA2	81	AP36
Donnies Brae, (Neil.) G78	98	AV44
Donohoe Ct, (Bishop.) G64	33	BW20
off Emerson Rd		
Don Path, Lark. ML9	144	DC61
Don Pl, John. PA5	79	AE37
Don St, G33	69	BZ29
Doon Cres, (Bears.) G61	29	BF18
Doonfoot Ct, (E.Kil.) G74	135	BZ51
off Doonfoot Gdns		
Doonfoot Gdns, (E.Kil.) G74	135	BZ51
Doonfoot Rd, G43	102	BM39
Doon Pl, (Kirk.) G66	17	CH11
Doon Rd, (Kirk.) G66	17	CH12
Doon Side, (Cumb.) G67	22	DD11
Doon St, Clyde. G81	27	AZ18
Doon St, Lark. ML9	145	DE59
Doon St, Moth. ML1	128	DC49
Doon Way, (Kirk.) G66	18	CJ12
Dorain Rd, Moth. ML1	113	DF42
Dora St, G40	88	BV34
Dorchester Av, G12	48	BJ23
Dorchester Ct, G12	48	BJ23
Dorchester Pl, G12	48	BJ23
Dorian Dr, (Clark.) G76	118	BK45
Dorlin Rd, G33	53	CG24
Dormanside Ct, G53	84	BD34
off Dormanside Rd		
Dormanside Gate, G53	84	BD34
off Dormanside Rd		
Dormanside Gro, G53	84	BD34
off Dormanside Rd		
Dormanside Pl, G53	85	BE35
off Dormanside Rd		
Dormanside Rd, G53	84	BD34
Dornal Av, G13	46	BA22
Dornford Av, G32	91	CF35
Dornford Rd, G32	91	CF35
Dornie Dr, G32	90	CD37
Dornie Dr, (Thornlie.) G46	101	BG42
Dornoch Av, (Giff.) G46	102	BL44
Dornoch Ct, Bell. ML4	111	CW40
Dornoch Pl, (Bishop.) G64	33	BY19
Dornoch Pl, (Chry.) G69	36	CM20
Dornoch Pl, (E.Kil.) G74	135	BY51
Dornoch Rd, (Bears.) G61	29	BF19
Dornoch Rd, Moth. ML1	112	DD40
Dornoch St, G40	68	BV32
Dornoch Way, (Cumb.) G68	9	DC8
Dornoch Way, Air. ML6	76	DB32
off Sutherland Dr		
Dorset Sq, G3	4	BP29
off Dorset St		
Dorset St, G3	4	BP29
Dosk Av, G13	46	BA21
Dosk Pl, G13	46	BB21
Double Hedges Rd, (Neil.) G78	114	AT47
Dougalston Av, (Miln.) G62	12	BK12
Dougalston Cres, (Miln.) G62	12	BK12
Dougalston Gdns N, (Miln.) G62	12	BK12
Dougalston Gdns S, (Miln.) G62	12	BK12
Dougalston Rd, G23	31	BN20
Douglas Av, G32	90	CD37
Douglas Av, (Giff.) G46	102	BL44
Douglas Av, (Lenz.) G66	35	CF15
Douglas Av, (Ruther.) G73	105	BY40
Douglas Av, (Elder.) John. PA5	80	AK35

Douglas Ct, (Lenz.) G66	35	CF16
Douglas Cres, (Udd.) G71	93	CR37
Douglas Cres, Air. ML6	76	DC31
Douglas Cres, Ersk. PA8	25	AP18
Douglas Cres, Ham. ML3	140	CT55
Douglasdale, (E.Kil.) G74	135	BZ51
Douglas Dr, G15	28	BB20
Douglas Dr, (Baill.) G69	71	CH32
Douglas Dr, (Both.) G71	109	CQ44
Douglas Dr, (Camb.) G72	106	CB40
Douglas Dr, (E.Kil.) G75	134	BU54
Douglas Dr, (Newt. M.) G77	117	BG47
Douglas Dr, Bell. ML4	111	CY41
Douglas Dr, (Ashgill) Lark. ML9	145	DH61
Douglas Gdns, (Giff.) G46	102	BL44
Douglas Gdns, (Bears.) G61	29	BH17
Douglas Gdns, (Lenz.) G66	35	CF16
Douglas Gdns, (Udd.) G71	109	CP40
Douglas Gate, (Camb.) G72	106	CB40
Douglas La, G2	4	BQ29
Douglas Muir Dr, (Miln.) G62	11	BE10
Douglas Muir Gdns, (Miln.) G62	11	BE10
Douglas Muir Pl, (Miln.) G62	11	BE10
Douglas Pk Cres, (Bears.) G61	30	BJ15
Douglas Pk La, Ham. ML3	126	CS49
Douglas Pl, (Bears.) G61	29	BG16
Douglas Pl, (Kirk.) G66	35	CF16
Douglas Pl, Coat. ML5	74	CV31
Douglas Pl, Ham. ML3	140	CT55
off Douglas Cres		
Douglas Rd, Renf. PA4	63	AW29
Douglas St, G2	4	BQ29
Douglas St, (Miln.) G62	12	BJ12
Douglas St, (Udd.) G71	93	CR38
Douglas St, (Blan.) G72	124	CL47
Douglas St, Air. ML6	76	DC31
Douglas St, Ham. ML3	126	CS48
Douglas St, Lark. ML9	144	DC57
Douglas St, Moth. ML1	127	CZ46
Douglas St, Pais. PA1	62	AS32
Douglas Ter, G41	87	BP34
off Glencairn Dr		
Douglas Ter, Pais. PA3	62	AU28
off Abbotsinch Rd		
Douglas Vw, Coat. ML5	94	CV34
Dougray Pl, (Barr.) G78	99	AY43
Dougrie Dr, G45	104	BT42
Dougrie Dr La, G45	104	BT42
off Dougrie Dr		
Dougrie Gdns, G45	104	BT43
Dougrie Pl, G45	104	BU42
Dougrie Rd, G45	104	BT42
Dougrie St, G45	104	BU42
Dougrie Ter, G45	104	BT42
Doune Cres, (Bishop.) G64	33	BX17
Doune Cres, (Newt. M.) G77	117	BH48
Doune Cres, (Chap.) Air. ML6	97	DF36
off Crieff Av		
Doune Gdns, G20	49	BN26
Doune Gdns La, G20	49	BN26
Doune Pk Way, Coat. ML5	94	CV33
Doune Quad, G20	49	BN26
Doune Ter, Coat. ML5	74	CT28
Dovecot, G43	86	BL37
Dovecote Vw, (Kirk.) G66	17	CH14
Dovecothall St, (Barr.) G78	99	AZ42
Dovecot Wd, (Kilsyth) G65	7	CT4
Dove Pl, (E.Kil.) G75	134	BV55
Dover St, G3	67	BN29
Dover St, Coat. ML5	74	CT27
Dove St, G53	100	BC40

Dove Wynd, (Strathclyde Bus. 94 CU38
Pk.) Bell. ML4
Dowanfield Rd, (Cumb.) G67 21 CZ12
Dowanhill St, G11 66 BL27
Dowanhill St, G12 48 BL26
Dowan Rd, (Miln.) G62 13 BN11
Dowanside La, G12 48 BM26
off Byres Rd
Dowanside Rd, G12 48 BL26
Downcraig Dr, G45 104 BT43
Downcraig Gro, G45 104 BT43
Downcraig Rd, G45 104 BS44
Downcraig Ter, G45 104 BT43
Downfield Dr, Ham. ML3 139 CR54
Downfield Gdns, (Both.) G71 109 CP43
Downfield St, G32 90 CA34
Downiebrae Rd, (Ruther.) G73 89 BX35
Downie Cl, (Udd.) G71 93 CR37
Downie St, Ham. ML3 140 CT52
Downs St, G21 50 BV25
Dowrie Cres, G53 84 BD36
Draffen Ct, Moth. ML1 128 DB46
off Draffen St
Draffen St, Moth. ML1 128 DB46
Drakemire Av, G45 104 BS41
Drakemire Dr, G44 104 BS42
Drakemire Dr, G45 104 BS42
Drake St, G40 68 BU32
Dreghorn St, G31 69 BY30
Drem Pl, G11 66 BK27
off Merkland St
Drimnin Rd, G33 53 CH24
Drive Rd, G51 65 BG29
Drochil St, G34 72 CJ28
Dromore St, (Kirk.) G66 17 CF14
Drove Hill, (Cumb.) G68 21 CX10
Drumbathie Rd, Air. ML6 76 DD29
Drumbathie Ter, Air. ML6 77 DE29
Drumbeg Dr, G53 100 BC39
Drumbeg Pl, G53 100 BC39
off Drumbeg Dr
Drumbeg Ter, (Miln.) G62 11 BF11
Drumbottie Rd, G21 51 BW24
Drumbowie Vw, (Cumb.) G68 21 CY10
Drumby Cres, (Clark.) G76 118 BM45
Drumby Dr, (Clark.) G76 118 BM45
Drumcarn Dr, (Miln.) G62 11 BH12
Drumcavel Rd, (Muir.) G69 54 CM22
Drumchapel Gdns, G15 28 BC19
Drumchapel Pl, G15 28 BD19
Drumchapel Rd, G15 28 BD19
Drumchapel Shop Cen, G15 28 BB18
Drumclair Pl, Air. ML6 77 DF30
Drumclog Av, (Miln.) G62 12 BJ9
Drumclog Gdns, G33 52 CB23
Drumcross Pl, G53 85 BE36
Drumcross Rd, G53 85 BE36
Drumcross Rd, Bish. PA7 24 AM18
Drumduff, (E.Kil.) G75 135 BZ56
Drumgelloch St, Air. ML6 77 DF29
Drumglass Vw, (Kilsyth) G65 20 CV9
Drumgray Gdns, (Green.) Air. 41 DF20
ML6
Drumgray La, (Green.) Air. 41 DF20
ML6
Drumhead La, G32 90 CB36
Drumhead Pl, G32 90 CB36
Drumhead Rd, G32 90 CB36
Drumhill, (Kirk.) G66 18 CK11
Drumilaw Cres, (Ruther.) G73 105 BW40
off Drumilaw Rd
Drumilaw Rd, (Ruther.) G73 105 BW40
Drumilaw Way, (Ruther.) G73 105 BW40

Drumlaken Av, G23 30 BL20
off Caldercuilt Rd
Drumlaken Ct, G23 30 BL20
off Arrochar St
Drumlaken Path, G23 30 BM20
off Littleton St
Drumlaken Pl, G23 30 BM20
off Chatton St
Drumlaken St, G23 30 BL20
Drumlanrig Av, G34 72 CL28
Drumlanrig Pl, G34 72 CM28
Drumlin Dr, (Miln.) G62 11 BH13
Drumloch Gdns, (E.Kil.) G75 136 CA56
Drumlochy Rd, G33 70 CC28
Drum Mains Pk, (Cumb.) G68 20 CS14
Drummond Av, (Ruther.) G73 88 BV37
Drummond Dr, Pais. PA1 83 AZ33
Drummond Hill, (E.Kil.) G74 122 CD49
Drummond Pl, (E.Kil.) G74 122 CD50
Drummond Way, (Newt. M.) 116 BC48
G77
Drummore Av, Coat. ML5 95 CZ34
Drummore Rd, G15 28 BD17
Drumnessie Ct, (Cumb.) G68 20 CV13
Drumnessie Rd, (Cumb.) G68 20 CV13
Drumnessie Vw, (Cumb.) G68 20 CV13
Drumore Av, (Chap.) Air. ML6 97 DF36
off Callander Rd
Drumover Dr, G31 90 CA33
Drumoyne Av, G51 65 BG29
Drumoyne Circ, G51 65 BG31
Drumoyne Dr, G51 65 BG30
Drumoyne Pl, G51 65 BG31
Drumoyne Quad, G51 65 BG31
Drumoyne Rd, G51 65 BG31
Drumoyne Sq, G51 65 BG30
Drumpark St, (Thornlie.) G46 101 BH41
Drumpark St, Coat. ML5 93 CR33
Drumpellier Av, (Cumb.) G67 39 CY15
Drumpellier Av, (Baill.) G69 92 CK34
Drumpellier Av, Coat. ML5 74 CS30
Drumpellier Ct, (Cumb.) G67 21 CY14
Drumpellier Cres, Coat. ML5 74 CT31
Drumpellier Gdns, (Cumb.) 21 CY14
G67
Drumpellier Gro, (Cumb.) G67 21 CY14
Drumpellier Pl, (Cumb.) G67 21 CY14
Drumpellier Pl, (Baill.) G69 92 CK33
Drumpellier Rd, (Baill.) G69 92 CJ34
Drumpellier St, G33 69 BZ27
Drumreoch Dr, G42 88 BU37
Drumreoch Pl, G42 88 BU37
Drumry Pl, G15 28 BA19
Drumry Rd, Clyde. G81 27 AY18
Drumry Rd E, G15 28 BA19
Drumsack Av, (Chry.) G69 54 CK21
Drumsargard Rd, (Ruther.) 105 BZ40
G73
Drums Av, Pais. PA3 61 AR31
Drums Cres, Pais. PA3 62 AS31
Drumshangie Pl, Air. ML6 76 DC27
Drumshangie St, Air. ML6 76 DC27
Drumshaw Dr, G32 91 CE37
Drums Rd, G53 84 BC34
Drumtrocher St, (Kilsyth) G65 7 CT5
Drumvale Dr, (Chry.) G69 37 CN19
Drury La Ct, (E.Kil.) G74 123 CE49
off Baillie Dr
Drury St, G2 4 BR30
Dryad St, (Thornlie.) G46 101 BG40
Dryburgh Av, (Ruther.) G73 89 BX38
Dryburgh Av, Pais. PA2 81 AQ36

Dryburgh Gdns, G20 49 BP26
off Wilton St
Dryburgh Hill, (E.Kil.) G74 135 BZ52
Dryburgh La, (E.Kil.) G74 135 BZ52
Dryburgh Pl, (Kirk.) G66 17 CH13
Dryburgh Pl, Coat. ML5 74 CV30
Dryburgh Rd, (Bears.) G61 29 BE15
Dryburgh St, Ham. ML3 125 CR47
Dryburgh Wk, (Mood.) G69 37 CQ18
Dryburgh Way, (Blan.) G72 124 CM46
off Winton Cres
Dryburn Av, G52 64 BC32
Dryden St, Ham. ML3 125 CR47
Drygate, G4 5 BU30
Drygate St, Lark. ML9 144 DC57
Drygrange Rd, G33 71 CE27
Drymen Pl, (Lenz.) G66 35 CF18
Drymen Rd, (Bears.) G61 29 BF15
Drymen St, G52 65 BG32
Drymen Wynd, (Bears.) G61 29 BH18
Drynoch Pl, G22 49 BR22
Drysdale St, G14 46 BB24
Duart Dr, (E.Kil.) G74 121 BZ50
Duart Dr, (Newt. M.) G77 118 BJ48
Duart Dr, (Elder.) John. PA5 80 AK36
Duart St, G20 48 BL21
Dubbs Rd, (Barr.) G78 100 BA42
Dubton Path, G34 72 CK28
Dubton St, G34 72 CK28
Duchall Pl, G14 46 BD25
Duchess Ct, Ham. ML3 141 CW51
off Royal Dr
Duchess Pl, (Ruther.) G73 89 BY37
Duchess Rd, (Ruther.) G73 89 BY36
Duchess Way, (Baill.) G69 73 CP31
off Park Rd
Duchray Dr, Pais. PA1 84 BB33
Duchray La, G33 69 BZ28
Duchray St, G33 69 BZ28
Dudhope St, G33 71 CF27
Dudley Dr, G12 48 BJ26
Dudley Dr, Coat. ML5 74 CS27
Dudley La, G12 48 BJ26
Duffus Pl, G32 91 CE37
Duffus St, G34 71 CH28
Duffus Ter, G32 91 CE37
Duich Gdns, G23 31 BN19
Duisdale Rd, G32 91 CE37
Dukes Gate, (Both.) G71 109 CN41
Dukes Pl, Ham. ML3 140 CT55
Dukes Rd, (Baill.) G69 73 CP32
Dukes Rd, (Camb.) G72 106 CA39
Dukes Rd, (Ruther.) G73 105 BY40
Duke St, G4 5 BU30
Duke St, G31 69 BW30
Duke St, Ham. ML3 126 CU50
Duke St, Lark. ML9 144 DC57
Duke St, Moth. ML1 128 DA45
Duke St, Pais. PA2 82 AU35
Duke St, (Linw.) Pais. PA3 60 AL31
Dullatur Rd, (Cumb.) G68 9 DA8
Dullatur Rd, (Dullatur) G68 9 CZ7
Dullatur Roundabout, (Cumb.) 9 DB8
G68
Dulnain St, (Camb.) G72 107 CF40
Dulsie Rd, G21 51 BY23
Dumbarton Rd, G11 66 BJ27
Dumbarton Rd, G14 65 BG27
Dumbarton Rd, G60 25 AQ15
Dumbarton Rd, Clyde. G81 26 AT17
Dumbarton Rd, (Dunt.) Clyde. 26 AV15
G81
Dumbreck Av, G41 86 BJ33

Dumbreck Ct, G41	86	BJ34
Dumbreck Path, G41	86	BJ33
off Dumbreck Av		
Dumbreck Pl, G41	86	BJ34
Dumbreck Pl, (Kirk.) G66	35	CG17
Dumbreck Rd, G41	86	BK34
Dumbreck Sq, G41	86	BJ33
Dumbreck Ter, (Kilsyth) G65	6	CP5
Dumbrock Rd, (Miln.) G62	11	BF11
Dumfries Cres, Air. ML6	76	DB32
Dumgoyne Av, (Miln.) G62	11	BH12
Dumgoyne Dr, (Bears.) G61	11	BF14
Dumgoyne Gdns, (Miln.) G62	11	BH12
Dumgoyne Pl, (Clark.) G76	118	BL46
off Lomondside Av		
Dunagoil Gdns, G45	104	BU43
Dunagoil Pl, G45	104	BU44
Dunagoil Rd, G45	104	BT43
Dunagoil St, G45	104	BU43
Dunagoil Ter, G45	104	BU44
Dunalistair Dr, G33	52	CD24
Dunan Pl, G33	71	CG30
Dunard Rd, (Ruther.) G73	89	BX38
Dunard St, G20	49	BP25
Dunard Way, Pais. PA3	62	AT30
off Mosslands Rd		
Dunaskin St, G11	66	BL28
Dunavon Pl, Coat. ML5	95	CZ33
off Paddock St		
Dunbar Av, (Ruther.) G73	89	BY38
Dunbar Av, Coat. ML5	94	CT33
Dunbar Av, John. PA5	79	AG37
Dunbar Dr, Moth. ML1	128	DC49
Dunbar Hill, (E.Kil.) G74	135	BY52
Dunbeath Av, (Newt. M.) G77	117	BH48
Dunbeith Pl, G20	48	BM24
Dunbeth Av, Coat. ML5	75	CX30
Dunbeth Ct, Coat. ML5	75	CX30
Dunbeth Rd, Coat. ML5	75	CX29
Dunblane Dr, (E.Kil.) G74	136	CB51
Dunblane Pl, (E.Kil.) G74	136	CB51
Dunblane Pl, Coat. ML5	94	CV33
Dunblane St, G4	4	BR28
Dunbrach Rd, (Cumb.) G68	21	CX10
Duncan Av, G14	47	BE26
Duncan Ct, Moth. ML1	111	CZ44
off Marmion Cres		
Duncan Graham St, Lark. ML9	144	DD57
Duncan La, G14	47	BE26
off Gleneagles La N		
Duncan La N, G14	47	BE25
off Duncan Av		
Duncan La S, G14	47	BE25
off Gleneagles La N		
Dun Cann, Ersk. PA8	43	AR22
Duncansby Rd, G33	71	CF31
Duncan St, Clyde. G81	27	AX18
Duncarnock Av, (Neil.) G78	114	AU46
Duncarnock Cres, (Neil.) G78	114	AU46
Dunchattan Pl, G31	68	BV30
Dunchattan St, G31	68	BV30
Dunchurch Rd, Pais. PA1	63	AZ32
Dunclutha Dr, (Both.) G71	109	CQ44
Dunclutha St, G40	89	BX35
Duncolm Pl, (Miln.) G62	11	BF11
off Dunellan Rd		
Duncombe St, G20	48	BM22

Duncombe Vw, Clyde. G81	27	AY18
off Kirkoswald Dr		
Duncraig Cres, John. PA5	79	AE36
Duncrub Dr, (Bishop.) G64	32	BU20
Duncruin St, G20	48	BM22
Duncryne Av, G32	91	CF33
Duncryne Gdns, G32	91	CG33
Duncryne Pl, (Bishop.) G64	50	BU21
Dundaff Hill, (Cumb.) G68	21	CY11
Dundas Av, (Torr.) G64	15	BX13
Dundas Ct, (E.Kil.) G74	136	CA51
Dundashill, G4	67	BR27
Dundas La, G1	5	BS29
Dundas Pl, (E.Kil.) G74	136	CA51
Dundas St, G1	5	BS29
Dundasvale Ct, G4	4	BR28
off Maitland St		
Dundasvale Rd, G4	4	BR28
off Maitland St		
Dundee Dr, G52	84	BD33
Dundee Path, G52	85	BE34
Dundonald Av, John. PA5	79	AF36
Dundonald Cres, (Newt. M.) G77	118	BJ49
Dundonald Dr, Ham. ML3	140	CT54
Dundonald Pl, (Neil.) G78	114	AT46
Dundonald Rd, G12	48	BL25
Dundonald Rd, Pais. PA3	63	AW30
Dundonald St, (Blan.) G72	124	CL45
Dundrennan Rd, G42	87	BP38
Dundyvan Gdns, Coat. ML5	75	CW32
Dundyvan Ind Est, Coat. ML5	74	CV32
Dundyvan La, Wis. ML2	129	DH50
Dundyvan Rd, Coat. ML5	74	CV31
Dundyvan Way, Coat. ML5	74	CV32
Dunearn Pl, Pais. PA2	83	AW34
Dunearn St, G4	67	BP27
Duneaton Wynd, Lark. ML9	144	DD60
off Carlisle Rd		
Dunedin Ct, (E.Kil.) G75	135	BW53
off Dunedin Dr		
Dunedin Dr, (E.Kil.) G75	135	BW52
Dunedin Rd, Lark. ML9	144	DD60
Dunedin Ter, Clyde. G81	45	AY21
Dunellan Av, (Mood.) G69	37	CQ19
Dunellan Cr, (Mood.) G69	37	CQ19
off Dunellan Av		
Dunellan Cres, (Mood.) G69	37	CQ19
Dunellan Gdns, (Mood.) G69	37	CQ19
off Dunellan Av		
Dunellan Rd, (Miln.) G62	11	BE11
Dunellan St, G52	65	BG32
Dungavel Gdns, Ham. ML3	140	CU53
Dungeonhill Rd, G34	72	CM29
Dunglass Av, G14	47	BE25
Dunglass Av, (E.Kil.) G74	122	CB50
Dunglass La, G14	47	BE25
off Dunglass Av		
Dunglass La N, G14	47	BE25
off Verona Av		
Dunglass La S, G14	47	BE25
off Verona Av		
Dunglass Pl, (Miln.) G62	11	BG10
Dunglass Pl, (Newt. M.) G77	116	BC48
Dunglass Rd, Bish. PA7	24	AL19
Dunglass Sq, (E.Kil.) G74	122	CB50
off Dunglass Av		
Dungoil Av, (Cumb.) G68	21	CX10
Dungoil Rd, (Lenz.) G66	35	CG17
Dungoyne St, G20	48	BL21
off Crosbie St		
Dunholme Pk, Clyde. G81	26	AT18
Dunira St, G32	90	CB34

Dunivaig St, G33	71	CG29
Dunkeld Av, (Ruther.) G73	89	BX38
Dunkeld Dr, (Bears.) G61	30	BK17
Dunkeld Gdns, (Bishop.) G64	33	BX19
Dunkeld La, (Chry.) G69	37	CQ19
off Burnbrae Av		
Dunkeld Pl, (Newt. M.) G77	118	BK49
Dunkeld Pl, Coat. ML5	94	CV33
Dunkeld Pl, Ham. ML3	125	CN50
Dunkeld St, G31	89	BY33
Dunkenny Pl, G15	28	BB17
Dunkenny Rd, G15	28	BA18
Dunkenny Sq, G15	28	BB18
Dunlin, G12	48	BJ23
off Ascot Av		
Dunlin, (E.Kil.) G74	122	CA50
Dunlin Ct, (Strathclyde Bus. Pk.) Bell. ML4	94	CU37
Dunlop Ct, Ham. ML3	140	CU54
Dunlop Cres, (Both.) G71	109	CQ44
Dunlop Cres, Renf. PA4	45	AZ25
off Fulbar St		
Dunlop Gro, (Udd.) G71	93	CQ36
Dunlop Pl, (Miln.) G62	11	BH10
Dunlop St, G1	5	BS31
Dunlop St, (Camb.) G72	107	CG39
Dunlop St, (Linw.) Pais. PA3	60	AL31
Dunlop St, Renf. PA4	45	AZ25
off Fulbar St		
Dunlop Twr, (E.Kil.) G75	136	CA53
off Telford Rd		
Dunmore Dr, (Miln.) G62	12	BL13
Dunmore La, G5	67	BR32
off Norfolk St		
Dunmore St, Clyde. G81	45	AY21
Dunnachie Dr, Coat. ML5	93	CR33
Dunnachie Pl, Coat. ML5	93	CR33
off Kenmuir St		
Dunnet Av, (Glenm.) Air. ML6	58	DB24
Dunnichen Gdns, (Bishop.) G64	33	BZ20
Dunnikier Wk, (Cumb.) G68	20	CU12
Dunnottar Ct, (E.Kil.) G74	121	BY50
off Dunnottar Cres		
Dunnottar Cres, (E.Kil.) G74	121	BY50
Dunnottar St, G33	70	CD27
Dunnottar St, (Bishop.) G64	33	BZ19
Dunn St, G40	89	BW33
Dunn St, Clyde. G81	26	AU18
Dunn St, (Dunt.) Clyde. G81	26	AV15
Dunn St, Pais. PA1	63	AW32
Dunolly Dr, (Newt. M.) G77	117	BH48
Dunolly St, G21	69	BW28
Dunottar Av, Coat. ML5	95	CX35
Dunottar Pl, Coat. ML5	95	CX34
Dun Pk, (Kirk.) G66	17	CG13
Dunphail Dr, G34	72	CM29
Dunphail Rd, G34	72	CM29
Dunragit St, G31	69	BY30
Dunrobin Av, (Elder.) John. PA5	80	AL36
Dunrobin Ct, (E.Kil.) G74	121	BZ50
off Dunrobin Cres		
Dunrobin Cres, (E.Kil.) G74	121	BZ50
Dunrobin Dr, (E.Kil.) G74	121	BZ50
Dunrobin Gdns, Air. ML6	77	DG31
off Fairhaven Av		
Dunrobin Pl, Coat. ML5	74	CV30
Dunrobin Rd, Air. ML6	77	DG30
Dunrobin St, G31	69	BX31
Dunrod Hill, (E.Kil.) G74	122	CB50
Dunrod St, G32	90	CD33
Dunscore Brae, Ham. ML3	139	CN51

Name	Page	Grid
Dunside Dr, G53	100	BC39
Dunskaith Pl, G34	72	CM30
Dunskaith St, G34	72	CM29
Dunsmuir St, G51	66	BK30
Duns Path, Coat. ML5	95	CZ34
Dunster Gdns, (Bishop.) G64	33	BX17
Dunswin Av, Clyde. G81	26	AU18
Dunswin Ct, Clyde. G81	26	AU18
off Dunswin Av		
Dunsyre Pl, G23	31	BN20
Dunsyre St, G33	70	CA29
Duntarvie Av, G34	72	CL29
Duntarvie Cl, G34	72	CL29
Duntarvie Cres, G34	72	CL29
Duntarvie Dr, G34	72	CK29
Duntarvie Gdns, G34	72	CL29
Duntarvie Gro, G34	72	CL29
Duntarvie Pl, G34	72	CK29
Duntarvie Rd, G34	72	CK29
Dunterlie Av, G13	46	BC23
Dunterlie Ct, (Barr.) G78	99	AY42
Duntiblae Rd, (Kirk.) G66	18	CJ14
Duntiglennan Rd, Clyde. G81	27	AW15
Duntocher Rd, (Bears.) G61	28	BC15
Duntocher Rd, Clyde. G81	26	AV18
Duntocher Rd, (Dunt.) Clyde. G81	27	AW15
Duntreath Av, G13	46	BA21
Duntreath Av, G15	28	BB20
Duntreath Dr, G15	28	BB20
Duntreath Gdns, G15	28	BB19
Duntreath Gro, G15	28	BB20
Duntreath Ter, (Kilsyth) G65	7	CT5
Duntroon Pl, Bell. ML4	111	CX42
Duntroon St, G31	69	BX29
Dunure Dr, (Ruther.) G73	104	BV40
Dunure Dr, (Newt. M.) G77	118	BJ48
Dunure Dr, Ham. ML3	138	CM51
Dunure Pl, (Newt. M.) G77	118	BJ48
Dunure Pl, Coat. ML5	94	CU34
Dunure St, G20	48	BM22
Dunure St, Coat. ML5	94	CU34
Dunvegan, (Glenm.) Air. ML6	58	DA25
Dunvegan Av, Coat. ML5	74	CT28
Dunvegan Av, (Elder.) John. PA5	80	AK36
Dunvegan Dr, (Bishop.) G64	33	BW17
Dunvegan Dr, (Newt. M.) G77	118	BJ48
Dunvegan Pl, (Udd.) G71	92	CM37
Dunvegan Pl, (E.Kil.) G74	121	BZ50
Dunvegan Quad, Renf. PA4	45	AX25
off Kirklandneuk Rd		
Dunwan Av, G13	46	BB22
Dunwan Pl, G13	46	BB22
Durban Av, Clyde. G81	26	AS17
Durham St, G41	66	BM32
Durisdeer Dr, Ham. ML3	139	CN52
Durness Av, (Bears.) G61	30	BK16
Durno Path, G33	71	CG30
Duror St, G32	70	CC31
Durris Gdns, G32	91	CF34
Durrockstock Cres, Pais. PA2	81	AP38
Durrockstock Rd, Pais. PA2	81	AP38
Durrockstock Way, Pais. PA2	81	AP38
off Durrockstock Cres		
Durward, (E.Kil.) G74	123	CG49
Durward Av, G41	86	BM36
Durward Ct, G41	86	BM36
Durward Ct, Moth. ML1	111	CZ43
off Marmion Cres		
Durward Cres, Pais. PA2	81	AP36
Durward Way, Pais. PA2	81	AP36
off Durward Cres		
Duthie Pk Gdns, G13	47	BF23
Duthie Pk Pl, G13	47	BF22
Duthil St, G51	65	BF31
Dyce Av, Air. ML6	96	DA33
Dyce La, G11	66	BJ27
Dyers Wynd, Pais. PA1	62	AU32
off Gilmour St		
Dyfrig St, (Blan.) G72	124	CL45
Dykebar Av, G13	46	BC23
Dykebar Cres, Pais. PA2	83	AX35
Dykehead Cres, Air. ML6	76	DB27
Dykehead La, G33	71	CF30
Dykehead Rd, G65	6	CN5
Dykehead Rd, (Dullatur) G68	8	CY7
Dykehead Rd, (Baill.) G69	73	CP32
Dykehead Rd, Air. ML6	76	DB27
Dykehead Sq, Ham. ML3	125	CP50
Dykehead St, G33	71	CF30
Dykemuir Pl, G21	51	BX25
off Dykemuir St		
Dykemuir Quad, G21	51	BW25
off Dykemuir St		
Dykemuir St, G21	51	BW25
Dyke Pl, G13	46	BC21
Dyke Rd, G13	46	BC22
Dyke Rd, G14	46	BB23
Dyke St, (Baill.) G69	72	CL32
Dyke St, Coat. ML5	93	CR33
Dysart Ct, (Cumb.) G68	20	CU12

E

Name	Page	Grid
Eagle Cres, (Bears.) G61	28	BD15
Eaglesham Ct, G51	67	BN31
off Blackburn St		
Eaglesham Path, (Glenb.) Coat. ML5 *off Gayne Dr*	56	CS23
Eaglesham Pl, G51	67	BN31
Eaglesham Rd, (E.Kil.) G75	135	BW52
Eaglesham Rd, (Clark.) G76	134	BS54
Eaglesham Rd, (Eagle.) G76	133	BP56
Eaglesham Rd, (Newt. M.) G77	117	BF49
Eagle St, G4	68	BS27
Earlbank Av, G14	47	BE25
Earlbank La N, G14	47	BE25
off Verona Av		
Earlbank La S, G14	47	BE25
off Verona Av		
Earl Haig Rd, G52	64	BB30
Earl La, G14	47	BE26
Earl Pl, G14	47	BE25
Earlsburn Rd, (Lenz.) G66	35	CG17
Earlscourt, (Mood.) G69	37	CP20
Earls Gate, (Both.) G71	109	CN42
Earls Hill, (Cumb.) G68	21	CX10
Earlspark Av, G43	87	BP38
Earlston Av, G21	68	BV28
Earlston Cres, Coat. ML5	95	CZ34
Earlston Pl, G21	5	BU28
Earl St, G14	47	BE26
Earl Vw, Moth. ML1	112	DC42
off Woodside St		
Earlybraes Dr, G32	71	CG31
Earlybraes Gdns, G33	71	CF31
Earn Av, (Bears.) G61	30	BK17
Earn Av, (Righead Ind. Est.) Bell. ML4	110	CU39
Earn Av, Renf. PA4	64	BA27
off Almond Av		
Earn Gdns, Lark. ML9	144	DC61
Earn La, Moth. ML1	112	DC40
off Howden Pl		
Earnock Av, Moth. ML1	127	CY47
Earnock Gdns, Ham. ML3	139	CQ51
Earnock Rd, Ham. ML3	139	CN51
Earnock St, G33	51	BZ25
Earnock St, Ham. ML3	125	CQ49
Earn Rd, (Newt. M.) G77	117	BF46
Earnside St, G32	70	CD32
Earn St, G33	70	CA28
Easdale, (E.Kil.) G74	136	CD54
Easdale Dr, G32	90	CC33
Easdale Path, (Carnbroe) Coat. ML5 *off Bellvue Way*	95	CZ33
Easdale Path, (Glenb.) Coat. ML5 *off The Oval*	56	CS23
Easdale Pl, (Newt. M.) G77	116	BD48
Easdale Ri, Ham. ML3	125	CN50
East Av, (Udd.) G71	110	CS39
East Av, (Blan.) G72	125	CN48
East Av, Moth. ML1	112	DC43
East Av, Renf. PA4	45	AZ26
Eastbank Dr, G32	71	CE32
Eastbank Pl, G32	71	CE32
Eastbank Ri, G32	71	CE32
East Barns St, Clyde. G81	45	AZ21
East Bath La, G2	5	BS29
off Sauchiehall St		
East Buchanan St, Pais. PA1	62	AV32
Eastburn Cres, G21	51	BX23
Eastburn Pl, G21	51	BX23
off Eastburn Cres		
Eastburn Rd, G21	51	BX24
East Burnside St, (Kilsyth) G65	7	CT5
East Campbell St, G1	5	BU31
Eastcote Av, G14	47	BG26
Eastcroft, (Ruther.) G73	89	BX37
Eastcroft Ter, G21	51	BW25
East Dean St, Bell. ML4	111	CX40
East End Av, Moth. ML1	112	DD44
off Montalto Av		
Easter Av, (Udd.) G71	109	CN39
Eastercraigs, G31	69	BX29
Easter Garngaber Rd, (Lenz.) G66	35	CG16
Eastergreens Av, (Kirk.) G66	17	CE14
Easterhill Pl, G32	90	CB34
Easterhill St, G32	90	CB34
Easterhouse Pl, G34	72	CL29
off Easterhouse Rd		
Easterhouse Quad, G34	72	CL30
Easterhouse Rd, G34	72	CL29
Easterhouse Rd, (Baill.) G69	72	CK32
Easterhouse Township Cen, G34	72	CJ29
Eastermains, (Kirk.) G66	18	CK11
Easter Ms, (Udd.) G71	109	CN39
Easter Queenslie Rd, G33	71	CG29
Easter Rd, (Clark.) G76	119	BQ48
Easterton Av, (Clark.) G76	119	BQ48
Easterwood Cres, (Udd.) G71	94	CT36
Eastfield Av, (Camb.) G72	106	CA39
Eastfield Rd, G21	50	BU25
Eastfield Rd, (Cumb.) G68	21	CX10
Eastfield Ter, Bell. ML4	111	CZ41
Eastgate, (Gart.) G69	55	CQ24
East Gate, (Glenb.) Coat. ML5	56	CT22
East George St, Coat. ML5	75	CX29
East Glebe Ter, Ham. ML3	140	CT51
East Greenlees Av, (Camb.) G72	107	CE42
East Greenlees Cres, (Camb.) G72	106	CD42
East Greenlees Dr, (Camb.) G72	107	CE42

East Greenlees Gro, (Camb.) G72	106	CC42
East Greenlees Rd, (Camb.) G72	106	CC42
Easthall Pl, G33	71	CH30
East High St, Air. ML6	76	DC29
East Kilbride Rd, (Ruther.) G73	105	BY40
East Kilbride Rd, (Clark.) G76	119	BQ48
East La, Pais. PA1	83	AW33
Eastlea Pl, Air. ML6	76	DD31
East Machan St, Lark. ML9	144	DD60
off Thistle Cres		
East Mains Rd, (E.Kil.) G74	122	CB49
East Milton Gro, (E.Kil.) G75	135	BX52
Eastmuir St, G32	70	CD32
East Nerston Rd, G72	123	CE46
Easton Pl, Coat. ML5	75	CX32
off Whifflet St		
East Queenslie Ind Est, G33	71	CG29
East Rd, (Kilb.) John. PA10	78	AC33
East Rd, Moth. ML1	112	DC41
East Scott Ter, Ham. ML3	140	CT52
Eastside, (Kirk.) G66	17	CE12
Eastside Ind Est, (Kirk.) G66	17	CF12
East Springfield Ter, (Bishop.) G64	51	BX21
East Sta Ind Est, Lark. ML9	144	DD57
East Stewart Gdns, Coat. ML5	75	CY30
off East Stewart St		
East Stewart Pl, Coat. ML5	75	CY30
off East Stewart St		
East Stewart St, Coat. ML5	75	CY31
East Thomson St, Clyde. G81	27	AX18
Eastvale Pl, G3	66	BL29
East Wellbrae Cres, Ham. ML3	139	CR52
East Wellington St, G31	69	BZ32
East Whitby St, G31	89	BY33
Eastwood Av, G41	86	BM37
Eastwood Av, (Giff.) G46	102	BL43
Eastwood Ct, (Thornlie.) G46	102	BJ41
off Crosslees Dr		
Eastwood Cres, (Thornlie.) G46	101	BH41
Eastwoodmains Rd, (Giff.) G46	102	BL44
Eastwoodmains Rd, (Clark.) G76	102	BL44
Eastwood Pk, (Giff.) G46	102	BJ43
Eastwood Pk, (Thornlie.) G46	102	BJ43
Eastwood Rd, (Mood.) G69	37	CP19
Eastwood Vw, (Camb.) G72	107	CG39
Eastwood Way, Lark. ML9	144	DD57
off Roselea St		
Easwald Bk, (Kilb.) John. PA10	78	AD35
Ebroch Dr, (Kilsyth) G65	7	CU5
Ebroch Pk, (Kilsyth) G65	7	CU5
Eccles St, G22	50	BU24
off Carron St		
Eckford St, G32	90	CC33
Eck Path, Moth. ML1	112	DC40
off Howden Pl		
Eday St, G22	50	BT23
Edderton Pl, G34	72	CJ30
Edderton Way, G34	72	CJ30
Eddington Dr, (Newt. M.) G77	117	BE50
Eddleston Pl, (Camb.) G72	107	CG40
off Montgomery St		
Eddlewood Ct, G33	72	CJ30
Eddlewood Path, G33	71	CH30
off Eddlewood Rd		
Eddlewood Pl, G33	71	CH30
Eddlewood Rd, G33	71	CH30
Edelweiss Ter, G11	66	BK27
off Gardner St		

Eden Dr, (E.Kil.) G75	134	BV55
Eden Gdns, (E.Kil.) G75	134	BV54
Eden Gro, (E.Kil.) G75	134	BV54
Edenhall Ct, (Newt. M.) G77	131	BF51
off Mearnskirk Rd		
Edenhall Gro, (Newt. M.) G77	131	BG51
Eden La, G33	69	BZ28
Eden Pk, (Both.) G71	109	CP43
Eden Pl, (Camb.) G72	107	CF40
Eden Pl, Renf. PA4	64	BA27
Eden St, G33	69	BZ28
Edenwood St, G31	70	CA32
Edgam Dr, G52	65	BE32
Edgefauld Av, G21	50	BV26
Edgefauld Dr, G21	50	BV25
Edgefauld Pl, G21	50	BV24
Edgefauld Rd, G21	50	BV25
Edgehill La, G11	48	BJ25
Edgehill Rd, G11	47	BH25
Edgehill Rd, (Bears.) G61	29	BG15
Edgemont Pk, Ham. ML3	140	CS53
Edgemont St, G41	87	BN37
Edinbeg Av, G42	88	BU37
Edinbeg Pl, G42	88	BU37
Edinburgh Rd, G33	69	BZ30
Edinburgh Rd, (Baill.) G69	71	CH31
Edinburgh Rd, Moth. ML1	113	DF39
Edington Gdns, (Mood.) G69	37	CP18
Edington St, G4	67	BR27
Edison St, G52	64	BA29
Edmiston Dr, G51	65	BH31
Edmonstone Ct, Clyde. G81	45	AZ22
off Hamilton Ter		
Edmonstone Dr, (Kilsyth) G65	7	CT6
Edmonton Ter, (E.Kil.) G75	135	BY53
Edmund Kean, (E.Kil.) G74	123	CE48
Edrom Ct, G32	70	CB32
Edrom Path, G32	70	CC32
off Edrom St		
Edrom St, G32	70	CB32
Edward Av, Renf. PA4	46	BA25
Edward St, (Kilsyth) G65	7	CT4
Edward St, (Baill.) G69	73	CP32
Edward St, Clyde. G81	45	AZ22
Edward St, Ham. ML3	140	CT51
Edward St, Moth. ML1	128	DB48
Edwin St, G51	66	BM32
Edzell Ct, G14	65	BF27
Edzell Dr, (Newt. M.) G77	117	BG49
Edzell Dr, (Elder.) John. PA5	80	AM35
Edzell Gdns, (Bishop.) G64	51	BY21
Edzell Pl, G14	47	BF26
Edzell St, G14	65	BF27
Edzell St, Coat. ML5	94	CT33
Egidia Av, (Giff.) G46	102	BL43
Egilsay Cres, G22	50	BS21
Egilsay Pl, G22	50	BS21
Egilsay St, G22	50	BS21
Egilsay Ter, G22	50	BS21
Eglinton Av, (Udd.) G71	109	CN39
off Lady Isle Cres		
Eglinton Ct, G5	67	BR32
Eglinton Dr, (Giff.) G46	102	BL43
Eglinton St, G5	67	BR32
Eglinton St, Coat. ML5	75	CX29
Egmont Pk, (E.Kil.) G75	135	BW54
Eider, G12	48	BJ22
off Ascot Av		
Eider Gro, (E.Kil.) G75	135	BW56
Eighth St, (Udd.) G71	93	CN36
Eildon Cres, (Chap.) Air. ML6	97	DH36
Eildon Dr, (Barr.) G78	99	AY44
Eildon Rd, (Kirk.) G66	17	CH13

Eileen Gdns, (Bishop.) G64	33	BX19
Elba La, G31	69	BY32
off Gallowgate		
Elcho St, G40	68	BV31
Elderbank, (Bears.) G61	29	BG18
Elder Cres, (Camb.) G72	107	CG41
Elder Gro, (Udd.) G71	93	CR38
Elder Gro Av, G51	65	BF30
Elder Gro Ct, G51	65	BF30
Elder Gro Pl, G51	65	BF30
Elderpark Gdns, G51	65	BH30
off Elderpark St		
Elderpark Gro, G51	65	BH30
Elderpark St, G51	65	BH30
Elderslie St, G3	4	BP28
Elder St, G51	65	BH29
Eldin Pl, (Elder.) John. PA5	80	AK35
Eldon Ct, G11	66	BK27
off Caird Dr		
Eldon Gdns, (Bishop.) G64	32	BU20
Eldon St, G3	67	BN27
Elgin Av, (E.Kil.) G74	122	CB50
Elgin Gdns, (Clark.) G76	119	BP45
Elgin Pl, (Kilsyth) G65	7	CT4
Elgin Pl, (E.Kil.) G74	122	CB50
Elgin Pl, Air. ML6	76	DA32
Elgin Pl, Coat. ML5	95	CX34
Elgin Rd, (Bears.) G61	11	BH14
Elgin St, G40	69	BW32
off Rowchester St		
Elgin Ter, Ham. ML3	125	CN49
Elgin Way, Bell. ML4	111	CW39
Elibank St, G33	70	CC28
Elie Ct, (Cumb.) G68	9	DB8
Elie St, G11	66	BL27
Eliot Cres, Ham. ML3	140	CT52
Eliot Ter, Ham. ML3	140	CT51
Elison Ct, Moth. ML1	128	DD49
off Dunbar Dr		
Elizabethan Way, Renf. PA4	63	AY28
Elizabeth Cres, (Thornlie.) G46	102	BJ42
Elizabeth Quad, Moth. ML1	112	DC40
off Sherry Av		
Elizabeth St, G51	66	BL32
Elizabeth Wynd, Ham. ML3	140	CT54
off Bankfield Dr		
Ella Gdns, Bell. ML4	111	CY41
Ellangowan Ct, (Miln.) G62	12	BJ11
Ellangowan Rd, G41	86	BL37
Ellangowan Rd, (Miln.) G62	12	BJ11
Ellergreen Rd, (Bears.) G61	29	BG17
Ellerslie St, John. PA5	80	AJ34
Ellesmere St, G22	49	BQ25
Ellinger Ct, Clyde. G81	26	AU17
off Scott St		
Elliot Av, (Giff.) G46	102	BL43
Elliot Av, Pais. PA2	80	AM38
Elliot Ct, Moth. ML1	111	CZ44
off Marmion Cres		
Elliot Cres, (E.Kil.) G74	136	CD51
Elliot Dr, (Giff.) G46	102	BL42
Elliot Pl, G3	67	BN29
off Finnieston St		
Elliot St, G3	67	BN30
Ellisland, (Kirk.) G66	18	CK11
Ellisland, (E.Kil.) G74	123	CF50
Ellisland Av, Clyde. G81	27	AY18
Ellisland Cres, (Ruther.) G73	104	BV40
Ellisland Dr, (Kirk.) G66	18	CJ11
Ellisland Dr, (Blan.) G72	124	CK47
Ellisland Rd, G43	102	BM39
Ellisland Rd, (Cumb.) G67	22	DD11
Ellisland Rd, (Clark.) G76	119	BN48

Name	Pg	Ref
Ellisland Wynd, Moth. ML1	113	DE42
Ellismuir Fm Rd, (Baill.) G69	92	CM33
off Bredisholm Ter		
Ellismuir Pl, (Baill.) G69	92	CL33
Ellismuir Rd, (Baill.) G69	92	CL33
Ellismuir St, Coat. ML5	94	CT34
Ellismuir Way, (Udd.) G71	93	CQ36
Ellis St, Coat. ML5	75	CW30
Elliston Av, G53	101	BE40
Elliston Cres, G53	101	BE40
Elliston Dr, G53	101	BE40
Ellis Way, Moth. ML1	128	DB48
off Toll St		
Ellon Dr, (Linw.) Pais. PA3	60	AJ32
Ellon Gro, Pais. PA3	62	AV30
off Ellon Way		
Ellon Way, Pais. PA3	62	AV30
Ellrig, (E.Kil.) G75	135	BZ56
Elm Av, (Lenz.) G66	35	CE15
Elm Av, Renf. PA4	45	AY25
Elm Bk, (Bishop.) G64	33	RX20
Elm Bk, (Kirk.) G66	17	CF12
Elmbank Av, (Udd.) G71	93	CR38
Elmbank Cres, G2	4	BQ29
Elmbank Cres, Ham. ML3	125	CQ49
Elmbank Dr, Lark. ML9	145	DE60
Elmbank La, G3	4	BP29
off North St		
Elmbank St, G2	4	BQ29
Elmbank St, Bell. ML4	111	CW40
Elmbank St La, G2	4	BQ29
Elm Cres, (Udd.) G71	94	CT38
Elm Dr, (Cumb.) G67	23	DH9
Elm Dr, (Camb.) G72	107	CE40
Elm Dr, (Chap.) Air. ML6	97	DG34
Elm Dr, John. PA5	80	AJ36
Elmfoot St, G5	88	BT35
Elm Gdns, (Bears.) G61	29	BG15
Elmhurst, Moth. ML1	127	CZ49
Elmira Rd, (Muir.) G69	54	CL22
Elm La E, G14	47	BF26
off Westland Dr		
Elm La W, G14	47	BF26
off Westland Dr		
Elm Lea, John. PA5	80	AK35
Elmore Av, G44	103	BR40
Elmore La, G44	103	BR40
Elm Pl, (E.Kil.) G75	135	BY55
Elm Quad, Air. ML6	77	DF31
Elm Rd, (Ruther.) G73	105	BX41
Elm Rd, Clyde. G81	27	AW16
Elm Rd, (Holytown) Moth. ML1	112	DD40
Elm Rd, (New Stev.) Moth. ML1	112	DC43
Elm Rd, Pais. PA2	83	AW36
Elmslie Ct, (Baill.) G69	92	CL33
Elm St, G14	47	BF26
Elm St, (Blan.) G72	125	CN46
Elm St, (Clark.) G76	119	BP47
Elm St, Coat. ML5	75	CY32
Elmtree Gdns, G45	104	BV41
Elmvale Row, G21	50	BU24
Elmvale Row E, G21	50	BU24
off Elmvale Row		
Elmvale Row W, G21	50	BU24
off Elmvale Row		
Elmvale St, G21	50	BU24
Elm Vw Ct, Bell. ML4	111	CZ41
Elm Wk, (Bears.) G61	29	BG15
Elm Way, (Camb.) G72	107	CG41
Elm Way, Lark. ML9	142	DC56
Elmwood, Wis. ML2	143	DG52
Elmwood Av, G11	47	BH25
Elmwood Av, (Newt. M.) G77	117	BH47
Elmwood Ct, (Both.) G71	109	CQ43
Elmwood Gdns, (Kirk.) G66	34	CC16
Elmwood La, G11	47	BH25
Elphinstone Cres, (E.Kil.) G75	136	CB54
Elphinstone Pl, G51	66	BL30
Elphinstone Rd, (Giff.) G46	118	BJ46
Elphin St, G23	30	BM20
off Invershiel Rd		
Elrig Rd, G44	103	BP40
Elsinore Path, (E.Kil.) G75	136	CA56
Elspeth Gdns, (Bishop.) G64	33	BY19
Eltham St, G22	49	BR26
off Bonhill St		
Elvan Ct, G32	70	CC32
off Edrom Ct		
Elvan Pl, (E.Kil.) G75	134	BU54
Elvan St, G32	70	CB32
Elvan St, Moth. ML1	127	CZ47
Embo Dr, G13	46	BD23
Emerald Ter, Bell. ML4	111	CW41
Emerson Rd, (Bishop.) G64	33	BW20
Emerson Rd W, (Bishop.) G64	33	BW20
off Crowhill Rd		
Emerson St, G20	49	BQ23
Emily Dr, Moth. ML1	128	DA49
Emma Jay Rd, Bell. ML4	111	CX40
Empire Way, Moth. ML1	111	CY44
Endfield Av, G12	48	BK23
Endrick Bk, (Bishop.) G64	33	BW17
Endrick Ct, Coat. ML5	74	CV31
off Kirk St		
Endrick Dr, (Bears.) G61	29	BH17
Endrick Dr, Pais. PA1	63	AX31
Endrick Gdns, (Miln.) G62	11	BG11
Endrick St, G21	50	BT26
English Row, (Calder.) Air. ML6	97	DE35
English St, Wis. ML2	129	DF50
Ennerdale, (E.Kil.) G75	134	BV55
Ennisfree Rd, (Blan.) G72	124	CM45
Ensay St, G22	50	BT22
Enterkin St, G32	90	CB33
Eriboll Pl, G22	49	BR22
Eriboll St, G22	49	BR22
Eribol Wk, Moth. ML1	113	DF42
off Loanhead Av		
Ericht Rd, G43	102	BL40
Eriska Av, G14	46	BC24
Eriskay Av, (Newt. M.) G77	116	BD48
Eriskay Av, Ham. ML3	139	CP51
Eriskay Cres, (Newt. M.) G77	116	BD48
Eriskay Dr, (Old Kil.) G60	26	AS15
Eriskay Pl, (Old Kil.) G60	26	AS15
Erradale St, G22	49	BQ22
Errogie St, G34	72	CK29
Errol Gdns, G5	88	BS33
Erskine Av, G41	86	BK33
Erskine Ct, Air. ML6	77	DG29
off Station Rd		
Erskine Cres, Air. ML6	76	DB32
Erskinefauld Rd, (Linw.) Pais. PA3	60	AJ31
Erskine Ferry Rd, (Old Kil.) G60	25	AQ16
Erskine Harbour, Ersk. PA8	25	AQ17
Erskine Rd, (Giff.) G46	118	BK47
Erskine Sq, G52	64	BB30
Erskine Vw, (Old Kil.) G60	25	AQ15
Erskine Vw, Clyde. G81	27	AX18
Ervie St, G34	72	CL30
Esdaile Ct, Moth. ML1	112	DC42
Esk Av, Renf. PA4	64	BA27
Eskbank St, G32	70	CC31
Eskbank Toll, (Giff.) G46	102	BK44
Esk Dale, (E.Kil.) G74	121	BY50
Eskdale, (Newt. M.) G77	118	BK48
off Kirkvale Ct		
Eskdale Dr, (Ruther.) G73	89	BZ38
Eskdale Rd, (Bears.) G61	29	BF19
Eskdale St, G42	87	BR36
Esk Dr, Pais. PA2	81	AN36
Esk St, G14	46	BB24
Esk Way, Pais. PA2	81	AN36
Esmond St, G3	66	BL28
Espedair St, Pais. PA2	82	AU34
Espieside Cres, Coat. ML5	74	CT29
Essenside Av, G15	29	BE19
Essex Dr, G14	47	BG25
Essex La, G14	47	BF25
Esslemont Av, G14	46	BD24
Estate Quad, G32	91	CE36
Estate Rd, G32	91	CE36
Etive Av, (Bears.) G61	30	BK17
Etive Av, Ham. ML3	139	CQ52
Etive Ct, (Cumb.) G67	39	CX15
Etive Ct, Clyde. G81	27	AY16
Etive Cres, (Bishop.) G64	33	BX20
Etive Cres, (Cumb.) G67	39	CX15
Etive Dr, (Giff.) G46	102	BM44
Etive Dr, (Cumb.) G67	39	CX15
Etive Dr, Air. ML6	77	DE32
Etive Dr, Bish. PA7	24	AL19
Etive Pl, (Cumb.) G67	39	CY15
Etive Pl, Lark. ML9	142	DB55
Etive St, G32	70	CC32
Etna Ind Est, Wis. ML2	129	DE49
Etna St, Wis. ML2	129	DE49
Eton La, G12	67	BN27
Etterby Wynd, (Blan.) G72	124	CL46
off Winton Cres		
Ettrick Av, Bell. ML4	95	CW38
off Rockburn Cres		
Ettrick Av, Renf. PA4	64	BB27
off Morriston Cres		
Ettrick Ct, (Camb.) G72	107	CG41
off Gateside Av		
Ettrick Cres, (Ruther.) G73	89	BY38
Ettrick Dr, (Bears.) G61	11	BE14
Ettrick Dr, Bish. PA7	24	AL19
Ettrick Hill, (E.Kil.) G74	122	CC50
off Cantieslaw Dr		
Ettrick Oval, Pais. PA2	81	AN37
Ettrick Pl, G43	86	BM38
Ettrick Sq, (Cumb.) G67	22	DB12
off Cumbernauld Shop Cen		
Ettrick Ter, John. PA5	79	AE37
Ettrick Wk, (Cumb.) G67	22	DB12
off Cumbernauld Shop Cen		
Ettrick Way, (Cumb.) G67	22	DB12
off Cumbernauld Shop Cen		
Ettrick Way, Renf. PA4	64	BB27
off Morriston Cres		
Evan Cres, (Giff.) G46	102	BM43
Evan Dr, (Giff.) G46	102	BM44
Evanton Dr, (Thornlie.) G46	101	BG43
Evanton Pl, (Thornlie.) G46	101	BG42
Everard Ct, G21	50	BU22
Everard Dr, G21	50	BU23
Everard Pl, G21	50	BU22
Everard Quad, G21	50	BU23
Everglades, The (Chry.) G69	54	CK21
Eversley St, G32	90	CC34
Everton Rd, G53	85	BE35
Ewart Cres, Ham. ML3	139	CQ51
Ewart Ter, Ham. ML3	139	CQ51
Ewing Ct, Ham. ML3	140	CS54

Ewing Pl, G31	69	BY32
Ewing St, (Ruther.) G73	89	BW38
Ewing St, (Kilb.) John. PA10	78	AC34
Ewing Wk, (Miln.) G62	12	BL12
Excelsior St, Wis. ML2	129	DF50
Exchange Pl, G1	5	BS30
off Buchanan St		
Exeter Dr, G11	66	BJ27
Exeter La, G11	66	BJ27
off Exeter Dr		
Exeter St, Coat. ML5	75	CW32
Eynort St, G22	49	BQ22
Eyrepoint Ct, G33	70	CC29
off Sutherness Dr		

F

Factory Rd, Moth. ML1	128	DA48
Fagan Ct, (Blan.) G72	109	CN44
Faifley Rd, Clyde. G81	27	AX15
Fairbairn Cres, (Thornlie.) G46	102	BJ43
Fairbairn Path, G40	89	BW33
off Ruby St		
Fairbairn St, G40	89	BW33
Fairburn St, G32	90	CB33
Fairfax Av, G44	104	BS40
Fairfield Ct, (Clark.) G76	119	BN48
Fairfield Dr, (Clark.) G76	119	BN48
Fairfield Dr, Renf. PA4	63	AZ28
Fairfield Gdns, G51	65	BH29
off Fairfield St		
Fairfield Pl, G51	65	BH29
off Fairfield St		
Fairfield Pl, (Both.) G71	109	CR43
Fairfield Pl, (E.Kil.) G74	135	BY51
Fairfield St, G51	65	BH29
Fairford Dr, (Cumb.) G67	39	CZ31
Fairhaven Av, Air. ML6	77	DG31
Fairhaven Rd, G23	49	BN21
Fairhill Av, G53	85	BE38
Fairhill Av, Ham. ML3	140	CS52
Fairhill Cres, Ham. ML3	140	CS52
Fairhill Pl, Ham. ML3	139	CR54
Fairholm Av, Ham. ML3	141	CY52
Fairholm St, G32	90	CB33
Fairholm St, Lark. ML9	144	DB57
Fairley St, G51	66	BK31
Fairlie, (E.Kil.) G74	121	BZ50
Fairlie Pk Dr, G11	66	BJ27
Fair Oaks, (Clark.) G76	120	BU45
Fairway, (Bears.) G61	28	BD16
Fairway Av, Pais. PA2	82	AT37
Fairways, Lark. ML9	145	DE58
Fairways Vw, Clyde. G81	27	AZ15
Fairweather Pl, (Newt. M.) G77	117	BE49
Fairyknowe Gdns, (Both.) G71	109	CR43
Falcon Cres, Pais. PA3	61	AR31
Falconer Ter, Ham. ML3	140	CS52
off Fairhill Av		
Falcon Rd, John. PA5	79	AF38
Falcon Ter, G20	48	BL21
Falcon Ter La, G20	48	BL21
Falfield St, G5	87	BQ33
Falkland Av, (Newt. M.) G77	118	BJ47
Falkland Cres, (Bishop.) G64	51	BZ21
Falkland Dr, (E.Kil.) G74	135	BY52
Falkland La, G12	48	BK26
Falkland Pk, (E.Kil.) G74	135	BZ52
Falkland Pl, (E.Kil.) G74	135	BZ52
Falkland Pl, Coat. ML5	95	CX34
Falkland St, G12	48	BK26
Falloch Rd, G42	87	BQ38
Falloch Rd, (Bears.) G61	29	BE19

Falloch Rd, (Miln.) G62	11	BF11
Fallside Av, (Udd.) G71	110	CS39
Fallside Rd, (Both.) G71	109	CQ43
Falside Av, Pais. PA2	82	AU36
Falside Rd, G32	90	CD35
Falside Rd, Pais. PA2	82	AT36
Falstaff, (E.Kil.) G74	123	CE48
Faraday Retail Pk, Coat. ML5	75	CX31
Fara St, G23	49	BP21
Farie St, (Ruther.) G73	88	BV37
Farm Ct, (Both.) G71	109	CR41
Farm Cres, Moth. ML1	113	DH41
Farme Castle Ct, (Ruther.) G73	89	BY36
Farme Castle Est, (Ruther.) G73	89	BY36
Farme Cross, (Ruther.) G73	89	BX36
Farmeloan Ind Est, (Ruther.) G73	89	BX36
Farmeloan Rd, (Ruther.) G73	89	BX37
Farmgate Sq, Bell. ML4	110	CV41
off Crofthead Cres		
Farmington Av, G32	71	CF32
Farmington Gdns, G32	71	CF32
Farmington Gate, G32	91	CF33
Farmington Gro, G32	71	CF32
Farm La, (Udd.) G71	109	CQ40
off Myers Cres		
Farm La, Bell. ML4	110	CV42
off Crofthead Cres		
Farm Pk, (Lenz.) G66	35	CF17
Farm Rd, G41	66	BK32
Farm Rd, (Blan.) G72	108	CM44
Farm Rd, (Dalmuir) Clyde. G81	26	AT18
Farm Rd, Ham. ML3	125	CP49
Farm St, Moth. ML1	127	CZ46
Farm Ter, Ham. ML3	125	CP49
Farndale, (E.Kil.) G74	121	BY50
Farne Dr, G44	103	BR41
Farnell St, G4	67	BR27
Farrier Ct, John. PA5	79	AH34
Faskally Av, (Bishop.) G64	32	BU18
Faskin Cres, G53	84	BB38
Faskine Av, Air. ML6	76	DB31
Faskine Av, (Calder.) Air. ML6	96	DD35
Faskine Cres, Air. ML6	76	DB31
Faskin Pl, G53	84	BB38
Faskin Rd, G53	84	BB38
Fasque Pl, G15	28	BA17
Fastnet St, G33	70	CC29
Fauldhouse St, G5	88	BT34
Faulds, (Baill.) G69	72	CL32
Faulds Gdns, (Baill.) G69	72	CL32
Fauldshead Rd, Renf. PA4	45	AY26
Faulds La, Coat. ML5	94	CV33
off Dunblane Pl		
Fauldspark Cres, (Baill.) G69	72	CL31
Faulds St, Coat. ML5	94	CU34
Fauldswood Cres, Pais. PA2	81	AR35
Fauldswood Dr, Pais. PA2	81	AR35
Faulkner Gro, Moth. ML1	129	DH45
off Morris Cres		
Fearnach Pl, G20	48	BK22
off Skaethorn Rd		
Fearnmore Rd, G20	48	BM22
Fellsview Av, (Kirk.) G66	17	CH12
Felton Pl, G13	46	BB22
Fendoch St, G32	90	CC33
Fenella St, G32	70	CD32
Fennsbank Av, (Ruther.) G73	105	BZ42
Fenwick Dr, (Barr.) G78	99	AZ44
Fenwick Pl, Ham. ML3	140	CU55
Fenwick Pl, (Giff.) G46	102	BK44
Fenwick Rd, (Giff.) G46	102	BL44
Fereneze Av, (Clark.) G76	118	BL45

Fereneze Av, (Barr.) G78	99	AX42
Fereneze Av, Renf. PA4	63	AW29
Fereneze Cres, G13	46	BC22
Fereneze Cres, Ham. ML3	125	CP50
Fereneze Dr, Pais. PA2	82	AS37
Fereneze Gro, (Barr.) G78	99	AX41
Fereneze Rd, (Neil.) G78	114	AS45
Fergus Av, Pais. PA3	61	AQ32
Fergus Ct, G20	49	BN25
off Fergus Dr		
Fergus Dr, G20	49	BN25
Fergus Dr, Pais. PA3	61	AQ32
Fergus Gdns, Ham. ML3	140	CV51
Fergus La, G20	49	BP25
Ferguslie, Pais. PA1	81	AQ33
Ferguslie Pk Av, Pais. PA3	61	AR31
Ferguslie Pk Cres, Pais. PA3	81	AQ33
off Ferguslie Pk Av		
Ferguslie Wk, Pais. PA1	81	AR33
Ferguson Av, (Miln.) G62	11	BH11
Ferguson Av, Renf. PA4	45	AZ26
Ferguson Dr, Moth. ML1	128	DA50
Ferguson St, John. PA5	79	AG34
Ferguson St, Renf. PA4	45	AZ26
Ferguson Way, Air. ML6	76	DC27
Fergusson Pl, (E.Kil.) G74	123	CF48
Fergusson Rd, (Cumb.) G67	22	DB11
Ferguston Rd, (Bears.) G61	29	BH17
Fernan St, G32	70	CB32
Fern Av, (Bishop.) G64	51	BX21
Fern Av, (Lenz.) G66	35	CE17
Fern Av, Ersk. PA8	43	AR22
Fernbank Av, (Camb.) G72	107	CE41
Fernbank St, G21	50	BU24
Fernbank St, G22	50	BU24
Fernbrae Av, (Ruther.) G73	105	BY42
Fernbrae Way, (Ruther.) G73	105	BX42
Fern Cotts, G13	47	BH24
off Fern La		
Ferncroft Dr, G44	104	BT40
Ferndale, Lark. ML9	144	DC60
Ferndale Ct, G23	48	BM21
Ferndale Dr, G23	30	BM20
Ferndale Gdns, G23	48	BM21
Ferndale Pl, G23	48	BM21
Fern Dr, (Barr.) G78	99	AX41
Ferness Oval, G21	51	BY22
Ferness Pl, G21	51	BY22
Ferness Rd, G21	51	BY23
Fern Gro, (Gart.) G69	55	CQ23
off Inchnock Av		
Ferngrove Av, G12	48	BK23
Fernhill Gra, (Both.) G71	109	CQ44
Fernhill Rd, (Ruther.) G73	105	BW41
Fernie Gdns, G20	49	BN22
Fern La, G13	47	BH24
Fernlea, (Bears.) G61	29	BG18
Fernleigh Pl, (Mood.) G69	37	CP19
Fernleigh Rd, G43	102	BM40
Fernside Wk, Ham. ML3	140	CU52
off Chatelherault Cres		
Fernslea Av, (Blan.) G72	124	CL45
Fern St, Moth. ML1	128	DC49
Ferryden Ct, G14	65	BG27
off Ferryden St		
Ferryden St, G14	65	BG28
Ferry Rd, G3	66	BK28
Ferry Rd, (Both.) G71	109	CQ43
Ferry Rd, (Udd.) G71	109	CN39
Ferry Rd, Renf. PA4	45	AZ25
Fersit Ct, G43	102	BL39
Fersit St, G43	102	BL39
Fetlar Dr, G44	104	BS40

Name	Page	Grid
Fettercairn Av, G15	28	BA18
Fettercairn Gdns, (Bishop.) G64	33	BY20
Fettes St, G33	70	CB29
Fidra St, G33	70	CB29
Fielden Pl, G40	69	BW32
Fielden St, G40	69	BW32
Field Gro, (Clark.) G76	119	BP48
Fieldhead Dr, G43	102	BJ40
Fieldhead Sq, G43	102	BJ40
Field Rd, (Clark.) G76	119	BP48
Field Rd, Lark. ML9	144	DD59
Field St, Ham. ML3	140	CT52
Fife Av, G52	84	BD33
Fife Av, Air. ML6	76	DC32
Fife Cres, (Both.) G71	109	CQ44
Fife Dr, Moth. ML1	111	CZ43
Fife Way, (Bishop.) G64	51	BZ21
Fifth Av, G12	47	BH24
Fifth Av, (Stepps) G33	52	CD24
Fifth Av, (Kirk.) G66	35	CF19
Fifth Av, Air. ML6	77	DE29
Fifth Av, Renf. PA4	63	AY27
Fifth Rd, (Blan.) G72	125	CN48
Fifty Pitches Pl, G51	64	BD30
Fifty Pitches Rd, G51	64	BD30
Fifty Pitches Way, G52	64	BD29
Finart Dr, Pais. PA2	83	AX36
Finaven Gdns, (Bears.) G61	10	BD13
Finch Dr, G13	46	BC21
Finch Pl, John. PA5	79	AF38
Findhorn, Ersk. PA8	25	AQ19
Findhorn Av, Pais. PA2	81	AP36
Findhorn Av, Renf. PA4	46	BA26
off Dee Av		
Findhorn Ct, (E.Kil.) G75	134	BT53
Findhorn Pl, (E.Kil.) G75	134	BT53
Findhorn St, G33	69	BZ29
Findlay Ct, Moth. ML1	127	CZ45
off Park Neuk St		
Findlay St, (Kilsyth) G65	7	CT5
off Backbrae St		
Findochty, Ersk. PA8	25	AQ18
Findochty St, G33	71	CG28
Fingal La, G20	48	BL22
off Fingal St		
Fingal St, G20	48	BM22
Fingalton Rd, (Newt. M.) G77	116	BA48
Fingask St, G32	91	CE33
Finglas Av, Pais. PA2	83	AX36
Finglen Gdns, (Miln.) G62	11	BG11
Finglen Pl, G53	100	BD41
Fingleton Av, (Barr.) G78	99	AZ44
Finhaven St, G32	90	CA34
Finlarig St, G34	72	CL30
Finlas St, G22	50	BT25
Finlay Dr, G31	69	BW30
Finlay Ri, (Miln.) G62	12	BL12
Finlayson Dr, Air. ML6	77	DG30
Finlayson Quad, Air. ML6	77	DG30
Finlaystone St, Coat. ML5	74	CU30
Finnart Sq, G40	88	BV34
Finnart St, G40	88	BV34
Finnieston Quay, G3	67	BN30
Finnieston Sq, G3	67	BN29
off Finnieston St		
Finnieston St, G3	67	BN30
Finnie Wynd, Moth. ML1	128	DD49
off Nelson Cres		
Finsbay St, G51	65	BF31
Fintrie Ter, Ham. ML3	125	CN49
off Fleming Way		
Fintry Av, Pais. PA2	82	AU37
Fintry Cres, (Bishop.) G64	51	BY21
Fintry Cres, (Barr.) G78	99	AY44
Fintry Dr, G44	88	BS38
Fintry Gdns, (Bears.) G61	11	BE13
Firbank Av, (Torr.) G64	15	BX13
Fir Bk Av, Lark. ML9	144	DD59
Firbank Quad, (Chap.) Air. ML6	97	DG34
Firbank Ter, (Barr.) G78	100	BA44
Fir Ct, (Camb.) G72	107	CG41
Fir Ct, Coat. ML5	94	CV33
off Ailsa Rd		
Firdon Cres, G15	28	BC20
Fir Dr, (E.Kil.) G75	135	BX56
Fir Gro, (Udd.) G71	93	CR38
Fir Gro, (New Stev.) Moth. ML1	112	DC43
Firhill Av, Air. ML6	76	DB31
Firhill Rd, G20	49	BQ25
Firhill St, G20	49	BQ25
Firlee, (E.Kil.) G75	134	BY53
Firpark Pl, G31	68	BV29
off Firpark St		
Firpark Rd, (Bishop.) G64	51	BX21
Firpark St, G31	68	BV29
Fir Pk St, Moth. ML1	128	DB49
Firpark Ter, G31	68	BV30
Fir Pl, (Baill.) G69	92	CJ34
Fir Pl, (Camb.) G72	107	CE39
Fir Pl, John. PA5	80	AJ35
First Av, (Millerston) G33	52	CD24
First Av, G44	103	BP43
First Av, (Bears.) G61	30	BJ18
First Av, (Kirk.) G66	35	CF20
First Av, (Udd.) G71	93	CN37
First Av, Renf. PA4	63	AY27
First Gdns, G41	86	BJ33
First Rd, (Blan.) G72	125	CN48
First St, (Udd.) G71	93	CP37
First Ter, Clyde. G81	27	AW18
Fir Vw, (Calder.) Air. ML6	96	DD35
Firwood Cts, (Newt. M.) G77	117	BG49
Firwood Dr, G44	104	BS39
Firwood Rd, (Newt. M.) G77	117	BG48
Fischer Gdns, Pais. PA1	81	AP33
Fisher Av, (Kilsyth) G65	7	CT5
Fisher Av, Pais. PA1	81	AP33
Fisher Ct, G31	68	BV30
Fisher Cres, Clyde. G81	27	AX15
Fisher Dr, Pais. PA1	81	AP33
Fishers Rd, Renf. PA4	45	AY23
Fisher St, Lark. ML9	144	DD60
Fisher Way, Pais. PA1	81	AP33
Fishescoates Av, (Ruther.) G73	105	BY40
Fishescoates Gdns, (Ruther.) G73	105	BY40
Fitzalan Dr, Pais. PA3	63	AW31
Fitzalan Rd, Renf. PA4	63	AW28
Fitzroy La, G3	67	BN29
Fitzroy Pl, G3	67	BN28
off Royal Ter		
Flakefield, (E.Kil.) G74	135	BX51
Flaxfield Gro, Moth. ML1	111	CZ43
Flaxmill Av, Wis. ML2	129	DF49
Flax Rd, (Udd.) G71	109	CQ40
Fleet Av, Renf. PA4	64	BA28
Fleet St, G32	90	CD33
Fleming Av, (Chry.) G69	54	CL22
Fleming Av, Clyde. G81	27	AZ20
Fleming Ct, Ham. ML3	125	CN49
Fleming Ct, Moth. ML1	128	DC49
Fleming Pl, (E.Kil.) G75	135	BZ53
Fleming Rd, (Cumb.) G67	22	DB11
Fleming Rd, Bell. ML4	111	CX39
Fleming Rd, Bish. PA7	24	AK18
Fleming St, G31	69	BX31
Fleming St, Pais. PA3	62	AU30
Flemington Ind Est, (Camb.) G72	107	CG41
Flemington Rd, (Camb.) G72	107	CH44
Flemington St, G21	50	BV26
Fleming Way, Ham. ML3	124	CM49
Fleming Way, Lark. ML9	145	DE59
off Bannockburn Dr		
Flenders Av, (Clark.) G76	118	BL47
Flenders Rd, (Clark.) G76	118	BL47
Fleurs Av, G41	86	BK33
Fleurs Rd, G41	86	BK33
Flinders Pl, (E.Kil.) G75	135	BX53
Flloyd St, Coat. ML5	74	CV30
Floorsburn Cres, John. PA5	79	AG35
Floors Rd, (Eagle.) G76	132	BL52
Floors St, John. PA5	79	AH35
Flora Gdns, (Bishop.) G64	33	BY19
Florence Dr, (Giff.) G46	102	BL43
Florence Gdns, (Ruther.) G73	105	BY41
Florence St, G5	68	BS32
Florida Av, G42	87	BR37
Florida Cres, G42	87	BR37
Florida Dr, G42	87	BQ37
Florida Gdns, (Baill.) G69	72	CJ32
Florida Sq, G42	87	BR37
Florida St, G42	87	BR37
Florish Rd, Ersk. PA8	44	AT21
Flowerdale Pl, G53	100	BD42
off Waukglen Dr		
Flowerhill Ind Est, Air. ML6	76	DD29
Flowerhill St, Air. ML6	76	DD29
Flures Av, Ersk. PA8	44	AU21
Flures Cres, Ersk. PA8	44	AU21
Flures Dr, Ersk. PA8	44	AU21
Flures Pl, Ersk. PA8	44	AU21
Fochabers Dr, G52	65	BE31
Fogo Pl, G20	48	BM23
Foinaven Dr, (Thornlie.) G46	101	BH39
Foinaven Gdns, (Thornlie.) G46	102	BJ39
Foinaven Way, (Thornlie.) G46	102	BJ40
Footfield Rd, Bell. ML4	110	CV41
Forbes Dr, G40	68	BV32
Forbes Dr, Moth. ML1	111	CX43
Forbes Pl, Pais. PA1	82	AU33
Forbes St, G40	68	BV31
Fordneuk St, G40	69	BW32
Fordoun St, G34	72	CM29
Ford Rd, G12	48	BM25
Ford Rd, (Newt. M.) G77	117	BF50
Fordyce Ct, (Newt. M.) G77	117	BF49
off Capelrig Rd		
Fordyce St, G11	66	BK27
Forehouse Rd, (Kilb.) John. PA10	78	AA34
Foremount Ter La, G12	48	BK26
Fore Row, Ham. ML3	126	CU49
off Muir St		
Forest Dr, (Both.) G71	109	CQ42
Forest Dr, Bell. ML4	111	CY42
Forest Gdns, (Kirk.) G66	34	CC17
Forest Gate, Ham. ML3	139	CR52
Foresthall Cres, G21	51	BW26
Foresthall Dr, G21	51	BW26
Forest La, Ham. ML3	140	CT55
Forest Pl, (Kirk.) G66	34	CC17
Forest Pl, Pais. PA2	82	AU35
Fore St, G14	47	BE26
Forest Rd, (Cumb.) G67	23	DE12
Forest Rd, Lark. ML9	144	DD59
Forest Vw, (Cumb.) G67	23	DE10
Forfar Av, G52	84	BD33

Forfar Cres, (Bishop.) G64	51	BY21
Forgan Gdns, (Bishop.) G64	51	BZ21
Forge, The (Giff.) G46	102	BM42
off Braidpark Dr		
Forge Dr, Coat. ML5	74	CV30
Forge Pl, G21	69	BX27
Forge Retail Pk, G31	69	BX31
Forge Rd, Air. ML6	77	DH31
Forge Row, (Calder.) Air. ML6	97	DE35
Forge Shop Cen, The, G31	69	BY32
Forge St, G21	69	BX27
Forgewood Path, Air. ML6	77	DH31
off Forge Rd		
Forgewood Rd, Moth. ML1	111	CY43
Forglen St, G34	72	CK28
Formby Dr, G23	30	BM20
Forres Av, (Giff.) G46	102	BL42
Forres Cres, Bell. ML4	111	CW39
Forres Gate, (Giff.) G46	102	BM43
Forres St, G23	31	BN20
off Tolsta St		
Forres St, (Blan.) G72	124	CL47
Forrest Av, Ham. ML3	140	CT55
Forrest Burn Ct, Air. ML6	75	CZ29
off Monkscourt Av		
Forrest Dr, (Bears.) G61	10	BD12
Forrester Ct, (Bishop.) G64	50	BV21
off Crowhill Rd		
Forrestfield Cres, (Newt. M.) G77	117	BF48
Forrestfield Gdns, (Newt. M.) G77 off Forrestfield Cres	117	BG48
Forrestfield St, G21	69	BW28
Forrest Gate, (Udd.) G71	93	CR36
Forrest St, G40	69	BW32
Forrest St, (Blan.) G72	125	CP46
Forrest St, Air. ML6	77	DF29
Forsyth St, Air. ML6	76	DD29
Forteviot Av, (Baill.) G69	72	CL32
Forteviot Pl, (Baill.) G69	72	CL32
Forth Av, Pais. PA2	81	AN36
Forth Ct, (E.Kil.) G75	134	BU54
Forth Cres, (E.Kil.) G75	134	BU53
Forth Gro, (E.Kil.) G75	134	BU54
Forth Pl, John. PA5	79	AE37
Forth Pl, Lark. ML9	144	DD61
off Glengonnar St		
Forth Rd, (Bears.) G61	29	BF19
Forth Rd, (Torr.) G64	15	BX13
Forth St, G41	87	BP34
Forth St, Clyde. G81	27	AY20
Forth Ter, Ham. ML3	139	CR53
Forth Wk, (Cumb.) G67	22	DB11
off Cumbernauld Shop Cen		
Forties Ct, (Thornlie.) G46	101	BH40
Forties Cres, (Thornlie.) G46	102	BJ40
Forties Gdns, (Thornlie.) G46	102	BJ40
Forties Way, (Thornlie.) G46	102	BJ40
Fortieth Av, (E.Kil.) G75	136	CB56
Fortingall Av, G12	48	BL23
Fortingall Pl, G12	48	BL23
Fortingall Rd, (Blan.) G72	125	CP48
Fortrose St, G11	66	BK27
Fort St, Moth. ML1	127	CY45
Forum Pl, Moth. ML1	111	CY44
Fossil Gro, (Kirk.) G66	18	CJ12
Foswell Dr, G15	28	BB16
Foswell Pl, G15	28	BB16
Fotheringay La, G41	86	BM35
Fotheringay Rd, G41	86	BM35
Foulis La, G13	47	BH23
Foulis St, G13	47	BH23
off Crow Rd		
Foundry La, (Barr.) G78	99	AY43
Foundry St, G21	50	BV25
Fountain Av, (Inch.) Renf. PA4	43	AR25
Fountain Cres, (Inch.) Renf. PA4	43	AR24
Fountain Dr, (Inch.) Renf. PA4	44	AS24
Fountainwell Av, G21	50	BT26
Fountainwell Dr, G21	68	BT27
Fountainwell Pl, G21	68	BT27
Fountainwell Rd, G21	68	BT27
Fountainwell Sq, G21	68	BU27
Fountainwell Ter, G21	68	BU27
Fourth Av, G33	52	CD24
Fourth Av, (Kirk.) G66	35	CF20
Fourth Av, Renf. PA4	63	AY27
Fourth Gdns, G41	86	BJ33
Fourth Rd, (Blan.) G72	125	CN48
Fourth St, (Udd.) G71	93	CP36
Fowlis Dr, (Newt. M.) G77	117	BE47
Foxbar Cres, Pais. PA2	81	AN38
Foxbar Dr, G13	46	BD23
Foxbar Dr, Pais. PA2	81	AN38
Foxbar Rd, (Elder.) John. PA5	80	AM38
Foxbar Rd, Pais. PA2	81	AP38
Foxes Gro, (Lenz.) G66	35	CG16
Foxglove Pl, G53	100	BD42
Fox Gro, Moth. ML1	127	CX46
Foxhills Pl, G23	31	BN20
Foxley St, G32	91	CE36
Fox St, G1	4	BR31
Foyers Ter, G21	51	BW25
Francis St, G5	87	BQ33
Frankfield Rd, G33	53	CG24
Frankfield St, G33	69	BZ27
Frankfort St, G41	87	BN36
Franklin Pl, (E.Kil.) G75	135	BX52
Franklin St, G40	88	BV34
Fraser Av, (Ruther.) G73	89	BY38
Fraser Av, (Newt. M.) G77	117	BG47
Fraser Av, Bish. PA7	24	AK17
Fraser Av, John. PA5	80	AJ35
Fraser Ct, Air. ML6	77	DG29
off Station Rd		
Fraser Cres, Ham. ML3	139	CR51
Fraser Gdns, (Kirk.) G66	16	CD13
Fraser River Twr, (E.Kil.) G75	135	BZ52
Fraser St, (Camb.) G72	106	CA39
Frazer St, G40	69	BW32
Frederick St, Coat. ML5	74	CU29
Freeland Ct, G53	101	BE39
off Freeland Cres		
Freeland Cres, G53	100	BD39
Freeland Dr, G53	100	BD39
Freeland Dr, (Inch.) Renf. PA4	44	AS23
Freeland La, (E.Kil.) G75	136	CB53
off Bell Grn E		
Freeland Pl, (Kirk.) G66	17	CF13
Freelands Ct, (Old Kil.) G60	26	AS16
off Freelands Rd		
Freelands Cres, (Old Kil.) G60	26	AS16
Freelands Pl, (Old Kil.) G60	26	AS17
off Freelands Rd		
Freelands Rd, (Old Kil.) G60	26	AS16
Freesia Ct, Moth. ML1	128	DA48
French St, G40	88	BV34
French St, Clyde. G81	26	AU18
French St, Renf. PA4	63	AX27
Freuchie St, G34	72	CK30
Frew St, Air. ML6	76	DC29
Friar Av, (Bishop.) G64	33	BX17
Friarscourt Av, G13	47	BF21
Friarscourt Rd, (Chry.) G69	36	CK20
Friars Cft, (Kirk.) G66	17	CG13
Friars Pl, G13	47	BF21
off Knightswood Rd		
Friars Way, Air. ML6	97	DE33
Friarton Rd, G43	103	BP39
Friendship Way, Renf. PA4	63	AZ28
Frood St, Moth. ML1	111	CY44
Fruin Av, (Newt. M.) G77	117	BG47
Fruin Pl, G22	50	BS25
Fruin Ri, Ham. ML3	139	CN51
Fruin Rd, G15	28	BB20
Fruin St, G22	50	BS25
Fulbar Av, Renf. PA4	45	AY25
Fulbar Ct, Renf. PA4	45	AZ25
off Fulbar Av		
Fulbar Cres, Pais. PA2	81	AP35
Fulbar Gdns, Pais. PA2	81	AP35
Fulbar La, Renf. PA4	45	AZ25
Fulbar Rd, G51	65	BE30
Fulbar Rd, Pais. PA2	81	AP34
Fulbar St, Renf. PA4	45	AZ25
Fullarton Av, G32	90	CC35
Fullarton Dr, G32	90	CC36
Fullarton La, G32	90	CC35
Fullarton Pl, Coat. ML5	94	CT34
Fullarton Rd, G32	90	CB37
Fullarton Rd, (Cumb.) G68	9	DA8
Fullarton St, Coat. ML5	94	CU34
Fullerton St, Pais. PA3	62	AT30
Fullerton Ter, Pais. PA3	62	AU30
Fulmar Ct, (Bishop.) G64	50	BV21
Fulmar Pk, (E.Kil.) G74	121	BZ50
Fulmar Pl, John. PA5	79	AE38
Fulton Cres, (Kilb.) John. PA10	78	AC34
Fulton St, G13	47	BF22
Fulwood Av, G13	46	BC22
Fulwood Av, (Linw.) Pais. PA3	60	AK31
Fulwood Pl, G13	46	BB22
Furlongs, The, Ham. ML3	126	CU48
Fyne Av, (Righead Ind. Est.) Bell. ML4	94	CU38
Fyne Ct, Ham. ML3	139	CQ52
Fyne Cres, Lark. ML9	142	DB56
Fyne Way, Moth. ML1	112	DC40
off Howden Pl		
Fyvie Av, G43	102	BK40
Fyvie Cres, Air. ML6	77	DH30
off Grantown Av		
G		
Gadie Av, Renf. PA4	64	BA27
Gadie St, G33	69	BZ29
Gadloch Av, (Kirk.) G66	35	CF19
Gadloch Gdns, (Kirk.) G66	35	CF18
Gadloch St, G22	50	BS23
Gadloch Vw, (Kirk.) G66	35	CF19
Gadsburn Ct, G21	51	BY23
Gadshill St, G21	68	BV28
Gailes Pk, (Both.) G71	109	CP43
Gailes Rd, (Cumb.) G68	9	DB8
Gailes St, G40	89	BX33
Gain & Shankburn Rd, G67	39	CX20
Gainburn Ct, (Cumb.) G67	38	CV15
Gainburn Cres, (Cumb.) G67	38	CV16
Gainburn Gdns, (Cumb.) G67	38	CV16
Gainburn Pl, (Cumb.) G67	38	CV15
Gainburn Vw, (Cumb.) G67	39	CW15
Gain Rd, G67	39	CW20
Gain Rd, Coat. ML5	39	CW20
Gainside Rd, (Glenb.) Coat. ML5	56	CS23
Gairbraid Av, G20	48	BL23
Gairbraid Ct, G20	48	BL23
Gairbraid Pl, G20	48	BM23

Gairbraid Ter, (Baill.) G69 73 CQ32
Gairloch Gdns, (Kirk.) G66 18 CK12
Gala Av, Renf. PA4 64 BA27
Gala St, G33 70 CA27
Galbraith Av, G51 65 BG29
  off Burghead Dr
Galbraith Dr, G51 65 BF29
  off Skipness Dr
Galbraith St, (Miln.) G62 11 BH13
Galbraith St, G51 65 BF29
  off Moss Rd
Galdenoch St, G33 70 CD27
Gallacher Av, Pais. PA2 81 AQ36
Gallacher Ct, Moth. ML1 128 DD50
Gallan Av, G23 31 BN20
Galloway Av, Ham. ML3 140 CS54
Galloway Dr, (Ruther.) G73 105 BX42
Galloway Rd, (E.Kil.) G74 123 CE50
Galloway Rd, Air. ML6 76 DB32
Galloway St, G21 50 BV23
Gallowflat St, (Ruther.) G73 89 BX37
Gallowgate, G1 5 BT31
Gallowgate, G4 5 BU31
Gallowgate, G31 69 BW31
Gallowgate, G40 5 BU31
Gallowhill, Lark. ML9 144 DC59
Gallowhill Av, (Lenz.) G66 35 CE15
Gallowhill Ct, Pais. PA3 63 AW29
  off Montgomery Rd
Gallowhill Gro, (Kirk.) G66 17 CE14
Gallowhill Rd, (Kirk.) G66 35 CE15
Gallowhill Rd, (Carm.) G76 120 BT45
Gallowhill Rd, Pais. PA3 63 AW31
Galston Av, (Newt. M.) G77 118 BJ48
Galston Ct, Ham. ML3 140 CU54
Galston St, G53 100 BB39
Galt Pl, (E.Kil.) G75 135 BZ54
Gamrie Dr, G53 84 BC38
Gamrie Gdns, G53 84 BC38
Gamrie Rd, G53 84 BC37
Gannochy Dr, (Bishop.) G64 33 BY20
Gantock Cres, G33 70 CD29
Gardenhall, (E.Kil.) G75 134 BT53
Gardenhall Ct, (E.Kil.) G75 134 BT53
Gardenside Av, G32 90 CD37
Gardenside Av, (Udd.) G71 109 CN39
Gardenside Cres, G32 90 CD37
Gardenside Gro, G32 90 CD37
Gardenside Pl, G32 90 CD37
Gardenside St, (Udd.) G71 109 CN39
Gardensquare Wk, Air. ML6 75 CZ29
Gardner Dr, (Udd.) G71 93 CQ37
Gardner St, G11 66 BK27
Gardyne St, G34 72 CJ28
  off Conisborough Rd
Gareloch Av, Air. ML6 76 DB27
Gareloch Av, Pais. PA2 81 AQ35
Garfield Av, Bell. ML4 111 CY40
Garfield Dr, Bell. ML4 111 CX41
Garfield St, G31 69 BW31
Garforth Rd, (Baill.) G69 91 CH33
Gargrave Av, (Baill.) G69 91 CH33
Garion Dr, G13 46 BD23
Garlieston Rd, G33 71 CH31
Garmouth Ct, G51 66 BJ29
Garmouth Gdns, G51 66 BJ29
  off Garmouth St
Garmouth St, G51 65 BH29
Garnet Ct, G4 4 BQ28
  off New City Rd
Garnethill St, G3 4 BQ28
Garnet St, G3 4 BQ28
Garngaber Av, (Lenz.) G66 35 CF16

Garngaber Ct, (Kirk.) G66 35 CG16
Garnie Av, Ersk. PA8 26 AT20
Garnie Cres, Ersk. PA8 26 AT20
Garnieland Rd, Ersk. PA8 26 AT20
Garnie La, Ersk. PA8 44 AT21
Garnie Oval, Ersk. PA8 26 AT20
Garnie Pl, Ersk. PA8 26 AT20
Garnkirk La, G33 53 CG24
Garnock Pk, (E.Kil.) G74 136 CG32
Garnock St, G21 68 BV27
Garrell Av, (Kilsyth) G65 7 CT4
Garrell Gro, (Kilsyth) G65 7 CT3
Garrell Pl, G65 7 CS5
Garrell Rd, (Kilsyth) G65 7 CS5
Garrell Way, G65 7 CS5
Garrell Way, (Cumb.) G67 22 DA11
Garrioch Av, (Newt. M.) G77 131 BF51
Garrick Ct, (Newt. M.) G77 131 BF51
  off Garrick Av
Garrioch Cres, G20 48 BM24
Garrioch Dr, G20 48 BM24
Garrioch Gate, G20 49 BN24
  off Garrioch Rd
Garriochmill Rd, G20 49 BN25
Garriochmill Way, G20 49 BP26
  off South Woodside Rd
Garrioch Quad, G20 48 BM24
Garrioch Rd, G20 48 BM25
Garrion Pl, (Ashgill) Lark. ML9 145 DH60
Garrowhill Dr, (Baill.) G69 91 CH33
Garry Av, (Bears.) G61 30 BJ18
Garry Dr, Pais. PA2 81 AQ35
Garry St, G44 87 BQ38
Garscadden Rd, G15 28 BC20
Garscadden Rd S, G13 46 BC21
Garscadden Vw, Clyde. G81 27 AZ18
  off Kirkoswald Dr
Garscube Cross, G4 67 BR27
Garscube Rd, G4 49 BQ26
Garscube Rd, G20 49 BQ26
Gartartan Rd, Pais. PA1 64 BB32
Gartcarron Hill, (Cumb.) G68 21 CY10
Gartcloss Rd, Coat. ML5 74 CS27
Gartconnell Dr, (Bears.) G61 29 BG15
Gartconnell Gdns, (Bears.) G61 29 BG15
Gartconnell Rd, (Bears.) G61 29 BG15
Gartconner Av, (Kirk.) G66 18 CK13
Gartcosh Rd, (Gart.) G69 73 CQ29
Gartcosh Wk, Bell. ML4 110 CV40
Gartcraig Path, G33 70 CC28
  off Gartcraig Pl
Gartcraig Pl, G33 70 CB28
Gartcraig Rd, G33 70 CA29
Gartferry Av, (Chry.) G69 37 CP19
Gartferry Rd, (Mood.) G69 37 CN19
Gartferry St, G21 50 BV25
Gartfield St, Air. ML6 76 DD31
Gartgill Rd, Coat. ML5 74 CU27
Garthamlock Dr, G31 69 BW30
Garthland La, Pais. PA1 62 AV32
Garth St, G1 5 BS30
  off Glassford St
Gartlea Av, Air. ML6 76 DC30
Gartlea Gdns, Air. ML6 76 DD30
  off South Nimmo St
Gartleahill, Air. ML6 76 DD31
Gartlea Rd, Air. ML6 76 DC30
Gartliston Rd, Coat. ML5 56 CV26
Gartliston Ter, (Baill.) G69 73 CQ32
Gartloch Cotts, (Gart.) G69 55 CN26
Gartloch Cotts, (Muir.) G69 54 CK24
Gartloch Rd, G33 70 BC27
Gartloch Rd, G34 71 CE28

Gartloch Rd, (Gart.) G69 54 CL26
Gartly St, G44 103 BP41
  off Clarkston Rd
Gartmore Gdns, (Udd.) G71 93 CN37
Gartmore La, (Mood.) G69 37 CQ19
Gartmore Rd, Pais. PA1 83 AX33
Gartmore Ter, (Camb.) G72 106 CA42
Gartness Dr, Air. ML6 77 DG32
Gartness St, G31 69 BX30
Gartocher Dr, G32 71 CE32
Gartocher Rd, G32 71 CE32
Gartocher Ter, G32 71 CE32
Gartons Rd, G21 51 BY24
Gartsherrie Av, (Glenb.) Coat. ML5 56 CV24
Gartsherrie Ind Est, Coat. ML5 74 CV28
Gartsherrie Rd, Coat. ML5 74 CU29
Gartshore Cres, (Kilsyth) G65 19 CP11
Gartshore Gdns, (Cumb.) G68 20 CU12
Gartshore Rd, (Kirk.) G66 37 CQ15
Gartshore Rd, (Cumb.) G68 37 CQ15
Garturk St, G42 87 BR36
Garturk St, Coat. ML5 95 CX33
Garvald Ct, G40 89 BW35
  off Baltic St
Garvald St, G40 89 BX34
Garve Av, G44 103 BQ41
Garvel Cres, G33 71 CG31
Garvel Pl, (Miln.) G62 11 BF11
Garvel Rd, G33 71 CG31
Garvel Rd, (Miln.) G62 11 BG11
Garvin Lea, Bell. ML4 95 CW37
Garvock Dr, G43 102 BJ40
Garwhitter Dr, (Miln.) G62 12 BK11
Gascoyne, (E.Kil.) G75 135 BY54
Gaskin Path, G33 53 CG24
Gask Pl, G13 46 BB21
Gas St, John. PA5 80 AJ34
Gatehouse St, G32 70 CD32
Gateside Av, (Kilsyth) G65 7 CR6
Gateside Av, (Camb.) G72 107 CF40
Gateside Cres, (Barr.) G78 99 AW44
Gateside Cres, Air. ML6 76 DC29
Gateside Pk, (Kilsyth) G65 7 CR5
Gateside Pl, (Kilb.) John. PA10 78 AC34
Gateside Rd, (Barr.) G78 98 AV44
Gateside Rd, Wis. ML2 129 DG49
Gateside St, G31 69 BX31
Gateside St, Ham. ML3 140 CU51
Gateway, The (E.Kil.) G74 122 CC49
Gaughan Quad, Moth. ML1 127 CZ48
  off Thomson Dr
Gauldry Av, G52 85 BE34
Gauze St, Pais. PA1 62 AU32
Gavell Rd, (Kilsyth) G65 6 CQ6
Gavins Mill Rd, (Miln.) G62 12 BJ12
Gavins Rd, Clyde. G81 27 AX16
Gavin St, Moth. ML1 128 DA48
Gavinton St, G44 103 BP40
Gayne Dr, (Glenb.) Coat. ML5 56 CS23
Gean Ct, (Cumb.) G67 23 DH9
Gear Ter, G40 89 BX35
Geary St, G23 30 BM20
  off Torrin Rd
Geddes Hill, (E.Kil.) G74 122 CD49
Geddes Rd, G21 51 BY22
Gelston St, G32 90 CD33
Gemini Gro, Moth. ML1 112 DD40
  off Glen Dr
Gemmel Pl, (Newt. M.) G77 116 BD49
Generals Gate, (Udd.) G71 109 CN39
General Terminus Quay, G51 4 BP31
Gentle Row, Clyde. G81 26 AV15

George Av, Clyde. G81 — 27 AY18
George Ct, Ham. ML3 — 125 CQ48
  off George St
George Ct, Pais. PA1 — 82 AT33
  off George St
George Cres, Clyde. G81 — 27 AY18
George Gray St, (Ruther.) G73 — 89 BY37
George La, Pais. PA1 — 82 AU33
George Mann Ter, (Ruther.) — 105 BW40
  G73
George Pl, Pais. PA1 — 82 AU33
George Reith Av, G12 — 47 BH24
George Sq, G2 — 5 BS30
George St, G1 — 5 BS30
George St, (Baill.) G69 — 92 CK33
George St, (Barr.) G78 — 99 AX42
George St, Air. ML6 — 76 DA30
George St, (Chap.) Air. ML6 — 97 DF34
George St, Ham. ML3 — 125 CQ48
George St, John. PA5 — 79 AH34
George St, Moth. ML1 — 128 DA49
George St, (New Stev.) Moth. — 112 DD41
  ML1
George St, Pais. PA1 — 82 AT33
George Way, Lark. ML9 — 144 DD57
  off Muirshot Rd
Gerard Pl, Bell. ML4 — 95 CW38
  off Mosshill Rd
Gertrude Pl, (Barr.) G78 — 99 AW43
Ghillies La, Moth. ML1 — 111 CY44
Gibbon Cres, (E.Kil.) G74 — 123 CE50
Gibb St, (Chap.) Air. ML6 — 97 DF34
Gibson Cres, John. PA5 — 79 AG35
Gibson Quad, Moth. ML1 — 111 CY44
  off Frood St
Gibson Rd, Renf. PA4 — 63 AX29
Gibson St, G12 — 67 BN27
Gibson St, G40 — 5 BU31
Giffnock Pk Av, (Giff.) G46 — 102 BL41
Gifford Dr, G52 — 64 BC32
Gifford Wynd, Pais. PA2 — 81 AP35
Gigha Quad, Wis. ML2 — 143 DG52
  off Montgomery Cres
Gilbertfield Path, G33 — 70 CD27
  off Gilbertfield St
Gilbertfield Pl, G33 — 70 CD27
Gilbertfield Rd, (Camb.) G72 — 107 CE42
Gilbertfield St, G33 — 70 CD27
Gilbert St, G3 — 66 BL29
Gilchrist St, Coat. ML5 — 75 CX29
Gilderdale, (E.Kil.) G74 — 135 BY51
Gilfillan Way, Pais. PA2 — 81 AN37
  off Spencer Dr
Gilhill St, G20 — 48 BM22
Gilia St, (Camb.) G72 — 106 CA39
Gillbank La, Lark. ML9 — 145 DE59
  off Carrick St
Gillies Cres, (E.Kil.) G74 — 123 CF48
Gillies La, (Baill.) G69 — 92 CL33
Gilmerton St, G32 — 90 CC33
Gilmour Av, (Thornton.) G74 — 133 BR51
Gilmour Av, Clyde. G81 — 27 AX16
Gilmour Cres, (Ruther.) G73 — 88 BV37
Gilmour Cres, (Eagle.) G76 — 133 BN56
Gilmour Dr, Ham. ML3 — 139 CP51
Gilmour Pl, G5 — 88 BS33
Gilmour Pl, Bell. ML4 — 110 CV40
Gilmour Pl, Coat. ML5 — 74 CU29
Gilmour Pl, (Eagle.) G76 — 133 BN56
Gilmour St, Clyde. G81 — 27 AY17
Gilmour St, Pais. PA1 — 62 AU32
Gilmourton Cres, (Newt. M.) — 117 BF49
  G77

Gimmerscroft Cres, Air. ML6 — 77 DH31
  off Ream Av
Girdons Way, (Udd.) G71 — 109 CN39
Girthon St, G32 — 91 CE33
Girvan Cres, (Chap.) Air. ML6 — 97 DF36
Girvan St, G33 — 69 BZ28
Glade, The, Lark. ML9 — 144 DD59
Gladney Av, G13 — 46 BA21
Gladsmuir Rd, G52 — 64 BD31
Gladstone Av, (Barr.) G78 — 99 AX43
Gladstone Av, John. PA5 — 79 AF38
Gladstone Ct, Ham. ML3 — 125 CQ48
Gladstone St, G4 — 67 BQ27
Gladstone St, Bell. ML4 — 111 CX40
Gladstone St, Clyde. G81 — 26 AV19
Glaive Rd, G13 — 29 BF20
Glamis Av, (Newt. M.) G77 — 117 BH48
Glamis Av, (Elder.) John. PA5 — 80 AK36
Glamis Ct, (New.) Moth. ML1 — 113 DE43
Glamis Dr, (E.Kil.) G74 — 122 CB50
Glamis Gdns, (Bishop.) G64 — 33 BX17
Glamis Rd, G31 — 89 BZ33
Glanderston Av, (Newt. M.) — 116 BD47
  G77
Glanderston Av, (Barr.) G78 — 100 BA43
  off Aurs Rd
Glanderston Ct, G13 — 46 BC21
Glanderston Dr, G13 — 46 BC22
Glanderston Gate, (Newt. M.) — 116 BD47
  G77
Glanderston Rd, (Newt. M.) — 115 AZ48
  G77
Glasgow Airport, (Abbots.) — 62 AT27
  Pais. PA3
Glasgow & Edinburgh Rd, — 93 CP33
  (Baill.) G69
Glasgow & Edinburgh Rd, — 97 DG37
  Moth. ML1
Glasgow Br, G1 — 4 BR31
Glasgow Br, G5 — 4 BR31
Glasgow Br, (Bishop.) G64 — 16 CB14
Glasgow Business Pk, (Baill.) — 72 CK30
  G69
Glasgow Cross, G1 — 5 BT31
Glasgow E Investment Pk, G32 — 90 CB36
Glasgow Grn, G1 — 68 BT32
Glasgow Grn, G40 — 68 BT32
Glasgow Rd, G53 — 99 AZ41
Glasgow Rd, (Miln.) G62 — 12 BK12
Glasgow Rd, (Kilsyth) G65 — 7 CR5
Glasgow Rd, (Kirk.) G66 — 16 CC13
Glasgow Rd, (Cumb.) G67 — 21 CY14
Glasgow Rd, (Cumb.V.) G67 — 22 DD9
Glasgow Rd, (Baill.) G69 — 91 CH33
Glasgow Rd, (Udd.) G71 — 93 CN38
Glasgow Rd, (Blan.) G72 — 108 CL44
Glasgow Rd, (Camb.) G72 — 106 CA39
Glasgow Rd, (Turnlaw) G72 — 106 CA84
Glasgow Rd, (Ruther.) G73 — 88 BV35
Glasgow Rd, (E.Kil.) G74 — 122 CC46
Glasgow Rd, (Eagle.) G76 — 118 BM50
Glasgow Rd, (Barr.) G78 — 99 AZ41
Glasgow Rd, Clyde. G81 — 45 AX21
Glasgow Rd, (Hardgate) Clyde. — 27 AY15
  G81
Glasgow Rd, Coat. ML5 — 74 CS32
Glasgow Rd, Ham. ML3 — 125 CP47
Glasgow Rd, Pais. PA1 — 63 AW32
Glasgow Rd, Renf. PA4 — 46 BA26
Glasgow Rd, Wis. ML2 — 129 DG50
Glasgow St, G12 — 49 BN26
Glassel Rd, G34 — 72 CM28
Glasserton Pl, G43 — 103 BP40

Glasserton Rd, G43 — 103 BP40
Glassford St, G1 — 5 BS30
Glassford St, (Miln.) G62 — 12 BK11
Glassford St, Moth. ML1 — 128 DC49
Glaudhall Av, (Gart.) G69 — 55 CN22
Glebe, The, (Both.) G71 — 109 CR43
Glebe Av, (Both.) G71 — 109 CR43
Glebe Av, (Carm.) G76 — 120 BT46
Glebe Av, Coat. ML5 — 94 CT34
Glebe Ct, G4 — 5 BT29
Glebe Cres, (E.Kil.) G74 — 136 CB52
Glebe Cres, Air. ML6 — 77 DF29
Glebe Cres, Ham. ML3 — 140 CS51
  off Glebe St
Glebe Hollow, (Both.) G71 — 109 CR43
Glebe La, (Newt. M.) G77 — 117 BF49
Glebe Pl, (Camb.) G72 — 106 CD40
Glebe Pl, (Ruther.) G73 — 88 BV37
Glebe Rd, (Newt. M.) G77 — 117 BF49
Glebe St, G4 — 5 BT28
Glebe St, (E.Kil.) G74 — 136 CB52
Glebe St, Bell. ML4 — 110 CV40
Glebe St, Ham. ML3 — 140 CS51
Glebe St, Renf. PA4 — 45 AZ26
Glebe Wynd, (Both.) G71 — 109 CR43
Gleddoch Rd, G52 — 64 BA31
Gledstane Rd, Bish. PA7 — 24 AK19
Glenacre Cres, (Udd.) G71 — 93 CN37
Glenacre Dr, G45 — 104 BT42
Glenacre Dr, Air. ML6 — 77 DF31
Glenacre Gdns, G45 — 104 BT42
Glenacre Gro, G45 — 104 BU41
Glenacre Rd, (Cumb.) G67 — 22 DB13
Glenacre St, G45 — 104 BT42
Glenacre Ter, G45 — 104 BT42
Glen Affric, (E.Kil.) G74 — 136 CD52
Glen Affric Av, G53 — 101 BE41
Glen Affric Way, (Chap.) Air. — 97 DF36
  ML6 *off Glenavon Dr*
Glenafton Vw, Ham. ML3 — 139 CR53
Glenallan Ter, Moth. ML1 — 111 CZ44
  off Marmion Cres
Glenallan Way, Pais. PA2 — 80 AM38
Glen Almond, (E.Kil.) G74 — 137 CF51
Glenalmond Rd, (Ruther.) G73 — 105 BZ42
  off Fennsbank Av
Glenalmond St, G32 — 90 CC33
Glenalva Ct, (Kilsyth) G65 — 7 CT4
Glenapp Av, Pais. PA2 — 83 AX36
Glenapp Pl, (Mood.) G69 — 37 CP18
  off Whithorn Cres
Glenapp Rd, Pais. PA2 — 83 AX36
Glenapp St, G41 — 87 BP34
Glenarklet Cres, Pais. PA2 — 83 AX36
Glenarklet Dr, Pais. PA2 — 83 AW36
Glen Arroch, (E.Kil.) G74 — 136 CD52
Glenartney Rd, (Chry.) G69 — 36 CL20
Glenashdale Way, Pais. PA2 — 83 AW36
Glen Av, G32 — 70 CD31
Glen Av, (Chry.) G69 — 37 CP19
Glen Av, (Neil.) G78 — 114 AU46
Glen Av, Lark. ML9 — 144 DB60
Glenavon Ct, Ham. ML3 — 139 CR52
  off Swisscot Av
Glenavon Dr, Air. ML6 — 97 DF36
Glenavon Rd, G20 — 48 BM22
Glenbank Av, (Lenz.) G66 — 35 CE17
Glenbank Ct, (Thornlie.) G46 — 101 BH43
  off Glenbank Dr
Glenbank Dr, (Thornlie.) G46 — 101 BH43
Glenbank Rd, (Lenz.) G66 — 35 CF17
Glenbarr St, G21 — 68 BV28
Glen Bervie, (E.Kil.) G74 — 136 CD51

Glenbervie Cres, (Cumb.) G68 22 DB9
off Lansdowne Dr
Glenbervie Pl, G23 31 BN20
off Hollinwell Rd
Glenbervie Pl, (Newt. M.) G77 116 BC48
Glenboig Fm Rd, (Glenb.) 56 CU23
Coat. ML5
Glenboig Rd, (Gart.) G69 55 CR21
Glenbrittle Dr, Pais. PA2 83 AW36
Glenbrittle Way, Pais. PA2 83 AW36
Glenbuck Av, G33 52 CB23
Glenbuck Dr, G33 52 CB23
Glenburn Av, (Baill.) G69 72 CL32
Glenburn Av, (Chry.) G69 37 CP19
Glenburn Av, (Camb.) G72 105 BZ40
Glenburn Av, Moth. ML1 113 DE41
Glenburn Ct, (Kirk.) G66 17 CF13
Glenburn Cres, (Udd.) G71 94 CS36
Glenburn Cres, Pais. PA2 82 AT37
Glenburn Gdns, (Bishop.) G64 32 BV19
Glenburn Gdns, (Glenb.) Coat. 56 CS23
ML5
Glenburnie Pl, G34 71 CH30
Glenburn La, G20 49 BN22
off Thornton St
Glenburn Rd, (Giff.) G46 102 BK44
Glenburn Rd, (Bears.) G61 29 BG16
Glenburn Rd, (E.Kil.) G74 121 BW50
Glenburn Rd, Ham. ML3 125 CR50
Glenburn Rd, Pais. PA2 81 AR37
Glenburn St, G20 49 BN22
Glenburn Ter, Moth. ML1 112 DD44
Glenburn Wk, (Baill.) G69 72 CL32
off Glenburn Av
Glenburn Way, (E.Kil.) G74 120 BV50
Glenburn Wynd, Lark. ML9 144 DD57
off Muirshot Rd
Glencairn Av, Wis. ML2 129 DF49
Glencairn Ct, Pais. PA3 63 AX29
off Montgomery Rd
Glencairn Dr, G41 86 BM35
Glencairn Dr, (Chry.) G69 37 CN19
Glencairn Dr, (Ruther.) G73 88 BV37
Glencairn Gdns, G41 87 BN35
Glencairn Gdns, (Camb.) G72 107 CF40
Glencairn La, G41 87 BP35
Glencairn Path, G32 71 CE31
off Hallhill Rd
Glencairn Rd, (Cumb.) G67 23 DE11
Glencairn Rd, Pais. PA3 63 AW29
Glencairn St, (Kirk.) G66 17 CF14
Glencairn St, Moth. ML1 128 DA48
Glencalder Cres, Bell. ML4 111 CX42
Glen Cally, (E.Kil.) G74 136 CD51
Glencally Av, Pais. PA2 83 AX36
Glen Cannich, (E.Kil.) G74 136 CD52
Glen Carron, (E.Kil.) G74 136 CD52
Glencart Gro, (Kilb.) John. 79 AE36
PA10 off Milliken Pk Rd
Glencleland Rd, Wis. ML2 129 DF49
Glenclora Dr, Pais. PA2 83 AW36
Glen Clova, (E.Kil.) G74 136 CD51
Glen Clova Dr, (Cumb.) G68 21 CY9
Glencloy St, G20 48 BL22
Glen Clunie, (E.Kil.) G74 137 CF51
Glen Clunie Dr, G53 101 BE41
Glen Clunie Pl, G53 101 BE41
off Glen Clunie Dr
Glencoats Dr, Pais. PA3 61 AQ32
Glencoe Dr, Moth. ML1 112 DC40
Glencoe Pl, G13 47 BG22
Glencoe Pl, Ham. ML3 139 CR53
Glencoe Rd, (Ruther.) G73 105 BZ42

Glencoe St, G13 47 BH22
Glen Cona Dr, G53 101 BE40
Glenconner Way, (Kirk.) G66 18 CJ12
Glencorse Rd, Pais. PA2 82 AS35
Glencorse St, G32 70 CA30
Glen Ct, Coat. ML5 74 CT32
Glen Ct, Moth. ML1 128 DD49
off Range Rd
Glencraig St, Air. ML6 76 DA30
Glen Creran Cres, (Neil.) G78 114 AS47
Glen Cres, G13 46 BA22
Glencroft Av, (Udd.) G71 93 CN37
Glencroft Rd, G44 104 BT40
Glencryan Rd, (Cumb.) G67 22 DD12
Glendale Av, Air. ML6 77 DF31
Glendale Cres, (Bishop.) G64 51 BY21
Glendale Dr, (Bishop.) G64 51 BY21
Glendale Gro, Coat. ML5 94 CU34
off Haddington Way
Glendale Pl, G31 69 BX31
Glendale Pl, (Bishop.) G64 51 BY22
Glendale St, G31 69 BX31
Glendaruel Av, (Bears.) G61 30 BK17
Glendaruel Rd, (Ruther.) G73 106 CA43
Glendarvel Gdns, G22 50 BT25
Glendee Gdns, Renf. PA4 63 AZ27
Glendee Rd, Renf. PA4 63 AZ27
Glen Dene Way, G53 101 BE41
Glen Derry, (E.Kil.) G74 137 CF51
Glen Dessary, (E.Kil.) G74 136 CD53
Glendeveron Way, (Carfin) 112 DC43
Moth. ML1
Glen Devon, (E.Kil.) G74 137 CF52
Glendevon Pl, Clyde. G81 26 AV18
Glendevon Pl, Ham. ML3 139 CR53
off Swisscot Av
Glendevon Sq, G33 70 CD27
Glen Dewar Pl, G53 101 BE41
Glendinning Rd, G13 29 BG20
Glendoick Pl, (Newt. M.) G77 116 BC48
Glen Doll, (E.Kil.) G74 136 CD52
Glendore St, G14 65 BG27
Glen Douglas Dr, (Cumb.) G68 21 CY9
Glendoune Rd, (Clark.) G76 119 BN48
Glendower Way, Pais. PA2 81 AN37
Glen Dr, Moth. ML1 112 DD40
Glenduffhill Rd, (Baill.) G69 71 CH32
Glen Dye, (E.Kil.) G74 136 CD51
Glen Eagles, (E.Kil.) G74 137 CE52
Gleneagles Av, (Cumb.) G68 9 DC8
Gleneagles Dr, (Bishop.) G64 33 BW18
Gleneagles Dr, (Newt. M.) G77 118 BK49
Gleneagles Gdns, (Bishop.) 32 BV18
G64
Gleneagles Gate, (Newt. M.) 118 BK49
G77
Gleneagles La N, G14 47 BE25
Gleneagles La S, G14 47 BE25
Gleneagles Pk, (Both.) G71 109 CP43
Glenelg Cres, (Kirk.) G66 18 CJ12
Glenelg Path, (Glenb.) Coat. 56 CS23
ML5 off Glenboig Rd
Glenelg Quad, G34 72 CM28
Glenelm Pl, Bell. ML4 111 CW39
Glen Esk, (E.Kil.) G74 137 CE51
Glen Esk Cres, G53 101 BE41
Glen Esk Dr, G53 101 BE41
Glen Esk Pl, G53 101 BE41
off Kennishead Rd
Glen Etive Pl, (Ruther.) G73 106 CA43
Glen Falloch, (E.Kil.) G74 137 CE52
Glen Falloch Cres, (Neil.) G78 114 AS48
Glen Farg, (E.Kil.) G74 137 CF52

Glenfarg Ct, Ham. ML3 139 CR53
Glenfarg Cres, (Bears.) G61 30 BK17
Glenfarg Rd, (Ruther.) G73 105 BX41
Glenfarg St, G20 67 BQ27
Glenfarm Rd, Moth. ML1 113 DG41
Glen Farrar, (E.Kil.) G74 136 CD52
Glen Feshie, (E.Kil.) G74 136 CD52
Glenfield Av, Pais. PA2 82 AT38
Glenfield Cres, Pais. PA2 98 AT39
Glenfield Gdns, Pais. PA2 98 AT39
Glenfield Gra, Pais. PA2 98 AU39
Glenfield Gro, Pais. PA2 98 AT39
Glenfield Rd, (E.Kil.) G75 136 CC55
Glenfield Rd, Pais. PA2 82 AS38
Glenfinnan Dr, G20 48 BM23
Glenfinnan Dr, (Bears.) G61 30 BK18
Glenfinnan Gro, Bell. ML4 111 CZ41
Glenfinnan Pl, G20 48 BM23
off Glenfinnan Rd
Glenfinnan Rd, G20 48 BM23
Glenfruin Cres, Pais. PA2 83 AX36
Glen Fruin Dr, Lark. ML9 145 DE60
Glen Fruin Pl, (Chap.) Air. ML6 97 DF36
off Glen Rannoch Dr
Glenfruin Rd, (Blan.) G72 124 CL46
Glen Fyne Rd, (Cumb.) G68 21 CX9
Glen Gairn, (E.Kil.) G74 137 CF51
Glen Gairn Cres, (Neil.) G78 114 AS47
Glen Gdns, (Elder.) John. PA5 80 AL34
Glen Garrel Pl, (Kilsyth) G65 7 CR4
Glengarriff Rd, Bell. ML4 95 CX37
Glen Garry, (E.Kil.) G74 136 CD53
Glengarry Dr, G52 65 BE32
Glengavel Cres, G33 52 CB23
Glen Gavin Way, Pais. PA2 83 AX36
Glengonnar St, Lark. ML9 144 DC61
Glen Gro, (Kilsyth) G65 7 CT3
Glen Gro, (E.Kil.) G75 135 BZ54
Glengyre St, G34 72 CL28
Glenhead Cres, G22 50 BS23
Glenhead Dr, Moth. ML1 128 DA49
Glenhead Rd, (Lenz.) G66 35 CE17
Glenhead Rd, Clyde. G81 26 AV16
Glenhead St, G22 50 BS23
Glenholme Av, Pais. PA2 81 AR36
off Corsebar Rd
Glenhove Rd, (Cumb.) G67 22 DC11
Gleniffer Av, G13 46 BC23
Gleniffer Ct, Pais. PA2 81 AR38
Gleniffer Cres, (Elder.) John. 80 AL36
PA5
Gleniffer Dr, (Barr.) G78 99 AW40
Gleniffer Rd, Pais. PA2 81 AR38
Gleniffer Rd, Renf. PA4 63 AX29
Gleniffer Vw, (Neil.) G78 114 AT45
Gleniffer Vw, Clyde. G81 27 AZ18
off Kirkoswald Dr
Glen Isla, (E.Kil.) G74 137 CE51
Glenisla Av, (Mood.) G69 37 CQ17
Glen Isla Av, (Neil.) G78 114 AS48
Glenisla St, G31 89 BZ34
Glenkirk Dr, G15 28 BD19
Glen Kyle Dr, G53 101 BE41
Glen La, Pais. PA3 62 AU32
Glen Lednock Dr, (Cumb.) G68 21 CX9
Glen Lee, (E.Kil.) G74 137 CE51
Glenlee Cres, G52 84 BB34
Glenlee St, Ham. ML3 125 CP48
Glen Lethnot, (E.Kil.) G74 137 CE51
Glen Livet Pl, G53 101 BE41
off Glen Moriston Rd
Glen Livet Rd, (Neil.) G78 114 AS47

Glen Lochay Gdns, (Cumb.) G68 — 21 — CX9
Glenlora Dr, G53 — 84 — BC38
Glenlora Ter, G53 — 84 — BD38
Glen Loy Pl, G53 — 101 — BE41
Glenluce Dr, G32 — 91 — CF34
Glenluce Gdns, (Mood.) G69 — 37 — CQ18
off Brady Cres
Glenluce Ter, (E.Kil.) G74 — 135 — BY51
Glenluggie Rd, (Kirk.) G66 — 18 — CJ14
Glenlui Av, (Ruther.) G73 — 105 — BX40
Glen Luss Gdns, (Cumb.) G68 — 21 — CX9
Glen Luss Pl, G53 — 101 — BE41
Glen Luss Rd, Coat. ML5 — 75 — CZ32
off Strathmore Wk
Glen Lyon, (E.Kil.) G74 — 137 — CE52
Glen Lyon Ct, (Cumb.) G68 — 21 — CX9
Glenlyon Ct, Ham. ML3 — 139 — CR53
Glen Lyon Pl, (Ruther.) G73 — 105 — BY42
Glen Lyon Rd, (Neil.) G78 — 114 — AS47
Glen Mallie, (E.Kil.) G74 — 137 — CE52
Glenmalloch Pl, (Elder.) John. PA5 — 80 — AL34
Glenmanor Av, (Mood.) G69 — 37 — CN19
Glenmanor Rd, (Chry.) G69 — 37 — CN19
Glenmare Av, (Kirk.) G66 — 18 — CJ14
Glen Mark, (E.Kil.) G74 — 137 — CE51
Glen Mark Rd, (Neil.) G78 — 114 — AS47
Glenmavis Rd, Air. ML6 — 58 — DA26
Glenmavis St, G4 — 4 — BR28
Glen More, (E.Kil.) G74 — 136 — CC52
Glenmore Av, G42 — 88 — BU37
Glenmore Av, Bell. ML4 — 111 — CX42
Glenmore Rd, Moth. ML1 — 113 — DE42
Glen Moriston, (E.Kil.) G74 — 136 — CD52
Glen Moriston Rd, G53 — 101 — BE41
Glen Moriston Rd, (Cumb.) G68 — 21 — CX9
Glenmoss Av, Ersk. PA8 — 25 — AP20
Glen Moy, (E.Kil.) G74 — 136 — CD52
Glenmuir Dr, G53 — 100 — BD40
Glen Muir Rd, (Neil.) G78 — 114 — AS47
Glen Nevis, (E.Kil.) G74 — 136 — CD53
Glen Nevis Pl, (Ruther.) G73 — 105 — BY43
Glen Ochil Rd, (Chap.) Air. ML6 — 97 — DF36
Glen Ogilvie, (E.Kil.) G74 — 137 — CE51
Glen Ogle St, G32 — 91 — CF33
Glenoran La, Lark. ML9 — 144 — DD57
off Station Rd
Glenorchard Rd, (Torr.) G64 — 14 — BU13
Glen Orchy Ct, (Cumb.) G68 — 8 — CX8
Glen Orchy Dr, G53 — 101 — BF41
Glen Orchy Dr, (Cumb.) G68 — 21 — CX9
Glen Orchy Gro, G53 — 101 — BE41
Glen Orchy Pl, G53 — 101 — BF41
off Glen Orchy Dr
Glen Orchy Pl, (Cumb.) G68 — 8 — CX8
Glen Orchy Pl, (Chap.) Air. ML6 — 97 — DF36
off Glen Rannoch Dr
Glen Orchy Way, G53 — 101 — BE42
Glen Orrin Way, (Neil.) G78 — 114 — AS47
Glen Pk, Air. ML6 — 77 — DG31
Glenpark Av, (Thornlie.) G46 — 101 — BH43
Glenpark Gdns, (Camb.) G72 — 90 — CA38
off Glenpark Ter
Glenpark Rd, G31 — 69 — BX31
Glenpark St, G31 — 69 — BX31
Glenpark Ter, (Camb.) G72 — 90 — CA38
Glenpatrick Bldgs, (Elder.) John. PA5 — 80 — AL36
Glenpatrick Rd, (Elder.) John. PA5 — 80 — AM35
Glen Pl, (Clark.) G76 — 119 — BN46

Glen Prosen, (E.Kil.) G74 — 137 — CE51
Glen Quoich, (E.Kil.) G74 — 123 — CF50
Glenraith Path, G33 — 52 — CD26
off Glenraith Rd
Glenraith Rd, G33 — 52 — CD26
Glenraith Sq, G33 — 52 — CD26
Glenraith Wk, G33 — 52 — CD26
Glen Rannoch Dr, (Chap.) Air. ML6 — 97 — DF36
Glen Rinnes Dr, (Neil.) G78 — 114 — AT47
Glen Rd, G32 — 70 — CD30
Glen Rd, (Old Kil.) G60 — 25 — AR15
Glen Rd, (Dullatur) G68 — 9 — CZ6
Glen Rd, (E.Kil.) G74 — 120 — BV49
Glen Rd, Air. ML6 — 77 — DG31
Glen Rosa Gdns, (Cumb.) G68 — 21 — CX9
Glen Roy Dr, (Neil.) G78 — 114 — AS47
Glen Sannox Dr, (Cumb.) G68 — 21 — CX9
Glen Sannox Gro, (Cumb.) G68 — 21 — CY9
Glen Sannox Ln, (Cumb.) G68 — 21 — CY9
Glen Sannox Vw, (Cumb.) G68 — 21 — CX9
Glen Sannox Way, (Cumb.) G68 — 21 — CY9
Glen Sannox Wynd, (Cumb.) G68 — 21 — CY9
Glen Sax Dr, Renf. PA4 — 64 — BA28
Glen Shee, (E.Kil.) G74 — 137 — CE51
Glen Shee Av, (Neil.) G78 — 114 — AS47
Glenshee Ct, G31 — 89 — BZ34
Glen Shee Cres, Air. ML6 — 97 — DF36
off Glenavon Dr
Glenshee Gdns, G31 — 90 — CA34
Glenshee St, G31 — 89 — BZ33
Glenshee Ter, Ham. ML3 — 139 — CR53
Glenshiel Av, Pais. PA2 — 83 — AW36
Glenshira Av, Pais. PA2 — 83 — AW36
Glen Shirva Rd, (Kilsyth) G65 — 19 — CP9
Glenside Av, G53 — 84 — BD35
Glenside Dr, (Ruther.) G73 — 105 — BZ39
Glenspean Pl, G43 — 86 — BM38
off Glenspean St
Glenspean Pl, Coat. ML5 — 75 — CZ32
off Strathmore Wk
Glenspean St, G43 — 102 — BL39
Glen St, (Camb.) G72 — 107 — CF41
Glen St, (Barr.) G78 — 99 — AY42
Glen St, Moth. ML1 — 112 — DA44
Glen St, (New.) Moth. ML1 — 113 — DF41
Glen St, Pais. PA3 — 62 — AT32
Glentanar Dr, (Mood.) G69 — 37 — CQ19
Glentanar Pl, G22 — 50 — BS21
Glentanar Rd, G22 — 49 — BR21
Glen Tanner, (E.Kil.) G74 — 123 — CF50
Glen Tarbert Dr, (Neil.) G78 — 114 — AS47
Glentarbert Rd, (Ruther.) G73 — 105 — BZ42
Glen Tennet, (E.Kil.) G74 — 137 — CE51
Glentore Quad, Air. ML6 — 76 — DC27
Glentrool Gdns, G22 — 50 — BS25
Glentrool Gdns, (Mood.) G69 — 37 — CQ18
Glen Turret, (E.Kil.) G74 — 137 — CE51
Glenturret St, G32 — 90 — CC33
Glentyan Av, (Kilb.) John. PA10 — 78 — AC33
Glentyan Dr, G53 — 84 — BC38
Glentyan Pl, G53 — 84 — BC38
Glen Urquhart, (E.Kil.) G74 — 136 — CD52
Glenview, (Kirk.) G66 — 17 — CF13
Glen Vw, (Cumb.) G67 — 23 — DE10
Glenview, Air. ML6 — 77 — DF31
off North Calder Dr
Glen Vw, Ham. ML3 — 140 — CT54
Glenview, Lark. ML9 — 144 — DB57
Glenview Cres, (Mood.) G69 — 37 — CP18
Glenview Pl, (Blan.) G72 — 108 — CM44
Glenview St, (Glenm.) Air. ML6 — 58 — DA25

Glenville Av, (Giff.) G46 — 102 — BK42
Glenville Gate, (Clark.) G76 — 119 — BQ48
Glenville Ter, (Clark.) G76 — 119 — BQ48
off The Paddock
Glenwell St, (Glenm.) Air. ML6 — 58 — DA26
Glenwood Av, Air. ML6 — 97 — DE33
Glenwood Business Pk, G45 — 104 — BU42
Glenwood Ct, (Kirk.) G66 — 34 — CC16
Glenwood Dr, (Thornlie.) G46 — 101 — BH43
Glenwood Gdns, (Kirk.) G66 — 34 — CC16
Glenwood Path, G45 — 104 — BU42
Glenwood Pl, G45 — 104 — BU42
Glenwood Pl, (Kirk.) G66 — 34 — CC16
Glenwood Rd, (Kirk.) G66 — 34 — CC16
Globe Ct, (E.Kil.) G74 — 123 — CF48
off Bosworth Rd
Gloucester Av, (Ruther.) G73 — 105 — BZ39
Gloucester Av, (Clark.) G76 — 118 — BM46
Gloucester St, G5 — 67 — BQ32
Gockston Rd, Pais. PA3 — 62 — AT30
Gogar Pl, G33 — 70 — CA29
Gogar St, G33 — 70 — CA29
Goil Av, (Righead Ind. Est.) Bell. ML4 — 110 — CT39
Goil Way, Moth. ML1 — 112 — DC40
off Howden Pl
Goldberry Av, G14 — 46 — BD24
Goldenacre Pl, (Plains) Air. ML6 — 59 — DH26
Goldie Rd, (Udd.) G71 — 109 — CQ41
Golf Av, Bell. ML4 — 111 — CX42
Golf Course Rd, (Torr.) G64 — 14 — BU13
Golf Ct, G44 — 103 — BN43
Golf Dr, G15 — 28 — BB20
Golf Dr, Pais. PA1 — 83 — AY33
Golf Gdns, Lark. ML9 — 145 — DE59
Golfhill Dr, G31 — 69 — BW29
Golfhill Quad, Air. ML6 — 76 — DC27
Golfhill Rd, Wis. ML2 — 129 — DF49
Golfhill Ter, G31 — 68 — BV29
off Firpark St
Golf Pl, Bell. ML4 — 111 — CX42
Golf Rd, (Ruther.) G73 — 105 — BX41
Golf Rd, (Clark.) G76 — 118 — BM46
Golf Vw, (Bears.) G61 — 28 — BD16
Golf Vw, Clyde. G81 — 26 — AV17
Golfview Dr, Coat. ML5 — 74 — CS30
Golfview Pl, Coat. ML5 — 74 — CS31
Golspie Av, Air. ML6 — 96 — DA33
Golspie St, G51 — 66 — BJ29
Goodview Gdns, Lark. ML9 — 145 — DE59
Goosedubbs, G1 — 5 — BS31
Gopher Av, (Udd.) G71 — 93 — CR37
Gorbals Cross, G5 — 68 — BS32
Gorbals La, G5 — 4 — BR31
off Oxford St
Gorbals St, G5 — 87 — BR33
Gordon Av, G44 — 103 — BN43
Gordon Av, G52 — 64 — BA29
Gordon Av, (Baill.) G69 — 71 — CH32
Gordon Ct, Air. ML6 — 77 — DG29
off Katherine St
Gordon Cres, (Newt. M.) G77 — 117 — BG47
Gordon Dr, G44 — 103 — BN42
Gordon Dr, (E.Kil.) G74 — 122 — CD50
Gordon La, G1 — 4 — BR30
off Mitchell St
Gordon Pl, Bell. ML4 — 110 — CV42
Gordon Rd, G44 — 103 — BN43
Gordon Rd, Ham. ML3 — 125 — CP49
Gordon St, G1 — 4 — BR30
Gordon St, Pais. PA1 — 82 — AU33
Gordon Ter, (Blan.) G72 — 108 — CL43

Gordon Ter, Ham. ML3 | 125 | CP50
Gorebridge St, G32 | 70 | CA30
Gorget Av, G13 | 29 | BE20
Gorget Pl, G13 | 29 | BE20
Gorget Quad, G13 | 28 | BD20
Gorse Dr, (Barr.) G78 | 99 | AX41
Gorse Pl, (Udd.) G71 | 93 | CR37
Gorsewood, (Bishop.) G64 | 32 | BU20
Gorstan Pl, G20 | 48 | BL24
off Wyndford Rd
Gorstan St, G23 | 48 | BM21
Gosford La, G14 | 46 | BC25
Goudie St, Pais. PA3 | 62 | AS30
Gough St, G33 | 69 | BZ29
Gourlay, (E.Kil.) G74 | 123 | CF48
Gourlay Path, G21 | 50 | BT26
off Endrick St
Gourlay St, G21 | 50 | BT26
Gourock St, G5 | 87 | BQ33
off Eglinton St
Govan Cross, G51 | 66 | BJ29
off Govan Rd
Govan Cross Shop Cen, G51 | 66 | BJ29
Govanhill St, G42 | 87 | BR35
Govan Rd, G51 | 66 | BL31
Gowanbank Gdns, John. PA5 | 79 | AG35
off Floors St
Gowan Brae, (Kirk.) G66 | 35 | CE15
off Marguerite Av
Gowanlea Av, G15 | 28 | BC20
Gowanlea Dr, (Giff.) G46 | 102 | BM41
Gowanlea Ter, (Udd.) G71 | 93 | CR38
Gower La, G51 | 66 | BM32
off North Gower St
Gower St, G41 | 86 | BL33
Gower St, G51 | 86 | BL33
Gower Ter, G41 | 66 | BL32
Gowkhall Av, Moth. ML1 | 113 | DH42
Goyle Av, G15 | 29 | BE18
Grace Av, (Baill.) G69 | 73 | CP32
Grace St, G3 | 4 | BP30
Graeme Ct, Moth. ML1 | 111 | CZ43
off Marmion Cres
Graffham Av, (Giff.) G46 | 102 | BM42
Grafton Pl, G1 | 5 | BS29
Graham Av, (Camb.) G72 | 107 | CF40
Graham Av, (E.Kil.) G74 | 136 | CA51
Graham Av, Clyde. G81 | 27 | AX18
Graham Av, Ham. ML3 | 140 | CT53
Graham Dr, (Miln.) G62 | 11 | BG11
Graham Pl, (Kilsyth) G65 | 7 | CS3
Graham Pl, (Ashgill) Lark. | 145 | DH60
ML9
Grahamsdyke Rd, (Kirk.) G66 | 17 | CG12
Grahamshill Av, Air. ML6 | 77 | DF29
Grahamshill St, Air. ML6 | 77 | DE29
Graham Sq, G31 | 68 | BV31
Grahamston Ct, Pais. PA2 | 83 | AY37
Grahamston Cres, Pais. PA2 | 83 | AY37
Grahamston Pk, (Barr.) G78 | 99 | AX40
Grahamston Pl, Pais. PA2 | 83 | AY37
Grahamston Rd, (Barr.) G78 | 99 | AX39
Grahamston Rd, Pais. PA2 | 99 | AX39
Graham St, (Barr.) G78 | 99 | AX42
Graham St, Air. ML6 | 76 | DC30
Graham St, Ham. ML3 | 126 | CU50
Graham St, John. PA5 | 79 | AG35
Graham St, Moth. ML1 | 112 | DC40
Graham Ter, (Bishop.) G64 | 51 | BX22
Graignestock Pl, G40 | 68 | BU32
off London Rd
Graignestock St, G40 | 68 | BU32
Grainger Rd, (Bishop.) G64 | 33 | BZ20

Grammar Sch Sq, Ham. ML3 | 126 | CU49
off Church St
Grampian Av, Pais. PA2 | 82 | AT37
Grampian Ct, (Bears.) G61 | 11 | BE13
Grampian Cres, G32 | 90 | CD33
Grampian Cres, (Chap.) Air. | 97 | DH36
ML6
Grampian Pl, G32 | 90 | CD33
Grampian Rd, Wis. ML2 | 129 | DH49
Grampian St, G32 | 90 | CD33
Grampian Way, (Bears.) G61 | 10 | BD13
Grampian Way, (Cumb.) G68 | 21 | CW11
Grampian Way, (Barr.) G78 | 99 | AY44
Granby La, G12 | 48 | BM26
Grandtully Dr, G12 | 48 | BL23
Grange Av, (Miln.) G62 | 12 | BK11
Grange Av, Wis. ML2 | 143 | DG52
Grange Gdns, (Both.) G71 | 109 | CR44
off Blairston Av
Grangeneuk Gdns, (Cumb.) | 21 | CY12
G68
Grange Rd, G42 | 87 | BQ37
Grange Rd, (Bears.) G61 | 29 | BH16
Grange St, Moth. ML1 | 128 | DC49
Grannoch Pl, Coat. ML5 | 95 | CZ35
Gran St, Clyde. G81 | 46 | BA21
Grant Ct, Air. ML6 | 77 | DG29
Grant Ct, Ham. ML3 | 140 | CS55
Grantholm Av, Moth. ML1 | 112 | DD39
Grantlea Gro, G32 | 91 | CF33
Grantlea Ter, G32 | 91 | CF33
Grantley Gdns, G41 | 86 | BM37
Grantley St, G41 | 86 | BM37
Grantoften Path, (E.Kil.) G75 | 135 | BZ55
Granton St, G5 | 88 | BU35
Grantown Av, Air. ML6 | 77 | DG31
Grantown Gdns, (Glenm.) Air. | 58 | DB24
ML6
Grants Av, Pais. PA2 | 82 | AS36
Grants Cres, Pais. PA2 | 82 | AT37
Grants Pl, Pais. PA2 | 82 | AS37
Grant St, G3 | 4 | BP28
Grants Way, Pais. PA2 | 82 | AS36
Granville St, G3 | 4 | BP29
Granville St, Clyde. G81 | 27 | AX18
Grasmere, (E.Kil.) G75 | 134 | BV56
Grasmere Ct, Ham. ML3 | 140 | CT55
off Ambleside Ri
Grathellen Ct, Moth. ML1 | 128 | DC45
Gray Dr, (Bears.) G61 | 29 | BH18
Grayshill Rd, (Cumb.) G68 | 38 | CU15
Gray's Rd, (Udd.) G71 | 109 | CR40
Gray St, G3 | 67 | BN28
Gray St, (Kirk.) G66 | 18 | CK14
Gray St, Lark. ML9 | 144 | DC57
Great Dovehill, G1 | 5 | BT31
Great George St, G12 | 48 | BM26
Great Hamilton St, Pais. PA2 | 82 | AU35
Great Kelvin La, G12 | 67 | BN27
off Glasgow St
Great Western Retail Pk, G15 | 28 | BB20
Great Western Rd, G4 | 49 | BN26
Great Western Rd, G12 | 48 | BK25
Great Western Rd, G13 | 28 | BB20
Great Western Rd, G15 | 28 | BB20
Great Western Ter, G12 | 48 | BL25
Great Western Ter La, G12 | 48 | BL25
Green, The, G40 | 68 | BU32
Greenacres, Moth. ML1 | 127 | CY48
Greenacres Ct, G53 | 101 | BE41
Greenacres Dr, G53 | 101 | BE41
Greenacres Vw, Moth. ML1 | 127 | CY48
off Greenacres

Greenacres Way, G53 | 101 | BE41
Greenan Av, G42 | 88 | BU38
Greenbank, (Blan.) G72 | 124 | CL46
off Moorfield Rd
Greenbank Av, (Giff.) G46 | 118 | BJ46
Greenbank Dr, Pais. PA2 | 82 | AT38
Greenbank Rd, (Cumb.) G68 | 21 | CY11
Greenbank St, (Ruther.) G73 | 89 | BW37
Greendyke St, G1 | 5 | BT31
Greenend Av, John. PA5 | 79 | AF36
Greenend Pl, G32 | 71 | CE30
Greenend Vw, Bell. ML4 | 110 | CV41
Greenfarm Rd, (Newt. M.) G77 | 116 | BD47
Greenfarm Rd, (Linw.) Pais. | 60 | AK31
PA3
Greenfaulds Cres, (Cumb.) G67 | 22 | DC13
Greenfaulds Rd, (Cumb.) G67 | 22 | DA14
Greenfield Av, G32 | 70 | CD31
Greenfield Pl, G32 | 70 | CD31
Greenfield Quad, Moth. ML1 | 113 | DH41
off Mossbank Cres
Greenfield Rd, G32 | 71 | CE30
Greenfield Rd, (Clark.) G76 | 119 | BN47
Greenfield Rd, Ham. ML3 | 125 | CQ47
Greenfield St, G51 | 65 | BH30
Greengairs Av, G51 | 65 | BF29
Greengairs Rd, (Green.) Air. | 58 | DD21
ML6
Greenhall Pl, (Blan.) G72 | 124 | CL47
Greenhead Rd, (Bears.) G61 | 29 | BH17
Greenhead Rd, (Inch.) Renf. | 44 | AS22
PA4
Greenhead St, G40 | 88 | BU33
Greenhill, (Bishop.) G64 | 51 | BY21
Greenhill Av, (Giff.) G46 | 102 | BK44
Greenhill Av, (Gart.) G69 | 55 | CN22
Greenhill Business Pk, Pais. | 62 | AS31
PA3
Greenhill Ct, (Ruther.) G73 | 89 | BW37
Greenhill Cres, (Elder.) John. | 80 | AM35
PA5
Greenhill Cres, (Linw.) Pais. | 60 | AK31
PA3
Greenhill Dr, (Linw.) Pais. PA3 | 60 | AL31
Greenhill Rd, (Ruther.) G73 | 89 | BW37
Greenhill Rd, Pais. PA3 | 62 | AS31
Greenhills Cres, (E.Kil.) G75 | 135 | BX56
Greenhills Rd, (E.Kil.) G75 | 134 | BU53
Greenhills Sq, (E.Kil.) G75 | 135 | BX56
off Greenhills Cres
Greenhill St, (Ruther.) G73 | 89 | BW38
Greenholm Av, (Udd.) G71 | 93 | CN38
Greenholm Av, (Clark.) G76 | 119 | BN46
Greenholme St, G44 | 103 | BQ39
Greenknowe Rd, G43 | 102 | BK39
Greenlaw Av, Pais. PA1 | 63 | AW32
Greenlaw Cres, Pais. PA1 | 63 | AW31
Greenlaw Dr, (Newt. M.) G77 | 117 | BE48
Greenlaw Dr, Pais. PA1 | 63 | AW32
Greenlaw Gdns, Pais. PA1 | 63 | AW31
Greenlaw Rd, G14 | 45 | AZ23
Greenlaw Rd, (Newt. M.) G77 | 117 | BE48
Greenlea Rd, (Chry.) G69 | 54 | CK21
Greenlea St, G13 | 47 | BG23
Greenlees Gdns, (Camb.) G72 | 106 | CB42
Greenlees Pk, (Camb.) G72 | 106 | CC42
Greenlees Rd, (Camb.) G72 | 106 | CC40
Greenless Gro, Coat. ML5 | 75 | CZ32
off Laxford Pl
Green Ln, Moth. ML1 | 112 | DC42
off Woodside St
Greenloan Av, G51 | 65 | BF29

Greenloan Vw, Lark. ML9	144	DD60
off Keir Hardie Rd		
Greenlodge Ter, G40	88	BU33
off Greenhead St		
Greenmoss Pl, Bell. ML4	111	CX40
Greenmount, G22	49	BQ22
Greenock Av, G44	103	BR40
Greenock Rd, Pais. PA3	62	AS29
Greenock Rd, (Inch.) Renf. PA4	43	AR23
Green Pl, (Both.) G71	109	CR43
Green Pl, (Calder.) Air. ML6	96	DD35
off Faskine Av		
Greenrig, (Udd.) G71	109	CP39
Greenrigg Rd, (Cumb.) G67	22	DC12
Greenrig St, G33	51	BZ26
Greenrig St, (Udd.) G71	109	CP39
Green Rd, (Ruther.) G73	89	BW37
Green Rd, Pais. PA2	81	AP34
Greens Av, (Kirk.) G66	17	CE14
Greens Cres, (Kirk.) G66	17	CE14
Greenshields Rd, (Baill.) G69	72	CK32
Greenside Cres, G33	52	CA26
Greenside Pl, (Bears.) G61	11	BE13
off Moorfoot Way		
Greenside Rd, (Clark.) G76	120	BT45
Greenside Rd, Moth. ML1	97	DE38
Greenside St, G33	52	CA26
Greenside St, Coat. ML5	75	CX28
Greenside St, Moth. ML1	113	DH41
off Manse Vw		
Greens Rd, (Cumb.) G67	40	DB15
Green St, G40	68	BU32
Green St, (Both.) G71	109	CR43
Green St, Clyde. G81	27	AW18
Greentree Dr, (Baill.) G69	91	CH34
Greenview St, G43	86	BL37
Greenway La, (Blan.) G72	124	CL47
off Hunthill Rd		
Greenways Av, Pais. PA2	81	AQ35
Greenways Ct, Pais. PA2	81	AQ35
Greenwood Av, (Chry.) G69	37	CP19
Greenwood Av, (Camb.) G72	107	CG39
Greenwood Ct, (Clark.) G76	119	BN47
Greenwood Cres, Coat. ML5	75	CY32
Greenwood Dr, (Bears.) G61	30	BJ17
Greenwood Dr, John. PA5	79	AG37
Greenwood Quad, Clyde. G81	27	AZ20
Greenwood Rd, (Clark.) G76	118	BM46
Greer Quad, Clyde. G81	27	AX17
Grenada Pl, (E.Kil.) G75	135	BW52
Grenadier Gdns, Moth. ML1	127	CZ50
Grenville Dr, (Camb.) G72	106	CB41
Gresham Vw, Moth. ML1	142	DD51
Gretna St, G40	89	BX33
Greyfriars Rd, (Udd.) G71	92	CL37
Greyfriars St, G32	70	CB30
Greystone Av, (Ruther.) G73	105	BY39
Greywood St, G13	47	BG22
Grier Path, G31	69	BZ32
off Crail St		
Grier Pl, Lark. ML9	144	DB59
Grierson La, G33	69	BZ29
off Lomax St		
Grierson St, G33	69	BZ29
Grieve Cft, (Both.) G71	109	CP44
Grieve Rd, (Cumb.) G67	22	DC10
Griffin Av, Pais. PA1	61	AN32
Griffin Pl, Bell. ML4	95	CW37
off Garvin Lea		
Griqua Ter, (Both.) G71	109	CR43
Grogarry Rd, G15	28	BC17
Grosvenor Cres, G12	48	BM26
Grosvenor Cres La, G12	48	BM26
off Byres Rd		

Grosvenor La, G12	48	BM26
Grosvenor Ter, G12	48	BM26
Grove, The (Giff.) G46	118	BK45
Grove, The (Neil.) G78	114	AS47
Grove, The (Kilb.) John. PA10	78	AC33
Groveburn Av, (Thornlie.) G46	102	BJ41
Grove Cres, Lark. ML9	145	DE59
Grove Pk, (Lenz.) G66	35	CF17
Grovepark Ct, G20	67	BQ27
Grovepark Gdns, G20	67	BQ27
Grovepark Pl, G20	49	BQ26
Grovepark St, G20	49	BQ26
Groves, The (Bishop.) G64	51	BY22
off Woodhill Gro		
Grove Way, Bell. ML4	110	CV41
off Caledonian Av		
Grove Wd, (Udd.) G71	94	CT36
Grovewood Business Pk, Bell. ML4	94	CU37
Grove Wynd, Moth. ML1	112	DC42
off Moore St		
Grudie St, G34	72	CJ29
Gryffe Av, Renf. PA4	45	AX24
Gryffe Cres, Pais. PA2	81	AP35
Gryffe St, G44	87	BQ38
Guildford St, G33	71	CE28
Gullane Ct, Ham. ML3	139	CR53
off Loch Grn		
Gullane Cres, (Cumb.) G68	9	DB7
Gullane St, G11	66	BK28
Gunn Quad, Bell. ML4	110	CU42
Guthrie Ct, Moth. ML1	127	CY47
off Malcolm St		
Guthrie Dr, (Udd.) G71	93	CQ36
Guthrie Pl, (Torr.) G64	15	BY13
Guthrie Pl, (E.Kil.) G74	136	CB51
Guthrie St, G20	48	BM23
Guthrie St, Ham. ML3	126	CT49

H

Haberlea Av, G53	101	BE42
Haberlea Gdns, G53	101	BE42
off Haberlea Av		
Haddington Way, Coat. ML5	94	CU34
Haddow Gro, (Udd.) G71	93	CQ37
Haddow St, Ham. ML3	126	CU50
Hadrian Ter, Moth. ML1	127	CY45
Hagen Dr, Moth. ML1	113	DG44
Hagg Cres, John. PA5	79	AG34
Hagg Pl, John. PA5	79	AG34
Hagg Rd, John. PA5	79	AG35
Haggs Rd, G41	86	BL36
Haggswood Av, G41	86	BL35
Haghill Rd, G31	69	BY31
Hagmill Cres, Coat. ML5	95	CY35
Hagmill Rd, Coat. ML5	95	CX35
Haig Dr, (Baill.) G69	91	CH33
Haig St, G21	50	BV25
Hailes Av, G32	71	CF32
Haining, The, Renf. PA4	63	AZ27
Haining Rd, Renf. PA4	45	AZ26
Hairmyres Dr, (E.Kil.) G75	134	BU53
Hairmyres La, (E.Kil.) G75	134	BU52
Hairmyres Pk, (E.Kil.) G75	134	BV53
Hairmyres Roundabout, (E.Kil.) G75	134	BV52
Hairst St, Renf. PA4	45	AZ25
Halbeath Av, G15	28	BB18
Halbert St, G41	87	BN36
Haldane La, G14	47	BF26
off Victoria Pk St		
Haldane Pl, (E.Kil.) G75	136	CB54

Haldane St, G14	47	BF26
Halfmerk N, (E.Kil.) G74	136	CC51
Halfmerk S, (E.Kil.) G74	136	CC51
Halgreen Av, G15	28	BA19
Halifax Way, Renf. PA4	63	AY28
off Britannia Way		
Hallbrae St, G33	70	CA27
Hallcraig St, Air. ML6	76	DC29
Halley Dr, G13	46	BA22
Halley Pl, G13	46	BA23
Halley Sq, G13	46	BA23
Halley St, G13	46	BA22
Hallforest St, G33	70	CD27
off Gartloch Rd		
Hallhill Cres, G33	71	CG31
Hallhill Rd, G32	71	CE31
Hallhill Rd, G33	71	CG31
Hallhill Rd, John. PA5	79	AE38
Halliburton Cres, G34	72	CJ30
off Ware Rd		
Halliburton Rd, G34	71	CH30
Halliburton Ter, G34	72	CJ30
Halldale Cres, Renf. PA4	64	BB27
Hallinan Gdns, Wis. ML2	143	DH51
Hallrule Dr, G52	65	BE32
Hallside Av, (Camb.) G72	107	CG40
Hallside Boul, (Camb.) G72	107	CH42
Hallside Cres, (Camb.) G72	107	CG40
Hallside Dr, (Camb.) G72	107	CG40
Hallside Pl, G5	88	BS33
Hallside Rd, (Camb.) G72	107	CH41
Hall St, Clyde. G81	27	AW20
Hall St, Ham. ML3	140	CT52
Hall St, Moth. ML1	112	DC41
Hallydown Dr, G13	47	BE24
Halpin Cl, Bell. ML4	110	CT40
Halton Gdns, (Baill.) G69	91	CH33
Hamersley Pl, (E.Kil.) G75	135	BX54
Hamilcomb Rd, Bell. ML4	111	CW42
Hamill Dr, (Kilsyth) G65	8	CV5
Hamilton Av, G41	86	BM34
Hamilton Business Pk, Ham. ML3	126	CT48
Hamilton Ct, Pais. PA2	82	AU35
Hamilton Cres, (Bears.) G61	11	BG14
Hamilton Cres, (Camb.) G72	107	CE41
Hamilton Cres, Coat. ML5	75	CW32
Hamilton Cres, Renf. PA4	45	AZ24
Hamilton Dr, G12	49	BN26
Hamilton Dr, (Giff.) G46	102	BM43
Hamilton Dr, (Both.) G71	109	CR44
Hamilton Dr, (Blan.) G72	124	CK48
Hamilton Dr, (Camb.) G72	106	CB40
Hamilton Dr, Air. ML6	76	DD28
Hamilton Dr, Ersk. PA8	25	AP18
Hamilton Dr, Moth. ML1	128	DB49
Hamiltonhill Cres, G22	49	BR25
off Hamiltonhill Rd		
Hamiltonhill Rd, G22	49	BR26
Hamilton Int Tech Pk, (Blan.) G72	124	CL48
Hamilton Pk Av, G12	49	BN26
Hamilton Pk N, Ham. ML3	126	CT47
Hamilton Pk S, Ham. ML3	126	CT47
Hamilton Pl, (E.Kil.) G75	136	CA54
Hamilton Pl, (Neil.) G78	114	AV46
Hamilton Pl, Ham. ML3	140	CT55
Hamilton Pl, (Holytown) Moth. ML1	112	DD41
Hamilton Rd, (New.) Moth. ML1	113	DE41
Hamilton Rd, G32	91	CF35
Hamilton Rd, (Both.) G71	109	CR44
Hamilton Rd, (Udd.) G71	92	CJ35

Hamilton Rd, (Blan.) G72   124   CJ47
Hamilton Rd, (Camb.) G72   106   CD40
Hamilton Rd, (Ruther.) G73   89   BX37
Hamilton Rd, (E.Kil.) G74   123   CF48
Hamilton Rd, Bell. ML4   110   CU42
Hamilton Rd, Lark. ML9   142   DB56
Hamilton Rd, Moth. ML1   127   CX48
Hamilton St, G42   88   BS36
Hamilton St, Clyde. G81   45   AZ22
Hamilton St, Lark. ML9   144   DC57
Hamilton St, Pais. PA3   62   AV31
Hamilton Ter, Clyde. G81   45   AZ22
Hamilton Vw, (Udd.) G71   93   CQ38
Hamlet, (E.Kil.) G74   122   CD49
Hampden Dr, G42   87   BR38
Hampden La, G42   87   BR37
Hampden Pk, G42   88   BS38
Hampden Ter, G42   87   BR37
Hampden Way, Renf. PA4   63   AZ28
  off Lewis Av
Handel Pl, G5   88   BS33
Hangingshaw Pl, G42   88   BS37
Hannover Ct, G1   5   BS29
Hanover Cl, G42   87   BQ37
  off Battlefield Gdns
Hanover Ct, Pais. PA1   63   AW32
  off Kelburne Gdns
Hanover Gdns, Pais. PA1   82   AS33
Hanover St, G1   5   BS30
Hanson Pk, G31   68   BV29
Hanson St, G31   68   BV29
Hapland Av, G53   85   BE35
Hapland Rd, G53   85   BE35
Harbour La, Pais. PA3   62   AU32
Harbour Rd, Pais. PA3   62   AU31
Harburn Pl, G23   31   BN19
Harbury Pl, G14   46   BB23
Harcourt Dr, G31   69   BX29
Hardgate Dr, G51   65   BE29
Hardgate Gdns, G51   65   BE29
Hardgate Path, G51   65   BE29
  off Hardgate Dr
Hardgate Pl, G51   65   BE29
  off Hardgate Dr
Hardgate Rd, G51   65   BE29
Hardie Av, (Ruther.) G73   89   BY37
Hardie St, (Blan.) G72   124   CM46
Hardie St, Ham. ML3   139   CR51
Hardie St, Moth. ML1   128   DA45
Hardmuir Gdns, (Kirk.) G66   17   CG12
Hardmuir Rd, (Kirk.) G66   17   CG12
Hardridge Av, G52   85   BF35
Hardridge Pl, G52   85   BG35
Hardridge Rd, G52   85   BF35
Harefield Dr, G14   46   BD24
Harelaw Av, G44   103   BP41
Harelaw Av, (Barr.) G78   99   AZ44
Harelaw Av, (Neil.) G78   114   AT47
Harelaw Cres, Pais. PA2   82   AS38
Hareleeshill Rd, Lark. ML9   145   DE59
Harestanes Gdns, (Kirk.) G66   18   CJ12
Harfield Dr, G32   71   CG31
Harfield Gdns, G32   71   CG31
Harhill St, G51   65   BH30
Harkins Av, (Blan.) G72   124   CL46
Harland Cotts, G14   47   BE26
  off South St
Harland St, G14   47   BE26
Harlaw Gdns, (Bishop.) G64   33   BZ19
Harley St, G51   66   BL32
Harmetray St, G22   50   BT23
Harmony Ct, G52   66   BJ30
Harmony Pl, G51   66   BJ30

Harmony Row, G51   66   BJ30
Harmony Sq, G51   66   BJ30
  off Harmony Row
Harmsworth St, G11   65   BG27
Harport St, (Thornlie.) G46   101   BG40
Harriet Pl, G43   102   BK39
Harriet St, (Ruther.) G73   89   BW37
Harrington Rd, (E.Kil.) G74   136   CA52
Harris Cl, (Newt. M.) G77   116   BD47
Harris Cres, (Old Kil.) G60   25   AR16
Harris Dr, (Old Kil.) G60   25   AR16
Harris Gdns, (Old Kil.) G60   26   AS16
Harrison Dr, G51   66   BK31
Harris Rd, G23   30   BM20
Harris Rd, (Old Kil.) G60   25   AR16
Harrow Ct, G15   28   BB18
  off Linkwood Dr
Harrow Pl, G15   28   BB18
Hartfield Cres, (Neil.) G78   114   AU46
Hartfield Ter, Pais. PA2   82   AV35
Hartlaw Cres, G52   64   BC31
Hartree Av, G13   46   BA21
Hartstone Pl, G53   84   BD38
Hartstone Rd, G53   84   BD38
Hartstone Ter, G53   84   BD38
Hart St, G31   70   CA32
Hart St, (Linw.) Pais. PA3   60   AK32
Hartwood Gdns, (Newt. M.)   131   BF51
  G77
Harvest Dr, Moth. ML1   127   CZ49
Harvey St, G4   68   BS27
Harvey Way, Bell. ML4   95   CY38
Harvie Av, (Newt. M.) G77   117   BF47
Harvie St, G51   66   BM31
Harwood Gdns, (Mood.) G69   37   CQ18
  off Dryburgh Wk
Harwood St, G32   70   CA30
Hastie St, G3   66   BM28
Hastings, (E.Kil.) G75   135   BW54
Hatfield Dr, G12   47   BH24
Hathaway Dr, (Giff.) G46   102   BK43
Hathaway La, G20   49   BN24
Hathaway St, G20   49   BN24
Hathersage Av, (Baill.) G69   72   CK32
Hathersage Dr, (Baill.) G69   72   CK32
Hathersage Gdns, (Baill.) G69   72   CK32
Hatton Dr, G52   84   BC33
Hatton Gdns, G52   84   BC33
Hatton Hill, Moth. ML1   113   DE43
Hatton Path, G52   84   BC33
Hatton Pl, Moth. ML1   113   DE43
Hattonrigg Rd, Bell. ML4   111   CW39
Hatton Ter, Moth. ML1   113   DE43
Haughburn Pl, G53   84   BD38
Haughburn Rd, G53   84   BD38
Haughburn Ter, G53   85   BE38
  off Haughburn Rd
Haugh Rd, G3   66   BM29
Haugh Rd, (Kilsyth) G65   7   CS5
Haughton Av, (Kilsyth) G65   7   CU5
Haughview Rd, Moth. ML1   127   CX47
  off Strathclyde Rd
Havelock La, G11   66   BL27
Havelock Pk, (E.Kil.) G75   135   BW52
Havelock St, G11   66   BL27
Haven Pl, (E.Kil.) G75   134   BV55
Hawbank Rd, (E.Kil.) G74   121   BW50
Hawick Av, Pais. PA2   81   AR36
Hawick Cres, Lark. ML9   144   DC59
Hawick Dr, Coat. ML5   95   CZ34
Hawick St, G13   46   BA22
Hawkhead Av, Pais. PA2   83   AX35

Hawkhead Rd, Air. ML6   58   DB25
  off Raebog Rd
Hawkhead Rd, Pais. PA1   83   AX33
Hawkhead Rd, Pais. PA2   83   AY36
Hawksland Wk, Ham. ML3   140   CU52
  off Silvertonhill Av
Hawkwood, (E.Kil.) G75   135   BZ56
Hawthorn Av, (Bears.) G61   12   BJ14
Hawthorn Av, (Bishop.) G64   51   BX21
Hawthorn Av, (Lenz.) G66   35   CE16
Hawthorn Av, Ersk. PA8   44   AU21
Hawthorn Av, John. PA5   80   AJ36
Hawthorn Ct, (Clark.) G76   119   BN47
  off Hawthorn Rd
Hawthorn Cres, Ersk. PA8   44   AU21
Hawthornden Gdns, G23   31   BN19
Hawthorn Dr, (Barr.) G78   115   AZ45
Hawthorn Dr, Air. ML6   77   DF30
Hawthorn Dr, Coat. ML5   75   CZ32
  off Southfield Cres
Hawthorn Dr, Moth. ML1   112   DD42
Hawthorn Gdns, (Camb.) G72   107   CG41
Hawthorn Gdns, (Clark.) G76   119   BN47
Hawthorn Gdns, Bell. ML4   111   CY41
Hawthorn Gdns, Lark. ML9   145   DE59
Hawthorn Hill, Ham. ML3   140   CU52
Hawthorn Pl, (Blan.) G72   125   CN46
Hawthorn Quad, G22   50   BS24
Hawthorn Rd, (Cumb.) G67   23   DH9
Hawthorn Rd, (Clark.) G76   119   BN47
Hawthorn Rd, Ersk. PA8   44   AU21
Hawthorn St, G22   50   BS24
Hawthorn St, (Torr.) G64   15   BY12
Hawthorn St, Clyde. G81   27   AW17
Hawthorn Ter, (Udd.) G71   93   CR38
Hawthorn Ter, (E.Kil.) G75   135   BX55
Hawthorn Wk, (Camb.) G72   105   BZ40
Hawthorn Way, Ersk. PA8   44   AU21
Hay Av, Bish. PA7   24   AL18
Hayburn Ct, G11   66   BK27
  off Hayburn St
Hayburn Cres, G11   48   BJ26
Hayburn Gate, G11   66   BK27
Hayburn La, G11   48   BJ26
Hayburn Pl, G11   66   BK27
  off Hayburn St
Hayburn St, G11   66   BK28
Hayfield Ct, G5   88   BT33
Hayfield St, G5   88   BT33
Hayhill Rd, (Thornton.) G74   133   BR54
Hayle Gdns, (Chry.) G69   37   CP18
Haylynn St, G14   65   BG27
Haymarket St, G32   70   CA30
Haystack Pl, (Lenz.) G66   35   CF17
Hayston Cres, G22   49   BR24
Hayston Rd, (Kirk.) G66   16   CC13
Hayston Rd, (Cumb.) G68   22   DA9
Hayston St, G22   49   BR24
Haywood St, G22   49   BR23
Hazel Av, G44   103   BP41
Hazel Av, (Bears.) G61   11   BH14
Hazel Av, (Lenz.) G66   35   CF15
Hazel Av, John. PA5   80   AJ36
Hazel Av La, G44   103   BP41
  off Hazel Av
Hazel Bk, (M. of Cam.) G66   16   CD9
Hazelbank, (Plains) Air. ML6   59   DH26
  off Arondale Rd
Hazelbank, Moth. ML1   112   DD40
  off Myrtle Dr
Hazelbank Wk, Air. ML6   75   CZ29
Hazel Dene, (Bishop.) G64   33   BX20
Hazeldene La, Lark. ML9   145   DE60
  off Dickson St

Hazelden Gdns, G44	103	BN41
Hazelden Pk, G44	103	BN41
Hazelden Rd, (Newt. M.) G77	131	BE53
Hazelfield Gro, (Chap.) Air. ML6	97	DG36
Hazel Gdns, Moth. ML1	127	CZ50
Hazel Gro, (Kirk.) G66	35	CF15
Hazelhead, (E.Kil.) G74	136	CD51
Hazellea Dr, (Giff.) G46	102	BM41
Hazel Pk, Ham. ML3	140	CU51
Hazel Rd, (Cumb.) G67	23	DF10
Hazel Ter, (Udd.) G71	93	CR38
Hazelton, Moth. ML1	127	CZ48
Hazelwood Av, (Newt. M.) G77	117	BG49
Hazelwood Av, Pais. PA2	81	AN38
Hazelwood Dr, (Blan.) G72	124	CL45
Hazelwood Gdns, (Ruther.) G73	105	BY41
Hazelwood Rd, G41	86	BL33
Hazlitt Gdns, G20	49	BQ23
off Bilsland Dr		
Hazlitt Pl, G20	49	BR23
off Hazlitt St		
Hazlitt St, G20	49	BR23
Headhouse Ct, (E.Kil.) G75	135	BZ53
Headhouse Grn, (E.Kil.) G75	136	CA53
off Mid Pk		
Heath Av, (Bishop.) G64	51	BX21
Heath Av, (Lenz.) G66	35	CE17
Heathcliff Av, (Blan.) G72	108	CL44
Heathcot Av, G15	28	BA19
Heathcot Pl, G15	27	AZ19
off Heathcot Av		
Heather Av, (Bears.) G61	11	BG13
Heather Av, (Barr.) G78	99	AW40
Heather Av, Moth. ML1	112	DC40
Heatherbank Wk, Air. ML6	75	CZ29
Heatherbrae, (Bishop.) G64	32	BU20
Heather Dr, (Kirk.) G66	34	CC16
Heather Gdns, (Kirk.) G66	34	CC17
Heather Gro, (E.Kil.) G75	136	CA54
off Strathcona La		
Heather Pl, (Kirk.) G66	34	CC16
Heather Pl, John. PA5	80	AJ35
Heather Way, Moth. ML1	112	DC41
off Thistle Rd		
Heathery Knowe, (E.Kil.) G75	136	CA54
Heatheryknowe Rd, (Baill.) G69	73	CN29
Heathery Lea Av, Coat. ML5	95	CZ34
Heathery Rd, Wis. ML2	129	DH50
Heathfield Av, (Mood.) G69	37	CQ19
Heathfield Dr, (Miln.) G62	12	BK10
Heathfield St, G33	71	CE29
Heath Rd, Lark. ML9	144	DD58
Heathside Rd, (Giff.) G46	102	BM42
Heathwood Dr, (Thornlie.) G46	102	BJ42
Hecla Av, G15	28	BB18
Hecla Pl, G15	28	BB18
Hecla Sq, G15	28	BB19
Hector Rd, G41	86	BM37
Heddle Pl, G2	4	BQ30
off Cadogan St		
Helena Pl, (Clark.) G76	119	BN45
off Busby Rd		
Helena Pl, Clyde. G81	27	AW15
off Chapel Rd		
Helensburgh Dr, G13	47	BF23
Helenslea, (Camb.) G72	107	CF41
Helenslea Pl, Bell. ML4	110	CV41
Helen St, G51	66	BJ30
Helen St, G52	65	BH32
Helenvale Ct, G31	89	BZ33
Helenvale St, G31	89	BY33
Helen Wynd, Lark. ML9	144	DC59
Helmsdale Av, (Blan.) G72	108	CL42
Helmsdale Ct, (Camb.) G72	107	CF40
Helmsdale Dr, Pais. PA2	81	AP35
Hemlock St, G13	47	BG22
Henderland Dr, (Bears.) G61	29	BG19
Henderland Rd, (Bears.) G61	29	BG19
Henderson Av, (Camb.) G72	107	CG39
Henderson St, G20	49	BP26
Henderson St, Air. ML6	76	DD29
Henderson St, Clyde. G81	46	BA21
Henderson St, Coat. ML5	74	CV31
Henderson St, Pais. PA1	62	AT32
Henrietta St, G14	47	BE26
Henry Bell Grn, (E.Kil.) G75	136	CB53
off Bell Grn E		
Henry St, (Barr.) G78	99	AX42
Hepburn Hill, Ham. ML3	139	CR53
Hepburn Rd, G52	64	BD30
Herald Av, G13	29	BF20
Herald Gro, Moth. ML1	127	CZ49
Herald Way, Renf. PA4	63	AY28
off Viscount Av		
Herbertson Gro, (Blan.) G72	108	CL44
Herbertson St, G5	67	BR32
Herbert St, G20	49	BP26
Herbison Ct, Lark. ML9	144	DD57
Hercules Way, Renf. PA4	63	AZ28
Heriot Av, Pais. PA2	81	AN37
Heriot Ct, Pais. PA2	81	AP37
off Heriot Av		
Heriot Cres, (Bishop.) G64	33	BW18
Heriot Rd, (Lenz.) G66	35	CE18
Heriot Way, Pais. PA2	81	AN37
off Heriot Av		
Heritage Ct, (Newt. M.) G77	117	BG48
Heritage Vw, Coat. ML5	74	CV29
Heritage Way, Coat. ML5	74	CV30
Herma St, G23	49	BN21
Hermes Way, Bell. ML4	112	DB40
Hermiston Av, G32	70	CD31
Hermiston Pl, G32	71	CE31
Hermiston Pl, Moth. ML1	112	DC40
off Windsor Rd		
Hermiston Rd, G32	70	CD30
Hermitage Av, G13	47	BE22
Hermitage Cres, Coat. ML5	95	CX34
Herndon Ct, (Newt. M.) G77	118	BJ47
Heron Ct, Clyde. G81	27	AX16
Heron Pl, John. PA5	79	AF38
Heron St, G40	88	BV33
Heron Way, Renf. PA4	63	AY28
off Britannia Way		
Herries Rd, G41	86	BL35
Herriet St, G41	87	BP34
Herriot St, Coat. ML5	74	CU29
Hertford Av, G12	48	BK23
Hexham Gdns, G41	86	BM36
Heys St, (Barr.) G78	99	AY43
Hickman St, G42	87	BR36
Hickman Ter, G42	88	BS35
Hickory Cres, (Udd.) G71	94	CS36
Hickory St, G22	50	BU24
High Avon St, Lark. ML9	144	DB57
High Barholm, (Kilb.) John. PA10	78	AC34
High Barrwood Rd, (Kilsyth) G65	7	CU5
High Beeches, (Carm.) G76	120	BU45
High Blantyre Rd, Ham. ML3	125	CP48
Highburgh Dr, (Ruther.) G73	105	BX40
Highburgh Rd, G12	48	BL26
High Burnside Av, Coat. ML5	74	CU32
High Calside, Pais. PA2	82	AT34
Highcoats, Coat. ML5	75	CX30
High Common Rd, (E.Kil.) G74	137	CE52
Highcraig Av, John. PA5	79	AF36
High Craigends, (Kilsyth) G65	7	CU5
High Craighall Rd, G4	67	BR27
Highcroft Av, G44	104	BT40
Highcross Av, Coat. ML5	94	CT33
Higher Ness Way, Coat. ML5	94	CT34
Highfield Av, (Kirk.) G66	17	CG13
Highfield Av, Pais. PA2	82	AS38
Highfield Ct, (Kirk.) G66	17	CH12
Highfield Cres, Moth. ML1	128	DC45
Highfield Cres, Pais. PA2	82	AT38
Highfield Dr, G12	48	BK23
Highfield Dr, (Ruther.) G73	105	BY42
Highfield Dr, (Clark.) G76	118	BM46
Highfield Gro, (Kirk.) G66	17	CG12
off Highfield Rd		
Highfield Pl, G12	48	BK23
Highfield Pl, (E.Kil.) G74	122	CB50
Highfield Rd, (Kirk.) G66	17	CG12
Highfield Rd, Lark. ML9	144	DD58
High Flenders Rd, (Clark.) G76	118	BM48
Highkirk Vw, John. PA5	79	AH35
Highland Av, (Blan.) G72	124	CL45
Highland La, G51	66	BL29
Highland Pk, (Kilsyth) G65	7	CS4
Highland Pl, (Kilsyth) G65	7	CS3
Highland Rd, (Miln.) G62	12	BJ11
High Mair, Renf. PA4	63	AY27
High Parksail, Ersk. PA8	44	AS21
High Parks Cres, Ham. ML3	140	CT55
High Patrick St, Ham. ML3	140	CU51
High Pleasance, Lark. ML9	144	DC58
High Rd, Moth. ML1	127	CZ46
High Rd, (Castlehead) Pais. PA2	82	AS34
High Row, (Bishop.) G64	33	BX16
Highstonehall Rd, Ham. ML3	139	CP53
High St, G1	5	BT31
High St, G4	5	BT31
High St, (Kirk.) G66	17	CE12
High St, (Ruther.) G73	89	BW37
High St, (Neil.) G78	114	AT46
High St, Air. ML6	76	DB29
High St, John. PA5	79	AH34
High St, Moth. ML1	113	DG41
High St, Pais. PA1	82	AT33
High St, Renf. PA4	45	AZ25
High Whitehills Rd, (E.Kil.) G75	135	BZ56
High Wd Gdns, Bell. ML4	110	CU40
Hilary Dr, (Baill.) G69	71	CH32
Hilda Cres, G33	52	CA25
Hillary Av, (Ruther.) G73	105	BZ39
Hill Av, (Newt. M.) G77	117	BE49
Hillbrae St, G51	65	BF31
Hill Cres, (Clark.) G76	119	BN47
Hillcrest, (Chry.) G69	54	CM21
Hillcrest, (Carm.) G76	120	BT45
Hillcrest Av, G32	90	CD37
Hillcrest Av, G44	103	BN41
Hillcrest Av, (Cumb.) G67	22	DB12
off North Carbrain Rd		
Hillcrest Av, Coat. ML5	75	CY31
Hillcrest Av, Pais. PA2	98	AS39
Hillcrest Av, Wis. ML2	129	DG50
Hillcrest Ct, (Cumb.) G67	22	DB12
Hillcrest Dr, (Newt. M.) G77	118	BJ48
Hillcrest Rd, G32	91	CE37

Hillcrest Rd, (Bears.) G61	29	BH17
Hillcrest Rd, (Kilsyth) G65	6	CN5
Hillcrest Rd, (Udd.) G71	93	CQ38
Hillcrest St, (Miln.) G62	12	BJ11
Hillcrest Ter, (Both.) G71	109	CR42
Hillcrest Vw, Lark. ML9	144	DD58
Hillcroft Ter, (Bishop.) G64	50	BV21
Hillend Cres, (Clark.) G76	118	BL47
Hillend Cres, Clyde. G81	26	AV15
Hillend Rd, G22	49	BQ22
Hillend Rd, (Ruther.) G73	105	BX40
Hillend Rd, (Clark.) G76	118	BL47
Hillfoot Av, (Bears.) G61	29	BH16
Hillfoot Av, (Ruther.) G73	89	BW38
Hillfoot Dr, (Bears.) G61	29	BH16
Hillfoot Dr, Coat. ML5	74	CT31
Hillfoot Gdns, (Udd.) G71	93	CN37
Hillfoot Rd, Air. ML6	76	DD31
Hillfoot St, G31	69	BW30
Hillhead Av, (Chry.) G69	37	CP19
Hillhead Av, (Ruther.) G73	105	BX41
Hillhead Av, Moth. ML1	112	DC43
Hillhead Cres, Ham. ML3	125	CN50
Hillhead Cres, Moth. ML1	112	DC43
Hillhead Dr, Air. ML6	76	DC31
Hillhead Dr, Moth. ML1	112	DC44
Hillhead Pl, G12	67	BN27
off Bank St		
Hillhead Pl, (Ruther.) G73	105	BX41
Hillhead Rd, G21	51	BZ22
Hillhead Rd, (Kirk.) G66	17	CF12
Hillhead St, G12	66	BM27
Hillhead St, (Miln.) G62	12	BJ11
Hillhead Ter, Ham. ML3	125	CN50
Hillhouse Cres, Ham. ML3	125	CP50
Hillhouse Pk Ind Est, Ham. ML3	125	CQ49
Hillhouse Rd, (Blan.) G72	124	CL48
Hillhouse Rd, Ham. ML3	125	CN49
Hillhouse St, G21	51	BW25
Hillhouse Ter, Ham. ML3	125	CP50
Hillington Gdns, G52	85	BE33
Hillington Ind Est, G52	64	BB29
Hillington Pk Circ, G52	65	BE32
Hillington Quad, G52	64	BC32
Hillington Rd, G52	64	BB27
Hillington Rd S, G52	64	BC32
Hillington Shop Cen, (Hillington Ind. Est.) G52	64	BB29
Hillington Ter, G52	64	BC32
Hillkirk Pl, G21	50	BU25
off Hillkirk St		
Hillkirk St, G21	50	BU25
Hillkirk St La, G21	50	BV25
off Hillkirk St		
Hillneuk Av, (Bears.) G61	29	BH16
Hillneuk Dr, (Bears.) G61	30	BJ16
Hillpark Av, Pais. PA2	82	AT36
Hillpark Dr, G43	102	BL39
Hill Path, G52	64	BC32
Hill Pl, G52	64	BC32
Hill Pl, Bell. ML4	110	CV42
Hill Pl, Moth. ML1	113	DE43
Hillrigg, (Green.) Air. ML6	41	DF20
Hillrigg Av, Air. ML6	77	DE29
Hill Rd, (Kilsyth) G65	7	CT3
Hill Rd, (Cumb.) G67	22	DA11
Hillsborough Rd, (Baill.) G69	71	CH32
Hillsborough Ter, G12	49	BN26
off Bower St		
Hillside, (Kilsyth) G65	8	CV8
Hillside Av, (Bears.) G61	29	BH16
Hillside Av, (Clark.) G76	118	BM46
Hillside Cotts, (Glenb.) Coat. ML5	56	CU23
Hillside Ct, (Thornlie.) G46	101	BH42
Hillside Cres, (Neil.) G78	114	AT46
Hillside Cres, Coat. ML5	94	CV33
Hillside Cres, Ham. ML3	140	CT51
Hillside Cres, Moth. ML1	113	DF41
Hillside Dr, (Bears.) G61	30	BJ16
Hillside Dr, (Bishop.) G64	33	BW19
Hillside Dr, (Barr.) G78	99	AW42
Hillside Gdns La, G11	48	BK26
off North Gardner St		
Hillside Gro, (Barr.) G78	99	AW42
Hillside La, Ham. ML3	140	CS51
Hillside Pk, Clyde. G81	27	AX15
Hillside Pl, Moth. ML1	113	DF42
Hillside Quad, G43	102	BK40
Hillside Rd, G43	102	BK40
Hillside Rd, (Barr.) G78	99	AW42
Hillside Rd, (Neil.) G78	114	AT46
Hillside Rd, Pais. PA2	83	AW35
Hillside Ter, (Old Kil.) G60	25	AR15
off Dalnottar Av		
Hillside Ter, Ham. ML3	140	CS51
Hill St, G3	4	BQ28
Hill St, G14	46	BC24
Hill St, (Chap.) Air. ML6	97	DF35
Hill St, Ham. ML3	125	CP50
Hill St, Lark. ML9	144	DC59
Hillsview, (Chry.) G69	54	CL21
Hillswick Cres, G22	49	BR21
Hill Ter, Moth. ML1	113	DE43
Hilltop Av, Bell. ML4	95	CW38
Hilltop Rd, (Mood.) G69	37	CP19
Hill Vw, (E.Kil.) G75	136	CA53
Hillview, (Green.) Air. ML6	41	DH19
Hillview Av, (Kilsyth) G65	7	CT6
Hillview Cres, (Udd.) G71	93	CN37
Hillview Cres, Bell. ML4	95	CW37
Hillview Cres, Lark. ML9	144	DD60
Hillview Dr, (Blan.) G72	108	CM43
Hillview Dr, (Clark.) G76	118	BM46
Hillview Gdns, (Bishop.) G64	51	BZ21
Hillview Pl, (Clark.) G76	119	BN46
Hillview Rd, (Elder.) John. PA5	80	AL35
Hillview St, G32	70	CB32
Hillview Ter, (Old Kil.) G60	25	AR15
off Station Rd		
Hiltonbank St, Ham. ML3	125	CR50
Hilton Ct, Ham. ML3	140	CU51
off Johnstone Rd		
Hilton Gdns, G13	47	BH22
Hilton Gdns La, G13	47	BG22
off Fulton St		
Hilton Pk, (Bishop.) G64	32	BV17
Hilton Rd, (Miln.) G62	11	BG11
Hilton Rd, (Bishop.) G64	32	BV18
Hilton Ter, G13	47	BG22
Hilton Ter, (Bishop.) G64	32	BV17
Hilton Ter, (Camb.) G72	106	CA42
Hindsland Rd, Lark. ML9	144	DD60
Hinshaw St, G20	49	BQ26
Hinshelwood Dr, G51	66	BJ31
Hirsel Pl, (Both.) G71	109	CR42
Hobart Cres, Clyde. G81	26	AT16
Hobart Rd, (E.Kil.) G75	135	BY54
Hobart St, G22	49	BR25
Hobden St, G21	51	BW26
Hoddam Av, G45	104	BW42
Hoddam Ter, G45	105	BW42
Hogan Ct, Clyde. G81	26	AV15
Hogan Way, Moth. ML1	129	DG45
off Morris Cres		
Hogarth Av, G32	69	BZ30
Hogarth Cres, G32	69	BZ30
Hogarth Dr, G32	69	BZ30
Hogarth Gdns, G32	69	BZ30
Hogganfield Ct, G33	69	BZ27
Hogganfield St, G33	69	BZ27
Hogg Av, John. PA5	79	AG36
Hogg Rd, Air. ML6	97	DF33
off Moncrieffe Rd		
Hogg St, Air. ML6	76	DC30
Holeburn La, G43	102	BL39
Holeburn Rd, G43	102	BL39
Holehills Dr, Air. ML6	76	DD27
Holehills Pl, Air. ML6	76	DD27
Holehouse Brae, (Neil.) G78	114	AS46
Holehouse Dr, G13	46	BC23
Holehouse Rd, (E.Kil.) G74	133	BQ54
Holehouse Rd, (Eagle.) G76	133	BN56
Holehouse Ter, (Neil.) G78	114	AS46
Hollandbush Gro, Ham. ML3	140	CS53
off Meikle Earnock Rd		
Hollandhurst Rd, Coat. ML5	74	CV28
Holland St, G2	4	BQ29
Hollinwell Rd, G23	48	BM21
Hollowglen Rd, G32	70	CD31
Hollows, The (Giff.) G46	102	BK44
off Ayr Rd		
Hollows Av, Pais. PA2	81	AP38
Hollows Cres, Pais. PA2	81	AP38
Hollybank Pl, (Camb.) G72	106	CD41
Hollybank St, G21	69	BW28
Hollybrook Pl, G42	88	BS35
off Hollybrook St		
Hollybrook St, G42	88	BS35
Hollybush Av, Pais. PA2	81	AR38
Hollybush Rd, G52	64	BB32
Holly Dr, G21	51	BW26
Hollymount, (Bears.) G61	29	BH19
Holly Pl, John. PA5	80	AJ37
Holly Rd, Air. ML6	77	DE30
Holly St, Clyde. G81	27	AW17
Holm Av, (Udd.) G71	109	CN39
Holm Av, Pais. PA2	82	AV35
Holmbank Av, G41	86	BM38
Holmbrae Av, (Udd.) G71	93	CP38
Holmbrae Rd, (Udd.) G71	93	CP38
Holmbyre Ct, G45	103	BR44
Holmbyre Rd, G45	104	BS44
Holmbyre Ter, G45	104	BS43
Holmes Av, Renf. PA4	63	AY28
Holmes Quad, Bell. ML4	111	CX41
off Sapphire Rd		
Holmfauldhead Dr, G51	65	BG29
Holmfauldhead Pl, G51	65	BG28
off Govan Rd		
Holmfauld Rd, G51	65	BG28
Holmfield, (Kirk.) G66	17	CG14
Holm Gdns, Bell. ML4	111	CY41
Holmhead Cres, G44	103	BQ39
Holmhead Pl, G44	103	BQ39
Holmhead Rd, G44	103	BQ40
Holmhill Av, (Camb.) G72	106	CC41
Holmhills Dr, (Camb.) G72	106	CB42
Holmhills Gdns, (Camb.) G72	106	CB41
Holmhills Gro, (Camb.) G72	106	CB41
Holmhills Pl, (Camb.) G72	106	CB41
Holmhills Rd, (Camb.) G72	106	CB42
Holmhills Ter, (Camb.) G72	106	CB41
Holm La, (E.Kil.) G74	136	CA52
Holmlea Rd, G44	87	BQ38
Holm Pl, Lark. ML9	144	DA59
off Clove Mill Wynd		

Holm Pl, (Linw.) Pais. PA3   60   AK30
Holms Cres, Ersk. PA8   25   AP19
Holms Pl, (Gart.) G69   55   CN22
Holm St, G2   4   BQ30
Holm St, Moth. ML1   112   DC42
Holmswood Av, (Blan.) G72   124   CM45
Holmwood Av, (Udd.) G71   93   CP38
Holmwood Gdns, (Udd.) G71   109   CP39
Holmwood Gro, G44   103   BQ41
Holyrood Cres, G20   67   BP27
Holyrood Quad, G20   67   BP27
Holyrood St, Ham. ML3   125   CQ48
Holytown Rd, Bell. ML4   112   DA40
Holytown Rd, Moth. ML1   112   DA40
Holywell St, G31   69   BX32
Homer Pl, Bell. ML4   112   DA40
Homeston Av, (Both.) G71   109   CQ42
Honeybog Rd, G52   64   BA30
Honeywell Cres, (Chap.) Air. ML6   97   DG36
Hood St, Clyde. G81   27   AY19
Hope Cres, Lark. ML9   144   DD58
Hopefield Av, G12   48   BL24
Hopehill Gdns, G20   49   BQ26
Hopehill Rd, G20   49   BQ26
Hopeman, Ersk. PA8   25   AQ18
Hopeman Av, (Thornlie.) G46   101   BG41
Hopeman Dr, (Thornlie.) G46   101   BG41
Hopeman Path, (Thornlie.) G46   101   BG40
   off Kennishead Pl
Hopeman Rd, (Thornlie.) G46   101   BG41
Hopeman St, (Thornlie.) G46   101   BG41
Hope St, G2   4   BR30
Hope St, Bell. ML4   111   CY40
Hope St, Ham. ML3   126   CU50
Hope St, Moth. ML1   128   DA46
Hopetoun Pl, G23   31   BN19
   off Broughton Rd
Hopetoun Ter, G21   51   BW26
Hopkins Brae, (Kirk.) G66   17   CF12
   off Hillhead Rd
Horatius St, Moth. ML1   111   CX44
Hornal Rd, (Udd.) G71   109   CP41
Hornbeam Dr, Clyde. G81   26   AV17
Hornbeam Rd, (Udd.) G71   93   CR37
Horndean Ct, (Bishop.) G64   33   BW17
Horndean Cres, G33   71   CF29
Horne St, G22   50   BU24
   off Hawthorn St
Hornock Cotts, Coat. ML5   74   CV29
   off Gartsherrie Rd
Hornock Rd, Coat. ML5   74   CV28
Hornshill Fm Rd, (Stepps) G33   53   CG22
Hornshill St, G21   51   BW25
Horsbrugh Av, (Kilsyth) G65   7   CT4
Horsburgh St, G33   71   CF27
   off Dudhope St
Horselethill Rd, G12   48   BL25
Horseshoe La, (Bears.) G61   29   BG17
Horseshoe Rd, (Bears.) G61   29   BG16
Hospital St, G5   68   BS32
Hospital St, Coat. ML5   95   CW33
Hotspur St, G20   49   BN24
Houldsworth La, G3   67   BN29
Houldsworth St, G3   67   BN29
Househillmuir Cres, G53   101   BE39
Househillmuir La, G53   85   BE38
   off Househillmuir Rd
Househillmuir Pl, G53   85   BE38
Househillmuir Rd, G53   100   BD39
Househillwood Cres, G53   84   BD38
Househillwood Rd, G53   100   BD39

Housel Av, G13   46   BD23
Houston Pl, G5   4   BP31
Houston Pl, (Elder.) John. PA5   80   AL35
Houston Rd, (Inch.) Renf. PA4   43   AP25
Houston St, G5   67   BP32
Houston St, Ham. ML3   140   CT52
Houston St, Renf. PA4   45   AZ25
Houston Ter, (E.Kil.) G74   135   BZ51
Houstoun Ct, John. PA5   79   AH34
   off William St
Houstoun Sq, John. PA5   79   AH34
Howard Av, (E.Kil.) G74   122   CC48
Howard Ct, (E.Kil.) G74   122   CC48
Howard St, G1   4   BR31
Howard St, Lark. ML9   145   DE60
Howard St, Pais. PA1   63   AW32
Howat St, G51   66   BJ29
Howcraigs Ct, Clyde. G81   45   AZ22
   off Mill Rd
Howden Av, Moth. ML1   97   DF37
Howden Dr, (Linw.) Pais. PA3   60   AJ32
Howden Pl, Moth. ML1   112   DC40
Howe Gdns, (Udd.) G71   93   CQ38
Howe Rd, (Kilsyth) G65   7   CT6
Howes St, Coat. ML5   95   CX33
Howford Rd, G52   84   BD33
Howgate Av, G15   28   BB18
Howgate Rd, Ham. ML3   139   CR53
Howie Bldgs, (Clark.) G76   119   BN45
   off Busby Rd
Howieshill Av, (Camb.) G72   106   CD40
Howieshill Rd, (Camb.) G72   107   CE40
Howie St, Lark. ML9   144   DD60
Howletnest Rd, Air. ML6   77   DF31
Howson Lea, Moth. ML1   128   DD49
   off Nelson Cres
Howson Vw, Moth. ML1   127   CX46
Howth Dr, G13   47   BH21
Howth Ter, G13   47   BH21
Hoxley Pl, G20   49   BP23
Hoylake Pk, (Both.) G71   109   CP43
Hoylake Pl, G23   31   BN20
Hozier Cres, (Udd.) G71   93   CP37
Hozier Ln, Lark. ML9   144   DD57
   off Muirshot Rd
Hozier Pl, (Both.) G71   109   CR42
Hozier St, Coat. ML5   95   CW33
Hudson Ter, (E.Kil.) G75   135   BX53
Hudson Way, (E.Kil.) G75   135   BY53
Hughenden Dr, G12   48   BK25
Hughenden Gdns, G12   48   BJ25
Hughenden La, G12   48   BK25
Hughenden Rd, G12   48   BK25
Hughenden Ter, G12   48   BK25
   off Hughenden Rd
Hugh Murray Gro, (Camb.) G72   107   CE40
Hugo St, G20   49   BP24
Hulks Rd, (Green.) Air. ML6   40   DD18
Humbie Ct, (Newt. M.) G77   131   BG51
Humbie Gate, (Newt. M.) G77   131   BG51
Humbie Gro, (Newt. M.) G77   117   BG50
Humbie Lawns, (Newt. M.) G77   131   BG51
Humbie Rd, (Eagle.) G76   132   BJ52
Humbie Rd, (Newt. M.) G77   131   BG51
Hume Dr, (Both.) G71   109   CQ42
Hume Dr, (Udd.) G71   93   CN38
Hume Pl, (E.Kil.) G75   135   BZ53
Hume Rd, (Cumb.) G67   22   DC10
Hume St, Clyde. G81   27   AX20
Hunter Dr, (Newt. M.) G77   116   BD49
Hunterfield Dr, (Camb.) G72   106   CA40

Hunterhill Av, Pais. PA2   82   AV34
Hunterhill Rd, Pais. PA2   82   AV34
Hunter Pl, (Miln.) G62   11   BG12
Hunter Pl, (Kilb.) John. PA10   78   AC35
Hunter Rd, (Miln.) G62   11   BG11
Hunter Rd, (Ruther.) G73   89   BY36
Hunter Rd, Ham. ML3   125   CR47
Huntersfield Rd, John. PA5   79   AE36
Hunters Hill Ct, G21   50   BV23
   off Belmont Rd
Huntershill Rd, (Bishop.) G64   51   BW21
Huntershill St, G21   50   BV23
   off Springburn Rd
Huntershill Way, (Bishop.) G64   50   BV22
Hunter St, G4   5   BU31
Hunter St, (E.Kil.) G74   136   CB51
Hunter St, Air. ML6   76   DB28
Hunter St, Bell. ML4   111   CW40
   off Motherwell Rd
Hunter St, Pais. PA1   62   AU32
Hunthill La, (Blan.) G72   124   CK47
Hunthill Pl, (Clark.) G76   119   BQ48
Hunt Hill Rd, (Cumb.) G68   20   CS12
Hunthill Rd, (Blan.) G72   124   CK46
Huntingdon Rd, G21   68   BU27
Huntingdon Sq, G21   68   BU27
Hunting Lo Gdns, Ham. ML3   141   CW51
Huntingtower Rd, (Baill.) G69   91   CH33
Huntley Rd, G52   64   BB29
Huntly Av, (Giff.) G46   102   BM43
Huntly Av, Bell. ML4   111   CW39
Huntly Ct, (Bishop.) G64   51   BW21
Huntly Dr, (Bears.) G61   11   BG14
   off Montrose Dr
Huntly Dr, (Camb.) G72   106   CD41
Huntly Dr, Coat. ML5   94   CT33
Huntly Gdns, G12   48   BL26
Huntly Path, (Chry.) G69   37   CP19
   off Burnbrae Av
Huntly Rd, G12   48   BL26
Huntly Ter, Pais. PA2   83   AW36
Hurlethill Ct, G53   84   BB38
Hurlet Rd, G53   83   AY37
Hurlet Rd, Pais. PA2   83   AY37
Hurlford Av, G13   46   BB22
Hurly Hawkin, (Bishop.) G64   51   BZ21
Hutcheson Rd, (Thornlie.) G46   102   BJ43
Hutcheson St, G1   5   BS30
Hutchinson Pl, (Camb.) G72   107   CG42
Hutchinsontown Ct, G5   88   BS33
Hutchison Ct, (Giff.) G46   102   BL44
   off Berryhill Rd
Hutchison Dr, (Bears.) G61   30   BJ19
Hutchison Pl, Coat. ML5   74   CV31
Hutchison St, Ham. ML3   140   CT53
Hutton, G12   48   BJ23
   off Ascot Av
Hutton Dr, G51   65   BG29
Hutton Dr, (E.Kil.) G74   122   CB49
Hydepark St, G3   4   BP30
Hyndal Av, G53   84   BD36
Hyndland Av, G11   66   BK27
Hyndland Rd, G12   48   BK25
Hyndland St, G11   66   BL27
Hyndlee Dr, G52   65   BE32
Hyslop Pl, Clyde. G81   27   AW18
Hyslop St, Air. ML6   76   DA29

I

Iain Dr, (Bears.) G61   29   BE15
Iain Rd, (Bears.) G61   29   BE15
Ian Smith Ct, Clyde. G81   45   AZ21

Ibroxholm Av, G51	66	BK32
Ibroxholm Oval, G51	66	BK32
Ibroxholm Pl, G51	66	BK32
off Paisley Rd W		
Ibrox Ind Est, G51	66	BL31
Ibrox St, G51	66	BL31
Ibrox Ter, G51	66	BK31
Ibrox Ter La, G51	66	BK31
Ida Quad, Bell. ML4	110	CV40
off St. Marys Rd		
Iddesleigh Av, (Miln.) G62	12	BJ11
Ilay Av, (Bears.) G61	47	BH21
Ilay Ct, (Bears.) G61	48	BJ21
Ilay Rd, (Bears.) G61	48	BJ21
Imlach Pl, Moth. ML1	127	CZ48
Imperial Dr, Air. ML6	76	DB32
Inchbrae Rd, G52	85	BE33
Inchcolm Gdns, (Mood.) G69	37	CQ18
off Culross Way		
Inchcolm Pl, (E.Kil.) G74	135	BY51
Inchcruin Pl, G15	28	BA17
Inchfad Cres, G15	28	BA18
Inchfad Dr, G15	28	BA18
Inchfad Pl, G15	28	BA18
Inch Garvie, (E.Kil.) G74	137	CF52
Inchholm La, G11	65	BG27
off Byron St		
Inchholm St, G11	65	BG27
Inchinnan Business Pk, (Inch.) Renf. PA4	44	AS25
Inchinnan Dr, (Inch.) Renf. PA4	44	AS25
Inchinnan Ind Est, (Inch.) Renf. PA4	43	AR24
Inchinnan Rd, Bell. ML4	94	CV38
Inchinnan Rd, Pais. PA3	62	AU30
Inchinnan Rd, Renf. PA4	45	AX25
Inchkeith, (E.Kil.) G74	137	CF52
Inchkeith Pl, G32	70	CD30
Inchlaggan Pl, G15	28	BA17
Inchlee St, G14	65	BG27
Inch Marnock, (E.Kil.) G74	137	CE53
Inch Meadow, Ersk. PA8	44	AT21
off Newshot Dr		
Inchmoan Pl, G15	28	BB17
Inch Murrin, (E.Kil.) G74	137	CF52
Inchmurrin Av, (Kirk.) G66	18	CK13
off Iona Way		
Inchmurrin Dr, (Ruther.) G73	105	BZ43
Inchmurrin Gdns, (Ruther.) G73	105	BZ43
Inchmurrin Pl, (Ruther.) G73	105	BZ43
Inchneuk Rd, (Glenb.) Coat. ML5	56	CU23
Inchnock Av, (Gart.) G69	55	CP23
Inchoch St, G33	71	CG27
Inchrory Pl, G15	28	BA17
Inchwood Ct, (Cumb.) G68	21	CW14
Inchwood Pl, (Cumb.) G68	20	CV14
Inchwood Rd, (Cumb.) G68	20	CV14
Incle St, Pais. PA1	62	AV32
India Dr, (Inch.) Renf. PA4	44	AS23
India St, G2	4	BQ29
Industry St, (Kirk.) G66	17	CF14
Inga St, G20	49	BN22
Ingerbreck Av, (Ruther.) G73	105	BZ41
Ingleby Dr, G31	69	BW30
Ingleby Pl, (Neil.) G78	114	AU46
Inglefield Ct, Air. ML6	76	DC30
Inglefield St, G42	87	BR34
Ingleneuk Av, G33	52	CD24
Ingleside, (Lenz.) G66	35	CE15
Inglestone Av, (Thornlie.) G46	102	BJ43
Inglewood Cres, (E.Kil.) G75	135	BW53
Inglewood Cres, Pais. PA2	81	AN35
Inglis Pl, (E.Kil.) G75	136	CB54
Inglis St, G31	69	BW31
Inglis St, Wis. ML2	143	DF51
Ingram St, G1	5	BS30
Inishail Rd, G33	71	CE28
Inkerman Rd, G52	64	BD32
Innellan Gdns, G20	48	BK22
Innellan Pl, G20	48	BK22
Innermanse Quad, Moth. ML1	113	DH40
off Manse Vw		
Innerwick Dr, G52	64	BD32
Innes Ct, (E.Kil.) G74	122	CA49
Innes Ct, Air. ML6	77	DG29
Innspark, (Kilsyth) G65	7	CT4
International Av, (Blan.) G72	124	CM49
Inveraray Dr, (Bishop.) G64	33	BX17
Inveraray Gdns, (New.) Moth. ML1	113	DE42
Inveravon Dr, Moth. ML1	127	CX48
Inverbervie, Ersk. PA8	25	AQ19
Invercanny Dr, G15	28	BC18
Invercanny Pl, G15	28	BC17
Invercargill, (E.Kil.) G75	135	BW54
Inverclyde Gdns, (Ruther.) G73	105	RZ42
Invercree Wk, (Glenb.) Coat. ML5 *off Dinyra Pl*	56	CS23
Inveresk Pl, Coat. ML5	75	CW29
Inveresk Quad, G32	70	CC31
Inveresk St, G32	70	CC31
Inverewe Av, (Thornlie.) G46	101	BF42
Inverewe Dr, (Thornlie.) G46	101	BF43
Inverewe Gdns, (Thornlie.) G46	101	BF43
Inverewe Pl, (Thornlie.) G46	101	BF42
Inverewe Way, (Newt. M.) G77	116	BC48
Invergarry Av, (Thornlie.) G46	101	BF44
Invergarry Ct, (Thornlie.) G46	101	BG44
Invergarry Dr, (Thornlie.) G46	101	BF43
Invergarry Gdns, (Thornlie.) G46	101	BF44
Invergarry Gro, (Thornlie.) G46	101	BF43
Invergarry Pl, (Thornlie.) G46 *off Invergarry Dr*	101	BG43
Invergarry Quad, (Thornlie.) G46	101	BG43
Invergarry Vw, (Thornlie.) G46	101	BG43
Inverglas Av, Renf. PA4 *off Morriston Cres*	64	BB28
Invergordon Av, G43	87	BP38
Invergyle Dr, G52	64	BD32
Inverkar Dr, Pais. PA2	81	AQ35
Inverlair Av, G43	103	BP39
Inverlair Av, G44	103	BP39
Inverleith St, G32	69	BZ31
Inverlochy St, G33	71	CF28
Inverness St, G51	65	BF31
Inveroran Dr, (Bears.) G61	30	BK17
Inver Rd, G33	71	CG30
Invershiel Rd, G23	30	BM20
Invershin Dr, G20	48	BM24
Inverurie St, G21	50	BT26
Invervale Av, Air. ML6	77	DH31
Inzievar Ter, G32	90	CD36
Iona, Air. ML6	77	DF32
Iona Av, (E.Kil.) G74	122	CC49
Iona Cres, (Old Kil.) G60	26	AT16
Iona Dr, (Old Kil.) G60	26	AS16
Iona Dr, Pais. PA2	82	AT38
Iona Gdns, (Old Kil.) G60	26	AS16
Iona La, (Mood.) G69	37	CQ19
Iona Path, (Blan.) G72	124	CL46
Iona Pl, (Old Kil.) G60	26	AS16
Iona Pl, Coat. ML5	74	CT28
Iona Ridge, Ham. ML3	139	CP52
Iona Rd, (Ruther.) G73	106	CA42
Iona Rd, Renf. PA4	63	AY28
Iona St, G51	66	BK30
Iona St, Moth. ML1	111	CZ44
Iona Wk, Coat. ML5	94	CU33
off Tarbert Way		
Iona Way, (Stepps) G33	53	CF25
Iona Way, (Kirk.) G66	18	CJ13
Iris Av, G45	105	BW42
Irongray St, G31	69	BY30
Irvine Cres, Coat. ML5	75	CY30
Irvine Pl, (Kilsyth) G65	7	CR4
Irvine St, G40	89	BX34
Irvine St, (Glenm.) Air. ML6	58	DB25
Irvine Ter, Ham. ML3	140	CT53
Irving Av, Clyde. G81	27	AX16
Irving Ct, Clyde. G81	27	AX15
off Stewart Dr		
Irving Quad, Clyde. G81	27	AX15
Isabella Gdns, Ham. ML3	141	CX52
Iser La, G41	87	BP37
Island Rd, (Cumb.) G67	21	CZ13
Islay, Air. ML6	77	DG31
Islay Av, (Ruther.) G73	106	CA42
Islay Ct, Ham. ML3	139	CP51
off Wellhall Rd		
Islay Cres, (Old Kil.) G60	26	AS16
Islay Cres, Pais. PA2	82	AT38
Islay Dr, (Old Kil.) G60	26	AS16
Islay Dr, (Newt.) Air. M.) G77	116	BD48
Islay Gdns, Lark. ML9	144	DD58
Islay Quad, Wis. ML2	143	DG52
Islay Rd, (Kirk.) G66	18	CJ13
Islay Way, Coat. ML5	94	CT33
Ivanhoe, (E.Kil.) G74	123	CF49
Ivanhoe Dr, (Kirk.) G66	17	CG13
Ivanhoe Pl, Moth. ML1	112	DD40
off Rowantree Ter		
Ivanhoe Rd, G13	47	BF21
Ivanhoe Rd, (Cumb.) G67	22	DA13
Ivanhoe Rd, Pais. PA2	81	AP36
Ivanhoe Way, Pais. PA2	81	AP36
off Ivanhoe Rd		
Ivybank Av, (Camb.) G72	107	CE41
Ivy Gro, Coat. ML5	75	CX31
Ivy Pl, (Blan.) G72	124	CL45
Ivy Pl, Moth. ML1	112	DC42
Ivy Rd, (Udd.) G71	94	CS37
Ivy Ter, Moth. ML1	112	DC40
Ivy Way, (Chap.) Air. ML6	97	DG34

J

Jackson Ct, Coat. ML5	75	CX31
Jackson Dr, G33	53	CH24
Jackson St, Coat. ML5	75	CX30
Jacks Rd, (Udd.) G71	109	CQ41
Jack St, Ham. ML3	140	CT53
Jack St, Moth. ML1	128	DD49
Jackton Rd, (E.Kil.) G75	134	BS55
Jacobite Pl, Bell. ML4	111	CZ41
Jade Ter, Bell. ML4	111	CW41
off Ruby Ter		
Jagger Gdns, (Baill.) G69	91	CH33
Jamaica Dr, (E.Kil.) G75	135	BW52
Jamaica St, G1	4	BR31
James Dempsey Ct, Coat. ML5	74	CV31
James Dempsey Gdns, Coat. ML5 *off James Dempsey Ct*	74	CV31

James Dunlop Gdns, (Bishop.) G64	51	BX22
James Gray St, G41	87	BN36
James Hamilton Dr, Bell. ML4	111	CX40
James Healy Dr, Ham. ML3	140	CS54
James Morrison St, G1	5	BT31
James Nisbet St, G21	5	BU29
James St, G40	88	BU33
James St, (Righead Ind. Est.) Bell. ML4	110	CU39
James St, Moth. ML1	127	CZ46
James Vw, Moth. ML1	112	DB42
James Watt Av, (E.Kil.) G75	136	CC53
James Watt La, G2	4	BQ30
off James Watt St		
James Watt Pl, (E.Kil.) G74	121	BX50
James Watt Rd, (Miln.) G62	11	BH10
James Watt St, G2	4	BQ30
Jamieson Ct, G42	87	BR35
Jamieson Dr, (E.Kil.) G74	136	CC51
Jamieson Path, G42	87	BR35
off Jamieson St		
Jamieson St, G42	87	BR35
Janebank Av, (Camb.) G72	107	CE41
Jane Ct, Lark. ML9	144	DC59
off Margaretvale Dr		
Janefield Av, John. PA5	79	AG35
Janefield Pl, (Blan.) G72	124	CL47
Janefield St, G31	69	BX32
Jane Pl, G5	88	BS33
Jane Rae Gdns, Clyde. G81	45	AZ21
Jane's Brae, (Cumb.) G67	22	DB13
Janesmith St, Wis. ML2	129	DE49
Janetta St, Clyde. G81	27	AW17
Jardine St, G20	49	BP26
off Tillie St		
Jardine Ter, (Gart.) G69	55	CP24
Jarvie Cres, (Kilsyth) G65	7	CT6
Jarvie Way, Pais. PA2	81	AN37
Jasmine Pl, (Cumb.) G67	21	CX14
Java St, Moth. ML1	111	CY44
Jean Armour Dr, Clyde. G81	27	AY18
Jeanette Av, Ham. ML3	140	CT54
Jean Maclean Pl, (Bishop.) G64	33	BX17
Jedburgh Av, (Ruther.) G73	89	BX38
Jedburgh Dr, Pais. PA2	81	AQ36
Jedburgh Gdns, G20	49	BP26
off Wilton St		
Jedburgh Pl, (E.Kil.) G74	136	CB51
Jedburgh Pl, Coat. ML5	94	CV34
Jedburgh St, (Blan.) G72	124	CM46
Jedworth Av, G15	28	BD18
Jedworth Pl, G15	29	BE18
off Tallant Rd		
Jedworth Rd, G15	28	BD18
Jeffrey Pl, (Kilsyth) G65	7	CS4
Jellicoe St, Clyde. G81	26	AU18
Jenny Lind Ct, G46	101	BG43
Jenny's Well Ct, Pais. PA2	83	AY35
Jenny's Well Rd, Pais. PA2	83	AX35
Jervis Ter, (E.Kil.) G75	135	BX54
Jerviston Ct, Moth. ML1	112	DC44
off Jerviston Rd		
Jerviston Rd, G33	71	CE27
Jerviston Rd, Moth. ML1	112	DC43
Jerviston St, Moth. ML1	128	DB45
Jerviston St, (Holytown)	112	DC41
Jerviston St, (New Stev.) Moth. ML1	112	DC43
Jerviswood, Moth. ML1	112	DC44
Jessie St, G42	88	BT35
Jessiman Sq, Renf. PA4	63	AX28
Jimmy Sneddon Way, Moth. ML1	111	CZ43
off Columba Cres		
Joanna Ter, (Blan.) G72	124	CM45
Jocelyn Sq, G1	5	BS31
John Bowman Gdns, Bell. ML4	111	CW39
John Brannan Way, Bell. ML4	110	CT39
John Brown Pl, (Chry.) G69	54	CL21
John Ewing Gdns, Lark. ML9	144	DC57
John Hendry Rd, (Udd.) G71	109	CQ41
John Jarvie Sq, (Kilsyth) G65	7	CT4
off Main St		
John Knox La, G4	5	BU30
off Drygate		
John Knox La, Ham. ML3	124	CM49
off Brankholm Brae		
John Knox St, G4	5	BU30
John Knox St, Clyde. G81	45	AY21
John Lang St, John. PA5	80	AJ34
John Marshall Dr, (Bishop.) G64	50	BU22
John McEwan Way, (Torr.) G64	15	BX13
John Murray Ct, Moth. ML1	128	DA50
Johnsburn Dr, G53	100	BD39
Johnsburn Rd, G53	100	BD39
Johnshaven, Ersk. PA8	25	AQ19
off North Barr Av		
Johnshaven St, G43	86	BL38
off Bengal St		
John Smith Ct, Air. ML6	76	DB29
John Smith Gdns, Coat. ML5	75	CZ32
John Smith Gate, (Barr.) G78	99	AY41
Johnson Dr, (Camb.) G72	106	CC40
Johnston Av, (Kilsyth) G65	7	CT6
Johnston Av, Clyde. G81	45	AZ21
Johnstone Av, G52	64	BD31
Johnstone Dr, (Ruther.) G73	89	BW38
Johnstone Rd, Ham. ML3	140	CU51
Johnstone St, Bell. ML4	111	CY40
Johnstone Ter, (Kilsyth) G65	19	CP10
Johnston Rd, (Gart.) G69	55	CQ23
Johnston St, Air. ML6	76	DD29
Johnston St, Pais. PA1	82	AU33
John St, G1	5	BS30
John St, (Kirk.) G66	17	CF12
John St, (Blan.) G72	125	CN46
John St, (Barr.) G78	99	AX42
John St, Bell. ML4	111	CW40
John St, Ham. ML3	126	CU50
John St, Lark. ML9	144	DC59
John St, Pais. PA1	82	AS33
off Broomlands St		
John St, Wis. ML2	129	DE49
John Wilson Dr, (Kilsyth) G65	7	CR4
Jones Wynd, Moth. ML1	113	DG44
off Morris Cres		
Joppa St, G33	70	CA30
Jordanhill Cres, G13	47	BF24
Jordanhill Dr, G13	47	BE24
Jordanhill La, G13	47	BG24
Jordan St, G14	65	BF27
Jordanvale Av, G14	65	BF27
Jowitt Av, Clyde. G81	27	AZ20
Jubilee Bk, (Kirk.) G66	35	CE18
off Heriot Rd		
Jubilee Ct, G52	64	BB30
Jubilee Gdns, (Bears.) G61	29	BH17
Jubilee Path, (Bears.) G61	29	BH17
off Jubilee Gdns		
Jubilee Ter, John. PA5	79	AF35
Julian Av, G12	48	BL25
Julian La, G12	48	BL25
Juniper Av, (E.Kil.) G75	135	BZ55
Juniper Ct, (Kirk.) G66	34	CD16
Juniper Dr, (M. of Cam.) G66	16	CD9
Juniper Gro, Ham. ML3	140	CV51
Juniper Pl, G32	91	CH33
Juniper Pl, (Udd.) G71	94	CT37
off Juniper Rd		
Juniper Pl, John. PA5	80	AJ37
Juniper Rd, (Udd.) G71	94	CT37
Juniper Ter, G32	91	CG33
Juniper Wynd, Moth. ML1	112	DD40
off Willow Gro		
Juno St, Moth. ML1	111	CZ44
Jupiter St, Moth. ML1	111	CZ44
Jura, (E.Kil.) G74	136	CD54
Jura Av, Renf. PA4	63	AZ28
Jura Ct, G52	65	BG32
Jura Dr, (Old Kil.) G60	26	AS16
Jura Dr, (Kirk.) G66	18	CJ13
Jura Dr, (Blan.) G72	108	CL42
Jura Dr, (Newt. M.) G77	116	BD47
Jura Gdns, (Old Kil.) G60	26	AS16
Jura Gdns, Ham. ML3	139	CQ51
Jura Gdns, Lark. ML9	145	DE58
Jura Pl, (Old Kil.) G60	26	AS16
Jura Quad, Wis. ML2	143	DG52
off Montgomery Cres		
Jura Rd, (Old Kil.) G60	26	AS16
Jura Rd, Pais. PA2	82	AT38
Jura St, G52	65	BH32
Jura Wynd, (Glenb.) Coat. ML5	56	CS23

K

Kaim Dr, G53	101	BE39
Karadale Gdns, Lark. ML9	144	DC59
Karol Path, G4	67	BQ27
off St. Peters St		
Kashmir Av, (Linw.) Pais. PA3	60	AK32
Katewell Av, G15	28	BA17
Katewell Pl, G15	28	BA17
Katherine St, Air. ML6	77	DG29
Katrine Av, (Bishop.) G64	33	BX20
Katrine Av, (Righead Ind. Est.) Bell. ML4	110	CT39
Katrine Cres, Air. ML6	76	DB28
off Ballochney St		
Katrine Dr, (Newt. M.) G77	118	BK49
Katrine Dr, Pais. PA2	81	AP35
Katrine Pl, (Camb.) G72	106	CC39
Katrine Pl, Coat. ML5	74	CT27
Katrine Way, (Both.) G71	109	CQ42
off Belstane Pl		
Katrine Wynd, Moth. ML1	112	DC40
off Howden Pl		
Katriona Path, Lark. ML9	145	DE60
off Stuart Dr		
Kay Gdns, Moth. ML1	127	CX47
Kaystone Rd, G15	28	BC20
Kay St, G21	50	BV25
Keal Av, G15	46	BC21
Keal Cres, G15	46	BC21
Keal Dr, G15	46	BC21
Keal Pl, G15	46	BC21
Keane Path, Moth. ML1	128	DD50
Kearn Av, G15	28	BD20
Kearn Pl, G15	28	BD20
Keats Pk, (Both.) G71	109	CR42
Keir Dr, (Bishop.) G64	32	BV30
Keir Hardie Av, Moth. ML1	112	DD40
Keir Hardie Ct, (Bishop.) G64	33	BW20
off Murray Av		
Keir Hardie Dr, (Kilsyth) G65	7	CT5
off Murray Av		
Keir Hardie Dr, Bell. ML4	110	CV41

Name	Page	Ref
Keir Hardie Pl, Bell. ML4	110	CV41
Keir Hardie Rd, Lark. ML9	145	DE60
Keir St, G41	87	BP34
Keirs Wk, (Camb.) G72	106	CC39
Keith Av, (Giff.) G46	102	BM42
Keith Ct, G11	66	BL28
Keith St, G11	66	BL27
Keith St, Bell. ML4	111	CW39
Keith St, Ham. ML3	126	CV50
Kelbourne Cres, Bell. ML4	110	CV40
off Cochrane St		
Kelbourne St, G20	49	BN25
Kelburne Dr, Pais. PA1	63	AX32
Kelburne Gdns, (Baill.) G69	92	CJ34
Kelburne Gdns, Pais. PA1	63	AW32
Kelburne Oval, Pais. PA1	63	AW32
Kelburn St, (Barr.) G78	99	AW44
Kelhead Av, G52	64	BB32
Kelhead Dr, G52	64	BB32
Kelhead Path, G52	64	BB32
Kelhead Pl, G52	64	BB32
Kellas St, G51	66	BJ30
Kellie Gro, (E.Kil.) G74	121	BZ50
Kellock Cres, Coat. ML5	94	CT33
Kells Pl, G15	28	BA17
Kelso Av, (Ruther.) G73	89	BX38
Kelso Av, Pais. PA2	81	AQ36
Kelso Dr, (E.Kil.) G74	122	CC50
Kelso Gdns, (Mood.) G69	37	CP18
off Whithorn Cres		
Kelso Pl, G14	46	BA23
Kelso Quad, Coat. ML5	74	CV29
Kelso St, G13	46	BB21
Kelso St, G14	46	BA23
Kelton St, G32	90	CD33
Kelty Pl, G5	67	BR32
off Bedford St		
Kelvin Av, G52	64	BB29
Kelvinbridge Roundabout, (Torr.) G64	15	BX13
Kelvin Ct, G12	47	BH23
Kelvin Cres, (Bears.) G61	29	BH19
Kelvindale, (Torr.) G64	15	BY12
Kelvindale Bldgs, G12	48	BL24
off Kelvindale Rd		
Kelvindale Gdns, G20	48	BL23
Kelvindale Pl, G20	48	BM23
off Kelvindale Rd		
Kelvindale Rd, G12	48	BK23
Kelvindale Rd, G20	48	BM23
Kelvin Dr, G20	48	BM25
Kelvin Dr, (Bishop.) G64	33	BW19
Kelvin Dr, (Kirk.) G66	16	CC13
Kelvin Dr, (Chry.) G69	37	CN19
Kelvin Dr, (E.Kil.) G75	136	CB54
Kelvin Dr, (Barr.) G78	99	AZ44
Kelvin Dr, Air. ML6	76	DD28
Kelvin Gdns, (Kilsyth) G65	7	CT6
Kelvin Gdns, Ham. ML3	125	CN49
Kelvingrove St, G3	67	BN29
Kelvinhaugh Gate, G3	66	BM29
Kelvinhaugh Pl, G3	66	BM29
off Kelvingrove St		
Kelvinhaugh St, G3	66	BL29
Kelvinhead Rd, (Kilsyth) G65	9	DA3
Kelvin Ind Est, (E.Kil.) G75	136	CB55
Kelvin Pl, (E.Kil.) G75	136	CC54
Kelvin Rd, (Miln.) G62	11	BG10
Kelvin Rd, (Cumb.) G67	22	DC13
Kelvin Rd, (Udd.) G71	93	CN38
Kelvin Rd, (E.Kil.) G75	136	CB54
Kelvin Rd, Bell. ML4	95	CX38
Kelvin Rd N, (Cumb.) G67	22	DC13
Kelvinside Av, G20	49	BN25
Kelvinside Dr, G20	49	BP25
Kelvinside Gdns, G20	49	BN25
Kelvinside Gdns E, G20	49	BP26
Kelvinside Gdns La, G20	49	BN25
Kelvinside Ter S, G20	49	BN26
Kelvinside Ter W, G20	49	BN26
Kelvin St, Coat. ML5	75	CY32
Kelvin Ter, (Kilsyth) G65	19	CP11
off Differ Av		
Kelvinvale, (Kirk.) G66	17	CF12
Kelvin Vw, (Torr.) G64	15	BY13
Kelvin Vw, (Kilsyth) G65	19	CP11
Kelvin Way, G3	66	BM28
Kelvin Way, (Kilsyth) G65	7	CS4
Kelvin Way, (Kirk.) G66	16	CC13
Kelvin Way, (Both.) G71	109	CQ42
Komp Av, Pais. PA3	63	AW20
Kemp Ct, Ham. ML3	126	CU50
Kempock St, G31	89	BY33
Kempsthorn Cres, G53	84	BC36
Kempsthorn Path, G53	84	BD36
off Kempsthorn Rd		
Kempsthorn Pl, G53	84	BD36
Kempsthorn Rd, G53	84	BC36
Kemp St, G21	50	BU25
Kemp St, Ham. ML3	126	CT50
Kendal Av, G12	48	BJ23
off Ripon Dr		
Kendal Av, (Giff.) G46	102	BL42
Kendal Dr, G12	48	BJ23
Kendal Rd, (E.Kil.) G75	134	BV55
Kendoon Av, G15	28	BA18
Kenilburn Av, Air. ML6	76	DD27
Kenilburn Cres, Air. ML6	76	DD27
Kenilworth, (E.Kil.) G74	123	CF49
Kenilworth Av, G41	86	BM37
Kenilworth Av, Pais. PA2	81	AP37
Kenilworth Ct, (Cumb.) G67	22	DA13
Kenilworth Ct, Moth. ML1	112	DD40
off Ivy Ter		
Kenilworth Cres, (Bears.) G61	29	BE15
Kenilworth Cres, Bell. ML4	111	CW39
Kenilworth Cres, Ham. ML3	125	CP49
Kenilworth Dr, Air. ML6	77	DE29
Kenilworth Rd, (Kirk.) G66	17	CG13
Kenilworth Way, Pais. PA2	81	AP37
off Kenilworth Av		
Kenmar Gdns, (Udd.) G71	93	CN37
Kenmar Rd, Ham. ML3	125	CR48
Kenmar Ter, Ham. ML3	125	CR48
Kenmore Gdns, (Bears.) G61	30	BK16
off Methven Av		
Kenmore Rd, (Cumb.) G67	22	DD11
Kenmore St, G32	70	CC32
Kenmuiraid Pl, Bell. ML4	110	CV42
Kenmuir Av, G32	91	CG34
Kenmuirhill Gdns, G32	91	CF35
Kenmuirhill Gate, G32	91	CF35
Kenmuirhill Rd, G32	91	CF35
Kenmuir Rd, G32	91	CE37
Kenmuir St, Coat. ML5	93	CR33
Kenmure Av, (Bishop.) G64	32	BU20
Kenmure Cres, (Bishop.) G64	32	BV20
Kenmure Dr, (Bishop.) G64	32	BV20
Kenmure Gdns, (Bishop.) G64	32	BU20
Kenmure La, (Bishop.) G64	32	BV20
Kenmure Rd, (Giff.) G46	118	BK47
Kenmure Row, G22	31	BR20
off Castlebay St		
Kenmure St, G41	87	BP35
Kenmure Way, (Ruther.) G73	105	BX42
Kennedar Dr, G51	65	BG29
Kennedy Av, (Kilsyth) G65	19	CQ10
Kennedy Ct, (Giff.) G46	102	BL41
Kennedy Dr, Air. ML6	76	DA30
Kennedy Path, G4	5	BT29
Kennedy St, G4	5	BT28
Kennelburn Rd, (Chap.) Air. ML6	97	DF36
Kenneth Rd, Moth. ML1	127	CY48
Kennet St, G21	69	BW28
Kennihill, Air. ML6	76	DC28
Kennihill Quad, Air. ML6	76	DC28
Kennishead Av, (Thornlie.) G46	101	BG40
Kennishead Path, (Thornlie.) G46 off Kennishead Pl	101	BG40
Kennishead Pl, (Thornlie.) G46	101	BG40
Kennishead Rd, G43	101	BH40
Kennishead Rd, (Thornlie.) G46	101	BG40
Kennishead Rd, G53	100	BD41
Kennisholm Av, (Thornlie.) G46	101	BG40
Kennisholm Path, (Thornlie.) G46 off Kennisholm Av	101	BG40
Kennisholm Pl, (Thornlie.) G46	101	BG40
Kennoway Dr, G11	65	BH27
Kennyhill Sq, G31	69	BX29
Kenshaw Av, Lark. ML9	144	DC61
Kenshaw Pl, Lark. ML9	144	DC61
Kensington Dr, (Giff.) G46	102	BM44
Kensington Gate, G12	48	BL25
off Kensington Rd		
Kensington Gate La, G12	48	BL25
Kensington Rd, G12	48	BL25
Kensington Sq, (Bears.) G61	30	BK18
Kentallen Rd, G33	71	CG31
Kent Dr, (Ruther.) G73	105	BZ40
Kentigern Ter, (Bishop.) G64	51	BW21
Kentmere Cl, (E.Kil.) G75	135	BW55
Kentmere Dr, (E.Kil.) G75	135	BW55
Kentmere Pl, (E.Kil.) G75	134	BV55
Kent Pl, (E.Kil.) G75	134	BV55
Kent Rd, G3	67	BN29
Kent St, G40	5	BU31
Keppel Dr, G44	88	BU38
Keppochhill Dr, G21	50	BT26
Keppochhill Pl, G21	68	BT27
Keppochhill Rd, G21	50	BT26
Keppochhill Rd, G22	50	BS26
Keppochhill Way, G21	68	BT27
Keppoch St, G21	50	BT26
Kerfield La, G15	28	BA17
Kerfield Pl, G15	28	BA17
Kerr Cres, Ham. ML3	140	CS52
Kerr Dr, G40	68	BV32
Kerrera Pl, G33	71	CF31
Kerrera Rd, G33	71	CF31
Kerr Gdns, (Udd.) G71	93	CQ37
Kerr Pl, G40	68	BV32
Kerr Rd, (Miln.) G62	11	BG10
off Craigton Gdns		
Kerr St, G40	68	BV32
Kerr St, (Kirk.) G66	17	CE13
Kerr St, (Blan.) G72	125	CN45
Kerr St, (Barr.) G78	99	AW43
Kerr St, Pais. PA3	62	AT32
Kerrycroy Av, G42	88	BT38
Kerrycroy Pl, G42	88	BT37
off Kerrycroy Av		
Kerrycroy St, G42	88	BT37
Kerrydale St, G40	89	BX33

Name	Page	Grid
Kerrylamont Av, G42	88	BU38
Kerry Pl, G15	28	BA18
Kersland Dr, (Miln.) G62	12	BK11
Kersland La, G12	48	BM26
Kersland St, G12	48	BM26
Kessington Dr, (Bears.) G61	30	BJ17
Kessington Rd, (Bears.) G61	30	BJ18
Kessock Dr, G22	49	BR26
Kessock Pl, G22	49	BR26
Kestrel Ct, Clyde. G81	27	AW16
Kestrel Pl, John. PA5	79	AF38
Kestrel Rd, G13	47	BE23
Kestrel Vw, (Strathclyde Bus. Pk.) Bell. ML4	94	CU36
Keswick Dr, Ham. ML3	140	CS55
Keswick Rd, (E.Kil.) G75	134	BV55
Kethers La, Moth. ML1	127	CX47
Kethers St, Moth. ML1	127	CY46
Kew Gdns, G12	48	BM26
off Ruthven St		
Kew Gdns, (Udd.) G71	93	CR38
Kew La, G12	48	BM26
Kew Ter, G12	48	BM26
Keynes Sq, Bell. ML4	111	CZ41
off Clydesdale Rd		
Keystone Av, (Miln.) G62	12	BJ12
Keystone Quad, (Miln.) G62	11	BH13
Keystone Rd, (Miln.) G62	12	BJ13
Kibbleston Rd, (Kilb.) John. PA10	78	AC34
Kidston Pl, G5	88	BS33
Kidston Ter, G5	88	BS33
Kierhill Rd, (Cumb.) G68	21	CY11
Kilbarchan Rd, John. PA5	79	AF35
Kilbarchan Rd, (Kilb.) John. PA10	79	AF35
Kilbarchan St, G5	67	BR32
off Bedford St		
Kilbeg Ter, (Thornlie.) G46	101	BF42
Kilberry St, G21	69	BW28
Kilbirnie Pl, G5	87	BQ33
Kilbirnie St, G5	87	BQ33
Kilbowie Ct, Clyde. G81	27	AX18
off Crown Av		
Kilbowie Pl, Air. ML6	77	DF32
Kilbowie Retail Pk, Clyde. G81	27	AY19
Kilbowie Rd, (Cumb.) G67	22	DC13
Kilbowie Rd, Clyde. G81	27	AX15
Kilbowie Roundabout, Clyde. G81	27	AX16
Kilbreck Gdns, (Bears.) G61	11	BE13
Kilbreck La, Moth. ML1	113	DE41
off Glenburn Av		
Kilbrennan Dr, Moth. ML1	127	CW46
Kilbrennan Rd, (Linw.) Pais. PA3	60	AK31
Kilbride St, G5	88	BT35
Kilbride Vw, (Udd.) G71	93	CQ38
Kilburn Gro, (Blan.) G72	108	CM44
Kilburn Pl, G13	46	BD23
Kilchattan Dr, G44	88	BS38
Kilchoan Rd, G33	71	CE27
Kilcloy Av, G15	28	BC17
Kildale Way, (Ruther.) G73	88	BV37
Kildary Av, G44	103	BQ40
Kildary Rd, G44	103	BQ40
Kildermorie Path, G34	72	CJ29
off Kildermorie Rd		
Kildermorie Rd, G34	71	CH29
Kildonan Dr, G11	66	BJ27
Kildonan Pl, Moth. ML1	127	CY46
Kildonan St, Coat. ML5	75	CX30
Kildrostan St, G41	87	BP35
Kildrummy Pl, (E.Kil.) G74	121	BZ50
Kildrum Rd, (Cumb.) G67	22	DD10
Kilearn Rd, Pais. PA3	63	AX30
Kilearn Sq, Pais. PA3	63	AX30
off Kilearn Rd		
Kilearn Way, Pais. PA3	63	AX30
Kilfinan St, G22	49	BR22
Kilgarth St, Coat. ML5	93	CR33
Kilkerran Ct, (Newt. M.) G77	116	BD49
Kilkerran Dr, G33	52	CB23
Kilkerran Way, (Newt. M.) G77	116	BD49
Killearn Dr, Pais. PA1	84	BB33
Killearn St, G22	49	BR25
Killermont Av, (Bears.) G61	30	BJ19
Killermont Ct, (Bears.) G61	30	BK18
Killermont Meadows, (Both.) G71	109	CN43
Killermont Rd, (Bears.) G61	30	BJ18
Killermont St, G2	5	BS29
Killermont Vw, G20	30	BJ19
Killiegrew Rd, G41	86	BM35
Killin St, G32	90	CD34
Killoch Av, Pais. PA3	61	AQ32
Killoch Dr, G13	46	BC22
Killoch Dr, (Barr.) G78	99	AZ44
Killoch La, Pais. PA3	61	AQ32
off Killoch Av		
Killoch Rd, Pais. PA3	61	AQ32
Killoch Way, Pais. PA3	61	AQ32
off Killoch Av		
Kilmailing Rd, G44	103	BR40
Kilmair Pl, G20	48	BM24
Kilmaluag Ter, (Thornlie.) G46	101	BG42
off Kyleakin Rd		
Kilmannan Gdns, (Miln.) G62	11	BF10
off Achray Pl		
Kilmany Dr, G32	70	CB32
Kilmany Gdns, G32	70	CB32
Kilmardinny Av, (Bears.) G61	29	BH15
Kilmardinny Cres, (Bears.) G61	29	BH15
Kilmardinny Dr, (Bears.) G61	29	BH15
Kilmardinny Gate, (Bears.) G61	29	BH15
off Kilmardinny Av		
Kilmardinny Gro, (Bears.) G61	29	BH15
Kilmari Gdns, G15	28	BA17
Kilmarnock Rd, G41	102	BM39
Kilmarnock Rd, G43	102	BM39
Kilmartin Pl, (Thornlie.) G46	101	BG41
Kilmartin Pl, (Udd.) G71	93	CQ36
Kilmartin Pl, Air. ML6	77	DF31
Kilmaurs Dr, (Giff.) G46	103	BN42
Kilmaurs St, G51	65	BH31
Kilmore Cres, G15	28	BA17
Kilmory Av, (Udd.) G71	93	CQ38
Kilmory Dr, (Newt. M.) G77	117	BG48
Kilmuir Cres, (Thornlie.) G46	101	BF41
Kilmuir Dr, (Thornlie.) G46	101	BG41
Kilmuir Rd, (Thornlie.) G46	101	BG41
Kilmuir Rd, (Udd.) G71	93	CP36
Kilmun St, G20	48	BM22
Kilnburn Rd, Moth. ML1	127	CY46
Kilncroft La, Pais. PA2	82	AU35
Kilnside Rd, Pais. PA1	62	AV32
Kilnwell Quad, Moth. ML1	127	CZ46
Kiloran Gro, (Newt. M.) G77	116	BC49
Kiloran Pl, (Newt. M.) G77	116	BC48
Kiloran St, (Thornlie.) G46	101	BH41
Kilpatrick Av, Pais. PA2	81	AR35
Kilpatrick Ct, (Old Kil.) G60	25	AQ15
Kilpatrick Cres, Pais. PA2	82	AT36
Kilpatrick Dr, (Bears.) G61	11	BE13
Kilpatrick Dr, Ersk. PA8	25	AR18
Kilpatrick Dr, Renf. PA4	63	AX29
Kilpatrick Gdns, (Clark.) G76	118	BL45
Kilpatrick Way, (Udd.) G71	93	CQ37
Kilsyth Rd, (Kilsyth) G65	6	CN6
Kilsyth Rd, (Kirk.) G66	17	CF12
Kiltarie Cres, Air. ML6	77	DH30
Kiltearn Rd, G33	71	CH30
Kiltongue Cotts, Air. ML6	75	CZ29
Kilvaxter Dr, (Thornlie.) G46	101	BG41
off Durisdeer Dr		
Kilwynet Way, Pais. PA3	63	AW30
Kimberley Gdns, (E.Kil.) G75	135	BY53
Kimberley St, Clyde. G81	26	AT16
Kimberley St, Wis. ML2	129	DE49
Kinalty Rd, G44	103	BQ40
Kinarvie Cres, G53	84	BB38
Kinarvie Gdns, G53	84	BB38
Kinarvie Pl, G53	84	BB38
Kinarvie Rd, G53	84	BB38
Kinarvie Ter, G53	84	BB38
Kinbuck St, G22	50	BT25
Kincaid Gdns, (Camb.) G72	90	CC38
Kincardine Dr, (Bishop.) G64	51	BX21
Kincardine Dr, (Bishop.) G64	51	BY22
off Kincardine Dr		
Kincardine Pl, (E.Kil.) G74	123	CE50
Kincardine Sq, G33	71	CF27
Kincath Av, (Ruther.) G73	105	BZ42
Kinclaven Av, G15	28	BC18
Kincraig St, G51	65	BF31
Kinellan Rd, (Bears.) G61	29	BH20
Kinellar Dr, G14	46	BC23
Kinfauns Dr, G15	28	BB18
Kinfauns Dr, (Newt. M.) G77	117	BH48
Kingarth La, G42	87	BQ35
Kingarth St, G42	87	BQ35
Kingarth St, Ham. ML3	140	CT53
King Edward La, G13	47	BG24
off King Edward Rd		
King Edward Rd, G13	47	BH24
Kingfisher Dr, G13	46	BB22
Kingfisher Gdns, G13	46	BC22
King George Ct, Renf. PA4	64	BA28
off King George Pk Av		
King George V Br, G1	4	BR31
King George V Br, G5	4	BR31
King George V Dock, G51	64	BD27
King George Gdns, Renf. PA4	64	BA27
King George Pk Av, Renf. PA4	64	BA28
King George Pl, Renf. PA4	64	BA28
off King George Pk Av		
King George Way, Renf. PA4	64	BA28
off King George Pk Av		
Kinghorn Dr, G44	104	BS39
Kinglass Rd, (Bears.) G61	29	BE19
King Pl, (Baill.) G69	73	CQ32
Kingsacre Rd, G44	88	BT38
Kingsacre Rd, (Ruther.) G73	88	BU38
Kingsbarns Dr, G44	87	BR38
Kingsborough Gdns, G12	48	BK26
Kingsborough Gate, G12	48	BK26
off Prince Albert Rd		
Kingsborough La, G12	48	BK26
Kingsborough La E, G12	48	BK26
Kingsbrae Av, G44	88	BS38
King's Br, G5	88	BT33
King's Br, G40	88	BT33
Kingsbridge Cres, G44	104	BT39
Kingsbridge Dr, G44	104	BT39
Kingsbridge Dr, (Ruther.) G73	104	BU34
Kingsbridge Pk Gdns, G44	104	BT39
Kingsburgh Dr, Pais. PA1	63	AX31

Kingsburn Dr, (Ruther.) G73 105 BW39
Kingsburn Gro, (Ruther.) G73 105 BW39
Kingscliffe Av, G44 104 BS39
Kingscourt Av, G44 88 BT38
Kings Cres, (Camb.) G72 106 CD40
Kings Cres, (Elder.) John. PA5 80 AL34
Kings Cross, G31 68 BV30
Kingsdale Av, G44 88 BS38
King's Dr, G40 88 BU33
King's Dr, (Cumb.) G68 9 DB7
Kings Dr, (Newt. M.) G77 117 BH49
Kings Dr, Moth. ML1 112 DB42
Kingsdyke Av, G44 88 BS38
Kingsford Av, G44 103 BN41
Kingsford Ct, (Newt. M.) G77 116 BD47
    off Greenfarm Rd
Kings Gdns, (Newt. M.) G77 118 BJ50
Kingsgate Retail Pk, (E.Kil.) 122 CC47
    G74
Kingsheath Av, (Ruther.) G73 104 BU39
Kingshill Av, (Cumb.) G68 20 CU12
Kingshill Dr, G44 104 BS39
Kingshouse Av, G44 88 BS38
Kingshurst Av, G44 88 BS38
Kings Inch Dr, G51 64 BD28
Kings Inch Pl, Renf. PA4 64 BB27
Kings Inch Rd, G51 46 BA25
Kings Inch Rd, Renf. PA4 46 BA25
Kingsknowe Dr, (Ruther.) G73 104 BU39
Kingsland Cres, G52 64 BD31
Kingsland Dr, G52 64 BD31
Kingsland La, G52 65 BE32
    off Berryknowes Rd
Kings La W, Renf. PA4 45 AZ25
    off Bell St
Kingsley Av, G42 87 BR36
Kingsley Ct, (Udd.) G71 93 CQ38
Kingslynn Dr, G44 104 BT39
Kingslynn La, G44 104 BT39
    off Kingslynn Dr
Kingsmuir Dr, (Ruther.) G73 104 BU39
    off King's Pk Av
Kings Pk, (Torr.) G64 15 BY12
King's Pk Av, G44 104 BS39
King's Pk Av, (Ruther.) G73 104 BU39
Kings Pk Rd, G44 87 BR38
Kings Pl, G22 49 BR22
Kings Rd, John. PA5 80 AK35
Kingston Av, (Udd.) G71 93 CQ37
Kingston Av, (Neil.) G78 114 AT47
Kingston Av, Air. ML6 77 DE30
    off Forrest St
Kingston Br, G3 4 BQ31
Kingston Br, G5 4 BQ31
Kingston Flats, (Kilsyth) G65 7 CT4
Kingston Gro, Bish. PA7 24 AK18
Kingston Ind Est, G5 67 BP32
Kingston Pl, Clyde. G81 26 AT17
Kingston Rd, (Kilsyth) G65 7 CT4
Kingston Rd, (Neil.) G78 114 AT48
Kingston Rd, Bish. PA7 24 AK19
Kingston St, G5 4 BQ31
King St, G1 5 BS31
King St, (Kilsyth) G65 7 CT5
King St, (Ruther.) G73 89 BX37
King St, Clyde. G81 45 AZ21
King St, Coat. ML5 74 CU31
King St, Ham. ML3 125 CP49
King St, Lark. ML9 144 DC58
King St, Pais. PA1 62 AS32
King's Vw, (Cumb.) G68 9 DB7
King's Vw, (Ruther.) G73 88 BV38
Kingsway, G14 46 BC24

Kingsway, (Kilsyth) G65 7 CT4
Kingsway, (Kirk.) G66 18 CK11
Kingsway, (E.Kil.) G74 122 CC48
Kingsway Ct, G14 46 BD24
Kingswood Dr, G44 104 BS39
Kingussie Dr, G44 104 BS39
Kiniver Dr, G15 28 BC20
Kinkell Gdns, (Kirk.) G66 18 CK12
Kinloch Av, (Camb.) G72 106 CD41
Kinloch Dr, Moth. ML1 111 CZ43
Kinloch Rd, (Newt. M.) G77 117 BE47
Kinloch Rd, Renf. PA4 63 AX28
Kinloch St, G40 89 BY33
Kinloss Pl, (E.Kil.) G74 136 CB51
Kinmount Av, G44 87 BR38
Kinnaird Av, (Newt. M.) G77 118 BJ48
Kinnaird Cres, (Bears.) G61 30 RK17
Kinnaird Dr, (Linw.) Pais. PA3 60 AK30
Kinnaird Pl, (Bishop.) G64 51 BX21
Kinnear Rd, G40 89 BX34
Kinneil Pl, Ham. ML3 139 CP51
Kinnell Av, G52 85 BE34
Kinnell Cres, G52 85 BE34
Kinnell Path, G52 85 BE34
    off Kinnell Cres
Kinnell Pl, G52 85 BF34
    off Mosspark Dr
Kinnell Sq, G52 85 BE34
Kinning Pk Ind Est, G5 67 BP32
Kinning St, G5 67 BQ32
Kinnoul Gdns, (Bears.) G61 11 BE14
Kinnoul La, G12 48 BL26
    off Downside Rd
Kinnoull Pl, (Blan.) G72 124 CM46
Kinpurnie Rd, Pais. PA1 63 AZ32
Kinross Av, G52 84 BD33
Kinross Pk, (E.Kil.) G74 123 CF50
Kinsail Dr, G52 64 BB31
Kinstone Av, G14 46 BC24
Kintail Gdns, (Kirk.) G66 18 CK12
Kintessack Pl, (Bishop.) G64 33 BZ19
Kintillo Dr, G13 46 BD23
Kintore Pk, Ham. ML3 139 CR54
Kintore Rd, G43 103 BP39
Kintra St, G51 66 BK30
Kintyre Av, (Linw.) Pais. PA3 60 AJ32
Kintyre Cres, (Newt. M.) G77 117 BE47
Kintyre Cres, (Plains) Air. ML6 59 DH26
Kintyre Gdns, (Kirk.) G66 18 CK11
Kintyre Rd, (Blan.) G72 124 CK45
    off Glenfruin Rd
Kintyre St, G21 69 BW28
Kipland Wk, Coat. ML5 75 CZ32
Kippen Dr, (Clark.) G76 119 BQ48
Kippen St, G22 50 BT23
Kippen St, Air. ML6 75 CZ31
Kippford Pl, (Chap.) Air. ML6 97 DG36
Kippford St, G32 91 CE33
Kipps Av, Air. ML6 76 DA29
Kippsbyre Ct, Air. ML6 75 CZ30
    off Monkscourt Av
Kirkaig Av, Renf. PA4 64 BB27
Kirkandrews Pl, Air. ML6 97 DH35
Kirkbean Av, (Ruther.) G73 105 BW41
Kirkburn Av, (Camb.) G72 106 CC41
Kirkcaldy Rd, G41 86 BM35
Kirkconnel Av, G13 46 BB22
Kirkconnel Av, (Cumb.) G68 20 CU12
Kirkconnel Dr, (Ruther.) G73 104 BV40
Kirkcudbright Pl, (E.Kil.) G74 123 CF50
Kirkdale Dr, G52 85 BG33
Kirkdene Av, (Newt. M.) G77 118 BK48

Kirkdene Bk, (Newt. M.) G77 118 BK48
Kirkdene Cres, (Newt. M.) G77 118 BK48
Kirkdene Gro, (Newt. M.) G77 118 BK48
Kirkdene Pl, (Newt. M.) G77 118 BK48
Kirkfieldbank Way, Ham. ML3 125 CQ50
    off Beattock Wynd
Kirkfield Rd, (Both.) G71 109 CQ42
Kirkford Rd, (Chry.) G69 37 CN19
    off Bridgeburn Dr
Kirk Glebe, (Neil.) G78 114 AU46
Kirkhall Rd, Moth. ML1 113 DF41
Kirkhill Av, (Camb.) G72 106 CC42
Kirkhill Cres, (Neil.) G78 114 AU45
Kirkhill Dr, G20 49 BN24
Kirkhill Gdns, (Camb.) G72 106 CC42
Kirkhill Gate, (Newt. M.) G77 118 BK49
Kirkhill Gro, (Camb.) G72 106 CC42
Kirkhill Pl, G20 48 BM24
    off Kirkhill Dr
Kirkhill Pl, Wis. ML2 143 DE51
Kirkhill Rd, (Gart.) G69 55 CP24
Kirkhill Rd, (Udd.) G71 93 CN37
Kirkhill Rd, (Newt. M.) G77 118 BK48
Kirkhill Rd, Wis. ML2 143 DE52
Kirkhill St, Wis. ML2 143 DF52
    off Clydesdale Av
Kirkhill Ter, (Camb.) G72 106 CC42
Kirkhope Dr, G15 28 RD19
Kirkinner Rd, G32 91 CF34
Kirkintilloch Rd, (Bishop.) G64 50 BV21
Kirkintilloch Rd, (Kirk.) G66 35 CE16
Kirkland Gro, John. PA5 79 AH34
Kirklandneuk Cres, Renf. PA4 45 AW25
    off Kirklandneuk Rd
Kirklandneuk Rd, Renf. PA4 45 AX25
Kirklands Cres, (Kilsyth) G65 7 CT6
Kirklands Cres, (Both.) G71 109 CQ42
Kirklands Dr, (Newt. M.) G77 131 BF51
Kirklands Pl, (Newt. M.) G77 131 BF51
Kirklands Rd, (Newt. M.) G77 131 BF51
Kirkland St, G20 49 BP26
Kirkland St, Moth. ML1 127 CZ46
Kirk La, G43 86 BL38
    off Riverbank St
Kirk La, (Bears.) G61 29 BG16
Kirklea Av, Pais. PA3 61 AQ31
    off Blackstone Rd
Kirklea Gdns, Pais. PA3 61 AQ32
Kirkle Dr, (Newt. M.) G77 118 BK48
Kirklee Circ, G12 48 BL25
Kirklee Gdns, G12 48 BL24
Kirklee Gdns La, G12 48 BM25
Kirklee Gate, G12 48 BM25
Kirklee Pl, G12 48 BM25
Kirklee Quad, G12 48 BM25
Kirklee Quad La, G12 48 BM25
    off Kirklee Quad
Kirklee Rd, G12 48 BL25
Kirklee Rd, Bell. ML4 112 DA43
Kirklee Ter, G12 48 BL25
Kirklee Ter La, G12 48 BL25
Kirkliston St, G32 70 CB31
Kirkmichael Av, G11 48 BJ26
    off Blairatholl Av
Kirkmichael Gdns, G11 48 BJ26
    off Blairatholl Av
Kirkmuir Dr, (Ruther.) G73 105 BX42
Kirkness St, Air. ML6 76 DC29
Kirknethan, Wis. ML2 143 DE52
Kirknewton St, G32 70 CC31
Kirkoswald, (E.Kil.) G74 123 CF50
Kirkoswald Dr, Clyde. G81 27 AY18

228

Kirkoswald Rd, G43	102	BM39
Kirkoswald Rd, Moth. ML1	113	DG41
Kirkpatrick Dr, G33	53	CG24
Kirkpatrick St, G40	69	BW32
Kirk Pl, (Bears.) G61	29	BG16
Kirk Pl, (Cumb.) G67	21	CW14
Kirk Pl, (Udd.) G71	109	CN40
Kirkriggs Av, (Ruther.) G73	105	BX40
Kirkriggs Gdns, (Ruther.) G73	105	BX40
Kirkriggs Vw, (Ruther.) G73	105	BX40
off Kirkriggs Av		
Kirkriggs Way, (Ruther.) G73	105	BX40
off Kirkriggs Gdns		
Kirk Rd, (Bears.) G61	29	BG16
Kirk Rd, (Carm.) G76	120	BT46
Kirk Rd, Moth. ML1	97	DF38
Kirkshaws Av, Coat. ML5	94	CU34
Kirkshaws Pl, Coat. ML5	94	CV34
off Kirkshaws Av		
Kirkshaws Rd, Coat. ML5	94	CV35
Kirkstall Gdns, (Bishop.) G64	33	BX17
Kirkstone, (Newt. M.) G77	118	BK48
off Kirkvale Ct		
Kirkstone Cl, (E.Kil.) G75	134	BV55
Kirk St, (Miln.) G62	11	BG11
Kirk St, Coat. ML5	74	CV31
Kirk St, Moth. ML1	128	DA46
Kirkstyle Cotts, Coat. ML5	94	CT34
Kirkstyle Cres, (Neil.) G78	114	AT46
Kirkstyle Cres, Air. ML6	76	DB27
Kirkstyle La, (Neil.) G78	114	AU46
off Main St		
Kirkstyle Pl, (Glenm.) Air. ML6	57	CZ25
Kirksyde Av, (Kirk.) G66	17	CF14
Kirkton, Ersk. PA8	25	AQ18
Kirkton Av, G13	46	BC23
Kirkton Av, (Blan.) G72	124	CM48
Kirkton Av, (Barr.) G78	99	AX43
Kirkton Cres, G13	46	BC23
Kirkton Cres, Coat. ML5	95	CZ33
Kirkton Dr, (Eagle.) G76	133	BN56
Kirktonfield Dr, (Neil.) G78	114	AV46
Kirktonfield Pl, (Neil.) G78	114	AV46
Kirktonfield Rd, (Neil.) G78	114	AU46
Kirkton Gate, (E.Kil.) G74	136	CA51
Kirktonholme Cres, (E.Kil.) G74	135	BZ51
Kirktonholme Rd, (E.Kil.) G74	135	BZ51
Kirkton Moor Rd, (Eagle.) G76	131	BH56
Kirkton Pk, (E.Kil.) G74	136	CB52
Kirkton Pl, (Blan.) G72	124	CM47
off Kirkton Av		
Kirkton Pl, (E.Kil.) G74	136	CB51
Kirkton Pl, Coat. ML5	95	CZ33
Kirkton Rd, (Camb.) G72	106	CD40
Kirkton Rd, (Neil.) G78	114	AU47
Kirktonside, (Barr.) G78	99	AX44
Kirkvale Ct, (Newt. M.) G77	118	BK48
Kirkvale Cres, (Newt. M.) G77	118	BK48
Kirkvale Dr, (Newt. M.) G77	118	BK48
Kirkview, (Cumb.) G67	39	CW15
Kirkview Ct, (Cumb.) G67	39	CW15
Kirkview Cres, (Newt. M.) G77	117	BG50
Kirkview Gdns, (Udd.) G71	93	CN37
Kirkville Pl, G15	28	BD20
Kirkwall, (Cumb.) G67	9	DC8
Kirkwall Av, (Blan.) G72	108	CL43
Kirkwell Rd, G44	103	BR40
Kirkwood Av, (Stepps) G33	53	CH24
Kirkwood Av, Clyde. G81	27	AZ20
Kirkwood Pl, Coat. ML5	94	CU33
Kirkwood Quad, Clyde. G81	27	AZ20
off Kirkwood Av		
Kirkwood Rd, (Udd.) G71	93	CQ37

Kirkwood St, G51	66	BL32
Kirkwood St, (Ruther.) G73	89	BW37
Kirkwood St, Coat. ML5	74	CU32
Kirn St, G20	48	BL21
Kirriemuir, (E.Kil.) G74	123	CF48
Kirriemuir Av, G52	85	BE34
Kirriemuir Gdns, (Bishop.) G64	33	BY19
Kirriemuir Pl, G52	85	BE33
Kirriemuir Rd, (Bishop.) G64	33	BY20
Kirtle Dr, Renf. PA4	64	BA27
Kirtle Pl, (E.Kil.) G75	134	BU54
Kishorn Pl, G33	71	CE28
Kittoch Pl, (E.Kil.) G74	136	CB51
off Kittoch St		
Kittochside Rd, (Clark.) G76	120	BV47
Kittoch St, (E.Kil.) G74	136	CA51
Klondike Ct, (New Stev.) Moth. ML1	112	DD42
Knapdale St, G22	49	BQ22
Knightsbridge St, G13	47	BF22
Knightscliffe Av, G13	47	BF21
Knights Gate, (Both.) G71	109	CN40
Knightswood Ct, G13	47	BF23
off Knightswood Rd		
Knightswood Cross, G13	47	BF22
Knightswood Rd, G13	29	BE20
Knightswood Ter, (Blan.) G72	109	CN44
Knivysbridge Pl, Bell. ML4	110	CV42
Knockburnie Rd, (Both.) G71	109	CQ41
Knockhall St, G33	71	CF27
Knockhill Dr, G44	87	BR38
Knockhill Rd, Renf. PA4	63	AW28
Knockside Av, Pais. PA2	82	AT38
Knock Way, Pais. PA3	63	AW30
Knollpark Dr, (Clark.) G76	118	BM46
Knowe Cres, Moth. ML1	113	DF41
Knowehead Dr, (Udd.) G71	109	CN39
Knowehead Gdns, G41	87	BN34
Knowehead Gdns, (Udd.) G71	109	CN39
Knowehead Ter, G41	87	BN34
Knowe Rd, (Chry.) G69	54	CL21
Knowe Rd, Pais. PA3	63	AX30
Knowes Av, (Newt. M.) G77	117	BG48
Knowes Rd, (Newt. M.) G77	117	BH48
Knowe St, (Miln.) G62	11	BH11
Knowetap St, G20	49	BN22
Knowetop Av, Moth. ML1	128	DB48
Knox Pl, (Newt. M.) G77	116	BD49
Knox St, Air. ML6	76	DD29
Knox St, Pais. PA1	81	AR33
Kronborg Way, (E.Kil.) G75	135	BZ56
Kyleakin Dr, (Blan.) G72	108	CK43
off Dalcraig Cres		
Kyleakin Rd, (Thornlie.) G46	101	BF42
Kyleakin Ter, (Thornlie.) G46	101	BF42
Kyle Ct, (Camb.) G72	106	CC39
Kyle Dr, (Giff.) G46	103	BN42
Kyle Gro, Moth. ML1	112	DC42
Kylemore Cres, Moth. ML1	111	CZ43
Kylepark Av, (Udd.) G71	108	CM39
Kylepark Cres, (Udd.) G71	92	CM38
Kylepark Dr, (Udd.) G71	92	CM38
Kyle Quad, Moth. ML1	113	DE41
off Lintie Rd		
Kyle Quad, Wis. ML2	143	DG52
Kylerhea Rd, (Thornlie.) G46	101	BF42
Kyle Rd, (Cumb.) G67	22	DD11
Kyle Sq, (Ruther.) G73	104	BV40
Kyle St, G4	5	BS28
Kyle St, Moth. ML1	127	CX46

L

La Belle Allee, G3	67	BN28

La Belle Pl, G3	67	BN28
Laberge Gdns, (New Stev.) Moth. ML1	112	DD42
Laburnum Av, (E.Kil.) G75	135	BY55
Laburnum Ct, (E.Kil.) G75	135	BY55
Laburnum Gdns, (Kirk.) G66	34	CD16
off Laburnum Gro		
Laburnum Gro, (Kirk.) G66	34	CD16
Laburnum Gro, Coat. ML5	75	CX31
Laburnum Lea, Ham. ML3	140	CU51
Laburnum Pl, John. PA5	80	AJ37
Laburnum Rd, G41	86	BL33
Laburnum Rd, (Cumb.) G67	23	DF11
Laburnum Rd, (Udd.) G71	94	CT38
Lachlan Cres, Ersk. PA8	24	AN20
La Crosse Ter, G12	49	BN26
Lacy St, Pais. PA1	63	AW32
Ladeside Cl, (Newt. M.) G77	117	BE47
Ladeside Dr, (Kilsyth) G65	7	CU4
Ladeside Dr, John. PA5	79	AF35
Lade Ter, G52	84	BC33
Ladhope Pl, G13	46	BA21
Ladyacres, (Inch.) Renf. PA4	44	AT23
Ladyacres Way, (Inch.) Renf. PA4	44	AT23
Lady Anne Cres, Air. ML6	77	DE31
Lady Anne St, G14	46	BB23
off Speirshall Cl		
Ladybank, (Cumb.) G68	9	DB7
Ladybank Ct, (E.Kil.) G74	136	CA51
off West Mains Rd		
Ladybank Dr, G52	85	BG33
Ladybank Gdns, (E.Kil.) G74	136	CA51
Ladybank Pl, (E.Kil.) G74	136	CA51
off Parkhall St		
Ladyburn St, Pais. PA1	83	AW33
Ladyhill Dr, (Baill.) G69	92	CJ33
Lady Isle Cres, (Udd.) G71	109	CN39
Lady Jane Gate, (Both.) G71	109	CN41
Ladykirk Cres, G52	64	BD31
Ladykirk Cres, Pais. PA2	82	AV34
Ladykirk Dr, G52	64	BD31
Lady La, Pais. PA1	82	AT33
Ladyloan Av, G15	28	BA17
Ladyloan Ct, G15	28	BB17
Ladyloan Gdns, G15	28	BB17
Ladyloan Gro, G15	28	BB17
Ladyloan Pl, G15	28	BA17
Lady Mary Wk, Ham. ML3	140	CU52
off Silvertonhill Av		
Ladymuir Circle, Ersk. PA8	25	AP20
Ladymuir Cres, G53	85	BE35
Ladysmith Av, (Kilb.) John. PA10	78	AD35
Ladysmith St, Wis. ML2	129	DE50
Lady Watson Gdns, Ham. ML3	139	CQ51
Ladywell Rd, Moth. ML1	127	CY47
Ladywell St, G4	5	BU30
Lady Wilson St, Air. ML6	76	DD31
Ladywood Est, (Miln.) G62	12	BK11
off Moor Rd		
Laggan Quad, Air. ML6	76	DA28
Laggan Rd, G43	103	BN40
Laggan Rd, (Bishop.) G64	33	BX20
Laggan Rd, (Newt. M.) G77	117	BF46
Laggan Rd, Air. ML6	76	DB28
Laggan Ter, Renf. PA4	45	AX25
Laidlaw Av, Moth. ML1	112	DB42
off Catherine Way		
Laidlaw Gdns, (Udd.) G71	93	CP36
Laidlaw St, G5	67	BQ32
Laidon Rd, Air. ML6	76	DB28
off Laggan Rd		

Laighcartside St, John. PA5	80	AJ34	Lane, The (Dullatur) G68	9	CZ7	Langside Gdns, G42	87	BQ38
Laighlands Rd, (Both.) G71	109	CR43	Lane Gdns, G11	48	BK26	Langside La, G42	87	BQ36
Laighmuir St, (Udd.) G71	109	CP40	off North Gardner St			Langside Pk, (Kilb.) John. PA10	78	AC35
Laighpark Av, Bish. PA7	24	AK18	Lanfine Rd, Pais. PA1	63	AX32	Langside Pl, G41	87	BP37
Laighpark Harbour, Pais. PA3	62	AU30	Langa St, G20	49	BN22	Langside Rd, G42	87	BQ36
Laighpark Vw, Pais. PA3	62	AU30	Lang Av, Bish. PA7	24	AL18	Langside Rd, (Both.) G71	109	CR44
Laigh Rd, (Newt. M.) G77	118	BK48	Lang Av, Renf. PA4	63	AY28	Langside St, Clyde. G81	28	BA15
Laighstonehall Rd, Ham. ML3	139	CR51	Langbank St, G5	67	BR32	Langstile Pl, G52	64	BB32
Laightoun Ct, (Cumb.) G67	39	CW15	off Eglinton St			Langstile Rd, G52	64	BB32
Laightoun Dr, (Cumb.) G67	39	CW15	Langbar Cres, G33	71	CG30	Lang St, Pais. PA1	83	AW33
Laightoun Gdns, (Cumb.) G67	39	CW15	Langbar Gdns, G33	71	CH30	Langton Cres, G53	85	BE36
Lainshaw Dr, G45	103	BQ43	Langbar Path, G33	71	CF30	Langton Cres, (Barr.) G78	99	AZ44
Laird Gro, (Udd.) G71	93	CQ37	off Bartiebeith Rd			Langton Gdns, (Baill.) G69	91	CH33
Laird Pl, G40	88	BV33	Langcraigs Dr, Pais. PA2	98	AS39	Langton Gate, (Newt. M.) G77	117	BE48
Lairds Gate, (Udd.) G71	108	CM40	Langcraigs Ter, Pais. PA2	98	AS39	Langton Pl, (Newt. M.) G77	117	BE48
Lairds Hill, (Cumb.) G67	22	DA11	Langcroft Dr, (Camb.) G72	107	CE41	Langton Rd, G53	85	BE37
Lairds Hill Ct, (Kilsyth) G65	6	CQ5	Langcroft Pl, G51	65	BF30	Langtree Av, (Giff.) G46	102	BJ44
Lairds Hill Pl, (Kilsyth) G65	6	CQ5	Langcroft Rd, G51	65	BF30	Lanrig Pl, (Chry.) G69	54	CL21
Laird St, Coat. ML5	75	CX30	Langcroft Ter, G51	65	BF30	Lanrig Rd, (Chry.) G69	54	CL21
Lairg Dr, (Blan.) G72	108	CL43	off Langcroft Rd			Lanrig Rd, (Newt. M.) G77	117	BE50
Lairhills Rd, (E.Kil.) G75	136	CB54	Langdale, (E.Kil.) G74	121	BY50	Lansbury Gdns, Pais. PA3	62	AT30
Lamberton Dr, G52	64	BD31	Langdale, (Newt. M.) G77	118	BK48	Lansbury Ter, Lark. ML9	145	DE60
Lambhill Quad, G41	67	BN32	off Kirkvale Ct			Lansdowne Cres, G20	67	BP27
Lambhill St, G41	66	BM32	Langdale Av, G33	52	CA26	Lansdowne Cres La, G20	67	BP27
Lambie Cres, (Newt. M.) G77	117	BE48	Langdale Rd, (Chry.) G69	37	CP19	Lansdowne Dr, (Cumb.) G68	9	DB8
Lamb St, G22	49	BR23	Langdale's Av, (Cumb.) G68	21	CY11	Lansdowne Gdns, Ham. ML3	126	CV50
Lamb St, Ham. ML3	126	CU50	Langdale St, G33	52	CA26	Lantana Gro, Moth. ML1	127	CZ45
Lamerton Rd, (Cumb.) G67	23	DE11	Langford Dr, G53	100	BC42	off Alyssum Cres		
Lamington Rd, G52	84	BD33	Langford Pl, G53	100	BD42	Lanton Dr, G52	64	BD32
Lamlash Cres, G33	70	CD29	Langhaul Pl, G53	84	BB36	Lanton Rd, G43	103	BN40
Lamlash Pl, G33	70	CD29	Langhaul Rd, G53	84	BB36	Lappin St, Clyde. G81	45	AZ21
off Lamlash Cres			Langhill Dr, (Cumb.) G68	21	CZ10	Larbert St, G4	4	BR28
Lamlash Pl, Moth. ML1	127	CY46	Langholm, (E.Kil.) G75	134	BV55	Larch Av, (Bishop.) G64	51	BX21
Lamlash Sq, G33	71	CE29	Langholm Ct, (Chry.) G69	37	CP19	Larch Av, (Lenz.) G66	35	CE15
Lammermoor, (E.Kil.) G74	123	CG49	off Heathfield Av			Larch Ct, (Cumb.) G67	23	DG9
Lammermoor Av, G52	85	BE33	Langholm Dr, (Linw.) Pais. PA3	60	AL32	Larch Ct, (Blan.) G72	124	CL45
Lammermoor Cres, (Kirk.) G66	17	CH13	Langholm Path, (Blan.) G72	124	CL46	Larch Ct, (E.Kil.) G75	135	BX56
Lammermoor Dr, (Cumb.) G67	22	DA14	off Broompark Rd			Larch Cres, (Kirk.) G66	35	CE15
Lammermoor Gdns, (Kirk.) G66	17	CH13	Langlands Av, G51	65	BF29	Larch Dr, (E.Kil.) G75	135	BX56
Lammermoor Rd, (Kirk.) G66	17	CH13	Langlands Ct, G51	65	BH29	Larches, The (Mood.) G69	37	CQ17
Lammermuir Ct, Pais. PA2	82	AU37	off Langlands Rd			Larchfield Av, G14	46	BD25
Lammermuir Dr, Pais. PA2	82	AT37	Langlands Dr, G51	65	BF30	Larchfield Av, (Newt. M.) G77	117	BG49
Lammermuir Gdns, (Bears.) G61	11	BE14	Langlands Rd, G51	65	BF30	Larchfield Ct, (Newt. M.) G77	117	BF49
Lammermuir Pl, Moth. ML1	112	DD41	Langlands-Seafar Interchange, (Cumb.) G67	22	DA13	Larchfield Dr, (Ruther.) G73	105	BY41
off Dornoch Rd			Langlea Av, (Camb.) G72	105	BZ41	Larchfield Pl, G14	46	BD25
Lammermuir Way, (Chap.) Air. ML6	97	DH36	Langlea Ct, (Camb.) G72	106	CA41	Larchfield Rd, (Bears.) G61	29	BH20
Lammermuir Wynd, Lark. ML9	142	DB56	Langlea Dr, (Camb.) G72	106	CA40	Larchfield Rd, (Mood.) G69	37	CP19
Lammer Wynd, Lark. ML9	145	DE60	Langlea Gdns, (Camb.) G72	106	CA40	Larch Gro, (Cumb.) G67	23	DG9
off Elmbank Dr			Langlea Gro, (Camb.) G72	106	CA41	Larch Gro, Ham. ML3	140	CU51
Lamont Av, Bish. PA7	24	AL18	Langlea Rd, (Camb.) G72	106	CA41	Larch Gro, Moth. ML1	112	DD40
Lamont Rd, G21	51	BX23	Langlea Way, (Camb.) G72	106	CA40	off Elm Rd		
Lanark Av, Air. ML6	96	DB33	Langlees Av, (Newt. M.) G77	118	BK48	Larchgrove Av, G32	71	CE31
Lanark Rd, Lark. ML9	142	DB54	Langley Av, G13	46	BD21	Larchgrove Pl, G32	71	CE30
Lanark Rd End, Lark. ML9	142	DA54	Langloan Cres, Coat. ML5	74	CU31	off Larchgrove Rd		
Lanark St, G1	5	BT31	Langloan Pl, Coat. ML5	74	CU31	Larchgrove Rd, G32	71	CE30
Lancaster Av, (Chap.) Air. ML6	97	DG37	Langloan St, Coat. ML5	74	CU32	Larch Pl, (Udd.) G71	94	CT37
Lancaster Cres, G12	48	BL25	Langlook Rd, G53	84	BB36	Larch Pl, (E.Kil.) G75	135	BX56
Lancaster Cres La, G12	48	BL25	Langmuir Av, (Kirk.) G66	17	CG12	Larch Pl, John. PA5	79	AH37
Lancaster Rd, (Bishop.) G64	33	BX17	Langmuirhead Rd, (Kirk.) G66	52	CC21	Larch Rd, G41	66	BK32
Lancaster Ter, G12	48	BL25	Langmuir Rd, (Kirk.) G66	17	CH12	Larch Rd, (Cumb.) G67	23	DF9
Lancaster Ter La, G12	48	BL25	Langmuir Rd, (Baill.) G69	73	CQ32	Larchwood Ter, (Barr.) G78	99	AZ44
off Westbourne Gdns W			Langmuir Way, (Baill.) G69	73	CQ32	off Newton Av		
Lancaster Way, Renf. PA4	63	AY28	Langness Rd, G33	70	CD29	Largie Rd, G43	103	BP40
off Tiree Av			Langoreth Av, Ham. ML3	139	CP51	Largo Pl, G51	65	BG30
Lancefield Quay, G3	67	BN30	Lang Pl, John. PA5	79	AG34	Largs St, G31	69	BX30
Lancefield St, G3	4	BP30	Langrig Rd, G21	51	BW25	Larkfield Ct, (Blan.) G72	124	CL47
Landemer Dr, (Ruther.) G73	104	BV39	Langshot St, G51	66	BM32	off Larkfield Dr		
Landressy Pl, G40	88	BU33	Langside Av, G41	87	BN36	Larkfield Dr, (Blan.) G72	124	CM47
Landressy St, G40	88	BV33	Langside Av, (Udd.) G71	110	CS39	Larkfield Rd, (Lenz.) G66	35	CG16
Landsdowne Rd, Lark. ML9	145	DE59	Langside Ct, (Both.) G71	109	CR44	Larkhill Ind Est, Lark. ML9	144	DD60
			Langside Dr, G43	103	BN40	Larkin Gdns, Pais. PA3	62	AT30
			Langside Dr, (Kilb.) John. PA10	78	AC35	Larkin Way, Bell. ML4	94	CV38
						Larkspur Dr, (E.Kil.) G74	121	BY49

Lark Way, (Strathclyde Bus. Pk.) Bell. ML4 — 94 CV37
Lasswade St, G14 — 46 BA23
Latherton Dr, G20 — 48 BM24
Latherton Pl, G20 — 48 BM24
off Latherton Dr
Latimer Gdns, G52 — 84 BC33
Latimer Path, G52 — 84 BC33
off Paisley Rd W
Lauchlin Pl, (Kirk.) G66 — 18 CK14
Lauchope Rd, Moth. ML1 — 97 DF38
Lauchope St, (Chap.) Air. ML6 — 97 DG35
Laudedale La, G12 — 48 BK26
Lauderdale Dr, (Newt. M.) G77 — 117 BE50
Lauderdale Gdns, G12 — 48 BK26
Lauder Dr, (Ruther.) G73 — 105 BZ39
Lauder Dr, (Linw.) Pais. PA3 — 60 AK32
Lauder Gdns, (Blan.) G72 — 108 CL43
Lauder Gdns, Coat. ML5 — 95 CZ34
Lauder Grn, (E.Kil.) G74 — 122 CD49
Lauder La, Ham. ML3 — 125 CN50
off Clarkwell Rd
Laughland Dr, Moth. ML1 — 113 DF42
Laundry La, G33 — 53 CE24
Lauranne Pl, Bell. ML4 — 110 CU40
Laurel Av, (Lenz.) G66 — 35 CF15
Laurel Av, Clyde. G81 — 26 AT17
Laurelbank, Coat. ML5 — 75 CW29
Laurel Bk, Ham. ML3 — 140 CS53
Laurelbank Rd, (Chry.) G69 — 54 CK22
Laurel Ct, (E.Kil.) G75 — 135 BZ56
Laurel Dr, (E.Kil.) G75 — 135 BZ56
Laurel Dr, Lark. ML9 — 145 DE59
Laurel Dr, Wis. ML2 — 129 DF49
Laurel Gdns, (Udd.) G71 — 93 CP37
Laurel Gdns, (Chap.) Air. ML6 — 97 DG35
Laurel Gro, (Green.) Air. ML6 — 41 DH19
Laurel La, Lark. ML9 — 145 DE60
off Dickson St
Laurel Pk Cl, G13 — 47 BE24
Laurel Pk Gdns, G13 — 47 BE24
Laurel Pl, G11 — 48 BJ26
Laurel Pl, (E.Kil.) G75 — 135 BZ56
Laurels, The (Newt. M.) G77 — 117 BF48
Laurels, The (Carfin) Moth. ML1 — 112 DD43
Laurel St, G11 — 66 BJ27
Laurel Wk, (Ruther.) G73 — 105 BY42
Laurel Way, (Barr.) G78 — 99 AX42
Laurence Ct, G15 — 28 BA18
off Laurence Dr
Laurence Dr, G15 — 28 BA18
Laurence Dr, (Bears.) G61 — 29 BF15
Laurence Gdns, G15 — 28 BA18
off Laurence Dr
Laurenstone Ter, (E.Kil.) G74 — 122 CD50
Lauren Way, Pais. PA2 — 81 AP36
Laurie Ct, (Udd.) G71 — 93 CQ38
Laurieston Cres, (Chap.) Air. ML6 — 97 DF36
Laurieston Rd, G5 — 87 BR33
Laurieston Way, (Ruther.) G73 — 105 BX41
Lauriston Gro, (Newt. M.) G77 — 116 BD48
Lavelle Dr, Coat. ML5 — 75 CY30
Lavender Dr, (E.Kil.) G75 — 135 BZ56
Laverock Av, Ham. ML3 — 141 CW51
Laverockhall St, G21 — 50 BV26
Laverock Rd, Air. ML6 — 76 DD27
Laverock Ter, (Chry.) G69 — 37 CP20
Law Dr, Moth. ML1 — 113 DE41
Lawers Dr, (Bears.) G61 — 29 BE15
Lawers La, Moth. ML1 — 113 DE41
off Hamilton Pl

Lawers Rd, G43 — 102 BK40
Lawers Rd, Renf. PA4 — 63 AX28
Lawfield Av, (Newt. M.) G77 — 118 BK48
Lawhill Av, G44 — 104 BT41
off Croftfoot Rd
Lawhope Mill Rd, Air. ML6 — 97 DH34
Lawmoor Av, G5 — 88 BS34
Lawmoor Pl, G5 — 88 BS35
Lawmoor Rd, G5 — 88 BS34
Lawmoor St, G5 — 88 BS34
Lawmuir Cres, Clyde. G81 — 10 BA14
Lawmuir Pl, Bell. ML4 — 111 CW43
Lawmuir Rd, Bell. ML4 — 111 CW42
Lawn Pk, (Miln.) G62 — 12 BL12
Lawn St, Pais. PA1 — 62 AV32
Law Pl, (E.Kil.) G74 — 122 CA49
Lawrence Av, (Giff.) G46 — 102 BL44
Lawrence St, G11 — 66 BL27
Lawrie St, G11 — 66 BK27
Lawrie Way, Lark. ML9 — 145 DE60
off Stuart Dr
Law Roundabout, (E.Kil.) G74 — 122 CA49
Lawson Av, Moth. ML1 — 128 DA50
Law St, G40 — 69 BW32
Laxford Av, G44 — 103 BQ41
Laxford Pl, Coat. ML5 — 75 CZ32
Laxford Rd, Ersk. PA8 — 24 AN20
Laxford Way, Moth. ML1 — 113 DE41
off Hamilton Pl
Laxton Dr, (Lenz.) G66 — 35 CG17
Lea Av, (Neil.) G78 — 114 AT46
Leabank Av, Pais. PA2 — 82 AU37
Leadburn Rd, G21 — 51 BY25
Leadburn St, G32 — 70 CA30
Leader St, G33 — 69 BZ28
Leaend Rd, Air. ML6 — 76 DA28
Leander Cres, Bell. ML4 — 112 DA40
Leander Cres, Renf. PA4 — 64 BA27
Learmont Pl, (Miln.) G62 — 11 BH11
Leathem Pl, Wis. ML2 — 143 DE52
Leathen Pl, Ersk. PA8 — 24 AN20
Leckethill Av, (Cumb.) G68 — 20 CV14
Leckethill Ct, (Cumb.) G68 — 20 CV14
Leckethill Pl, (Cumb.) G68 — 20 CU14
Leckethill Vw, (Cumb.) G68 — 20 CV14
Leckie Dr, Ham. ML3 — 126 CS49
Leckie St, G43 — 86 BL37
Ledaig Pl, G31 — 69 BY30
Ledaig St, G31 — 69 BY30
Ledard Rd, G42 — 87 BP37
Ledcameroch Cres, (Bears.) G61 — 29 BF17
Ledcameroch Pk, (Bears.) G61 — 29 BF17
Ledcameroch Rd, (Bears.) G61 — 29 BF17
Ledgate, (Kirk.) G66 — 17 CF12
Ledgowan Pl, G20 — 48 BM21
Ledi Dr, (Bears.) G61 — 10 BD14
Ledi Path, Moth. ML1 — 113 DE41
off Martin Pl
Ledi Rd, G43 — 102 BL40
Ledmore Dr, G15 — 28 BB17
Lednock Rd, (Stepps) G33 — 53 CE24
Lednock Rd, G52 — 64 BC32
Lee Av, G33 — 70 CA28
Leebank Dr, G44 — 103 BP44
Leechlee Rd, Ham. ML3 — 126 CU50
Lee Cres, (Bishop.) G64 — 51 BW21
Leefield Dr, G44 — 103 BP43
Leehill Rd, G21 — 50 BU22
Lee Pl, Bell. ML4 — 111 CZ41
Leesburn Pl, (E.Kil.) G74 — 122 CB49
Lees Ct, Coat. ML5 — 75 CW32
Leeside Rd, G21 — 50 BU22

Leesland, (Udd.) G71 — 93 CQ37
Leeward Circle, (E.Kil.) G75 — 135 BW52
Leewood Dr, G44 — 103 BQ43
Le Froy Gdns, (E.Kil.) G75 — 135 BY53
Le Froy La, (E.Kil.) G75 — 135 BY53
Lefroy St, Coat. ML5 — 74 CU30
Legbrannock Cres, Moth. ML1 — 113 DF41
Legbrannock Rd, Moth. ML1 — 113 DG39
Leggatston Dr, G53 — 101 BE42
Leggatston Rd, G53 — 101 BE43
Leglen Wd Cres, G21 — 51 BZ23
Leglen Wd Dr, G21 — 51 BZ23
Leglen Wd Pl, G21 — 51 BZ23
Leglen Wd Rd, G21 — 51 BZ23
Leicester Av, G12 — 48 BK24
Leighton St, G20 — 49 BN23
Leitchland Rd, (Elder.) John. PA5 — 80 AM37
Leitchland Rd, Pais. PA2 — 80 AM37
Leithland Av, G53 — 84 BD36
Leithland Rd, G53 — 84 BD36
Leith St, G33 — 69 BZ29
Lembert Dr, (Clark.) G76 — 118 BM45
Lendale La, (Bishop.) G64 — 33 BW18
Lendalfoot Gdns, Ham. ML3 — 138 CM51
Lendal Pl, (E.Kil.) G75 — 134 BU55
Lendel Pl, G51 — 66 BM32
off Paisley Rd W
Lenihall Dr, G45 — 104 BU43
Lenihall Ter, G45 — 104 BU43
Lennox Av, G14 — 47 BE26
Lennox Av, (Miln.) G62 — 12 BJ12
Lennox Av, Bish. PA7 — 24 AK18
Lennox Av, Coat. ML5 — 74 CU30
Lennox Ct, (Bears.) G61 — 11 BG14
off Montrose Dr
Lennox Cres, (Bishop.) G64 — 50 BV21
Lennox Dr, (Bears.) G61 — 29 BH15
Lennox Dr, (Newt. M.) G77 — 131 BG51
Lennox Gdns, G14 — 47 BF25
Lennox La E, G14 — 47 BF26
Lennox La W, G14 — 47 BF25
off Lennox Av
Lennox Pl, G14 — 47 BE26
off Scotstoun St
Lennox Pl, Clyde. G81 — 26 AU18
Lennox Rd, (Cumb.) G67 — 22 DB11
Lennox St, G20 — 48 BL22
off Maryhill Rd
Lennox Ter, Pais. PA3 — 63 AW29
Lennox Vw, Clyde. G81 — 27 AX18
off Granville St
Lentran St, G34 — 72 CM30
Leny St, G20 — 49 BP25
Lenziemill Ind Est, (Cumb.) G67 — 22 DC13
Lenziemill Rd, (Cumb.) G67 — 22 DD13
Lenzie Pl, G21 — 50 BV23
Lenzie Rd, (Stepps) G33 — 53 CF23
Lenzie Rd, (Kirk.) G66 — 35 CF15
Lenzie St, G21 — 50 BV24
Lenzie Ter, G21 — 50 BV24
Lenzie Way, G21 — 50 BV23
Lesley Quad, Bell. ML4 — 110 CV43
off McLean Dr
Leslie Av, (Newt. M.) G77 — 117 BG46
Leslie Av, Bish. PA7 — 24 AK18
Leslie Rd, G41 — 87 BN34
Leslie St, G41 — 87 BP34
Leslie St, Moth. ML1 — 128 DB46
Lesmuir Dr, G14 — 46 BB24
Lesmuir Pl, G14 — 46 BB23
Letham Ct, G43 — 103 BN40
Letham Dr, G43 — 103 BN40

Letham Dr, (Bishop.) G64	51	BY21
Letham Gra, (Cumb.) G68	22	DB9
Lethamhill Cres, G33	70	CB28
Lethamhill Pl, G33	70	CA28
Lethamhill Rd, G33	70	CA28
Letham Oval, (Bishop.) G64	51	BZ21
Lethbridge Pl, (E.Kil.) G75	135	BY53
off Edmonton Ter		
Letherby Dr, G42	87	BR38
Letherby Dr, G44	87	BR38
Lethington Av, G41	87	BN37
Lethington Pl, G41	87	BN37
Lethington Rd, (Giff.) G46	118	BJ46
Letterfearn Dr, G23	31	BN20
Letterickhills Cres, (Camb.) G72	107	CG42
Lettoch St, G51	66	BJ30
Leven Av, (Bishop.) G64	33	BX20
Leven Ct, (Barr.) G78	99	AX40
off Linnhe Dr		
Leven Dr, (Bears.) G61	29	BH17
Leven Path, Moth. ML1	112	DC40
off Graham St		
Leven Pl, Ersk. PA8	24	AN20
Leven Quad, Air. ML6	76	DB27
Leven Rd, Coat. ML5	74	CT28
Leven Sq, Renf. PA4	45	AX25
Leven St, G41	87	BP34
Leven St, Moth. ML1	128	DA49
Leven Ter, Moth. ML1	113	DE43
Leven Vw, Clyde. G81	27	AX18
off Crown Av		
Leven Way, (Cumb.) G67	22	DB12
off Cumbernauld Shop Cen		
Leven Way, (E.Kil.) G75	134	BV55
Leven Way, Pais. PA2	81	AN36
Levern Br Ct, G53	84	BB38
Levern Br Gro, G53	84	BB38
Levern Br Pl, G53	100	BB39
Levern Br Rd, G53	100	BB39
Levern Br Way, G53	100	BB39
Levern Cres, (Barr.) G78	99	AX44
Leverndale Ct, G53	84	BB36
Leverndale Ind Cen, G53	84	BB37
Leverndale Rd, G53	84	BB36
Levern Gdns, (Barr.) G78	99	AX42
Levernside Av, G53	85	BE37
off Levernside Cres		
Levernside Av, (Barr.) G78	99	AW43
Levernside Cres, G53	84	BD36
Levernside Rd, G53	85	BE36
Lewis Av, Renf. PA4	63	AZ28
Lewis Cres, (Old Kil.) G60	25	AR16
Lewis Cres, (Kilb.) John. PA10	79	AE35
Lewis Dr, (Old Kil.) G60	25	AR16
Lewis Gdns, (Old Kil.) G60	26	AS16
Lewis Gdns, (Bears.) G61	28	BD15
Lewis Gro, (Old Kil.) G60	26	AS16
Lewis Pl, (Old Kil.) G60	26	AS16
Lewis Pl, (Newt. M.) G77	116	BD47
off Tiree Pl		
Lewis Pl, Air. ML6	77	DF31
Lewiston Dr, G23	30	BM20
off Lewiston Rd		
Lewiston Pl, G23	30	BM20
off Lewiston Rd		
Lewiston Rd, G23	30	BM20
Lexwell Av, (Elder.) John. PA5	80	AM34
Leyden Ct, G20	49	BN24
Leyden Gdns, G20	49	BN24
Leyden St, G20	49	BN24
Leys, The (Bishop.) G64	33	BW20
Leys Pk, Ham. ML3	125	CQ49
Libberton Way, Ham. ML3	125	CQ50
Liberton St, G33	69	BZ29
Liberty Av, (Baill.) G69	73	CQ32
Liberty Path, (Blan.) G72	124	CM46
off Burnbrae Rd		
Liberty Rd, Bell. ML4	111	CW41
Libo Av, G53	85	BF36
Libo Pl, Ersk. PA8	24	AN19
Library Gdns, (Camb.) G72	106	CB39
Lickprivick Rd, (E.Kil.) G75	135	BX55
Liddell Gro, (E.Kil.) G75	135	BZ54
Liddells Ct, (Bishop.) G64	51	BW21
Liddell St, G32	91	CE36
Liddel Rd, (Cumb.) G67	22	DA12
Liddesdale Av, Pais. PA2	80	AM38
Liddesdale Pl, G22	50	BU21
Liddesdale Rd, G22	50	BS22
Liddesdale Sq, G22	50	BU22
Liddesdale Ter, G22	50	BU22
Liddoch Way, (Ruther.) G73	88	BV37
Liff Gdns, (Bishop.) G64	51	BZ21
Liff Pl, G34	72	CL28
Lightburn Pl, G32	70	CD30
Lightburn Rd, G31	69	BY31
Lightburn Rd, (Camb.) G72	107	CF41
Lilac Av, Clyde. G81	26	AT16
Lilac Cres, (Udd.) G71	93	CR37
Lilac Gdns, (Bishop.) G64	51	BX21
Lilac Hill, Ham. ML3	140	CV51
Lilac Pl, John. PA5	80	AJ36
off Spruce Av		
Lilac Way, Moth. ML1	112	DD40
off Myrtle Dr		
Lilac Wynd, (Camb.) G72	107	CG41
Lillyburn Pl, G15	28	BA16
Lilybank Av, (Muir.) G69	54	CL22
Lilybank Av, (Camb.) G72	107	CE41
Lilybank Av, Air. ML6	76	DD27
Lilybank Gdns, G12	66	BM27
Lilybank Gdns La, G12	66	BM27
Lilybank La, G12	66	BM27
off Lilybank Gdns		
Lilybank St, Ham. ML3	126	CS49
Lilybank Ter, G12	66	BM27
off Great George St		
Lily St, G40	89	BX34
Limecraigs Av, Pais. PA2	82	AS38
Limecraigs Cres, Pais. PA2	82	AS38
Limecraigs Rd, Pais. PA2	81	AR38
Lime Cres, (Cumb.) G67	23	DG10
Lime Cres, Air. ML6	77	DE30
Lime Gro, (Lenz.) G66	35	CF16
Lime Gro, (Blan.) G72	108	CL44
Lime Gro, Moth. ML1	128	DA49
off Ferguson St		
Limegrove St, Bell. ML4	95	CW38
off Primrose Av		
Limekilns Rd, (Cumb.) G67	40	DB15
Lime La, G14	47	BF26
off Westland Dr		
Lime Ln, Moth. ML1	112	DD41
Limeside Av, (Ruther.) G73	89	BX38
Limeside Gdns, (Ruther.) G73	89	BY38
Lime St, G14	47	BF26
Limetree Av, (Udd.) G71	93	CR37
Limetree Ct, Ham. ML3	125	CQ48
Limetree Cres, (Newt. M.) G77	117	BF49
Limetree Dr, Clyde. G81	27	AW17
Limetree Quad, (Udd.) G71	94	CS37
Limetree Wk, (M. of Cam.) G66	16	CD9
Limeview Av, Pais. PA2	81	AR38
Limeview Cres, Pais. PA2	81	AR38
Limeview Rd, Pais. PA2	81	AR38
Limeview Way, Pais. PA2	81	AR38
off Limeview Av		
Linacre Dr, G32	71	CE32
Linacre Gdns, G32	71	CF32
Linburn Pl, G52	64	BC31
Linburn Rd, G52	64	BA30
Linburn Rd, Ersk. PA8	24	AN20
Linclive Interchange, (Linw.) Pais. PA3	60	AM32
Linclive Link Rd, (Linw.) Pais. PA3	61	AN31
Linclive Ter, (Linw.) Pais. PA3	60	AM32
off Candren Rd		
Lincluden Path, G41	87	BP33
off McCulloch St		
Lincoln Av, G13	47	BE22
Lincoln Av, (Udd.) G71	93	CP36
Lincuan Av, (Giff.) G46	102	BL44
Lindams, (Udd.) G71	109	CP40
Linden Ct, Clyde. G81	27	AW15
off Linden Dr		
Linden Dr, Clyde. G81	27	AW15
Linden Lea, Ham. ML3	125	CR49
Linden Pl, G13	47	BH22
Linden St, G13	47	BH22
Linden Way, G13	47	BH22
off Sutcliffe Rd		
Lindores Av, (Ruther.) G73	89	BX38
Lindores Dr, (E.Kil.) G74	135	BY52
Lindores Pl, (E.Kil.) G74	135	BY52
off Lindores Dr		
Lindores St, G42	87	BR38
off Somerville Dr		
Lindrick Dr, G23	31	BN20
Lindsaybeg Ct, (Chry.) G69	54	CL21
Lindsaybeg Rd, (Lenz.) G66	35	CH17
Lindsaybeg Rd, (Chry.) G69	36	CK19
Lindsay Dr, G12	48	BK23
Lindsay Gro, (E.Kil.) G74	136	CB51
Lindsay Pl, G12	48	BK23
Lindsay Pl, (Lenz.) G66	35	CF18
Lindsay Pl, (E.Kil.) G74	136	CC52
Lindsay Pl, John. PA5	80	AJ34
off Thorn Brae		
Lindsay Rd, (E.Kil.) G74	136	CB52
Lindum Cres, Moth. ML1	127	CX45
Lindum St, Moth. ML1	127	CX45
Linfern Rd, G12	48	BL26
Lingley Av, Air. ML6	76	DC31
Linhope Pl, (E.Kil.) G75	134	BU54
Links Rd, G32	91	CF34
Links Rd, G44	104	BS41
Links Vw, Lark. ML9	145	DE59
Linksview Rd, Moth. ML1	112	DD44
Linkwood Av, G15	28	BB18
Linkwood Cres, G15	28	BC18
Linkwood Dr, G15	28	BB18
Linkwood Gdns, G15	28	BD18
Linkwood Gro, G15	28	BD18
Linkwood Pl, G15	28	BB18
Linlithgow Gdns, G32	71	CF32
Linn Brae, John. PA5	79	AH35
Linn Cres, Pais. PA2	82	AS38
Linndale Dr, G51	104	BS44
Linndale Gdns, G51	104	BS44
Linndale Gro, G51	104	BS44
Linndale Rd, G51	104	BS44
Linn Dr, G44	103	BP42
Linnet Av, John. PA5	79	AE38
Linnet Pl, G13	46	BB22
Linnet Rd, Bell. ML4	111	CX41
Linnet Way, (Strathclyde Bus. Pk.) Bell. ML4	94	CV37

Linn Gdns, (Cumb.) G68 20 CV11
Linnhead Dr, G53 100 BD39
Linnhead Pl, G14 46 BD25
Linnhe Av, G44 103 BQ41
Linnhe Av, (Bishop.) G64 33 BX20
Linnhe Av, Ham. ML3 139 CQ52
Linnhe Ct, Lark. ML9 142 DB56
Linnhe Dr, (Barr.) G78 99 AX40
Linnhe Pl, (Blan.) G72 108 CL43
Linnhe Pl, Ersk. PA8 24 AN20
Linn Pk, G44 103 BR42
Linnpark Av, G44 103 BP43
Linnpark Ct, G44 103 BP43
Linn Pk Gdns, John. PA5 79 AH35
Linn Pk Ind Est, G45 103 BR43
Linnvale Way, (Dullatur) G68 8 CY7
Linn Valley Vw, G45 104 BT42
Linnwell Cres, Pais. PA2 82 AT37
Linnwood Ct, G44 103 BQ40
Linside Av, Pais. PA1 83 AW33
Lint Butts, (Blan.) G72 124 CL46
off Stewart Av
Lintfield Ln, (Udd.) G71 109 CQ40
off Myers Cres
Linthaugh Rd, G53 84 BC35
Linthaugh Ter, G53 85 BF36
off Linthaugh Rd
Linthouse Bldgs, G51 65 BG29
Linthouse Rd, G51 65 BG28
Lintie Rd, Moth. ML1 113 DE41
Lintlaw, (Blan.) G72 108 CM44
Lintlaw Dr, G52 64 BD31
Lintmill Ter, (Neil.) G78 114 AS47
Linton Pl, Coat. ML5 94 CU34
off Ellismuir St
Linton St, G33 70 CA29
Linwood Av, (E.Kil.) G74 134 BV51
Linwood Av, (Clark.) G76 119 BP46
Linwood Ind Est, (Linw.) Pais. 80 AL33
PA3
Linwood Rd, Pais. PA1 60 AM32
Linwood Rd, (Linw.) Pais. PA3 60 AL32
Linwood Ter, Ham. ML3 125 CR49
Lion Bk, (Kirk.) G66 17 CF12
Lismore, (E.Kil.) G74 137 CE53
Lismore Av, Moth. ML1 127 CX45
Lismore Av, Renf. PA4 63 AZ28
Lismore Dr, Coat. ML5 94 CT33
Lismore Dr, Pais. PA2 82 AT38
Lismore Gdns, (Kilb.) John. 79 AE35
PA10
Lismore Hill, Ham. ML3 124 CM50
Lismore Pl, (Mood.) G69 37 CQ18
off Altnacreag Gdns
Lismore Pl, (Newt. M.) G77 116 BD48
Lismore Rd, G12 48 BK24
Lister Gdns, (Clark.) G76 119 BQ48
Lister Pl, G52 64 BC30
off Lister Rd
Lister Rd, G52 64 BC30
Lister St, G4 5 BT28
Lister Twr, (E.Kil.) G75 136 CB53
off Telford Rd
Lister Wk, Bell. ML4 95 CY38
off Harvey Way
Lithgow Av, (Kirk.) G66 17 CF14
Lithgow Cres, Pais. PA2 83 AW35
Lithgow Pl, (E.Kil.) G74 135 BX51
Little Dovehill, G1 5 BT31
Little Drum Rd, (Cumb.) G68 19 CR13
Littleholm Pl, Clyde. G81 26 AU17
Littlemill Av, (Cumb.) G68 20 CU12
Littlemill Cres, G53 84 BC37

Littlemill Dr, G53 84 BC37
Littlemill Gdns, G53 84 BC37
Littlemill Way, (Carfin) Moth. 112 DD44
ML1
Littleston Gdns, Ersk. PA8 25 AP20
Little St, G3 4 BP30
off McIntyre St
Littleton Dr, G23 30 BL20
off Littleton St
Littleton St, G23 30 BM20
Lively Pl, (Blan.) G72 124 CL46
off Burnbrae Rd
Livingstone Av, G52 64 BC29
Livingstone Boul, (Blan.) G72 124 CM48
Livingstone Cres, (Blan.) G72 108 CM44
Livingstone Cres, (E.Kil.) G75 135 BZ54
off Livingstone Dr
Livingstone Dr, (E.Kil.) G75 135 BZ53
Livingstone Gdns, Lark. ML9 144 DD58
Livingstone La, (Both.) G71 109 CQ42
off Appledore Cres
Livingstone Pk, (Kilsyth) G65 7 CR3
Livingstone St, Clyde. G81 27 AY20
Livingstone St, Ham. ML3 125 CP49
Livingston Pl, Air. ML6 76 DD31
Lloyd Av, G32 90 CC35
Lloyd Dr, Moth. ML1 112 DC44
Lloyds St, Coat. ML5 75 CW32
Lloyd St, G31 69 BW29
Lloyd St, (Ruther.) G73 89 BX36
Lloyd St, Moth. ML1 112 DC44
Loan, (The Miln.) G62 11 BE9
Loanbank Quad, G51 65 BH30
Loancroft Av, (Baill.) G69 92 CL34
Loancroft Gdns, (Udd.) G71 109 CN40
Loancroft Gate, (Udd.) G71 109 CN40
Loancroft Pl, (Baill.) G69 92 CK34
Loanend Cotts, (Camb.) G72 107 CH44
Loanfoot Av, G13 46 BC22
Loanfoot Av, (Neil.) G78 114 AT47
Loanfoot Rd, (Blan.) G72 124 CM47
off Kirkton Av
Loanhead Av, Moth. ML1 113 DF42
Loanhead Av, (Linw.) Pais. PA3 60 AJ31
Loanhead Av, Renf. PA4 45 AZ26
Loanhead Cres, Moth. ML1 113 DF42
Loanhead La, (Linw.) Pais. PA3 60 AJ31
Loanhead Rd, Moth. ML1 113 DE42
Loanhead Rd, (Linw.) Pais. PA3 60 AJ31
Loanhead St, G32 70 CB30
Loanhead St, Coat. ML5 94 CU34
Loaning, Lark. ML9 145 DE59
off Shawrigg Rd
Loaning, The (Giff.) G46 118 BJ45
Loaning, The (Bears.) G61 29 BG16
off Manse Rd
Loaning, The (Kirk.) G66 17 CE14
Loaning, The, Moth. ML1 127 CY46
Loan Lea Cres, Lark. ML9 144 DD60
Lobnitz Av, Renf. PA4 45 AZ26
Lochaber Dr, (Ruther.) G73 105 BZ41
Lochaber Path, (Blan.) G72 124 CM46
off Burnbrae Rd
Lochaber Pl, (E.Kil.) G74 122 CB50
Lochaber Rd, (Bears.) G61 30 BJ19
Loch Achray Gdns, G32 91 CE33
Loch Achray St, G32 91 CE33
Lochaline Av, Pais. PA2 81 AQ35
Lochaline Dr, G44 103 BQ41
Lochalsh Dr, Pais. PA2 81 AP35
Lochalsh Pl, (Blan.) G72 108 CK43
Lochar Cres, G53 85 BF35
Lochard Dr, Pais. PA2 81 AQ35

Lochar Pl, (E.Kil.) G75 134 BU54
Loch Assynt, (E.Kil.) G74 136 CD53
Loch Awe, (E.Kil.) G74 136 CC53
Loch Awe Pl, Coat. ML5 74 CV31
off Loch Brora Cres
Lochay St, G32 91 CE33
Lochbrae Dr, (Ruther.) G73 105 BZ41
Lochbridge Rd, G34 72 CJ30
Lochbroom Ct, (Newt. M.) G77 117 BH47
off Lochbroom Dr
Lochbroom Dr, (Newt. M.) G77 118 BJ47
Lochbroom Dr, Pais. PA2 81 AQ35
Loch Brora Cres, Coat. ML5 74 CU31
Lochbuie La, (Glenm.) Air. ML6 58 DA25
Lochburn Cres, G20 49 BN22
Lochburn Gro, G20 49 BN22
off Cadder Rd
Lochburn Pas, G20 49 BN22
Lochburn Rd, G20 48 BM23
Lochdochart Path, G34 72 CL30
off Lochdochart Rd
Lochdochart Rd, G34 72 CL30
Lochearn Cres, Air. ML6 76 DB27
Lochearn Cres, Pais. PA2 81 AQ35
Lochearnhead Rd, G33 52 CD24
Lochend Av, (Gart.) G69 55 CN23
Lochend Cres, (Bears.) G61 29 BF18
Lochend Dr, (Bears.) G61 29 BF18
Lochend Path, G34 72 CK28
off Dubton St
Lochend Rd, G34 72 CK28
Lochend Rd, (Bears.) G61 29 BG18
Lochend Rd, G69 73 CN27
Lochend Rd, (Gart.) G69 55 CP24
Lochend Rd, Coat. ML5 73 CN27
Lochend St, Moth. ML1 128 DB47
Lochfauld Rd, G23 31 BQ19
Lochfield Cres, Pais. PA2 82 AV36
Lochfield Dr, Pais. PA2 83 AW36
Lochfield Gdns, G34 72 CL28
Lochfield Rd, Pais. PA2 82 AV36
Lochgarry Way, Coat. ML5 94 CU33
off Newton St
Lochgilp St, G20 48 BL22
Loch Goil, (E.Kil.) G74 136 CC52
Lochgoin Av, G15 28 BA17
Lochgoin Gdns, G15 28 BA17
Loch Grn, Ham. ML3 139 CR53
Lochgreen Pl, Coat. ML5 74 CS27
Lochgreen St, G33 51 BZ26
Lochhead Av, (Linw.) Pais. PA3 60 AK32
Lochiel Ct, Air. ML6 75 CZ30
off Monkscourt Av
Lochiel La, (Ruther.) G73 105 BZ41
Lochiel Rd, (Thornlie.) G46 101 BH41
Lochinch Pl, (Newt. M.) G77 116 BC48
Lochinvar Rd, (Cumb.) G67 21 CZ14
Lochinver Cres, Pais. PA2 81 AQ35
Lochinver Dr, G44 103 BQ41
Lochinver Gro, (Camb.) G72 106 CD40
off Andrew Sillars Av
Loch Katrine St, G32 91 CE33
Loch Laidon St, G32 91 CF33
Loch Laxford, (E.Kil.) G74 136 CD53
Loch Lea, (Kirk.) G66 17 CH11
Lochlea, (E.Kil.) G74 123 CF49
Lochlea Av, Clyde. G81 27 AY18
Lochlea Av, Lark. ML9 145 DE59
off Shawrigg Rd
Lochlea Rd, G43 102 BM39
Lochlea Rd, (Cumb.) G67 22 DD10
Lochlea Rd, (Ruther.) G73 104 BV40
Lochlea Rd, (Clark.) G76 119 BN48

Name	Page	Ref
Lochlea Way, Moth. ML1	113	DG41
Lochleven La, G42	87	BQ38
Lochleven Rd, G42	87	BQ38
Lochlibo Av, G13	46	BB23
Lochlibo Cres, (Barr.) G78	99	AW44
Lochlibo Rd, (Barr.) G78	114	AU45
Lochlibo Ter, (Barr.) G78	99	AW44
Loch Long, (E.Kil.) G74	136	CC53
Loch Loyal, (E.Kil.) G74	136	CD53
Lochmaben Rd, G52	84	BB33
Lochmaddy Av, G44	103	BQ40
Loch Maree, (E.Kil.) G74	136	CD53
Loch Meadie, (E.Kil.) G74	136	CD53
Lochnagar Dr, (Bears.) G61	10	BD14
Lochnagar Way, Lark. ML9	145	DE60
off Bannockburn Dr		
Loch Naver, (E.Kil.) G74	136	CD53
off Loch Loyal		
Lochore Av, Pais. PA3	62	AV30
Loch Pk Pl, Lark. ML9	144	DC60
Lochranza Ct, (Carfin) Moth.	112	DD43
ML1		
Loch Rd, (Stepps) G33	53	CF24
Loch Rd, (Miln.) G62	12	BK10
Loch Rd, (Kirk.) G66	17	CG14
Loch Rd, (Chap.) Air. ML6	97	DF35
Loch Shin, (E.Kil.) G74	136	CD53
Lochside, (Bears.) G61	29	BH18
Lochside, (Gart.) G69	55	CP23
Lochside St, G41	87	BN36
off Minard Rd		
Lochsloy Ct, G22	50	BT25
Loch Striven, (E.Kil.) G74	136	CC52
Loch St, (Calder.) Air. ML6	96	DD35
Loch Torridon, (E.Kil.) G74	136	CD53
Loch Vw, (Calder.) Air. ML6	96	DD35
Lochview Cotts, (Gart.) G69	55	CN26
Lochview Cres, G33	52	CB26
Lochview Dr, G33	52	CB26
Lochview Gdns, G33	52	CB26
Lochview Pl, G33	52	CB26
Lochview Quad, Bell. ML4	110	CV42
off Dempsey Rd		
Lochview Rd, (Bears.) G61	29	BG18
Lochview Rd, Coat. ML5	74	CS28
Lochview Ter, (Gart.) G69	55	CP24
Loch Voil St, G32	91	CF33
Lochwood Ln, (Mood.) G69	37	CQ18
Lochwood St, G33	70	CA27
Lochy Av, Renf. PA4	64	BB28
Lochy Gdns, (Bishop.) G64	33	BX20
Lochy Pl, Ersk. PA8	24	AN20
Locke Gro, Moth. ML1	113	DH44
Lockerbie Av, G43	103	BP39
Locket Yett Vw, Bell. ML4	110	CU40
Lockhart Av, (Camb.) G72	107	CF39
Lockhart Ct, (Newt. M.) G77	131	BF51
Lockhart Dr, (Camb.) G72	107	CF39
Lockhart Dr, (Newt. M.) G77	131	BF51
Lockhart St, G21	69	BX27
Lockhart St, Ham. ML3	140	CS55
Lockhart Ter, (E.Kil.) G74	136	CD51
Locksley Av, G13	47	BE21
Locksley Av, (Cumb.) G67	40	DA15
Locksley Ct, (Cumb.) G67	40	DA15
Locksley Cres, (Cumb.) G67	40	DA15
Locksley Pl, (Cumb.) G67	40	DA15
Locksley Rd, (Cumb.) G67	40	DA15
Locksley Rd, Pais. PA2	81	AP36
Locksley Way, Pais. PA2	81	AP36
off Locksley Rd		
Locks St, Coat. ML5	75	CZ31
Logan Av, (Newt. M.) G77	117	BE47
Logan Dr, (Cumb.) G68	21	CZ10
Logan Dr, Pais. PA3	62	AS31
Loganlea Dr, Moth. ML1	112	DC44
Logans Rd, Moth. ML1	127	CX46
Logan St, G5	88	BT34
Logan St, (Blan.) G72	125	CN46
Loganswell Dr, (Thornlie.) G46	101	BG43
Loganswell Gdns, (Thornlie.)	101	BG43
G46		
Loganswell Pl, (Thornlie.) G46	101	BG43
Loganswell Rd, (Thornlie.) G46	101	BG43
Logan Twr, (Camb.) G72	107	CG41
off Claude Av		
Logie Pk, (E.Kil.) G74	122	CC50
Logie Sq, (E.Kil.) G74	122	CC50
Lomax St, G33	69	BZ29
Lomond Av, Renf. PA4	63	AX28
Lomond Ct, (Cumb.) G67	21	CY14
Lomond Ct, (Barr.) G78	99	AY43
off Eildon Dr		
Lomond Cres, (Cumb.) G67	21	CY14
Lomond Cres, Pais. PA2	82	AT37
Lomond Dr, (Bishop.) G64	32	BV18
Lomond Dr, (Cumb.) G67	21	CX14
Lomond Dr, (Both.) G71	109	CR42
Lomond Dr, (Newt. M.) G77	117	BF46
Lomond Dr, (Barr.) G78	99	AX41
Lomond Dr, Air. ML6	76	DA28
Lomond Gdns, (Elder.) John.	80	AL35
PA5		
Lomond Gro, (Cumb.) G67	21	CY14
Lomond Pl, (Stepps) G33	53	CG25
Lomond Pl, (Cumb.) G67	21	CX14
Lomond Pl, Coat. ML5	74	CU28
Lomond Pl, Ersk. PA8	24	AN20
Lomond Rd, (Bears.) G61	29	BG19
Lomond Rd, (Lenz.) G66	35	CF16
Lomond Rd, (Udd.) G71	93	CP36
Lomond Rd, Coat. ML5	74	CT27
Lomondside Av, (Clark.) G76	118	BL45
Lomond St, G22	49	BR24
Lomond Vw, (Cumb.) G67	21	CY14
Lomond Vw, Clyde. G81	27	AX18
off Granville St		
Lomond Vw, Ham. ML3	139	CP51
Lomond Wk, Lark. ML9	144	DD57
off Muirshot Rd		
Lomond Wk, Moth. ML1	113	DE41
Lomond Way, Moth. ML1	112	DC40
off Graham St		
London Arc, G1	5	BT31
off London Rd		
London La, G1	5	BT31
off London Rd		
London Rd, G1	5	BT31
London Rd, G31	89	BX33
London Rd, G32	90	CA35
London Rd, G40	68	BU32
London St, Lark. ML9	144	DC57
London St, Renf. PA4	45	AZ24
London Way, G1	5	BT31
Lonend, Pais. PA1	82	AV33
Longay Pl, G22	50	BS21
Longay St, G22	50	BS21
Longcroft Dr, Renf. PA4	45	AY25
Longden St, Clyde. G81	45	AZ21
Long Dr, (E.Kil.) G75	136	CC54
Longford St, G33	69	BZ29
Longlee, (Baill.) G69	92	CK33
Longmeadow, John. PA5	79	AE36
Long Row, (Kirk.) G66	18	CK14
off Burnbrae Rd		
Long Row, (Baill.) G69	72	CL31
Longstone Pl, G33	70	CD29
off Longstone Rd		
Longstone Rd, G33	70	CD29
Longwill Ter, (Cumb.) G67	22	DD9
Lonmay Rd, G33	71	CF29
Lonsdale Av, (Giff.) G46	102	BL42
Loom Wk, (Kilb.) John. PA10	78	AC34
Lora Dr, G52	85	BG33
Lord Way, (Baill.) G69	73	CP32
off Dukes Rd		
Loretto Pl, G33	70	CB29
Loretto St, G33	70	CB29
Lorimer Cres, (E.Kil.) G75	135	BZ54
Lorn Av, (Chry.) G69	54	CM21
Lorne Cres, (Bishop.) G64	33	BZ19
Lorne Dr, Moth. ML1	111	CZ43
Lorne Dr, (Linw.) Pais. PA3	60	AJ32
Lorne Pl, Coat. ML5	75	CZ32
Lorne Rd, G52	64	BB29
Lorne St, G51	66	BM31
Lorne St, Ham. ML3	126	CS49
Lorne Ter, (Camb.) G72	106	CB42
Lorn Pl, (Kirk.) G66	18	CL12
Lorraine Gdns, G12	48	BL25
off Kensington Rd		
Lorraine Gdns La, G12	48	BL25
off Westbourne Gdns La		
Lorraine Rd, G12	48	BL25
off Kensington Rd		
Loskin Dr, G22	50	BS22
Lossie Cres, Renf. PA4	64	BB27
Lossie St, G33	69	BZ28
Lothian Cres, Pais. PA2	82	AT36
Lothian Dr, (Clark.) G76	118	BM45
Lothian Gdns, G20	49	BN26
off Wilton St		
Lothian St, G52	64	BA29
Lothian Way, (E.Kil.) G74	123	CE50
Louden Hill Dr, G33	52	CA23
off Louden Hill Rd		
Louden Hill Gdns, G33	52	CA23
off Louden Hill Rd		
Louden Hill Pl, G33	52	CA23
off Louden Hill Rd		
Louden Hill Rd, G33	52	CA23
off Louden Hill Rd		
Louden Hill Way, G33	51	BZ23
off Louden Hill Rd		
Loudon, (E.Kil.) G75	136	CA56
Loudon Gdns, John. PA5	80	AJ34
Loudonhill Av, Ham. ML3	140	CT53
Loudon Rd, G33	52	CD24
Loudon St, Air. ML6	76	DC30
Loudon Ter, G12	48	BM26
off Observatory Rd		
Loudon Ter, (Bears.) G61	11	BF13
Louise Gdns, (Holytown) Moth.	112	DB40
Lounsdale Av, Pais. PA2	81	AR34
Lounsdale Cres, Pais. PA2	81	AQ35
Lounsdale Dr, Pais. PA2	81	AR35
Lounsdale Gro, Pais. PA2	81	AR34
Lounsdale Ho, Pais. PA2	81	AQ36
Lounsdale Pl, G14	46	BD25
Lounsdale Rd, Pais. PA2	81	AR35
Lounsdale Way, Pais. PA2	81	AR34
Lourdes Av, G52	85	BF33
Lourdes Ct, G52	85	BF33
Lovat Av, (Bears.) G61	11	BG14
Lovat Dr, (Kirk.) G66	16	CD13
Lovat Path, Lark. ML9	145	DE59
off Shawrigg Rd		
Lovat Pl, G52	64	BA30
Lovat Pl, (Ruther.) G73	105	BZ41

Lovat St, G4 68 BS27
off Borron St
Love St, Pais. PA3 62 AU30
Low Barholm, (Kilb.) John. 78 AD35
PA10
Low Broadlie Rd, (Neil.) G78 114 AT45
Low Craigends, (Kilsyth) G65 7 CU5
Low Cres, Clyde. G81 45 AZ21
Lower Auchingramont Rd, 126 CU49
Ham. ML3 off Muir St
Lower Bourtree Dr, (Ruther.) 105 BY41
G73
Lower Millgate, (Udd.) G71 109 CP39
Lower Mill Rd, (Clark.) G76 119 BP47
Low Flenders Rd, (Clark.) G76 118 BM48
Low Moss Ind Est, (Bishop.) 33 BX17
G64
Lowndes St, (Barr.) G78 99 AY43
Low Parksail, Ersk. PA8 44 AS21
Low Patrick St, Ham. ML3 126 CV50
Low Pleasance, Lark. ML9 144 DC58
Low Quarry Gdns, Ham. ML3 140 CT51
Low Rd, (Castlehead) Pais. PA2 82 AS34
Lowther Av, (Bears.) G61 11 BE14
Lowther Ter, G12 48 BL25
off Redlands La
Low Waters Rd, Ham. ML3 140 CT53
Low Wd Interchange, (Cumb.) 21 CX13
G67
Loyal Av, Ersk. PA8 25 AP20
Loyal Gdns, (Bears.) G61 10 BD13
Loyal Pl, Ersk. PA8 25 AP20
Loyne Dr, Renf. PA4 64 BB27
Luath St, G51 66 BJ29
Lubas Av, G42 88 BT38
Lubas Pl, G42 88 BT38
Lubnaig Dr, Ersk. PA8 25 AP20
Lubnaig Gdns, (Bears.) G61 11 BE14
Lubnaig Pl, Air. ML6 76 DA27
Lubnaig Rd, G43 103 BN39
Lubnaig Wk, Moth. ML1 112 DC40
off Graham St
Luckiesfauld, (Neil.) G78 114 AT46
Luckingsford Av, (Inch.) Renf. 44 AT22
PA4
Luckingsford Dr, (Inch.) Renf. 44 AS22
PA4
Luckingsford Rd, (Inch.) Renf. 44 AS22
PA4
Lucy Brae, (Udd.) G71 93 CN37
Ludovic Sq, John. PA5 79 AH34
Luffness Gdns, G32 90 CD35
Lugar Dr, G52 85 BG33
Lugar Pl, G44 104 BU40
Lugar St, Coat. ML5 75 CX29
Luggiebank Pl, (Baill.) G69 93 CQ33
Luggiebank Rd, (Kirk.) G66 17 CF13
Luggie Gro, (Kirk.) G66 18 CJ14
Luggie Vw, (Cumb.) G67 39 CW15
Luing, Air. ML6 77 DG31
Luing Rd, G52 65 BG32
Luma Gdns, G51 65 BE30
Lumloch St, G21 51 BW25
Lumsden St, G3 66 BM29
Lunan Dr, (Bishop.) G64 51 BY21
Lunan Pl, G51 65 BG30
Lunar Path, (Chap.) Air. ML6 97 DF36
off Michael Ter
Luncarty Pl, G32 90 CC34
Luncarty St, G32 90 CC34
Lunderston Cl, G53 100 BD39
Lunderston Dr, G53 84 BC38
Lunderston Gdns, G53 100 BD39

Lundie Gdns, (Bishop.) G64 51 BZ21
Lundie St, G32 90 CA34
Luss Brae, Ham. ML3 139 CN51
Lusset Glen, (Old Kil.) G60 25 AR15
Lusset Rd, (Old Kil.) G60 25 AR15
Lusset Vw, Clyde. G81 27 AX18
Lusshill Ter, (Udd.) G71 92 CK35
Luss Rd, G51 65 BH30
Lybster Cres, (Ruther.) G73 105 BZ42
Lye Brae, (Cumb.) G67 22 DD11
Lyell Ct, (E.Kil.) G74 122 CA50
Lyell Gro, (E.Kil.) G74 122 CA50
Lyle Pl, Pais. PA2 82 AV35
Lyle Rd, Air. ML6 77 DH30
Lylesland Ct, Pais. PA2 82 AU35
Lyle Sq, (Miln.) G62 11 BG11
Lymburn St, G3 66 BM28
Lymekilns Rd, (E.Kil.) G74 135 BZ51
Lyndale Pl, G20 48 BM21
Lyndale Rd, G20 48 BM21
Lyndhurst Gdns, G20 49 BP26
Lyndhurst Gdns La, G20 49 BN25
Lynebank Gro, (Newt. M.) G77 131 BF51
Lynebank Pl, (Newt. M.) G77 131 BF51
Lyne Cft, (Bishop.) G64 33 BW17
Lynedoch Cres, G3 4 BP28
Lynedoch Cres La, G3 4 BP28
Lynedoch Pl, G3 4 BP28
Lynedoch St, G3 4 BP28
Lynedoch Ter, G3 4 BP28
Lyne Dr, G23 31 BN20
Lynnburn Av, Bell. ML4 111 CW40
Lynn Ct, Lark. ML9 144 DC59
Lynn Dr, (Miln.) G62 12 BL12
Lynn Dr, (Eagle.) G76 133 BN55
Lynnhurst, (Udd.) G71 93 CP38
Lynn Wk, (Udd.) G71 109 CQ40
off Flax Rd
Lynton Av, (Giff.) G46 102 BJ44
Lyoncross Av, (Barr.) G78 99 AZ43
Lyoncross Cres, (Barr.) G78 99 AZ42
off Lyoncross Av
Lyoncross Rd, G53 84 BD35
Lyon Rd, Ersk. PA8 24 AN20
Lyon Rd, Pais. PA2 81 AP36
Lyon Rd, (Linw.) Pais. PA3 80 AK33
Lyons Quad, Wis. ML2 129 DF49
off Charles St
Lysander Way, Renf. PA4 63 AZ28
off Lewis Av
Lysa Vale Pl, Bell. ML4 110 CU40
Lytham Dr, G23 31 BN20
Lytham Meadows, (Both.) G71 109 CN43
Lyttleton, (E.Kil.) G75 135 BX55

M

Mabel St, Moth. ML1 128 DA48
Macadam Gdns, Bell. ML4 111 CW39
Macadam Pl, (E.Kil.) G75 136 CA53
McAllister Av, Air. ML6 77 DF29
McAlpine St, G2 4 BQ30
McArdle Av, Moth. ML1 127 CX46
McArthur Av, (Glenm.) Air. 57 CZ26
ML6
Macarthur Ct, (E.Kil.) G74 121 BY50
Macarthur Cres, (E.Kil.) G74 121 BY50
Macarthur Dr, (E.Kil.) G74 121 BY50
Macarthur Gdns, (E.Kil.) G74 121 BY50
McArthur Pk, (Kirk.) G66 17 CE14
McArthur St, G43 86 BL37
off Pleasance St

Macarthur Wynd, (Camb.) G72 107 CE40
McAslin Ct, G4 5 BT29
McAslin St, G4 5 BU29
Macbeth, (E.Kil.) G74 122 CD48
off Bosworth Rd
Macbeth Pl, G31 89 BZ33
Macbeth St, G31 89 BZ33
McBride Av, (Kirk.) G66 17 CE14
McCallum Av, (Ruther.) G73 89 BX38
McCallum Ct, (E.Kil.) G74 121 BX49
Maccallum Dr, (Camb.) G72 107 CE40
McCallum Gdns, Bell. ML4 110 CV43
McCallum Gro, (E.Kil.) G74 121 BW49
McCallum Pl, (E.Kil.) G74 121 BX49
McCallum Rd, Lark. ML9 144 DD60
McCash Pl, (Kirk.) G66 17 CE14
off Greens Av
McCloy Gdns, G53 100 BB39
McClue Av, Renf. PA4 45 AX25
McClue Rd, Renf. PA4 45 AY25
McClurg Ct, Moth. ML1 128 DA48
off Albion St
McCourt Gdns, Bell. ML4 111 CY40
off Unitas Rd
McCracken Av, Renf. PA4 63 AX27
McCracken Dr, (Udd.) G71 94 CS37
McCreery St, Clyde. G81 45 AZ21
Maccrimmon Pk, (E.Kil.) G74 121 BX49
McCrorie Pl, (Kilb.) John. PA10 78 AC34
McCulloch Av, (Udd.) G71 110 CS39
McCulloch St, G41 87 BP33
McCulloch Way, (Neil.) G78 114 AT46
Macdairmid Dr, Ham. ML3 139 CR54
Macdonald Av, (E.Kil.) G74 121 BW49
McDonald Av, John. PA5 79 AG36
McDonald Cres, (Kilsyth) G65 19 CP10
McDonald Cres, Clyde. G81 45 AZ21
Macdonald Gro, Bell. ML4 110 CV42
McDonald Pl, (Neil.) G78 114 AU46
McDonald Pl, Moth. ML1 112 DC40
off Graham St
Macdonald St, (Ruther.) G73 89 BW38
off Greenhill Rd
Macdonald St, Moth. ML1 128 DB48
Macdougall Dr, (Camb.) G72 107 CE40
Macdougall Quad, Bell. ML4 110 CV43
off McCallum Gdns
Macdougall St, G43 86 BL38
Macdowall St, John. PA5 79 AH34
Macdowall St, Pais. PA3 62 AT31
Macduff, Ersk. PA8 25 AQ19
Macduff Pl, G31 89 BZ33
Macduff St, G31 89 BZ33
Macedonian Gro, (New.) Moth. 113 DE41
ML1
Mace Rd, G13 29 BE20
McEwan Gdns, (E.Kil.) G74 121 BW49
Macfarlane Cres, (Camb.) G72 107 CE40
Macfarlane Rd, (Bears.) G61 29 BH18
McFarlane St, G4 5 BU31
McFarlane St, Pais. PA3 62 AS38
Macfie Pl, (E.Kil.) G74 121 BX49
McGhee St, Clyde. G81 27 AX17
McGowan Pl, Ham. ML3 125 CQ48
McGown St, Pais. PA3 62 AT31
Macgregor Av, Air. ML6 77 DF29
McGregor Av, Renf. PA4 63 AX27
Macgregor Ct, (Camb.) G72 107 CE40
off Macarthur Wynd
McGregor Path, (Glenb.) Coat. 56 CS23
ML5 off Gayne Dr
McGregor Rd, (Cumb.) G67 22 DA12
McGregor St, G51 65 BH31

McGregor St, Clyde. G81	45	AZ21
McGregor St, Wis. ML2	129	DF49
off Ladysmith St		
McGrigor Rd, (Miln.) G62	11	BH10
Machan Av, Lark. ML9	144	DC58
Machanhill, Lark. ML9	144	DD59
Machanhill Vw, Lark. ML9	144	DD59
Machan Rd, Lark. ML9	144	DC59
Machrie Dr, G45	104	BV41
Machrie Dr, (Newt. M.) G77	117	BG47
Machrie Rd, G45	104	BV41
Machrie St, G45	104	BV41
Machrie St, Moth. ML1	127	CX46
McIntosh Ct, G31	68	BV30
McIntosh Quad, Bell. ML4	110	CV43
off McCallum Gdns		
McIntosh St, G31	68	BV30
McIntosh Way, Moth. ML1	127	CY48
McIntyre Pl, Pais. PA2	82	AU35
McIntyre St, G3	4	BP30
McIntyre Ter, (Camb.) G72	106	CC39
off Keirs Wk		
McIver St, (Camb.) G72	107	CG39
Macivor Cres, (E.Kil.) G74	121	BW49
McKay Cres, John. PA5	80	AJ35
McKay Gro, Bell. ML4	110	CV40
McKay Pl, (E.Kil.) G74	121	BW49
McKay Pl, (Newt. M.) G77	117	BE49
Mackean St, Pais. PA3	62	AS31
McKechnie St, G51	66	BJ29
Mackeith St, G40	88	BV33
McKenna Dr, Air. ML6	76	DA30
McKenzie Av, Clyde. G81	27	AX17
Mackenzie Dr, (Kilb.) John. PA10	78	AD36
Mackenzie Gdns, (E.Kil.) G74	121	BW49
McKenzie St, Pais. PA3	62	AS32
Mackenzie Ter, Bell. ML4	111	CW39
McKeown Gdns, Bell. ML4	111	CZ41
McKerrell St, Pais. PA1	63	AW32
Mackiesmill Rd, (Elder.) John. PA5	80	AM37
Mackie St, G4	68	BS27
off Borron St		
McKinlay Pl, (Newt. M.) G77	117	BF49
off School Rd		
Mackinlay St, G5	87	BR33
Mackintosh Pl, (E.Kil.) G75	135	BY54
Mack St, Air. ML6	76	DC29
McLaren Av, Renf. PA4	63	AY28
McLaren Ct, (Giff.) G46	102	BK44
off Fenwick Pl		
McLaren Cres, G20	49	BN22
McLaren Dr, Bell. ML4	111	CZ41
McLaren Gdns, G20	49	BN22
McLaren Pl, (E.Kil.) G74	121	BW49
Maclaren Pl, G44	103	BP43
off Clarkston Rd		
McLaurin Cres, John. PA5	79	AF36
Maclay Av, (Kilb.) John. PA10	78	AC35
Maclean Ct, (E.Kil.) G74	121	BX49
McLean Dr, Bell. ML4	110	CV43
Maclean Gro, (E.Kil.) G74	121	BX49
Maclean Pl, (E.Kil.) G74	121	BX49
McLean Pl, Pais. PA3	62	AT30
off Gockston Rd		
Maclean Sq, G51	66	BM31
Maclean St, G51	66	BM31
Maclean St, Clyde. G81	46	BA21
McLees La, Moth. ML1	127	CX46
Maclehose Rd, (Cumb.) G67	23	DE10
Maclellan Rd, (Neil.) G78	114	AU47
Maclellan St, G41	66	BL32
McLennan St, G42	87	BQ37
Macleod Pl, (E.Kil.) G74	122	CD50
Macleod St, G4	5	BU29
Macleod Way, (Camb.) G72	107	CE40
McMahon Gro, Bell. ML4	111	CX39
Macmillan Gdns, (Udd.) G71	93	CQ37
McMillan Rd, (Netherton Ind. Est.) Wis. ML2	143	DF51
Macmillan St, Lark. ML9	144	DB59
McNair St, G32	70	CC32
McNeil Av, Clyde. G81	28	BA20
McNeil Dr, (Holytown) Moth. ML1	96	DB37
McNeil Gdns, G5	88	BT33
Macneill Dr, (E.Kil.) G74	121	BX49
Macneill Gdns, (E.Kil.) G74	121	BW49
McNeil St, G5	88	BT33
McNeil St, Lark. ML9	144	DB58
Macneish Way, (E.Kil.) G74	121	BX49
Macnicol Ct, (E.Kil.) G74	121	BW49
Macnicol Pl, (E.Kil.) G74	121	BW49
Macnicol Pl, (E.Kil.) G74	121	BW49
McPhail Av, (New.) Moth. ML1	113	DH40
McPhail St, G40	88	BU33
McPhater St, G4	4	BR28
McPherson Cres, (Chap.) Air. ML6	97	DG36
McPherson Dr, (Both.) G71	109	CR42
Macpherson Pk, (E.Kil.) G74	121	BY50
McPherson St, Bell. ML4	111	CZ40
Macrae Gdns, (E.Kil.) G74	121	BY50
Macrimmon Pl, (E.Kil.) G75	136	CA53
McShannon Gro, Bell. ML4	111	CW42
off Sapphire Rd		
McSparran Rd, (Kilsyth) G65	20	CV9
Mactaggart Rd, (Cumb.) G67	22	DA13
Madison Av, G44	103	BR40
Madison Path, (Blan.) G72	124	CM46
off Burnbrae Rd		
Madras Pl, G40	88	BV34
Madras Pl, (Neil.) G78	114	AU46
Madras St, G40	88	BV34
Mafeking St, G51	66	BK31
Mafeking St, Wis. ML2	129	DF49
Mafeking Ter, (Neil.) G78	114	AS46
Magdalen Way, Pais. PA2	80	AM38
Magna St, Moth. ML1	127	CX45
Magnolia Dr, (Camb.) G72	107	CH42
Magnolia Gdns, Moth. ML1	113	DE42
Magnolia Pl, (Udd.) G71	94	CS37
Magnus Cres, G44	103	BR41
Mahon Ct, (Mood.) G69	37	CP20
Maidens, (E.Kil.) G74	121	BZ50
Maidens Av, (Newt. M.) G77	118	BJ48
Maidland Rd, G53	85	BE37
Mailerbeg Gdns, (Mood.) G69	37	CP18
Mailie Wk, Moth. ML1	113	DE42
off Clarinda Pl		
Mailing Av, (Bishop.) G64	33	BY19
Mainhill Av, (Baill.) G69	72	CM32
Mainhill Dr, (Baill.) G69	72	CL32
Mainhill Pl, (Baill.) G69	72	CL32
Mainhill Rd, (Baill.) G69	73	CP32
Main Rd, (Cumb.) G67	39	CW15
Main Rd, (Elder.) John. PA5	80	AL34
Main Rd, (Millarston) Pais. PA1	81	AN34
Main Rd, (Castlehead) Pais. PA2	82	AT33
Mains Av, (Giff.) G46	102	BK44
Mainscroft, Ersk. PA8	26	AS20
Mains Dr, Ersk. PA8	26	AS20
Mains Hill, Ersk. PA8	25	AR20
Mainshill Av, Ersk. PA8	25	AR20
Mainshill Gdns, Ersk. PA8	25	AR20
Mains Pl, Bell. ML4	111	CW42
Mains River, Ersk. PA8	26	AS20
Mains Rd, (E.Kil.) G74	122	CA48
Main St, G40	88	BV34
Main St, (Thornlie.) G46	101	BH42
Main St, (Miln.) G62	12	BJ12
Main St, (Torr.) G64	15	BX13
Main St, (Kilsyth) G65	7	CT5
Main St, (Twechar) G65	19	CQ9
Main St, (Baill.) G69	92	CL33
Main St, (Chry.) G69	54	CL21
Main St, (Both.) G71	109	CQ43
Main St, (Udd.) G71	109	CP39
Main St, (Blan.) G72	124	CM47
Main St, (Camb.) G72	106	CC39
Main St, (Ruther.) G73	89	BW37
Main St, (E.Kil.) G74	136	CB51
Main St, (Clark.) G76	119	BP47
Main St, (Barr.) G78	99	AX43
Main St, (Neil.) G78	114	AT46
Main St, (Calder.) Air. ML6	97	DE35
Main St, (Chap.) Air. ML6	97	DG34
Main St, Bell. ML4	110	CV40
Main St, Coat. ML5	75	CW30
Main St, (Glenb.) Coat. ML5	56	CU23
Main St, (Holytown) Moth. ML1	112	DC39
Mains Wd, Ersk. PA8	26	AT20
Mair St, G51	67	BN31
Maitland Bk, Lark. ML9	145	DE58
Maitland Dr, (Torr.) G64	15	BX12
Maitland Pl, Renf. PA4	63	AX27
Maitland St, G4	4	BR28
Malcolm Gdns, (E.Kil.) G74	135	BY51
Malcolm St, Moth. ML1	127	CY47
Maleny Gro, (Newt. M.) G77	116	BD50
Malin Pl, G33	70	CB29
Mallaig Path, G51	65	BF30
off Moss Rd		
Mallaig Pl, G51	65	BF30
off Mallaig Rd		
Mallaig Rd, G51	65	BF30
Mallard Cres, (E.Kil.) G75	135	BW56
Mallard La, (Both.) G71	109	CR42
off Fallside Rd		
Mallard Pl, (E.Kil.) G75	135	BW56
Mallard Rd, Clyde. G81	27	AX16
Mallard Ter, (E.Kil.) G75	135	BW56
Mallard Way, (Strathclyde Bus. Pk.) Bell. ML4	94	CV36
Malleable Gdns, Moth. ML1	111	CY43
Malletsheugh Rd, (Newt. M.) G77	116	BD50
Malloch Cres, (Elder.) John. PA5	80	AK35
Malloch Pl, (E.Kil.) G74	136	CD51
off Angus Av		
Malloch St, G20	49	BN24
Mallots Vw, (Newt. M.) G77	116	BD50
Malov Ct, (E.Kil.) G75	136	CA56
Malta Ter, G5	87	BR33
Maltbarns St, G20	49	BQ26
Malvaig La, (Blan.) G72	124	CL47
off Moorfield Rd		
Malvern Ct, G31	69	BW31
Malvern Way, Pais. PA3	62	AT29
Mambeg Dr, G51	65	BG29
off St. Kenneth Dr		
Mamore Pl, G43	102	BL39
Mamore St, G43	102	BL39
Manchester Dr, G12	48	BJ23
Manitoba Cres, (E.Kil.) G75	135	BX52

Mannering, (E.Kil.) G74	123	CF49
Mannering Ct, G41	86	BL37
Mannering Rd, G41	86	BL37
Mannering Rd, Pais. PA2	81	AN37
Mannering Way, Pais. PA2	81	AN37
off Brediland Rd		
Mannoch Pl, Coat. ML5	95	CZ34
Mannofield, (Bears.) G61	29	BE17
Manor Dr, Air. ML6	76	DA29
Manor Gate, (Newt. M.) G77	117	BH50
Manor Pk Av, Pais. PA2	81	AR36
Manor Rd, G14	47	BG25
Manor Rd, G15	28	BB20
Manor Rd, (Gart.) G69	55	CP24
Manor Rd, Pais. PA2	81	AP36
Manor Vw, (Calder.) Air. ML6	96	DD35
Manor Vw, Lark. ML9	145	DE59
Manor Way, (Ruther.) G73	105	BY41
Manresa Pl, G4	67	BR27
Manse Av, (Bears.) G61	29	BH16
Manse Av, (Both.) G71	109	CQ43
Manse Av, Coat. ML5	94	CT33
Manse Brae, G44	103	BR39
Manse Brae, (Camb.) G72	108	CJ40
Manse Ct, (Kilsyth) G65	7	CT6
Manse Ct, (Barr.) G78	99	AZ42
Mansefield Av, (Camb.) G72	106	CC41
Mansefield Cres, (Clark.) G76	118	BM47
Mansefield Rd, (Clark.) G76	118	BM47
Mansefield Rd, Ham. ML3	140	CT54
Manse Gdns, G32	91	CF33
Manse La, (E.Kil.) G74	122	CB50
Mansel St, G21	50	BV24
Manse Pl, Air. ML6	76	DC30
Manse Rd, G32	91	CF33
Manse Rd, (Bears.) G61	29	BG16
Manse Rd, (Kilsyth) G65	7	CT6
Manse Rd, (Baill.) G69	73	CN31
Manse Rd, (Clark.) G76	120	BT46
Manse Rd, (Neil.) G78	114	AT46
Manse Rd, Moth. ML1	128	DB49
Manse Rd Gdns, (Bears.) G61	29	BG16
Manse St, Coat. ML5	74	CV31
Manse St, Renf. PA4	45	AZ25
Manse Vw, Lark. ML9	144	DD59
Manse Vw, Moth. ML1	113	DH41
Manseview Ter, (Eagle.) G76	133	BN56
off Pollock Av		
Mansewood Rd, G43	102	BK39
Mansfield Dr, (Udd.) G71	109	CP39
Mansfield Rd, G52	64	BB30
Mansfield Rd, Bell. ML4	110	CV42
Mansfield St, G11	66	BL27
Mansion Ct, (Camb.) G72	106	CC39
Mansionhouse Av, G32	91	CE37
Mansionhouse Dr, G32	71	CE31
Mansionhouse Gdns, G41	87	BN38
Mansionhouse Gro, G32	91	CG34
Mansionhouse Rd, G32	91	CG33
Mansionhouse Rd, G41	87	BN38
Mansionhouse Rd, Pais. PA1	63	AW32
Mansion St, G22	50	BS24
Mansion St, (Camb.) G72	106	CC39
Manson Pl, (E.Kil.) G75	136	CC56
Manus Duddy Ct, (Blan.) G72	124	CM45
Maple Av, (Newt. M.) G77	117	BF49
Maple Bk, Ham. ML3	140	CV51
Maple Ct, Coat. ML5	94	CV33
off Ailsa Rd		
Maple Cres, (Camb.) G72	107	CH42
Maple Dr, (Kirk.) G66	34	CC16
Maple Dr, (Barr.) G78	115	AZ45
off Oakbank Dr		
Maple Dr, Clyde. G81	26	AV16
Maple Dr, John. PA5	79	AH37
Maple Dr, Lark. ML9	142	DC56
Maple Gro, (E.Kil.) G75	135	BX55
Maple Pl, (Udd.) G71	94	CT37
Maple Pl, (E.Kil.) G75	135	BX55
Maple Quad, Air. ML6	77	DF31
Maple Rd, G41	86	BK33
Maple Rd, Moth. ML1	112	DD40
Maple Ter, (E.Kil.) G75	135	BX55
Maple Way, (Blan.) G72	124	CL46
off Moorfield Rd		
Maplewood, Wis. ML2	143	DF52
Mar Av, Bish. PA7	24	AK18
Marchbank Gdns, Pais. PA1	83	AZ33
Marchfield, (Bishop.) G64	32	BU18
Marchfield Av, Pais. PA3	62	AT29
Marchglen Pl, G51	65	BF30
off Mallaig Rd		
March La, G41	87	BP35
off Nithsdale Dr		
Marchmont Gdns, (Bishop.)	32	BV18
G64		
Marchmont Ter, G12	48	BL26
off Observatory Rd		
March St, G41	87	BP35
Mardale, (E.Kil.) G74	121	BY50
Mar Dr, (Bears.) G61	11	BH14
Maree Dr, G52	85	BG33
Maree Dr, (Cumb.) G67	21	CX14
Maree Gdns, (Bishop.) G64	33	BX20
Maree Rd, Pais. PA2	81	AQ35
Maree Way, (Blan.) G72	124	CM45
off Clyde Cres		
Marfield St, G32	70	CA30
Mar Gdns, (Ruther.) G73	105	BZ41
Margaret Pl, Bell. ML4	110	CU40
Margaret Rd, Ham. ML3	125	CR47
Margaret's Pl, Lark. ML9	144	DC58
Margaret St, Coat. ML5	95	CW33
Margaretta Bldgs, G44	103	BQ39
off Clarkston Rd		
Margaretvale Dr, Lark. ML9	144	DC59
Marguerite Av, (Lenz.) G66	35	CE15
Marguerite Dr, (Kirk.) G66	35	CE15
Marguerite Gdns, (Kirk.) G66	35	CE15
Marguerite Gdns, (Both.) G71	109	CR43
Marguerite Gro, (Kirk.) G66	35	CE15
Marian Dr, Moth. ML1	113	DE43
Marigold Av, Moth. ML1	128	DA45
Marina Ct, Bell. ML4	110	CV42
off Hamilton Rd		
Marine Cres, G51	67	BN31
Marine Gdns, G51	4	BP31
Marion St, Bell. ML4	111	CZ40
Mariscat Rd, G41	87	BN35
Marjory Dr, Pais. PA3	63	AW30
Marjory Rd, Renf. PA4	63	AW28
Markdow Av, G53	84	BC36
Market Cl, (Kilsyth) G65	7	CT5
off Main St		
Market Ct, (Kilsyth) G65	7	CT5
off Market St		
Markethill Rd, (E.Kil.) G74	121	BZ47
Markethill Roundabout, (E.Kil.)	122	CA50
G74		
Market Pl, (Kilsyth) G65	7	CT5
off Market St		
Market Pl, (Udd.) G71	94	CS38
off Market St		
Market Rd, (Kirk.) G66	18	CJ14
Market Rd, (Udd.) G71	94	CS38
Market Sq, (Kilsyth) G65	7	CT5
off Market St		
Market St, (Kilsyth) G65	7	CT5
Market St, (Udd.) G71	94	CS38
Marlach Pl, G53	84	BC36
Marlborough Av, G11	47	BH26
Marlborough La N, G11	47	BH26
Marlborough La S, G11	47	BH26
Marlborough Pk, (E.Kil.) G75	135	BW54
Marldon La, G11	47	BH26
Marlfield Gdns, Bell. ML4	95	CW38
off Merlin Av		
Marlow St, G41	87	BN33
Marmion Ct, Pais. PA2	81	AP37
off Heriot Av		
Marmion Cres, Moth. ML1	111	CZ43
Marmion Dr, (Kirk.) G66	17	CH13
Marmion Pl, (Cumb.) G67	22	DA14
Marmion Rd, (Cumb.) G67	22	DA14
Marmion Rd, Pais. PA2	81	AN37
Marne St, G31	69	BX30
Marnoch Dr, (Glenb.) Coat. ML5	56	CT23
Marnoch Way, (Mood.) G69	37	CP19
off Braeside Av		
Marnock Ter, Pais. PA2	83	AW34
Marquis Gate, (Udd.) G71	109	CN40
Marrswood Grn, Ham. ML3	125	CQ49
Marshall Gro, Ham. ML3	125	CR50
Marshall's La, Pais. PA1	82	AU33
Marshall St, Lark. ML9	144	DC58
Marshall St, Wis. ML2	143	DH51
Martha Pl, Lark. ML9	144	DD59
Martha St, G1	5	BS29
Martin Ct, Ham. ML3	126	CS50
off Bent Rd		
Martin Cres, (Baill.) G69	72	CL32
Martin Pl, Moth. ML1	113	DE42
Martinside, (E.Kil.) G75	136	CA56
Martin St, G40	88	BV34
Martin St, Coat. ML5	75	CZ30
Martlet Dr, John. PA5	79	AE38
Mart St, G1	5	BS31
Martyn St, Air. ML6	76	DA30
Martyrs Pl, (Bishop.) G64	51	BW21
Marwick St, G31	69	BX30
Mary Dr, Bell. ML4	110	CU42
Maryhill Rd, (Bears.) G61	30	BJ19
Maryhill Shop Cen, G20	49	BN24
Maryknowe Rd, Moth. ML1	113	DE44
Maryland Dr, G52	85	BG33
Maryland Gdns, G52	65	BG32
Mary Rae Rd, Bell. ML4	110	CU42
Mary Sq, (Baill.) G69	73	CP32
Maryston Pl, G33	69	BZ27
Maryston St, G33	69	BZ27
Mary St, G4	67	BR27
Mary St, Ham. ML3	140	CS51
Mary St, John. PA5	80	AJ34
Mary St, Pais. PA2	82	AU35
Maryville Av, (Giff.) G46	102	BL43
Maryville Gdns, (Giff.) G46	102	BL43
Maryville Vw, (Udd.) G71	92	CM36
Marywood Sq, G41	87	BP35
Mary Young Pl, (Clark.) G76	119	BP47
off Riverside Ter		
Masonfield Av, (Cumb.) G68	21	CZ11
Mason La, Moth. ML1	128	DA47
Mason St, Lark. ML9	145	DE60
Mason St, Moth. ML1	128	DA47
Masterton St, G21	50	BS26
Masterton Way, (Udd.) G71	93	CR36
Matherton Av, (Newt. M.) G77	118	BK48

Mathew McWhirter Pl, Lark. ML9	144	DD57
Mathieson Rd, (Ruther.) G73	89	BY36
Mathieson St, Pais. PA1	63	AX32
Matilda Rd, G41	87	BN34
Mauchline, (E.Kil.) G74	123	CF50
off Alloway Rd		
Mauchline Av, (Kirk.) G66	18	CJ11
Mauchline Ct, (Kirk.) G66	18	CJ11
Mauchline Ct, Ham. ML3	138	CM51
Mauchline St, G5	87	BQ33
Maukinfauld Ct, G32	89	BZ34
Maukinfauld Gdns, G31	90	CA33
Maukinfauld Rd, G32	90	CA34
Mauldslie Pl, (Ashgill) Lark. ML9	145	DH61
Mauldslie St, G40	89	BX33
Mauldslie St, Bell. ML4	111	CW41
off Cross Gates		
Mauldslie St, Coat. ML5	75	CW32
Maule Dr, G11	66	BJ27
Mavis Bk, (Bishop.) G64	50	BV21
Mavis Bk, (Blan.) G72	124	CL46
off Moorfield Rd		
Mavisbank Gdns, G51	67	BN31
Mavisbank Gdns, Bell. ML4	111	CW39
Mavisbank St, Air. ML6	76	DB29
Mavisbank Ter, John. PA5	79	AH35
off Campbell St		
Mavisbank Ter, Pais. PA1	82	AV34
Mavor Av, (E.Kil.) G74	122	CC48
Mavor Roundabout, (E.Kil.) G74	122	CB50
Maxton Av, (Barr.) G78	99	AW42
Maxton Gro, (Barr.) G78	99	AW43
Maxton Ter, (Camb.) G72	106	CB42
Maxwell Av, G41	87	BN33
Maxwell Av, (Bears.) G61	29	BG18
Maxwell Av, (Baill.) G69	92	CJ33
Maxwell Ct, G41	87	BN33
off St. John's Rd		
Maxwell Cres, (Blan.) G72	124	CM47
Maxwell Dr, G41	86	BL33
Maxwell Dr, (Baill.) G69	72	CJ32
Maxwell Dr, (E.Kil.) G74	136	CB51
Maxwell Dr, Ersk. PA8	25	AP18
Maxwell Gdns, G41	86	BM33
Maxwell Gro, G41	86	BM33
Maxwell La, G41	87	BN33
off Maxwell Dr		
Maxwell Oval, G41	87	BP33
Maxwell Path, Lark. ML9	145	DE59
off Wallace Dr		
Maxwell Pl, G41	87	BQ34
Maxwell Pl, (Kilsyth) G65	7	CT4
off Charles St		
Maxwell Pl, (Udd.) G71	109	CQ39
off North British Rd		
Maxwell Pl, Coat. ML5	74	CV31
Maxwell Rd, G41	87	BP33
Maxwell Rd, Bish. PA7	24	AK18
Maxwell St, G1	5	BS31
Maxwell St, (Baill.) G69	92	CK33
Maxwell St, Clyde. G81	26	AV17
Maxwell St, Pais. PA3	62	AU32
Maxwell Ter, G41	87	BN33
Maxwellton Av, (E.Kil.) G74	136	CC51
Maxwellton Ct, Pais. PA1	81	AS33
Maxwellton Pl, (E.Kil.) G74	122	CD50
Maxwellton Rd, (E.Kil.) G74	122	CD49
Maxwellton Rd, Pais. PA1	81	AR33
Maxwellton St, Pais. PA1	82	AS34
Maxwelton Rd, G33	69	BZ27
Maybank La, G42	87	BQ36
Maybank St, G42	87	BQ36
off Albert Av		
Mayberry Cres, G32	71	CF32
Mayberry Gdns, G32	71	CF32
Mayberry Gro, G32	71	CF32
Mayberry Pl, (Blan.) G72	124	CM45
Maybole Cres, (Newt. M.) G77	118	BJ49
Maybole Dr, Air. ML6	96	DC33
Maybole Gdns, Ham. ML3	138	CM51
off Barnhill Dr		
Maybole Gro, (Newt. M.) G77	118	BJ49
Maybole Pl, Coat. ML5	95	CZ34
Maybole St, G53	100	BB39
Mayfield Av, (Clark.) G76	119	BN46
Mayfield Pl, Coat. ML5	95	CW34
Mayfield Rd, Ham. ML3	125	CP49
Mayfield St, G20	49	BP23
May Gdns, Ham. ML3	126	CS48
May Rd, Pais. PA2	82	AU38
May St, Ham. ML3	126	CT48
May Ter, G42	87	BR37
May Ter, (Giff.) G46	102	BL42
Meadow Av, (Blan.) G72	124	CM47
Meadowbank La, (Udd.) G71	109	CN39
Meadowbank Pl, (Newt. M.) G77	117	BF48
Meadowburn, (Bishop.) G64	32	BV17
Meadowburn Av, (Lenz.) G66	35	CG16
Meadowburn Av, (Newt. M.) G77	117	BF48
Meadowhead Av, (Chry.) G69	37	CP19
Meadowhead Rd, (Plains) Air. ML6	59	DH26
Meadowhead Rd, Wis. ML2	129	DE49
Meadowhill, (Newt. M.) G77	117	BF48
Meadowhill St, Lark. ML9	144	DD58
Meadow La, (Both.) G71	109	CX43
Meadow La, Renf. PA4	45	AZ24
Meadowpark St, G31	69	BX30
Meadow Path, (Chap.) Air. ML6	97	DF36
off Timmons Ter		
Meadow Ri, (Newt. M.) G77	117	BE48
Meadow Rd, G11	66	BJ27
Meadow Rd, Moth. ML1	128	DC48
Meadows Av, Ersk. PA8	26	AS20
Meadows Av, Lark. ML9	144	DD58
Meadows Dr, Ersk. PA8	26	AS20
Meadowside, Ham. ML3	140	CT55
off Parks Vw		
Meadowside Av, (Elder.) John. PA5	80	AL35
Meadowside Gdns, Air. ML6	77	DF30
off Castle Quad		
Meadowside Ind Est, Renf. PA4	45	AZ23
Meadowside Pl, Air. ML6	77	DF30
Meadowside Quay, G11	65	BG28
Meadowside Rd, (Kilsyth) G65	6	CN5
Meadowside St, G11	66	BJ28
Meadowside St, Renf. PA4	45	AZ24
Meadow St, Coat. ML5	95	CX33
Meadow Vw, (Cumb.) G67	23	DE10
Meadow Wk, Coat. ML5	75	CX31
Meadow Way, (Newt. M.) G77	117	BF48
Meadowwell St, G32	70	CD32
Meadside Av, (Kilb.) John. PA10	78	AC33
Meadside Rd, (Kilb.) John. PA10	78	AC33
Mearns Ct, Ham. ML3	140	CU54
Mearnscroft Gdns, (Newt. M.) G77	117	BH50
Mearnscroft Rd, (Newt. M.) G77	117	BH50
Mearnskirk Ho, (Newt. M.) G77	131	BF52
off Mearnskirk Rd		
Mearnskirk Rd, (Newt. M.) G77	131	BF51
Mearns Rd, (Clark.) G76	118	BL46
Mearns Rd, (Newt. M.) G77	131	BG51
Mearns Rd, Moth. ML1	127	CY45
Mearns Way, (Bishop.) G64	33	BZ19
Medlar Ct, (Camb.) G72	107	CH42
off Maple Cres		
Medlar Rd, (Cumb.) G67	23	DF10
Medrox Gdns, (Cumb.) G67	38	CV16
Medwin Ct, (E.Kil.) G75	134	BU54
Medwin Gdns, (E.Kil.) G75	134	BU54
Medwin St, (Camb.) G72	107	CF40
Medwyn St, G14	47	BF26
Meek Pl, (Camb.) G72	106	CD40
Meetinghouse La, Pais. PA1	62	AU32
off Moss St		
Megan Gate, G40	88	BV33
off Megan St		
Megan St, G40	88	BV33
Meigle Rd, Air. ML6	96	DB33
Meikle Av, Renf. PA4	63	AY27
Meikle Cres, (Green.) Air. ML6	59	DF21
Meikle Cres, Ham. ML3	140	CS54
Meikle Drumgray Rd, (Green.) Air. ML6	59	DF21
Meikle Earnock Rd, Ham. ML3	139	CQ55
Meiklehill Ct, (Kirk.) G66	17	CG12
Meiklehill Rd, (Kirk.) G66	17	CG12
Meiklem St, Bell. ML4	111	CY40
Meiklerig Cres, G53	85	BE35
Meikleriggs Dr, Pais. PA2	81	AQ36
Meikle Rd, G53	85	BE37
Meiklewood Rd, G51	65	BF31
Melbourne Av, (E.Kil.) G75	135	BY54
Melbourne Av, Clyde. G81	26	AT16
Melbourne Ct, (Giff.) G46	102	BM42
Melbourne Grn, (E.Kil.) G75	135	BY53
Melbourne St, G31	68	BV31
Meldon Pl, G51	65	BG30
off Mallaig Rd		
Meldrum Gdns, G41	86	BM35
Meldrum Mains, (Glenm.) Air. ML6	58	DA25
Meldrum St, Clyde. G81	45	AZ21
Melford Av, (Giff.) G46	102	BM43
Melford Av, (Kirk.) G66	16	CD13
Melford Rd, (Righead Ind. Est.) Bell. ML4	110	CU39
Melford Way, Pais. PA3	63	AW30
off Knock Way		
Melfort Av, G41	86	BK33
Melfort Av, Clyde. G81	27	AX18
Melfort Ct, Clyde. G81	27	AY19
Melfort Gdns, (Kilb.) John. PA10	79	AE36
off Milliken Pk Rd		
Melfort Quad, Moth. ML1	113	DF42
off Glenmore Rd		
Melfort Rd, Ham. ML3	125	CN50
Mellerstain Dr, G14	46	BA23
Mellerstain Gro, G14	46	BB23
off Mellerstain Dr		
Melness Pl, G51	65	BF30
off Mallaig Rd		
Melrose Av, (Baill.) G69	73	CP32
off Roslyn Dr		
Melrose Av, (Ruther.) G73	89	BX38
Melrose Av, (Chap.) Air. ML6	97	DF35
Melrose Av, Moth. ML1	112	DD39
Melrose Av, Pais. PA2	81	AQ36
Melrose Av, (Linw.) Pais. PA3	60	AK32
Melrose Ct, (Ruther.) G73	89	BX38

Name	Page	Ref
Melrose Gdns, G20	49	BP26
Melrose Gdns, (Kilsyth) G65	19	CN9
Melrose Gdns, (Udd.) G71	93	CP36
Melrose Pl, (Blan.) G72	108	CL44
Melrose Pl, Coat. ML5	74	CV30
Melrose Pl, Lark. ML9	144	DC60
Melrose Rd, (Cumb.) G67	22	DA14
Melrose St, G4	67	BP27
off Queens Cres		
Melrose St, Ham. ML3	125	CR48
Melrose Ter, (E.Kil.) G74	136	CB51
Melrose Ter, Ham. ML3	125	CR47
Melvaig Pl, G20	48	BM24
Melvick Pl, G51	65	BF30
off Mallaig Rd		
Melville Ct, G1	5	BT31
off Brunswick St		
Melville Dr, Moth. ML1	128	DB47
Melville Gdns, (Bishop.) G64	33	BW19
Melville Pk, (E.Kil.) G74	122	CD50
Melville St, G41	87	BP34
Memel St, G21	50	BU24
Memus Av, G52	85	BE33
Mennock Ct, Ham. ML3	139	CN51
Mennock Dr, (Bishop.) G64	33	BW17
Menock Rd, G44	103	BR39
Menteith Av, (Bishop.) G64	33	BX20
Menteith Ct, Moth. ML1	128	DA47
off Melville Dr		
Menteith Dr, (Ruther.) G73	105	BZ43
Menteith Gdns, (Bears.) G61	11	BE13
Menteith Ln, Moth. ML1	112	DC40
off Windsor Rd		
Menteith Pl, (Ruther.) G73	105	BZ43
Menteith Rd, Moth. ML1	128	DA46
Menzies Dr, G21	51	BW24
Menzies Pl, G21	51	BW24
Menzies Rd, G21	51	BW24
Merchant La, G1	5	BS31
Merchants Cl, (Kilb.) John. PA10	78	AC34
Merchiston St, G32	70	CA30
Merkland Ct, G11	66	BK28
off Vine St		
Merkland Ct, (Kirk.) G66	18	CJ12
Merkland Dr, (Kirk.) G66	18	CJ12
Merkland Pl, (Kirk.) G66	18	CJ12
Merkland Rd, Coat. ML5	74	CS27
Merkland St, G11	66	BK27
Merksworth Way, Pais. PA3	62	AU30
off Mosslands Rd		
Merlewood Av, (Both.) G71	109	CR41
Merlin Av, Bell. ML4	95	CW37
Merlinford Av, Renf. PA4	46	BA26
Merlinford Cres, Renf. PA4	46	BA26
Merlinford Dr, Renf. PA4	46	BA26
Merlinford Way, Renf. PA4	46	BA26
Merlin Way, Pais. PA3	63	AX30
Merrick Ct, Air. ML6	76	DD27
Merrick Gdns, G51	66	BK32
Merrick Gdns, (Bears.) G61	11	BE13
Merrick Path, G51	66	BK32
off Merrick Gdns		
Merrick Ter, (Udd.) G71	93	CR38
Merrick Way, (Ruther.) G73	105	BX42
Merryburn Av, (Giff.) G46	102	BM40
Merrycrest Av, (Giff.) G46	102	BM41
Merrycroft Av, (Giff.) G46	102	BM41
Merryflats, (Kilsyth) G65	19	CP9
Merryland Pl, G51	66	BK30
Merryland St, G51	66	BK30
Merrylee Cres, (Giff.) G46	102	BL40
Merrylee Pk Av, (Giff.) G46	102	BM41
Merrylee Pk La, (Giff.) G46	102	BL41
Merrylee Pk Ms, (Giff.) G46	102	BM40
Merrylee Rd, G43	102	BM40
Merrylee Rd, G44	103	BN40
Merrylees Rd, (Blan.) G72	124	CL46
Merryston Ct, Coat. ML5	74	CU31
Merry St, Moth. ML1	128	DA46
Merryton Av, G15	28	BD18
Merryton Av, (Giff.) G46	102	BL41
Merryton Pl, G15	28	BD18
Merryton Rd, Lark. ML9	142	DB55
Merryton Rd, Moth. ML1	142	DD51
Merryton St, Lark. ML9	142	DB56
Merryvale Av, (Giff.) G46	102	BM41
Merryvale Pl, (Giff.) G46	102	BL40
Merton Dr, G52	64	BC32
Meryon Gdns, G32	91	CF35
Meryon Rd, G32	91	CF34
off Dornford Av		
Methil St, G14	47	BE26
Methlick Av, Air. ML6	96	DA33
Methuen Rd, Pais. PA3	62	AV28
Methven Av, (Bears.) G61	30	BK16
Methven Pl, (E.Kil.) G74	135	BY51
Methven Rd, (Giff.) G46	118	BJ47
Methven St, G31	89	BZ34
Methven St, Clyde. G81	26	AV17
Metropole La, G1	5	BS31
off Clyde St		
Mews La, Pais. PA3	62	AV30
Mey Ct, (Newt. M.) G77	116	BC49
Mey Pl, (Newt. M.) G77	116	BC49
Michael McParland Dr, (Torr.) G64	15	BX12
Michael Ter, (Chap.) Air. ML6	97	DF36
Micklehouse Oval, (Baill.) G69	72	CK31
Micklehouse Pl, (Baill.) G69	72	CK31
Micklehouse Rd, (Baill.) G69	72	CK31
Micklehouse Wynd, (Baill.) G69	72	CK31
Midas Pl, Bell. ML4	112	DA40
Mid Barwood Rd, (Kilsyth) G65	8	CV5
Mid Carbarns, Wis. ML2	143	DF52
off Carbarns		
Mid Cotts, (Gart.) G69	54	CL26
Midcroft, (Bishop.) G64	32	BU18
Midcroft Av, G44	104	BT40
Middlefield, (E.Kil.) G75	136	CA56
Middlemuir Av, (Kirk.) G66	35	CF15
Middlemuir Rd, (Lenz.) G66	35	CF15
Middle Pk, Pais. PA2	82	AT35
Middlerigg Rd, (Cumb.) G68	21	CZ11
Middlesex Gdns, G41	67	BN31
Middlesex St, G41	67	BN32
Middleton Av, (Strutherhill Ind. Est.) Lark. ML9	144	DD61
Middleton Cres, Pais. PA3	61	AR31
Middleton Dr, (Miln.) G62	12	BK11
Middleton Rd, Pais. PA3	61	AR31
Middleton Rd, (Linw.) Pais. PA3	60	AM30
Middleton St, G51	66	BL31
Midfaulds Av, Renf. PA4	64	BA27
off King George Pk Av		
Midland St, G1	4	BR30
Midlem Dr, G52	65	BE32
Midlem Oval, G52	65	BE32
Midlock St, G51	66	BL32
Midlothian Dr, G41	86	BM36
Mid Pk, (E.Kil.) G75	136	CA53
Mid Rd, (Cumb.) G67	40	DB15
Midton Cotts, (Mood.) G69	37	CQ20
Midton St, G21	50	BV26
Midwharf St, G4	68	BS27
Migvie Pl, G20	48	BM24
off Wyndford Rd		
Milan St, G41	87	BQ34
Milford, (E.Kil.) G75	135	BX54
Milford St, G33	70	CC29
Millands Av, (Blan.) G72	108	CL44
Millarbank St, G21	50	BU25
Millar Gro, Ham. ML3	125	CR49
Millarston Av, Pais. PA1	81	AQ33
Millarston Ct, Pais. PA1	81	AR33
Millarston Dr, Pais. PA1	81	AQ33
Millarston Ind Est, Pais. PA1	81	AQ34
Millar St, Pais. PA1	62	AV32
off Christie St		
Millar Ter, (Ruther.) G73	89	BX36
Millbank Av, Bell. ML4	111	CX42
Millbank Rd, Wis. ML2	143	DH51
Millbeg Cres, G33	71	CH31
Millbeg Pl, G33	71	CG32
Millbrae Av, (Chry.) G69	54	CM21
Millbrae Ct, G42	87	BP38
Millbrae Ct, Coat. ML5	74	CT32
Millbrae Cres, G42	87	BN38
Millbrae Cres, Clyde. G81	45	AZ22
Millbrae Gdns, G42	87	BP38
Millbrae Rd, G42	87	BN38
Millbrix Av, G14	46	BC24
Millbrook, (E.Kil.) G74	135	BX52
Millburn Av, (Ruther.) G73	105	BW39
Millburn Av, Clyde. G81	46	BA21
Millburn Av, Renf. PA4	45	AZ26
Millburn Ct, (E.Kil.) G75	134	BU54
Millburn Dr, Renf. PA4	46	BA26
Millburn Gdns, (E.Kil.) G75	134	BU54
Millburn La, Lark. ML9	145	DE59
off Afton St		
Millburn Pl, Lark. ML9	144	DD61
Millburn Rd, Renf. PA4	45	AZ26
Millburn St, G21	68	BV28
Millburn St, Moth. ML1	128	DA46
Millburn Way, (E.Kil.) G75	134	BU54
Millburn Way, Renf. PA4	46	BA26
Mill Ct, (Ruther.) G73	89	BW37
Mill Ct, Ham. ML3	140	CS51
Mill Cres, G40	88	BV34
Mill Cres, (Torr.) G64	15	BY12
Millcroft Rd, (Cumb.) G67	22	DD12
Millcroft Rd, (Ruther.) G73	88	BV35
Millcroft Rd, Air. ML6	40	DC17
Millennium Ct, G34	72	CL29
Millennium Gdns, G34	72	CL30
Miller Cl, (Bishop.) G64	51	BZ21
Miller Dr, (Bishop.) G64	51	BZ21
Millerfield Pl, G40	89	BX34
Millerfield Pl, Ham. ML3	126	CV50
off Miller St		
Millerfield Rd, G40	89	BX34
Miller Gdns, (Bishop.) G64	51	BZ21
Miller La, Clyde. G81	27	AX20
Miller Pl, (Bishop.) G64	51	BZ21
Millersneuk Av, (Lenz.) G66	35	CF18
Millersneuk Cres, G33	52	CC24
Millersneuk Dr, (Lenz.) G66	35	CF17
Millersneuk Rd, (Kirk.) G66	35	CF17
Millers Pl, (Lenz.) G66	35	CF17
Millers Pl, Air. ML6	76	DD30
Millerston St, G31	69	BW31
Miller St, G1	5	BS30
Miller St, (Baill.) G69	92	CK33
Miller St, Clyde. G81	27	AX20
Miller St, Coat. ML5	75	CX32
Miller St, Ham. ML3	126	CV50
Miller St, John. PA5	80	AK34
Miller St, Lark. ML9	144	DD58
Miller Wk, (Bishop.) G64	51	BZ21

Millfield Av, Ersk. PA8	25	AP20
Millfield Av, Moth. ML1	128	DB45
Millfield Cres, Ersk. PA8	25	AQ20
Millfield Dr, Ersk. PA8	43	AQ21
Millfield Gdns, Ersk. PA8	25	AQ20
Millfield Hill, Ersk. PA8	25	AP20
Millfield La, Ersk. PA8	25	AP20
Millfield Meadows, Ersk. PA8	25	AP20
Millfield Pl, Ersk. PA8	25	AP20
Millfield Vw, Ersk. PA8	25	AP20
Millfield Wk, Ersk. PA8	43	AQ21
Millfield Wynd, Ersk. PA8	25	AP20
Millford Dr, (Linw.) Pais. PA3	60	AK32
Millgate, (Udd.) G71	93	CP37
Millgate Av, (Udd.) G71	93	CP37
Millgate Ct, (Udd.) G71	93	CP38
Millgate Rd, Ham. ML3	140	CS52
Millgate Ter, Ham. ML3	140	CS51
off Millgate Rd		
Mill Gro, Ham. ML3	140	CS51
Millheugh, Lark. ML9	144	DA59
Millheugh Brae, Lark. ML9	144	DA59
Millheugh Pl, (Blan.) G72	124	CL47
Millholm Rd, G44	103	BR41
Millhouse Cres, G20	48	BL22
Millhouse Dr, G20	48	BK22
Millichen Rd, G23	30	BM16
Milliken Dr, (Kilb.) John. PA10	79	AE35
Milliken Pk Rd, (Kilb.) John. PA10	79	AE36
Milliken Rd, (Kilb.) John. PA10	79	AE35
Mill Pk, Ham. ML3	140	CS51
off Mill Ct		
Mill Pl, (Linw.) Pais. PA3	60	AJ31
Millport Av, G44	88	BS38
Mill Rig, (E.Kil.) G75	135	BZ56
Mill Ri, (Lenz.) G66	35	CF17
Mill Rd, (Queenzieburn) G65	6	CN6
Mill Rd, (Both.) G71	109	CQ44
Mill Rd, (Camb.) G72	107	CF40
Mill Rd, Air. ML6	76	DC28
Mill Rd, (Riggend) Air. ML6	40	DC20
Mill Rd, Clyde. G81	45	AZ22
Mill Rd, Ham. ML3	140	CS52
Mill Rd, Moth. ML1	128	DB46
Millroad Dr, G40	5	BU31
Millroad Gdns, G40	68	BV31
Millroad St, G40	5	BU31
Millstream Ct, Pais. PA1	82	AV33
Mill St, G40	88	BV34
Mill St, (Ruther.) G73	89	BW37
Mill St, Pais. PA1	82	AV33
Mill Vennel, Renf. PA4	45	AZ26
off Pearson Dr		
Millview, (Barr.) G78	99	AZ42
Millview Meadows, (Neil.) G78	114	AS46
Millview Pl, G53	100	BD41
Millview Ter, (Neil.) G78	114	AS46
Mill Way, (Kirk.) G66	18	CJ14
Millwood St, G41	87	BN37
Milnbank St, G31	69	BW29
Milncroft Pl, G33	70	CC28
Milncroft Rd, G33	70	CC28
Milner La, G13	47	BG24
Milner Rd, G13	47	BG24
Milngavie Rd, (Bears.) G61	29	BH18
Milnpark Gdns, G41	66	BM32
Milnpark St, G41	67	BN32
Milnwood Dr, Bell. ML4	111	CY41
Milnwood Dr, Moth. ML1	111	CY43
Milovaig Av, G23	30	BM20
Milovaig St, G23	30	BM20
Milrig Rd, (Ruther.) G73	88	BV38
Milroy Gdns, Bell. ML4	95	CW37
off Caldwell Gro		
Milton Av, (Camb.) G72	106	CA40
Milton Ct, Air. ML6	76	DC29
off Milton St		
Milton Douglas Rd, Clyde. G81	27	AW15
Milton Dr, (Bishop.) G64	50	BU22
Milton Gdns, (Udd.) G71	93	CN37
Milton Mains Rd, Clyde. G81	27	AW16
Milton Rd, (Kirk.) G66	17	CE11
Milton Rd, (E.Kil.) G74	135	BW51
Milton St, G4	5	BS28
Milton St, Air. ML6	76	DC29
Milton St, Ham. ML3	125	CQ49
Milton St, Moth. ML1	128	DA46
Milton Ter, Ham. ML3	125	CQ48
Milverton Av, (Bears.) G61	29	BE15
Milverton Rd, (Giff.) G46	102	BJ44
Minard Rd, G41	87	BN36
Minard Way, (Udd.) G71	93	CQ30
off Newton Dr		
Mincher Cres, Moth. ML1	128	DA49
Minch Way, Air. ML6	77	DF32
Minella Gdns, Bell. ML4	95	CW37
Minerva St, G3	67	BN29
Minerva Way, G3	67	BN29
Mingarry La, G20	49	BN25
off Clouston St		
Mingarry St, G20	49	BN25
Mingulay Cres, G22	50	BT21
Mingulay Pl, G22	50	BU21
Mingulay St, G22	50	BT21
Minister Wk, (Baill.) G69	73	CP32
off Dukes Rd		
Minmoir Rd, G53	84	BB38
Minsters Pk, (E.Kil.) G74	120	BV49
Minstrel Rd, G13	29	BF20
Minto Av, (Ruther.) G73	105	BZ41
Minto Cres, G52	65	BH32
Minto St, G52	65	BH32
Mireton St, G22	49	BR24
Mirrlees Dr, G12	48	BL25
Mirrlees La, G12	48	BL25
Mitchell Arc, (Ruther.) G73	89	BX37
off Stonelaw Rd		
Mitchell Av, (Camb.) G72	107	CG39
Mitchell Av, Renf. PA4	63	AX27
Mitchell Ct, (E.Kil.) G74	135	BY51
Mitchell Dr, (Miln.) G62	12	BL12
Mitchell Dr, (Ruther.) G73	105	BX39
Mitchell Gro, (E.Kil.) G74	135	BY51
Mitchellhill Rd, G45	104	BV43
Mitchell La, G1	4	BR30
Mitchell Rd, (Cumb.) G67	22	DB11
Mitchell St, G1	4	BR30
Mitchell St, Air. ML6	76	DB29
Mitchell St, Coat. ML5	73	CR32
Mitchison Rd, (Cumb.) G67	22	DC10
Mitre Ct, G11	47	BH25
Mitre Gate, G11	47	BH25
Mitre La, G14	47	BF25
Mitre La W, G14	47	BF25
Mitre Rd, G11	47	BH25
Mitre Rd, G14	47	BG25
Moat Av, G13	47	BE22
Mochrum Rd, G43	103	BN39
Moffat Ct, (E.Kil.) G75	134	BU54
Moffat Gdns, (E.Kil.) G75	134	BU54
Moffathill, Air. ML6	77	DG32
Moffat Pl, (Blan.) G72	108	CM44
Moffat Pl, (E.Kil.) G75	134	BT54
Moffat Pl, Air. ML6	77	DH29
Moffat Pl, Coat. ML5	95	CZ33
Moffat Rd, Air. ML6	77	DH30
Moffat St, G5	88	BT33
Mogarth Av, Pais. PA2	81	AP37
Moidart Av, Renf. PA4	45	AX25
Moidart Ct, (Barr.) G78	99	AX40
Moidart Cres, G52	65	BG32
Moidart Gdns, (Kirk.) G66	18	CK12
Moidart Gdns, (Newt. M.) G77	117	BG47
Moidart Pl, G52	65	BG32
Moidart Rd, G52	65	BG32
Moir St, G1	5	BT31
Molendinar Cl, G33	70	CA27
Molendinar Gdns, G33	69	BZ27
Molendinar St, G1	5	BT31
Molendinar Ter, (Neil.) G78	114	AS46
Mollinsburn Rd, (Glenm.) Air. ML6	57	CX22
Mollinsburn Rd, (Glenb.) Coat. ML5	38	CU18
Mollinsburn St, G21	50	BU26
Mollins Ct, (Cumb.) G68	38	CT16
Mollins Rd, G68	20	CS14
Monach Rd, G33	71	CE29
Monar Dr, G22	49	BR26
off Monar St		
Monar Pl, G22	49	BR26
off Monar St		
Monar St, G22	49	BR26
Monart Pl, G20	49	BP24
Moncrieff Av, (Lenz.) G66	35	CE16
Moncrieffe Rd, Air. ML6	97	DF33
Moncrieff Gdns, (Kirk.) G66	35	CF16
off Moncrieff Av		
Moncrieff St, Pais. PA3	62	AU32
off Back Sneddon St		
Moncur St, G40	5	BU31
Moness Dr, G52	85	BG33
Money Gro, Moth. ML1	128	DD49
Monieburgh Cres, (Kilsyth) G65	7	CU4
Monieburgh Rd, (Kilsyth) G65	7	CU4
Monifieth Av, G52	85	BF34
Monikie Gdns, (Bishop.) G64	33	BZ20
Monkcastle Dr, (Camb.) G72	106	CC39
Monkland Av, (Kirk.) G66	17	CF14
Monkland La, Coat. ML5	94	CU33
Monkland St, Air. ML6	76	DD30
Monkland Ter, (Glenb.) Coat. ML5	56	CT23
Monkland Vw, (Udd.) G71	93	CQ36
off Lincoln Av		
Monkland Vw, (Calder.) Air. ML6	96	DD35
off Woodhall Av		
Monkland Vw Cres, (Baill.) G69	93	CP33
Monksbridge Av, G13	29	BE20
Monkscourt Av, Air. ML6	76	DA29
Monkscroft Av, G11	48	BJ26
Monkscroft Ct, G11	66	BJ27
off Crow Rd		
Monkscroft Gdns, G11	48	BJ26
off Monkscroft Av		
Monks Rd, Air. ML6	97	DE33
Monkton Dr, G15	28	BD19
Monkton Gdns, (Newt. M.) G77	118	BJ49
off Maybole Cres		
Monmouth Av, G12	48	BJ23
Monreith Av, (Bears.) G61	29	BF19
Monreith Rd, G43	103	BN39
Monreith Rd E, G44	103	BQ40
Monroe Dr, (Udd.) G71	93	CP36
Monroe Pl, (Udd.) G71	93	CP36
Montague La, G12	48	BK25
Montague St, G4	67	BP27

Montalto Av, Moth. ML1	112	DC44
Montclair Pl, (Linw.) Pais. PA3	60	AJ31
Montego Grn, (E.Kil.) G75	135	BW52
off Leeward Circle		
Monteith Dr, (Clark.) G76	119	BP45
Monteith Gdns, (Clark.) G76	119	BP45
Monteith Pl, G40	68	BU32
Monteith Pl, (Blan.) G72	125	CN45
Monteith Row, G40	68	BU32
Monteith Row La, G40	68	BU32
off Monteith Pl		
Montford Av, G44	88	BT38
Montford Av, (Ruther.) G73	88	BU38
Montfort Gate, (Barr.) G78	100	BA42
Montgarrie St, G51	65	BF31
Montgomery Av, Coat. ML5	74	CV29
Montgomery Av, Pais. PA3	63	AX29
Montgomery Ct, Pais. PA3	63	AX30
off Montgomery Av		
Montgomery Cres, Wis. ML2	143	DG52
Montgomery Dr, (Giff.) G46	102	BL44
Montgomery Dr, (Kilb.) John.	78	AC33
PA10 off Meadside Av		
Montgomery Pl, (E.Kil.) G74	136	CB51
Montgomery Pl, Lark. ML9	144	DD59
off John St		
Montgomery Rd, Pais. PA3	63	AW29
Montgomery St, G40	89	BW33
Montgomery St, (Camb.) G72	107	CG40
Montgomery St, (E.Kil.) G74	136	CB51
Montgomery St, Lark. ML9	144	DC58
Montraive St, (Ruther.) G73	89	BY36
Montrave Path, G52	85	BF33
off Montrave St		
Montrave St, G52	65	BF32
Montreal Ho, Clyde. G81	26	AT15
off Perth Cres		
Montreal Pk, (E.Kil.) G75	135	BY52
Montrose Av, G32	91	CE36
Montrose Av, G52	64	BB29
Montrose Ct, Pais. PA2	81	AP37
off Montrose Rd		
Montrose Cres, Ham. ML3	126	CT49
Montrose Dr, (Bears.) G61	11	BG14
Montrose Gdns, (Miln.) G62	12	BJ10
Montrose Gdns, (Kilsyth) G65	7	CS4
Montrose Gdns, (Blan.) G72	108	CL43
Montrose Pl, (Linw.) Pais. PA3	60	AJ31
Montrose Rd, Pais. PA2	81	AP37
Montrose St, G1	5	BT30
Montrose St, G4	5	BT29
Montrose St, Clyde. G81	27	AX19
Montrose St, Moth. ML1	111	CZ44
Montrose Ter, (Bishop.) G64	51	BY22
Monument Dr, G33	52	CA24
Monymusk Gdns, (Bishop.) G64	33	BZ19
Monymusk Pl, G15	28	BA16
Moodiesburn St, G33	69	BZ27
Moorburn Av, (Giff.) G46	102	BK42
Moorcroft Dr, Air. ML6	77	DG30
Moorcroft Rd, (Newt. M.) G77	117	BE50
Moore Dr, (Bears.) G61	29	BH18
Moore Gdns, Ham. ML3	140	CU54
Moore St, G31	68	BV31
off Gallowgate		
Moore St, Moth. ML1	112	DC42
Moorfield Cres, Air. ML6	77	DH30
Moorfield Rd, (Blan.) G72	124	CL47
Moorfoot, (Bishop.) G64	33	BY19
Moorfoot Av, (Thornlie.) G46	102	BJ42
Moorfoot Av, Pais. PA2	82	AT36
Moorfoot Dr, Wis. ML2	129	DH50
Moorfoot Path, Pais. PA2	82	AT37
off Moorfoot Av		
Moorfoot St, G32	70	CA31
Moorfoot Way, (Bears.) G61	11	BE13
Moorhill Cres, (Newt. M.) G77	117	BE50
Moorhill Rd, (Newt. M.) G77	117	BE49
Moorhouse Av, G13	46	BB23
Moorhouse Av, Pais. PA2	81	AR35
Moorhouse St, (Barr.) G78	99	AY43
Moorings, The, Pais. PA2	81	AR34
Moorland Dr, Air. ML6	77	DG30
Moorpark Av, G52	64	BB31
Moorpark Av, (Muir.) G69	54	CL22
Moorpark Av, Air. ML6	77	DG30
off Moorcroft Dr		
Moorpark Dr, G52	64	BC31
Moorpark Pl, G52	64	BB31
Moorpark Sq, Renf. PA4	63	AX27
Moor Rd, (Miln.) G62	12	BK11
Morag Av, (Blan.) G72	108	CL44
Moraine Av, G15	28	BD20
Moraine Circ, G15	28	BC20
Moraine Dr, G15	28	BC20
Moraine Dr, (Clark.) G76	118	BL45
Moraine Pl, G15	28	BD20
off Moraine Av		
Morar Av, Clyde. G81	27	AX17
Morar Ct, (Cumb.) G67	21	CX13
Morar Ct, Clyde. G81	27	AX17
Morar Ct, Ham. ML3	139	CQ52
Morar Ct, Lark. ML9	142	DB56
off Etive Pl		
Morar Cres, (Bishop.) G64	32	BV19
Morar Cres, Air. ML6	76	DA28
Morar Cres, Bish. PA7	24	AL19
Morar Cres, Clyde. G81	27	AX17
Morar Cres, Coat. ML5	74	CT28
Morar Dr, (Bears.) G61	30	BK18
Morar Dr, (Cumb.) G67	21	CX14
Morar Dr, (Ruther.) G73	105	BX42
Morar Dr, Clyde. G81	27	AX17
Morar Dr, Pais. PA2	81	AP35
Morar Dr, (Linw.) Pais. PA3	60	AJ32
Morar Pl, (E.Kil.) G74	122	CB50
Morar Pl, (Newt. M.) G77	117	BF46
Morar Pl, Clyde. G81	27	AX17
Morar Pl, Renf. PA4	45	AX25
Morar Rd, G52	65	BG32
Morar Rd, Clyde. G81	27	AX17
Morar Ter, (Udd.) G71	93	CR38
Morar Ter, (Ruther.) G73	105	BZ42
Morar Way, Moth. ML1	113	DE42
off Clarinda Pl		
Moravia Av, (Both.) G71	109	CQ42
Moray Av, Air. ML6	76	DC32
Moray Ct, (Ruther.) G73	89	BW37
Moray Dr, (Torr.) G64	15	BX12
Moray Dr, (Clark.) G76	119	BP46
Moray Gdns, (Cumb.) G68	9	DB8
Moray Gdns, (Udd.) G71	93	CP37
Moray Gdns, (Clark.) G76	119	BP45
Moray Gate, (Both.) G71	109	CN41
Moray Pl, G41	87	BN35
Moray Pl, (Bishop.) G64	33	BY20
Moray Pl, (Kirk.) G66	18	CJ12
Moray Pl, (Chry.) G69	54	CM21
Moray Pl, (Blan.) G72	124	CL47
Moray Pl, (Linw.) Pais. PA3	60	AJ31
Moray Quad, Bell. ML4	111	CW40
Moray Way, Moth. ML1	112	DC40
off Ivy Ter		
Mordaunt St, G40	89	BW34
Moredun Cres, G32	71	CE30
Moredun Dr, Pais. PA2	81	AR36
Moredun Rd, Pais. PA2	81	AR36
Moredun St, G32	71	CE30
Morefield Rd, G51	65	BF30
Morgan Ms, G42	87	BR34
Morgan St, Ham. ML3	140	CT51
Morgan St, Lark. ML9	144	DB58
Morina Gdns, G53	101	BE42
off Waukglen Cres		
Morion Rd, G13	47	BF21
Morland, (E.Kil.) G74	123	CF48
Morley St, G42	87	BQ38
Morna Pl, G14	65	BG27
off Victoria Pk Dr S		
Morningside St, G33	69	BZ29
Morrin Path, G21	50	BU25
off Crichton St		
Morrin Sq, G4	5	BU29
off Collins St		
Morrin St, G21	50	BU25
Morris Cres, (Blan.) G72	124	CM46
Morris Cres, Moth. ML1	113	DG44
Morrishall Rd, (E.Kil.) G74	123	CE49
Morrison Ct, G2	4	BR30
Morrison Gdns, (Torr.) G64	15	BY13
Morrison Quad, Clyde. G81	28	BA19
Morrison St, G5	4	BQ31
Morrison St, Clyde. G81	26	AV15
Morris St, Ham. ML3	140	CT52
Morris St, Lark. ML9	145	DE60
Morriston Cres, Renf. PA4	64	BB28
Morriston Pk Dr, (Camb.) G72	106	CC39
Morriston St, (Camb.) G72	106	CC39
Morton Gdns, G41	86	BL36
Morton St, Moth. ML1	128	DA45
Morven Av, (Bishop.) G64	33	BY20
Morven Av, (Blan.) G72	108	CL44
Morven Av, Pais. PA2	82	AT37
Morven Dr, (Clark.) G76	118	BM45
Morven Dr, (Linw.) Pais. PA3	60	AJ32
Morven Gait, Ersk. PA8	44	AU21
Morven Gdns, (Udd.) G71	93	CP37
Morven La, (Blan.) G72	108	CL44
Morven Rd, (Bears.) G61	29	BG15
Morven Rd, (Camb.) G72	106	CB42
Morven St, G52	65	BG32
Morven St, Coat. ML5	75	CW29
Morven Way, (Kirk.) G66	18	CK13
off Gartconner Av		
Morven Way, (Both.) G71	109	CR42
Mosesfield St, G21	50	BV24
Mosque Av, G5	68	BS32
Moss Av, (Linw.) Pais. PA3	60	AK31
Mossbank, (Blan.) G72	124	CM47
Mossbank, (E.Kil.) G75	134	BV53
Mossbank Av, G33	52	CB25
Mossbank Cres, Moth. ML1	113	DH40
Mossbank Dr, G33	52	CB25
Mossbell Rd, (Bellshill Ind. Est.) Bell. ML4	110	CU39
Mossblown St, Lark. ML9	144	DB58
off Burnbrae St		
Mosscastle Rd, G33	71	CE27
off Mossvale Rd		
Mossdale, (E.Kil.) G74	121	BY50
Mossdale Ct, Bell. ML4	111	CZ40
off Christie St		

Mossdale Gdns, Ham. ML3	139	CN51
Moss Dr, (Barr.) G78	99	AW40
Moss Dr, Ersk. PA8	43	AR22
Mossedge Ind Est, (Linw.) Pais. PA3	60	AL31
Mossend La, G33	71	CF29
Mossend St, G33	71	CF30
Mossgeil La, Lark. ML9 *off Lansbury Ter*	145	DE60
Mossgiel, (E.Kil.) G75	135	BX54
Mossgiel Av, (Ruther.) G73	105	BW40
Mossgiel Cres, (Clark.) G76	119	BP48
Mossgiel Dr, Clyde. G81	27	AY18
Mossgiel Gdns, (Kirk.) G66	17	CH12
Mossgiel Gdns, (Udd.) G71	93	CN37
Mossgiel Pl, (Ruther.) G73	105	BW40
Mossgiel Rd, G43	86	BM38
Mossgiel Rd, (Cumb.) G67	22	DD10
Mossgiel Ter, (Blan.) G72	108	CL43
Mossgiel Way, Moth. ML1	113	DE41
Mosshall Gro, Moth. ML1	113	DH41
Mosshall Rd, Moth. ML1	97	DF38
Mosshall St, Moth. ML1	113	DH41
Mosshead Rd, (Bears.) G61	11	BH14
Moss Hts Av, G52	65	BF32
Mosshill Rd, Bell. ML4	95	CX38
Moss Knowe, (Cumb.) G67	23	DE11
Mossland Rd, G52	64	BA29
Mosslands Rd, Pais. PA3	62	AT29
Mosslingal, (E.Kil.) G75	136	CA56
Mossmulloch, (E.Kil.) G75	135	BZ56
Mossneuk Av, (E.Kil.) G75	134	BU53
Mossneuk Dr, (E.Kil.) G75	134	BV54
Mossneuk Dr, Pais. PA2	82	AS37
Mossneuk Rd, (E.Kil.) G75	134	BV53
Mossneuk St, Coat. ML5	94	CV34
Mosspark Av, G52	85	BH34
Mosspark Av, (Miln.) G62	12	BJ10
Mosspark Boul, G52	85	BG33
Mosspark Dr, G52	85	BE33
Mosspark La, G52 *off Mosspark Dr*	85	BG34
Mosspark Oval, G52	85	BG34
Mosspark Rd, (Miln.) G62	12	BJ10
Mosspark Rd, Coat. ML5	74	CT29
Mosspark Sq, G52	85	BG34
Moss Path, (Baill.) G69	91	CH34
Moss Rd, G51	65	BE31
Moss Rd, (Kirk.) G66	34	CD15
Moss Rd, (Cumb.) G67	23	DG10
Moss Rd, (Muir.) G69	54	CL22
Moss Rd, Air. ML6	76	DC31
Moss Rd, (Hous.) John. PA6	60	AK27
Moss Rd, (Linw.) Pais. PA3	60	AL29
Moss Side Av, Air. ML6	76	DA29
Moss-Side Rd, G41	86	BM36
Moss St, Pais. PA1	62	AU32
Mossvale Cres, G33	71	CE27
Mossvale La, Pais. PA3	62	AT31
Mossvale Path, G33	53	CE26
Mossvale Rd, G33	52	CD26
Mossvale Sq, G33	52	CD26
Mossvale Sq, Pais. PA3	62	AT31
Mossvale St, Pais. PA3	62	AT30
Mossvale Ter, (Chry.) G69	37	CQ18
Mossvale Wk, G33	71	CE27
Mossvale Way, G33 *off Mossvale Rd*	53	CE26
Mossview Cres, Air. ML6	76	DC31
Mossview Quad, G52	65	BE32
Mossview Rd, G33	53	CG24
Mosswell Rd, (Miln.) G62	12	BK10
Mossywood Ct, (Cumb.) G68	20	CV14
Mossywood Pl, (Cumb.) G68	20	CV14
Mossywood Rd, (Cumb.) G68	20	CU14
Mote Hill, Ham. ML3	126	CU48
Mote Hill Rd, Pais. PA3	63	AW31
Motherwell Rd, Bell. ML4	111	CX41
Motherwell Rd, Moth. ML1	113	DE44
Motherwell Roundabout, Ham. ML3	126	CV50
Motherwell St, Air. ML6	77	DE28
Moulin Circ, G52	84	BC33
Moulin Pl, G52	84	BC33
Moulin Rd, G52	84	BC33
Moulin Ter, G52	84	BC33
Mount, The, Moth. ML1	127	CZ47
Mountainblue St, G31	69	BW32
Mount Annan Dr, G44	87	BR38
Mountblow Ho, Clyde. G81 *off Melbourne Av*	26	AT16
Mountblow Rd, Clyde. G81	26	AU15
Mount Cameron Dr N, (E.Kil.) G74	136	CC53
Mount Cameron Dr S, (E.Kil.) G74	136	CC53
Mountgarrie Path, G51 *off Mountgarrie Rd*	65	BF30
Mountgarrie Rd, G51	65	BF30
Mount Harriet Av, (Stepps) G33	53	CG23
Mount Harriet Dr, (Stepps) G33	53	CF23
Mountherrick, (E.Kil.) G75	136	CA56
Mount Lockhart, (Udd.) G71	92	CK35
Mount Lockhart Gdns, (Udd.) G71 *off Mount Lockhart*	92	CK35
Mount Lockhart Pl, (Udd.) G71 *off Mount Lockhart*	92	CK35
Mount Pleasant Pl, (Old Kil.) G60 *off Station Rd*	25	AR15
Mount St, G20	49	BP26
Mount Stuart St, G41	87	BN37
Mount Vernon Av, G32	91	CG34
Mount Vernon Av, Coat. ML5	74	CU30
Mournian Way, Ham. ML3	140	CT52
Mowbray, (E.Kil.) G74	123	CE49
Mowbray Av, (Gart.) G69	55	CP24
Moyne Rd, G53	84	BC35
Moy St, G11 *off Church St*	66	BL27
Muckcroft Rd, (Mood.) G69	36	CK17
Mugdock Rd, (Miln.) G62	12	BJ11
Muirbank Av, (Ruther.) G73	88	BV38
Muirbank Gdns, (Ruther.) G73	88	BV38
Muirbrae Rd, (Ruther.) G73	105	BX41
Muirbrae Way, (Ruther.) G73 *off Muirbrae Rd*	105	BX41
Muirburn Av, G44	103	BN41
Muir Ct, G44 *off Strathdon Av*	103	BP43
Muirdrum Av, G52	85	BF34
Muirdyke Rd, Air. ML6	57	CX24
Muirdyke Rd, Coat. ML5	74	CT29
Muirdyke Rd, (Glenb.) Coat. ML5	56	CV25
Muirdykes Av, G52	64	BC32
Muirdykes Cres, Pais. PA3	61	AR31
Muirdykes Rd, G52	64	BC32
Muirdykes Rd, Pais. PA3	61	AR31
Muiredge Ct, (Udd.) G71	109	CP39
Muiredge Ter, (Baill.) G69	92	CK33
Muirend Av, G44	103	BP40
Muirend Rd, G44	103	BN41
Muirfield Ct, G44 *off Muirend Rd*	103	BN41
Muirfield Cres, G23	31	BN20
Muirfield Meadows, (Both.) G71	109	CN43
Muirfield Rd, (Cumb.) G68	9	DC8
Muirhead-Braehead Roundabout, (Cumb.) G67	22	DD10
Muirhead Cotts, (Kirk.) G66	18	CK14
Muirhead Ct, (Baill.) G69	92	CL33
Muirhead Dr, Moth. ML1	113	DH41
Muirhead Dr, (Linw.) Pais. PA3	60	AJ32
Muirhead Gdns, (Baill.) G69	92	CL33
Muirhead Gate, (Udd.) G71	93	CR37
Muirhead Gro, (Baill.) G69	92	CL33
Muirhead Rd, (Baill.) G69	92	CK34
Muirhead St, G11 *off Purdon St*	66	BK27
Muirhead St, (Kirk.) G66	17	CE14
Muirhead Ter, Moth. ML1	128	DA48
Muirhead Way, (Bishop.) G64	33	BZ20
Muirhill Av, G44	103	BN41
Muirhill Cres, G13	46	BC22
Muirhouse Av, Moth. ML1	128	DD50
Muirhouse Dr, Moth. ML1	143	DE51
Muirhouse La, (E.Kil.) G75 *off Bell Grn W*	136	CA53
Muirhouse Pk, (Bears.) G61	11	BF13
Muirhouse Rd, Moth. ML1	142	DD51
Muirkirk Dr, G13	47	BH22
Muirkirk Dr, Ham. ML3	138	CM51
Muirlees Cres, (Miln.) G62	11	BG11
Muirmadkin Rd, Bell. ML4	111	CX40
Muirpark Av, Renf. PA4	63	AY27
Muirpark Dr, (Bishop.) G64	51	BW21
Muirpark St, G11	66	BK27
Muir Pk Ter, (Bishop.) G64	50	BV21
Muirshiel Av, G53	101	BE39
Muirshiel Cres, G53	101	BE39
Muirshot Rd, Lark. ML9	144	DD57
Muirside Av, G32	91	CG34
Muirside Av, (Kirk.) G66	18	CJ13
Muirside Rd, (Baill.) G69	92	CK33
Muirside Rd, Pais. PA3	61	AR30
Muirside St, (Baill.) G69	92	CK33
Muirskeith Cres, G43	103	BP39
Muirskeith Pl, G43	103	BP39
Muirskeith Rd, G43	103	BP39
Muir St, (Bishop.) G64	33	BW20
Muir St, (Blan.) G72	124	CM47
Muir St, Coat. ML5	74	CU30
Muir St, Ham. ML3	126	CU49
Muir St, Lark. ML9	144	DC58
Muir St, Moth. ML1	127	CZ45
Muir St, Renf. PA4	45	AZ25
Muir Ter, Pais. PA3	63	AW30
Muirton Dr, (Bishop.) G64	32	BV18
Muiryfauld Dr, G31	90	CA33
Muiryhall St, Coat. ML5	75	CW30
Muiryhall St E, Coat. ML5	75	CY30
Mulben Cres, G53	84	BB38
Mulben Pl, G53	84	BB38
Mulben Ter, G53	84	BB38
Mulberry Cres, (Chap.) Air. ML6	97	DG34
Mulberry Dr, (E.Kil.) G75	135	BY56
Mulberry Rd, G43	102	BM40
Mulberry Rd, (Udd.) G71	94	CS36
Mulberry Way, (E.Kil.) G75	135	BY56
Mulberry Wynd, (Camb.) G72	107	CH42
Mull, (E.Kil.) G74	137	CE53

Mull, Air. ML6	77	DF32
Mullardoch St, G23	30	BM20
Mull Av, Pais. PA2	82	AT38
Mull Av, Renf. PA4	63	AY28
Mull Ct, Ham. ML3	139	CP52
Mull St, G21	69	BX27
Mulvey Cres, Air. ML6	76	DA30
Mungo Pk, (E.Kil.) G75	135	BZ53
Mungo Pl, (Udd.) G71	93	CQ36
off Lincoln Av		
Munlochy Rd, G51	65	BF30
Munro Ct, Clyde. G81	26	AV15
Munro La, G13	47	BG24
Munro La E, G13	47	BG24
Munro Pl, G13	47	BG22
Munro Pl, (E.Kil.) G74	122	CD50
Munro Rd, G13	47	BG24
Murano St, G20	49	BP25
Murchison, G12	47	BH23
off Ascot Av		
Murchison Dr, (E.Kil.) G75	135	BX53
Murdoch Dr, (Miln.) G62	12	BL13
off Finlay Ri		
Murdoch Pl, Moth. ML1	112	DB42
Murdoch Rd, (E.Kil.) G75	136	CA53
Murdoch St, G21	50	BV24
off Lenzie St		
Murdock Sq, Bell. ML4	95	CY38
Muriel St, (Barr.) G78	99	AY42
Muriel St Ind Est, (Barr.) G78	99	AY41
Murray Av, (Kilsyth) G65	7	CT6
Murray Business Area, Pais. PA3	62	AT31
Murrayfield, (Bishop.) G64	33	BW18
Murrayfield Dr, (Bears.) G61	29	BG20
Murrayfield St, G32	70	CA30
Murray Gro, (Bears.) G61	10	BD13
Murrayhill, (E.Kil.) G75	135	BZ53
Murray Path, (Udd.) G71	109	CN39
Murray Pl, (Barr.) G78	99	AZ41
Murray Pl, (Righead Ind. Est.) Bell. ML4	94	CU38
Murray Rd, (Both.) G71	109	CQ42
Murray Rd, The (E.Kil.) G75	136	CA53
Murray Roundabout, The (E.Kil.) G75	136	CB53
Murray Sq, The (E.Kil.) G75	135	BZ54
off The Murray Rd		
Murray St, Pais. PA3	62	AS31
Murray St, Renf. PA4	45	AY26
Murray Ter, Moth. ML1	127	CX46
Murrin Av, (Bishop.) G64	33	BZ20
Murroes Rd, G51	65	BF30
Musgrove Pl, (E.Kil.) G75	135	BY53
Muslin St, G40	88	BV33
Muttonhole Rd, Ham. ML3	138	CM54
Mybster Pl, G51	65	BF30
off Mallaig Rd		
Mybster Rd, G51	65	BF30
Myers Cres, (Udd.) G71	109	CQ40
Myreside Pl, G32	69	BZ31
Myreside St, G32	69	BZ31
Myres Rd, G53	85	BF37
Myrie Gdns, (Bishop.) G64	33	BX19
Myroch Pl, G34	72	CL28
Myrtle Av, (Lenz.) G66	35	CE16
Myrtle Dr, Moth. ML1	112	DD40
Myrtle Dr, Wis. ML2	129	DF49
Myrtle Hill La, G42	88	BS37
Myrtle La, Lark. ML9	144	DD60
Myrtle Pk, G42	87	BR36

Myrtle Pl, G42	88	BS36
Myrtle Rd, (Udd.) G71	93	CR37
Myrtle Rd, Clyde. G81	26	AT17
Myrtle Sq, (Bishop.) G64	51	BW21
Myrtle St, (Blan.) G72	108	CM44
Myrtle Vw Rd, G42	88	BS37
Myrtle Wk, (Camb.) G72	106	CB39
Myvot Av, (Cumb.) G67	39	CX15
Myvot Rd, (Cumb.) G67	39	CW17

N

Naburn Gate, G5	88	BS33
Nagle Gdns, Moth. ML1	129	DH45
Nairn Av, (Blan.) G72	108	CL43
Nairn Av, Bell. ML4	111	CW39
Nairn Cres, Air. ML6	76	DC32
Nairn Pl, (E.Kil.) G74	123	CE50
Nairn Pl, Clyde. G81	26	AV18
Nairnside Rd, G21	51	BY22
Nairn St, G3	66	BM28
Nairn St, (Blan.) G72	124	CL47
Nairn St, Clyde. G81	26	AV18
Nairn St, Lark. ML9	144	DB59
Nairn Way, (Cumb.) G68	9	DC8
Naismith St, G32	91	CE36
Naismith Wk, Bell. ML4	95	CY38
Nansen St, G20	49	BQ26
Napier Ct, (Old Kil.) G60	26	AS16
off Freelands Rd		
Napier Dr, G51	66	BK29
Napier Gdns, (Linw.) Pais. PA3	60	AL31
Napier Hill, (E.Kil.) G75	136	CA53
Napier La, (E.Kil.) G75	136	CA53
Napier Pl, G51	66	BK29
Napier Pl, (Old Kil.) G60	26	AS16
Napier Rd, G51	66	BK29
Napier Rd, G52	64	BB28
Napiershall La, G20	67	BP27
Napiershall Pl, G20	67	BP27
off Napiershall St		
Napiershall St, G20	67	BP27
Napier Sq, Bell. ML4	95	CX38
Napier St, Clyde. G81	45	AY22
Napier St, John. PA5	79	AG34
Napier St, (Linw.) Pais. PA3	60	AL31
Napier Ter, G51	66	BK29
Naproch Pl, (Newt. M.) G77	118	BL48
Naseby Av, G11	47	BH26
Naseby La, G11	47	BH26
Nasmyth Av, (Bears.) G61	10	BD13
Nasmyth Av, (E.Kil.) G75	136	CB54
Nasmyth Pl, G52	64	BC30
Nasmyth Pl, (E.Kil.) G75	136	CB54
off Nasmyth Av		
Nasmyth Rd, G52	64	BC30
Nasmyth Rd N, G52	64	BC30
Nasmyth Rd S, G52	64	BC30
Nassau Pl, (E.Kil.) G75	135	BW52
Navar Pl, Pais. PA2	83	AW35
Naver St, G33	70	CA28
Naylor La, Air. ML6	76	DD29
Naysmyth Bk, (E.Kil.) G75	136	CB54
Neidpath, (Baill.) G69	92	CJ33
Neidpath Av, Coat. ML5	95	CX34
Neidpath E, (E.Kil.) G74	135	BZ52
off Kirktonholme Rd		
Neidpath Pl, Coat. ML5	95	CW34
Neidpath Rd E, (Giff.) G46	118	BJ47
Neidpath Rd W, (Giff.) G46	118	BJ46

Neidpath W, (E.Kil.) G74	135	BZ52
off Kirktonholme Rd		
Neilsland Dr, Ham. ML3	139	CR54
Neilsland Dr, Moth. ML1	127	CX47
Neilsland Oval, G53	85	BF37
Neilsland Rd, Ham. ML3	139	CR52
Neilsland Sq, G53	85	BF36
Neilsland Sq, Ham. ML3	140	CS52
off Neilsland Rd		
Neilsland St, Ham. ML3	140	CS52
Neilson Ct, Ham. ML3	140	CU51
off Portland Pl		
Neilson St, Bell. ML4	111	CW40
Neilston Av, G53	101	BE40
Neilston Ct, G53	101	BE40
Neilston Pl, (Kilsyth) G65	7	CR4
Neilston Rd, (Barr.) G78	114	AV45
Neilston Rd, Pais. PA2	82	AU34
Neilston Wk, (Kilsyth) G65	7	CR4
off Balmalloch Rd		
Neil St, Pais. PA1	82	AS33
Neil St, Renf. PA4	45	AZ24
Neilvaig Dr, (Ruther.) G73	105	BY42
Neistpoint Dr, G33	70	CC29
Nelson Av, Coat. ML5	94	CU33
Nelson Cres, Moth. ML1	128	DD50
Nelson Mandela Pl, G2	5	BS29
Nelson Pl, (Baill.) G69	92	CK33
Nelson St, G5	4	BQ31
Nelson St, (Baill.) G69	92	CK33
Nelson Ter, (E.Kil.) G74	136	CC53
Neptune St, G51	66	BK30
Neptune Way, Bell. ML4	112	DA40
Nerston Ind Est, (E.Kil.) G74	122	CB49
Nerston Rd, (E.Kil.) G74	122	CB47
Ness Av, John. PA5	79	AE37
Ness Dr, (Blan.) G72	109	CN44
Ness Dr, (E.Kil.) G74	136	CD52
Ness Gdns, (Bishop.) G64	33	BX20
off Wester Cleddens Rd		
Ness Gdns, Lark. ML9	144	DC60
Ness Rd, Renf. PA4	45	AX25
Ness St, G33	70	CA28
Ness Ter, Ham. ML3	139	CQ52
Ness Way, Moth. ML1	112	DC40
off Graham St		
Nethan Av, Wis. ML2	143	DE51
Nethan Gate, Ham. ML3	126	CS50
Nethan Path, Lark. ML9	144	DC61
off Riverside Rd		
Nethan Pl, Ham. ML3	140	CT55
Nethan St, G51	66	BJ29
Nethan St, Moth. ML1	111	CY43
Nether Auldhouse Rd, G43	86	BK38
Netherbank Rd, (Netherton Ind. Est.) Wis. ML2	143	DF51
Netherburn Av, G44	103	BP43
Netherby Dr, G41	86	BM33
Nethercairn Pl, (Newt. M.) G77	118	BL48
Nethercairn Rd, G43	102	BL41
Nethercliffe Av, G44	103	BP43
Nethercommon Harbour, Pais. PA3	62	AU30
Nethercraigs Ct, Pais. PA2	81	AR38
Nethercraigs Dr, Pais. PA2	82	AS37
Nethercraigs Rd, Pais. PA2	81	AR38
Nethercroy Rd, (Kilsyth) G65	7	CU8
Netherdale, (Newt. M.) G77	118	BK48
off Kirkvale Ct		
Netherdale Cres, Wis. ML2	143	DE51
Netherdale Dr, Pais. PA1	84	BB34

Netherdale Rd, (Netherton Ind. 143 DG51
Est.) Wis. ML2
Netherfield St, G31 69 BY31
Nethergreen Cres, Renf. PA4 45 AX26
Nethergreen Rd, Renf. PA4 45 AX26
Nethergreen Wynd, Renf. PA4 45 AX26
Netherhall Rd, (Netherton Ind. 143 DF51
Est.) Wis. ML2
Netherhill Av, G44 103 BP44
Netherhill Cotts, Pais. PA3 63 AX30
off Netherhill Rd
Netherhill Cres, Pais. PA3 63 AW31
Netherhill Rd, (Mood.) G69 37 CP20
Netherhill Rd, Pais. PA3 62 AV31
Netherhill Way, Pais. PA3 63 AX30
Netherhouse Av, (Lenz.) G66 35 CG17
Netherhouse Av, Coat. ML5 94 CV34
Netherhouse Pl, G34 73 CN29
Netherhouse Rd, (Baill.) G69 72 CM30
Nether Kirkton Av, (Neil.) G78 114 AU45
Nether Kirkton Vw, (Neil.) G78 114 AU45
Nether Kirkton Way, (Neil.) G78 114 AU45
Nether Kirkton Wynd, (Neil.) 114 AU45
G78
Netherlee Pl, G44 103 BQ41
Netherlee Rd, G44 103 BP42
Nethermains Rd, (Miln.) G62 12 BJ13
Netherpark Av, G44 103 BP44
Netherplace Cres, G53 84 BD37
Netherplace Cres, (Newt. M.) 117 BE49
G77
Netherplace Rd, G53 84 BD37
Netherplace Rd, (Newt. M.) 116 BD50
G77
Netherton Av, G13 47 BG21
Netherton Ct, G45 104 BV43
Netherton Ct, (Newt. M.) G77 118 BJ46
Netherton Dr, (Barr.) G78 99 AZ43
Netherton Fm La, (Bears.) G61 47 BH21
Netherton Ind Est, Wis. ML2 143 DG51
Netherton Rd, G13 47 BG21
Netherton Rd, (E.Kil.) G75 135 BY55
Netherton Rd, (Newt. M.) G77 117 BH47
Netherton Rd, Wis. ML2 143 DE51
Netherton St, G13 47 BH22
Netherton St, Wis. ML2 143 DH51
Nethervale Av, G44 103 BP44
Netherview Rd, G44 103 BQ44
Netherway, G44 103 BP44
Netherwood Av, (Cumb.) G68 20 CV13
Netherwood Ct, (Cumb.) G68 21 CW13
Netherwood Ct, Moth. ML1 142 DD51
Netherwood Gro, (Cumb.) G68 21 CW13
Netherwood Pl, (Cumb.) G68 20 CV13
Netherwood Rd, (Cumb.) G68 20 CV13
Netherwood Rd, Moth. ML1 128 DD50
Netherwood Way, (Cumb.) G68 21 CW13
Nethy Way, Renf. PA4 64 BB28
off Teith Av
Neuk, The, Wis. ML2 129 DG50
Neuk Av, (Muir.) G69 54 CL22
Neuk Way, G32 91 CE37
Neville, (E.Kil.) G74 123 CE48
Nevis Av, Ham. ML3 139 CQ51
Nevis Ct, (Barr.) G78 99 AY44
Nevis Ct, Moth. ML1 128 DA49
off Glenhead Dr
Nevis Dr, (Torr.) G64 15 BX12
Nevison St, Lark. ML9 144 DD59
Nevis Rd, G43 102 BK40
Nevis Rd, (Bears.) G61 10 BD14

Nevis Rd, Renf. PA4 63 AX28
Nevis Way, (Abbots.) Pais. PA3 62 AU28
Newark Dr, G41 86 BM34
Newark Dr, Pais. PA2 82 AS37
Newarthill Rd, Moth. ML1 113 DE43
New Ashtree St, Wis. ML2 129 DF50
Newbank Ct, G31 90 CA33
Newbank Gdns, G31 89 BZ33
Newbank Rd, G31 90 CA33
Newbattle Av, (Calder.) Air. 96 DD35
ML6
Newbattle Ct, G32 90 CD35
Newbattle Gdns, G32 90 CD35
Newbattle Pl, G32 90 CD35
Newbattle Rd, G32 90 CC36
Newbold Av, G21 50 BU22
Newburgh, Ersk. PA8 25 AQ18
Newburgh St, G43 86 BM38
Newcastleton Dr, G23 31 BN20
off Broughton Rd
New City Rd, G4 4 BR28
Newcraigs Dr, (Clark.) G76 120 BT46
Newcroft Dr, G44 104 BT40
Newdyke Av, (Kirk.) G66 17 CG13
Newdyke Rd, (Kirk.) G66 17 CG13
New Edinburgh Rd, (Udd.) G71 93 CP38
New Edinburgh Rd, Bell. ML4 93 CP38
Newfield Cres, Ham. ML3 125 CR49
Newfield La, (Both.) G71 109 CR42
Newfield Pl, (Thornlie.) G46 101 BH43
Newfield Pl, (Ruther.) G73 88 BU38
Newfield Sq, G53 100 BC39
Newford Gro, (Clark.) G76 119 BN48
Newgrove Gdns, (Camb.) G72 106 CC39
Newhall St, G40 88 BU34
Newhaven Rd, G33 70 CD29
Newhaven St, G32 70 CC30
Newhills Rd, G33 71 CG30
Newhouse Ind Est, Moth. ML1 97 DE38
Newhousemill Rd, (E.Kil.) G74 137 CF54
New Inchinnan Rd, Pais. PA3 62 AU30
Newington St, G32 70 CB31
New Kirk Pl, (Bears.) G61 29 BG16
off New Kirk Rd
New Kirk Rd, (Bears.) G61 29 BG16
New Lairdsland Rd, (Kirk.) G66 17 CE12
Newlands Dr, Ham. ML3 140 CT53
Newlandsfield Rd, G43 86 BM38
Newlands Gdns, (Elder.) John. 80 AL36
PA5
Newlandsmuir Rd, (E.Kil.) G75 135 BW55
Newlands Pl, (E.Kil.) G74 136 CA52
Newlands Rd, G43 103 BN39
Newlands Rd, G44 103 BQ39
Newlands Rd, (Udd.) G71 93 CP37
Newlands Rd, (E.Kil.) G75 134 BU56
Newlands St, Coat. ML5 95 CW33
New La, (Calder.) Air. ML6 96 DD35
New Luce Dr, G32 91 CF34
Newmains Av, (Inch.) Renf. PA4 43 AQ24
Newmains Rd, Renf. PA4 63 AX27
Newmill Rd, G21 51 BY24
Newmilns St, G53 100 BB39
Newnham Rd, Pais. PA1 83 AZ33
Newpark Cres, (Camb.) G72 90 CC38
off Morriston Pk Dr
New Pk St, Ham. ML3 126 CS48
New Plymouth, (E.Kil.) G75 135 BW54
New Rd, (Camb.) G72 107 CG41
New Rd, (Glenb.) Coat. ML5 56 CV23
Newrose Av, Bell. ML4 95 CX38

Newshot Ct, Clyde. G81 45 AZ22
off Clydeholm Ter
Newshot Dr, Ersk. PA8 26 AS20
New Sneddon St, Pais. PA3 62 AU32
Newstead Gdns, G23 31 BN20
New Stevenston Rd, Moth. 112 DD43
ML1
New St, (Blan.) G72 124 CL46
New St, Clyde. G81 27 AW15
New St, (Kilb.) John. PA10 78 AC34
New St, Pais. PA1 82 AU33
Newton Av, (Camb.) G72 107 CF39
Newton Av, (Barr.) G78 99 AY44
Newton Av, (Elder.) John. PA5 81 AN34
Newton Brae, (Camb.) G72 107 CG39
Newton Ct, (Newt. M.) G77 117 BF50
Newton Dr, (Udd.) G71 93 CQ38
Newton Dr, (Elder.) John. PA5 81 AN34
Newton Fm Rd, (Camb.) G72 91 CH38
Newtongrange Av, G32 90 CD34
Newtongrange Gdns, G32 90 CD35
Newton Gro, (Newt. M.) G77 117 BF50
Newtonlea Av, (Newt. M.) G77 117 BG49
Newton Pl, G3 4 BP28
Newton Pl, (Newt. M.) G77 117 BG50
Newton Rd, (Lenz.) G66 35 CG18
Newton Sta Rd, (Camb.) G72 107 CG41
Newton St, G3 4 BQ29
off Argyle St
Newton St, Coat. ML5 94 CU33
Newton St, Pais. PA1 82 AS33
Newton Ter, G3 4 BP29
off Sauchiehall St
Newton Ter, Pais. PA1 81 AP34
Newton Ter La, G3 4 BP29
Newton Way, Pais. PA3 63 AX30
off Merlin Way
Newtown St, (Kilsyth) G65 7 CT5
Newtyle Dr, G53 84 BB36
Newtyle Pl, G53 84 BB36
Newtyle Pl, (Bishop.) G64 33 BZ20
Newtyle Rd, Pais. PA1 83 AX33
New Vw Cres, Bell. ML4 111 CW42
off New Vw Dr
New Vw Dr, Bell. ML4 111 CW42
New Vw Pl, Bell. ML4 111 CW42
New Wynd, G1 5 BS31
Niamh Ct, (Inch.) Renf. PA4 44 AS22
Nicholas St, G1 5 BT30
Nicholson La, G5 4 BR31
off Nicholson St
Nicholson St, G5 4 BR31
Nicolson Ct, (Stepps) G33 53 CG24
Nicol St, Air. ML6 77 DE28
Niddrie Rd, G42 87 BP35
Niddrie Sq, G42 87 BP35
Niddry St, Pais. PA3 62 AV32
Nigel Gdns, G41 86 BM36
Nigel St, Moth. ML1 127 CZ47
Nigg Pl, G34 72 CJ29
Nimmo Dr, G51 65 BG30
Ninian Rd, Air. ML6 77 DE32
Ninians Ri, (Kirk.) G66 17 CH14
Nisbet St, G31 69 BZ32
Nisbett Pl, (Chap.) Air. ML6 97 DG34
Nisbett St, (Chap.) Air. ML6 97 DG35
Nissen Pl, G53 84 BB36
Nith Av, Pais. PA2 81 AP35
off Don Dr
Nith Dr, Renf. PA4 64 BA27
Nith Pl, John. PA5 79 AE37

Name	Page	Ref
Nith Quad, Moth. ML1	113	DE42
Nithsdale, (E.Kil.) G74	123	CF50
Nithsdale Cres, (Bears.) G61	29	BE15
Nithsdale Dr, G41	87	BP35
Nithsdale Pl, G41	87	BP34
off Nithsdale Rd		
Nithsdale Rd, G41	87	BP35
Nithsdale St, G41	87	BP35
Nith St, G33	69	BZ28
Nitshill Rd, (Thornlie.) G46	101	BF42
Nitshill Rd, G53	100	BB39
Niven St, G20	48	BL23
Noble Rd, Bell. ML4	111	CW40
Nobles Pl, Bell. ML4	110	CV41
Nobles Vw, Bell. ML4	110	CV41
Noldrum Av, G32	91	CE37
Noldrum Gdns, G32	91	CE37
off Park Rd		
Norbreck Dr, (Giff.) G46	102	BL41
Norby Rd, G11	47	BH26
Noremac Way, (Bellshill Ind. Est.) Bell. ML4	94	CV38
Norfield Dr, G44	87	BR38
Norfolk Ct, G5	67	BR32
Norfolk Cres, (Bishop.) G64	32	BU18
Norfolk Ho, (E.Kil.) G74	136	CA52
off The Plaza Shop Cen		
Norfolk La, G5	67	BR32
off Norfolk St		
Norfolk St, G5	68	BS32
Norham St, G41	87	BN36
Norman St, G40	88	BV34
Norse La N, G14	47	BE25
off Verona Av		
Norse La S, G14	47	BE25
off Verona Av		
Norse Pl, G14	47	BE25
Norse Rd, G14	47	BE25
Northall Quad, Moth. ML1	112	DD44
off Clapperhow Rd		
Northampton Dr, G12	48	BK23
Northampton La, G12	48	BK23
North Av, (Camb.) G72	106	CB39
North Av, Clyde. G81	27	AW19
North Av, Moth. ML1	112	DC43
Northbank Av, (Kirk.) G66	17	CE13
Northbank Av, (Camb.) G72	107	CF39
North Bk Pl, Clyde. G81	45	AY21
Northbank La, (Kirk.) G66	17	CE13
Northbank St, (Camb.) G72	107	CF39
off Westburn Rd		
North Bk St, Clyde. G81	45	AY21
North Barr Av, Ersk. PA8	25	AQ18
North Berwick Av, (Cumb.) G68	9	DB8
North Berwick Cres, (E.Kil.) G75	135	BW55
North Berwick Gdns, (Cumb.) G68	9	DB8
North Biggar Rd, Air. ML6	76	DD29
North Brae Pl, G13	46	BD22
North Br St, Air. ML6	76	DB29
North British Rd, (Udd.) G71	109	CP39
Northburn Av, Air. ML6	76	DD28
Northburn Pl, Air. ML6	76	DD27
Northburn Rd, Coat. ML5	75	CY28
North Bute St, Coat. ML5	95	CX33
North Caldeen Rd, Coat. ML5	75	CY32
North Calder Dr, Air. ML6	77	DF31
North Calder Gro, (Udd.) G71	92	CK35
North Calder Pl, (Udd.) G71	92	CK35
North Calder Rd, (Udd.) G71	94	CS36
North Campbell Av, (Miln.) G62	11	BH12
North Canal Bk, G4	68	BS27
North Canal Bk St, G4	68	BS27
North Carbrain Rd, (Cumb.) G67	22	DB13
North Claremont St, G3	67	BN28
off Royal Ter		
North Corsebar Rd, Pais. PA2	82	AS35
North Ct, G1	5	BS30
off St. Vincent Pl		
North Ct La, G1	5	BS30
Northcroft Rd, G21	50	BV25
Northcroft Rd, (Chry.) G69	37	CN19
North Cft St, Pais. PA3	62	AV32
North Dean Pk Av, (Both.) G71	109	CQ42
North Douglas St, Clyde. G81	45	AY21
North Dr, G1	4	BR30
North Dr, (Linw.) Pais. PA3	60	AK31
North Dumgoyne Av, (Miln.) G62	11	BH11
North Elgin Pl, Clyde. G81	45	AY22
North Elgin St, Clyde. G81	45	AY22
North Erskine Pk, (Bears.) G61	29	BF16
Northfield, (E.Kil.) G75	134	BV54
Northfield Rd, (Kilsyth) G65	7	CR4
Northfield St, Moth. ML1	128	DA45
North Frederick St, G1	5	BS30
North Gardner St, G11	66	BK27
Northgate Quad, G21	51	BY23
Northgate Rd, G21	51	BY22
North Gower St, G51	66	BL32
North Gra Rd, (Bears.) G61	29	BG15
North Hanover Pl, G4	5	BS29
off North Hanover St		
North Hanover St, G1	5	BS29
North Hillhead Rd, (Newt. M.) G77	130	BC52
Northinch Ct, G14	65	BF27
off Northinch St		
Northinch St, G14	65	BF27
North Iverton Pk Rd, John. PA5	80	AK34
Northland Av, G14	47	BE24
Northland Dr, G14	47	BE24
Northland Gdns, G14	47	BE24
off Northland Dr		
Northland La, G14	47	BE25
off Northland Dr		
North La, (Linw.) Pais. PA3	60	AL31
North Lo Av, Moth. ML1	128	DA49
North Lo Rd, Renf. PA4	45	AY25
North Moraine La, G15	29	BE19
off Moraine Av		
Northmuir Rd, G15	28	BD17
North Orchard St, Moth. ML1	127	CZ46
North Pk Av, (Thornlie.) G46	101	BH41
North Pk Av, (Barr.) G78	99	AX42
Northpark St, G20	49	BP25
North Pk Vil, (Thornlie.) G46	101	BH41
off North Pk Av		
North Pl, G3	4	BP29
off North St		
North Portland St, G1	5	BT30
North Rd, (Cumb.) G68	21	CW13
North Rd, Bell. ML4	111	CW39
North Rd, John. PA5	79	AG35
North Sq, Coat. ML5	74	CU29
North St, G3	4	BP29
North St, Lark. ML9	144	DC57
North St, Moth. ML1	128	DB45
North St, Pais. PA3	62	AU31
Northumberland St, G20	49	BN25
North Vw, (Bears.) G61	29	BF19
North Wallace St, G4	5	BT28
Northway, (Blan.) G72	108	CL44
North Woodside Rd, G20	49	BP26
Norval St, G11	66	BJ27
Norwich Dr, G12	48	BK24
Norwood Av, (Kirk.) G66	16	CD12
Norwood Dr, (Giff.) G46	102	BJ44
Norwood Pk, (Bears.) G61	29	BH18
Norwood Ter, (Udd.) G71	93	CQ38
Nottingham Av, G12	48	BJ23
off Northampton Dr		
Nottingham La, G12	48	BK23
off Northampton Dr		
Novar Dr, G12	48	BJ25
Novar Gdns, (Bishop.) G64	32	BU19
Novar St, Ham. ML3	140	CT51
Nuneaton St, G40	89	BW34
Nuneaton St Ind Est, G40	89	BW34
Nurseries Rd, (Baill.) G69	71	CH31
Nursery Av, (Erskine Hosp.) Bish. PA7	24	AN17
Nursery La, G41	87	BP35
Nursery Pl, (Blan.) G72	124	CM47
Nursery St, G41	87	BQ34
off Pollokshaws Rd		
Nutberry Ct, G42	87	BR36

O

Name	Page	Ref
Oak Av, (Bears.) G61	11	BH14
Oak Av, (E.Kil.) G75	135	BX55
Oakbank Av, Wis. ML2	143	DG52
Oakbank Dr, (Barr.) G78	115	AZ45
Oakbank Ind Est, G20	49	BR26
Oakbank St, Air. ML6	77	DF30
Oakburn Av, (Miln.) G62	11	BH12
Oakburn Cres, (Miln.) G62	11	BH12
Oak Cres, (Baill.) G69	92	CJ33
Oakdene Av, (Udd.) G71	93	CR38
Oakdene Av, Bell. ML4	95	CW38
Oakdene Cres, (New.) Moth. ML1	113	DE42
Oak Dr, (Kirk.) G66	34	CD16
Oak Dr, (Camb.) G72	107	CE41
Oak Fern Dr, (E.Kil.) G74	121	BZ49
Oak Fern Gro, (E.Kil.) G74	121	BZ49
Oakfield Av, G12	67	BN27
Oakfield Dr, Moth. ML1	128	DB47
off Brandon St		
Oakfield La, G12	67	BN27
Oakfield Rd, Moth. ML1	128	DA47
Oak Gro, (Chap.) Air. ML6	97	DG34
Oakhill Av, (Baill.) G69	91	CH34
Oak Lea, Ham. ML3	140	CV51
Oaklea Cres, (Blan.) G72	124	CL45
Oakley Dr, G44	103	BP42
Oakley Ter, G31	68	BV30
Oak Pk, (Bishop.) G64	33	BX20
Oak Pk, Moth. ML1	127	CZ48
Oak Path, Moth. ML1	112	DD40
off Myrtle Dr		
Oak Pl, (Udd.) G71	94	CS38
Oak Pl, (E.Kil.) G75	135	BX55
Oak Pl, Coat. ML5	75	CY32
Oakridge Cres, Pais. PA3	61	AR32
Oakridge Rd, (Baill.) G69	73	CQ31
Oak Rd, (Cumb.) G67	23	DG9
Oak Rd, Clyde. G81	26	AV16
Oak Rd, Pais. PA2	83	AW36

Oaks, The, John. PA5	79	AG35
Oakshaw Brae, Pais. PA1	62	AT32
Oakshawhead, Pais. PA1	62	AT32
Oakshaw St E, Pais. PA1	62	AT32
Oakshaw St W, Pais. PA1	62	AT32
Oakside Pl, Ham. ML3	140	CT54
off Chriss Av		
Oak St, G2	4	BQ30
Oaktree Gdns, G45	104	BV41
Oakwood Av, Pais. PA2	81	AR36
Oakwood Cres, G34	72	CM28
Oakwood Dr, G34	72	CM29
Oakwood Dr, (Newt. M.) G77	117	BH49
Oakwood Dr, Coat. ML5	74	CT32
off Rowanwood Cres		
Oak Wynd, (Camb.) G72	107	CH42
Oates Gdns, Moth. ML1	128	DD49
Oatfield St, G21	51	BX25
Oban Ct, G20	49	BN25
off Kelvinside Gdns		
Oban Dr, G20	49	BN25
Oban La, G20	49	BN25
Observatory La, G12	48	BM26
off Observatory Rd		
Observatory Rd, G12	48	BL26
Ochel Path, (Chap.) Air. ML6	97	DH36
Ochil Dr, (Barr.) G78	99	AX44
Ochil Dr, Pais. PA2	82	AU37
Ochil Pl, G32	90	CC33
Ochil Rd, (Bears.) G61	10	BD14
Ochil Rd, (Bishop.) G64	33	BY20
Ochil Rd, Renf. PA4	63	AX28
Ochil St, G32	90	CC33
Ochil St, Wis. ML2	129	DH49
Ochiltree Av, G13	47	BH22
Ochiltree Dr, Ham. ML3	139	CN52
Ochil Vw, (Udd.) G71	93	CQ37
Odense Ct, (E.Kil.) G75	136	CA55
Ogilvie Ct, Air. ML6	77	DG29
off Station Rd		
Ogilvie Pl, G31	89	BZ33
Ogilvie St, G31	89	BZ33
Old Aisle Rd, G66	17	CG14
Old Avon Rd, Ham. ML3	141	CW51
Old Biggar Rd, (Chap.) Air. ML6	97	DH37
Old Biggar Rd, (Riggend) Air. ML6	40	DD20
Old Bore Rd, Air. ML6	77	DF29
Old Bothwell Rd, (Both.) G71	109	CR44
Old Castle Gdns, G44	103	BR39
Old Castle Rd, G44	103	BR39
Old Ch Gdns, (Baill.) G69	73	CQ32
Old Coach Rd, (E.Kil.) G74	122	CB50
Old Cotts, Pais. PA2	83	AY37
off Grahamston Rd		
Old Dalmarnock Rd, G40	88	BV33
Old Dalnottar Rd, (Old Kil.) G60	25	AR16
Old Dullatur Rd, (Dullatur) G68	9	CZ7
Old Dumbarton Rd, G3	66	BL28
Old Edinburgh Rd, (Udd.) G71	93	CN36
Old Edinburgh Rd, Bell. ML4	93	CQ38
Old Fm La, (Bears.) G61	47	BH21
Old Fm Rd, Pais. PA2	83	AZ36
Old Ferry Rd, Ersk. PA8	25	AQ17
Old Gartloch Rd, (Gart.) G69	55	CP25
Old Glasgow Rd, (Udd.) G71	92	CM37
Old Govan Rd, Renf. PA4	46	BB26
Old Greenock Rd, Bish. PA7	24	AK18
Old Greenock Rd, Ersk. PA8	24	AN20
Old Greenock Rd, (Inch.) Renf. PA4	44	AT22
Oldhall Rd, Pais. PA1	63	AY32
Old Humbie Rd, (Newt. M.) G77	131	BG51
Old Manse Rd, G32	91	CF33
Old Manse Rd, Wis. ML2	143	DG53
Old Mill Ct, (Dunt.) Clyde. G81	27	AW16
Old Mill Pk Ind Est, (Kirk.) G66	17	CE12
Old Mill Rd, (Both.) G71	109	CQ44
Old Mill Rd, (Udd.) G71	109	CP40
Old Mill Rd, (Camb.) G72	107	CF39
Old Mill Rd, (E.Kil.) G74	136	CB51
Old Mill Rd, Clyde. G81	27	AW15
Old Mill Rd, Pais. PA2	81	AR34
Old Mill Vw, (Kilsyth) G65	20	CV9
Old Monkland Rd, Coat. ML5	94	CT34
Old Playfield Rd, (Carm.) G76	120	BT45
Old Quarry Rd, (Cumb.) G68	38	CT16
Old Rd, (Elder.) John. PA5	80	AL34
Old Rutherglen Rd, G5	88	BS33
Old Sch Ct, Coat. ML5	95	CW33
Old Shettleston Rd, G32	70	CC32
Old Sneddon St, Pais. PA3	62	AU32
Old Stable Row, Coat. ML5	75	CX30
Old Sta Ct, (Both.) G71	109	CQ43
Old St, Clyde. G81	26	AV15
Old Union St, Air. ML6	76	DD30
Old Vic Ct, (E.Kil.) G74	122	CD49
Old Wd Rd, (Baill.) G69	92	CJ34
Old Wynd, G1	5	BS31
Olifard Av, (Both.) G71	109	CR42
Oliphant Ct, Pais. PA2	81	AP37
off Heriot Av		
Oliphant Cres, (Clark.) G76	119	BN48
Oliphant Cres, Pais. PA2	81	AN37
Oliphant Oval, Pais. PA2	81	AN37
off Bothwell Pl		
Olive Bk, (Udd.) G71	94	CS36
Olive Ct, Moth. ML1	112	DD40
off Poplar Pl		
Olive St, G33	51	BZ25
Olympia, (E.Kil.) G74	136	CB53
off The Plaza Shop Cen		
Olympia Arc, (E.Kil.) G74	136	CB53
off The Plaza Shop Cen		
Olympia Ct, (E.Kil.) G74	136	CB53
off The Plaza Shop Cen		
Olympia St, G40	68	BV32
Olympia Way, (E.Kil.) G74	136	CB53
off The Plaza Shop Cen		
O'Neill Av, (Bishop.) G64	51	BX21
Onslow, (E.Kil.) G75	135	BY54
Onslow Dr, G31	69	BW30
Onslow Rd, Clyde. G81	27	AY19
Onslow Sq, G31	69	BW30
Ontario Pk, (E.Kil.) G75	135	BX52
Ontario Pl, (E.Kil.) G75	135	BX52
Onyx St, Bell. ML4	111	CW41
Oran Gdns, G20	49	BN24
Oran Gate, G20	49	BN24
Oran Pl, G20	49	BN25
Oran St, G20	49	BN24
Orbiston Dr, Moth. ML1	128	DC48
off Orbiston St		
Orbiston Dr, Bell. ML4	111	CX41
Orbiston Gdns, G32	70	CC32
Orbiston Rd, Bell. ML4	110	CV41
Orbiston Sq, Bell. ML4	110	CV42
off Busby Rd		
Orbiston St, Moth. ML1	128	DC48
Orcades Dr, G44	103	BR41
Orchard Av, (Both.) G71	109	CR44
Orchard Brae, (Lenz.) G66	35	CG17
off Lindsaybeg Rd		
Orchard Ct, G32	90	CD37
Orchard Ct, (Thornlie.) G46	102	BJ42
Orchard Ct, Renf. PA4	45	AZ25
Orchard Dr, (Giff.) G46	102	BK42
Orchard Dr, (Blan.) G72	124	CL45
Orchard Dr, (Ruther.) G73	88	BV37
Orchardfield, (Lenz.) G66	35	CG17
Orchard Gate, Lark. ML9	144	DC59
Orchard Grn, (E.Kil.) G74	122	CD49
Orchard Gro, (Giff.) G46	102	BK41
Orchard Gro, Coat. ML5	75	CX31
Orchard Pk, (Giff.) G46	102	BL42
Orchard Pk Av, (Giff.) G46	102	BJ41
Orchard Pl, (Kirk) G66	18	CJ14
Orchard Pl, Bell. ML4	110	CV42
Orchard Pl, Ham. ML3	126	CT50
Orchard St, (Baill.) G69	91	CH34
Orchard St, Ham. ML3	126	CT50
Orchard St, Moth. ML1	127	CZ46
Orchard St, Pais. PA1	82	AU33
Orchard St, Renf. PA4	45	AZ25
Orchardton Rd, (Cumb.) G68	20	CT14
Orchardton Wds Ind Pk, (Cumb.) G68	20	CS13
Orchy Av, (Clark.) G76	103	BP44
Orchy Ct, Clyde. G81	27	AY16
Orchy Cres, (Bears.) G61	29	BF19
Orchy Cres, Air. ML6	77	DE32
Orchy Cres, Pais. PA2	81	AP36
Orchy Dr, (Clark.) G76	103	BP44
Orchy Gdns, (Clark.) G76	103	BP44
Orchy St, G44	103	BQ39
Orchy Ter, (E.Kil.) G74	136	CC52
Orefield Pl, (E.Kil.) G74	122	CA50
Oregon Pl, G5	88	BS33
Orion Pl, Bell. ML4	112	DA40
Orion Way, (Camb.) G72	106	CC39
Orkney Pl, G51	66	BJ30
off Orkney St		
Orkney St, G51	66	BK30
Orlando, (E.Kil.) G74	123	CE48
Orleans Av, G14	47	BG26
Orleans La, G14	47	BG26
Orlington Ct, Coat. ML5	74	CV29
off Gilmour Pl		
Ormiston Av, G14	47	BE25
Ormiston Dr, Ham. ML3	140	CS53
Ormiston La, G14	47	BE25
off Ormiston Av		
Ormiston La N, G14	47	BE25
off Ormiston Av		
Ormiston La S, G14	47	BE25
off Ormiston Av		
Ormonde Av, G44	103	BP42
Ormonde Ct, G44	103	BN42
Ormonde Cres, G44	103	BP42
Ormonde Dr, G44	103	BP42
Ornsay St, G22	50	BT22
Oronsay Ct, (Old Kil.) G60	26	AS15
Oronsay Cres, (Old Kil.) G60	26	AS15
Oronsay Cres, (Bears.) G61	30	BK18
Oronsay Gdns, (Old Kil.) G60	26	AS15
Oronsay Pl, (Old Kil.) G60	26	AS15
Oronsay Sq, (Old Kil.) G60	26	AS15
Orr Sq, Pais. PA1	62	AU32
Orr St, G40	68	BV32
Orr St, Pais. PA1	62	AT32
Orr St, Pais. PA2	82	AU34
Orr Ter, (Neil.) G78	114	AS47

Orton Pl, G51 66 BJ31
Osborne Cres, (Thornton.) G74 119 BR50
Osborne St, G1 5 BS31
Osborne St, Clyde. G81 27 AW18
Osborne Vil, G44 103 BQ40
  off Holmhead Rd
Osprey Dr, (Udd.) G71 93 CQ38
Ossian Av, Pais. PA1 64 BB32
Ossian Rd, G43 103 BN39
Oswald St, G1 4 BR31
Oswald Wk, (Miln.) G62 12 BL13
Otago La, G12 67 BN27
Otago La N, G12 67 BN27
  off Otago St
Otago Pk, (E.Kil.) G75 135 BW52
Otago St, G12 67 BN27
Othello, (E.Kil.) G74 122 CD48
Ottawa Cres, Clyde. G81 26 AT17
Otterburn Dr, (Giff.) G46 102 BL43
Otterswick Pl, G33 71 CE27
Oval, The (Clark.) G76 103 BP44
Oval, The (Glenb.) Coat. ML5 56 CS23
Overbrae Gdns, G15 28 BB16
Overbrae Pl, G15 28 BB16
Overdale Av, G42 87 BP37
Overdale Gdns, G42 87 BP37
Overdale St, G42 87 BP37
Overdale Vil, G42 87 BP37
  off Overdale St
Overjohnstone Dr, Wis. ML2 129 DE49
Overlea Av, (Ruther.) G73 105 BZ39
Overlee Rd, (Clark.) G76 119 BN46
Overnewton Pl, G3 66 BM29
  off Kelvinhaugh St
Overnewton Sq, G3 66 BM28
  off Blackie St
Overnewton St, G3 66 BM28
Overton Cres, John. PA5 80 AK35
Overton Rd, (Camb.) G72 107 CF41
Overton Rd, John. PA5 80 AJ35
Overton St, (Camb.) G72 107 CF41
Overtoun Ct, Clyde. G81 26 AU18
  off Dunswin Av
Overtoun Dr, (Ruther.) G73 89 BW38
Overtoun Dr, Clyde. G81 26 AV17
Overtoun Rd, Clyde. G81 26 AU17
Overtown Av, G53 100 BC39
Overtown Pl, G31 69 BW32
Overtown St, G31 69 BW32
Overwood Dr, G44 104 BS39
Owen Av, (E.Kil.) G75 135 BZ54
Owendale Av, Bell. ML4 95 CX38
Owen Pk, (E.Kil.) G75 135 BY54
Owen St, Moth. ML1 128 DA45
O'Wood Av, Moth. ML1 112 DD39
Oxford Dr, (Linw.) Pais. PA3 60 AK31
Oxford La, G5 67 BR32
Oxford La, Renf. PA4 45 AY26
Oxford Rd, Renf. PA4 45 AY26
Oxford St, G5 4 BR31
Oxford St, (Kirk.) G66 17 CE13
Oxford St, Coat. ML5 74 CV31
Oxgang Pl, (Kirk.) G66 17 CG14
Oxton Dr, G52 64 BD32

P

Pacific Dr, G51 66 BL31
Pacific Quay, G51 66 BM30
Paddock, The (Clark.) G76 119 BQ48
Paddock, The, Ham. ML3 126 CT47

Paddock St, Coat. ML5 95 CZ33
Paidmyre Cres, (Newt. M.) G77 117 BF50
Paidmyre Gdns, (Newt. M.) 117 BF50
  G77
Paidmyre Rd, (Newt. M.) G77 117 BE50
Paisley Rd, G5 4 BQ31
Paisley Rd, (Barr.) G78 99 AX40
Paisley Rd, Renf. PA4 63 AX28
Paisley Rd W, G51 66 BL32
Paisley Rd W, G52 66 BJ32
Palacecraig St, Coat. ML5 95 CW34
Palace Grds Rd, Ham. ML3 126 CV49
Paladin Av, G13 46 BD21
Palermo St, G21 50 BU25
  off Atlas Rd
Palladium Pl, G14 47 BF26
  off Dumbarton Rd
Palmer Av, G13 29 BF20
Palmerston, (E.Kil.) G75 135 BW54
Palmerston Pl, G3 66 BM29
  off Kelvinhaugh St
Palmerston Pl, John. PA5 79 AE38
Palm Pl, (Udd.) G71 93 CR36
Pandora Way, (Udd.) G71 93 CQ38
Pankhurst Pl, (E.Kil.) G74 136 CB51
Panmure Cl, G22 49 BQ25
Panmure St, G20 49 BQ25
Park Av, G3 67 BP27
Park Av, (Miln.) G62 12 BJ12
Park Av, (Bishop.) G64 33 BW18
Park Av, (Kilsyth) G65 19 CN9
Park Av, (Kirk.) G66 17 CE13
Park Av, (Barr.) G78 99 AX44
Park Av, (Elder.) John. PA5 80 AL35
Park Av, Moth. ML1 112 DC40
Park Av, Pais. PA2 82 AS36
Park Bk, Ersk. PA8 25 AR20
Park Brae, Ersk. PA8 44 AS21
Parkbrae Gdns, G20 49 BQ23
Parkbrae Pl, G20 49 BQ23
Parkburn Av, (Kirk.) G66 16 CD14
Parkburn Ind Est, Ham. ML3 125 CQ47
Parkburn Rd, (Kilsyth) G65 7 CT4
Park Circ, G3 67 BN28
Park Circ La, G3 67 BN28
Park Circ Pl, G3 4 BP28
Park Ct, (Giff.) G46 102 BL43
Park Ct, (Bishop.) G64 33 BX18
Park Ct, Clyde. G81 26 AU17
Park Cres, (Bears.) G61 28 BD16
Park Cres, (Bishop.) G64 33 BW18
Park Cres, (Torr.) G64 15 BY12
Park Cres, (Blan.) G72 124 CL47
Park Cres, (Eagle.) G76 133 BN56
Park Cres, Air. ML6 76 DA29
Park Cres, (Inch.) Renf. PA4 44 AS22
Park Dr, G3 67 BN27
Park Dr, (Ruther.) G73 89 BW38
Park Dr, (Thornton.) G74 120 BS50
Park Dr, Bell. ML4 111 CW41
Park Dr, Ersk. PA8 44 AS21
Park Dr, Ham. ML3 141 CY52
Parker Pl, (Kilsyth) G65 7 CT5
Parker Pl, Lark. ML9 144 DD57
Parker St, G14 65 BG27
  off Dumbarton Rd
Parkfield, (E.Kil.) G75 136 CA56
Parkfoot St, (Kilsyth) G65 7 CT4
Park Gdns, G3 67 BN28
Park Gdns, (Kilb.) John. PA10 78 AD33
Park Gdns La, G3 67 BN28
Park Gate, G3 67 BN28

Park Gate, Ersk. PA8 43 AR21
Park Gate Pl, Bell. ML4 110 CV40
Park Glade, Ersk. PA8 43 AR21
Park Grn, Ersk. PA8 43 AR21
Park Gro, Ersk. PA8 44 AS21
Parkgrove Av, (Giff.) G46 102 BM42
Parkgrove Ct, (Giff.) G46 102 BM42
Parkgrove Ter, G3 67 BN28
Parkgrove Ter La, G3 67 BN28
  off Derby St
Parkhall Rd, Clyde. G81 26 AV17
Parkhall St, (E.Kil.) G74 136 CB51
Parkhall Ter, Clyde. G81 26 AV16
Parkhead Cross, G31 69 BZ32
Parkhead La, Air. ML6 76 DC29
  off Parkhead St
Parkhead St, Air. ML6 76 DC29
Parkhead St, Moth. ML1 128 DB48
Parkhill, Ersk. PA8 25 AR20
Parkhill Dr, (Ruther.) G73 89 BW38
Parkhill Rd, G43 86 BM37
Park Holdings, Ersk. PA8 43 AR22
Parkhouse Path, G53 100 BD41
  off Woodfoot Quad
Parkhouse Rd, G53 100 BB41
Parkhouse Rd, (Barr.) G78 100 BB41
Parkinch, Ersk. PA8 44 AS21
Parklands Rd, G44 103 BP42
Parklands Vw, G53 84 BB35
Park La, (Kilsyth) G65 7 CT5
Park La, (Blan.) G72 124 CM45
Parklea, (Bishop.) G64 32 BU18
  off Westfields
Parklee Dr, (Carm.) G76 120 BU46
Park Moor, Ersk. PA8 43 AR21
Parkneuk Rd, G43 102 BL41
Parkneuk Rd, (Blan.) G72 138 CJ51
Park Neuk St, Moth. ML1 128 DA45
Parknook Way, Lark. ML9 144 DD57
  off Muirshot Rd
Park Pl, (Thornton.) G74 120 BS50
Park Pl, Bell. ML4 110 CU42
Park Pl, Coat. ML5 95 CZ33
  off Kirkton Cres
Park Pl, John. PA5 79 AH35
  off Park Rd
Park Quad, G3 67 BN28
Park Quad, Wis. ML2 143 DG52
  off Montgomery Cres
Park Ridge, Ersk. PA8 25 AR20
Park Rd, G4 67 BN27
Park Rd, G32 91 CE37
Park Rd, (Giff.) G46 102 BL43
Park Rd, (Miln.) G62 12 BJ12
Park Rd, (Bishop.) G64 33 BW19
Park Rd, (Baill.) G69 73 CP32
Park Rd, (Muir.) G69 54 CL21
Park Rd, (Calder.) Air. ML6 96 DD35
Park Rd, Bell. ML4 111 CW41
Park Rd, Clyde. G81 26 AV17
Park Rd, Ham. ML3 126 CT50
Park Rd, John. PA5 79 AH35
Park Rd, Moth. ML1 112 DD43
Park Rd, Pais. PA2 82 AT36
Park Rd, (Inch.) Renf. PA4 44 AT22
Parksail, Ersk. PA8 44 AS22
Parksail Dr, Ersk. PA8 44 AS21
Parkside Gdns, G20 49 BQ23
Parkside Pl, G20 49 BQ23
Parkside Rd, Moth. ML1 127 CX47
Park St, (Kirk.) G66 18 CK14

Name	Page	Grid
Park St, Air. ML6	76	DA29
Park St, Coat. ML5	75	CX29
Park St, Moth. ML1	128	DA46
Park St, (New Stev.) Moth. ML1	112	DB42
Park St S, G3	67	BN28
Parks Vw, Ham. ML3	140	CT55
Park Ter, G3	67	BN28
Park Ter, (Giff.) G46	102	BL43
Park Ter, (E.Kil.) G74	136	CA52
Park Ter E La, G3	67	BN28
Park Ter La, G3	67	BN28
Park Top, Ersk. PA8	26	AS20
Parkvale Av, Ersk. PA8	26	AT20
Parkvale Cres, Ersk. PA8	44	AT21
Parkvale Dr, Ersk. PA8	44	AT21
Parkvale Gdns, Ersk. PA8	26	AT20
Parkvale Pl, Ersk. PA8	26	AT20
Parkvale Way, Ersk. PA8	44	AT21
Park Vw, (Kilb.) John. PA10	78	AC33
Park Vw, Lark. ML9	144	DD59
Park Vw, Pais. PA2	82	AT35
Parkview Av, (Kirk.) G66	17	CF14
Parkview Ct, (Kirk.) G66	17	CF14
Parkview Dr, (Stepps) G33	53	CG23
Parkview Dr, Coat. ML5	74	CU30
Parkville Dr, (Blan.) G72	125	CN47
Parkville Rd, Bell. ML4	95	CY38
off Rosebank Rd		
Park Way, G32	91	CE37
off Park Rd		
Park Way, (Cumb.) G67	22	DD9
Parkway Pl, Coat. ML5	74	CU32
Park Winding, Ersk. PA8	44	AS21
Park Wd, Ersk. PA8	26	AS20
Parnell St, Air. ML6	76	DB32
Parnie St, G1	5	BS31
Parry Ter, (E.Kil.) G75	135	BX52
Parsonage Row, G1	5	BT30
Parsonage Sq, G4	5	BT30
Parson St, G4	5	BU29
Partick Br St, G11	66	BL27
Partickhill Av, G11	66	BK27
Partickhill Ct, G11	48	BK26
Partickhill Rd, G11	48	BK26
Patchy Pk, Lark. ML9	144	DC61
Paterson Pl, (Bears.) G61	11	BE13
Paterson's Laun, (Torr.) G64	14	BU14
Paterson St, G5	67	BQ32
Paterson St, Moth. ML1	128	DA46
Paterson Ter, (E.Kil.) G75	135	BZ54
Pathhead Gdns, G33	52	CB23
Pathhead Rd, (Carm.) G76	120	BT46
Patna Ct, Ham. ML3	139	CN52
off Ochiltree Dr		
Patna St, G40	89	BX34
Paton Ct, Wis. ML2	143	DF52
off Shaw Cres		
Paton St, G31	69	BX30
Patrickbank Cres, John. PA5	80	AM36
Patrickbank Gdns, John. PA5	80	AM36
Patrickbank Vw, John. PA5	80	AM36
Patrickbank Wynd, John. PA5	80	AM36
Patrick St, Pais. PA2	82	AV34
Patterton Dr, (Barr.) G78	99	AZ43
Pattison St, Clyde. G81	26	AU17
Paxton Ct, (E.Kil.) G74	122	CB49
off Canonbie Av		
Paxton Cres, (E.Kil.) G74	122	CB49
off Canonbie Av		
Payne St, G4	68	BS27
Peacock Av, Pais. PA2	81	AP35
Peacock Cross Ind Pk, Ham. ML3	126	CS49
Peacock Dr, Ham. ML3	126	CS49
Peebles Dr, Pais. PA2	81	AP34
Pearce La, G51	66	BJ29
off Pearce St		
Pearce St, G51	66	BJ29
Pearl Rd, Bell. ML4	111	CX42
off Sapphire Rd		
Pearson Dr, Renf. PA4	63	AZ27
Pearson Pl, (Linw.) Pais. PA3	60	AK32
Peathill Av, (Chry.) G69	36	CK20
Peathill St, G21	50	BS26
Peat Pl, G53	100	BC40
off Peat Rd		
Peat Rd, G53	100	BD39
Pedmyre La, (Carm.) G76	120	BS46
Peebles Dr, (Ruther.) G73	89	BZ38
Peebles Path, Coat. ML5	95	CZ34
Peel Av, Moth. ML1	128	DA49
Peel Glen Gdns, G15	28	BC16
Peel Glen Rd, G15	28	BC17
Peel Glen Rd, (Bears.) G61	28	BC15
Peel La, G11	66	BK27
Peel Pk Pl, (E.Kil.) G74	134	BV51
Peel Pl, (Both.) G71	109	CQ42
Peel Pl, Coat. ML5	74	CT32
Peel Rd, (Thornton.) G74	133	BR51
Peel St, G11	66	BK27
Peel Vw, Clyde. G81	27	AZ18
off Kirkoswald Dr		
Pegasus Av, Bell. ML4	112	DA40
Pegasus Rd, Pais. PA1	60	AM32
Peinchorran, Ersk. PA8	44	AS22
Peiter Pl, (Blan.) G72	124	CL46
off Burnbrae Rd		
Pembroke, (E.Kil.) G74	123	CF49
Pembroke St, G3	4	BP29
Pencaitland Dr, G32	90	CC34
Pencaitland Gro, G32	90	CC35
Pencaitland Pl, G23	31	BN20
Pendale Ri, G45	104	BT42
Pendeen Cres, G33	71	CG32
Pendeen Pl, G33	71	CH31
Pendeen Rd, G33	71	CG32
Pendicle Cres, (Bears.) G61	29	BF18
Pendicle Rd, (Bears.) G61	29	BF18
Pendle Ct, (Gart.) G69	55	CP23
Pendreich Cres, (E.Kil.) G75	135	BZ53
Penicuik St, G32	69	BZ31
Penilee Rd, G52	63	AZ29
Penilee Rd, Pais. PA1	64	BA32
Penilee Ter, G52	64	BA31
Peninver Dr, G51	65	BF29
Penman Av, (Ruther.) G73	88	BV37
Pennan, Ersk. PA8	25	AQ19
Pennan Pl, G14	46	BC24
Penneld Rd, G52	64	BB32
Pennine Gro, (Chap.) Air. ML6	97	DH36
Pennyroyal Ct, (E.Kil.) G74	121	BZ50
Penrith Av, (Giff.) G46	102	BL42
Penrith Dr, G12	48	BJ23
Penrith Pl, (E.Kil.) G75	134	BV55
Penryn Gdns, G32	91	CF34
Penston Rd, G33	71	CF29
Pentland Av, (Linw.) Pais. PA3	60	AJ31
Pentland Ct, (Barr.) G78	99	AX44
off Pentland Dr		
Pentland Ct, Air. ML6	76	DD27
Pentland Cres, Lark. ML9	142	DB56
Pentland Cres, Pais. PA2	82	AT37
Pentland Dr, (Bishop.) G64	33	BZ19
Pentland Dr, (Barr.) G78	99	AX44
Pentland Dr, Renf. PA4	63	AX29
Pentland Pl, (Bears.) G61	10	BD14
Pentland Rd, G43	102	BL40
Pentland Rd, (Chry.) G69	36	CM20
Pentland Rd, Wis. ML2	129	DG49
Penzance Way, (Chry.) G69	37	CN18
Peockland Gdns, John. PA5	80	AJ34
Peockland Pl, John. PA5	80	AJ34
off Thorn Brae		
Peploe Dr, (E.Kil.) G74	123	CF48
Percy Dr, (Giff.) G46	102	BL44
Percy Rd, Renf. PA4	63	AW29
Percy St, G51	66	BM31
off Clifford St		
Percy St, Lark. ML9	144	DC57
Perran Gdns, (Chry.) G69	37	CN19
Perth Av, Air. ML6	76	DC32
Perth Cres, Clyde. G81	26	AT16
Perth St, G3	4	BP30
off Argyle St		
Peter D Stirling Rd, (Kirk.) G66	17	CF12
Petersburn Pl, Air. ML6	77	DF31
off Petersburn Rd		
Petersburn Rd, Air. ML6	77	DE31
Petershill Ct, G21	51	BY25
Petershill Dr, G21	51	BX25
Petershill Pl, G21	51	BX25
Petershill Rd, G21	50	BV26
Peterson Dr, G13	46	BA21
Peterson Gdns, G13	46	BA21
Petition Pl, (Udd.) G71	109	CQ40
Pettigrew St, G32	70	CC32
Peveril Av, G41	86	BM36
Peveril Av, (Ruther.) G73	105	BY40
Peveril Ct, (Ruther.) G73	105	BY40
Pharonhill St, G31	70	CA32
off Quarrybrae St		
Philip Murray Rd, Bell. ML4	110	CT39
Philipshill Gate, (E.Kil.) G74	120	BU50
Philipshill Rd, (Clark.) G76	120	BU50
Phoenix Business Pk, Pais. PA1	61	AN32
Phoenix Ct, (E.Kil.) G74	123	CE48
off Bosworth Rd		
Phoenix Cres, (Strathclyde Bus. Pk.) Bell. ML4	94	CU37
Phoenix Ind Est, Pais. PA3	62	AU29
Phoenix Pk Ter, G4	67	BR27
off Corn St		
Phoenix Pl, (Elder.) John. PA5	80	AM34
Phoenix Pl, Moth. ML1	112	DC42
Phoenix Retail Pk, The, Pais. PA1	81	AN33
Phoenix Rd, G4	4	BQ28
off Great Western Rd		
Phoenix Rd, Bell. ML4	112	DA40
Piccadilly St, G3	4	BP30
Pickerstonhill, Moth. ML1	113	DG41
Picketlaw Dr, (Carm.) G76	120	BT46
Picketlaw Fm Rd, (Carm.) G76	120	BS46
Piershill St, G32	70	CB30
Pikeman Rd, G13	47	BE23
Pillans Ct, Ham. ML3	125	CQ
Pilmuir Av, G44	103	BF
Pilmuir Av, (Newt. M.) G77	130	B
Pilrig St, G32	70	
Pilton Rd, G15	28	
Pine Av, (Camb.) G72	107	
Pine Cl, (Cumb.) G67	23	
Pine Ct, (Cumb.) G67	2	

Name	Page	Grid
Pine Ct, (E.Kil.) G75	135	BX56
Pine Ct, Coat. ML5	94	CV33
off Ailsa Rd		
Pine Cres, (Cumb.) G67	23	DG9
Pine Cres, (E.Kil.) G75	135	BX56
Pine Cres, John. PA5	80	AJ36
Pine Gro, (Cumb.) G67	23	DG9
Pine Gro, (Baill.) G69	73	CQ31
Pine Gro, (Udd.) G71	93	CR37
Pinegrove, (Calder.) Air. ML6	96	DD35
Pinelands, (Bishop.) G64	33	BW17
Pine Pk, Ham. ML3	140	CU52
Pine Pl, G5	88	BS33
Pine Pl, (Cumb.) G67	23	DG9
Pine Quad, (Chap.) Air. ML6	97	DG34
Pine Rd, (Cumb.) G67	23	DG9
Pine Rd, Clyde. G81	26	AT17
Pine St, Air. ML6	77	DF30
Pine St, Pais. PA2	83	AW35
Pineview Ct, G15	28	BD18
Pinewood Av, (Kirk.) G66	34	CC16
Pinewood Ct, (Kirk.) G66	34	CC16
Pinewood Pl, (Kirk.) G66	34	CC16
Pinewood Sq, G15	28	BD17
Pinkerton Av, (Ruther.) G73	88	BU37
Pinkerton La, Renf. PA4	63	AZ28
Pinkston Dr, G21	68	BU27
Pinkston Rd, G4	50	BT26
Pinkston Rd, G21	50	BT26
Pinmore Path, G53	100	BB40
off Seamill St		
Pinmore Pl, G53	100	BB39
Pinmore St, G53	100	BB39
Pinwherry Dr, G33	52	CB23
Pinwherry Pl, (Both.) G71	109	CQ42
Piper Rd, Air. ML6	77	DE32
Pirnie Pl, (Kilsyth) G65	7	CT5
Pirnmill Av, Moth. ML1	127	CX46
Pitcairn Cres, (E.Kil.) G75	134	BV53
Pitcairn Gro, (E.Kil.) G75	135	BW53
Pitcairn Pl, (E.Kil.) G75	134	BV53
Pitcairn St, G31	90	CA33
Pitcairn Ter, Ham. ML3	125	CQ49
Pitcaple Dr, G43	102	BK39
Pitlochry Dr, G52	84	BD33
Pitlochry Dr, Lark. ML9	145	DE60
Pitmedden Rd, (Bishop.) G64	33	BZ19
Pitmilly Rd, G15	29	BE17
Pitreavie Ct, Ham. ML3	139	CR53
Pitreavie Pl, G33	71	CE27
Pit Rd, (Kirk.) G66	18	CK14
Pit Rd, (Bellshill Ind. Est.) Bell. ML4	110	CV39
Pitt St, G2	4	BQ30
Pladda Rd, Renf. PA4	63	AZ28
Pladda St, Moth. ML1	127	CX45
Plaintrees Ct, Pais. PA2	82	AU35
Plane Pl, (Udd.) G71	93	CR36
Planetree Pl, John. PA5	80	AJ36
Planetree Rd, Clyde. G81	27	AW17
Plantation Av, Moth. ML1	112	DD39
Plantation Pk Gdns, G51	66	BM32
off Clifford La		
...ntation Sq, G51	67	BN31
...t St, G31	69	BY31
...horn Dr, (E.Kil.) G74	136	CB52
...orn Rd, (E.Kil.) G74	136	CB52
...Avondale Av		
...St, G40	89	BW34
...p Cen, The (E.Kil.)	136	CB52
Pleaknowe Cres, (Chry.) G69	37	CN19
Pleamuir Pl, (Cumb.) G68	21	CY12
Plean St, G14	46	BC24
Pleasance La, G43	86	BL38
off Pleasance St		
Pleasance St, G43	86	BL37
Pleasance Way, G43	86	BM38
Plover Dr, (E.Kil.) G75	135	BW56
Plover Pl, John. PA5	79	AE38
Pochard Way, (Strathclyde Bus. Pk.) Bell. ML4	94	CV37
Poets Vw, (Kirk.) G66	17	CH14
Pointhouse Rd, G3	67	BN30
Polbae Cres, (Eagle.) G76	132	BM56
Pollock Av, (Eagle.) G76	133	BN56
Pollock Av, (Hillhouse Ind. Est.) Ham. ML3	125	CQ49
Pollock Rd, (Bears.) G61	30	BJ18
Pollock Rd, (Newt. M.) G77	117	BE49
Pollock St, Moth. ML1	128	DA46
Pollok Av, G43	86	BK37
Pollok Castle Est, (Newt. M.) G77	116	BC47
Pollok Dr, (Bishop.) G64	32	BU20
Pollok La, (E.Kil.) G74	122	CD50
Pollok Pl, (E.Kil.) G74	122	CD50
Pollokshaws Rd, G41	87	BQ35
Pollokshaws Rd, G43	86	BK38
Pollokshields Sq, G41	87	BP35
off Glencairn Dr		
Pollok Shop Cen, G53	85	BE38
Polmadie Av, G5	88	BT35
Polmadie Ind Est, G5	88	BU35
Polmadie Rd, G5	88	BU34
Polmadie Rd, G42	88	BS36
Polmadie St, G42	88	BS36
Polnoon Av, G13	46	BC23
Polnoon Dr, (Eagle.) G76	133	BN56
Polquhap Ct, G53	84	BC37
Polquhap Gdns, G53	84	BC37
Polquhap Pl, G53	84	BC37
Polquhap Rd, G53	84	BC37
Polson Dr, John. PA5	79	AG35
Polsons Cres, Pais. PA2	82	AT35
Polwarth La, G12	48	BK25
Polwarth St, G12	48	BK26
Pomona Pl, Ham. ML3	139	CP51
off Gilmour Dr		
Poplar Av, G11	47	BH25
off Crow Rd		
Poplar Av, (Newt. M.) G77	117	BG50
Poplar Av, Bish. PA7	24	AK19
Poplar Av, John. PA5	79	AH36
Poplar Ct, Coat. ML5	94	CV33
off Ailsa Rd		
Poplar Cres, Bish. PA7	24	AK19
Poplar Dr, (Kirk.) G66	34	CC16
Poplar Dr, Clyde. G81	26	AV16
Poplar Gdns, (E.Kil.) G75	135	BY56
Poplar Pl, (Udd.) G71	94	CT37
off Laburnum Rd		
Poplar Pl, (Blan.) G72	108	CL44
Poplar Pl, (Holytown) Moth. ML1	112	DD41
Poplar Rd, G41	66	BK32
off Urrdale Rd		
Poplars, The (Bears.) G61	11	BF13
Poplar St, Air. ML6	77	DF30
Poplar Way, (Camb.) G72	107	CH42
Poplin St, G40	88	BV34
Porchester St, G33	71	CF27
Portal Rd, G13	47	BE21
Port Dundas Ind Est, G4	68	BS27
Port Dundas Pl, G2	5	BS29
Port Dundas Rd, G4	4	BR28
Port Dundas Trd Centres, G4	68	BS27
Porterfield Rd, Renf. PA4	45	AX26
Porters La, (Chap.) Air. ML6	97	DF35
off Aitkenhead Rd		
Porter St, G51	66	BL32
Porters Well, (Udd.) G71	109	CN40
Portessie, Ersk. PA8	25	AQ19
Portland Pk, Ham. ML3	140	CU51
Portland Pl, Ham. ML3	140	CU51
Portland Rd, (Cumb.) G68	9	DB8
Portland Sq, Ham. ML3	140	CU51
off Portland Pl		
Portland St, Coat. ML5	75	CX29
Portland St, Pais. PA2	83	AX34
Portland Wynd, Lark. ML9	144	DD57
off Muirshot Rd		
Portlethen, Ersk. PA8	25	AQ19
Portman Pl, G12	67	BN27
off Cowan St		
Portman St, G41	67	BN32
Portmarnock Dr, G23	49	BN21
off Fairhaven Rd		
Portreath Rd, (Chry.) G69	37	CP18
Portree Av, Coat. ML5	94	CU33
Portree Pl, G15	28	BA17
Portsoy, Ersk. PA8	25	AQ19
Portsoy Av, G13	46	BB21
off Wyvis Av		
Portsoy Pl, G13	46	BA21
Port St, G3	4	BP29
Portugal La, G5	67	BR32
off Bedford St		
Portugal St, G5	67	BR32
Portwell, Ham. ML3	126	CU49
off Church St		
Possil Cross, G22	50	BS26
Possil Rd, G4	67	BR27
Postgate, Ham. ML3	126	CU49
Potassels Rd, (Muir.) G69	54	CL22
Potrail Pl, Ham. ML3	125	CQ50
Potter Cl, G32	90	CA34
Potter Gro, G32	90	CA34
Potterhill Av, Pais. PA2	82	AU37
Potterhill Rd, G53	84	BD35
Potter Path, G32	90	CA34
off Rattray St		
Potter Pl, G32	90	CA34
Potter St, G32	90	CA34
Potts Way, Moth. ML1	111	CY44
Powbrone, (E.Kil.) G75	136	CA56
Powburn Cres, (Udd.) G71	92	CM38
Powfoot St, G31	69	BZ32
Powforth Cl, Lark. ML9	144	DA58
Powrie St, G33	53	CE26
Prentice La, (Udd.) G71	93	CQ37
Prentice Rd, Moth. ML1	127	CX48
Prestonfield, (Miln.) G62	11	BG12
Preston Pl, G42	87	BR35
Preston St, G42	87	BR35
Prestwick Ct, (Cumb.) G68	22	DB9
Prestwick Pl, (Newt. M.) G77	118	BJ49
Prestwick St, G53	100	BC39
Priestfield Ind Est, (Blan.) G72	124	CM48
Priestfield St, (Blan.) G72	124	CL47
Priesthill Av, G53	101	BE39
Priesthill Cres, G53	101	BE39
Priesthill Gdns, G53	101	BE39

Priesthill Rd, G53 100 BD39
Primrose Av, Bell. ML4 95 CW38
Primrose Av, Lark. ML9 144 DC60
Primrose Ct, G14 47 BF26
   off Dumbarton Rd
Primrose Cres, Moth. ML1 128 DB48
   off Gavin St
Primrose Pl, (Cumb.) G67 21 CX14
Primrose Pl, (Udd.) G71 94 CS37
Primrose St, G14 47 BE26
Prince Albert Rd, G12 48 BK26
Prince Edward St, G42 87 BQ35
Prince of Wales Gdns, G20 48 BL21
   off Crosbie St
Prince's Dock, G51 66 BL30
Princes Gdns, G12 48 BK26
Princes Gate, (Both.) G71 109 CN41
Princes Gate, (Ruther.) G73 89 BW37
Princes Mall, (E.Kil.) G74 136 CB52
   off The Plaza Shop Cen
Princes Pl, G12 48 BL26
Princess Anne Quad, Moth. 112 DB40
   ML1 off Woodhall Av
Princess Cres, Pais. PA1 63 AX32
Princess Dr, (Baill.) G69 73 CQ32
Princess Pk, (Erskine Hosp.) 24 AN17
   Bish. PA7
Princes Sq, G1 5 BS30
   off Buchanan St
Princes Sq, (E.Kil.) G74 136 CA52
   off The Plaza Shop Cen
Princes Sq, (Barr.) G78 99 AZ42
Princess Rd, Moth. ML1 112 DB41
Princes St, (Ruther.) G73 89 BW37
Princes St, Moth. ML1 128 DA45
Princes Ter, G12 48 BL26
Printers Land, (Clark.) G76 119 BQ47
   off Main St
Priorwood Ct, G13 47 BF23
Priorwood Gdns, G13 47 BE23
Priorwood Gate, (Newt. M.) 116 BC49
   G77
Priorwood Pl, G13 47 BF23
Priorwood Rd, (Newt. M.) G77 116 BC49
Priorwood Way, (Newt. M.) G77 116 BC49
Priory Av, Pais. PA3 63 AW30
Priory Dr, (Udd.) G71 92 CM38
Priory Pl, G13 47 BF22
Priory Pl, (Cumb.) G68 20 CU12
Priory Rd, G13 47 BF22
Priory St, (Blan.) G72 124 CM46
Priory Ter, Wis. ML2 143 DE51
Professors Sq, G12 66 BM27
Prosen St, G32 90 CB34
Prospect Av, (Udd.) G71 109 CN39
Prospect Av, (Camb.) G72 106 CB39
Prospect Ct, (Blan.) G72 124 CM48
Prospect Dr, (Ashgill) Lark. 145 DH61
   ML9
Prospecthill Circ, G42 88 BT36
Prospecthill Cres, G42 88 BU37
Prospecthill Dr, G42 88 BS37
Prospecthill Gro, G42 87 BQ37
Prospecthill Pl, G42 88 BU37
Prospecthill Rd, G42 87 BQ37
Prospecthill Sq, G42 88 BT37
Prospecthill Way, G42 87 BQ37
   off Prospecthill Gro
Prospect Rd, G43 86 BM37
Prospect Rd, (Dullatur) G68 8 CY7
Provand Hall Cres, (Baill.) G69 92 CK34

Provanhill St, G21 68 BV28
Provanmill Pl, G33 51 BZ26
   off Provanmill Rd
Provanmill Rd, G33 51 BZ26
Provan Rd, G33 69 BY28
Provan Wk, G34 71 CG28
Provost Cl, John. PA5 79 AH34
   off High St
Provost Driver Ct, Renf. PA4 63 AZ27
Provost Gate, Lark. ML9 144 DC58
Purdie, (E.Kil.) G74 123 CF48
Purdie St, Ham. ML3 125 CQ48
Purdon St, G11 66 BK27
Pyatshaw Rd, Lark. ML9 144 DD60

Q

Quadrant, The (Clark.) G76 119 BP45
Quadrant Rd, G43 103 BN40
Quadrant Shop Cen, Coat. ML5 75 CW30
Quarrelton Rd, John. PA5 79 AG35
Quarry Av, (Camb.) G72 107 CG42
Quarrybank, (Kilb.) John. PA10 79 AE35
Quarrybrae Av, (Clark.) G76 118 BM46
Quarrybrae Gdns, (Udd.) G71 110 CS39
   off Roman Way
Quarrybrae St, G31 69 BZ32
Quarry Dr, (Kirk.) G66 17 CH13
Quarryknowe, (Ruther.) G73 88 BV38
Quarryknowe Pl, Bell. ML4 110 CV42
Quarryknowe St, G31 70 CA32
Quarryknowe St, Clyde. G81 10 BA14
Quarry Pk, (E.Kil.) G75 136 CA53
Quarry Pl, (Camb.) G72 106 CA39
Quarry Pl, Ham. ML3 126 CU50
   off Quarry St
Quarry Rd, (E.Kil.) G75 135 BZ56
Quarry Rd, (Barr.) G78 99 AX41
Quarry Rd, Air. ML6 76 DC28
Quarry Rd, Lark. ML9 144 DC59
Quarry Rd, Pais. PA2 82 AV36
Quarryside St, (Glenm.) Air. 57 CZ25
   ML6
Quarry St, Coat. ML5 75 CZ30
Quarry St, Ham. ML3 126 CU50
Quarry St, John. PA5 79 AH34
Quarry St, Lark. ML9 144 DD60
Quarry St, Moth. ML1 112 DC41
Quarrywood Av, G21 51 BY25
Quarrywood Rd, G21 51 BZ25
Quay Rd, (Ruther.) G73 89 BW36
Quay Rd N, (Ruther.) G73 89 BW36
Quebec Dr, (E.Kil.) G75 135 BY52
Quebec Grn, (E.Kil.) G75 135 BY52
Quebec Ho, Clyde. G81 26 AT15
   off Perth Cres
Quebec Wynd, G32 91 CE37
Queen Elizabeth Av, G52 64 BA30
Queen Elizabeth Ct, Clyde. G81 27 AW18
Queen Elizabeth Ct, Moth. ML1 127 CZ46
   off Ladywell Rd
Queen Elizabeth Gdns, G5 88 BS33
Queen Elizabeth Sq, G5 88 BT33
Queen Margaret Ct, G20 49 BN25
   off Fergus Dr
Queen Margaret Dr, G12 48 BM26
Queen Margaret Dr, G20 48 BM26
Queen Margaret Rd, G20 49 BN25
Queen Mary Av, G42 87 BR36
Queen Mary Av, Clyde. G81 27 AZ19
Queen Mary Gdns, Clyde. G81 27 AW18

Queen Mary St, G40 88 BV33
Queens Av, (Camb.) G72 106 CD39
Queensbank Av, (Gart.) G69 55 CN22
Queensberry Av, (Bears.) G61 11 BG14
Queensberry Av, (Clark.) G76 119 BN46
Queensborough Gdns, G12 48 BJ25
Queensbury Av, G52 64 BB30
Queensby Av, (Baill.) G69 72 CK31
Queensby Dr, (Baill.) G69 72 CK31
Queensby Pl, (Baill.) G69 72 CL31
Queensby Rd, (Baill.) G69 72 CK31
Queens Ct, (Miln.) G62 12 BJ13
Queens Cres, G4 67 BP27
Queen's Cres, (Baill.) G69 73 CP32
Queens Cres, (Chap.) Air. ML6 97 DF34
Queens Cres, Bell. ML4 110 CV41
   off Hamilton Rd
Queens Cres, Moth. ML1 112 DB41
Queensdale Av, Lark. ML9 144 DD61
Queensdale Rd, Lark. ML9 144 DD61
Queens Dr, G42 87 BP35
Queens Dr, (Cumb.) G68 9 DB7
Queens Dr, Bish. PA7 24 AK17
Queens Dr, Ham. ML3 140 CT55
Queens Dr La, G42 87 BR36
Queensferry St, G5 88 BU35
Queens Gdns, G12 48 BL26
   off Victoria Cres Rd
Queens Gate, (Clark.) G76 119 BN45
Queens Gate La, G12 48 BL26
   off Victoria Cres Rd
Queens Gro, (Lenz.) G66 35 CE17
Queenside Cres, Ersk. PA8 25 AP20
Queensland Ct, G52 65 BE31
Queensland Dr, G52 65 BE31
Queensland Gdns, G52 65 BE31
Queensland La E, G52 65 BE31
Queensland La W, G52 65 BE31
Queenslie Ind Est, G33 71 CE29
Queenslie St, G33 69 BZ27
Queens Pk Av, G42 87 BR36
Queens Pl, G12 48 BL26
Queens Rd, (Elder.) John. PA5 80 AL35
Queens St, Ham. ML3 125 CQ48
Queen St, G1 5 BS30
Queen St, (Kirk.) G66 17 CE13
Queen St, (Ruther.) G73 89 BW37
Queen St, Ham. ML3 125 CQ48
Queen St, Moth. ML1 128 DA46
Queen St, Pais. PA1 82 AS33
Queen St, Renf. PA4 45 AZ26
Queen's Vw, (Torr.) G64 15 BX13
Queensway, (E.Kil.) G74 135 BY52
Queensway, (E.Kil.) G75 136 CA53
Queen Victoria Ct, G14 47 BE25
   off Queen Victoria Dr
Queen Victoria Dr, G13 47 BE24
Queen Victoria Dr, G14 47 BE25
Queen Victoria Gate, G13 47 BE24
Queen Victoria St, Air. ML6 76 DB30
Queenzieburn Ind Est, (Kilsyth) 6 CP6
   G65
Quendale Dr, G32 90 CB34
Quentin St, G41 87 BN36
Quinton Gdns, (Baill.) G69 72 CJ32

R

Raasay Cres, Air. ML6 77 DG31
Raasay Dr, Pais. PA2 82 AT38

Raasay Gdns, (Newt. M.) G77 116 BD48
Raasay Pl, G22 50 BS21
Raasay St, G22 50 BS21
Radnor St, G3 66 BM29
  off Argyle St
Radnor St, Clyde. G81 27 AW18
Raeberry St, G20 49 BP26
Raebog Cres, Air. ML6 76 DB27
Raebog Rd, (Glenm.) Air. ML6 58 DA25
Raeburn Av, (E.Kil.) G74 122 CD49
Raeburn Av, Pais. PA1 83 AW33
Raeburn Cres, Ham. ML3 125 CN50
Raeburn Pl, (E.Kil.) G74 122 CD49
Raeburn Wk, Bell. ML4 95 CW38
  off Hattonrigg Rd
Raeside Av, (Newt. M.) G77 117 BF50
Raeswood Dr, G53 84 BB37
Raeswood Gdns, G53 84 BB37
Raeswood Pl, G53 84 BC37
Raeswood Rd, G53 84 BB37
Raewell Cres, Bell. ML4 110 CV42
Rafford St, G51 66 BJ30
Raglan St, G4 67 BQ27
Railway Rd, Air. ML6 75 CZ30
Raith Av, G44 104 BT41
  off Croftfoot Rd
Raithburn Av, G45 104 BS42
Raithburn Rd, G45 104 BS42
Raith Dr, (Cumb.) G68 20 CT12
Raith Dr, Bell. ML4 111 CX41
Ralston Av, G52 84 BB33
Ralston Av, Pais. PA1 84 BB34
Ralston Ct, G52 84 BB33
Ralston Dr, G52 84 BB33
Ralston Path, G52 84 BB33
Ralston Pl, G52 84 BB33
Ralston Rd, (Bears.) G61 29 BG16
Ralston Rd, (Barr.) G78 99 AY43
Ralston St, Air. ML6 76 DA30
Ralston St, Pais. PA1 83 AW33
Ramillies Ct, Clyde. G81 27 AY19
Rampart Av, G13 46 BC21
Ramsay Av, John. PA5 79 AG36
Ramsay Ct, (Newt. M.) G77 117 BG50
Ramsay Cres, (Kilb.) John. 78 AD35
  PA10
Ramsay Hill, (E.Kil.) G74 122 CC50
Ramsay Ind Est, G66 16 CD12
Ramsay Pl, Coat. ML5 74 CS32
Ramsay Pl, John. PA5 79 AG36
Ramsay St, Clyde. G81 26 AV18
Ramsey Wynd, Bell. ML4 95 CX38
  off Kelvin Rd
Ram St, G32 70 CB32
Ranald Gdns, (Ruther.) G73 105 BZ42
Randolph Av, (Clark.) G76 103 BQ44
Randolph Dr, (Clark.) G76 103 BP44
Randolph Gdns, (Clark.) G76 103 BP44
Randolph Gate, G11 47 BH25
Randolph La, G11 47 BH26
Randolph Rd, G11 47 BH25
Ranfurly Dr, (Cumb.) G68 22 DA9
Ranfurly Rd, G52 64 BB32
Rangerhouse Rd, (E.Kil.) G75 136 CB56
Range Rd, Moth. ML1 128 DD49
Range Rd Ind Est, Moth. ML1 129 DE50
Range St, Moth. ML1 128 DD49
Rankin Cres, (Green.) Air. ML6 41 DH19
Rankin Dr, (Newt. M.) G77 117 BE47
Rankine Av, (E.Kil.) G75 136 CC54

Rankine Pl, (E.Kil.) G75 136 CC54
  off Rankine Av
Rankine Pl, John. PA5 79 AH34
Rankines La, Renf. PA4 45 AZ25
  off Manse St
Rankine St, John. PA5 79 AH34
Rankin Way, (Barr.) G78 99 AZ42
Rannoch Av, (Bishop.) G64 33 BX20
Rannoch Av, (Newt. M.) G77 117 BF46
Rannoch Av, Coat. ML5 74 CT28
Rannoch Av, Ham. ML3 139 CQ52
Rannoch Ct, (Cumb.) G67 39 CX15
Rannoch Ct, (Blan.) G72 125 CP48
  off Fortingall Rd
Rannoch Dr, (Bears.) G61 30 BJ19
Rannoch Dr, (Kirk.) G66 18 CK12
Rannoch Dr, (Cumb.) G67 39 CX15
Rannoch Dr, Renf. PA4 45 AY25
Rannoch Gdns, (Bishop.) G64 33 BY19
Rannoch Grn, (E.Kil.) G74 122 CB50
Rannoch La, (Chry.) G69 37 CQ19
  off Heathfield Av
Rannoch Pl, Pais. PA2 83 AW34
Rannoch Rd, (Udd.) G71 93 CN36
Rannoch Rd, Air. ML6 76 DB28
Rannoch Rd, John. PA5 79 AH36
Rannoch St, G44 103 BQ39
Rannoch Ter, Lark. ML9 145 DE60
Rannoch Way, (Both.) G71 109 CQ42
  off Appledore Cres
Raploch Av, G14 46 BD25
Raploch La, G14 46 BD25
Raploch Rd, Lark. ML9 144 DB59
Raploch St, Lark. ML9 144 DB58
Rashieburn, Ersk. PA8 25 AQ19
Rashieglen, Ersk. PA8 25 AQ19
Rashiehill, Ersk. PA8 25 AQ19
Rashielee Av, Ersk. PA8 25 AR19
Rashielee Rd, Ersk. PA8 25 AQ19
Rashiewood, Ersk. PA8 25 AR19
Rathlin St, G51 66 BJ29
Ratho Dr, G21 50 BU24
Ratho Dr, (Cumb.) G68 9 DA8
Ratho Pk, Ham. ML3 139 CR54
Rattray, Ersk. PA8 25 AU18
Rattray St, G32 90 CA34
Ravel Row, G31 69 BZ32
Ravelston Rd, (Bears.) G61 29 BG19
Ravelston St, G32 69 BZ31
Ravel Wynd, (Udd.) G71 93 CQ37
Ravenscliffe Dr, (Giff.) G46 102 BK42
Ravens Ct, (Bishop.) G64 50 BV21
  off Lennox Cres
Ravenscourt, (Thornton.) G74 134 BS51
Ravenscraig Av, Pais. PA2 82 AS35
Ravenscraig Ct, Bell. ML4 111 CX40
Ravenscraig Dr, G53 100 BD39
Ravenscraig Ter, G53 101 BE40
  off Ravenscraig Dr
Ravenshall Rd, G41 86 BL37
Ravenstone Dr, (Giff.) G46 102 BL40
Ravenswood Av, Pais. PA2 81 AN38
Ravenswood Dr, G41 86 BM36
Ravenswood Rd, (Baill.) G69 92 CL33
Rawyards Av, Air. ML6 76 DD27
Raymond Pl, (E.Kil.) G75 135 BY52
Rayne Pl, G15 28 BD17
Ream Av, Air. ML6 77 DH31
Reay Av, (E.Kil.) G74 135 BX51
Reay Gdns, (E.Kil.) G74 135 BX51
  off Reay Av

Redan St, G40 68 BV32
Redbrae Pl, (Kirk.) G66 17 CF12
Redbrae Rd, (Kirk.) G66 17 CG13
Red Br Ct, Coat. ML5 75 CW29
Redburn Av, (Giff.) G46 118 BK45
Redcastle Sq, G33 71 CF28
Redcliffe Dr, (E.Kil.) G75 135 BX53
Red Deer Rd, (E.Kil.) G75 135 BY53
  off Westwood Rd
Rederech Cres, Ham. ML3 139 CP51
Redford St, G33 69 BZ29
Redgate Pl, G14 46 BD25
Redgrave, (E.Kil.) G74 123 CE48
Redhill Rd, (Cumb.) G68 21 CZ10
Redholm Path, Lark. ML9 144 DD60
  off Fisher St
Redhurst Cres, Pais. PA2 81 AR38
Redhurst La, Pais. PA2 81 AR38
Redhurst Way, Pais. PA2 81 AR38
Redlands La, G12 48 BL25
Redlands Rd, G12 48 BL25
Redlands Ter, G12 48 BL25
  off Julian Av
Redlands Ter La, G12 48 BL25
Redlawood Pl, (Camb.) G72 108 CJ39
Redlawood Rd, (Camb.) G72 108 CJ39
Redmoss St, G22 49 BR24
Rednock St, G22 50 BS25
Redpath Dr, G52 65 BE32
Red Rd, G21 51 BX25
Red Rd Ct, G21 51 BX26
Redwood Av, (E.Kil.) G74 134 BU52
Redwood Ct, (E.Kil.) G74 134 BU52
Redwood Cres, (Udd.) G71 94 CS37
Redwood Cres, (Camb.) G72 107 CH42
Redwood Cres, (E.Kil.) G74 134 BU51
Redwood Cres, Bish. PA7 24 AL18
Redwood Dr, G21 51 BW26
Redwood Dr, (Thornton.) G74 134 BU51
Redwood Gro, Coat. ML5 75 CX31
Redwood Pl, (Kirk.) G66 34 CD16
  off Almond Dr
Redwood Pl, (Udd.) G71 94 CS37
  off Redwood Cres
Redwood Pl, (E.Kil.) G74 134 BU51
Redwood Rd, (Cumb.) G67 23 DF11
Redwood Rd, Moth. ML1 112 DD40
Redwood Way, (Camb.) G72 107 CH42
Reelick Av, G13 46 BA21
Reelick Quad, G13 46 BA21
Reema Rd, Bell. ML4 111 CX39
Reen Pl, (Both.) G71 109 CR41
Regency Ct, Ham. ML3 141 CW51
Regency Shop Cen, Ham. ML3 126 CV50
  off Princess Rd
Regency Way, Moth. ML1 112 DB41
Regent Dr, (Ruther.) G73 89 BW37
  off King St
Regent Moray St, G3 66 BM28
Regent Pk Sq, G41 87 BP35
Regent Pl, Clyde. G81 26 AU17
Regents Gate, (Both.) G71 108 CM41
Regent Sq, (Lenz.) G66 35 CE17
Regent St, (Kirk.) G66 17 CE13
Regent St, Clyde. G81 26 AU17
Regent St, Pais. PA1 63 AX32
Regent Way, Ham. ML3 126 CV50
Register Av, Bell. ML4 111 CW42
Register Rd, (Kilsyth) G65 7 CU5
Regwood St, G41 86 BM37
Reid Av, (Bears.) G61 30 BJ15

Name	Page	Grid
Reid Av, (Linw.) Pais. PA3	60	AK32
Reid Gro, Moth. ML1	128	DD49
Reidhouse St, G21	50	BV25
Reid Pl, G40	88	BV33
Reid St, G40	88	BV34
Reid St, (Ruther.) G73	89	BX37
Reid St, Air. ML6	76	DD28
Reid St, Coat. ML5	75	CX29
Reid St, Ham. ML3	125	CP48
Reidvale St, G31	68	BV31
Reith Dr, (E.Kil.) G75	135	BZ54
Remus Pl, Bell. ML4	112	DA40
Renfield La, G2	4	BR30
Renfield St, G2	4	BR30
Renfield St, Renf. PA4	45	AZ25
Renfrew Ct, G2	4	BR29
Renfrew La, G2	4	BR29
Renfrew Rd, G51	64	BD29
Renfrew Rd, Pais. PA3	62	AV32
Renfrew Rd, Renf. PA4	64	BC28
Renfrew St, G2	4	BR29
Renfrew St, G3	4	BQ28
Renfrew St, Coat. ML5	94	CS33
Rennie Pl, (E.Kil.) G74	121	BW50
Rennie Rd, (Kilsyth) G65	6	CQ4
Rennies Rd, (Inch.) Renf. PA4	44	AS22
Renshaw Dr, G52	64	BD31
Renshaw Rd, Bish. PA7	24	AK18
Renshaw Rd, (Elder.) John. PA5	80	AL35
Renton St, G4	5	BS28
Resipol St, (Stepps) G33	53	CG24
Reston Dr, G52	64	BD31
Reuther Av, (Ruther.) G73	89	BX38
Revoch Dr, G13	46	BC22
Reynolds Av, (E.Kil.) G75	136	CC54
Rhannan Rd, G44	103	BQ40
Rhannan Ter, G44	103	BQ40
Rhindhouse Pl, (Baill.) G69	72	CM32
Rhindhouse Rd, (Baill.) G69	72	CM32
Rhindmuir Av, (Baill.) G69	72	CL32
Rhindmuir Ct, (Baill.) G69	72	CL31
Rhindmuir Cres, (Baill.) G69	72	CM31
Rhindmuir Dr, (Baill.) G69	72	CL31
Rhindmuir Gdns, (Baill.) G69	72	CL31
Rhindmuir Gro, (Baill.) G69	72	CM31
Rhindmuir Path, (Baill.) G69	72	CM31
Rhindmuir Pl, (Baill.) G69	72	CM31
Rhindmuir Rd, (Baill.) G69	72	CL31
Rhindmuir Vw, (Baill.) G69	72	CM31
Rhindmuir Wynd, (Baill.) G69	72	CM31
Rhinds St, Coat. ML5	93	CR33
Rhinsdale Cres, (Baill.) G69	72	CL32
Rhumhor Gdns, (Kilb.) John. PA10 *off Ladysmith Av*	78	AD35
Rhymer St, G21	5	BU28
Rhymie Rd, G32	91	CF34
Rhynie Dr, G51	66	BK32
Riach Gdns, Moth. ML1	111	CY44
Ribblesdale, (E.Kil.) G74	121	BY50
Riccarton, (E.Kil.) G75	135	BX54
Riccarton St, G42	88	BS35
Riccartsbar Av, Pais. PA2	82	AS34
Rice Way, Moth. ML1	128	DD49
Richard St, G2 *off Cadzow St*	4	BQ30
Richard St, Renf. PA4	45	AZ25
Richmond Av, (Clark.) G76	119	BN46
Richmond Ct, (Ruther.) G73	89	BY37
Richmond Dr, (Bishop.) G64	33	BX17
Richmond Dr, (Camb.) G72	106	CA40
Richmond Dr, (Ruther.) G73	89	BY38
Richmond Dr, (Linw.) Pais. PA3	60	AJ30
Richmond Gdns, (Chry.) G69	36	CK20
Richmond Gro, (Ruther.) G73	89	BY38
Richmond Pl, (Ruther.) G73	89	BY37
Richmond St, G1	5	BT30
Richmond St, Clyde. G81	27	AY20
Riddell St, Clyde. G81	27	AY18
Riddell St, Coat. ML5	75	CY30
Riddon Av, G13	46	BA21
Riddon Av, Clyde. G81	46	BA21
Riddon Pl, G13	46	BA21
Riddrie Cres, G33	70	CA29
Riddrie Knowes, G33	70	CA29
Riddrievale Ct, G33	70	CA28
Riddrievale St, G33	70	CA28
Rigby St, G32	70	CA31
Rigg Pl, G33	71	CG30
Riggs, The (Miln.) G62	12	BJ10
Riggside Rd, G33	71	CE27
Righead Gate, (E.Kil.) G74 *off The Plaza Shop Cen*	136	CA52
Righead Ind Est, Bell. ML4	94	CT38
Righead Roundabout, (E.Kil.) G75	135	BZ52
Riglands Gate, Renf. PA4	45	AY25
Riglands Way, Renf. PA4	45	AY25
Riglaw Pl, G13	46	BC22
Rigmuir Rd, G51	65	BE30
Rimsdale St, G40	69	BW32
Ringford St, G21	50	BV26
Ripon Dr, G12	48	BJ23
Risk St, Clyde. G81	26	AV17
Ristol Rd, G13 *off Anniesland Rd*	46	BD24
Ritchie Cres, (Elder.) John. PA5	80	AL34
Ritchie Pk, John. PA5	80	AK34
Ritchie Pl, (Newt. M.) G77	117	BE49
Ritchie St, G5	87	BQ33
Ritchie St, Wis. ML2	129	DF50
Riverbank Dr, Bell. ML4	111	CY42
Riverbank St, G43	86	BL38
River Cart Wk, Pais. PA1 *off Marshall's La*	82	AU33
River Dr, (Inch.) Renf. PA4	44	AS24
Riverford Rd, G43	86	BL38
Riverford Rd, (Ruther.) G73	89	BY36
River Rd, G32 *off Mansionhouse Rd*	91	CE37
Riversdale La, G14	46	BC25
Riverside, (Miln.) G62	12	BJ11
Riverside Ct, G44	103	BP43
Riverside Gdns, (Clark.) G76	119	BP48
Riverside Ind Est, Clyde. G81	27	AW20
Riverside Pk, G44	103	BQ42
Riverside Pl, (Camb.) G72	107	CG39
Riverside Rd, G43	87	BN38
Riverside Rd, (Eagle.) G76	133	BN53
Riverside Rd, Lark. ML9	144	DC61
Riverside Ter, (Clark.) G76	119	BP48
Riverside Way, Ersk. PA8	25	AQ16
Riverton Dr, (E.Kil.) G75	135	BX53
Riverview Dr, G5	4	BQ31
Riverview Gdns, G5	4	BQ31
Riverview Pl, G5	4	BQ31
Roaden Av, Pais. PA2	81	AP38
Roaden Rd, Pais. PA2	81	AP38
Roadside Pl, (Green.) Air. ML6	59	DF21
Robb Ter, (Kirk.) G66	36	CJ15
Robert Burns Av, Clyde. G81	27	AY18
Robert Burns Av, Moth. ML1	113	DG41
Robert Burns Quad, Bell. ML4	110	CV40
Robert Dr, G51	66	BJ29
Robert Gilson Gdns, Coat. ML5	75	CX32
Roberton Av, G41	86	BL35
Roberton St, (Chap.) Air. ML6	97	DG34
Robert Smillie Cres, Lark. ML9	144	DC61
Robertson Av, Renf. PA4	45	AX26
Robertson Cl, Renf. PA4	45	AY26
Robertson Cres, (Neil.) G78	114	AT45
Robertson Dr, (E.Kil.) G74	136	CD51
Robertson Dr, Bell. ML4	111	CW41
Robertson Dr, Renf. PA4 *off Motherwell Rd*	45	AX26
Robertson La, G2	4	BQ30
Robertson's Gait, Pais. PA2	82	AU34
Robertson St, G2	4	BR30
Robertson St, (Barr.) G78	99	AX42
Robertson St, Air. ML6	76	DA29
Robertson St, Ham. ML3	125	CP48
Robertson Ter, (Baill.) G69 *off Edinburgh Rd*	72	CL32
Roberts Quad, Bell. ML4 *off Sapphire Rd*	111	CX42
Roberts St, Clyde. G81	26	AU18
Robert St, G51	66	BJ29
Robert Templeton Dr, (Camb.) G72	106	CD40
Robin Way, G32	91	CE37
Robroyston Av, G33	52	CA26
Robroyston Dr, G33	52	CA25
Robroyston Rd, G33	52	CA23
Robroyston Rd, (Bishop.) G64	34	CB20
Robshill Ct, (Newt. M.) G77 *off Capelrig Rd*	117	BF49
Robslee Cres, (Giff.) G46	102	BJ42
Robslee Dr, (Giff.) G46	102	BK42
Robslee Rd, (Thornlie.) G46	102	BJ43
Robson Gro, G42	87	BR34
Rochdale Pl, (Kirk.) G66 *off New Lairdsland Rd*	17	CE12
Rochsoles Cres, Air. ML6 *off Rochsoles Dr*	76	DC27
Rochsoles Dr, Air. ML6	76	DB27
Rochsolloch Fm Cotts, Air. ML6 *off Victoria Pl*	76	DA30
Rochsolloch Rd, Air. ML6	75	CZ31
Rockall Dr, G44	104	BS41
Rockbank Pl, Clyde. G81 *off Glasgow Rd*	27	AY15
Rockbank St, G40	69	BW32
Rockburn Cres, Bell. ML4	95	CW38
Rockburn Dr, (Clark.) G76	118	BL45
Rockcliffe Path, (Chap.) Air. ML6	97	DG37
Rockcliffe St, G40	88	BV34
Rock Dr, (Kilb.) John. PA10	78	AD35
Rockfield Pl, G21	51	BY24
Rockfield Rd, G21	51	BY24
Rockhampton Av, (E.Kil.) G75	135	BX54
Rockmount Av, (Thornlie.) G46	102	BJ41
Rockmount Av, (Barr.) G78	99	AZ44
Rock St, G4	49	BR26
Rockwell Av, Pais. PA2	82	AS37
Roddinghead Rd, (Giff.) G46	118	BJ4
Rodger Av, (Newt. M.) G77	117	BE
Rodger Dr, (Ruther.) G73	105	BV
Rodger Pl, (Ruther.) G73	105	B
Rodil Av, G44	104	
Rodney St, G4	67	
Roebank Dr, (Barr.) G78	99	

Roebank St, G31	69	BX29
Roffey Pk Rd, Pais. PA1	63	AZ32
Rogart St, G40	68	BV32
Rogerfield Rd, (Baill.) G69	72	CL30
Roland Cres, (Newt. M.) G77	117	BH50
Roman Av, G15	28	BC20
Roman Av, (Bears.) G61	29	BH16
Roman Ct, (Bears.) G61	29	BH16
Roman Dr, (Bears.) G61	29	BH16
Roman Dr, Bell. ML4	111	CX41
Roman Gdns, (Bears.) G61	29	BH16
Roman Pl, Bell. ML4	110	CU42
Roman Rd, (Bears.) G61	29	BG16
Roman Rd, (Kirk.) G66	16	CD13
Roman Rd, Clyde. G81	27	AW15
Roman Rd, Moth. ML1	128	DA46
Roman Way, (Udd.) G71	110	CS39
Romney Av, G44	104	BS40
Romulus Ct, Moth. ML1	111	CY44
Ronaldsay Dr, (Bishop.) G64	33	BZ19
Ronaldsay Pas, G22	50	BT22
off Scalpay St		
Ronaldsay Pl, (Cumb.) G67	21	CZ13
Ronaldsay St, G22	50	BS22
Ronald St, Coat. ML5	75	CW29
off Stewart St		
Rona St, G21	69	BX27
Rona Ter, (Camb.) G72	106	CB42
Ronay St, G22	50	BT21
Rooksdell Av, Pais. PA2	82	AS36
Ropework La, G1	5	BS31
off Clyde St		
Rorison Pl, (Ashgill) Lark. ML9	145	DH60
Rosebank Av, (Kirk.) G66	17	CG13
Rosebank Av, (Blan.) G72	109	CN44
Rosebank Dr, (Udd.) G71	94	CS38
Rosebank Dr, (Camb.) G72	107	CE41
Rosebank Gdns, (Udd.) G71	92	CK35
Rosebank Gdns, John. PA5	80	AJ35
Rosebank La, (Both.) G71	109	CR42
off Lomond Dr		
Rosebank Pl, (Dullatur) G68	8	CY7
Rosebank Pl, (Udd.) G71	92	CK35
Rosebank Pl, Ham. ML3	125	CQ50
Rosebank Rd, Bell. ML4	95	CX37
Rosebank Ter, (Baill.) G69	93	CP33
Roseberry La, Air. ML6	97	DG34
Roseberry Pl, Ham. ML3	125	CQ49
Roseberry Rd, Air. ML6	97	DF33
Roseberry St, G5	88	BU34
Rose Cres, Ham. ML3	125	CP49
Rosedale, (Bishop.) G64	51	BX21
off Woodfield Av		
Rosedale, (E.Kil.) G74	121	BY50
Rosedale Av, Pais. PA2	80	AM38
Rosedale Dr, (Baill.) G69	92	CJ33
Rosedale Gdns, G20	48	BL21
Rosedene Ter, Bell. ML4	111	CW39
off Airlie Dr		
Rosefield Gdns, (Udd.) G71	93	CN38
Rosegreen Cres, Bell. ML4	95	CW37
Rosehall Av, Coat. ML5	95	CX33
Rosehall Ind Est, Coat. ML5	95	CW34
Rosehall Rd, (Bellshill Ind. Est.)	110	CV39
Bell. ML4		
Rosehall Ter, Wis. ML2	143	DG52
Rosehill Dr, (Cumb.) G67	21	CW14
Rosehill Rd, (Torr.) G64	15	BY13
Roselea Rd, G42	88	BT36

Roseland Brae, Ersk. PA8	44	AT21
off Newshot Dr		
Roselea Dr, (Miln.) G62	12	BK10
Roselea Gdns, G13	47	BH22
Roselea Pl, (Blan.) G72	108	CL44
Roselea St, Lark. ML9	144	DD57
Rosemary Cres, (E.Kil.) G74	121	BZ49
Rosemary Pl, (E.Kil.) G74	121	BZ49
Rosemount, (Cumb.) G68	9	DB8
Rosemount Av, (Newt. M.) G77	131	BF51
Rosemount Ct, (Newt. M.) G77	131	BF52
Rose Mt Ct, Air. ML6	77	DE29
Rosemount Cres, G21	68	BV29
Rosemount La, Lark. ML9	145	DE60
off Dickson St		
Rosemount Meadows, (Both.)	109	CP43
G71		
Rosemount St, G21	68	BV28
Rosendale Way, (Blan.) G72	125	CN46
Roseneath Gate, (E.Kil.) G74	135	BY51
Roseness Pl, G33	70	CC29
Rosepark Av, (Udd.) G71	110	CS39
Rose Pk Cotts, Coat. ML5	94	CV34
Rose Pl, (E.Kil.) G74	123	CE50
Rose St, G3	4	BR29
Rose St, (Kirk.) G66	17	CF13
Rose St, (Cumb.) G67	39	CX15
Rose St, Moth. ML1	128	DC48
Rosevale Cres, Bell. ML4	111	CY41
Rosevale Cres, Ham. ML3	139	CR51
Rosevale Rd, (Bears.) G61	29	BG17
Rosevale St, G11	66	BJ27
Rosewood Av, Bell. ML4	95	CX38
Rosewood Av, Pais. PA2	81	AR36
Rosewood Path, Bell. ML4	110	CU40
Rosewood St, G13	47	BG22
Roslea Dr, G31	69	BW30
Roslin Twr, (Camb.) G72	106	CA42
Roslyn Dr, (Baill.) G69	73	CP32
Rosneath St, G51	66	BJ29
Ross Av, (Kirk.) G66	17	CH13
Ross Av, Renf. PA4	63	AW26
Ross Cres, Moth. ML1	127	CY48
Ross Dr, (Udd.) G71	94	CS36
Ross Dr, Air. ML6	96	DA33
Ross Dr, Moth. ML1	127	CY48
Rossendale Ct, G43	86	BL37
Rossendale Rd, G41	86	BL37
Rossendale Rd, G43	86	BL37
Ross Gdns, Moth. ML1	127	CY48
Rosshall Av, Pais. PA1	83	AY33
Ross Hall Pl, Renf. PA4	45	AZ26
Rosshill Av, G52	64	BB32
Rosshill Rd, G52	64	BB32
Rossie Cres, (Bishop.) G64	51	BY21
Rossie Gro, (Newt. M.) G77	116	BD48
Rosslea Dr, (Giff.) G46	102	BL43
Rosslyn Av, (Ruther.) G73	89	BY38
Rosslyn Av, (E.Kil.) G74	122	CB50
Rosslyn Ct, Ham. ML3	125	CQ49
Rosslyn Rd, (Bears.) G61	28	BD15
Rosslyn Rd, (Ashgill) Lark. ML9	145	DH61
Rosslyn Ter, G12	48	BL25
Ross Pl, (Ruther.) G73	105	BZ41
Ross St, G40	5	BT31
Ross St, Coat. ML5	75	CW30
Ross St, Pais. PA1	82	AV34
Ross Ter, Ham. ML3	141	CY52
Rostan Rd, G43	102	BL40
Rosyth Rd, G5	88	BU35
Rosyth St, G5	88	BU35

Rotherwick Dr, Pais. PA1	84	BA33
Rotherwood Av, G13	29	BE20
Rotherwood Av, Pais. PA2	81	AP37
Rotherwood La, G13	29	BE19
Rotherwood Pl, G13	47	BG21
Rotherwood Way, Pais. PA2	81	AP37
off Rotherwood Av		
Rothesay Cres, Coat. ML5	95	CX33
Rothesay Pl, (E.Kil.) G74	136	CA53
Rothesay Pl, Coat. ML5	95	CX33
off Rothesay Cres		
Rothesay St, (E.Kil.) G74	136	CA53
Rothes Dr, G23	30	BM20
Rothes Pl, G23	30	BL20
off Rothes Dr		
Rottenrow, G4	5	BT29
Rottenrow E, G4	5	BT30
Roughcraig St, Air. ML6	76	DC27
Roukenburn St, (Thornlie.)	101	BG41
G46		
Rouken Glen Pk, (Thornlie.)	101	BH44
G46		
Rouken Glen Rd, (Thornlie.)	101	BH43
G46		
Roundhill Dr, (Elder.) John. PA5	81	AN34
Roundknowe Rd, (Udd.) G71	92	CL36
Rowallan Gdns, G11	48	BJ26
Rowallan La, G11	47	BH26
Rowallan La, (Clark.) G76	119	BN46
Rowallan La E, G11	48	BJ26
Rowallan Rd, (Thornlie.) G46	101	BH43
Rowallan Ter, G33	52	CD25
Rowan Av, Moth. ML1	97	DF38
Rowan Av, Renf. PA4	45	AY25
Rowanbank Pl, Air. ML6	75	CZ29
Rowan Ct, (Camb.) G72	107	CH41
Rowan Ct, Pais. PA2	82	AU35
Rowan Ct, Wis. ML2	143	DF51
off Netherton Rd		
Rowan Cres, (Lenz.) G66	35	CE16
Rowan Cres, (Chap.) Air. ML6	97	DG34
Rowandale Av, (Baill.) G69	92	CJ33
Rowand Av, (Giff.) G46	102	BL43
Rowanden Av, Bell. ML4	111	CW39
Rowan Dr, (Bears.) G61	11	BH14
Rowan Dr, Clyde. G81	26	AV17
Rowan Gdns, G41	86	BK33
Rowan Gate, Pais. PA2	82	AV35
Rowan La, Moth. ML1	112	DC43
Rowanlea, (Plains) Air. ML6	59	DH26
off Silverdale Ter		
Rowanlea Av, Pais. PA2	80	AM38
Rowanlea Dr, (Giff.) G46	102	BM41
Rowanpark Dr, (Barr.) G78	99	AW40
Rowan Pl, (Blan.) G72	124	CM45
Rowan Pl, (Camb.) G72	107	CE39
Rowan Pl, Coat. ML5	94	CU33
off Old Monkland Rd		
Rowan Rd, G41	86	BK33
Rowan Rd, (Cumb.) G67	23	DF10
Rowans, The (Bishop.) G64	32	BV19
Rowans Gdns, (Both.) G71	109	CR41
Rowans St, Pais. PA2	82	AU35
Rowantree Av, (Udd.) G71	94	CS38
Rowantree Av, (Ruther.) G73	105	BX40
Rowantree Gdns, (Ruther.) G73	105	BX40
Rowantree Pl, John. PA5	79	AH36
off Rowantree Rd		
Rowantree Rd, Lark. ML9	145	DF59
Rowantree Rd, John. PA5	79	AH36
Rowantree Ter, Moth. ML1	112	DD40

253

Rowanwood Cres, Coat. ML5	74	CT32
Rowchester St, G40	69	BW32
Rowena Av, G13	29	BF20
Roxburgh Dr, (Bears.) G61	11	BG14
Roxburgh Dr, Coat. ML5	95	CZ33
Roxburgh La, G12	48	BM26
off Saltoun St		
Roxburgh Pk, (E.Kil.) G74	136	CB52
Roxburgh Pl, (Blan.) G72	124	CM46
off Coldstream St		
Roxburgh Rd, Pais. PA2	80	AM38
Roxburgh St, G12	48	BM26
Royal Bk Pl, G1	5	BS30
off Buchanan St		
Royal Cres, G3	67	BN29
Royal Cres, G42	87	BQ36
off Queens Dr		
Royal Dr, Ham. ML3	141	CW51
Royal Ex Bldgs, G1	5	BS30
off Royal Ex Sq		
Royal Ex Ct, G1	5	BS30
Royal Ex Sq, G1	5	BS30
Royal Gdns, (Both.) G71	109	CN43
Royal Inch Cres, Renf. PA4	45	AZ24
off Campbell St		
Royal Ter, G3	67	BN28
Royal Ter La, G3	67	BN28
Royellen Av, Ham. ML3	139	CP51
Roystonhill, G21	68	BV28
Roystonhill Pl, G21	68	BV28
Royston Rd, G21	5	BU28
Royston Rd, G33	52	CA26
Royston Sq, G21	5	BU28
Roy St, G21	50	BT26
Rozelle Av, G15	28	BD18
Rozelle Av, (Newt. M.) G77	116	BD49
Rozelle Dr, (Newt. M.) G77	116	BD49
Rozelle Pl, (Newt. M.) G77	116	BD49
Rubislaw Dr, (Bears.) G61	29	BG17
Ruby St, G40	89	BW33
Ruby Ter, Bell. ML4	111	CW41
Ruchazie Pl, G33	70	CB29
Ruchazie Rd, G32	70	CB30
Ruchazie Rd, G33	70	CB30
Ruchill Pl, G20	49	BP24
off Ruchill St		
Ruchill St, G20	49	BN24
Ruel St, G44	87	BQ38
Rufflees Av, (Barr.) G78	99	AZ41
Rugby Av, G13	46	BD21
Rullion Pl, G33	70	CB29
Rumford St, G40	88	BV34
Runciman Pl, (E.Kil.) G74	122	CD49
Rupert St, G4	67	BP27
Rushyhill St, G21	51	BW25
Ruskin La, G12	49	BN26
Ruskin Pl, G12	49	BN26
Ruskin Pl, (Kilsyth) G65	7	CT5
off Murray Av		
Ruskin Sq, (Bishop.) G64	33	BW20
Ruskin Ter, G12	49	BN26
Ruskin Ter, (Ruther.) G73	89	BX37
Russellcolt St, Coat. ML5	75	CW29
Russell Cres, (Baill.) G69	92	CM33
Russell Dr, (Bears.) G61	29	BG15
Russell Gdns, (Udd.) G71	93	CQ37
off Kingston Av		
Russell Pl, (Newt. M.) G77	117	BE49
Russell Pl, (E.Kil.) G75	135	BY54
Russell Pl, (Clark.) G76	119	BR48
Russell St, G11	66	BK27
off Vine St		
Russell St, (Chap.) Air. ML6	97	DG35
Russell St, Bell. ML4	111	CZ40
Russell St, Ham. ML3	125	CP48
Russell St, John. PA5	80	AJ34
Russell St, Pais. PA3	62	AT30
Rutherford Av, (Bears.) G61	10	BD13
Rutherford Av, (Kirk.) G66	36	CK15
Rutherford Gra, (Kirk.) G66	35	CE15
Rutherford La, (E.Kil.) G75	136	CB53
off Murdoch Rd		
Rutherford Sq, (E.Kil.) G75	136	CA53
Rutherglen Br, G40	88	BV34
Rutherglen Br, G42	88	BV34
Rutherglen Ind Est, (Ruther.) G73	89	BW36
Rutherglen Rd, G5	88	BT34
Rutherglen Rd, (Ruther.) G73	88	BT34
Ruthven Av, (Giff.) G46	102	BM44
Ruthven La, G12	48	BM26
Ruthven La, (Glenb.) Coat. ML5	56	CS23
off Chapman Av		
Ruthven Pl, (Bishop.) G64	51	BY21
Ruthven St, G12	48	BM26
Rutland Ct, G51	67	BN31
off Govan Rd		
Rutland Cres, G51	67	BN31
Rutland Pl, G51	67	BN31
Ryan Rd, (Bishop.) G64	33	BX20
Ryan Way, (Ruther.) G73	105	BY42
Ryat Dr, (Newt. M.) G77	117	BE47
Ryat Grn, (Newt. M.) G77	117	BE48
Ryat Linn, Ersk. PA8	25	AP20
Rydal Gro, (E.Kil.) G75	134	BV55
Rydal Pl, (E.Kil.) G75	134	BV55
Ryden Mains Rd, (Glenm.) Air. ML6	57	CZ25
Ryebank Rd, G21	51	BY24
Rye Cres, G21	51	BX24
Ryecroft Dr, (Baill.) G69	72	CK32
Ryedale Pl, G15	28	BC17
Ryefield Av, Coat. ML5	74	CT30
Ryefield Av, John. PA5	79	AF36
Ryefield Pl, John. PA5	79	AF36
Ryefield Rd, G21	51	BX24
Ryehill Pl, G21	51	BY24
Ryehill Rd, G21	51	BY24
Ryemount Rd, G21	51	BY24
Rye Rd, G21	51	BX24
Rye Way, Pais. PA2	81	AN36
Ryewraes Rd, (Linw.) Pais. PA3	60	AK32
Rylands Dr, G32	91	CF33
Rylands Gdns, G32	91	CG33
Rylees Cres, G52	64	BA31
Rylees Pl, G52	64	BA31
Rylees Rd, G52	64	BA31
Rysland Av, (Newt. M.) G77	117	BG48
Rysland Cres, (Newt. M.) G77	117	BG48
Ryvra Rd, G13	47	BF23

S

Sachelcourt Av, Bish. PA7	24	AK19
Sackville Av, G13	47	BH24
Sackville La, G13	47	BH23
Saddell Rd, G15	28	BD17
Sadlers Wells Ct, (E.Kil.) G74	122	CD49
Saffron Cres, Wis. ML2	143	DF52
Saffronhall Cres, Ham. ML3	126	CT49
off Almada St		
Saffronhall La, Ham. ML3	126	CT49
off Montrose Cres		
St. Abbs Dr, Pais. PA2	81	AQ36
St. Andrews Av, (Bishop.) G64	32	BU19
St. Andrew's Av, (Both.) G71	109	CO44
St. Andrews Ct, (E.Kil.) G75	135	BY55
St. Andrews Cres, G41	87	BN33
St. Andrews Cres, Pais. PA3	62	AS28
St. Andrews Cross, G41	87	BQ34
St. Andrews Dr, G41	87	BN33
St. Andrews Dr, (Bears.) G61	11	BF14
St. Andrews Dr, Coat. ML5	74	CU31
St. Andrews Dr, Ham. ML3	124	CM49
St. Andrews Dr, (Abbots.) Pais. PA3	62	AT29
St. Andrews Dr W, (Abbots.) Pais. PA3	62	AS28
St. Andrews Gate, Bell. ML4	110	CV40
off Cochrane St		
St. Andrews La, G1	5	BT31
off Gallowgate		
St. Andrews Path, Lark. ML9	145	DE60
off Glen Fruin Dr		
St. Andrews Pl, (Kilsyth) G65	7	CS4
St. Andrews Rd, G41	87	BP33
St. Andrews Rd, Renf. PA4	45	AY26
St. Andrews Sq, G1	5	BT31
St. Andrews St, G1	5	BT31
St. Andrews St, Moth. ML1	112	DC40
St. Annes Av, Ersk. PA8	44	AT21
off St. Annes Wynd		
St. Annes Wynd, Ersk. PA8	44	AS21
St. Anns Dr, (Giff.) G46	102	BL43
St. Barchan's Rd, (Kilb.) John. PA10 *off Easwald Bk*	78	AD35
St. Blanes Dr, (Ruther.) G73	104	BU39
St. Boswell's Cres, Pais. PA2	81	AQ36
St. Boswells Dr, Coat. ML5	95	CZ33
St. Brides Av, (Udd.) G71	94	CS38
St. Brides Rd, G43	102	BM39
St. Brides Way, (Both.) G71	109	CQ42
St. Bryde St, (E.Kil.) G74	136	CB51
St. Catherines Rd, (Giff.) G46	102	BL43
St. Clair Av, (Giff.) G46	102	BL42
St. Clair St, G20	67	BP27
off North Woodside Rd		
St. Columba Dr, (Kirk.) G66	17	CG14
St. Cyrus Gdns, (Bishop.) G64	33	BY20
St. Cyrus Rd, (Bishop.) G64	33	BY20
St. Davids Dr, Air. ML6	97	DE33
St. Davids Pl, Lark. ML9	144	DC58
off McNeil St		
St. Denis Way, Coat. ML5	74	CV29
off Heritage Vw		
St. Edmunds Gro, (Miln.) G62	12	BJ10
St. Edmunds La, (Miln.) G62	12	BJ10
St. Enoch Av, (Udd.) G71	94	CS37
St. Enoch Shop Cen, G1	5	BS31
St. Enoch Sq, G1	4	BR31
St. Fillans Rd, G33	53	CE24
St. Francis Rigg, G5	88	BS33
St. Georges Pl, G20	4	BQ28
off St. Georges Rd		
St. Georges Rd, G3	67	BQ27
St. Germains, (Bears.) G61	29	BG17
St. Giles Pk, Ham. ML3	139	CR51
St. Giles Way, Ham. ML3	139	CR51
St. Helena Cres, Clyde. G81	27	AY15
St. Ives Rd, (Mood.) G69	37	CP18

St. James Av, Pais. PA3	61	AR30	St. Ronans Dr, G41	86	BM36	Sandholm Pl, G14	46	BB24
St. James Business Cen, (Linw.)	81	AN33	St. Ronans Dr, (Ruther.) G73	105	BY39	Sandholm Ter, G14	46	BB24
Pais. PA3			St. Ronan's Dr, Ham. ML3	140	CS53	Sandiefield Rd, G5	88	BS33
St. James Ct, Coat. ML5	94	CU34	St. Stephens Av, (Ruther.) G73	105	BZ42	Sandielands Av, Ersk. PA8	44	AT22
St. James Rd, G4	5	BT29	St. Stephens Cres, (Ruther.)	106	CA42	Sandilands Cres, Moth. ML1	127	CX48
St. James St, Pais. PA3	62	AU32	G73			Sandilands St, G32	70	CD32
St. James Way, Coat. ML5	94	CU34	St. Valentine Ter, G5	88	BT33	Sandmill St, G21	69	BW28
St. John's Ct, G41	87	BN33	St. Vigeans Av, (Newt. M.) G77	116	BD49	Sandpiper Dr, (E.Kil.) G75	135	BW56
St. John's Quad, G41	87	BN33	St. Vigeans Pl, (Newt. M.) G77	117	BE50	Sandpiper Pl, (E.Kil.) G75	135	BW56
St. John's Rd, G41	87	BN34	St. Vincent Cres, G3	66	BM29	Sandpiper Way, (Strathclyde	94	CU37
St. John St, Coat. ML5	75	CW30	St. Vincent Cres La, G3	66	BM29	Bus. Pk.) Bell. ML4		
St. Joseph's Ct, G21	68	BV28	St. Vincent La, G2	4	BQ29	Sandra Rd, (Bishop.) G64	33	BY19
St. Joseph's Pl, G21	68	BV28	St. Vincent Pl, G1	5	BS30	Sandringham Av, (Newt. M.)	118	BJ47
St. Joseph's Vw, G21	68	BV28	St. Vincent Pl, (E.Kil.) G75	135	BW52	G77		
St. Kenneth Dr, G51	65	BF29	St. Vincent Pl, Moth. ML1	128	DA46	Sandringham Ct, (Newt. M.)	118	BJ48
St. Kilda Dr, G14	47	BG25	off Milton St			G77 off Duart Dr		
St. Lawrence Pk, (E.Kil.) G75	135	BY52	St. Vincent St, G2	4	BQ29	Sandringham Dr, (Elder.) John.	80	AK36
St. Leonards Dr, (Giff.) G46	102	BL42	St. Vincent St, G3	4	BP29	PA5 off Glamis Av		
St. Leonards Rd, (E.Kil.) G74	137	CE51	St. Vincent Ter, G3	4	BP29	Sandringham La, G12	48	BM26
St. Leonards Sq, (E.Kil.) G74	137	CE52	Salamanca St, G31	69	BZ32	off Kersland St		
off Blacklaw Dr			Salasaig Ct, G33	70	CC30	Sandwood Cres, G52	64	BC32
St. Leonards Wk, Coat. ML5	95	CY34	off Sutherness Dr			Sandwood Path, G52	64	BC32
St. Luke's Pl, G5	68	BS32	Salen St, G52	65	BH32	off Hillington Rd S		
St. Luke's Ter, G5	68	BS32	Salford Pl, (Kirk.) G66	17	CE12	Sandwood Rd, G52	84	BC33
St. Margaret's Av, Pais. PA3	63	AW30	off West High St			Sandyford Av, Moth. ML1	97	DF37
St. Margaret's Ct, Bell. ML4	111	CX40	Saline St, Air. ML6	75	CZ31	Sandyford Pl, G3	4	BP29
St. Margaret's Ct, Pais. PA3	63	AW30	Salisbury, (E.Kil.) G74	123	CF49	off Sauchiehall St		
St. Margaret's Dr, Wis. ML2	143	DG52	Salisbury Pl, G5	87	BR33	Sandyford Pl La, G3	67	BN29
St. Margarets Pl, G1	5	BS31	Salisbury Pl, Clyde. G81	26	AT16	Sandyford Rd, Moth. ML1	97	DF38
off Bridgegate			Salisbury St, G5	87	BR33	Sandyford Rd, Pais. PA3	62	AV29
St. Mark Gdns, G32	70	CB32	Salkeld St, G5	87	BR33	Sandyford St, G3	66	BL29
St. Mark St, G32	70	CA32	Salmona St, G22	49	BR25	Sandyhills Cres, G32	90	CD34
St. Marnock St, G40	69	BW32	Saltaire Av, (Udd.) G71	109	CQ40	Sandyhills Dr, G32	90	CD34
St. Martins Gate, Coat. ML5	95	CW33	Salterland Rd, G53	100	BA40	Sandyhills Gro, G32	91	CE35
St. Mary's Cres, (Barr.) G78	99	AY43	Salterland Rd, (Barr.) G78	100	BA40	Sandyhills Pl, G32	90	CD34
St. Mary's Gdns, (Barr.) G78	99	AZ43	Saltire Cres, Lark. ML9	145	DE58	Sandyhills Rd, G32	90	CD34
St. Marys La, G2	4	BR30	Saltmarket, G1	5	BS31	Sandyknowes Rd, (Cumb.) G67	22	DB13
St. Marys Rd, (Bishop.) G64	32	BU19	Saltmarket Pl, G1	5	BS31	Sandy La, G11	66	BJ27
St. Marys Rd, Bell. ML4	110	CU40	off Bridgegate			off Crawford St		
St. Maurice's Roundabout,	20	CV12	Saltoun Gdns, G12	48	BM26	Sandy Rd, G11	66	BJ28
(Cumb.) G68			off Roxburgh St			Sandy Rd, Renf. PA4	63	AY28
St. Michael Rd, Wis. ML2	143	DE52	Saltoun La, G12	48	BM26	Sannox Rd, Moth. ML1	127	CX46
St. Michael's Ct, G31	69	BY32	Saltoun St, G12	48	BL26	Sannox Gdns, G31	69	BX29
off St. Michael's La			Salvia St, (Camb.) G72	106	CB39	Sanquhar Dr, G53	84	BC37
St. Michael's La, G31	69	BY32	Sandaig Rd, G33	71	CG31	Sanquhar Gdns, G53	84	BC37
St. Mirrens Rd, (Kilsyth) G65	7	CU5	Sandale Path, (Blan.) G72	124	CL47	Sanquhar Gdns, (Blan.) G72	108	CK43
St. Mirren St, Pais. PA1	62	AU32	off Moorfield Rd			Sanquhar Pl, G53	84	BC37
St. Monance St, G21	50	BV24	Sandalwood Av, (E.Kil.) G74	121	BZ49	Sanquhar Rd, G53	84	BC37
St. Monica's Way, Coat. ML5	94	CT33	Sandalwood Ct, (E.Kil.) G74	121	BZ49	Sapphire Rd, Bell. ML4	111	CW42
St. Mungo Av, G4	5	BS29	Sanda St, G20	49	BN25	Saracen Head La, G1	5	BU31
St. Mungo Pl, G4	5	BT29	Sandbank Av, G20	48	BM22	off Gallowgate		
St. Mungo Pl, Ham. ML3	124	CM49	Sandbank Cres, G20	48	BM23	Saracen St, G22	50	BS26
off Fleming Way			Sandbank Dr, G20	48	BM22	Sarazen Ct, Moth. ML1	129	DG45
St. Mungos Ct, Moth. ML1	112	DD44	Sandbank St, G20	48	BM23	off Morris Cres		
St. Mungo's Rd, (Cumb.) G67	22	DB11	Sandbank Ter, G20	48	BM22	Sardinia La, G12	48	BM26
St. Mungo St, (Bishop.) G64	50	BV21	Sandend, Ersk. PA8	25	AQ18	Sardinia Ter, G12	48	BM26
St. Mungos Wk, (Cumb.) G67	22	DB12	Sandend Rd, G53	84	BC38	off Cecil St		
off Cumbernauld Shop Cen			Sanderling Pl, (E.Kil.) G75	135	BW56	Saskatoon Pl, (E.Kil.) G75	135	BX52
St. Ninians Cres, Pais. PA2	82	AV35	Sanderling Rd, Pais. PA3	62	AT29	Saturn Av, Pais. PA1	81	AN33
St. Ninian's Pl, Ham. ML3	125	CP50	Sanderson Av, (Udd.) G71	110	CT39	Saucelhill Ter, Pais. PA2	82	AV34
off St. Ninian's Rd			Sandfield Av, (Miln.) G62	12	BJ10	Saucel St, Pais. PA1	82	AU33
St. Ninian's Rd, Ham. ML3	125	CN50	Sandfield St, G20	49	BN24	Sauchenhall Rd, (Kirk.) G66	37	CN16
St. Ninians Rd, Pais. PA2	82	AV35	Sandford Gdns, (Baill.) G69	72	CK32	Sauchiehall La, G2	4	BQ29
St. Ninian Ter, G5	68	BS32	off Scott St			Sauchiehall St, G2	4	BQ29
off Ballater St			Sandgate Av, G32	91	CF34	Sauchiehall St, G3	66	BM28
St. Peters La, G2	4	BQ30	Sandhaven Pl, G53	84	BC38	Saughs Av, G33	52	CB23
St. Peter's Path, G4	67	BQ27	off Sandhaven Rd			Saughs Dr, G33	52	CB23
off Braid St			Sandhaven Rd, G53	84	BC38	Saughs Gate, G33	52	CB23
St. Peters St, G4	67	BQ27	Sandhead Cres, (Chap.) Air.	97	DG36	Saughs Pl, G33	52	CB23
St. Roberts Gdns, G53	101	BF40	ML6 off Honeywell Cres			Saughs Rd, G33	52	CA24
St. Rollox Brae, G21	68	BU27	Sandholes St, Pais. PA1	82	AS33	Saughton St, G32	70	CA30

Saunders Ct, (Barr.) G78	99	AX42
off John St		
Savoy St, G40	88	BV33
Sawmillfield St, G4	67	BR27
Sawmill Rd, G11	65	BH27
off South St		
Saxon Rd, G13	47	BF22
Scadlock Rd, Pais. PA3	61	AR31
Scalpay, (E.Kil.) G74	137	CE52
Scalpay Pas, G22	50	BT22
Scalpay Pl, G22	50	BT22
Scalpay St, G22	50	BS22
Scapa St, G23	49	BN21
Scaraway Dr, G22	50	BT21
Scaraway Pl, G22	50	BT21
Scaraway St, G22	50	BS21
Scaraway Ter, G22	50	BT21
Scarba Dr, G43	102	BK40
Scarba Quad, Wis. ML2	143	DG52
Scarhill Av, Air. ML6	76	DB32
Scarhill La, Air. ML6	76	DC32
off Scarhill Av		
Scarhill St, Coat. ML5	94	CV34
Scarrel Dr, G45	105	BW41
Scarrel Gdns, G45	105	BW41
Scarrel Pl, G45	105	BW41
Scarrel Rd, G45	105	BW41
Scarrel Ter, G45	105	BW41
Scavaig Cres, G15	28	BA17
Schaw Ct, (Bears.) G61	29	BG15
Schaw Dr, (Bears.) G61	29	BG15
Schaw Rd, Pais. PA3	63	AW31
Schipka Pas, G1	5	BT31
off Gallowgate		
Scholar's Gate, (E.Kil.) G75	135	BZ55
School Av, (Camb.) G72	106	CD40
Schoolhouse La, (Blan.) G72	124	CL47
School Quad, Air. ML6	76	DB27
School Rd, (Stepps) G33	53	CG23
School Rd, (Torr.) G64	15	BY12
School Rd, (Newt. M.) G77	117	BF49
School Rd, Pais. PA1	64	BA32
School St, (Chap.) Air. ML6	97	DF35
School St, Coat. ML5	95	CW33
School St, Ham. ML3	140	CT52
School Wynd, Pais. PA1	62	AU32
Scioncroft Av, (Ruther.) G73	89	BY38
Scone Pl, (E.Kil.) G74	121	BZ50
Scone Pl, (Newt. M.) G77	118	BK49
Scone St, G21	50	BS26
Scone Wk, (Baill.) G69	92	CJ34
Sconser St, G23	31	BN20
Scorton Gdns, (Baill.) G69	91	CG33
off Danby Rd		
Scotia Cres, Lark. ML9	144	DC60
Scotia Gdns, Ham. ML3	140	CS54
Scotia St, Moth. ML1	127	CY46
Scotland St, G5	67	BP32
Scotland St W, G41	67	BN32
Scotsblair Av, (Kirk.) G66	17	CE14
Scotsburn Rd, G21	51	BY25
Scotstoun Mill Rd, G11	66	BL28
off Partick Br St		
Scotstoun Pl, G14	47	BE26
off Scotstoun St		
Scotstoun St, G14	47	BE26
Scott Av, John. PA5	79	AG37
Scott Cres, (Cumb.) G67	21	CZ14
Scott Dr, (Bears.) G61	29	BE15
Scott Dr, (Cumb.) G67	21	CZ14
Scott Gro, Ham. ML3	140	CT51
Scott Hill, (E.Kil.) G74	122	CC50
off Cantieslaw Dr		
Scott Pl, Bell. ML4	95	CX38
Scott Pl, John. PA5	79	AG37
Scott Rd, G52	64	BB29
Scott's Pl, Air. ML6	76	DD29
Scotts Rd, Pais. PA2	83	AY34
Scott St, G3	4	BQ29
Scott St, (Baill.) G69	92	CK33
Scott St, Clyde. G81	26	AU17
Scott St, Ham. ML3	140	CT52
Scott St, Lark. ML9	144	DD59
Scott St, Moth. ML1	128	DA46
Seafar Rd, (Cumb.) G67	22	DA13
Seafield Av, (Bears.) G61	11	BH14
Seafield Cres, (Cumb.) G68	20	CU12
Seafield Dr, (Ruther.) G73	105	BZ42
Seaforth Cres, (Barr.) G78	99	AX40
Seaforth La, (Mood.) G69	37	CQ19
off Burnbrae Av		
Seaforth Pl, Bell. ML4	110	CV42
Seaforth Rd, G52	64	BC30
Seaforth Rd, Clyde. G81	27	AX20
Seaforth Rd N, G52	64	BC30
Seaforth Rd S, G52	64	BC30
Seagrove St, G32	69	BZ31
Seamill Gdns, (E.Kil.) G74	135	BZ51
Seamill Path, G53	100	BB40
off Seamill St		
Seamill St, G53	100	BB40
Seamore St, G20	67	BP27
Seath Av, Air. ML6	76	DA30
Seath Rd, (Ruther.) G73	89	BW36
Seath St, G42	88	BS35
Seaton Ter, Ham. ML3	125	CQ49
Seaward La, G41	67	BN31
Seaward Pl, G41	87	BN33
Seaward St, G41	67	BP32
Second Av, (Millerston) G33	52	CD24
Second Av, G44	103	BR39
Second Av, (Bears.) G61	30	BJ18
Second Av, (Kirk.) G66	35	CE20
Second Av, (Udd.) G71	93	CN36
Second Av, Clyde. G81	26	AV18
Second Av, Renf. PA4	63	AY27
Second Gdns, G41	86	BJ33
Second Rd, (Blan.) G72	125	CN48
Second St, (Udd.) G71	93	CP37
Seedhill, Pais. PA1	82	AV33
Seedhill Rd, Pais. PA1	82	AV33
Seggielea La, G13	47	BF23
off Helensburgh Dr		
Seggielea Rd, G13	47	BF23
Seil Dr, G44	103	BR41
Selborne Pl, G13	47	BG24
off Selborne Rd		
Selborne Pl La, G13	47	BG24
Selborne Rd, G13	47	BG24
Selby Gdns, G32	71	CF32
off Hailes Av		
Selby Pl, Coat. ML5	74	CT27
Selby St, Coat. ML5	74	CT27
Selkirk Av, G52	85	BE33
Selkirk Av, Pais. PA2	81	AQ36
Selkirk Dr, (Ruther.) G73	89	BY38
Selkirk Pl, (E.Kil.) G74	123	CF50
Selkirk St, (Blan.) G72	124	CM46
Selkirk St, Ham. ML3	140	CU51
Selkirk Way, Bell. ML4	95	CX38
off Bell St		
Selkirk Way, Coat. ML5	96	DA34
Sella Rd, (Bishop.) G64	33	BZ19
Selvieland Rd, G52	64	BB32
Semphill Gdns, (E.Kil.) G74	136	CD51
Sempie St, Ham. ML3	125	CP49
Sempill Av, Ersk. PA8	25	AP19
Semple Av, Bish. PA7	24	AK18
Semple Pl, (Linw.) Pais. PA3	60	AK30
Senga Cres, Bell. ML4	95	CW38
off Oakdene Av		
Seres Rd, (Clark.) G76	118	BM45
Seton Ter, G31	68	BV30
Settle Gdns, (Baill.) G69	91	CH33
off Danby Rd		
Seven Sisters, (Kirk.) G66	35	CG16
Seventh Av, (Udd.) G71	93	CP37
Seventh Rd, (Blan.) G72	125	CN48
Severn Rd, (E.Kil.) G75	134	BV54
Seymour Grn, (E.Kil.) G75	135	BX53
Seyton Av, (Giff.) G46	102	BL44
Seyton La, (E.Kil.) G74	122	CA50
Shaftesbury Ct, (E.Kil.) G74	123	CE48
off Bosworth Rd		
Shaftesbury Cres, Moth. ML1	113	DF42
Shaftesbury St, G3	4	BP29
Shaftesbury St, Clyde. G81	26	AV19
Shafton Pl, G13	47	BG21
Shafton Rd, G13	47	BG21
Shakespeare Av, Clyde. G81	26	AV17
Shakespeare St, G20	49	BN24
Shamrock St, G4	4	BQ28
Shamrock St, (Kirk.) G66	17	CF13
Shandon Cres, Bell. ML4	95	CW38
Shandon Ter, Ham. ML3	139	CP51
Shandwick Sq, G34	72	CJ29
off Bogbain Rd		
Shandwick St, G34	72	CJ29
Shanks Av, (Barr.) G78	99	AY43
Shanks Cres, John. PA5	79	AG35
Shanks Ind Pk, (Barr.) G78	99	AY40
Shanks St, G20	49	BN24
Shanks St, Air. ML6	76	DC28
Shanks Way, (Barr.) G78	99	AY41
off Blackbyres Rd		
Shannon St, G20	49	BP24
Shapinsay St, G22	50	BT21
Sharp Av, Coat. ML5	94	CS33
Sharp St, Moth. ML1	127	CX46
Shaw Av, Bish. PA7	24	AL18
Shawbridge Arc, G43	86	BL37
off Ashtree Rd		
Shawbridge St, G43	86	BK38
Shawburn Cres, Ham. ML3	125	CR49
off Shawburn St		
Shawburn St, Ham. ML3	125	CQ49
Shaw Ct, Ersk. PA8	25	AP18
Shaw Cres, Wis. ML2	143	DF52
Shawfield Dr, G5	88	BU35
Shawfield Ind Est, (Ruther.) G73	88	BV3
Shawfield Rd, G5	88	B
Shawhead Av, Coat. ML5	95	
Shawhead Cotts, Coat. ML5	95	
off Dunottar Av		
Shawhead Ind Est, Coat. ML5	9	
Shawhill Cres, (Newt. M.) G77		
Shawhill Rd, G41		
Shawhill Rd, G43		
Shawholm Cres, G43		
Shawlands Arc, G41		
Shawlands Sq, G41		
Shawmoss Rd, G41		

Shawpark St, G20	49	BN23
Shaw Pl, (Linw.) Pais. PA3	60	AK32
Shawrigg Rd, Lark. ML9	145	DE59
Shaw Rd, (Miln.) G62	12	BJ13
Shaw Rd, (Newt. M.) G77	117	BG49
Shaws Rd, Lark. ML9	145	DF60
Shaw St, G51	66	BJ29
Shaw St, Lark. ML9	144	DD61
Shawwood Cres, (Newt. M.) G77	117	BG50
Shearer Dr, Ham. ML3	140	CS54
Shearers La, Renf. PA4	45	AZ26
off Fauldshead Rd		
Shearer Dr, G5	4	BP31
off Paisley Rd		
Sheddens Pl, G32	70	CB32
Sheddens Roundabout, (Clark.) G76	119	BN46
Sheepburn Rd, (Udd.) G71	93	CN38
Sheila St, G33	52	CA25
Sheilinghill, Ham. ML3	126	CU49
off Church St		
Shelley Ct, G12	48	BJ24
Shelley Dr, (Both.) G71	109	CR42
Shelley Dr, Clyde. G81	27	AW17
Shelley Rd, G12	47	BH24
Shells Rd, (Kirk.) G66	17	CG12
Sheppard St, G21	50	BU25
off Cowlairs Rd		
Sherbrooke Av, G41	86	BL34
Sherbrooke Dr, G41	86	BL33
Sherbrooke Gdns, G41	86	BL34
Sherbrooke Pl, (E.Kil.) G75	135	BY52
Sherburn Gdns, (Baill.) G69	91	CH33
Sherdale Av, (Chap.) Air. ML6	97	DF35
Sheriff Pk Av, (Ruther.) G73	89	BW38
Sherry Av, Moth. ML1	112	DB40
Sherry Dr, Ham. ML3	139	CP52
Sherry Hts, (Camb.) G72	106	CC39
Sherwood Av, (Udd.) G71	109	CQ40
Sherwood Av, Pais. PA1	63	AW31
Sherwood Dr, (Thornlie.) G46	102	BJ42
Sherwood Pl, G15	28	BD18
Shetland Dr, G44	103	BR41
Shettleston Rd, G31	69	BY31
Shettleston Rd, G32	70	CC32
Shettleston Sheddings, G31	70	CA32
Shiel Av, (E.Kil.) G74	122	CB50
Shielbridge Gdns, G23	31	BN19
Shiel Ct, (Barr.) G78	99	AX40
Shieldaig Dr, (Ruther.) G73	105	BX41
Shieldaig Rd, G22	49	BR21
Shieldburn Rd, G51	65	BE30
Shieldhall Gdns, G51	65	BE30
Shieldhall Rd, G51	65	BE29
Shieldhill, (E.Kil.) G75	136	CB54
off Kelvin Dr		
…muir St, Wis. ML2	129	DF49
…el Dr, Lark. ML9	142	DB56
…ds Ct, Moth. ML1	128	DD50
…s Dr, Moth. ML1	128	DD50
…Rd, G41	67	BP32
…d, Moth. ML1	143	DE51
…Kil.) G74	122	CB50
…at. ML5	75	CZ32
…hop.) G64	33	BX20
…3	46	BC22
	50	BU21
	101	BE40
…A7	24	AN17
…G81	27	AZ20

Shipbank La, G1	5	BS31
off Clyde St		
Shira Ter, (E.Kil.) G74	136	CD52
Shirley Quad, Moth. ML1	127	CZ50
Shirrel Av, Bell. ML4	95	CW38
off North Rd		
Shirrel Rd, Moth. ML1	112	DD41
Shirvalea, (Kilsyth) G65	19	CP9
off Burnbrae		
Shiskine Dr, G20	48	BL22
Shiskine Pl, G20	48	BL21
Shiskine St, G20	48	BL21
Sholto Cres, (Righead Ind. Est.) Bell. ML4	94	CT38
Shore St, G40	88	BV35
Shortridge St, G20	49	BN24
Shortroods Av, Pais. PA3	62	AT30
Shortroods Cres, Pais. PA3	62	AT30
Shortroods Rd, Pais. PA3	62	AT30
Shotts St, G33	71	CF29
Showcase Leisure Pk, (Baill.) G69	93	CR33
Shuna Gdns, G20	49	BP24
Shuna Pl, G20	49	BN24
Shuna Pl, (Newt. M.) G77	116	BD47
Shuna St, G20	49	BN23
Shuttle La, G1	5	BT30
off George St		
Shuttle St, G1	5	BT30
Shuttle St, (Kilsyth) G65	7	CT5
Shuttle St, (Kilb.) John. PA10	78	AC33
Shuttle St, Pais. PA1	82	AU33
Sidland Rd, G21	51	BY24
Sidlaw Av, (Barr.) G78	99	AY44
off Ochil Dr		
Sidlaw Av, Ham. ML3	139	CP51
Sidlaw Dr, Wis. ML2	129	DH50
Sidlaw Rd, (Bears.) G61	28	BD15
Sidlaw Way, (Chap.) Air. ML6	97	DH36
Sidlaw Way, Lark. ML9	142	DB56
off Pentland Cres		
Sielga Pl, G34	72	CJ29
Siemens Pl, G21	69	BX27
Siemens St, G21	69	BX27
Sievewright St, (Ruther.) G73	89	BY36
off Hunter Rd		
Sighthill Ln, Lark. ML9	144	DD57
off Muirshot Rd		
Sikeside Pl, Coat. ML5	75	CZ32
Sikeside St, Coat. ML5	75	CZ32
Silkin Av, Clyde. G81	27	AZ20
Silk St, Pais. PA1	62	AV32
Silvan Pl, (Clark.) G76	119	BQ48
Silver Birch Dr, G51	65	BF30
Silver Birch Gdns, G51	65	BE30
Silverburn Cres, Moth. ML1	113	DF42
Silverburn St, G33	70	CA29
Silverdale, (E.Kil.) G74	121	BY50
Silverdale St, G31	89	BY33
Silverdale Ter, (Plains) Air. ML6	59	DH26
Silverfir Ct, G5	88	BT34
Silverfir Pl, G5	88	BT34
Silver Firs, Moth. ML1	112	DD42
Silverfir St, G5	88	BT34
Silvergrove St, G40	68	BU32
Silvertonhill Av, Ham. ML3	140	CU52
Silvertonhill Pl, Ham. ML3	140	CT54
off Chriss Av		
Silverwells, (Both.) G71	109	CR44
Silverwells Ct, (Both.) G71	109	CQ44
Silverwells Cres, (Both.) G71	109	CQ44

Simons Cres, Renf. PA4	45	AZ24
Simpson Ct, (Udd.) G71	109	CP39
Simpson Ct, Clyde. G81	27	AW19
Simpson Dr, (E.Kil.) G75	135	BZ54
Simpson Gdns, (Barr.) G78	99	AX43
Simpson Pl, (E.Kil.) G75	135	BZ54
off The Murray Rd		
Simpson St, G20	49	BP26
Simpson Way, Bell. ML4	95	CY38
Simshill Rd, G44	103	BR42
Sinclair Av, (Bears.) G61	29	BG15
Sinclair Dr, G42	87	BP38
Sinclair Dr, Coat. ML5	74	CT30
Sinclair Gdns, (Bishop.) G64	51	BW21
Sinclair Gro, Bell. ML4	110	CV43
Sinclair Pk, (E.Kil.) G75	136	CB53
off Telford Rd		
Sinclair Pl, (E.Kil.) G75	136	CB53
Sinclair St, (Miln.) G62	12	BJ11
Sinclair St, Clyde. G81	45	AZ21
Singer Rd, (E.Kil.) G75	136	CB55
Singer Rd, Clyde. G81	26	AV18
Singer St, Clyde. G81	27	AX18
Sir Michael Pl, Pais. PA1	82	AT33
Sixth Av, Renf. PA4	63	AY28
Sixth St, (Udd.) G71	93	CN36
Skaethorn Rd, G20	48	BK22
Skaterigg Dr, G13	47	BH24
Skaterigg Gdns, G13	47	BH24
Skaterig La, G13	47	BG24
Skelbo Path, G34	72	CM28
off Auchingill Rd		
Skelbo Pl, G34	72	CM28
Skellyton Cres, Lark. ML9	144	DD59
Skene Rd, G51	66	BK32
Skerne Gro, (E.Kil.) G75	134	BV55
Skerray Quad, G22	50	BS21
Skerray St, G22	50	BS21
Skerryvore Pl, G33	70	CD29
Skerryvore Rd, G33	70	CD29
Skibo Dr, (Thornlie.) G46	101	BG42
Skibo La, (Thornlie.) G46	101	BG42
Skimmers Hill, (M. of Cam.) G66	16	CD9
Skipness Dr, G51	65	BG29
Skirsa Ct, G23	49	BQ21
off Skirsa St		
Skirsa Pl, G23	49	BP22
Skirsa Sq, G23	49	BQ22
Skirsa St, G23	49	BP21
Skirving St, G41	87	BN37
Skovlunde Way, (E.Kil.) G75	136	CA55
Skye, (E.Kil.) G74	137	CE52
Skye Av, Renf. PA4	63	AY28
Skye Ct, (Cumb.) G67	21	CZ13
Skye Cres, (Old Kil.) G60	26	AS16
Skye Cres, Pais. PA2	82	AT38
Skye Dr, (Old Kil.) G60	26	AS16
Skye Dr, (Cumb.) G67	21	CZ13
Skye Gdns, (Bears.) G61	28	BD15
Skye Pl, (Cumb.) G67	21	CZ13
Skye Rd, (Cumb.) G67	21	CZ13
Skye Rd, (Ruther.) G73	105	BZ42
Skye Wynd, Ham. ML3	139	CP52
Slakiewood Av, (Gart.) G69	55	CN22
Slatefield Ct, G31	69	BW31
off Slatefield St		
Slatefield St, G31	69	BW31
Sleaford Av, Moth. ML1	127	CZ49
Slenavon Av, (Ruther.) G73	105	BZ42
Slessor Dr, (E.Kil.) G75	136	CA54

Slioch Sq, Moth. ML1	113	DE41
off Law Dr		
Sloy St, G22	50	BT25
Small Cres, (Blan.) G72	124	CM46
Smeaton Av, (Torr.) G64	15	BX13
Smeaton Dr, (Bishop.) G64	33	BW17
Smeaton Gro, G20	49	BP23
Smeaton St, G20	49	BP23
Smith Cl, (Bishop.) G64	51	BZ21
Smith Cres, Clyde. G81	27	AX16
Smith Gdns, (Bishop.) G64	51	BZ21
Smith Gro, (Bishop.) G64	51	BZ21
Smithhills St, Pais. PA1	62	AU32
Smith Quad, Coat. ML5	75	CY30
Smiths La, Pais. PA3	62	AU31
Smithstone Cres, (Kilsyth) G65	7	CU8
Smithstone Rd, (Cumb.) G68	20	CV11
Smith St, G14	65	BG27
Smith Ter, (Ruther.) G73	89	BX36
Smith Way, (Bishop.) G64	51	BZ21
Smithycroft, Ham. ML3	141	CW51
Smithycroft Rd, G33	70	CA28
Snaefell Av, (Ruther.) G73	105	BY41
Snaefell Cres, (Ruther.) G73	105	BY40
Sneddon St, Ham. ML3	125	CP47
Sneddon Ter, Ham. ML3	125	CP47
Snowdon Pl, G5	88	BT33
off Benthall St		
Snowdon St, G5	88	BT33
off Benthall St		
Snuff Mill Rd, G44	103	BR40
Society St, G31	69	BX32
Solar Ct, Lark. ML9	144	DD61
Sollas Pl, G13	46	BA21
Solway St, Ham. ML3	139	CR53
Solway Pl, (Chry.) G69	36	CM20
Solway Rd, (Bishop.) G64	33	BZ19
Solway St, G40	88	BV35
Somerford Rd, (Bears.) G61	29	BH20
Somerled Av, Pais. PA3	62	AV28
Somerset Av, Ham. ML3	125	CR49
Somerset Pl, G3	4	BP28
Somerset Pl Ms, G3	4	BP28
Somervell St, (Camb.) G72	106	CB39
Somerville Dr, G42	87	BR37
Somerville Dr, (E.Kil.) G75	136	CB54
Somerville La, (E.Kil.) G75	136	CB54
Somerville Ter, (E.Kil.) G75	136	CB54
off The Murray Rd		
Sorby St, G31	69	BZ32
Sorley St, G11	65	BH27
off Dumbarton Rd		
Sorn St, G40	89	BX34
Souterhouse Rd, Coat. ML5	74	CV32
Southampton Dr, G12	48	BK23
Southampton La, G12	48	BK23
South Annandale St, G42	87	BR35
South Av, (Blan.) G72	124	CM48
South Av, Clyde. G81	27	AW19
South Av, Pais. PA2	82	AV37
South Av, Renf. PA4	45	AZ26
Southbank Dr, (Kirk.) G66	17	CE13
Southbank Rd, (Kirk.) G66	17	CE14
Southbank St, G31	69	BZ32
South Bk St, Clyde. G81	45	AY22
Southbar Av, G13	46	BC22
Southbar Rd, Ersk. PA8	43	AQ23
Southbar Rd, Renf. PA4	43	AQ23
South Barrwood Rd, (Kilsyth) G65	7	CU6
South Biggar Rd, Air. ML6	76	DD30
Southbrae Dr, G13	47	BE24
Southbrae La, G13	47	BG24
off Milner Rd		
South Br St, Air. ML6	76	DC29
Southburn Rd, Air. ML6	75	CZ30
South Caldeen Rd, Coat. ML5	75	CX32
South Calder, Moth. ML1	128	DB45
South Campbell St, Pais. PA2	82	AU34
South Carbrain Rd, (Cumb.) G67	22	DB13
South Chester St, G32	70	CC32
South Circular Rd, Coat. ML5	75	CW30
South Commonhead Av, Air. ML6	76	DC28
Southcroft Rd, (Ruther.) G73	88	BU36
Southcroft St, G51	66	BK30
South Cft St, Pais. PA1	62	AV32
off Lawn St		
South Crosshill Rd, (Bishop.) G64	33	BW20
South Dean Pk Av, (Both.) G71	109	CQ43
Southdeen Av, G15	28	BD18
Southdeen Gro, G15	28	BD18
Southdeen Rd, G15	28	BC18
South Douglas St, Clyde. G81	45	AY21
South Dr, (Linw.) Pais. PA3	60	AK31
South Dumbreck Rd, (Kilsyth) G65	7	CR5
South Elgin Pl, Clyde. G81	45	AY22
South Elgin St, Clyde. G81	45	AY22
Southend Pl, Bell. ML4	110	CV41
Southend Rd, Clyde. G81	27	AX16
Southern Av, (Ruther.) G73	105	BX40
Southerness Dr, (Cumb.) G68	9	DC8
off Letham Gra		
South Erskine Pk, (Bears.) G61	29	BF16
Southesk Av, (Bishop.) G64	32	BV18
Southesk Gdns, (Bishop.) G64	32	BV18
South Ex Ct, G1	5	BS30
Southfield Av, Pais. PA2	82	AU37
Southfield Cres, G53	85	BE37
Southfield Cres, Coat. ML5	75	CY32
Southfield Rd, (Cumb.) G68	21	CY12
South Frederick St, G1	5	BS30
Southgate, (Miln.) G62	12	BJ12
off Park Rd		
Southgate, (E.Kil.) G74	136	CA53
off The Plaza Shop Cen		
South Glassford St, (Miln.) G62	12	BK12
South Hallhill Rd, G32	70	CD32
Southhill Av, (Ruther.) G73	105	BY40
Southinch Av, G14	46	BA23
Southinch La, G14	46	BA23
Southlea Av, (Thornlie.) G46	102	BJ42
South Ln, (Chry.) G69	55	CN21
Southloch Gdns, G21	50	BV26
Southloch St, G21	50	BV26
South Mains Rd, (Miln.) G62	11	BH12
South Medrox St, (Glenb.) Coat. ML5	56	CS22
South Moraine La, G15	29	BE19
off Moraine Av		
South Muirhead Rd, (Cumb.) G67	22	DC11
Southmuir Pl, G20	48	BM24
South Nimmo St, Air. ML6	76	DD30
South Nitshill Ind Est, G53	100	BC40
Southpark Av, G12	66	BM27
South Pk Av, (Barr.) G78	99	AX42
South Pk Dr, Pais. PA2	82	AU35
South Pk Gro, Ham. ML3	126	CT50
Southpark La, G12	67	BN27
South Pk Rd, Ham. ML3	126	CT50
Southpark Ter, G12	67	BN27
off Southpark Av		
South Pl, Bell. ML4	110	CV41
South Portland St, G5	67	BR32
South Rd, (Clark.) G76	119	BQ48
South Robertson Pl, Air. ML6	76	DA30
South Scott St, (Baill.) G69	92	CK33
Southside Cres, G5	87	BR33
South St, G11	65	BF27
South St, G14	65	BF27
South St, (Inch.) Renf. PA4	43	AR25
South Vesalius St, G32	70	CC32
off Shettleston Rd		
South Vw, (Blan.) G72	108	CL44
South Vw, Bell. ML4	110	CU41
South Vw, Clyde. G81	26	AV18
Southview Av, (Clark.) G76	119	BN48
Southview Ct, (Bishop.) G64	50	BV22
off Southview Ter		
Southview Dr, (Bears.) G61	29	BE16
Southview Gro, (Bears.) G61	29	BE16
Southview Pl, (Gart.) G69	55	CN23
Southview Ter, (Bishop.) G64	50	BV22
South William St, John. PA5	79	AH35
Southwold Rd, Pais. PA1	64	BA32
Southwood Dr, G44	104	BS40
Southwood Pl, (Newt. M.) G77	131	BF51
South Woodside Rd, G4	67	BN27
South Woodside Rd, G20	49	BP26
Soutra Pl, G33	70	CD29
Spairdrum Rd, (Cumb.) G67	40	DA17
Spairdrum Rd, Air. ML6	40	DC17
Spalehall Dr, Moth. ML1	113	DH42
Spateston Rd, John. PA5	79	AE38
Spean Av, (E.Kil.) G74	136	CD52
Spean St, G44	103	BQ39
Speirsfield Ct, Pais. PA2	82	AT34
Speirsfield Gdns, Pais. PA2	82	AU34
Speirshall Cl, G14	46	BB23
Speirshall Ter, G14	46	BA23
Speirs Rd, (Bears.) G61	30	BJ18
Speirs Rd, John. PA5	80	AK34
Spencer Dr, Pais. PA2	80	AM37
Spencerfield Gdns, Ham. ML3	126	CV50
Spencer St, G13	47	BH22
Spencer St, Clyde. G81	27	AW18
Spence St, G20	48	BL21
Spey Av, Pais. PA2	81	AN36
Spey Ct, Air. ML6	77	DE32
off Etive Dr		
Spey Dr, Coat. ML5	94	CU33
Spey Dr, Renf. PA4	64	BA27
Spey Gdns, Ham. ML3	139	CR53
Spey Gro, (E.Kil.) G75	134	BU54
Spey Pl, John. PA5	79	AE37
Spey Rd, (Bears.) G61	29	BE19
Spey St, G33	70	CB29
Spey Ter, (E.Kil.) G75	134	BV54
Spey Wk, (Cumb.) G67	22	DB12
off Cumbernauld Shop Cen		
Spey Wk, Moth. ML1	113	DE39
off Redwood Rd		
Spey Wynd, Lark. ML9	144	DC61
off Riverside Rd		
Spiersbridge Av, (Thornlie.) G46	10?	
Spiersbridge La, (Thornlie.) G46		

Spiersbridge Rd, (Thornlie.) G46 101 BH42
Spiersbridge Ter, (Thornlie.) G46 101 BG42
Spiersbridge Toll, (Thornlie.) G46 101 BH43
Spiers Gro, (Thornlie.) G46 101 BH42
Spiers Pl, (Linw.) Pais. PA3 60 AL30
Spiers Wf, G4 67 BR27
Spindlehowe Rd, (Udd.) G71 109 CP39
Spinners Gdns, Pais. PA2 81 AR34
Spinners Row, John. PA5 79 AF35
Spittal Rd, (Ruther.) G73 104 BV41
Spittal Ter, (Camb.) G72 108 CJ43
Spoolers Rd, Pais. PA1 82 AS34
Spoutmouth, G1 5 BT31
Springbank Rd, Pais. PA3 62 AT30
Springbank St, G20 49 BP25
Springbank Ter, Pais. PA3 62 AT30
Springbank Vw, (Plains) Air. ML6 59 DH26
Springboig Av, G32 71 CE31
Springboig Rd, G32 71 CE30
Springburn Pl, (E.Kil.) G74 121 BW50
Springburn Rd, G21 68 BU27
Springburn Rd, (Bishop.) G64 50 BU24
Springburn Shop Cen, G21 50 BV25
Springburn Way, G21 50 BU25
Springcroft Av, (Baill.) G69 72 CK31
Springcroft Cres, (Baill.) G69 72 CK31
Springcroft Dr, (Baill.) G69 72 CJ31
Springcroft Gdns, (Baill.) G69 72 CL31
Springcroft Gro, (Baill.) G69 72 CK31
Springcroft Rd, (Baill.) G69 72 CK31
Springcroft Wynd, (Baill.) G69 72 CK31
Springfield Av, (Bishop.) G64 51 BW21
Springfield Av, (Udd.) G71 109 CP40
Springfield Av, Pais. PA1 83 AX33
Springfield Ct, G1 5 BS30
Springfield Cres, (Bishop.) G64 51 BW21
Springfield Cres, (Udd.) G71 109 CP40
Springfield Cres, (Blan.) G72 124 CL46
Springfield Dr, (Barr.) G78 100 BA44
Springfield Gro, (Barr.) G78 115 AZ45
Springfield Pk, John. PA5 80 AJ35
Springfield Pk Rd, (Ruther.) G73 105 BY39
Springfield Quay, G5 4 BP31
Springfield Rd, G31 89 BY33
Springfield Rd, G40 89 BX34
Springfield Rd, (Bishop.) G64 33 BW20
Springfield Rd, (Cumb.) G67 22 DC9
Springfield Rd, (Barr.) G78 115 AY45
Springfield Rd, Air. ML6 77 DG29
Springfield Sq, (Bishop.) G64 51 BW21
Springfield Wds, John. PA5 80 AJ35
off Springfield Pk
Springhall Ct, (Ruther.) G73 105 BZ42
off Cruachan Rd
Springhill Av, Air. ML6 76 DD29
Springhill Av, Coat. ML5 94 CS33
Springhill Dr N, (Baill.) G69 72 CJ30
Springhill Dr S, (Baill.) G69 72 CJ30
Springhill Fm Gro, (Baill.) G69 72 CJ31
Springhill Fm Pl, (Baill.) G69 72 CJ31
Springhill Fm Rd, (Baill.) G69 72 CJ31
Springhill Fm Way, (Baill.) G69 72 CJ31
Springhill Gdns, G41 87 BN36
Springhill Parkway, (Baill.) G69 72 CJ31
Springhill Pl, Coat. ML5 94 CS33
Springhill Rd, (Baill.) G69 71 CH32

Springhill Rd, (Clark.) G76 119 BP46
Springhill Rd, (Barr.) G78 99 AX43
Springholm Dr, Air. ML6 76 DB27
Springkell Av, G41 86 BL34
Springkell Dr, G41 86 BK35
Springkell Gdns, G41 86 BL35
Springkell Gate, G41 86 BM35
Spring La, G5 88 BS34
off Lawmoor St
Springside Gdns, G15 28 BC16
Springside Pl, G15 28 BC17
Springvale Dr, Pais. PA2 81 AP35
Springvale Ter, G21 50 BU25
Springwell Cres, (Blan.) G72 125 CP46
Springwells Av, Air. ML6 77 DE29
Springwells Cres, Air. ML6 77 DE29
Spring Wynd, G5 88 BS33
Spruce Av, (Blan.) G72 124 CL45
Spruce Av, Ham. ML3 140 CU52
Spruce Av, John. PA5 80 AJ35
Spruce Ct, Coat. ML5 94 CV33
off Ailsa Rd
Spruce Ct, Ham. ML3 140 CU52
Spruce Dr, (Kirk.) G66 34 CC16
Spruce Dr, (Camb.) G72 107 CH41
Spruce Rd, (Cumb.) G67 23 DF9
Spruce Rd, (Udd.) G71 94 CS36
off Laburnum Rd
Spruce St, G22 50 BT24
Spruce Way, (Camb.) G72 107 CH41
Spruce Way, Moth. ML1 112 DD41
off Shirrel Rd
Spynie Pl, (Bishop.) G64 33 BZ19
Squire St, G14 65 BF27
Stable Gro, Pais. PA1 81 AR33
Stable Pl, (Miln.) G62 11 BH10
Stable Rd, (Miln.) G62 11 BH10
Staffa, (E.Kil.) G74 137 CE53
Staffa Av, Renf. PA4 63 AY28
Staffa Dr, (Kirk.) G66 18 CK13
Staffa Dr, Air. ML6 77 DH30
Staffa Dr, Pais. PA2 82 AU38
Staffa Rd, (Camb.) G72 106 CB42
Staffa St, G31 69 BX29
Staffa Ter, (Camb.) G72 106 CB42
Staffin Dr, G23 30 BM20
Staffin Path, G23 31 BN20
Staffin St, G23 31 BN20
Stafford St, G4 5 BT28
Stafford St, Bell. ML4 110 CV41
Stag St, G51 66 BK30
Staig Wynd, Moth. ML1 128 DC49
off Dunbar Dr
Staineybraes Pl, Air. ML6 76 DB27
Stair St, G20 49 BP25
Stamford Pl, G31 69 BX32
Stamford Rd, G31 69 BX32
Stamford St, G31 69 BX32
Stamford St, G40 69 BX32
Stamperland Av, (Clark.) G76 119 BP45
Stamperland Cres, (Clark.) G76 119 BN45
off Stamperland Hill
Stamperland Dr, (Clark.) G76 119 BP45
Stamperland Gdns, (Clark.) G76 103 BP44
Stamperland Hill, (Clark.) G76 119 BN45
Stanalane St, (Thornlie.) G46 101 BH41
Standburn Rd, G21 51 BY22
Staneacre Pk, Ham. ML3 126 CV50
Stanefield Dr, Moth. ML1 113 DG41
Stanely Av, Pais. PA2 81 AR36

Stanely Cres, Pais. PA2 81 AR37
Stanely Dr, Pais. PA2 82 AS36
Stanely Gra, Pais. PA2 81 AQ38
Stanely Gro, Pais. PA2 81 AR37
Stanely Rd, Pais. PA2 82 AS36
Stanford St, Clyde. G81 27 AY20
Stanhope Dr, (Ruther.) G73 105 BZ40
Stanley Boul, (Blan.) G72 124 CM49
Stanley Dr, (Bishop.) G64 33 BX19
Stanley Dr, Bell. ML4 111 CW39
Stanley Pl, (Blan.) G72 108 CM44
Stanley St, G41 67 BN32
Stanley St, Ham. ML3 125 CP49
Stanley St La, G41 67 BN32
Stanmore Rd, G42 87 BR37
Stark Av, Clyde. G81 26 AU15
Starling Way, Bell. ML4 94 CU37
Startpoint St, G33 70 CC29
Station Brae, (Neil.) G78 114 AS45
Station Cres, Renf. PA4 45 AZ25
off Station Rd
Station Pk, (Baill.) G69 92 CL33
Station Rd, G20 48 BL21
Station Rd, (Millerston) G33 52 CC24
Station Rd, (Stepps) G33 53 CF24
Station Rd, (Giff.) G46 102 BL42
off Fenwick Rd
Station Rd, (Old Kil.) G60 25 AR15
Station Rd, (Bears.) G61 29 BE18
Station Rd, (Bardowie) G62 13 BQ14
Station Rd, (Miln.) G62 12 BJ12
Station Rd, (Kilsyth) G65 7 CT4
Station Rd, (Lenz.) G66 35 CE17
Station Rd, (Baill.) G69 92 CL33
Station Rd, (Muir.) G69 54 CL23
Station Rd, (Both.) G71 109 CQ43
Station Rd, (Udd.) G71 109 CN39
Station Rd, (Blan.) G72 109 CN44
Station Rd, (Clark.) G76 119 BQ48
Station Rd, (Neil.) G78 114 AT46
Station Rd, Air. ML6 77 DG29
Station Rd, Bish. PA7 24 AK19
Station Rd, (Kilb.) John. PA10 78 AC34
Station Rd, Lark. ML9 144 DD57
Station Rd, Moth. ML1 112 DC42
Station Rd, Pais. PA1 81 AQ34
Station Rd, Renf. PA4 45 AZ25
Station Way, (Udd.) G71 109 CP39
Station Wynd, (Kilb.) John. PA10 78 AD35
Staybrae Dr, G53 84 BB36
Staybrae Gro, G53 84 BB36
Steel St, G1 5 BT31
Steeple Sq, (Kilb.) John. PA10 78 AC34
off Ewing St
Steeple St, (Kilb.) John. PA10 78 AC34
Stenhouse Av, (Muir.) G69 54 CL22
Stenton Cres, Wis. ML2 143 DF52
Stenton Pl, Wis. ML2 143 DF52
off Carbarns Rd
Stenton St, G32 70 CA30
Stepford Pl, G33 71 CH30
Stepford Rd, G33 71 CH30
Stephen Cres, (Baill.) G69 71 CH32
Stephenson Pl, (E.Kil.) G75 135 BZ53
Stephenson Sq, (E.Kil.) G75 135 BZ53
off Simpson Dr
Stephenson St, G52 64 BA29
Stephenson Ter, (E.Kil.) G75 135 BZ53
Steppshill Ter, G33 53 CE24
Stepps Rd, G33 71 CE28

Stepps Rd, (Kirk.) G66	35	CG19
Stevens La, Moth. ML1	112	DC42
off Jerviston St		
Stevenson Pl, Bell. ML4	95	CX38
off Kelvin Rd		
Stevenson St, G40	5	BU31
Stevenson St, Clyde. G81	26	AV17
Stevenson St, Pais. PA2	82	AU34
Stevenson Ct, (New Stev.)	112	DC41
Moth. ML1		
Stevenston St, Moth. ML1	112	DC41
Stewart Av, (Blan.) G72	124	CL46
Stewart Av, (Newt. M.) G77	117	BG47
Stewart Av, Renf. PA4	63	AX28
Stewart Ct, (Ruther.) G73	89	BY38
Stewart Ct, (Barr.) G78	99	AY41
off Stewart St		
Stewart Cres, (Barr.) G78	99	AZ41
Stewart Dr, (Baill.) G69	73	CR31
Stewart Dr, (Clark.) G76	118	BM45
Stewart Dr, Clyde. G81	27	AX15
Stewartfield Cres, (E.Kil.) G74	121	BY49
Stewartfield Dr, (E.Kil.) G74	121	BZ49
Stewartfield Rd, (E.Kil.) G74	121	BY50
Stewartfield Way, (E.Kil.) G74	121	BW49
Stewartgill Pl, (Ashgill) Lark.	145	DH60
ML9 off Auldton Ter		
Stewarton Dr, (Camb.) G72	106	CA40
Stewarton Rd, (Thornlie.) G46	101	BG43
Stewarton Rd, (Newt. M.) G77	117	BE46
Stewart Pl, (Barr.) G78	99	AZ41
Stewart Rd, Pais. PA2	82	AV37
Stewart St, G4	4	BR28
Stewart St, (Miln.) G62	12	BJ12
Stewart St, (Barr.) G78	99	AZ41
Stewart St, Bell. ML4	111	CY40
Stewart St, Clyde. G81	26	AU18
Stewart St, Coat. ML5	75	CW29
Stewart St, Ham. ML3	125	CQ48
Stewartville St, G11	66	BK27
Stirling Av, (Bears.) G61	29	BG19
Stirling Av, (E.Kil.) G74	122	CC50
Stirling Dr, (Bears.) G61	29	BE15
Stirling Dr, (Bishop.) G64	32	BU18
Stirling Dr, (Ruther.) G73	105	BX40
Stirling Dr, Ham. ML3	125	CN49
Stirling Dr, John. PA5	79	AF35
Stirlingfauld Pl, G5	67	BR32
Stirling Gdns, (Bishop.) G64	32	BU18
Stirling Rd, G4	5	BT29
Stirling Rd, (Kilsyth) G65	8	CV4
Stirling Rd, (Cumb.) G67	40	DC15
Stirling Rd, Air. ML6	58	DD26
Stirling Rd, (Riggend) Air. ML6	40	DC20
Stirling Rd Ind Est, Air. ML6	59	DE26
Stirling St, (Cumb.) G67	22	DD9
Stirling St, Air. ML6	76	DB30
Stirling St, Coat. ML5	94	CT33
Stirling St, Moth. ML1	128	DD49
Stirling Way, (Baill.) G69	92	CJ33
off Huntingtower Rd		
Stirling Way, Renf. PA4	63	AZ28
off York Way		
Stirrat St, G20	48	BL23
Stirrat St, Pais. PA3	61	AR30
Stobcross Rd, G3	66	BM29
Stobcross St, G3	4	BP30
Stobcross St, Coat. ML5	75	CW31
Stobcross Wynd, G3	66	BL29
Stobhill Cotts, G21	51	BW22
off Stobhill Rd		

Stobhill Rd, G21	50	BV22
Stobo, (E.Kil.) G74	123	CE49
Stobo Ct, (E.Kil.) G74	123	CE49
Stobs Dr, (Barr.) G78	99	AX40
Stobs Pl, G34	72	CL28
Stock Av, Pais. PA2	82	AU34
Stockholm Cres, Pais. PA2	82	AU34
Stockiemuir Av, (Bears.) G61	11	BF14
Stockiemuir Rd, (Bears.) G61	11	BE12
Stock St, Pais. PA2	82	AU34
Stockwell Pl, G1	5	BS31
Stockwell St, G1	5	BS31
Stoddard Sq, (Elder.) John.	80	AM34
PA5		
Stonebank Gro, G45	104	BT42
Stonebyres Ct, Ham. ML3	125	CQ50
Stonedyke Gro, G15	28	BD19
Stonefield Av, G12	48	BK23
Stonefield Av, Pais. PA2	82	AV36
Stonefield Cres, (Blan.) G72	124	CK47
Stonefield Cres, (Clark.) G76	118	BL45
off Dorian Dr		
Stonefield Cres, Pais. PA2	82	AV36
Stonefield Dr, Pais. PA2	82	AV36
Stonefield Gdns, Pais. PA2	82	AV36
Stonefield Grn, Pais. PA2	82	AU36
Stonefield Gro, Pais. PA2	82	AU36
Stonefield Pk, Pais. PA2	82	AU37
Stonefield Pk Gdns, (Blan.)	124	CM45
G72		
Stonefield Pl, (Blan.) G72	124	CK47
Stonefield Rd, (Blan.) G72	124	CL46
Stonefield St, Air. ML6	76	DC28
Stonehall Av, Ham. ML3	139	CR51
Stonehaven Cres, Air. ML6	76	DA32
Stonelaw Dr, (Ruther.) G73	89	BX38
Stonelaw Rd, (Ruther.) G73	89	BX38
Stonelaw Twrs, (Ruther.) G73	105	BY39
Stoneside Dr, G43	102	BJ39
Stoneside Sq, G43	102	BJ39
Stoney Brae, Pais. PA1	62	AU32
Stoney Brae, Pais. PA2	82	AU30
Stoneyetts Cotts, (Chry.) G69	37	CN17
Stoneyetts Rd, (Mood.) G69	37	CP18
Stoneymeadow Rd, (Blan.)	123	CF48
G72		
Stoneymeadow Rd, (E.Kil.)	122	CD49
G74		
Stonyhurst St, G22	49	BR25
Stonylee Rd, (Cumb.) G67	22	DC12
Storie St, Pais. PA1	82	AU33
Stormyland Way, (Barr.) G78	99	AY43
Stornoway St, G22	50	BS21
Stow Brae, Pais. PA1	82	AU33
Stow St, Pais. PA1	82	AU33
Strachan St, Bell. ML4	111	CW41
Strachur St, G22	49	BQ22
Straiton Dr, Ham. ML3	138	CM51
Straiton Pl, (Blan.) G72	124	CM45
Straiton St, G32	70	CA30
Stranka Av, Pais. PA2	82	AS34
Stranraer Dr, G15	29	BE19
Stratford, (E.Kil.) G74	123	CF48
Stratford St, G20	48	BM24
Strathallan Cres, Air. ML6	58	DC26
Strathallandale Ct, (E.Kil.) G75	134	BU53
Strathallan Gdns, (Kirk.) G66	17	CF13
off Willowbank Gdns		
Strathallon Pl, (Ruther.) G73	105	BZ42
off Ranald Gdns		

Strathaven Rd, (E.Kil.) G75	136	CC53
Strathavon Cres, Air. ML6	76	DC27
Strathblane Cres, Air. ML6	58	DC26
Strathblane Dr, (E.Kil.) G75	134	BU53
Strathblane Gdns, G13	47	BH21
Strathblane Rd, (Miln.) G62	12	BL10
Strathbran St, G31	89	BZ33
Strathcairn Cres, Air. ML6	58	DC26
Strathcarron Cres, Pais. PA2	83	AX36
Strathcarron Dr, Pais. PA2	83	AX36
Strathcarron Pl, G20	49	BN23
off Glenfinnan Rd		
Strathcarron Pl, Pais. PA2	83	AX36
Strathcarron Rd, Pais. PA2	83	AX37
Strathcarron Way, Pais. PA2	83	AX36
Strathclyde Business Pk, Bell.	94	CV37
ML4		
Strathclyde Dr, (Ruther.) G73	89	BW38
Strathclyde Path, (Udd.) G71	109	CN39
Strathclyde Rd, Moth. ML1	127	CX47
Strathclyde St, G40	89	BW35
Strath Clyde Vw, (Both.) G71	109	CR44
Strathclyde Way, Bell. ML4	95	CY38
off Clay Cres		
Strathcona Dr, G13	47	BH22
Strathcona Gdns, G13	48	BJ22
Strathcona La, (E.Kil.) G75	136	CA54
Strathcona Pl, (Ruther.) G73	105	BZ41
off Ross Pl		
Strathcona Pl, (E.Kil.) G75	136	CA54
Strathcona St, G13	47	BH22
Strathconon Gdns, (E.Kil.)	134	BU52
G75 off Strathnairn Dr		
Strathdearn Gro, (E.Kil.) G75	134	BU53
Strathdee Av, Clyde. G81	27	AX16
Strathdee Rd, G44	103	BN43
Strathdon Av, G44	103	BP43
Strathdon Av, Pais. PA2	82	AS35
Strathdon Dr, G44	103	BP43
Strathdon Pl, (E.Kil.) G75	134	BU53
off Strathnairn Dr		
Strathearn Gro, (Kirk.) G66	18	CK11
Strathearn Rd, (Clark.) G76	119	BN47
Strathendrick Dr, G44	103	BN41
Strathfillan Rd, (E.Kil.) G74	135	BZ51
Strathgoil Cres, Air. ML6	58	DC26
Strathkelvin Av, (Bishop.) G64	50	BV22
off Southview Ter		
Strathkelvin La, (E.Kil.) G75	134	BU53
Strathkelvin Pl, (Kirk.) G66	17	CE14
Strathkelvin Retail Pk,	33	BY16
(Bishop.) G64		
Strathmiglo Ct, (E.Kil.) G75	134	BU53
Strathmore Av, (Blan.) G72	108	CL44
Strathmore Av, Pais. PA1	83	AZ33
Strathmore Cres, Air. ML6	76	DC27
off Broompark Cres		
Strathmore Gdns, (Ruther.)	105	BZ41
G73		
Strathmore Gro, (E.Kil.) G75	134	BU53
Strathmore Ho, (E.Kil.) G74	136	CA52
off Cornwall St		
Strathmore Pl, Coat. ML5	75	CZ32
off Strathmore Wk		
Strathmore Rd, G22	49	BR22
Strathmore Rd, Ham. ML3	126	CU50
Strathmore Wk, Coat. ML5	75	CZ32
Strathmungo Cres, Air. ML6	76	DB27
off Springholm Dr		
Strathnairn Av, (E.Kil.) G75	134	BU53

Strathnairn Ct, (E.Kil.) G75	134	BU53
off Strathnairn Dr		
Strathnairn Dr, (E.Kil.) G75	134	BU53
Strathnairn Way, (E.Kil.) G75	134	BU53
Strathnaver Cres, Air. ML6	58	DC26
Strathnaver Gdns, (E.Kil.) G75	134	BU53
off Strathnairn Av		
Strathord Pl, (Mood.) G69	37	CQ18
Strathord St, G32	90	CC34
Strathpeffer Cres, Air. ML6	76	DC27
Strathpeffer Dr, (E.Kil.) G75	134	BU52
off Strathnairn Dr		
Strathrannoch Way, (E.Kil.) G75	134	BU53
Strathspey Av, (E.Kil.) G75	134	BU53
Strathspey Cres, Air. ML6	58	DC26
Strathtay Av, G44	103	BP43
Strathtay Av, (E.Kil.) G75	134	BU53
Strathtummel Cres, Air. ML6	58	DC26
Strathview Gdns, (Bears.) G61	29	BF17
Strathview Gro, G44	103	BN43
Strathview Pk, G44	103	BP43
Strathview Rd, Bell. ML4	110	CU42
Strathvithie Gro, (E.Kil.) G75	134	BU53
Strathy Pl, G20	48	BM24
off Glenfinnan Rd		
Strathyre Ct, (E.Kil.) G75	134	BU53
Strathyre Gdns, (Bears.) G61	30	BK16
Strathyre Gdns, (Mood.) G69	37	CQ18
off Heathfield Av		
Strathyre Gdns, (E.Kil.) G75	134	BU53
Strathyre Gdns, (Glenm.) Air. ML6 off Banchory Av	58	DB24
Strathyre Rd, (Blan.) G72	125	CP47
Strathyre St, G41	87	BN37
Stratton Dr, (Giff.) G46	102	BK43
Strauss Av, Clyde. G81	28	BA20
Stravaig Path, Pais. PA2	81	AQ38
Stravaig Wk, Pais. PA2	81	AQ38
Stravanan Av, G45	104	BU43
Stravanan Ct, G45	104	BU43
Stravanan Gdns, G45	104	BT43
Stravanan Pl, G51	104	BT43
Stravanan Rd, G45	104	BT43
Stravanan St, G45	104	BT43
Stravanan Ter, G45	104	BT43
Strawhill Rd, (Clark.) G76	119	BN46
Streamfield Gdns, G33	51	BZ22
Streamfield Gate, G33	51	BZ22
off Brookfield Dr		
Streamfield Lea, G33	51	BZ22
Streamfield Pl, G33	51	BZ22
Strenabey Av, (Ruther.) G73	105	BZ41
Striven Gdns, G20	49	BP26
Striven Ter, Ham. ML3	139	CQ51
Stroma St, G21	69	BX27
Stromness St, G5	87	BQ33
Strone Gdns, (Kilsyth) G65	7	CR5
Stronend St, G22	49	BR24
Strone Path, (Glenb.) Coat. ML5	56	CS23
off Dinyra Pl		
Strone Pl, Air. ML6	77	DE32
Strone Rd, G33	70	CD30
Stronsay Pl, (Bishop.) G64	33	BZ19
Stronsay St, G21	69	BX27
Stronvar Dr, G14	46	BD25
Stronvar La, G14	46	BD25
off Larchfield Av		
Stroud Rd, (E.Kil.) G75	135	BZ55
Strowan Cres, G32	90	CD33
Strowan St, G32	90	CD33
Struan Av, (Giff.) G46	102	BK42
Struan Gdns, G44	103	BQ40
Struan Rd, G44	103	BQ40
Struie St, G34	72	CJ29
Struma Dr, (Clark.) G76	118	BL45
Strutherhill Ind Est, Lark. ML9	145	DE61
Struthers Cres, (E.Kil.) G74	122	CD49
Struther St, Lark. ML9	144	DD61
Stuart Av, (Old Kil.) G60	25	AR16
Stuart Av, (Ruther.) G73	105	BX40
Stuart Dr, (Bishop.) G64	50	BU21
Stuart Dr, Lark. ML9	145	DE60
Stuarton Pk, (E.Kil.) G74	136	CA51
Stuart Quad, (Holytown) Moth. ML1	112	DD39
Stuart Quad, Wis. ML2	143	DF52
Stuart Rd, (Carm.) G76	120	BT45
Stuart Rd, Bish. PA7	24	AK17
Stuart St, (Old Kil.) G60	25	AR16
Stuart St, (E.Kil.) G74	136	CB51
Succoth St, G13	47	BH22
Sudbury Cres, (E.Kil.) G75	135	BX52
Suffolk St, G40	5	BU31
off Kent St		
Sugworth Av, (Baill.) G69	72	CK32
Suisnish, Ersk. PA8	44	AS22
Sumburgh St, G33	70	CB29
Summerfield Cotts, G14	65	BG27
Summerfield Rd, (Cumb.) G67	39	CW15
Summerfield St, G40	89	BX35
Summerhill & Garngibbock Rd, G67	39	CY18
Summerhill Av, Lark. ML9	144	DC59
Summerhill Dr, G15	28	BD17
Summerhill Gdns, G15	28	BD17
Summerhill Pl, G15	28	BD17
Summerhill Rd, G15	28	BC17
Summerhill Rd, (Clark.) G76	119	BP46
Summerhill Way, Bell. ML4	110	CV41
Summerlea Rd, (Thornlie.) G46	101	BH41
Summerlee Cotts, Coat. ML5	74	CV30
off Melrose Pl		
Summerlee Rd, Lark. ML9	142	DB56
Summerlee St, G33	71	CE29
Summerlee St, Coat. ML5	74	CV30
Summer St, G40	68	BV32
Summertown Rd, G51	66	BK30
Sunart Av, Renf. PA4	45	AX25
Sunart Ct, Ham. ML3	139	CQ52
off Etive Av		
Sunart Gdns, (Bishop.) G64	33	BY20
Sunart Rd, G52	65	BG32
Sunart Rd, (Bishop.) G64	33	BY20
Sunbury Av, (Clark.) G76	118	BL46
Sundale Av, (Clark.) G76	118	BM46
Sunflower Gdns, Moth. ML1	127	CZ45
off Park Neuk St		
Sunningdale Av, (Newt. M.) G77	117	BH48
Sunningdale Rd, G23	48	BM21
Sunningdale Wynd, (Both.) G71	109	CN42
Sunnybank Dr, (Clark.) G76	118	BM47
Sunnybank Gro, (Clark.) G76	118	BM47
Sunnybank St, G40	89	BX34
Sunnyhill, (Kilsyth) G65	19	CP10
Sunnylaw Dr, Pais. PA2	81	AQ35
Sunnylaw St, G22	49	BR25
Sunnyside Av, (Udd.) G71	109	CP40
Sunnyside Av, Moth. ML1	112	DD40
Sunnyside Cres, Moth. ML1	112	DC40
Sunnyside Dr, G15	28	BC20
Sunnyside Dr, (Baill.) G69	73	CP32
Sunnyside Dr, (Clark.) G76	118	BM45
Sunnyside Oval, Pais. PA2	82	AU36
Sunnyside Pl, G15	28	BC20
Sunnyside Pl, (Barr.) G78	99	AX43
Sunnyside Pl, Moth. ML1	112	DC40
Sunnyside Rd, Coat. ML5	75	CW30
Sunnyside Rd, Pais. PA2	82	AT35
Sunnyside St, Lark. ML9	144	DB57
Sunnyside Ter, Moth. ML1	112	DC40
Surrey St, G5	87	BR33
Sussex St, G41	67	BN32
Sutcliffe Ct, G13	47	BG22
off Sutcliffe Rd		
Sutcliffe Rd, G13	47	BG22
Sutherland Av, G41	86	BK34
Sutherland Av, (Bears.) G61	11	BG14
Sutherland Cres, Ham. ML3	125	CQ49
Sutherland Dr, (Giff.) G46	102	BM44
Sutherland Dr, Air. ML6	76	DB32
Sutherland La, G12	66	BL27
Sutherland Pl, Bell. ML4	110	CV43
Sutherland Rd, Clyde. G81	27	AX19
Sutherland St, (Blan.) G72	124	CL48
Sutherland St, Pais. PA1	62	AT32
Sutherland Way, (E.Kil.) G74	123	CE50
Sutherness Dr, G33	70	CC30
Swaledale, (E.Kil.) G74	121	BY50
Swallow Gdns, G13	46	BB22
Swan Pl, John. PA5	79	AE38
Swanston St, G40	89	BW35
Swan St, G4	5	BS28
Swan St, Clyde. G81	26	AV18
Sween Av, G44	103	BQ41
Sween Dr, Ham. ML3	139	CQ52
Sween Path, Bell. ML4	111	CY42
off Millbank Av		
Sweethill Ter, Coat. ML5	95	CZ34
off Selkirk Way		
Sweethill Wk, Bell. ML4	95	CY38
off Harvey Way		
Sweethope Gdns, (Both.) G71	109	CR43
Sweethope Pl, (Both.) G71	109	CQ42
Swift Bk, Ham. ML3	139	CN52
Swift Cres, G13	46	BB22
Swift Pl, (E.Kil.) G75	134	BU55
Swift Pl, John. PA5	79	AF38
Swindon St, Clyde. G81	26	AU18
Swinton Av, (Baill.) G69	72	CL32
Swinton Cres, (Baill.) G69	72	CL32
Swinton Cres, Coat. ML5	93	CR33
Swinton Dr, G52	64	BD32
Swinton Gdns, (Baill.) G69	72	CM32
off Swinton Av		
Swinton Path, (Baill.) G69	72	CM32
Swinton Pl, G52	64	BD32
Swinton Pl, Coat. ML5	93	CR33
off Dunnachie Dr		
Swinton Rd, (Baill.) G69	72	CL32
Swinton Vw, (Baill.) G69	72	CL32
Swisscot Av, Ham. ML3	139	CR53
Swisscot Wk, Ham. ML3	139	CR53
off Glencoe Pl		
Switchback Rd, (Bears.) G61	29	BH19
Swordale Path, G34	72	CJ29
off Swordale Pl		
Swordale Pl, G34	72	CJ29
Sword St, G31	68	BV31
Sword St, Air. ML6	76	DB30

Sycamore Av, (Lenz.) G66	35	CF15
Sycamore Av, (Udd.) G71	94	CS37
Sycamore Av, John. PA5	80	AJ36
Sycamore Ct, (E.Kil.) G75	135	BZ55
Sycamore Ct, Coat. ML5	94	CV33
off Ailsa Rd		
Sycamore Cres, (E.Kil.) G75	135	BY55
Sycamore Cres, Air. ML6	77	DF31
Sycamore Dr, Air. ML6	77	DF31
Sycamore Dr, Clyde. G81	26	AV17
Sycamore Dr, Ham. ML3	140	CV51
Sycamore Gro, (Blan.) G72	124	CL45
Sycamore Pl, (E.Kil.) G75	135	BZ55
Sycamore Pl, Moth. ML1	112	DD42
Sycamore Way, (Camb.) G72	107	CH41
Sycamore Way, (Carm.) G76	120	BU46
off Manse Rd		
Sydenham La, G12	48	BK26
off Crown Rd S		
Sydenham Rd, G12	48	BL26
Sydes Brae, (Blan.) G72	124	CK49
Sydney Dr, (E.Kil.) G75	135	BY54
Sydney Pl, (E.Kil.) G75	135	BY53
Sydney St, G31	5	BU31
Sydney St, Clyde. G81	26	AT17
Sykehead Av, Bell. ML4	111	CX40
Sykeside St, Air. ML6	96	DA33
Sykes Ter, (Neil.) G78	114	AV46
Sylvania Way, Clyde. G81	27	AX19
Sylvania Way S, Clyde. G81	27	AX20
Symington Dr, Clyde. G81	27	AW19
Symington Sq, (E.Kil.) G75	136	CB53
off Naysmyth Bk		
Syriam Pl, G21	50	BV25
off Syriam St		
Syriam St, G21	50	BV25

T

Tabard Pl, G13	47	BE21
Tabard Pl N, G13	47	BE21
off Tabard Rd		
Tabard Pl S, G13	47	BE21
off Tabard Rd		
Tabard Rd, G13	47	BE21
Tabernacle La, (Camb.) G72	106	CC40
Tabernacle St, (Camb.) G72	106	CC40
Taggart Rd, (Kilsyth) G65	20	CV10
Taig Rd, (Kirk.) G66	18	CK14
Tain Pl, G34	72	CM29
Tait Av, (Barr.) G78	99	AZ41
Tak ma doon Rd, (Kilsyth) G65	7	CU4
Talbot, (E.Kil.) G74	123	CE49
Talbot Ct, G13	46	BD24
Talbot Dr, G13	46	BD24
Talbot Pl, G13	46	BD24
Talbot Ter, G13	46	BD24
off Kintillo Dr		
Talbot Ter, (Udd.) G71	93	CN37
Talisman, Clyde. G81	27	AZ19
off Onslow Rd		
Talisman Cres, Moth. ML1	111	CZ43
Talisman Rd, G13	47	BE23
Talisman Rd, Pais. PA2	81	AN38
Tallant Rd, G15	28	BD18
Tallant Ter, G15	29	BE18
Talla Rd, G52	64	BD32
Tamarack Cres, (Udd.) G71	94	CS36
Tamar Dr, (E.Kil.) G75	134	BV55
Tambowie Av, (Miln.) G62	11	BH11
Tambowie Cres, (Miln.) G62	11	BH11
Tambowie St, G13	47	BG22
Tamshill St, G20	49	BP23
Tamworth St, G40	69	BW32
off Rimsdale St		
Tanar Av, Renf. PA4	64	BB28
Tanar Way, Renf. PA4	64	BA28
off Afton Dr		
Tandlehill Rd, (Kilb.) John. PA10	78	AD36
Tanera Av, G44	104	BS40
Tanfield Pl, G32	71	CE30
off Tanfield St		
Tanfield St, G32	71	CE30
Tankerland Rd, G44	103	BQ39
Tannadice Av, G52	85	BE34
Tannadice Path, G52	85	BE33
off Tannadice Av		
Tanna Dr, G52	85	BH34
Tannahill Cres, John. PA5	79	AG36
Tannahill Dr, (E.Kil.) G74	123	CE50
Tannahill Rd, G43	103	BP39
Tannahill Rd, Pais. PA3	61	AR31
Tannahill Ter, Pais. PA3	61	AR31
Tannoch Dr, (Miln.) G62	12	BK10
Tannoch Dr, (Cumb.) G67	22	DB14
Tannoch Pl, (Cumb.) G67	22	DB14
Tannochside Business Pk, (Udd.) G71	93	CQ36
Tannochside Dr, (Udd.) G71	93	CQ36
Tannock St, G22	49	BR25
Tantallon Dr, Coat. ML5	74	CS28
Tantallon Dr, Pais. PA2	81	AQ36
Tantallon Pk, (E.Kil.) G74	135	BZ51
Tantallon Rd, G41	87	BN38
Tantallon Rd, (Baill.) G69	92	CJ34
Tantallon Rd, (Both.) G71	109	CR42
off Olifard Av		
Tanzieknowe Av, (Camb.) G72	106	CD41
Tanzieknowe Dr, (Camb.) G72	106	CD42
Tanzieknowe Pl, (Camb.) G72	106	CD42
Tanzieknowe Rd, (Camb.) G72	106	CD42
Taransay Ct, G22	50	BT22
off Liddesdale Sq		
Taransay St, G51	66	BJ29
Tarbert Av, (Blan.) G72	108	CL43
Tarbert Ct, Ham. ML3	139	CQ52
Tarbert Way, Coat. ML5	94	CU33
Tarbolton, (E.Kil.) G74	123	CF50
Tarbolton Cres, (Chap.) Air. ML6	97	DF37
Tarbolton Dr, Clyde. G81	27	AY18
Tarbolton Path, Lark. ML9	144	DB58
off Annbank St		
Tarbolton Rd, G43	102	BM39
Tarbolton Rd, (Cumb.) G67	22	DD11
Tarbolton Sq, Clyde. G81	27	AY18
off Tarbolton Dr		
Tarbrax Way, Ham. ML3	125	CQ50
Tarff Av, (Eagle.) G76	133	BN56
Tarfside Av, G52	85	BE33
Tarfside Gdns, G52	85	BF33
Tarfside Oval, G52	85	BF33
Target Rd, Air. ML6	76	DD31
Tarland St, G51	65	BH31
Tarn Gro, G33	51	BZ22
Tarras Dr, Renf. PA4	64	BA28
Tarras Pl, (Camb.) G72	107	CF40
Tasman Dr, (E.Kil.) G75	135	BX54
Tassie Pl, (E.Kil.) G74	136	CC51
Tassie St, G41	86	BM37
Tattershall Rd, G33	71	CE27
Tavistock Dr, G43	102	BM40
Tay Av, Pais. PA2	81	AP36
off Don Dr		
Tay Av, Renf. PA4	46	BA26
Tay Ct, (Mood.) G69	37	CQ19
off Deepdene Rd		
Tay Ct, (E.Kil.) G75	134	BU54
Tay Cres, G33	70	CA28
Tay Cres, (Bishop.) G64	33	BX20
Tay Gdns, Ham. ML3	139	CR53
Tay Gro, (E.Kil.) G75	134	BU54
Tay Ln, Moth. ML1	112	DC40
off Windsor Rd		
Taylor Av, (Kilb.) John. PA10	78	AB34
Taylor Av, Moth. ML1	113	DF43
Taylor Pl, G4	5	BT29
Taylor St, G4	5	BT30
Taylor St, Clyde. G81	45	AY21
Taymouth St, G32	90	CD34
Taynish Dr, G44	103	BK41
Tay Pl, (E.Kil.) G75	134	BU54
Tay Pl, John. PA5	79	AE37
Tay Pl, Lark. ML9	144	DC61
Tay Rd, (Bears.) G61	29	BF19
Tay Rd, (Bishop.) G64	33	BX20
Tayside, Air. ML6	76	DB28
Tay St, Coat. ML5	74	CS28
Tay Ter, (E.Kil.) G75	134	BU53
Tay Wk, (Cumb.) G67	22	DB11
off Cumbernauld Shop Cen		
Teak Pl, (Udd.) G71	94	CT36
Teal Ct, (Strathclyde Bus. Pk.) Bell. ML4	94	CU37
Teal Cres, (E.Kil.) G75	134	BV56
Teal Dr, G13	46	BC22
Tealing Av, G52	85	BE33
Tealing Cres, G52	85	BE33
Teasel Av, G53	100	BD42
Teawell Rd, (Newt. M.) G77	117	BF48
Technology Av, (Blan.) G72	124	CL48
Teesdale, (E.Kil.) G75	121	BY50
Teign Gro, (E.Kil.) G75	134	BV55
Teith Av, Renf. PA4	64	BB27
Teith Dr, (Bears.) G61	29	BF18
Teith Pl, (Camb.) G72	107	CF40
Teith St, G33	70	CA28
Telephone La, G12	48	BL26
Telford Av, (Strutherhill Ind. Est.) Lark. ML9	145	DE61
Telford Ct, Clyde. G81	27	AW19
Telford Pl, (Cumb.) G67	22	DC14
Telford Rd, (Cumb.) G67	22	DC13
Telford Rd, (E.Kil.) G75	136	CB53
Telford St, Bell. ML4	111	CW39
Telford Ter, (E.Kil.) G75	136	CB53
off Bell Grn E		
Teme Pl, (E.Kil.) G75	134	BV54
Templar Av, G13	47	BF2?
Temple Gdns, G13	47	BH?
Templeland Av, G53	85	B?
Templeland Rd, G53	85	B?
Temple Locks Ct, G13	48	
Temple Locks Pl, G13	47	
Temple Rd, G13	4?	
Templetons Business Cen, G40		
Templeton St, G40		
Tennant Av, (E.Kil.) G74		
Tennant Rd, Pais. PA3		
Tennant St, Renf. PA4		
Tennent St, Coat. ML5		

Tennyson Dr, G31	90	CA33
Tenters Way, Pais. PA2	81	AR34
Tern Pl, John. PA5	79	AF38
Terrace Pl, (Camb.) G72	107	CG40
Terregles Av, G41	86	BK35
Terregles Cres, G41	86	BK35
Terregles Dr, G41	86	BL35
Teviot Av, (Bishop.) G64	33	BW18
Teviot Av, Pais. PA2	81	AN37
Teviot Cres, (Bears.) G61	29	BF19
Teviot Dale, (E.Kil.) G74	135	BZ51
off Strathfillan Rd		
Teviotdale, (Newt. M.) G77	118	BK48
off Kirkvale Ct		
Teviot Dr, Bish. PA7	24	AL19
Teviot Pl, (Camb.) G72	107	CF40
Teviot Sq, (Cumb.) G67	22	DB11
Teviot St, G3	66	BL29
Teviot St, Coat. ML5	74	CT27
Teviot Ter, G20	49	BN25
off Sanda St		
Teviot Ter, John. PA5	79	AE37
Teviot Wk, (Cumb.) G67	22	DB12
off Cumbernauld Shop Cen		
Teviot Way, (Blan.) G72	124	CL46
off Stonefield Rd		
Tewkesbury Rd, (E.Kil.) G74	123	CF48
Thane Rd, G13	47	BE23
Thanes Gate, (Udd.) G71	109	CN40
Thankerton Av, Moth. ML1	112	DB40
Thankerton Rd, Lark. ML9	144	DD60
Tharsis St, G21	68	BV28
Third Av, (Millerston) G33	52	CD24
Third Av, G44	87	BR38
Third Av, (Kirk.) G66	35	CF20
Third Av, Renf. PA4	63	AY27
Third Gdns, G41	86	BJ33
Thirdpart Cres, G13	46	BA22
Third Rd, (Blan.) G72	125	CN48
Third St, (Udd.) G71	93	CP37
Thirlmere, (E.Kil.) G75	134	BV56
off Windermere		
Thistle Bk, (Lenz.) G66	35	CF17
Thistlebank Gro, Coat. ML5	94	CU34
Thistle Cres, Lark. ML9	144	DD59
Thistledown Gro, Coat. ML5	75	CY32
Thistle Gdns, Moth. ML1	112	DC40
Thistle Pl, (E.Kil.) G74	121	BZ50
Thistle Quad, Air. ML6	76	DD28
off Thistle St		
Thistle Rd, Moth. ML1	112	DC41
Thistle St, G5	68	BS32
Thistle St, (Kirk.) G66	17	CF13
Thistle St, Air. ML6	76	DD28
Thistle St, Pais. PA2	82	AS35
Thistle Ter, G5	88	BS33
Thomas Muir Av, (Bishop.) G64	51	BW21
...homas St, Pais. PA1	81	AR33
...ompson Brae, Pais. PA2	80	AJ34
...mpson Pl, Clyde. G81	27	AY15
...eson Av, (Kirk.) G66	17	CG13
...on Av, John. PA5	79	AG34
...n Av, Wis. ML2	143	DF51
... Dr, (Bears.) G61	29	BH15
...Dr, Air. ML6	76	DB31
..., Bell. ML4	110	CT40
... Moth. ML1	127	CZ48
... (Camb.) G72	90	CC38
...n Pk Dr		
...	69	BW31
Thomson St, John. PA5	79	AG35
Thomson St, Renf. PA4	63	AY27
Thorn Av, (Thornton.) G74	120	BS50
Thornbank St, G3	66	BL28
Thorn Brae, John. PA5	80	AJ34
Thornbridge Av, G12	48	BL24
off Balcarres Av		
Thornbridge Av, (Baill.) G69	72	CK32
off Bannercross Dr		
Thornbridge Gdns, (Baill.) G69	72	CJ32
Thornbridge Rd, (Baill.) G69	72	CJ32
Thorncliffe Gdns, G41	87	BN35
Thorncliffe La, G41	87	BN35
Thorn Ct, John. PA5	80	AK35
off Thornhill		
Thorncroft Dr, G44	104	BT41
Thorndean Av, Bell. ML4	111	CX41
Thorndean Cres, Bell. ML4	111	CX41
Thorndene, (Elder.) John. PA5	80	AK35
Thorndene Av, Moth. ML1	113	DE43
Thornden La, G14	46	BC25
Thorn Dr, (Bears.) G61	29	BF16
Thorn Dr, (Ruther.) G73	105	BY41
Thorndyke, (E.Kil.) G74	123	CE48
Thornhill, John. PA5	80	AK35
Thornhill Av, (Blan.) G72	124	CM45
Thornhill Av, (Elder.) John. PA5	80	AK35
Thornhill Dr, (Elder.) John. PA5	80	AK35
Thornhill Gdns, (Newt. M.) G77	131	BF51
Thornhill La, (Both.) G71	109	CR42
off Churchill Cres		
Thornhill Path, G31	89	BZ33
off Crail St		
Thornhill Rd, Ham. ML3	125	CN49
Thornhill Way, Coat. ML5	95	CZ33
Thorniecroft Dr, (Cumb.) G67	39	CY15
Thorniecroft Pl, (Cumb.) G67	39	CY15
Thornielee, (E.Kil.) G74	136	CD51
Thorniewood Gdns, (Udd.) G71	93	CQ38
Thorniewood Rd, (Udd.) G71	93	CP37
Thornkip Pl, Coat. ML5	75	CZ32
off Strathmore Wk		
Thornlea Dr, (Giff.) G46	102	BM41
Thornley Av, G13	46	BD23
Thornliebank Ind Est, (Thornlie.) G46	101	BG42
Thornliebank Rd, G43	102	BJ40
Thornliebank Rd, (Deac.) G46	117	BF45
Thornliebank Rd, (Thornlie.) G46	102	BJ41
Thornly Pk Av, Pais. PA2	82	AV37
Thornly Pk Dr, Pais. PA2	82	AV37
Thornly Pk Gdns, Pais. PA2	82	AU36
Thornly Pk Rd, Pais. PA2	82	AU36
Thorn Rd, (Bears.) G61	29	BE16
Thorn Rd, Bell. ML4	111	CX40
Thornside Rd, John. PA5	80	AJ34
Thornton La, G20	49	BN22
Thornton Pl, Ham. ML3	140	CT55
off High Parks Cres		
Thornton Rd, (Thornton.) G74	134	BS51
Thornton St, G20	49	BN22
Thornton St, Coat. ML5	74	CT27
Thorntree Av, Ham. ML3	125	CP48
Thorntree Way, (Both.) G71	109	CR42
Thornwood Av, G11	66	BJ27
Thornwood Av, (Kirk.) G66	34	CC16
Thornwood Cres, G11	47	BH26
Thornwood Dr, G11	65	BH27
Thornwood Dr, Pais. PA2	81	AR35
Thornwood Gdns, G11	66	BJ27
Thornwood Pl, G11	48	BJ26
Thornwood Quad, G11	47	BH26
off Thornwood Dr		
Thornwood Rd, G11	65	BH27
Thornwood Ter, G11	65	BH27
Thornyburn Dr, (Baill.) G69	92	CM33
Thornyburn Pl, (Baill.) G69	92	CL33
Thrashbush La, Air. ML6	76	DD27
off Thrashbush Rd		
Thrashbush Quad, Air. ML6	76	DC27
Thrashbush Rd, Air. ML6	76	DC27
Threave Pl, (Newt. M.) G77	116	BD48
Three Rivers Wk, (E.Kil.) G75	135	BX53
off Hudson Ter		
Threestonehill Av, G32	70	CD31
Threshold, (E.Kil.) G74	136	CC51
Threshold Pk, (E.Kil.) G74	136	CC51
Thrums, (E.Kil.) G74	123	CF48
Thrums Av, (Bishop.) G64	33	BY20
Thrums Gdns, (Bishop.) G64	33	BY20
Thrushcraig Cres, Pais. PA2	82	AV35
Thrush Pl, John. PA5	79	AF38
Thurso St, G11	66	BL28
Thurston Rd, G52	64	BC32
Thyme Sq, Moth. ML1	128	DA45
off Alyssum Cres		
Tianavaig, Ersk. PA8	44	AS22
Tibbermore Rd, G11	48	BJ26
Tiber Av, Moth. ML1	111	CY44
Tighnasheen Way, (Blan.) G72	124	CM45
Tillanburn Rd, Moth. ML1	113	DH42
Tillet Oval, Pais. PA3	62	AT30
Tillie St, G20	49	BP26
Tillycairn Av, G33	71	CF27
Tillycairn Dr, G33	71	CF27
Tillycairn Pl, G33	71	CG27
Tillycairn Rd, G33	71	CG27
Tillycairn St, G33	71	CG27
Tilt St, G33	70	CA27
Time Capsule Leisure Cen, Coat. ML5	74	CV31
Timmons Gro, Bell. ML4	111	CZ40
Timmons Ter, (Chap.) Air. ML6	97	DF36
Tinkers La, Moth. ML1	127	CY47
Tintagel Gdns, (Chry.) G69	37	CP18
Tintock Dr, (Kirk.) G66	17	CH12
Tintock Pl, (Dullatur) G68	9	CZ7
Tintock Rd, G66	18	CK11
Tinto Dr, (Barr.) G78	99	AX44
Tinto Gro, (Baill.) G69	73	CR31
Tinto Rd, G43	102	BL40
Tinto Rd, (Bears.) G61	28	BD15
Tinto Rd, (Bishop.) G64	33	BY20
Tinto Rd, Air. ML6	76	DD31
Tinto Sq, Renf. PA4	63	AX28
off Ochil Rd		
Tinto Vw, Ham. ML3	140	CU53
Tinto Vw Rd, Lark. ML9	145	DG61
Tinto Way, (E.Kil.) G75	135	BX56
Tinwald Path, G52	64	BC32
Tiree, (E.Kil.) G74	137	CE54
Tiree Av, Pais. PA2	82	AT38
Tiree Av, Renf. PA4	63	AY29
Tiree Ct, (Cumb.) G67	21	CZ13
Tiree Dr, (Cumb.) G67	21	CZ13
Tiree Gdns, (Old Kil.) G60	26	AS15
Tiree Gdns, (Bears.) G61	28	BD15

Tiree Gdns, (Glenm.) Air. ML6 58 DB24
off Balmoral Av
Tiree Gra, Ham. ML3 139 CP52
Tiree Pl, (Old Kil.) G60 26 AS15
Tiree Pl, (Newt. M.) G77 116 BD48
Tiree Pl, Coat. ML5 94 CU33
off Newton St
Tiree Rd, (Cumb.) G67 21 CZ13
Tiree St, G21 69 BY27
Tirry Av, Renf. PA4 64 BB27
Tirry Way, Renf. PA4 64 BB27
off Morriston Cres
Titwood Rd, G41 87 DN36
Titwood Rd, (Newt. M.) G77 131 BF52
Tiverton Av, G32 91 CF34
Tivoli Ct, (E.Kil.) G75 136 CA55
Tobago Pl, G40 68 BV32
Tobago Pl, (E.Kil.) G75 135 BW52
Tobago St, G40 68 BU32
Tobermory Rd, (Ruther.) G73 105 BZ43
Todburn Dr, Pais. PA2 82 AV37
Todd St, G31 69 BY30
Todhills, (E.Kil.) G75 136 CB53
off Todhills N
Todhills N, (E.Kil.) G75 136 CB53
Todhills S, (E.Kil.) G75 136 CB53
Todholm Cres, Pais. PA2 83 AX35
Todholm Rd, Pais. PA2 83 AX35
Todholm Ter, Pais. PA2 83 AW35
Tofthill Av, (Bishop.) G64 32 BV19
Tofthill Gdns, (Bishop.) G64 32 BU19
Tollbrae Av, Air. ML6 76 DD30
Toll Ct, G51 67 BN31
Tollcross Pk Gdns, G32 90 CA34
off Tollcross Pk Vw
Tollcross Pk Gro, G32 90 CB34
off Tollcross Pk Vw
Tollcross Pk Vw, G32 90 CA34
Tollcross Rd, G31 69 BZ32
Tollcross Rd, G32 90 CA33
Tollhouse Gdns, Bell. ML4 111 CY42
Toll St, Moth. ML1 128 DB48
Toll Wynd, Ham. ML3 140 CS54
Tolsta St, G23 31 BN20
Tomtain Brae, (Cumb.) G68 20 CV14
Tomtain Ct, (Cumb.) G68 20 CV14
Tontine La, G1 5 BT31
Tontine Pl, (Ruther.) G73 106 CA41
Topaz Ter, Bell. ML4 111 CW42
Toppersfield, (Kilb.) John. PA10 79 AE35
Torbreck St, G52 65 BH32
Torbrex Rd, (Cumb.) G67 22 DC12
Torburn Av, (Giff.) G46 102 BK41
Tordene Path, (Cumb.) G68 21 CZ10
Torgyle St, G23 30 BM20
Tormeadow Rd, (Newt. M.) 117 BF48
G77
Tormore St, G51 65 BF31
Tormusk Dr, G45 105 BW41
Tormusk Gdns, G45 105 BW41
Tormusk Gro, G45 105 BW41
Tormusk Rd, G45 105 BW41
Torness St, G11 66 BL27
Torogay Pl, G22 50 BU21
Torogay St, G22 50 BS22
Torogay Ter, G22 50 BS21
Toronto Wk, G32 91 CE37
Torphin Cres, G32 70 CC30
Torphin Wk, G32 70 CD31
Torrance Av, Air. ML6 77 DF30
Torrance Rd, (Torr.) G64 15 BY14

Torrance Rd, (E.Kil.) G74 136 CA51
Torrance St, G21 50 BV25
Torran Dr, Ersk. PA8 44 AU22
Torran Rd, G33 71 CH30
Torranyard Ter, Ham. ML3 139 CN52
Torr Gdns, G22 50 BT25
Torriden Ct, Coat. ML5 74 CU32
off Torriden St
Torriden Pl, Coat. ML5 74 CU32
Torriden St, Coat. ML5 74 CU32
Torridon Av, G41 86 BK34
Torridon Av, Moth. ML1 113 DF42
Torridon Gdns, (Bears.) G61 11 BF14
Torridon Gdns, (Newt. M.) G77 118 BK49
Torridon Path, G41 86 BJ34
off Dumbreck Av
Torrington Av, (Giff.) G46 118 BJ45
Torrington Cres, G32 91 CF34
Torrin Rd, G23 30 BM20
Torrisdale Pl, Coat. ML5 74 CU30
Torrisdale St, G42 87 BP35
Torrisdale St, Coat. ML5 74 CU30
Torr Pl, G22 50 BT25
Torr Rd, (Bishop.) G64 33 BZ20
Torr St, G22 50 BT25
Torryburn Rd, G21 51 BY25
Torwood Brae, Ham. ML3 139 CP51
Torwood La, (Mood.) G69 37 CQ19
off Burnbrae Av
Toryglen Rd, (Ruther.) G73 88 BU37
Toryglen St, G5 88 BT35
Tourmaline Rd, Bell. ML4 111 CX42
off Sapphire Rd
Tournai Path, (Blan.) G72 124 CM46
off Burnbrae Rd
Toward Ct, (Blan.) G72 109 CN44
Toward Rd, G33 71 CE30
Tower Av, (Barr.) G78 99 AZ41
Tower Cres, Renf. PA4 63 AX27
Tower Dr, Renf. PA4 63 AX27
Towerhill Rd, G13 29 BE20
Tower Pl, (Miln.) G62 12 BK11
Tower Pl, John. PA5 79 AH36
Tower Rd, (Torr.) G64 14 BV11
Tower Rd, (Cumb.) G67 40 DC15
Tower Rd, John. PA5 79 AH36
Towerside Cres, G53 84 BC35
Towerside Rd, G53 84 BC35
Towers Pl, Air. ML6 77 DH30
Towers Rd, Air. ML6 77 DG29
Tower St, G41 67 BN32
Tower Ter, Pais. PA1 82 AT33
Towie Pl, G20 48 BM23
off Glenfinnan Dr
Towie Pl, (Udd.) G71 109 CP39
Town Cen, (Cumb.) G67 22 DC12
off Cumbernauld Shop Cen
Townhead, (Kirk.) G66 17 CF13
Townhead Av, (Holytown) 96 DB38
Moth. ML1
Townhead Dr, Moth. ML1 113 DH42
Townhead Pl, (Udd.) G71 93 CQ37
Townhead Rd, (Newt. M.) G77 117 BF49
Townhead Rd, Coat. ML5 73 CQ28
Townhead St, (Kilsyth) G65 7 CT5
Townhead Ter, Ham. ML3 126 CV50
Townhead Ter, Pais. PA1 82 AT33
Townhill Rd, Ham. ML3 125 CN50
Townhill Ter, Ham. ML3 125 CN50
off Townhill Rd
Townmill Rd, G31 68 BV29

Townsend St, G4 5 BS28
Tradeston St, G5 67 BQ32
Trafalgar Ct, (Dullatur) G68 9 CZ7
Trafalgar St, G40 88 BV34
Trafalgar St, Clyde. G81 26 AV18
Trainard Av, G32 90 CB33
Tranent Pl, G33 70 CA29
Traquair Av, Pais. PA2 81 AN37
Traquair Dr, G52 84 BD33
Traquair Wynd, (Blan.) G72 124 CM46
off Burnbrae Rd
Treeburn Av, (Giff.) G46 102 BK42
Treemain Rd, (Giff.) G46 118 BJ45
Trees Pk Av, (Barr.) G78 99 AX41
Trefoil Av, G41 86 BM37
Trent Pl, (E.Kil.) G75 134 BU55
Trent St, Coat. ML5 74 CT27
Tresta Rd, G23 49 BP21
Tribboch St, Lark. ML9 144 DB58
off Watson St
Trident Way, Renf. PA4 63 AY28
off Newmains Rd
Trinidad Grn, (E.Kil.) G75 135 BW52
off Leeward Circle
Trinidad Way, (E.Kil.) G75 135 BW52
Trinity Av, G52 85 BE33
Trinity Dr, (Camb.) G72 107 CE42
Trinity Way, Lark. ML9 145 DE60
off Blair Atholl Dr
Trinley Brae, G13 29 BE20
Trinley Rd, G13 29 BF20
Triton Pl, Bell. ML4 112 DB40
Trondra Path, G34 71 CH29
Trondra Pl, G34 71 CH30
Trondra Rd, G34 71 CH29
Trongate, G1 5 BS31
Troon Av, (E.Kil.) G75 135 BW55
Troon Ct, (E.Kil.) G75 135 BX55
Troon Gdns, (Cumb.) G68 9 DB/
Troon Pl, (Newt. M.) G77 118 BJ49
Troon St, G40 89 BX34
Trossachs Av, Moth. ML1 112 DC40
off Howden Pl
Trossachs Ct, G20 49 BQ26
off Trossachs St
Trossachs Rd, (Ruther.) G73 105 BZ43
Trossachs St, G20 49 BQ26
Troubridge Av, (Kilb.) John. 78 AD36
PA10
Troubridge Cres, (Kilb.) John. 78 AD35
PA10
Truce Rd, G13 46 BD21
Truro Av, (Chry.) G69 37 CP18
Tryst Rd, (Cumb.) G67 22 DB12
Tudor Rd, G14 47 BG26
Tudor St, (Baill.) G69 91 CH34
Tulley Wynd, Moth. ML1 111 CZ43
off Dinmont Cres
Tulliallan Pl, (E.Kil.) G74 136 CC53
Tullis Ct, G40 88 BU33
Tullis St, G40 88 BU33
Tulloch-Ard Pl, (Ruther.) G73 105 BZ41
off Lochbrae Dr
Tulloch Gdns, Moth. ML1 128 DD49
Tulloch St, G44 103 BQ39
Tullymet Rd, Ham. ML3 140 CT53
Tummel Dr, Air. ML6 76 DB27
Tummel Grn, (E.Kil.) G74 122 CA50
Tummell Way, Pais. PA2 81 AP36
Tummel St, G33 70 CA27

Tummel Wk, (Cumb.) G67   22   DB11
   off Cumbernauld Shop Cen
Tunnel St, G3   67   BN30
Tuphall Rd, Ham. ML3   140   CT51
Tureen St, G40   68   BV31
Turnberry Av, G11   48   BK26
   off Turnberry Rd
Turnberry Cres, (Chap.) Air.   97   DG36
   ML6 *off Honeywell Cres*
Turnberry Cres, Coat. ML5   94   CU33
Turnberry Dr, (Ruther.) G73   104   BV41
Turnberry Dr, (Newt. M.) G77   118   BJ48
Turnberry Dr, Ham. ML3   138   CM51
Turnberry Gdns, (Cumb.) G68   9   DB8
Turnberry Pl, (Ruther.) G73   104   BV41
   off Turnberry Dr
Turnberry Pl, (E.Kil.) G75   135   BX55
Turnberry Rd, G11   48   BJ26
Turnberry Wynd, (Both.) G71   109   CN42
Turnbull St, G1   5   BT31
Turner Rd, G21   68   BV27
Turner Rd, Pais. PA3   62   AV29
Turners Av, Pais. PA1   81   AR34
Turner St, Coat. ML5   74   CV31
Turnhill Av, Ersk. PA8   43   AR22
Turnhill Cres, Ersk. PA8   43   AR22
Turnhill Dr, Ersk. PA8   43   AR22
Turnhill Gdns, Ersk. PA8   43   AR22
Turnlaw, (E.Kil.) G75   135   BZ56
Turnlaw Rd, (Camb.) G72   106   CC43
Turnlaw St, G5   88   BT33
Turnyland Meadows, Ersk.   43   AR22
   PA8
Turnyland Way, Ersk. PA8   43   AR22
Turquoise Ter, Bell. ML4   111   CX42
Turret Cres, G13   47   BE21
Turret Rd, G13   47   BE21
Turriff St, G5   87   BR33
Twechar Enterprise Pk,   19   CP9
   (Kilsyth) G65
Tweed Av, Pais. PA2   81   AP35
Tweed Ct, Air. ML6   77   DE32
   off Etive Dr
Tweed Cres, G33   69   BZ28
Tweed Cres, Renf. PA4   46   BA26
Tweed Dr, (Bears.) G61   29   BF18
Tweed La, Moth. ML1   112   DD40
   off Redwood Rd
Tweed Pl, John. PA5   79   AE37
Tweedsmuir, (Bishop.) G64   33   BY19
Tweedsmuir Cres, (Bears.) G61   11   BG14
Tweedsmuir Pk, Ham. ML3   140   CS53
Tweedsmuir Rd, Coat. ML5   95   CY34
Tweedsmuir Rd, G52   84   BD33
Tweed St, (E.Kil.) G75   134   BV54
Tweed St, Coat. ML5   95   CW34
Tweed St, Lark. ML9   144   DC60
Tweedvale Av, G14   46   BA23
Tweedvale Pl, G14   46   BA23
   off Tweedvale Av
Tweed Wk, (Cumb.) G67   22   DB12
   off Cumbernauld Shop Cen
Twinlaw St, G34   72   CM28
Tylney Rd, Pais. PA1   63   AZ32
Tyndrum Rd, (Bears.) G61   30   BK16
   off Rannoch Dr
Tyndrum St, G4   5   BS28
Tynecastle Cres, G32   70   CD30
Tynecastle Path, G32   70   CD30
   off Lightburn Pl
Tynecastle Pl, G32   70   CD30

Tynecastle St, G32   70   CD30
Tyne Pl, (E.Kil.) G75   134   BU55
Tyne St, G14   65   BF27
Tynron Ct, Ham. ML3   139   CN52
Tynwald Av, (Ruther.) G73   105   BZ41

U

Uddingston Rd, (Both.) G71   109   CP42
Udston Rd, Ham. ML3   125   CN49
   off Udston Ter
Udston Ter, Ham. ML3   125   CP48
Uig Pl, G33   71   CG32
Uist Cres, (Stepps) G33   53   CG25
Uist Dr, (Kirk.) G66   18   CJ13
Uist Pl, Air. ML6   77   DF31
Uist St, G51   65   BH30
Ullswater, (E.Kil.) G75   134   BV56
Ulundi Rd, John. PA5   79   AF35
Ulva St, G52   65   BH32
Ulverston Ter, Ham. ML3   140   CT55
Umachan, Ersk. PA8   44   AS22
Underwood Ct, Pais. PA3   62   AT32
Underwood La, Pais. PA1   62   AT32
Underwood Rd, (Ruther.) G73   105   BY39
Underwood Rd, Pais. PA3   62   AS32
Underwood St, G41   87   BN37
Union Ct, Pais. PA2   82   AU35
Union Pl, G1   4   BR30
   off Gordon St
Union St, G1   4   BR30
Union St, (Kirk.) G66   17   CE13
Union St, Clyde. G81   45   AY21
Union St, Ham. ML3   126   CT49
Union St, Lark. ML9   144   DC58
Union St, Moth. ML1   112   DC41
Union St, Pais. PA2   82   AU35
Unitas Rd, Bell. ML4   111   CY40
Unity Pl, G4   67   BQ27
University Av, G12   66   BM27
University Gdns, G12   66   BM27
University of Glasgow, G12   66   BM27
University Pl, G12   66   BM27
Unsted Pl, Pais. PA1   83   AW33
Unthank Rd, Bell. ML4   111   CY40
Uphall Pl, G33   70   CA29
Upland Rd, G14   47   BE25
Up La, (Kilsyth) G65   7   CT5
   off Up Rd
Upper Bourtree Ct, (Ruther.)   105   BY41
   G73
Upper Bourtree Dr, (Ruther.)   105   BX41
   G73
Upper Glenburn Rd, (Bears.)   29   BE16
   G61
Upper Mill St, Air. ML6   76   DC29
Up Rd, (Kilsyth) G65   7   CT5
Urquhart Cres, Renf. PA4   63   AY27
Urquhart Dr, (E.Kil.) G74   122   CC50
Urrdale Rd, G41   66   BK32
Usmore Pl, G33   71   CG32
   off Pendeen Cres

V

Vaila Pl, G23   49   BQ22
Vaila St, G23   49   BP22
Valerio Ct, (Blan.) G72   124   CM45
Valetta Pl, Clyde. G81   26   AT17
Valeview Ter, G42   87   BQ37
Vale Wk, (Bishop.) G64   51   BY21

Vallantine Cres, (Udd.) G71   93   CQ37
Vallay St, G22   50   BT21
Valley Ct, Ham. ML3   140   CS51
Valleyfield, (E.Kil.) G75   135   BZ52
Valleyfield Dr, (Cumb.) G68   20   CU12
Valleyfield St, G21   50   BU26
   off Ayr St
Valley Vw, (Camb.) G72   107   CE39
Valley Vw, Moth. ML1   128   DD50
Vancouver Dr, (E.Kil.) G75   135   BX52
Vancouver La, G14   47   BF25
   off Vancouver Rd
Vancouver Pl, Clyde. G81   26   AT17
Vancouver Rd, G14   47   BE25
Vanguard St, Clyde. G81   27   AY19
Vanguard Way, Renf. PA4   63   AY28
Vardar Av, (Clark.) G76   118   BL45
Vardon Lea, Moth. ML1   113   DG44
Varna La, G14   47   BG26
Varna Rd, G14   47   BG25
Varnsdorf Way, Air. ML6   77   DG31
Vasart Pl, G20   49   BP24
Veitches Ct, Clyde. G81   27   AW15
Vennacher Rd, Renf. PA4   45   AW25
Vennard Gdns, G41   87   BN35
Vermont Av, (Ruther.) G73   89   BW38
Vermont St, G41   67   BN32
Vernon Bk, (E.Kil.) G74   122   CA50
Vernon Dr, (Linw.) Pais. PA3   60   AJ31
Verona Av, G14   47   BE25
Verona Gdns, G14   47   BE25
Verona La, G14   47   BE25
Vesalius St, G32   70   CC32
Veterans Cotts, (Erskine Hosp.)   25   AP16
   Bish. PA7
Viaduct Rd, (Clark.) G76   119   BP46
Vicarfield Pl, G51   66   BK30
   off Vicarfield St
Vicarfield St, G51   66   BK30
Vicarland Pl, (Camb.) G72   106   CC41
Vicarland Rd, (Camb.) G72   106   CC40
Vicars Wk, (Camb.) G72   106   CD40
Vickers St, Moth. ML1   127   CX45
Victoria Av, (Barr.) G78   99   AX41
Victoria Br, G1   5   BS31
Victoria Br, G5   5   BS31
Victoria Circ, G12   48   BL26
Victoria Ct, (Newt. M.) G77   131   BF51
Victoria Cres, G12   48   BL26
   off Dowanside Rd
Victoria Cres, (Kilsyth) G65   7   CR5
Victoria Cres, (Clark.) G76   119   BP46
Victoria Cres, (Barr.) G78   99   AX41
Victoria Cres, Air. ML6   76   DA31
Victoria Cres, Wis. ML2   129   DF49
   off Shieldmuir St
Victoria Cres La, G12   48   BL26
Victoria Cres Pl, G12   48   BL26
   off Bowmont Ter
Victoria Cres Rd, G12   48   BL26
Victoria Cross, G42   87   BQ35
Victoria Dr, (Barr.) G78   99   AX41
Victoria Dr E, Renf. PA4   63   AY27
Victoria Dr W, Renf. PA4   45   AX26
Victoria Gdns, (Barr.) G78   99   AX41
   off Victoria Rd
Victoria Gdns, Air. ML6   76   DB30
Victoria Gdns, Pais. PA2   82   AS35
Victoria Glade, (Dullatur) G68   9   CZ7
Victoria Gro, (Barr.) G78   99   AX41
Victoria La, (Newt. M.) G77   131   BF51

265

Victoria Pk, (Kilsyth) G65 — 7 — CR5
Victoria Pk Cor, G14 — 47 — BF25
Victoria Pk Dr N, G14 — 47 — BF25
Victoria Pk Dr S, G14 — 47 — BE26
Victoria Pk Gdns N, G11 — 47 — BH26
Victoria Pk Gdns S, G11 — 47 — BH26
Victoria Pk La N, G14 — 47 — BF26
Victoria Pk La S, G14 — 47 — BF26
off Westland Dr
Victoria Pk St, G14 — 47 — BF26
Victoria Pl, (Miln.) G62 — 12 — BK12
off Glasgow Rd
Victoria Pl, (Kilsyth) G65 — 7 — CR5
Victoria Pl, (Ruther.) G73 — 89 — BW37
off Greenbank St
Victoria Pl, (Barr.) G78 — 99 — AY41
Victoria Pl, Air. ML6 — 76 — DA31
Victoria Pl, Bell. ML4 — 110 — CV41
Victoria Quad, Moth. ML1 — 112 — DB40
Victoria Rd, (Stepps) G33 — 53 — CF24
Victoria Rd, G42 — 87 — BQ36
Victoria Rd, (Lenz.) G66 — 35 — CE17
Victoria Rd, (Dullatur) G68 — 9 — CZ7
Victoria Rd, (Ruther.) G73 — 105 — BX39
Victoria Rd, (Barr.) G78 — 99 — AX41
Victoria Rd, Pais. PA2 — 82 — AS35
Victoria Sq, (Newt. M.) G77 — 131 — BF51
Victoria St, (Kirk.) G66 — 17 — CE13
Victoria St, (Blan.) G72 — 124 — CM47
Victoria St, (Ruther.) G73 — 89 — BW37
Victoria St, Ham. ML3 — 125 — CR47
Victoria St, Lark. ML9 — 144 — DC58
Victoria Ter, (Dullatur) G68 — 8 — CY7
Victory Dr, (Kilb.) John. PA10 — 78 — AC33
Victory Way, (Baill.) G69 — 92 — CK33
Viewbank, (Thornlie.) G46 — 102 — BJ42
Viewbank Av, (Calder.) Air. ML6 — 96 — DD35
Viewbank St, (Glenb.) Coat. ML5 — 56 — CV24
Viewfield, Air. ML6 — 76 — DA30
Viewfield Av, (Bishop.) G64 — 50 — BU21
Viewfield Av, (Lenz.) G66 — 35 — CE16
Viewfield Av, (Baill.) G69 — 71 — CH32
Viewfield Av, (Blan.) G72 — 109 — CN44
Viewfield Dr, (Bishop.) G64 — 50 — BU21
Viewfield Dr, (Baill.) G69 — 71 — CH32
Viewfield La, G12 — 67 — BN27
Viewfield Rd, (Bishop.) G64 — 50 — BU21
Viewfield Rd, Bell. ML4 — 110 — CV42
Viewfield Rd, Coat. ML5 — 93 — CR33
Viewglen Ct, G45 — 104 — BT44
Viewmount Dr, G20 — 48 — BM22
Viewpark, (Miln.) G62 — 12 — BK12
off Crossveggate
Viewpark Av, G31 — 69 — BX29
Viewpark Dr, (Ruther.) G73 — 105 — BX39
Viewpark Gdns, Renf. PA4 — 63 — AX27
Viewpark Pl, Moth. ML1 — 127 — CY47
off Viewpark Rd
Viewpark Rd, Moth. ML1 — 127 — CY47
Viewpark Shop Cen, (Udd.) G71 — 94 — CT38
Viewpoint Pl, G21 — 50 — BV23
Viewpoint Rd, G21 — 50 — BV23
Viking Rd, (Thornlie.) G46 — 101 — BH41
Viking Rd, Air. ML6 — 76 — DD32
Viking Ter, (E.Kil.) G75 — 136 — CA55
Viking Way, Renf. PA4 — 63 — AY28
off Vanguard Way
Villafield Av, (Bishop.) G64 — 33 — BW18

Villafield Dr, (Bishop.) G64 — 33 — BW18
Villafield Ln, (Bishop.) G64 — 33 — BW18
off Villafield Av
Village Gdns, (Blan.) G72 — 109 — CN44
Village Rd, (Camb.) G72 — 107 — CG40
Vincent Ct, Bell. ML4 — 111 — CW41
off Strachan St
Vine St, G11 — 66 — BK27
Vinicombe La, G12 — 48 — BM26
Vinicombe St, G12 — 48 — BM26
Vintner St, G4 — 68 — BS27
Viola Pl, (Torr.) G64 — 15 — BY13
Violet Pl, Moth. ML1 — 112 — DD39
Violet St, Pais. PA1 — 83 — AW33
Virginia Bldgs, G1 — 5 — BS30
off Virginia St
Virginia Ct, G1 — 5 — BS30
off Virginia St
Virginia Gdns, (Miln.) G62 — 12 — BL13
Virginia Pl, G1 — 5 — BS30
Virginia St, G1 — 5 — BS30
Viscount Av, Renf. PA4 — 63 — AY28
Viscount Gate, (Both.) G71 — 109 — CN40
Vivian Av, (Miln.) G62 — 11 — BH12
Voil Dr, G44 — 103 — BQ41
Vorlich Ct, (Barr.) G78 — 99 — AY44
off Eildon Dr
Vorlich Gdns, (Bears.) G61 — 11 — BE14
Vorlich Wynd, Moth. ML1 — 113 — DE41
off Glenburn Av
Vulcan St, G21 — 50 — BU25
off Springburn Way
Vulcan St, Moth. ML1 — 128 — DA45

W

Waddell Av, (Glenm.) Air. ML6 — 57 — CZ25
Waddell Ct, G5 — 68 — BT32
Waddell St, G5 — 88 — BT33
Waddell St, Air. ML6 — 76 — DC28
Waid Av, (Newt. M.) G77 — 117 — BE47
Waldemar Rd, G13 — 47 — BE22
Waldo St, G13 — 47 — BH22
Walkerburn Rd, G52 — 84 — BD33
Walker Ct, G11 — 66 — BK28
Walker Dr, (Elder.) John. PA5 — 80 — AK35
Walker Path, (Udd.) G71 — 93 — CQ37
Walker St, G11 — 66 — BK28
Walker St, Pais. PA1 — 82 — AT33
Walkinshaw Cres, Pais. PA2 — 61 — AR31
Walkinshaw Rd, Renf. PA4 — 44 — AS26
Walkinshaw St, G40 — 89 — BW33
Walkinshaw St, John. PA5 — 79 — AH34
Wallace Av, Bish. PA7 — 24 — AK18
Wallace Av, (Elder.) John. PA5 — 80 — AL34
Wallace Dr, (Bishop.) G64 — 51 — BZ22
Wallace Dr, Lark. ML9 — 145 — DE59
Wallace Gdns, (Torr.) G64 — 15 — BX12
Wallace Gate, (Bishop.) G64 — 51 — BZ22
Wallace Pl, (Bishop.) G64 — 51 — BZ22
Wallace Pl, (Blan.) G72 — 109 — CN44
Wallace Pl, Ham. ML3 — 141 — CW51
Wallace Rd, Moth. ML1 — 112 — DD43
off Park Rd
Wallace Rd, Renf. PA4 — 63 — AW28
Wallace St, G5 — 4 — BQ31
Wallace St, (Ruther.) G73 — 89 — BW38
Wallace St, Clyde. G81 — 45 — AX21
Wallace St, Coat. ML5 — 75 — CW32
Wallace St, Moth. ML1 — 127 — CZ46
Wallace St, Pais. PA3 — 62 — AU31

Wallacewell Cres, G21 — 51 — BX24
Wallacewell Pl, G21 — 51 — BX24
Wallacewell Quad, G21 — 51 — BY23
Wallacewell Rd, G21 — 51 — BX24
Wallbrae Rd, (Cumb.) G67 — 22 — DB13
Wallneuk, Pais. PA1 — 62 — AV32
off Incle St
Wallneuk Rd, Pais. PA3 — 62 — AV32
Walls St, G1 — 5 — BT30
Walmer Cres, G51 — 66 — BL31
Walnut Cres, G22 — 50 — BT24
Walnut Cres, John. PA5 — 80 — AK36
Walnut Dr, (Kirk.) G66 — 34 — CD15
Walnut Gate, (Camb.) G72 — 107 — CH41
Walnut Pl, G22 — 50 — BT24
Walnut Pl, (Udd.) G71 — 94 — CS36
Walnut Rd, G22 — 50 — BT24
Walpole Pl, John. PA5 — 79 — AF38
off Hallhill Rd
Walter St, G31 — 69 — BX30
Walton Av, (Newt. M.) G77 — 117 — BE47
Walton Ct, (Giff.) G46 — 102 — BL43
Walton St, G41 — 87 — BN37
Walton St, (Barr.) G78 — 99 — AY42
Wamba Av, G13 — 47 — BG21
Wamba Pl, G13 — 47 — BG21
Wamphray Pl, (E.Kil.) G75 — 134 — BT54
Wandilla Av, Clyde. G81 — 27 — AZ19
Wanlock St, G51 — 66 — BJ29
Wardend Rd, (Torr.) G64 — 15 — BX12
Warden Rd, G13 — 47 — BF22
Wardhill Rd, G21 — 51 — BX24
Wardhouse Rd, Pais. PA2 — 82 — AS38
Wardie Path, G33 — 71 — CH30
Wardie Pl, G33 — 71 — CH30
Wardie Rd, G33 — 71 — CH30
Wardie Rd, G34 — 72 — CJ29
Wardlaw Av, (Ruther.) G73 — 89 — BX38
Wardlaw Cres, (E.Kil.) G75 — 136 — CB54
Wardlaw Dr, (Ruther.) G73 — 89 — BX37
Wardlaw Rd, (Bears.) G61 — 29 — BH20
Wardrop Pl, (E.Kil.) G74 — 122 — CB50
Wardrop St, G51 — 66 — BJ29
Wardrop St, Pais. PA1 — 82 — AU33
Wards Cres, Coat. ML5 — 74 — CU32
Ware Path, G34 — 72 — CJ30
Ware Rd, G34 — 71 — CH30
Warilda Av, Clyde. G81 — 27 — AY19
Warnock Cres, Bell. ML4 — 111 — CX41
Warnock Rd, (Newt. M.) G77 — 117 — BE47
Warnock St, G31 — 5 — BU29
Warren Rd, Ham. ML3 — 140 — CT53
Warren St, G42 — 87 — BR36
Warriston Cres, G33 — 69 — BZ29
Warriston Pl, G32 — 70 — CD30
Warriston St, G33 — 69 — BZ29
Warriston Way, (Ruther.) G73 — 105 — BZ41
off Lochaber Dr
Warroch St, G3 — 4 — BP30
Warwick, (E.Kil.) G74 — 123 — CE49
Warwick Gro, Ham. ML3 — 125 — CN48
off Stirling Dr
Washington Rd, (Kirk.) G66 — 16 — CD12
Washington Rd, Pais. PA3 — 62 — AV29
Washington St, G3 — 4 — BQ30
Waterbank Rd, (Carm.) G76 — 120 — BT48
Water Brae, Pais. PA1 — 82 — AU33
off Forbes Pl
Waterfoot Av, G53 — 85 — BE?
Waterfoot Rd, (Thornton.) G74 — 133 — BC?
Waterfoot Rd, (Clark.) G76 — 118 — ?

Waterfoot Rd, (Newt. M.) G77	117	BH50
Waterfoot Row, (Clark.) G76	118	BM50
off Waterfoot Rd		
Waterfoot Ter, G53	85	BE37
off Waterfoot Av		
Waterford Rd, (Giff.) G46	102	BK42
Waterhaughs Gdns, G33	51	BZ22
Waterhaughs Gro, G33	51	BZ22
Waterhaughs Pl, G33	51	BZ22
Waterloo Cl, (Kirk.) G66	17	CF12
Waterloo Gdns, (Kirk.) G66	17	CF12
off John St		
Waterloo La, G2	4	BR30
Waterloo St, G2	4	BQ30
Watermill Av, (Lenz.) G66	35	CF17
Water Rd, (Barr.) G78	99	AY42
Water Row, G51	66	BJ29
Waterside Av, (Newt. M.) G77	117	BE49
Waterside Ct, (Clark.) G76	120	BT45
off Waterside Rd		
Waterside Dr, (Newt. M.) G77	117	BE49
Waterside Gdns, (Camb.) G72	107	CG42
Waterside Gdns, (Carm.) G76	120	BT46
Waterside Gdns, Ham. ML3	140	CU52
Waterside La, (Kilb.) John. PA10	79	AE36
Waterside Pl, G5	88	BT33
Waterside Rd, (Kirk.) G66	17	CG14
Waterside Rd, (Carm.) G76	120	BT45
Waterside St, G5	88	BT33
Waterside Ter, (Kilb.) John. PA10 off Kilbarchan Rd	79	AE35
Watling Pl, (E.Kil.) G75	135	BW52
off Leeward Circle		
Watling St, (Udd.) G71	93	CN37
Watling St, Moth. ML1	111	CX44
Watson Av, (Ruther.) G73	88	BV38
Watson Av, (Linw.) Pais. PA3	60	AK31
Watson Cres, (Kilsyth) G65	7	CU5
Watson Pl, (Blan.) G72	124	CK46
Watson St, G1	5	BT31
Watson St, (Udd.) G71	109	CP40
Watson St, (Blan.) G72	124	CK46
Watson St, Lark. ML9	144	DB58
Watson St, Moth. ML1	128	DA48
Watsonville Pk, Moth. ML1	128	DA47
off Oakfield Rd		
Watt Av, G33	53	CH24
Watt Cres, Bell. ML4	95	CX38
Watt Low Av, (Ruther.) G73	104	BV39
Watt Pl, (Miln.) G62	11	BH10
Watt Pl, (Blan.) G72	124	CL49
Watt Rd, G52	64	BB30
Watt St, G5	4	BP31
Watt St, Air. ML6	76	DD28
Waukglen Av, G53	100	BD43
Waukglen Cres, G53	101	BE42
Waukglen Dr, G53	100	BD42
Waukglen Gdns, G53	100	BD42
Waukglen Path, G53	100	BD42
off Waukglen Dr		
Waukglen Pl, G53	100	BD42
Waukglen Rd, G53	100	BD42
Waulkmill Av, (Barr.) G78	99	AZ41
Waulkmill St, (Thornlie.) G46	101	BG41
Waulkmill Way, (Barr.) G78	99	AZ41
off Waulkmill Av		
Waverley, (E.Kil.) G74	123	CF49
Waverley, Clyde. G81	27	AY19
off Onslow Rd		
Waverley Ct, (Both.) G71	109	CQ43
Waverley Cres, (Kirk.) G66	17	CG13
Waverley Cres, (Cumb.) G67	21	CZ14
Waverley Cres, Ham. ML3	125	CP49
Waverley Dr, (Ruther.) G73	89	BY38
Waverley Dr, Air. ML6	76	DD28
Waverley Gdns, G41	87	BN36
Waverley Gdns, (Elder.) John. PA5	80	AM35
Waverley Pk, (Kirk.) G66	17	CF12
Waverley Rd, Pais. PA2	81	AP37
Waverley St, G41	87	BN36
Waverley St, Coat. ML5	75	CX28
Waverley St, Ham. ML3	125	CP49
Waverley St, Lark. ML9	144	DC61
Waverley Ter, G31	69	BW31
off Whitevale St		
Waverley Ter, (Blan.) G72	124	CL48
Waverley Way, Pais. PA2	81	AP38
off Waverley Rd		
Weardale La, G33	71	CE29
Weardale St, G33	71	CE29
Weaver Av, (Newt. M.) G77	117	BE46
Weaver Cres, Air. ML6	76	DC32
Weaver La, (Kilb.) John. PA10	78	AC33
off Glentyan Av		
Weaver Pl, (E.Kil.) G75	134	BU54
Weavers Av, Pais. PA2	81	AR34
Weavers Gate, Pais. PA1	81	AQ34
Weavers Rd, Pais. PA2	81	AR34
Weaver St, G4	5	BT30
Weaver Ter, Pais. PA2	83	AW34
Webster St, G40	89	BW34
Webster St, Clyde. G81	46	BA21
Wedderlea Dr, G52	64	BC32
Weensmoor Pl, G53	100	BC41
off Willowford Rd		
Weensmoor Rd, G53	100	BC40
Weeple Dr, (Linw.) Pais. PA3	60	AJ31
Weighhouse Cl, Pais. PA1	82	AU33
Weir Av, (Barr.) G78	99	AY43
Weir St, Coat. ML5	75	CW30
Weir St, Pais. PA3	62	AU32
Weirwood Av, (Baill.) G69	91	CH33
Weirwood Gdns, (Baill.) G69	91	CH33
Welbeck Rd, G53	100	BD40
Weldon Pl, (Kilsyth) G65	20	CV10
Welfare Av, (Camb.) G72	107	CF41
Welland Pl, (E.Kil.) G75	134	BU54
Wellbank Pl, (Udd.) G71	109	CP40
off Church St		
Well Brae, Lark. ML9	144	DC59
Wellbrae Rd, Ham. ML3	139	CR52
Wellbrae Ter, (Mood.) G69	37	CP19
Wellcroft Pl, G5	87	BR33
Wellcroft Rd, Ham. ML3	125	CN50
Wellcroft Ter, Ham. ML3	125	CN50
Wellesley Cres, (Cumb.) G68	20	CU13
Wellesley Cres, (E.Kil.) G75	134	BV54
Wellesley Dr, (Cumb.) G68	20	CU12
Wellesley Dr, (E.Kil.) G75	134	BV53
Wellesley Pl, (Cumb.) G68	20	CT12
Wellfield Av, (Giff.) G46	102	BK42
Wellfield Ct, (Giff.) G46	102	BK42
off Wellfield Av		
Wellfield St, G21	50	BV25
Wellgate Ct, Lark. ML9	144	DC57
off Wellgate St		
Wellgate St, Lark. ML9	144	DC57
Well Grn, G43	86	BL37
Wellgreen Ct, G43	86	BL37
off Well Grn		
Wellhall Ct, Ham. ML3	125	CR49
Wellhall Rd, Ham. ML3	139	CP51
Wellhouse Cres, G33	71	CG30
Wellhouse Gdns, G33	71	CH30
Wellhouse Gro, G33	71	CH30
Wellhouse Path, G34	71	CH30
Wellhouse Rd, G33	71	CH29
Wellington, (E.Kil.) G75	135	BX54
Wellington La, G2	4	BQ30
Wellington Path, (Baill.) G69	92	CK33
off Nelson Pl		
Wellington Pl, Clyde. G81	26	AT17
Wellington Pl, Coat. ML5	74	CS32
Wellington Rd, (Bishop.) G64	33	BX17
Wellington St, G2	4	BR30
Wellington St, Air. ML6	76	DC28
Wellington St, Pais. PA3	62	AT32
Wellington Way, Renf. PA4	63	AY28
off Tiree Av		
Wellknowe Av, (Thornton.) G74	134	BS51
Wellknowe Pl, (Thornton.) G74	120	BS50
Wellknowe Rd, (Thornton.) G74	120	BS50
Wellmeadow Cl, (Newt. M.) G77	117	BF48
Wellmeadow Grn, (Newt. M.) G77	117	BF47
Wellmeadow Rd, G43	102	BJ39
Wellmeadow St, Pais. PA1	82	AT33
Wellmeadow Way, (Newt. M.) G77	117	BF48
Wellpark Rd, Moth. ML1	127	CY47
off Viewpark Rd		
Wellpark St, G31	5	BU30
Wellpark Ter, (Neil.) G78	114	AT47
Well Rd, (Kilb.) John. PA10	78	AC34
Wellshot Dr, (Camb.) G72	106	CB40
Wellshot Rd, G32	90	CB34
Wellside Av, Air. ML6	76	DC28
Wellside Dr, (Camb.) G72	107	CE41
Wellside La, Air. ML6	76	DD28
Wellside Quad, Air. ML6	76	DC28
Wellsquarry Rd, (Kittochside) G76	121	BY48
Wells St, Clyde. G81	26	AV18
Well St, Pais. PA1	62	AS32
Wellview Dr, Moth. ML1	127	CZ47
Wellwynd, Air. ML6	76	DB29
Wellwynd Gdns, Air. ML6	76	DB29
off Wellwynd		
Welsh Dr, (Blan.) G72	124	CM47
Welsh Dr, Ham. ML3	140	CS54
Welsh Row, (Calder.) Air. ML6	97	DE35
Wemyss Av, (Newt. M.) G77	117	BE46
Wemyss Dr, (Cumb.) G68	20	CU12
Wemyss Gdns, (Baill.) G69	92	CJ34
Wendur Way, Pais. PA3	62	AU29
off Abbotsburn Way		
Wenlock Rd, Pais. PA2	82	AV35
Wensleydale, (E.Kil.) G74	121	BY50
Wentworth Dr, G23	31	BN20
off Dougalston Rd		
Wesley St, Air. ML6	76	DB30
Westacres Rd, (Newt. M.) G77	116	BD49
West Av, (Stepps) G33	53	CF24
West Av, (Udd.) G71	109	CR39
West Av, (Blan.) G72	125	CN48
West Av, Moth. ML1	112	DC43
West Av, Renf. PA4	45	AZ26
West Balgrochan Rd, (Torr.) G64	15	BX12

Westbank Ct, G12   67   BN27
Westbank La, G12   67   BN27
Westbank Quad, G12   67   BN27
Westbourne Cres, (Bears.) G61   29   BE16
Westbourne Dr, (Bears.) G61   29   BE16
Westbourne Gdns La, G12   48   BL25
Westbourne Gdns N, G12   48   BL25
Westbourne Gdns S, G12   48   BL25
Westbourne Gdns W, G12   48   BL25
Westbourne Rd, G12   48   BK25
Westbourne Shop Cen, (Barr.) G78   99   AX43
Westbourne Ter La, G12   48   BK25
  off Westbourne Rd
West Brae, Pais. PA1   82   AT33
Westbrae Dr, G14   47   BG25
Westbrae Rd, (Newt. M.) G77   117   BH47
West Buchanan Pl, Pais. PA1   82   AT33
  off Sir Michael Pl
Westburn Av, (Camb.) G72   107   CF39
Westburn Av, Pais. PA3   61   AQ32
Westburn Cres, (Ruther.) G73   88   BV38
Westburn Dr, (Camb.) G72   90   CD38
Westburn Fm Rd, (Camb.) G72   106   CD39
Westburn Rd, (Camb.) G72   107   CE39
West Burnside St, (Kilsyth) G65   7   CT5
  off Main St
Westburn Way, Pais. PA3   61   AR32
  off Westburn Av
West Campbell St, G2   4   BQ30
West Campbell St, Pais. PA1   81   AR33
West Canal St, Coat. ML5   74   CV31
Westcastle Ct, G45   104   BS42
  off Westcastle Cres
Westcastle Cres, G45   104   BT42
Westcastle Gdns, G45   104   BT42
Westcastle Gro, G45   104   BS42
  off Westcastle Cres
West Chapelton Av, (Bears.) G61   29   BH17
West Chapelton Cres, (Bears.) G61   29   BH17
West Chapelton Dr, (Bears.) G61   29   BH17
West Chapelton La, (Bears.) G61   29   BH17
West Clyde St, Lark. ML9   144   DD59
Westclyffe St, G41   87   BN36
West Coats Rd, (Camb.) G72   106   CB40
West Cotts, (Gart.) G69   54   CK26
West Ct, Clyde. G81   26   AU17
West Ct, Pais. PA1   81   AQ33
West Dr, Air. ML6   77   DG31
Westend, (Bears.) G61   30   BJ19
West End Dr, Bell. ML4   110   CV41
West End Pk St, G3   4   BP28
West End Pl, Bell. ML4   110   CV41
Westerburn St, G32   70   CB31
Wester Carriagehill, Pais. PA2   82   AU35
Wester Cleddens Rd, (Bishop.) G64   33   BW19
Wester Common Dr, G22   49   BQ24
Wester Common Rd, G22   49   BQ25
Wester Common Ter, G22   49   BR25
Westercraigs, G31   68   BV30
Westercraigs Ct, G31   68   BV30
  off Westercraigs
Westerdale, (E.Kil.) G74   121   BY50
Westerfield Rd, (Cumb.) G68   38   CT15
Westerfield Rd, (Carm.) G76   120   BU48

Westergill Av, Air. ML6   77   DG31
Westergreens Av, (Kirk.) G66   35   CE15
Westerhill Rd, (Bishop.) G64   33   BY17
Westerhouse Path, G34   71   CH29
  off Kildermorie Rd
Westerhouse Rd, G34   72   CJ28
Westerkirk Dr, G23   31   BN20
Westerlands, G12   47   BH23
  off Ascot Av
Westerlands Dr, (Newt. M.) G77   116   BD49
Westerlands Gdns, (Newt. M.) G77   116   BD49
Westerlands Gro, (Newt. M.) G77   116   BD49
Westerlands Pl, (Newt. M.) G77   116   BD48
  off Westacres Rd
Westermains Av, (Kirk.) G66   16   CD14
Wester Mavisbank Av, Air. ML6   76   DA29
Wester Moffat Av, Air. ML6   77   DG30
Wester Moffat Cres, Air. ML6   77   DG30
Wester Myvot Rd, (Cumb.) G67   39   CW17
Western Av, (Ruther.) G73   88   BV37
Western Isles Rd, (Old Kil.) G60   26   AS16
Western Rd, (Camb.) G72   106   CA41
Wester Rd, G32   91   CF33
Westerton Av, (Bears.) G61   47   BH21
Westerton Av, (Clark.) G76   119   BQ48
Westerton Av, Lark. ML9   144   DC60
Westerton Ct, (Clark.) G76   119   BQ48
Westerton La, (Clark.) G76   119   BQ48
Westerton Rd, (Dullatur) G68   8   CY7
West Fairholm St, Lark. ML9   142   DB56
Westfield, (Cumb.) G68   38   CT15
Westfield Av, (Ruther.) G73   88   BV38
Westfield Cres, (Bears.) G61   29   BG19
Westfield Dr, G52   64   BC32
Westfield Dr, (Bears.) G61   29   BG19
Westfield Dr, (Cumb.) G68   20   CU14
Westfield Ind Est, (Cumb.) G68   38   CT15
Westfield Pl, (Cumb.) G68   38   CT15
Westfield Rd, (Thornlie.) G46   102   BJ43
Westfield Rd, (Kilsyth) G65   7   CR4
Westfields, (Bishop.) G64   32   BU18
Westfield Vil, (Ruther.) G73   88   BU38
Westgarth Pl, (E.Kil.) G74   121   BW50
Westgate Way, Bell. ML4   110   CV40
  off West End Dr
West George La, G2   4   BQ29
West George St, G2   4   BQ29
West George St, Coat. ML5   75   CW29
West Glebe Ter, Ham. ML3   140   CS51
  off Glebe St
West Graham St, G4   4   BQ28
West Greenhill Pl, G3   67   BN29
West Hamilton St, Moth. ML1   128   DA47
West High St, (Kirk.) G66   17   CE12
Westhorn Dr, G32   90   CC36
Westhouse Av, (Ruther.) G73   88   BU38
Westhouse Gdns, (Ruther.) G73   88   BU38
West Kirk St, Air. ML6   76   DB30
Westknowe Gdns, (Ruther.) G73   105   BX40
Westland Dr, G14   47   BF26
Westland Dr La, G14   47   BF26
  off Westland Dr
Westlands Gdns, Pais. PA2   82   AT35

West La, Pais. PA1   81   AR33
Westlea Pl, Air. ML6   76   DC31
West Lo Rd, Renf. PA4   45   AX25
West Mains Rd, (E.Kil.) G74   135   BX51
Westminster Gdns, G12   48   BM26
  off Kersland St
Westminster Ter, G3   67   BN29
  off Royal Ter
Westmoreland St, G42   87   BQ35
Westmuir Pl, (Ruther.) G73   88   BU37
Westmuir St, G31   69   BZ32
West Nile St, G1   4   BR30
Westpark, (Miln.) G62   12   BK13
Westpark Dr, Pais. PA3   61   AR32
Westport, (E.Kil.) G75   135   BW52
West Princes St, G4   67   BP27
Westray Av, (Newt. M.) G77   117   BE46
Westray Circ, G22   50   BT23
Westray Ct, (Cumb.) G67   22   DA13
Westray Pl, G22   50   BT23
Westray Pl, (Bishop.) G64   33   BZ19
Westray Rd, (Cumb.) G67   22   DA13
Westray Sq, G22   50   BS22
Westray St, G22   50   BS22
West Regent La, G2   4   BR29
West Regent St, G2   4   BQ29
West Rd, (Torr.) G64   15   BX12
West Rd, (Kilb.) John. PA10   78   AC33
West Scott Ter, Ham. ML3   140   CT52
Westside Gdns, G11   66   BK27
West Stewart St, Ham. ML3   126   CS49
West St, G5   67   BQ32
West St, Clyde. G81   46   BA21
West St, Pais. PA1   82   AS33
West Thomson St, Clyde. G81   27   AW17
West Wellbrae Cres, Ham. ML3   139   CR52
West Whitby St, G31   89   BY33
Westwood Av, (Giff.) G46   102   BK42
Westwood Cres, Ham. ML3   140   CS52
Westwood Gdns, Pais. PA3   61   AR32
Westwood Hill, (E.Kil.) G75   135   BX53
Westwood Quad, Clyde. G81   27   AZ20
Westwood Rd, G43   102   BK39
Westwood Rd, (E.Kil.) G75   135   BX53
Westwood Sq, (E.Kil.) G75   135   BX53
  off Westwood Rd
Weymouth Dr, G12   48   BJ23
Whamflet Av, (Baill.) G69   72   CL30
Wheatfield Rd, (Bears.) G61   29   BF18
Wheatholm Cres, Air. ML6   76   DD28
  off Wheatholm St
Wheatholm St, Air. ML6   76   DD28
Wheatland Av, (Blan.) G72   124   CL45
Wheatlandhead Ct, (Blan.) G72   124   CL45
Wheatlands Dr, (Kilb.) John. PA10   78   AC33
Wheatlands Fm Rd, (Kilb.) John. PA10   78   AC33
Wheatley Ct, G32   70   CC32
Wheatley Cres, (Kilsyth) G65   7   CT6
Wheatley Dr, G32   70   CC32
Wheatley Ln, (Bishop.) G64   51   BY21
Wheatley Pl, G32   70   CC32
Wheatley Rd, G32   70   CC32
Whifflet Ct, Coat. ML5   95   CX33
  off Whifflet St
Whifflet St, Coat. ML5   95   CW34
Whin Av, (Barr.) G78   99   AW41
Whinfell Dr, (E.Kil.) G75   135   BW55

Whinfell Gdns, (E.Kil.) G75	135	BW55
Whinfield Av, (Camb.) G72	89	BZ38
off Cambuslang Rd		
Whinfield Path, G53	100	BC41
off Parkhouse Rd		
Whinfield Rd, G53	100	BC41
off Parkhouse Rd		
Whinhall Av, Air. ML6	76	DB28
Whinhall Rd, Air. ML6	76	DA28
Whin Hill, (E.Kil.) G74	122	CD49
Whinhill Gdns, G53	84	BC34
Whinhill Pl, G53	84	BC34
Whinhill Rd, G53	84	BC34
Whinhill Rd, Pais. PA2	83	AX35
Whinknowe, (Ashgill) Lark. ML9	145	DH61
Whin Ln, G65	6	CM5
Whinnie Knowe, Lark. ML9	144	DB60
Whinpark Av, Bell. ML4	110	CV42
Whin Pl, (E.Kil.) G74	122	CD48
Whins Rd, G41	86	BL36
Whin St, Clyde. G81	27	AW17
Whirlies Roundabout, The (E.Kil.) G74	122	CC49
Whirlow Gdns, (Baill.) G69	72	CJ32
Whirlow Rd, (Baill.) G69	72	CJ32
Whistleberry Cres, Ham. ML3	125	CQ46
Whistleberry Dr, Ham. ML3	125	CR46
Whistleberry Ind Pk, Ham. ML3	125	CQ46
Whistleberry Pk, Ham. ML3	125	CQ46
Whistleberry Rd, (Blan.) G72	125	CP46
Whistleberry Rd, Ham. ML3	125	CP46
Whistlefield Ct, (Bears.) G61	29	BH18
Whitacres Path, G53	100	BC41
off Wiltonburn Rd		
Whitacres Pl, G53	100	BC41
off Whitacres Rd		
Whitacres Rd, G53	100	BB41
Whitburn St, G32	70	CB30
Whiteadder Pl, (E.Kil.) G75	134	BT54
Whitecart Rd, (Abbots.) Pais. PA3 off Sanderling Rd	62	AU29
White Cart Twr, (E.Kil.) G74	136	CD54
Whitecraigs Ct, (Giff.) G46	118	BJ45
Whitecraigs Pl, G23	49	BN21
off Fairhaven Rd		
Whitecrook St, Clyde. G81	45	AX21
Whitefield Av, (Camb.) G72	106	CC41
Whitefield Rd, G51	66	BL32
Whitefield Ter, (Camb.) G72	106	CD40
off Croft Rd		
Whiteford Ct, Ham. ML3	140	CS55
Whiteford Rd, (Stepps) G33	53	CH24
Whiteford Rd, Pais. PA2	83	AW35
Whitehall St, G3	4	BP30
Whitehaugh Av, Pais. PA1	63	AX32
Whitehaugh Cres, G53	100	BC41
Whitehaugh Dr, Pais. PA1	63	AX32
Whitehaugh Path, G53	100	BC40
off Wiltonburn Rd		
Whitehaugh Rd, G53	100	BC41
Whitehill Av, (Stepps) G33	53	CF23
Whitehill Av, (Kirk.) G66	17	CH12
Whitehill Av, (Cumb.) G68	21	CZ11
Whitehill Av, Air. ML6	76	DC27
Whitehill Ct, G31	69	BW30
Whitehill Ct, (Kirk.) G66	17	CH12
Whitehill Cres, (Kirk.) G66	17	CH12
Whitehill Cres, Clyde. G81	10	BA14
Whitehill Fm Rd, (Stepps) G33	53	CF24

Whitehill Gdns, G31	69	BW30
Whitehill Gro, (Newt. M.) G77	131	BH51
Whitehill La, (Bears.) G61	29	BF16
Whitehill Pl, G31	69	BW30
Whitehill Rd, (Stepps) G33	53	CF21
Whitehill Rd, (Bears.) G61	29	BF16
Whitehill Rd, (Kirk.) G66	53	CF22
Whitehill Rd, Ham. ML3	125	CR48
Whitehills, Ersk. PA8	25	AQ19
Whitehills Dr, (E.Kil.) G75	136	CA54
Whitehills Pl, (E.Kil.) G75	136	CA54
Whitehills Ter, (E.Kil.) G75	136	CA55
Whitehill St, G31	69	BW30
Whitehill St La, G31	69	BW30
Whitehill Ter, (Gart.) G69	55	CP25
Whitehorse Wk, (E.Kil.) G75	135	BX53
off Winnipeg Dr		
Whitehurst, (Bears.) G61	29	BE15
Whitehurst Pk, (Bears.) G61	29	BE15
Whitekirk Pl, G15	28	BC19
Whitelaw Av, (Glenb.) Coat. ML5	56	CV24
Whitelaw Cres, Bell. ML4	111	CZ41
Whitelaw Gdns, (Bishop.) G64	33	BW18
Whitelaw St, G20	48	BL22
Whitelaw Ter, (Kilsyth) G65	19	CP9
Whitelee, (E.Kil.) G75	135	BZ56
Whitelee Cres, (Newt. M.) G77	116	BD47
Whitelee Gate, (Newt. M.) G77	116	BD47
Whiteloans, (Both.) G71	109	CR42
Whitemoss Av, G44	103	BP41
Whitemoss Av, (E.Kil.) G74	136	CB52
Whitemoss Gro, (E.Kil.) G74	136	CC51
Whitemoss Rd, (E.Kil.) G74	136	CB52
Whitemoss Roundabout, (E.Kil.) G74	136	CC52
Whitepond Av, Bell. ML4	110	CV42
off Footfield Rd		
Whiterigg Ct, Air. ML6	75	CZ29
off Monkscourt Av		
Whitesbridge Av, Pais. PA3	81	AP33
Whitesbridge Cl, Pais. PA3	61	AQ32
off Whitesbridge Av		
Whitestone Av, (Cumb.) G68	21	CX11
White St, G11	66	BK27
White St, Clyde. G81	45	AZ22
Whitevale St, G31	69	BW31
Whithope Rd, G53	100	BB40
Whithope Ter, G53	100	BB40
Whithorn Cres, (Mood.) G69	37	CP18
Whitlawburn Av, (Camb.) G72	106	CA41
Whitlawburn Rd, (Camb.) G72	106	CA41
Whitlawburn Ter, (Camb.) G72	106	CA41
Whitriggs Rd, G53	100	BB40
Whitslade Pl, G34	71	CH28
Whitslade St, G34	72	CJ28
Whitsun Dale, (E.Kil.) G74	121	BY50
Whittagreen Av, Moth. ML1	113	DF42
Whittagreen Ct, Moth. ML1	113	DF42
off Carfin Rd		
Whittagreen Cres, Moth. ML1	113	DF42
Whittingehame Dr, G12	47	BH24
Whittingehame Dr, G13	47	BH24
Whittingehame Gdns, G12	48	BJ24
Whittingehame La, G13	47	BH24
Whittingehame Pk, G12	47	BH24
Whittington St, Coat. ML5	75	CW31
off Ellis St		
Whittliemuir Av, G44	103	BP41
Whitton Dr, (Giff.) G46	102	BM41
Whitton St, G20	48	BL21

Whitworth Dr, G20	49	BQ23
Whitworth Dr, Clyde. G81	27	AW19
Whitworth Gdns, G20	49	BP23
Whitworth Gate, G20	49	BQ24
Whyte Av, (Camb.) G72	106	CA39
Wick Av, Air. ML6	96	DA33
Wickets, The, Pais. PA1	83	AW34
Wickham Av, (Newt. M.) G77	117	BF47
Wigton Av, (Newt. M.) G77	117	BE46
Wigtoun Pl, (Cumb.) G67	22	DD9
Wilderness Brae, (Cumb.) G67	22	DD9
Wilfred Av, G13	47	BF22
Wilkie Cres, Lark. ML9	144	DD59
Wilkie Ln, Bell. ML4	95	CX38
off Fleming Rd		
Wilkie Rd, (Udd.) G71	109	CQ40
William Dr, Ham. ML3	140	CT54
William Mann Dr, (Newt. M.) G77	116	BD49
Williamsburgh Ct, Pais. PA1	83	AW33
off Lacy St		
Williamsburgh Ter, Pais. PA1	63	AW32
off Lacy St		
Williamson Pl, John. PA5	80	AK35
Williamson St, G31	89	BY33
Williamson St, Clyde. G81	27	AX17
William Spiers Pl, Lark. ML9	144	DD60
William St, G3	4	BP29
William St, (Kilsyth) G65	7	CT5
off Backbrae St		
William St, Clyde. G81	27	AW15
William St, Coat. ML5	95	CX33
William St, Ham. ML3	125	CR48
William St, John. PA5	79	AH34
William St, Pais. PA1	82	AS33
William Ure Pl, (Bishop.) G64	33	BX16
Williamwood Dr, G44	103	BP43
Williamwood Pk, G44	103	BP43
Williamwood Pk W, G44	103	BP43
Willock Pl, G20	49	BN22
Willoughby Dr, G13	47	BH23
Willoughby La, G13	47	BH23
off Willoughby Dr		
Willow Av, (Bishop.) G64	51	BW21
Willow Av, (Lenz.) G66	35	CE15
Willow Av, (Elder.) John. PA5	80	AL35
Willow Av, (New Stev.) Moth. ML1	112	DC43
Willowbank, Lark. ML9	142	DC56
Willowbank Cres, G3	67	BP27
off Woodlands Rd		
Willowbank Gdns, (Kirk.) G66	17	CF13
Willowbank St, G3	67	BP27
Willow Ct, (E.Kil.) G75	135	BX55
Willow Cres, Coat. ML5	95	CW33
Willowdale Cres, (Baill.) G69	92	CJ33
Willowdale Gdns, (Baill.) G69	92	CJ33
Willow Dr, (Blan.) G72	124	CL45
Willow Dr, Air. ML6	77	DF30
Willow Dr, John. PA5	79	AH36
Willowford Rd, G53	100	BB41
Willow Gro, Moth. ML1	112	DD40
Willow La, G32	90	CD35
Willow Pl, (Udd.) G71	94	CT37
off Laburnum Rd		
Willow Pl, John. PA5	80	AJ35
Willows, The, (Carm.) G76	120	BT45
Willow St, G13	47	BH22
Willow Way, Ham. ML3	140	CU52
Wilmot Rd, G13	47	BF23
Wilson Av, (Linw.) Pais. PA3	60	AJ31

Wilson Ct, Bell. ML4 110 CV40
off Main St
Wilson Pl, (E.Kil.) G74 122 CC49
Wilson Pl, (Newt. M.) G77 117 BE49
Wilsons Pl, Pais. PA1 82 AV33
off Seedhill
Wilson St, G1 5 BS30
Wilson St, Air. ML6 76 DB29
Wilson St, Coat. ML5 75 CY30
Wilson St, Ham. ML3 125 CQ48
Wilson St, Lark. ML9 144 DD60
Wilson St, Moth. ML1 128 DB46
Wilson St, Pais. PA1 82 AS33
Wilson St, Renf. PA4 45 AZ25
Wiltonburn Path, G53 100 BC41
off Wiltonburn Rd
Wiltonburn Rd, G53 100 BC41
Wilton Cres, G20 49 BP26
Wilton Cres La, G20 49 BP26
Wilton Dr, G20 49 BP26
Wilton Gdns, G20 49 BP26
Wilton St, G20 49 BN26
Wilton St, Coat. ML5 74 CT27
Wilverton Rd, G13 47 BG21
Winburne Cres, Ham. ML3 125 CR49
off Clearfield Av
Winchester Dr, G12 48 BK23
Windermere, (E.Kil.) G75 134 BV56
Windermere Gdns, Ham. ML3 140 CS55
Windermere St, Bell. ML4 110 CV41
off West End Dr
Windhill Cres, G43 102 BK40
Windhill Pk, (Eagle.) G76 133 BN51
Windhill Pl, G43 102 BK40
off Windhill Rd
Windhill Rd, G43 102 BK40
Windlaw Ct, G45 104 BT43
Windlaw Gdns, G44 103 BP42
Windlaw Pk Gdns, G44 103 BP41
Windlaw Rd, G45 104 BT44
Windlaw Rd, (Carm.) G76 120 BT45
Windmill Ct, Moth. ML1 128 DB47
Windmillcroft Quay, G5 4 BQ31
Windmillhill St, Moth. ML1 128 DB48
Windmill Rd, Ham. ML3 126 CT49
Windsor Av, (Newt. M.) G77 117 BH48
Windsor Cres, Clyde. G81 27 AW18
Windsor Cres, (Elder.) John. 80 AK36
PA5
Windsor Cres, Pais. PA1 63 AW31
Windsor Dr, (Glenm.) Air. ML6 58 DB25
Windsor Gdns, Ham. ML3 125 CQ48
Windsor Path, (Baill.) G69 73 CP31
off Park Rd
Windsor Path, Lark. ML9 145 DE59
off Afton St
Windsor Rd, Moth. ML1 112 DC40
Windsor Rd, Renf. PA4 63 AY27
Windsor St, G20 67 BQ27
Windsor St, G32 71 CE31
Windsor St, Coat. ML5 94 CU34
Windsor Ter, G20 67 BQ27
Windsor Wk, (Udd.) G71 93 CR38
Windward Rd, (E.Kil.) G75 135 BW52
Windyedge Cres, G13 47 BE24
Windyedge Pl, G13 47 BE24
Windyetts, (Kilsyth) G65 19 CP10
Windyridge, Ham. ML3 140 CU52
off Chatelherault Cres
Windyridge Pl, (Blan.) G72 124 CL46
off Ansdell Av
Wingate Cres, (E.Kil.) G74 123 CE49

Wingate Dr, (E.Kil.) G74 123 CE49
Wingate Pk, (E.Kil.) G74 123 CE49
off Boswell Pk
Wingate St, Wis. ML2 129 DF49
Wingfield Gdns, (Both.) G71 109 CR44
off Blairston Av
Winifred St, G33 51 BZ25
Winning Ct, (Blan.) G72 109 CN44
Winning Quad, Wis. ML2 129 DF50
off English St
Winning Row, G31 69 BZ32
Winnipeg Dr, (E.Kil.) G75 135 BX53
Wintergreen Ct, (E.Kil.) G74 121 BZ49
Wintergreen Dr, (E.Kil.) G74 121 BZ49
off Stewartfield Dr
Winton Av, (Giff.) G46 102 BL43
Winton Cres, (Blan.) G72 124 CM46
Winton Dr, G12 48 BL24
Winton Gdns, (Udd.) G71 93 CP38
Winton La, G12 48 BL24
Winton Pk, (E.Kil.) G75 135 BW52
Wirran Pl, G13 46 BA21
Wishart St, G31 5 BU30
Wishawhill St, Wis. ML2 129 DH50
Wisner Ct, (Thornlie.) G46 101 BH42
Wiston St, (Camb.) G72 107 CF40
Witchwood Ct, Coat. ML5 74 CT27
off Lomond Rd
Witcutt Way, Wis. ML2 143 DG52
Woddrop St, G40 89 BX35
Wolcott Dr, (Blan.) G72 124 CM45
off Ansdell Av
Wolfe Av, (Newt. M.) G77 117 BE46
Wolseley St, G5 88 BT34
Woodale, Moth. ML1 127 CZ49
Wood Aven Dr, (E.Kil.) G74 121 BZ49
Woodbank Cres, (Clark.) G76 119 BN47
Woodbank Cres, John. PA5 79 AH35
Woodburn Av, (Blan.) G72 125 CN45
Woodburn Av, (Clark.) G76 119 BN47
Woodburn Av, Air. ML6 76 DB31
Woodburn Ct, (Ruther.) G73 105 BX39
Woodburn Rd, G43 102 BM40
Woodburn St, Moth. ML1 128 DA45
Woodburn Ter, Lark. ML9 145 DE59
off Lansbury Ter
Woodburn Way, (Cumb.) G68 21 CY11
Wood Cres, Moth. ML1 112 DA44
Woodcroft Av, G11 47 BH26
Woodend, (Blan.) G72 124 CM47
off Muir St
Woodend Ct, G32 91 CG35
Woodend Dr, G13 47 BG24
Woodend Dr, Air. ML6 77 DE28
Woodend Dr, Pais. PA1 83 AZ33
Woodend Gdns, G32 91 CG35
Woodend La, G13 47 BG24
Woodend La, Lark. ML9 145 DE60
off Rannoch Ter
Woodend Pl, (Elder.) John. 80 AK35
PA5
Woodend Rd, G32 91 CF35
Woodend Rd, (Ruther.) G73 105 BX41
Wood Fm Rd, (Thornlie.) G46 102 BJ43
Woodfield, (Udd.) G71 110 CS39
Woodfield Av, (Bishop.) G64 33 BX20
Woodfoot Path, G53 100 BC41
off Woodfoot Quad
Woodfoot Pl, G53 100 BB41
off Woodfoot Rd
Woodfoot Quad, G53 100 BD41

Woodfoot Rd, G53 100 BC41
Woodfoot Rd, Ham. ML3 139 CR51
Woodford Pl, (Linw.) Pais. 60 AJ31
PA3
Woodford St, G41 87 BN38
Woodgreen Av, G44 103 BR39
Woodhall Av, (Calder.) Air. 96 DD35
ML6
Woodhall Av, Coat. ML5 94 CU34
Woodhall Av, Ham. ML3 125 CR49
Woodhall Av, Moth. ML1 112 DB40
Woodhall Est, (Calder.) Air. 96 DD36
ML6
Woodhall Pl, Coat. ML5 94 CV34
Woodhall Rd, (Calder.) Air. 96 DD35
ML6
Woodhall St, G40 89 BX35
Woodhall St, (Chap.) Air. ML6 97 DF36
Woodhead Av, (Kirk.) G66 17 CF14
Woodhead Av, (Cumb.) G68 20 CV14
Woodhead Av, (Both.) G71 125 CR45
Woodhead Ct, (Cumb.) G68 20 CV14
Woodhead Cres, (Udd.) G71 93 CP38
Woodhead Cres, Ham. ML3 139 CR53
Woodhead Gdns, (Both.) G71 125 CR45
Woodhead Grn, Ham. ML3 139 CR53
Woodhead Gro, (Cumb.) G68 20 CV14
Woodhead Ind Est, (Chry.) 54 CK23
G69
Woodhead Path, G53 100 BC40
off Woodhead Rd
Woodhead Pl, (Cumb.) G68 20 CV14
Woodhead Rd, G53 100 BB40
Woodhead Rd, (Cumb.) G68 20 CV14
Woodhead Rd, (Chry.) G69 54 CK24
Woodhead Ter, (Chry.) G69 54 CK22
Woodhead Vw, (Cumb.) G68 20 CV14
Woodhill Gro, (Bishop.) G64 51 BY21
Woodhill Rd, G21 51 BX23
Woodhill Rd, (Bishop.) G64 33 BY20
Woodholm Av, G44 104 BS39
Woodhouse Ct, (Clark.) G76 119 BQ48
off East Kilbride Rd
Woodhouse St, G13 47 BG22
Woodilee Cotts, (Kirk.) G66 35 CH15
Woodilee Ind Est, (Kirk.) G66 35 CG15
Woodilee Rd, (Kirk.) G66 35 CG16
Woodilee Rd, Moth. ML1 113 DG41
Woodland Av, (Kirk.) G66 16 CD13
Woodland Av, Air. ML6 97 DE33
Woodland Av, Pais. PA2 82 AU37
Woodland Cres, (Camb.) G72 106 CD41
Woodland Cres, (Eagle.) G76 132 BM56
Woodland Gdns, (Carm.) G76 120 BT46
Woodland Gdns, Ham. ML3 140 CU51
Woodlands, The, Bell. ML4 111 CZ42
off Forest Dr
Woodlands Av, (Gart.) G69 55 CN23
Woodlands Av, (Both.) G71 109 CQ42
Woodlands Ct, (Thornlie.) G46 101 BH43
Woodlands Ct, (Old Kil.) G60 25 AR16
off Dumbarton Rd
Woodlands Cres, (Thornlie.) 101 BH42
G46
Woodlands Cres, (Both.) G71 109 CP42
Woodlands Cres, John. PA5 79 AF36
Woodlands Dr, G4 67 BP27
Woodlands Dr, Coat. ML5 74 CT30
Woodlands Dr, Moth. ML1 112 DB40
Woodlands Gdns, (Both.) G71 109 CP41
Woodlands Gate, G3 4 BP28

Woodlands Gate, (Thornlie.) G46	101	BH42
Woodlands Gro, (Miln.) G62	12	BJ10
Woodlands Pk, (Thornlie.) G46	101	BH43
Woodlands Pl, Coat. ML5	74	CT30
Woodlands Rd, G3	67	BP27
Woodlands Rd, (Thornlie.) G46	101	BH43
Woodlands Rd, Moth. ML1	128	DB50
Woodlands St, (Miln.) G62	12	BJ11
Woodlands St, Moth. ML1	128	DB49
off Manse Rd		
Woodlands Ter, G3	67	BN28
Woodlands Ter, (Both.) G71	109	CP42
Woodland Ter, Lark. ML9	145	DE60
Woodland Way, (Cumb.) G67	22	DD10
Wood La, (Bishop.) G64	51	BY21
Woodlea Av, Air. ML6	97	DE33
Woodlea Dr, (Giff.) G46	102	BM41
Woodlea Dr, Ham. ML3	140	CT53
Woodlea Pl, Air. ML6	77	DE28
Woodlinn Av, G44	103	BR40
Woodmill Dr, (Torr.) G64	15	BY12
Woodmill Gdns, (Cumb.) G67	38	CV15
Woodneuk Ct, Pais. PA1	81	AR33
Woodneuk La, (Gart.) G69	55	CQ24
Woodneuk Rd, G53	100	BD41
Woodneuk Rd, (Gart.) G69	55	CP24
Woodneuk St, (Chap.) Air. ML6	97	DF36
Woodneuk Ter, (Gart.) G69	55	CQ24
Wood Quad, Clyde. G81	46	BA21
Woodrow Av, (Holytown) Moth. ML1	112	DD43
Woodrow Circ, G41	86	BM33
Woodrow Pl, G41	86	BL33
Woodrow Rd, G41	86	BM33
Woodside Av, (Thornlie.) G46	102	BJ42
Woodside Av, (Kilsyth) G65	8	CV5
Woodside Av, (Lenz.) G66	35	CF15
Woodside Av, (Ruther.) G73	89	BY38
Woodside Av, Ham. ML3	140	CU51
off Woodside Wk		
Woodside Ct, Coat. ML5	74	CT32
off Torriden St		
Woodside Cres, G3	4	BP28
Woodside Cres, (Barr.) G78	99	AZ43
Woodside Cres, Pais. PA1	82	AS33
Woodside Dr, (Eagle.) G76	132	BM51
Woodside Dr, (Calder.) Air. ML6	96	DD35
Woodside Gdns, (Carm.) G76	120	BT46
Woodside Gdns, (Clark.) G76	118	BM46
Woodside Gdns, Coat. ML5	94	CT33
Woodside Gro, (Ruther.) G73	89	BY38
Woodside Pl, G3	4	BP28
Woodside Pl, (Udd.) G71	94	CS37
Woodside Pl La, G3	4	BP28
Woodside Rd, (Carm.) G76	120	BT46
Woodside St, (Chap.) Air. ML6	97	DF35
Woodside St, Coat. ML5	94	CT33
Woodside St, Moth. ML1	128	DD49
Woodside St, (Holytown) Moth. ML1	96	DA37
Woodside St, (New Stev.) Moth. ML1	112	DC42

Woodside Ter, G3	4	BP28
Woodside Ter La, G3	4	BP28
Woodside Wk, Ham. ML3	126	CU50
Woodstock Av, G41	86	BM37
Woodstock Av, (Kirk.) G66	17	CH13
Woodstock Av, Pais. PA2	81	AN37
Woodstock Way, Pais. PA2	81	AN37
off Woodstock Av		
Wood St, G31	69	BX29
Wood St, Air. ML6	76	DD28
Wood St, Coat. ML5	74	CU30
Wood St, Moth. ML1	128	DB45
Wood St, Pais. PA2	83	AX34
Woodvale Av, (Giff.) G46	118	BK45
Woodvale Av, (Bears.) G61	30	BK19
Woodvale Av, Air. ML6	97	DE33
Woodvale Dr, Pais. PA3	61	AQ32
Woodview, (Udd.) G71	94	CT37
Wood Vw, Moth. ML1	112	DD40
off Myrtle Dr		
Woodview Dr, Air. ML6	76	DC32
Woodview Dr, Bell. ML4	95	CY38
Woodview La, Air. ML6	76	DC32
off Woodview Dr		
Woodview Rd, Lark. ML9	144	DC61
Woodview Ter, Ham. ML3	125	CR49
Woodville Pk, G51	66	BK31
Woodville St, G51	66	BK31
Woodyett Pk, (Clark.) G76	119	BP48
Woodyett Rd, (Clark.) G76	119	BP48
Wordsworth Way, (Both.) G71	109	CR42
Works Av, (Camb.) G72	107	CG40
Worsley Cres, (Newt. M.) G77	117	BE47
Wraes Av, (Barr.) G78	99	AZ41
Wraes Vw, (Barr.) G78	98	AV44
Wrangholm Cres, Moth. ML1	112	DD42
Wrangholm Dr, Moth. ML1	112	DD42
Wren Ct, (Strathclyde Bus. Pk.) Bell. ML4	94	CU37
Wren Pl, John. PA5	79	AF38
Wright Av, (Barr.) G78	99	AW43
Wrightlands Cres, Ersk. PA8	44	AU21
Wright St, Renf. PA4	63	AW28
Wright Way, Moth. ML1	112	DC42
off Woodside St		
Wye Cres, Coat. ML5	74	CT27
Wykeham Pl, G13	47	BE23
Wykeham Rd, G13	47	BE23
Wylie, (E.Kil.) G74	123	CF48
Wylie Av, (Newt. M.) G77	117	BF46
Wylie St, Ham. ML3	140	CT51
Wyndford Dr, G20	48	BM24
Wyndford Pl, G20	48	BM24
off Wyndford Rd		
Wyndford Rd, G20	48	BL24
Wyndham Ct, G12	48	BM25
off Wyndham St		
Wyndham St, G12	48	BM25
Wynford Ter, (Udd.) G71	93	CR38
Wynyard Grn, (E.Kil.) G75	135	BX53
Wyper Pl, G40	68	BV31
Wyvil Av, G13	29	BG20
Wyvis Av, G13	46	BA21

Wyvis Av, (Bears.) G61	11	BE14
Wyvis Ct, (Newt. M.) G77	131	BE51
Wyvis Pl, G13	46	BB21
Wyvis Pl, (Newt. M.) G77	131	BE51
Wyvis Quad, G13	46	BB21

Y

Yair Dr, G52	64	BC31
Yarrow Ct, (Camb.) G72	107	CG41
Yarrow Cres, Bish. PA7	24	AL19
Yarrow Gdns, G20	49	BP26
Yarrow Gdns La, G20	49	BP26
Yarrow Pk, (E.Kil.) G74	136	CC52
Yarrow Rd, (Bishop.) G64	33	BW17
Yarrow Way, (Blan.) G72	125	CN45
off Ennisfree Rd		
Yate Gro, G31	69	BX32
Yate Rd, G31	69	BX32
Yate St, G31	69	BX32
Yetholm Gdns, (E.Kil.) G74	122	CB49
Yetholm St, G14	46	BA23
off Speirshall Ter		
Yetholm Ter, Ham. ML3	125	CN50
Yett Rd, Moth. ML1	113	DF42
Yetts Cres, (Kirk.) G66	17	CH13
Yetts Hole Rd, G67	39	CX20
Yetts Hole Rd, Air. ML6	57	CX26
Yew Dr, G21	51	BW26
Yew Pl, John. PA5	79	AH36
Yews Cres, Ham. ML3	125	CR48
Yoker Burn Pl, G13	46	BA22
off Yoker Mill Gdns		
Yokerburn Ter, Clyde. G81	45	AZ22
Yoker Ferry Rd, G14	46	BA23
Yoker Mill Gdns, G13	46	BA22
Yoker Mill Rd, G13	46	BA22
York Dr, (Ruther.) G73	105	BZ40
Yorkhill Par, G3	66	BL28
Yorkhill Quay, G3	66	BL29
Yorkhill St, G3	66	BM29
York Pl, Bell. ML4	111	CW40
off Neilson St		
York Rd, (Chap.) Air. ML6	97	DF37
York St, G2	4	BQ31
York St, Clyde. G81	27	AZ19
York Way, Renf. PA4	63	AZ28
Younger Quad, (Bishop.) G64	33	BW20
off Springfield Rd		
Young Pl, (Udd.) G71	93	CQ37
Young Pl, (E.Kil.) G75	136	CC56
Young St, Clyde. G81	27	AX17
Young Ter, G21	51	BW25
Young Wynd, Bell. ML4	95	CW37
Yukon Ter, (E.Kil.) G75	135	BX53

Z

Zambesi Dr, (Blan.) G72	108	CL44
Zena Cres, G33	51	BY25
Zena Pl, G33	51	BZ25
Zena St, G33	51	BZ25
Zetland Rd, G52	64	BB29